European Food Law Handbook

European Food Law Handbook

Bernd van der Meulen
Menno van der Velde

with contributions from
Anna Szajkowska and Ronald Verbruggen
and a foreword by Robert Madelin

Wageningen Academic
Publishers

ISBN 978-90-8686-082-1

First published, 2008

Wageningen Academic Publishers
The Netherlands, 2008

Foreword

European food law has evolved tremendously in the recent years. In its early days, European law concerning food focussed on setting the right framework for the better functioning of the internal market. Food was primarily a good that had to move freely. Prevention of the distortion of competition was key. The tool of the time was harmonisation of compositional or processing standards for individual foods. Directives provided certain prohibitions and gradual harmonisation in specific areas. Rules on food of animal origin were swiftly developed through a sector by sector approach and the so called vertical veterinary directives.

Several important rulings of the European Court of Justice addressing unjustified discrimination, in particular the *Dassonville* and *Cassis de Dijon* cases, had a significant influence on the shape of Community food law at this time. The Court made mutual recognition of national regulations a principle of food law and thus defined minimum protective standards. There was some reluctance to develop the necessary trust for mutual recognition. Public sensitivity in this field led Member States to defend passionately national measures on public health and consumer protection, which obstructed the internal market. The resulting disputes highlighted the need for Community harmonisation. Increased harmonisation in the field of food safety then resulted in a shift of the centre of gravity from national to Community level.

The Single European Act (1986) modified voting rules to qualified majority. As a result, harmonisation on a more horizontal level was intensified. Directives on e.g. additives, labelling, hygiene and official controls were adopted. With the Treaty of Maastricht (1992), the then Article 100a (now Article 95) was amended to require a '*high level of health protection*' as a general objective of food law. The BSE crisis in the late 1980s led to an irrevocable shift in the political focus of food law - food safety was now a prerequisite for proper functioning of the internal market in food. The Treaty of Amsterdam (1997) granted the European Parliament a more active participation by making the co-decision procedure compulsory.

These developments resulted in a call for a fundamental overhaul of food law and a comprehensive integrated approach. The General Food Law (Regulation 178/2002) was adopted. The objective of the General Food Law was to provide a basic framework of overarching principles for all food legislation, at Community and national level. As a regulation, it was directly applicable without transposition. The General Food Law closed gaps that resulted from the internal market approach. Along with the definition of food, the concept of risk analysis and the precautionary principle were formally introduced as principles of food law. Existing food law had consequently to be adapted in order to comply.

The introduction of a more structured approach to risk analysis was also the result of the ever increasing importance of international trade in food. Parallel to the developments in the Community, a risk analysis approach to food safety was developed in Codex Alimentarius, a long standing joint initiative of two United Nations institutions. This approach had gained importance and momentum through the Agreement on Sanitary and Phytosanitary Measures (SPS), a consequence of the finalisation of the Uruguay Round on world trade. Risk analysis with a clear separation of risk assessment and risk management was integrated in the new EU framework and led, among other things, to the establishment of the European Food Safety Authority (EFSA).

This serves to illustrate that food law will never be static - there will always be a need to adapt the rules to new circumstances and challenges.

Today, the European Union consists of twenty-seven independent states, which not only share a single market, but aim to strengthen their economic, political and social co-operation. The role of the European Commission is significant as it makes proposals for new legislation by Parliament and Council, implements EU policy, monitors adherence to European Treaties and represents the European Union at international level including at the World Trade Organisation and Codex Alimentarius.

This is very much a role of designer and co-ordinator. Like any designer we have to pay attention to trends, i.e. developments within the Community, in the Member States and at international level. In food law this means observing and analysing developments in science, law, business, trade and politics in order to evaluate their potential impact on measures in place and to consider possible adaptations. This role means that our success depends on input from others - institutions, organisations, business, citizens ... - both inside and outside the EU, as well as on our capacity to co-ordinate and foster sustainable consensus. Stakeholder contributions are even more significant when they take into account the relevant legal framework.

Rules on food are designed to protect us from harm or fraud. They need to be based on the best science available and should at best be acceptable to the citizens of all Member States. It is not always easy to take account of scientific knowledge (or uncertainty) and strike the right balance between feasibility of controls, legitimate expectations of the food business and consumer protection. Even the best rules need to be properly monitored to be fully effective. This task is the responsibility of the competent authorities of the Member States - that is, the control authorities and judiciary.

This book provides a comprehensive introduction to current food law in the EU, its objectives and provisions. It covers the relevant areas of international trade law, and looks at food law from different legal perspectives such as criminal law or intellectual property law. This is beneficial because even though food safety and quality are at the centre of food law in the EU, the legislative frameworks governing other aspects of our society often have an impact on food law or are impacted on by food law. It is important that the objectives of food safety and food quality are well understood. This book should contribute to a better appreciation of the relation of food law to other legal disciplines.

Robert Madelin

Director-General

Health and Consumer Directorate General of the European Commission

Preface

This book is a successor to 'Food Safety Law in the European Union. An introduction' (2004). What started out as an update changed so much in content, scope and ambition that 'handbook' now seems a more appropriate label than 'introduction', and 'food law' more than 'food safety law' even thought food safety is still a core subject.

The aim of this book is fourfold:
- to provide a background in food law to both lawyers and non-lawyers who take an interest in the field of food and its regulatory framework;
- to assign the functional field of food law its proper place within European law;
- to uncover the system of EU food law;
- to provide a framework for further research in this exciting area.

This book is about food and food safety in European Union law. Food safety is a topic that at present attracts a considerable amount of interest from all kinds of different scientific angles. In the mid-1990's food safety scares brought food safety to the top of the European policy agenda. There it has remained ever since. On the one hand this is due to the persistence of food safety problems, on the other hand to the fact that an atmosphere of crisis has been mobilised and sustained to achieve policy goals.

This state of affairs contributed to the flourishing of technical sciences concerned with food safety: microbiology and food chemistry to name but a few. All those who contribute to dealing with food safety problems do so within the framework of an applicable set of rules. We could call the rules that are concerned with food 'food law'. The aim of this book is to present this framework. We encounter such rules at different levels: the global level, the regional level and the national level. This book focuses on the European Union.

We address the subject matter from the presumption that food law is not a world of its own. There is no clear distinction between rules that concern food safety and other rules. For this reason, and for the benefit of readers who do not have a background in (European) law, Chapters 2-5 introduce the reader to legal methodology, international law and European law. In doing this, the perspective of food has been kept in mind. Chapter 6 connects the general aspects of EU law to the specific domain of food. Chapters 7-15 are dedicated to EU food law in a strict sense. These are the rules that have been devised with the subject matter of food (safety) in mind.

Chapters 16 and 17 take account of the fact that the European Union is not an island in the world. Chapter 16 briefly explains the place of European food law in the global context of WTO, SPS and Codex Alimentarius. Chapter 17 addresses food regulation by the private sector.

We have applied several techniques to make law accessible to the food sector. The text is straightforward. Quotes from legal sources are presented in law text boxes to make them stand out. Diagrams have been used. The table of contents, indexes, and list of abbreviations give entries from different sides.

The reference list, as far as possible, gives the hyperlinks to sources cited in the book. This list is available in electronic form on the websites of Wageningen Academic Publishers (www.wageningenacademic.com/foodlaw) and the European Institute for Food Law (www.food-law.nl).

We would like to thank:
Martha Cecilia Kühn, Maria Litjens, Isabel Cachapa Rodrigues and Maryvon Noordam for critical comments on draft chapters;
Mike Jacobs and his team at Wageningen Academic Publishers, in particular: Marijn van der Gaag (desk editing), Jessica van Wijngaarden and Enrico Kunst (cover design and desktop publishing) and Sandra McElroy (language editing).

This book is the second publication in the series of the European Institute for Food Law.

Menno van der Velde
Associate Professor of European Law, Law and Governance Group, (www.law.wur.nl) Wageningen University (www.wur.nl).

Bernd van der Meulen
Professor of Law and Governance at Wageningen University (www.law.wur.nl); director of the European Institute for Food Law (www.food-law.nl).

Comments are welcome at: Bernd.vanderMeulen@wur.nl.

Table of contents

Abbreviations

AB	Appellate Body (WTO)
ADI	Acceptable Daily Intake
AFC	Panel on additives, flavourings, processing aids and materials in contact with food (EFSA)
AGRI	Agriculture and Rural Development Committee of the European Parliament
AHAW	Panel on animal health and welfare (EFSA)
ALARA	As low as reasonably achievable
ANS	Panel on food additives and nutrient sources added to food (EFSA)
ARfD	Acute Reference Dose
Art.	Article
BIOHAZ	Panel on biological hazards (EFSA)
BIPs	EU Border Inspections Posts
BRC	British Retail Consortium
BSE	Bovine spongiform encephalopathy
B-to-B (B2B)	Business to business
B-to-C (B2C)	Business to consumer
CAC	Codex Alimentarius Commission
CCD	Colony Collapse Disorder
CCP	Critical Control Point
CEF	Panel on food contact materials, enzymes, flavourings, and processing aids (EFSA)
CEN	Comité Européen de Normalisation (the European Committee for Standardization)
CENELEC	Comité Européen de Normalisation Electrotechnique (European Committee for Electrotechnical Standardization)
CFI	Court of First Instance (EU)
CFSP	Common Foreign and Security Policy of the European Union
CIES	Comité International d'Entreprise à Succursales; The Food Business Forum
CIF	Costs, Insurance, Freight
CISG	United Nations Convention on Contracts for the International Sale of Goods
cm	centimetre
CMO	Common Market Organisation
CN	Combined Nomenclature (Customs tariff numbers)
COE	Council of Europe
CONTAM	Panel on contaminants in the food chain (EFSA)
COOL	Country of origin labeling
COREPER	Comité de Représentants Permanent, Committee of Permanent Representatives (EU)

CSA	Comité Special d'Agriculture; Special Agriculture Committee
DCFR	Draft common frame of reference
DDT	Dichloro-Diphenyl-Trichloroethane
DES	Diethylstilbestrol
DG	Directorate General of the European Commission's civil service
DG Agri	EC Directorate General Agriculture and Rural Development
DG Entr	EC Directorate General Enterprise and Industry
DG Sanco	EC Directorate General Health and Consumer Protection
DM	Deutsche Mark
DNA	Deoxyribonucleic acid
DOI	Declarations of Interests
DSB	Dispute Settlement Body (WTO)
DSU	Dispute Settlement Understanding (WTO)
EC	European Community
ECE	United Nations' Economic Commission for Europe
ECHR	European Court of Human Rights (COE)
Ecofin	Economic and Financial Affairs (EU)
ECOSOC	Economic and Social Council (UN)
ECJ	European Court of Justice (EU)
ECR	European Court Reports
ECSC	European Coal and Steel Community
ECU	European Currency Unit (now EURO)
EEA	European Economic Area
EEC	European Economic Community
EFFL	European Food & Feed Law Review
EFLA	European Food Law Association
EFSA	European Food Safety Authority
E.L.rev.	European Law review
ENVI	Environment, Public Health and Consumer Policy Committee of the European Parliament
EP	European Parliament
EPO	European Patent Office
EU	European Union
Euratom	European Atomic Energy Community
EUREP	Euro-Retailer Produce Working Group
FAO	Food and Agriculture Organisation (a United Nations' Specialised Agency)
FCD	Fédération des entreprises du Commerce et de la Distribution
FDA	Food and Drug Administration (the food regulatory agency in the USA)
FEEDAP	Panel on additives and products or substances used in animal feed (EFSA)
FFV	Fresh fruit and vegetables
FIAP	Food improvement agents package

FMI	Food Marketing Institute
FOB	Free On Board
FSMS	Food Safety Management System
FSO	Food Safety Objective
FVO	Food and Veterinary Office (EU)
g	grams
GATS	General Agreement on trade in Services (WTO)
GATT	General Agreement on Tariffs and Trade (WTO)
GFL	General Food Law; Regulation 178/2002
GFSI	Global Food Safety Initiative
GM-food	Genetically Modified Organisms used for human consumption
GMO	Genetically Modified Organism
GMO	Panel on Genetically Modified Organisms (EFSA)
GMP	Good Manufacturing Practice
GTZ	Gesellschaft für Technische Zusammenarbeit
HACCP	Hazard Analysis and Critical Control Points
HCH	Hexachlorocyclohexane
HDE	Hauptverband des Deutschen Einzelhandels
ICC	International Chamber of Commerce
ICESCR	International Covenant on Economic, Social and Cultural Rights (UN)
ICJ	International Court of Justice (UN)
ICTSD	International Centre for Trade and Sustainable Development
ICUMSA	International Commission for Uniform Methods of Sugar Analysis
IEC	International Electrotechnical Commission
IFAD	International Fund for Agricultural Development (UN)
IFIC	International Food Information Council
IFS	International Food Standard
INFOSAN	International Food Safety Authorities Network (WHO)
IPPC	International Plant Protection Convention
IPR	Intellectual property rights
ISBN	International Standard Book Number
ISO	International Organization of Standardization
ISSN	International Standard Serial Number
JECFA	Joint FAO/WHO Expert Committee on Food Additives
kg.	kilogram
L	Lot
LCB	Licensed certification Body
LOD	Limit of determination
MB	Management board (EFSA))
MCPDs	Monochloropropanediols
mg.	microgram
MRL	Maximum Residue Level

MS	Member state(s)
NACMCF	National Advisory Committee on Microbiological Criteria for Foods (USA)
NDA	Panel on dietetic products, nutrition and allergies (EFSA)
NFR	Novel foods regulation (Regulation 258/97)
NGO	Non-Governmental Organisation
NHCR	Nutrition and Health Claims Regulation (Regulation 1924/2006)
NOAEL	No observed adverse effects level
NS	Non-numerical Acceptable Daily Intake 'Not Specified'
NVLR	Nederlandse Vereniging voor Levensmiddelenrecht (Dutch Food Law Association)
OECD	Organization for Economic Cooperation and Development
OIE	International Office of Epizootics
OIML	Organisation internationale de métrologie légale
OJ	Official Journal of the European Union
OJ C	Official Journal Communication Series
OJ L	Official Journal Legislation Series
OLFs	Other legitimate factors
PAHs	Polycyclic aromatic hydrocarbons
PC	Performance Criterion
PCA	Permanent Court of Arbitration
PCBs	Polychlorinated biphenyls
PCT	Patent Cooperation Treaty
PDO	Protected Designation of Origin
PGI	Protected Geographical Indication
PLH	Panel on Plant health (EFSA)
PO	Performance Objective
PPR	Panel on plant protection products and their residues (EFSA)
PRAC	Regulatory procedure with scrutiny (procédure de réglementation avec contrôle)
QS	Quantum Satis (the required quantity and no more)
QUID	QUantitative Ingredients Declaration
RDA	Recommended daily allowance
SARS	Severe acute respiratory syndrome
SCFCAH	Standing Committee on the Food Chain and Animal Health (EU)
SQF	Safe Quality Food
SQFI	SQF Institute
RASFF	Rapid Alert System for Food and Feed (EU)
REACH	Registration, Evaluation, Authorisation and Restriction of Chemical substances (Regulation 1907/2006)
SCF	Scientific Committee on Food (EU)
SG	Secretary-General

SPS	Agreement on the Application of Sanitary and Phytosanitary Measures (WTO)
STMR	Supervised Trial Median Residue Level
TBR	Trade Barriers Regulation (Regulation 3286/94)
TBT	Agreement on Technical Barriers to Trade (WTO)
TEC	EC Treaty
TEU	Treaty on European Union (Lisbon)
TFEU	Treaty on the Functioning of the European Union (Lisbon)
Trb.	Tractatenblad, the official Dutch publication medium for treaties
TRIPs	Agreement on Trade Related Aspects of Intellectual Property Rights (WTO)
TSE	Transmissible spongiform encephalopathy
TSG	Traditional Speciality Guaranteed
UK	United Kingdom
UN	United Nations
UNCITRAL	United Nations Commission on International Trade Law
UNECE	United Nations Economic Commission for Europe
UNGA	United Nations' General Assembly
UNTS	United Nations Treaty Series
US / USA	United States of America
USDA	US Department of Agriculture
v.	versus (against)
vCJD	Variant Creutzfeldt-Jakob disease
WFP	World Food Programme (UN)
WHO	World Health Organisation (a United Nations' Specialised Agency)
WIPO	World Intellectual Property Organization
WTO	World Trade Organisation
ZLR	Zeitschrift für das gesamte Lebensmittelrecht

List of law text boxes

List of diagrams

1. Introduction

1.1 The food sector and its law

The food sector is in size the first production sector in the European Union. It is a heavily regulated sector. According to the EU's directorate general for Enterprise and Industry, the food Industry is the third most regulated industrial sector following automobiles and chemicals.

The motives for regulating the food sector have developed over time. Initially the focus was on creating a level playing field for a well-functioning internal market. Currently the emphasis is on protecting consumer health and other interests.

European food law has an impact on interests of many stakeholders: consumers, officials and civil servants at European as well as at national level in the member states of the EU, candidate members and neighbouring countries, businesses in the EU or trading with EU partners, legal and regulatory affairs advisors, consultants and many more.

1.2 Multi-layered food law

Eating and drinking are necessities of life. From the beginning of time the gathering, production and distribution of food has been central to many human relations. And in all societies rules and regulations concerning this primary human activity have developed. As those relations have become more complex, stretched across borders and ecosystems, organisation has become increasingly necessary. Food law is now formulated and used at many levels: from the international community to several smaller parts of the world. The European Union plays a key role, as it provides the legal framework and substance for rules applied on a continental scale to societies that belong to the most developed in the world, that are integrating with societies that have only recently become free to participate, and who have to develop a new infrastructure to accommodate the style and standard of the Union's food law. At the national level there is enough left to work on and assist the implementation of EC law into the national law. And there are enough reminiscences of the old style of action by national states, to colour the step now taken to integrate and leave the old fragmentation behind. By focussing on European food law, this book limits itself to a small but important part of the larger story.

1.3 This book

This book gives an account of European[1] food law from the perspective of European Union (EU) law. After 2000 an overhaul of European food law was undertaken. The blueprint was laid down in the White Paper on Food Safety (2000). The general concepts and principles have been enacted in Regulation 178/2002, known as the General Food Law. In 2003 there followed a package of regulations regarding genetically modified foods, in 2004 a package regarding food hygiene and enforcement, in 2005 legislation on packaging[2] and allergen labelling, and in 2006 a regulation on nutrition and health claims. At the moment of writing these lines, proposals are in procedure regarding food additives, flavourings, enzymes, novel foods and labelling.

This large-scale reformulation of food law in the European Community (EC) is driven by several concerns, two of which stand out: the intimate connection of food law with the internal market, and the lessons learned from the major food scares of the 1990's. The innovated body of European food law is at the centre of this book. It is described and analysed. It is situated in the midst of those elements of European Community law that determine the conditions and restrictions for food law in the Community and in the Union's member states. Food law on the level of the European Community is flanked by many legal rules from the wider international plane, from the national legal systems of the member states and from self-regulation by the private sector. This book presents just a few excursions into these flanks. Our main attention is focussed on the food law of the EU itself, whilst the excursions serve to fit EU food law to these surroundings, or to underline its specific characteristics.

The development of European Communities' food law is traced over the three decades of its history since the end of the transition period used to create the common market. Knowledge of certain aspects of this development is necessary to understand the present situation of the internal market, harmonisation of national legislation, and food law. Readers will learn how law is used as an instrument to achieve food safety and to deal with food safety problems.

[1] Strictly speaking the European Union does not stand for all of Europe, but we take the freedom to write 'Europe' when we mean a major part of it with great influence on food law, even outside the territory of the European Union, even outside the European Economic Area. We feel this to be at least as justified as the habit of using the word 'America' when only a part of that continent is meant.
Legally speaking we would have to differentiate clearly when to use the term European Union, and when European Community, as these are quite different entities. Nevertheless, we will freely interchange these terms, using European Community especially when the specific characteristics of that Community are decisive for the subject matter at hand.

[2] Not discussed in this book.

1.4 Overview

This European Food Law Handbook opens with a rather concise introduction to some basic notions on law, national and international (Chapter 2 and 3). After this bird's eye excursion elementary aspects of European Union law are introduced with an ever increasing focus on food (Chapters 4, 5 and 6). Against this background the turbulent development of food law in Europe from the beginnings of the European Community to the release of the White Paper on Food Safety in 2000 is described in Chapter 7. Chapters 8-15 are dedicated to the content of European food law based on the design laid down in the White Paper. Chapter 8 discusses the general provisions laid down in the General Food Law. The following chapters deal with substantive matters of food law: the product (premarket approval requirements in Chapter 9 and food safety criteria in Chapter 10), the process (handling of food, Chapter 11). Chapter 12 addresses communication on food through labelling from the angle of informed choice. Chapter 13 analyses public powers regarding enforcement of food law and incident management. In the short Chapter 14 some aspects are discussed regarding the position of the consumer in EU food law. Chapter 15 deals with marketing standards and quality standards for fresh fruit and vegetables. Chapter 16 on international food law addresses the Codex Alimentarius and the WTO. Chapter 17 is about the contribution the private sector makes to the development of food law in the form of so-called private standards. Some concluding remarks are made in the final chapter.

Writing about law is reciting, describing, comparing and analysing the law. To separate the original instrument of law from description, analysis and comments, the legal texts as such, like articles from treaties, legislation, or case law appear in Law text boxes. In this way the reader is invited to look at the original and to develop personal views on the description and analysis made by the authors. To further stimulate recourse to the sources, references to the official documents are often made, especially to readily available sources on the world wide web. We have included some specific web sites although access to almost all the information is assured simply by googling. A consolidated version of the central General Food Law produced by the CONSLEG system of the Office for Official Publications of the European Communities is included at the end of the book. The account is supported by Diagrams that give a more or less graphical image of these basics and provide some additional information in a nutshell.

2. Introduction to law

Food law is a specialisation in law. Since not all readers will be familiar with legal science, its vocabulary and methods, this chapter provides a brief introduction to the science of law. Readers with a background in law may want to skip it.

2.1 Introduction to legal science

The word 'law' refers to limits set on various forms of human behaviour. Legal science does not concern itself with so-called descriptive laws, such as those found in natural sciences and economics, which describe how people or natural phenomena usually behave. Legal science is concerned with prescriptive laws, which are rules governing how people ought to behave. The rule that food shall not be placed on the market if it is unsafe,[3] does not say that this does not happen but that it should not happen. It imposes a duty on those who put food on the market. Likewise there are rules prescribing what is to be done if - despite this rule - unsafe food does appear on the market. Law in this sense is intended to prevent and resolve conflict by organising and describing the rights and duties in our society. Those rights and duties are overseen and interpreted by a system of courts, which is backed by the enforcement powers of police services.[4]

To a very large extent law is national. It is closely linked to the political structure of a given society. Political debates in parliaments, for example, often result in legislation. Obviously, this results in different laws from one country to the next, even where such laws are intended to regulate or define the same fields of activity.

Diagram 2.1. Law as a multifunctional word.

Law, a word about a word
Readers may have noted that already in the few lines above we have used the word 'law' with two different meanings, one referring to a system or academic discipline and one to a text. Other languages have different words for these two meanings. Law as a system is called *ius* in Latin, *le droit* in French, *das Recht* in German, *het recht* in Dutch. The law (the article is rarely used when referring to the system) as a text that forms part of legislation also known as 'act' or 'enactment' is *lex* in Latin, *la loi* in French, *das Gesetz* in German and *de wet* in Dutch.

---

[3] Article 14 (1) General Food Law. Discussed repeatedly in this book.

[4] Other means to promote the observance of the law, such as arbitration or mediation, are ultimately based on the public court system, for persons participating in these voluntary proceedings to apply the law know that ultimately the public power will back up the decisions reached in the voluntary proceedings, unless they are blatantly unjust (in which case the public court system can provide a solution itself).

Most national legal systems in the world can be grouped into one of two basic systems: the common law system, used in England and most of the former British colonies including the USA, India and Australia; and the civil law system, which is used across most of continental Europe and in its former colonies like parts of Latin America. English law is called common law because it was common to the whole of England. This uniformity was achieved at a very early stage. It began soon after the Norman Conquest of England in 1066, when King and Court travelled around the country hearing grievances. Because the same people sat in different courts, the same understanding of the law applied whichever court made the decision.

The common law system is based on the principle of deciding cases by reference to previous judicial decisions (known as 'precedent'), rather than by reference to written statutes drafted by legislative bodies. English law has evolved from the 12th century onwards in this way, through a body of reported cases, which present specific problems out of which specific points of law are extracted. Formulation of the law is bottom-up from a specific event to a general principle. Judicial decisions accumulate around a particular kind of dispute and general rules or precedents emerge. These precedents are binding on other courts at the same or a lower level in the hierarchy. The same decision must result from each situation in which the material or relevant facts are the same. The law evolves when opinions change as to which facts are relevant, and when novel situations arise.

The civil[5] law system is used by most of continental Europe and parts of Latin America. The main body of the law is written down in statutes or codes in a more or less logical and organised (codified) way across all the subject areas. Many modern codifications find their origins in the Napoleonic (civil[6] and criminal) codes of the 18th century.

In such systems, precedents are not normally recognised as binding on the courts, although they may have a strong influence through the quality of their reasoning and the authority of the courts that gave them. The civil law system results in a top-down system of codified law books, which are based upon broad principles and then broken into legal topics similar to those of the common law countries.

Generally speaking, civil law approaches are more cautious than common law approaches.[7] For almost a millennium, common law has developed in reaction to problems that took place and were dealt with in terms of liability. In civil law on the other hand, legislatures make it their business to foresee and prevent societal

[5] The word is derived from Latin. It referred to the law for the Roman citizens. Roman law has strongly influenced the development of legal thinking and scholarship in continental Europe.

[6] In the sense of 'private law', see section 2.7.

[7] John C. Coffee, Jr., The Rise of Dispersed Ownership: The Roles of Law & the State in the Separation of Ownership and Control, 111 Yale Law Journal 1 (2001): 62-63.

problems. In other words, civil law lays down the rules before the game is started, while common law invents the rules while the game is in progress.

In practice the differences between common law and civil law systems are not as big as they used to be. In common law countries the amount of statutory legislation is rapidly increasing and in civil law countries the courts take it upon themselves to fill in the gaps that have been left open by the legislators and to give authoritative interpretation to the written enactments. Changes in interpretation may have effects similar to changes in legislation.

This book reflects the civil law tradition in that it takes legislation and its underlying structure as frame of analysis.[8]

2.2 Sources of law

Rules do not just 'exist', they must originate from a body that is accepted by doctrine and the courts as having rule-making powers. These are the so-called sources of law.

Although differing in relative weight, in both common law and civil law systems statutory legislation ('written law') and case law[9] are the most important primary sources of law, with textbooks, journal articles, encyclopaedias, indices and digests making up a body of secondary sources. Primary sources of law are those sources where the rules are found. Other primary sources of law are international treaties and so-called unwritten law (like legal custom and general principles of law). Secondary sources provide tools that may help to understand the primary sources. They themselves do not give law, only opinions about law.

Diagram 2.2. Sources of law.

Written law	International treaties Legislation
Unwritten law	Case law Customary law Principles of law

European Community law resembles the civil law system more than the common law system. Legislation (treaties, regulations and directives) is the major source

[8] The abundant use of footnotes for references and additional information is typical for legal literature.
[9] We avoid the word 'jurisprudence'. It may be used to refer to case law, but also to legal science.

of European Community law. However, the importance of the case law of the European Court of Justice can hardly be overestimated.

The sources of international law are listed in the Statute of the International Court of Justice, presented in Law text box 2.1. The Statute is an integral part of the Charter of the United Nations, the world's largest international organisation. Therefore, the statement of Article 38 carries some authority.

Law text box 2.1. Sources of public international law, Article 38 Statute of the International Court of Justice (Source: www.icj-cij.org).

1. The Court, whose function is to decide in accordance with international law such disputes as are submitted to it, shall apply:
   a. international conventions, whether general or particular, establishing rules expressly recognised by the contesting states;
   b. international custom, as evidence of a general practice accepted as law;
   c. the general principles of law recognised by civilised nations;
   d. subject to the provisions of Article 59, judicial decisions and the teachings of the most highly qualified publicists of the various nations, as subsidiary means for the determination of rules of law.
2. This provision shall not prejudice the power of the Court to decide a case ex aequo et bono, if the parties agree thereto.

2.3 Branches of law

In legal doctrine different branches of law are distinguished. Most novices think first of criminal law, but there is more to law than just crimes and punishment. A first distinction is between public and private law. Private law is concerned with relations between parties who have no public power or do not exercise it. There are different kinds of private parties with different legal status. Among them are natural persons, associations of persons without legal personality, and various legal persons. National private law can be subdivided in several ways; one of them is an important division in the law of persons, law of property, contract law and non-contractual liability law (or tort law). Public law covers relations in which public authorities are involved as such: they are using their public powers. National public law can be subdivided into constitutional law, administrative law and criminal law. Diagram 2.3 presents an overview of the branches of law that are most relevant for food law.

2.4 Constitutional law

Constitutional law is concerned with the recognition of human rights and the organisational structure of the state and its government. Most countries have a written constitution defining the legislator, the executive, the powers of the courts, etcetera. For the European Union the founding treaties fulfil the function of constitution. Countries that do not have a written constitution still have parts of their customary law and legislation that deal with constitutional issues and define one way or another the legislator and the other essential organs of their state. Many constitutions create a balance of power between the organs or institutions of the state. By dividing the powers of the state over several organs they aim to protect freedom of the citizens. Constitutions also differentiate several basic functions of the state, such as maintenance of public order and peace, rule making, execution of policies, and impartial appraisal of conflicts about facts and law, and settlement of those conflicts by an authoritative judgement. All constitutions differentiate the functions of legislator, executive and judiciary, but differ in how they attribute these functions to different organs. The question 'who creates rules on food' is thus a question of constitutional law, and may be answered differently in different national systems.

In most countries and in the European Union (EU) public authorities - especially the executive branch - only have those powers that have been explicitly conferred on them by the legislator. This means that only the legislator can create new powers. When the powers involved touch the essentials of the state that are protected by the constitution, only the constitutional legislator can create new powers or re-arrange existing powers. A system of limited powers that guarantees the protection of human rights to the population and provide the people with instruments to defend themselves against abuse of power by the authorities, is often referred to as applying 'the rule of law'.[10] A consequence of the rule of law is that the government who makes the law is itself bound by these laws. If these authorities want to act in a way that the law does not allow, they have to follow the procedures for legislation to change the law first, before they can act.

Legislation is an important means of organising the law and expressing the opinions of society. Legislation is the name of a specific procedure for decision making by the legislator. The procedure is often used for different purposes: to decide on the budget, to make rules for general application or to take a solemn decision about a particular issue.

In general, legislation is equated with making rules, the decision that prescribes a certain set of consequences for situations that occur generally. The legislator decides on a formula that will be used each time when the conditions of the rule are fulfilled. The legislator does not know when this will be the case, nor how many times. The legislator has decided that all situations that belong to the scope of the legislation will be treated the same way for as long as the legislation is valid. This general application is one of the cornerstones of the rule of law

[10] Also the German expression '*Rechtsstaat*' is well known.

Diagram 2.3. An overview of the branches of law that are most relevant for food law. The most relevant branches for food have a lighter shade.

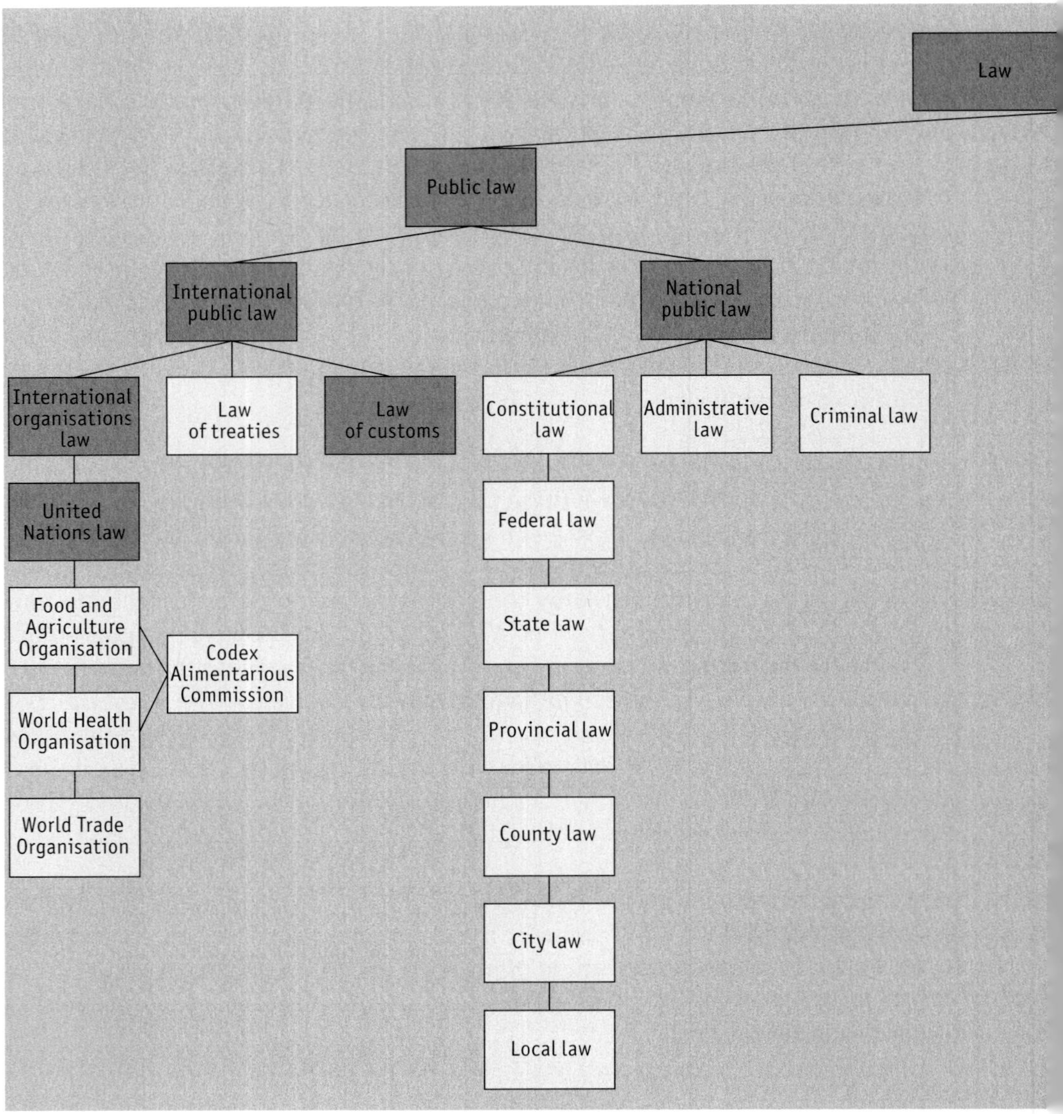

and a breach with the system of privilege where some or all have their private legislation, given only to them.

Common law countries use the terms Bill and Act. Bill indicates a proposal which the legislature can decide to make into binding law, the Act. The Acts that contain general prescripts, rules, are often called statutes. The word legislation is used primarily to indicate the process of making these statutes.

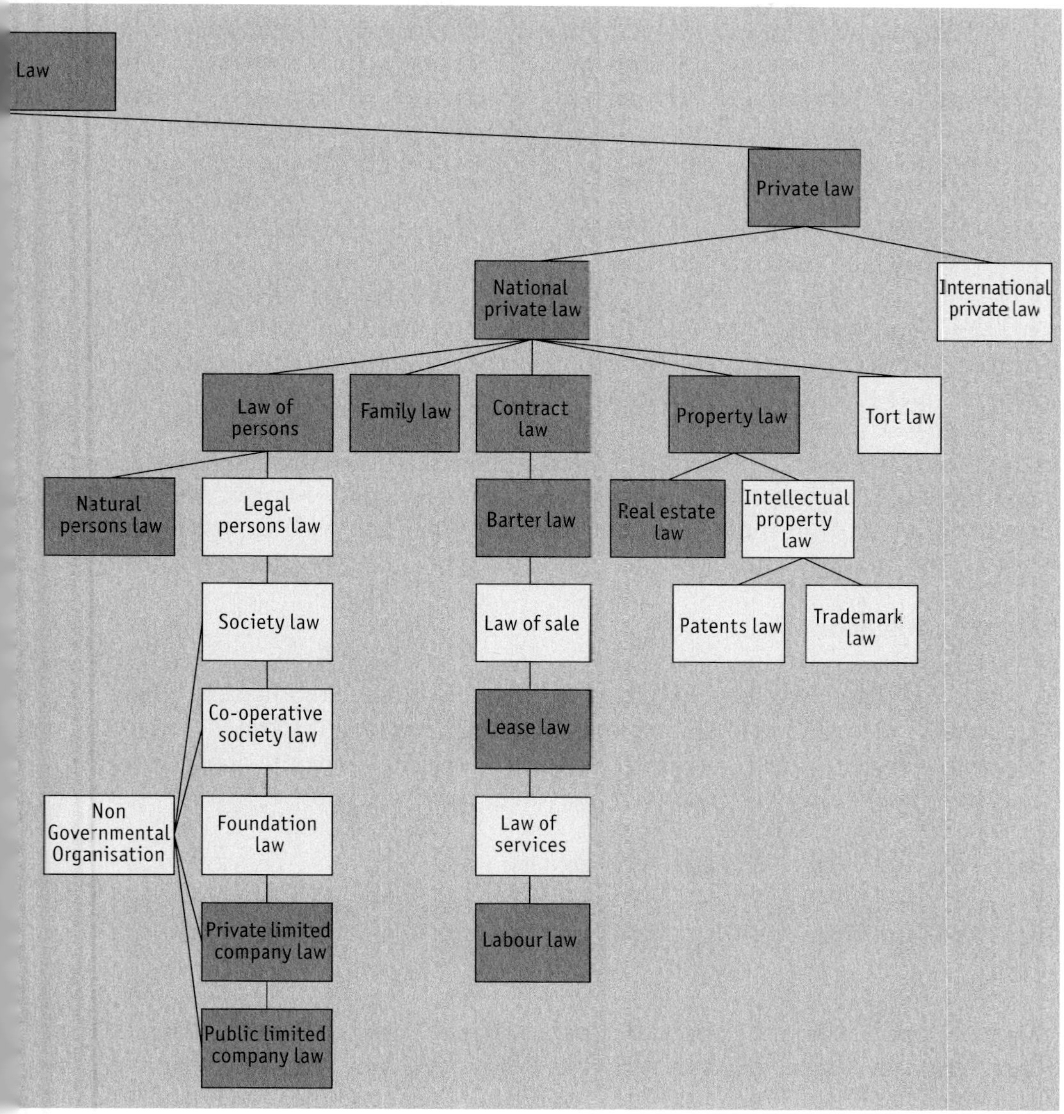

Within the confines of this book the word legislation has the meaning that is common to the civil law traditions: the rules made by the legislature.

2.5 Administrative law

Administrative law deals with the exercise of public powers by the executive in relation to private persons (including companies), and provides systems of legal protection for these persons. The exercise of public powers changes the legal position of persons irrespective of their consent. Therefore these persons need special protection attuned to the one-sided use of public, administrative, powers. Administrative law provides the rules for the legitimate use of public power and offers procedures to deal with complaints. For instance, rules concerning the process of obtaining authorisation to bring novel foods to the market, or how to contest such an authorisation granted to a competitor, belong to the field of administrative law.

The European Union has its own administrative law. The examples in the description below will be taken from the EU.

The (administrative) decision is a central concept in administrative law. A large part of the work of the executive branch of government is to apply in individual cases the rules that are laid down in legislation.

In food businesses it is usually the responsibility of the regulatory affairs department to deal with public authorities acting under administrative law. The legal department of businesses concerns itself more often with contracts and other private law matters.

2.5.1 The decision

A special way of applying legislation is to give administrative authorities the power to apply the rules in individual cases on situations or persons whose identity is known. The rule can make certain actions unlawful but provide the opportunity to ask permission for those actions in individual cases.

Law text box 2.2. Article 110(2) EC Treaty on decisions.

> A decision shall be binding in its entirety upon those to whom it is addressed.

The decision to give permission and the decision to refuse permission are examples of administrative decisions. Administrative law contains the rules that determine the types of administrative decisions, the rights and obligations they can prescribe, the way the authorities have to make these decisions, and the objections or appeals that can be lodged against the decision. Some legislation contains rules that can be applied to individual persons by administrative authorities. These authorities apply the legislation to the individual person when they take an administrative decision that specifies his rights or obligations. The legislation is not made to be applied only once, its rules have to be applied time and again, every time the conditions specified by the rules are fulfilled.

The administrative decision is made for one person whose name and address are known, and applies the general provisions to the individual case. The administrative decision can be made on request or on the initiative of the authority.

The decision is binding for the person to whom it is addressed. A decision can do many things. It can refuse a request by an individual person to apply the general legislation, it can impose an obligation and it can grant a right.

Diagram 2.4. The Administrative decisions: contents, initiative and example.

Administrative decisions	Contents	Initiative	Example from book
License	Permits an identified individual to do what is otherwise forbidden	Interested person requests	Market authorisation of a food (Chapter 9)
Subsidy	A grant of money from a public authority for a specified activity	Interested person requests or initiative of authorities	
Enforcement action	The authorities restore the lawful situation by removing illegal objects or restoring a missing object	Initiative of the public authority	Suspension of an unsafe food; closure of a food business (Chapter 13)
Administrative sanctions	Take away a right as punishment	Initiative of the public authority	
Other administrative decision	Varies	Varies	

2.5.2 License

The license is made on request, it gives permission to a person to do what is generally forbidden. The government wants to keep a close watch on some developments. The legislator makes a statutory regulation that declares specified activities illegal. But interested persons can request the executive power to grant an exception by a license. The license is an explicit decision that allows the activity to the person to whom the decision is addressed. The granting of a licence is subject to the administrative law rules on decision making. The licence may be granted under conditions and for a specified period of time. The conditions give the authorities the opportunity to make prescriptions and terms that apply the general conditions set by the legislation to the specific situation that the authorities know from the request and their information gathering.

Chapter 9 of this book deals with pre-market approval schemes. For certain types of foods like food additives, food supplements, genetically modified foods and novel foods a ban applies to bring them to the market. This ban can be lifted for certain foods after they have been proven to be safe.

2.5.3 Subsidy

A subsidy is an example of an administrative decision that determines a right for a specific person. The subsidy is an entitlement to a sum of money provided by an administrative authority for a specific activity for the benefit of a specific group of people, or the general interest of society. The subsidy is not a payment for goods or services supplied to the authority. The granting of a subsidy may contain obligations.

2.5.4 Administrative enforcement

An enforcement action is a set of physical acts taken by the administrative authority to end an infringement on the law.

Such infringement can be the presence of an object or situation that is not allowed. In food law this will mainly apply to unsafe foods. The authorities will remove the object or change the situation. An infringement can be an omission to do what legislation prescribes. The public authorities will end the omission. The offender will have to pay the costs in either case.

The authorities have to put the decision to take enforcement action in writing. It is an administrative decision that has to be notified to the persons responsible for the infringement before the measures are taken. The decision contains the following information:

- A specification of the action that will be taken.
- The legislation or statutory regulation that has been breached.
- The fact that the offender will have to pay the costs.
- The final period granted to the offenders to take the required measures themselves.

2.5.5 Injunction

An alternative for the enforcement action is to send the offender an administrative decision with the specification of his duty combined with a sum of money that he will have to pay for each day he fails to do his duty. Decisions of this type are sometimes called injunctions. Such a payment of money is not a sanction but a coercive sum of money. The offender can end the obligation to pay it by doing what s/he has to do. The sum of money will become larger for every period s/he fails to do that.

A sanction is a fixed sum of money that has to be paid for an offence already committed. The offender cannot undo the sanction by performing his duties.

2.5.6 General principles of good governance

In most legal systems, administrative authorities have to observe general principles of proper public administration or good governance in their contacts with persons and organisations. The principles are part of the legislation in some countries or have been created by administrative courts and accumulate in their case law. See Diagram 2.5. Examples of important principles and duties for administrative authorities.

Diagram 2.5. Examples of important principles and duties for administrative authorities.

Name	Content	Example
	Every administrative authority has the following obligations:	
Impartiality	Perform its duties without prejudice	
Integrety transparancy	Ensure that a personal interest of the public authority's decision makers does not influence its decision making on the matter	
Good decision making	Gather the necessary information concerning the relevant facts and the interests to be weighed	
Detournement de pouvoir	The authority may not use the power to make a decision for a purpose other than that for which it was given	Article 5 EC Treaty
Proportionality	The adverse consequences of a decision for one or more interested parties may not be disproportionate to the purposes to be served by the order	EC Treaty Protocol (30) on the application of the principles of subsidiarity and proportionality
Accountability transparancy	Administrative decisions must be based on reasons that carry the decision and have to state those reasons	Article 253 EC Treaty Article 41(2) 3rd indent of the Charter of Fundamental Rights of the European Union

2.5.7 Administrative procedure

The time limit for taking a decision on a request is determined by the legislation that the request wants to be applied. If that legislation does not provide a time limit a reasonable period must be respected. The authority must give the person who requests the decision the opportunity to state his views.

2.5.8 Administrative review

In some countries, the person to whom the administrative decision is addressed has the right to submit a notice of objection to the administrative authority which made the decision. The same right can be used against a written refusal to make a decision and the failure to make a decision in a reasonable period of time.

Such an objection gives the authority the obligation to reconsider its decision. The authority will change its decision when it is convinced by the objections or a part of them. The authority can also change its decision based on arguments that are not part of the objections.

When the authority rejects the objections, it is sometimes possible to appeal to a higher administrative authority by submitting a notice of appeal to the appeals authority.[11] This authority has the power to make a decision that changes the decisions of lower authorities.

2.5.9 Appeal to a judge

As a consequence of the rule of law it is always possible to appeal to an administrative court by submitting a notice of appeal to that court. The court is independent of the administrative authorities. It can declare the administrative decision null and void. The authority that made the decision will have to make a new one.

Law text box 2.3. Article 230 EC Treaty on the right to appeal an institution's decisions.

> Any natural or legal person may (...) institute proceedings against a decision addressed to that person or against a decision which, although in the form of a regulation or a decision addressed to another person, is of direct and individual concern to the former.

The fundamental difference between an administrative decision and legislation is indicated by the fact that appeal against such a decision is guaranteed and appeal against a particular act of legislation is usually refused. The separation of powers and the balance of power between the legislator and the judiciary makes it impossible for a judge to deal with general objections against an Act of the legislator. The judge has to decide on the internal consistency of the collection

[11] For example Article 36 of Regulation 1829/2003 on genetically modified foods gives the European Commission the power to review decisions and failures to act by the European Food Safety Authority.

of legislation, and has to strike down a piece of legislation that is in conflict with higher legislation. But this assistance of the judiciary to the legislator to preserve the intended meaning of two conflicting pieces of legislation is different from a court case that sets out to test all legislation.

The administrative decision must be tested against the legislation that was made to provide the rules for that kind of decision. Occasionally the test will reveal that the administrative authority made a mistake. In some of these cases it turns out that there are different opinions about what a rule means. The judge will select or construct the valid meaning of the rule from the history of the making of the rule, or from the place of the rule in the system of law. In some of these cases it will become clear that the rule is in contradiction to a higher rule. The judge will base his decision on the higher legislation which makes the disregarded rule meaningless.

The person for whom the decision is made has the rights of objection and appeal. The same rights are given to interested parties, persons whose interest is directly affected by the decision. The criterion of 'directly affected interest' separates the persons who are entitled to object from persons in the general public to whom this right is denied. The interests that qualify a person as directly affected are, for instance, his activities in the same line of business or property rights that will be affected. If the authority gives one person a licence and refuses to give the same licence to another person, this last person is an interested party if his circumstances are comparable.

2.6 Criminal law

Criminal law is the branch of law that defines crimes and fixes punishments for them. Criminal law also includes rules and procedures for preventing and investigating crimes and prosecuting suspected criminals, as well as provisions governing the constitution of courts, the conduct of trials, the organisation of police forces and the administration of penal institutions. A crime is an offence against the collective interest, and is prosecuted by the state. Punishments for criminal acts include fines or a prison sentence, but also probation or community service which are seen as alternatives for a prison sentence.[12]

Countries in the civil law tradition have a Criminal Code. It is an inventory of crimes and punishments. It contains the definitions of crimes, for example fraud, and states the limits to the punishment that a judge can give. In several countries

[12] In most countries capital punishment is considered contrary to human rights and has therefore been abolished. See for example Article 2(2) of the Charter of Fundamental Rights of the European Union: No one shall be condemned to the death penalty, or executed.

criminal rulings on poisoning and fraud provided a basis for early developments in food law.

The Code does not contain all the offences and crimes. The legislator makes laws on other issues and includes the definitions of new crimes for behaviour that is relevant for that issue and rejected by society.[13]

European Community legislation gives rules for several aspects of food law. Some of these are enforced with the weapons of criminal justice. The Community does not have its own criminal law nor the authority to prosecute and try suspects. The Community relies on the member states to provide these remedies. Article 17 of the General Food Law (Regulation 178/2002) on responsibilities lays the first responsibility to ensure that foods or feeds satisfy the requirements of food law on food and feed business operators. The member states are ordered to enforce food law, and monitor and verify that the relevant requirements of food law are fulfilled. In addition, 'Member States shall also lay down the rules on measures and penalties applicable to infringements of food and feed law. The measures and penalties provided for shall be effective, proportionate and dissuasive'.[14]

Traditionally criminal law has been used for the enforcement of legal obligations. Increasingly, however, enforcement powers are also granted under administrative law as described above. Even private law may play a role in enforcement. For instance, the rule that unsafe food may not be brought to the market may be enforced under criminal law if in (national) legislation it is defined as a crime to sell unsafe food. The legislator may also choose to apply administrative law sanctions instead of criminal law sanctions. Regardless of the system of sanctioning that has been chosen, the victim of unsafe food may claim compensation for damages under private liability law (see section 2.7.5 and Chapter 14, section 14.7).

2.7 Private law

Private law[15] deals with the enjoyment of rights and obligations, relations and disputes between individuals or organisations without public power. Public authorities wielding public power, (lawyers use the terminology 'public authorities as such'), are not involved in these relations and disputes.[16] A public authority can be a party in a private law contract, for instance when a ministry of the national government hires a caterer to provide daily lunches for its civil servants. In such

[13] An example is the legislation on road traffic. To drive away after an accident without taking care of the possible victims, and without identifying yourself is a crime that is defined in the traffic legislation. The same legislator has made the Criminal Code and the traffic legislation, and there is no special procedure for Codes, so there is no difference in hierarchy between the two.

[14] See Appendix A for the full text of this regulation.

[15] Also referred to as 'civil law', but not to be confused with civil law as distinct from common law.

[16] The use of public power is ruled by constitutional or administrative law.

a case the state represented by the government is treated as any other private contract partner, and public powers can not be used in this relationship. For private law, the role of public power is merely to provide the means and forum through which private disputes are resolved. If need be, the state provides an armed 'strong arm' (the police) to enforce the verdict of a judge in a private law suit.

The structure of private law can be described briefly by focussing on four complexes which each have their own character: the law of persons defining the status of a person, law of property defining the claims of persons on goods (including intellectual property on ideas), contract law defining legal agreements between persons, and non-contractual liability law (or tort law) for injuries and damages caused by other persons that have no other pre-existing relevant legal relation with the victim. In tort it is the act that caused the damage that created the legal relation.

2.7.1 Law of persons

In law persons can have two distinctly different characters: natural persons and legal persons together represent all there is on personality. Human beings are called natural persons in contrast to the legal person which is an artificial construct made by law.

Natural persons
The status of persons is directly connected to their existence as human beings, even before they are born. The rights of the person are confirmed and protected by human rights law and find many of their aspects regulated by private law. The right to a name, inviolability, family life, marriage, upbringing, protection of a minor by limiting his capacities to enter into binding legal arrangements and recognition of the full legal capacities of the natural person who comes of age, these are all part of private law. Countries with a civil law system usually have a Civil Code that provides the law of persons.

Legal persons
Legal personality is a legal construction that enables organisations to act and be treated in law like a human being. An organisation with legal personality can own property, make contracts, be liable and so on. Examples of legal personality are an association, a foundation, a limited company. The constructions that are possible and necessary to create a legal person are part of private law, usually a part of the Civil Code on persons.

Diagram 2.6 depicts the essential building blocks of a legal person: the need of a recognisable design of the entity, the need for an internal organisation, based on internal rules,[17] the need of representation and the need for rules on external relations and liabilities (Diagram 2.6). Representation is a legal construct that defines that the acts and omissions of one person are deemed to be the acts and omissions of another person. The law takes regard solely of the legal consequences for the person who is represented. The representative does not bind himself and so liabilities or contractual obligations do not entitle the creditors to demand compensation from the representative: their rights are rights in the relation to the person who was represented. Representation can be based on a contract. For

Diagram 2.6. A Legal person. The legal person is a fiction that enables organisation and the separation of rights and liabilities of the legal person from those of the (natural) persons who act on behalf of the legal person. The basis structure of the legal person is rather simple: replace the general meeting of the shareholders by the same meeting of the members of an association and the diagram turns into a scheme of a society. Most Civil Code countries have similar basic sets of possible legal persons. Public law legal persons have the same structure, although they are founded by special public legislation. That legislation provides their charter for the organisation and the internal and external rules.

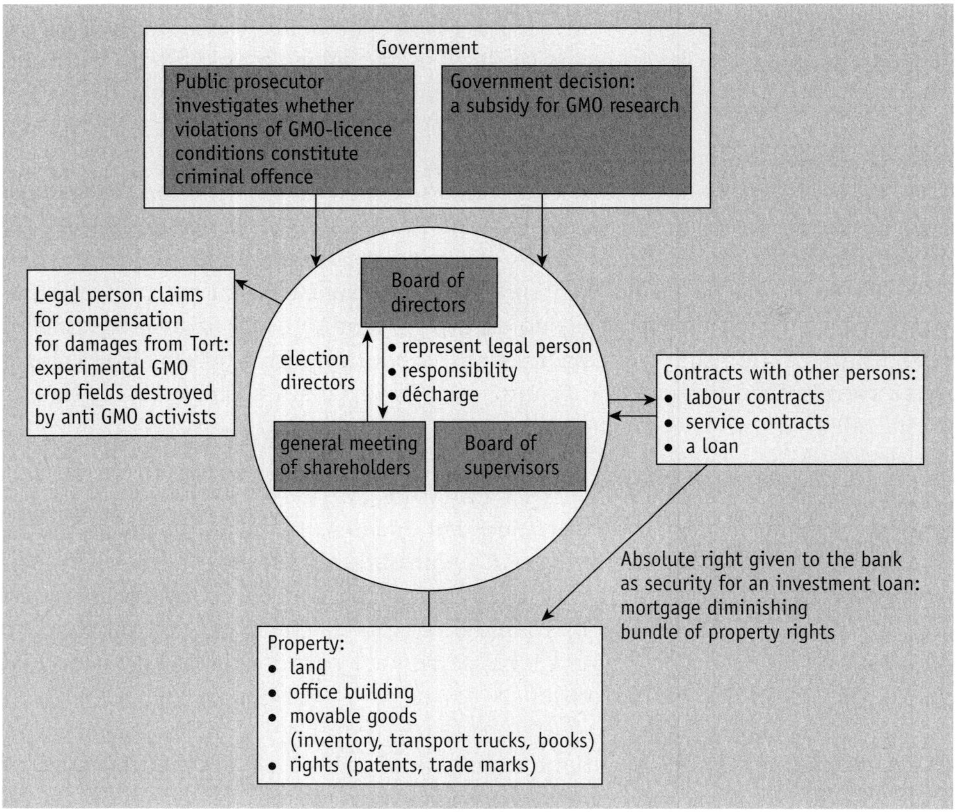

[17] The so-called Articles of Association.

the legal person representation is a necessity which has to be an element of the legal construct. Although legal persons can be created or directed by other legal persons, ultimately there must be one or more natural persons to create the construction and act on behalf of it.

Public law has its own legal persons such as the local communities, intermediate bodies like counties or provinces, special bodies like universities (these can also be private law legal persons) or the states of a federation and the state itself. The European Community is a legal person, the European Union is not. The consequence of this arrangement is that the EU can not be a party to treaties or any other relation, because the Union is literally a nobody.

2.7.2 Property law

In civil law countries the Civil Code prescribes a closed system for property law. Contrary to contract law (discussed in section 2.7.4), where the parties are free to use their creativity to design new types of contracts, the possible types of property rights are known. They are circumscribed by the Code. Property of tangibles, material goods like land, this book or a delivery van, is an absolute right.[18] It is absolute because it gives the owner rights that s/he can maintain against all other persons. Everyone has the obligation not to disturb the owner in his enjoyment of his property. Property right is not absolute in the sense that it would provide limitless powers. There are and always have been laws that limit the rights of the property owner. If you own a piece of land, your property right does not automatically allow you to build a factory or plant an orchard.

The Civil Code provides rules for certain other absolute rights, which are split-offs from property law. You may own the land, but someone else may own the (private law) right to build on that land. You may create the absolute right of a way for someone else to walk or drive over your land. Alternatively you could have made a contract with this person giving the same right to walk or drive over your land. Only it will turn out to be not quite the same right. The contract you made is a legal relation between the two persons involved. It is a personal obligation. If you sell your land and someone else becomes the owner, you are no longer able to allow your contract partner to pass over the land. If you create the absolute right of way, that right continues to exist even when you transfer the property of the land to someone else, or when you die. As an absolute right it has to be recognised by everyone, including the person who bought the land. Because of these consequences, private law has attached heavy formal demands on absolute rights. If you want to transfer ownership, everyone has to have the opportunity to know about the transfer. Therefore the law requires a deed made by a notary

[18] It is also called a 'real' right because it defines the relationship between a person and (not another person but) a thing (*'res'* in Latin).

public to describe which property is handed over. The transfer of property, as a result of a contractual obligation, can only be made by this deed and by the entry of the deed describing the transfer into a public register.

Diagram 2.7. Rights included in property.

Property: a bundle of rights
Right to access the property
Right to use
Right to consume (e.g. destroy)
Right to exclude use by others
Right to transfer

Special laws have created special property rights which are collectively known as intellectual property rights. Copyright, patent right, trademarks give the person who first entered them in the prescribed register the exclusive rights related to these creations. Like 'conventional' property rights, they give the owner absolute rights to be respected by everyone. Because of its importance for the food sector we will dwell on intellectual property a little bit longer than on the other elements of law discussed in this chapter.

2.7.3 Intellectual property

General

Intellectual property rights (IPRs) are like any other property rights – they allow the creator, or owner, of a patent, trademark, or copyright to benefit[19] from his or her own work or investment and to protect his or her new creations from others. The legal protection of these new creations is thought to encourage the expenditure of additional resources, which leads to further innovation.

The importance of intellectual property was first recognised in the Paris Convention for the Protection of Industrial Property in 1883 and the Berne Convention for the Protection of Literary and Artistic Works in 1886. Both treaties are administered by the World Intellectual Property Organization (WIPO).[20]

[19] Not necessarily, however, to use the invention. Somebody else's intellectual property right may prevent this.

[20] This section is based on texts and information published on WIPO's website: www.wipo.int, in particular the brochure 'What is intellectual property?'. On this website WIPO provides an e-book that provides a wealth of information on IPR: WIPO Intellectual Property Handbook: Policy, Law and Use, WIPO Publication No.489 (E). See the reference list for the hyperlink.

Intellectual property refers to creations of the mind: inventions, literary and artistic works, and symbols, names, and images used in commerce. Intellectual property is divided into two categories (Diagram 2.8):

- Industrial Property includes patents for inventions, trademarks, industrial designs and geographical indications.
- Copyright includes literary works such as novels, poems and plays, films, musical works, artistic works such as drawings, paintings, photographs and sculptures, and architectural designs. The book you are holding in your hands is also protected by copyright.[21] Rights related to copyright include those of performing artists in their performances, producers of phonograms, and those of broadcasters in their radio and television programs.

Diagram 2.8. Intellectual property rights.

Copy rights ©	Literature Art Music
Industrial property	Patent Trademark ® / ™ Industrial design Geographical indications

Some texts are by principle not protected by copyrights. Legislation for example must be accessible to all. Private standards by contrast may well be copyrighted and be made available only on condition of payment. See Chapter 17. This section will limit its attention to industrial property as these IPRs are the most important for the food industry.

Patents

A patent is an exclusive right granted for an invention, which is a product or a process that provides a new way of doing something, or offers a new technical solution to a problem. A patent provides protection for the invention to the owner of the patent. The protection is granted for a limited period, generally 20 years.

A patent owner has the right to decide who may – or may not – use the patented invention for the period in which the invention is protected. The patent owner may give permission, or a license, to other parties to use the invention on mutually agreed terms. The owner may also sell the right to the invention to someone else, who will then become the new owner of the patent. Once a patent expires, the protection ends, and an invention enters the public domain, that is, the owner

[21] The previous footnote respects the copy rights of WIPO by admitting that we made use of materials they made.

no longer holds exclusive rights to the invention, which becomes available to commercial exploitation by others.

All patent owners are obliged, in return for patent protection, to publicly disclose information on their invention in order to enrich the total body of technical knowledge in the world. Such an ever-increasing body of public knowledge is thought to promote further creativity and innovation in others. In this way, patents provide not only protection for the owner but also valuable information and inspiration for future generations of researchers and inventors.

Acquiring a patent

To acquire a patent the inventor needs to file a patent application. The patent application generally contains the title of the invention, as well as an indication of its technical field; it must include the background and a description of the invention, in clear language and enough detail that an individual with an average understanding of the field could use or reproduce the invention. Such descriptions are usually accompanied by visual materials such as drawings, plans, or diagrams to better describe the invention. The application also contains various 'claims', that is, information which determines the extent of protection granted by the patent.[22]

Innovative food business operators may acquire patents both on new food products and on new food production techniques.

An invention must, in general, fulfil the following conditions to be protected by a patent:

- It must be of practical use.
- It must show an element of novelty, that is, some new characteristic that is not known in the body of existing knowledge in its technical field.

This body of existing knowledge is called 'prior art'. The invention must show an inventive step that could not be deduced by a person with average knowledge of the technical field.[23]

Finally, its subject matter must be accepted as 'patentable' under law. In many countries, scientific theories, mathematical methods, plant or animal varieties, discoveries of natural substances, commercial methods, or methods for medical treatment (as opposed to medical products) are generally not patentable.

---

[22] In law the word 'claim' can be encountered in different meanings. Here it is an expression of a feature of an invention. In liability law it may be the amount of money the party to a conflict demands the other party to pay. In the context of 'nutrition and health claims' – see Chapter 12 – claim is the feature a food possesses according to its label or other communication.

[23] See for example Article 56 of the European Patent Convention.

Although heavily subject to ethical debate, the patentability of GMOs is recognised in a widening circle of countries and in the EU.[24]

A patent is granted by a national patent office or by a regional office that does the work for a number of countries, such as the European Patent Office (EPO). Under such regional systems, an applicant requests protection for the invention in one or more countries, and each country decides as to whether to offer patent protection within its borders. The WIPO-administered Patent Cooperation Treaty (PCT) provides for the filing of a single international patent application, which has the same effect as national applications filed in the designated countries. An applicant seeking protection may file one application and request protection in as many signatory states as needed.

Trademarks
A trademark is a distinctive sign, which identifies certain goods or services as those produced or provided by a specific person or enterprise. A trademark provides protection to the owner of the mark by ensuring the exclusive right to use it to identify goods or services, or to authorise another to use it in return for payment. The period of protection varies, but a trademark can be renewed indefinitely on payment of corresponding fees.

The possibilities are almost limitless. Trademarks may be one or a combination of words, letters, and numerals. They may consist of drawings, symbols, three-dimensional signs such as the shape and packaging of goods, audible signs such as music or vocal sounds, fragrances, or colours used as distinguishing features.

Example trademark

A well-known example of a trademark in the world of food is Coca Cola. This trademark encompasses words, the design of the letters used to write them, the colour of the background and the shape of the bottle in which the product is offered for sale.

In addition to trademarks identifying the commercial source of goods or services, several other categories of marks exist.

Collective marks are owned by an association whose members use them to identify themselves with a level of quality and other requirements set by the association.

[24] See Directive 88/44 on the legal protection of biotechnological inventions, Official Journal L 213, 30 July 1998, p. 13.

Certification marks are given for compliance with defined standards, but are not confined to any membership. They may be granted to anyone who can certify that the products involved meet certain established standards. The internationally accepted 'ISO 22.000' food safety and quality standards are an example of such widely recognised certifications.

Acquiring a trademark

First, an application for registration of a trademark must be filed with the appropriate national or regional trademark office. The application must contain a clear reproduction of the sign filed for registration, including any colours, forms, or three-dimensional features. The application must also contain a list of goods or services to which the sign would apply. The sign must fulfil certain conditions in order to be protected as a trademark or other type of mark. The trademark must be distinctive, so that consumers can distinguish it from other trademarks identifying other products, as well as identify a particular product with it. It must neither mislead nor deceive customers or violate public order or morality.

Finally, the rights applied for can not be the same as, or similar to, rights already granted to another trademark owner. This may be determined through search and examination by the national office, or by the opposition of third parties who claim similar or identical rights.

Almost all countries in the world register and protect trademarks. Each national or regional office maintains a Register of Trademarks, which contains full application information on all registrations and renewals, facilitating examination, search, and potential opposition by third parties. The effects of such a registration are, however, limited to the country (or, in the case of a regional registration, countries) concerned.

In order to avoid the need to register separately with each national or regional office, WIPO administers a system of international registration of marks. This system is governed by two treaties, the Madrid Agreement Concerning the International Registration of Marks and the Madrid Protocol. A person who has a link (through nationality, domicile, or establishment) with a country party to one or both of these treaties may, on the basis of a registration or application with the trademark office of that country, obtain an international registration having effect in some or all of the other countries of the Madrid Union.

Industrial design

Instead of or in addition to a trademark, a company may protect the distinctive features of its brand as industrial design. An industrial design is the ornamental or aesthetic aspect of an article. The design may consist of three-dimensional features, such as the shape or surface of an article, or of two-dimensional features, such as patterns, lines or colour.

To be protected under most national laws, an industrial design must be new or original and non-functional. This means that an industrial design is primarily of an aesthetic nature and any technical features of the article to which it is applied are not protected.

Example industrial design

> Again the shape of the Coca Cola bottle can be mentioned as an example of a feature which can be protected.

When an industrial design is protected, the owner – the person or entity that has registered the design – is assured an exclusive right against unauthorised copying or imitation of the design by third parties.

In most countries, an industrial design must be registered in order to be protected under industrial design law. As a general rule, to be eligible for registration, the design must be 'new' or 'original'. Different countries have varying definitions of such terms, as well as variations in the registration process itself. Generally, 'new' means that no identical or very similar design is known to have existed before.

Once a design is registered, a registration certificate is issued. Following that, the term of protection is generally five years, with the possibility of further periods of renewal up to, in most cases, 15 years.

Generally, industrial design protection is limited to the country in which protection is granted. Under The Hague Agreement Concerning the International Deposit of Industrial Designs, a WIPO-administered treaty, a procedure for an international registration is offered. An applicant can file a single international deposit either with WIPO or the national office of a country which is party to the treaty. The design will then be protected in as many member countries of the treaty as the applicant wishes.

Geographical indication

A geographical indication is a sign used on goods that have a specific geographical origin and possess qualities, reputation or characteristics that are essentially attributable to that place of origin. Most commonly, a geographical indication includes the name of the place of origin of the goods. Agricultural products typically have qualities that derive from their place of production and are influenced by specific local factors, such as climate and soil. Whether a sign is recognised as a geographical indication is a matter of national law. Geographical indications may be used for a wide variety of products, whether natural, agricultural or manufactured.

Geographical indications differ from trademarks. A trademark is a sign used by an enterprise to distinguish its goods and services from those of other enterprises. It gives its owner the right to exclude others from using the trademark. A trademark will often consist of a fanciful or arbitrary name or device. A geographical indication tells consumers that a product is produced in a certain place and has certain characteristics that are due to that place of production. It may be used by all producers who make their products in the place designated by a geographical indication and whose products share specified qualities. Unlike a trademark, the name used as a geographical indication will usually be predetermined by the name of the place of production.

See also Chapter 12, section 12.10 on protected designation of origin and protected geographical indication. An important difference between a trademark and a geographical indication is that a trademark is usually individual – the owner enjoys exclusive rights to it – and a geographical indication is collective – every company in the region that meets the requirements may use it.

2.7.4 Contract law

A contract, in law, is an agreement that creates binding obligations between the parties involved. It is a mutual exchange of promises, which the law will enforce. In general, to make a valid contract, there must be two or more separate and definite parties, an offer, an acceptance, the intention to create legal relations, and a capacity to do so.[25] The protection of public morality, public policy or public security is part of the demands for a valid contract. In general, contracts may be either oral or written. Certain classes of contracts, however, must be concluded in writing in order to be enforceable. These may include contracts involving the sale and transfer of real estate.

The obligation to fulfil the promise made in the contract, can be upheld in a court of law. In case of non-fulfilment the debtor (the one who made the promise) is liable for the damages suffered by the creditor (the one to whom the promise was made).

To a large extent food safety is ensured through so-called self-regulation or private standards. Contract law is a legal instrument for this self-regulation. Companies may for instance make contracts with other companies, or a foundation promoting food quality, to apply certain measures to prevent contamination of food during its production and to submit to third party audits to prove that they have adhered to their contracts.

[25] In most jurisdictions young children are considered incapable of concluding contracts.

2.7.5 Non-contractual liability law (tort law)

The fourth main complex of private law is tort law, the law of wrongful acts that have to be prevented, and if they occur have to be stopped and for which compensation of damages has to be paid.[26] In the civil law tradition this category has a name that varies with the language. The name indicates that it is an unlawful occurrence that must be restored by the use of private law, irrespective of the criminal law relevance of the act. Private law contains several types of liabilities, but the most prominent liability is non-contractual liability.

The name non-contractual liability for this separate category is the result of a negative selection. The common law tradition uses the word 'tort'. The crucial aspect of this category is the absence of a legal relation between the persons who get involved in a non-contractual liability situation. The event that brings them within the reach of this part of the law is itself the trigger of the sequence: event > unlawful > duty to restore lawful situation with compensation of damages.

Torts mainly encompass those obligations and duties of care which we all owe to others who may foreseeably be affected by our actions, balanced by a standard test of reasonableness that is applied so as not to extend torts to remote and generalised effects. To pass that test, a defendant must demonstrate that s/he has taken all reasonable care to avoid acts and omissions, which could reasonably be foreseen to cause injury or harm to others. Torts are essentially civil wrongs that provide individuals with a course of action (that is, a wrong which the courts recognise and are willing to judge) for damages to atone for the breach of a legal duty of care. Damages for torts may include economic as well as physical damage, but will not include prison terms or fines, as such remedies are reserved for public authorities. A consumer who suffers ill health due to a food company neglecting its duty of care with respect to food safety could thus seek compensation both for damage to health, and for economic damage in the form of medical costs or income losses. A special type of tort is based on EC and national legislation on product liability.[27]

The same behaviour that caused the tort with its private law consequences may also be defined as a criminal act. Then the public prosecutor for crimes will start criminal proceedings to obtain a conviction and punishment

[26] The word tort comes via Old French from the Latin *tortus*, the past participle of *torquere* which means to twist. So tort is (something) twisted.
[27] See Chapter 14, section 14.7.

Law text box 2.4. DCFR on liability.[28]

1:101: Basic rule
(1) A person who suffers legally relevant damage has a right to reparation from a person who caused the damage intentionally or negligently or is otherwise accountable for the causation of the damage.

2.8 Substantive and procedural law

Many branches of law can be subdivided into substantive law and procedural law. Substantive law are the rules that define a particular right or duty. Property right is an example of substantive private law, theft is substantive criminal law. The civil law states separate substantive law from procedural law and present them in different law books. They have a Code Civil with a Code of Civil Procedure, and a Criminal Code with a Criminal Procedural Code.

2.8.1 Code of Civil Procedure

The Code of Civil Procedure provides the rules for court cases to solve conflicts about private law. The rules prescribe how to begin a case and how to proceed before the court of first instance and to appeal to higher courts. Civil procedures depend to a large extent on the action and reactions of the parties. One of them serves a writ of summons to the other to state his claims and to announce that he has put the case on the court's agenda. The other party has three options. He can end the conflict by doing what the writ of summons demands. He can contest the claims in court, or not react at all.

The judge follows the steps taken by the parties:
- When the summoned party does not appear in court, the judge will decide the case on the basis of the writ, unless the demands are evidently unreasonable.
- When both parties present their case in court the judge will consider the claims and the offers of the parties to provide evidence. The judge will direct who will present evidence in court and will determine its value. The parties in the case can reach an agreement to settle the conflict out of court at any time.

[28] European Union law is mainly administrative law. The EU has no criminal and private (civil) law system. For criminal and civil issues the EU depends on the national legal systems in the member states. For this reason EU legislation often relates to national civil law. To acquire a better understanding of the common aspects and differences in civil law in the member states, a group of scholars has been asked to devise a common frame of reference. In 2008 these scholars published a draft common frame of reference (DCFR) setting out the common principles found in civil law in the member states in the *form* of a code. This DCFR is not (EU) law but a description of national law in the member states. For a hyperlink see the reference list.

The Code of Civil Procedure determines the rules for every step in court cases, but the parties decide first whether they want to take that step. They put each other in positions that ask for a reaction.

2.8.2 Execution of judgements in private law cases

The decision of the court becomes final when all possibilities for appeal are exhausted or parties decide to refrain from appeal. In most cases the parties will carry out the orders of the court. They know that the final decision of the court is an enforceable title that provides a writ of execution. This writ can be used by the party whose rights are recognised and affirmed by the court to force the other party to do what the judge ordered. The writ of execution is brought by a bailiff. His position can vary according to the national system of law. A bailiff is either a public law officer or a private person who has made it a business to carry out the provisions of the Code of Civil Procedure to force obedience to court decisions.

He will serve the writ to the party that has to pay or surrender an object. When that party still refuses to do that, the bailiff will take the step to execute the judgement. He will take possession of the assets and sell them to raise the money determined by the court. In some cases he can take the disputed object and hand it over to the winning party. Police forces will protect the bailiff if necessary.

2.8.3 Criminal Procedural Code

The substantive law on major and minor crimes can be found in the Criminal Code and other legislation in civil law countries. The way to determine whether a specific person has committed a particular crime is determined by procedural criminal law. The Criminal Procedural Code sets the rules for when and under what conditions a suspect can be apprehended, how long he may be interrogated, when he has to be brought before a judge. The Code likewise contains the rights of an accused person to have the assistance of a lawyer, and access to a judge to guard the time limits set for the different periods of detention. It prescribes how the court proceedings are properly run.

The judge can apply the substantive law (Is a crime committed? Is the defendant guilty? Which punishment is right?) only when the proceedings follow the prescripts of procedural criminal law. The judges who try criminal cases lead the proceedings actively.

2.9 International private law

The national private law of each country has its own characteristics that make it different from the other national private law systems. It develops in the national system of law, changes under its influence and exerts its influences on it. Society adapts to changing ideas, some lead to changes in legislation. Private law that was the same in different countries does not remain the same under diverging developments. Legal transactions that remain in one system are not involved with divergent law, and as far as their own system is changing, they adapt. But legal transactions that have effects in more than one legal system are bound to encounter an impossible situation.

2.9.1 Conflict rules

A contract that was negotiated in London between a Chinese and an American company, after the Chinese invitation to open negotiations during a business faire in Milano, was finally agreed on by an exchange of signed documents in Amsterdam. What contract law will be applied when some differences of opinion between the contract parties have to be settled? Who determines the choice of the national private law, especially when the result depends on the chosen system?

The answer is that these complications are very old and familiar and have lead to a system of so-called conflict rules.[29] That central part of private international law has a set of solutions like the rule that the law on contract follows the place where the contract was closed. So when the last offer was accepted by the other party and this acceptance has been communicated to the party that made the last offer. The second part of the answer is that many contract parties who close contracts across national borders know this. They can accept it, but they can not know in advance where the negotiations will end. So it is more likely that the choice of the national law system is a part of the contract. Private parties have this freedom because national governments generally accept the rule that the conflict rule will give way to a choice of the applicable law.

This is different when real estate is involved. When, for example, a French person buys a piece of land from a Polish person who lives in Paris. They have closed the deal in Spain and the land property lies in Poland. Here the conflict rule is simple: Polish law does not accept any choice of a legal system to transfer property rights on land in Poland. Only Polish law can be applied. Real estate is governed by the law of the land where it is situated (this principle is known as '*lex loci*').

See Law text box 2.5. Convention on the law applicable to contractual obligations for a treaty made to clarify the Freedom of choice. See Law text box 2.6. Convention on the law applicable to contractual obligations, Title II Uniform rules, Article 4 Applicable law in the absence of choice, for another solution when the contract parties made no choice.

[29] In this expression the word 'conflict' does not refer to a conflict between the parties but between different legal systems. Which system applies and which has to give way? The conflict rule decides.

Law text box 2.5. Convention on the law applicable to contractual obligations (Source: Official Journal C 027, 26 January 1998, pp. 34-46).

Title II Uniform rules, Article 3 Freedom of choice

1. A contract shall be governed by the law chosen by the parties. The choice must be expressed or demonstrated with reasonable certainty by the terms of the contract or the circumstances of the case. By their choice the parties can select the law applicable to the whole or a part only of the contract.
2. The parties may at any time agree to subject the contract to a law other than that which previously governed it, whether as a result of an earlier choice under this Article or of other provisions of this Convention. Any variation by the parties of the law to be applied made after the conclusion of the contract shall not prejudice its formal validity under Article 9 or adversely affect the rights of third parties.
3. The fact that the parties have chosen a foreign law, whether or not accompanied by the choice of a foreign tribunal, shall not, where all the other elements relevant to the situation at the time of the choice are connected with one country only, prejudice the application of rules of the law at the country which cannot be derogated from by contract, hereinafter called 'mandatory rules'.
4. The existence and validity of the consent of the parties as to the choice of the applicable law shall be determined in accordance with the provisions of Articles 8, 9 and 11.

Law text box 2.6. Convention on the law applicable to contractual obligations (Source: Official Journal C 027, 26 January 1998, pp. 34-46).

Title II Uniform rules, Article 4 Applicable law in the absence of choice

1. To the extent that the law applicable to the contract has not been chosen in accordance with Article 3, the contract shall be governed by the law of the country with which it is most closely connected. Nevertheless, a separable part of the contract which has a closer connection with another country may by way of exception be governed by the law of that other country.
2. Subject to the provisions of paragraph 5 of this Article, it shall be presumed that the contract is most closely connected with the country where the party who is to effect the performance which is characteristic of the contract has, at the time of conclusion of the contract, his habitual residence, or, in the case of a body corporate or unincorporate, its central administration. However, if the contract is entered into in the course of that party's trade or profession, that country shall be the country in which the principal place of business is situated or, where under the terms of the contract the performance is to be effected through a place of business other than the principal place of business, the country in which that other place of business is situated.

2.9.2 Harmonisation of different national private law

In practice different systems of law operating simultaneously are not convenient. They can make transactions quite complicated. A basic value of law is its function to settle conflicts by clarity of rules.

One of the ways to provide more transparent law is to make the law of different systems more alike. This can be done by negotiating treaties that determine the rules for a particular part of the law. There are many treaties on this subject, the 'Convention on the law applicable to contractual obligations' is one example, the 'United Nations Convention on Contracts for the International Sale of Goods (CISG)' is another.

The CISG gives legal rules on how to make a contract for the international sale of goods. It specifies the obligations of the buyer and seller, remedies for breach of contract and other aspects of the contract. The Convention entered into force on 1 January 1988. It is one of the results of the United Nations Commission on International Trade Law (UNCITRAL). This Commission was established by the General Assembly in 1966.[30]

The International Chambers of Commerce sponsored the Incoterms 2000, the INternational COmmercial TERMS like FOB (Free On Board) and CIF (Costs, Insurance, Freight) that determine who pays the costs.[31]

An International Code Civil is unlikely to occur. Nevertheless, the EU has taken a seemingly small step in the direction of such a code. The European commissioned scholars to draft the Common Frame of Reference mentioned above. In theory this text has no legal significance. It will however be on the table when legislators in the EU member states work on their national Civil Code and in this way inspire them to at least consider the ideas laid down in the Common Frame of Reference.

2.10 International public law

International public law is the subject of the next chapter.

2.11 European Union law

European law is not included in the diagram representing the branches of law. It started as international law with special traits setting it apart on the edge between international law and the law of a new type of federation of national states. In the fifty years of its existence, European law acquired a Union and

[30] UNGA Resolution 2205 (XXI) of 17 December 1966.

[31] ICC Official Rules for the Interpretation of Trade Terms, ICC Publication No. 560, 2000 Edition.

several branches of law combining international, constitutional, administrative and a little private law; in short it is all over the place, a system of its own. This is the subject of Chapter 4.

2.12 Food law

The scheme representing the branches of law as applied in legal scholarship does not depict a part of law called food law. Much of food law is national and European administrative law, the rules safeguarding the relationships between public authorities and private persons, when authorities apply public power to limit or enable certain actions by private persons. So food law might be presented as a subdivision of administrative law. However that classification would lose sight of other important traits of food law. Next to administrative law, food law can also be private law. Self-regulation by food producers to set quality standards or to give certain methods of producing food a special place in the market uses private law contracts or private law legal persons in addition to, or in lieu of, action by public authorities. Food law is concerned with intellectual property rights when patents or trade marks are used in the production or sale of feed or food. These rights are also part of private law. Food law is involved with state or constitutional law when a Food Authority is founded to perform certain functions essential for a proper food law system (see Chapter 5). Food law provides instruments that make reality of human rights guaranteed by national constitutions and international treaties (see Chapter 3). Food law is also assisted by criminal law when the government classifies certain actions detrimental to the common good (e.g. food safety) as punishable offences (see Chapter 13). In short food law is a functional part of law that combines parts of several branches of law in a coherent body of law to serve its goals.

To illustrate this in Diagram 2.3, food law would be a contorted line or some other bend figure collecting parts of several branches. The lighter shades in the diagram indicate those branches that are most important for food law.

A functional part of law is defined not by the scholarly distinctions but by the function rules have in relation to a societal phenomenon regardless of the place of these rules within the legal system. All rules relating to environmental issues together form the functional domain of environmental law; all rules relating to food together form the functional domain of food law.

2.13 The intertwining branches of law

The branches of law are tools that enable specialisation. They are separated to understand their particularities and to organise the court system, the lawyers' practice and education. In practice the law from different branches operates at the same time and together determine a particular situation. The *Vitis vinifera* L. case illustrates a part of these twines (Diagram 2.9).

Diagram 2.9. The law and Vitis vinifera L., *of the* Vitaceae *family.*

The vines: stages in the development of a grape	Interactions with law	Branch of law	Treated in this book
Selecting plants	Plant breeders' rights	Intellectual property rights	section 2.7.3
Cultivar, variety	Patent	Intellectual property rights	section 2.7.3
List of varieties	UNECE Standard FFV-19 Table grapes, 2007 Exhaustive list of small-berry varieties	International public law	Chapter 15
Genetically modified: not yet	Regulation (EC) No 1829/2003 of the European Parliament and of the Council of 22 September 2003 on genetically modified food and feed. Regulation (EC) No 1830/2003 concerning traceability and labelling of GMOs.	EU law	Chapter 9, section 9.5 GM foods Chapter 11, section 11.2.5 GMO-traceability Chapter 12, section 12.12 GM Labelling
Grapes grown		Private law	section 2.7
The regulated grape	Planted in vineyard. Property land	Property rights private law	section 2.7.2 Property law
Grape pest	EU supports producers who replant their vineyards to combat phylloxera	EU law Administrative law	section 2.5.3
Grape harvest		Private law	
Transport		Private law	
International trade		Private law	
Sea freight			
Crossing borders	Export /import	Customs law	

Fresh table grapes	Regulation 1234/2007 Single Common Market Organisation Part IX: Fruit and vegetables	EU law	Chapter 15
	UNECE Standard FFV-19 Table grapes, 2007 Geneva Protocol	International public law	Chapter 3
	EU Regulation 2789/1999 Marketing standard for table grapes	EU law	Chapter 5
	Codex standard for table grapes (Codex Stan. 255-2007)	International substantive law	Chapter 16
	OECD Brochure Table Grapes	Legal position not clear: soft law?	
Dried grapes	UNECE DDP-11 Standard Dry and Dried Produce. International Quality Standard	EU law Transformed into national law	Chapter 5
Σταφίδα Ζακύνθου	'(Stafida Zakynthou)' Sun-dried grapes, Greece PGI entered in Register of Protected Designations of Origin (PDO) and Protected Geographical Indications (PGI):.	EU law	Chapter 12
Fruit juices[1]	EU Marketing standard Regulation 2200/96/EC	EU law	
Grape juice (including grape must)	EU Marketing standards Regulation 2201/96	EU law	
Other grape musts[2]	Directive 2001/112/EC fruit juices and certain similar products	EU law	
Wine of fresh grapes	Council Regulation (EC) No 1493/1999 of 17 May 1999. CMO wine		
	Commission proposal to reform CMO wine COM(2007) 372 final		
Fortified wines	Part XII: Wine OJ L 299/75 L 299/75		
Grape must other[3]			

Grape jams			
Grape jellies	Directive 2001/113/EC		
Grape marmalades	Directive 2001/113/EC		
Fresh grapes other than table grapes	Directive 2001/113/EC		
Wine vinegar			
Piquette			
Wine lees			
Grape marc			
	Sale to trader	Contract law	section 2.7.4
	Export	Contract law	section 2.7.4
	Distribution	Contract law	section 2.7.4
	Retail sales to consumer	Contract law	section 2.7.4

The European Union occupies a leading position on the world wine market, accounting for 45% of wine-growing areas, 65% of production, 57% of global consumption and 70% of exports in global terms (http://ec.europa.eu/agriculture/markets/wine/index_en.htm)

[1] Excluding grape juice and grape must of subheadings 2009 61 and 2009 69.

[2] Other than those in fermentation or with fermentation arrested otherwise than by the addition of alcohol.

[3] Than that of heading 2009, excluding other grape must of subheadings 2204 30 92, 2204 30 94, 2204 30 96 and 2204 30 98.

3. International public law

3.1 Basic characteristics of international law: the nation state[32]

European nation state dominance left a profound mark on current international law. Every state is sovereign; it does not recognise any higher authority that could bind it against its will with legal rules or measures. Every state is equal in this respect. The preponderant position of the nation state has been such as to determine the words and concepts that we use to describe law. For law that is valid all over the world, the term is not 'global law' or 'world law' but 'international law'. The laws of local or regional communities are always subsumed by the national law that is valid in the territories of these communities. National law has become the benchmark used to position all other layers of law. See for this terminology Diagram 3.1 'Different levels of law'. In an international system with

Diagram 3.1. Different levels of law. The terminology for different levels of law, and one concrete example of regulation of the same subject on most, if not all, levels.

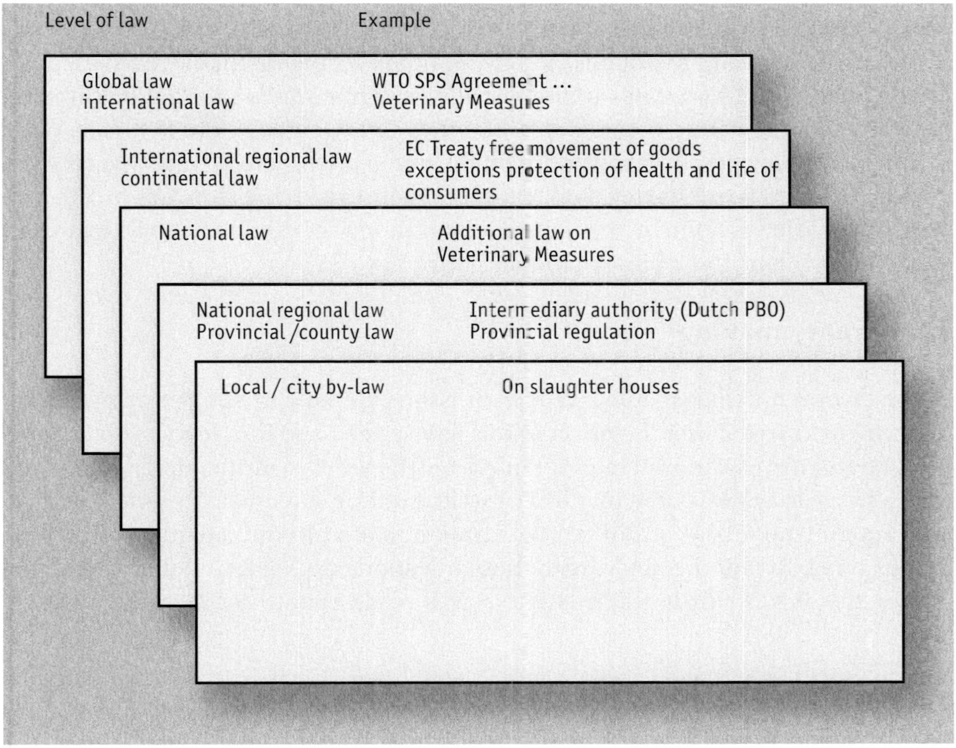

[32] Literature: Malanczuk, Peter, Akehurst's Modern Introduction to International Law, 7th ed London, 1997.

sovereign states the only possible law is the kind that is based on the agreement of all participating states. There are two types of law that fulfil this condition: customary law and treaty.

3.1.1 Customary law

The oldest type of law is customary law, the way of doing things as they were traditionally done. Tradition alone, however, is not enough to create law. It must be combined with the conviction that it is an obligation to behave as tradition requires. The consent of the states is shown by their behaviour. Customary law can exist on a regional scale but also worldwide.

3.1.2 Treaty

The second type is an explicit agreement binding the state to the other states that participate in creating this contract. In international law such a contract is called a treaty (an agreement, charter, convention, covenant, protocol; many names are used). It can be created in many ways, ranging from a simple telephone conversation between two Ministers of Foreign Affairs, to an extended negotiation process lasting a decade and involving almost all states of the world.[33] Treaties can be made between two states, and every other arrangement of treaty partners up to the current 192[34] states in the world, from trilateral to multilateral binding documents. Given the sovereignty of the individual states, there is no separate, higher overseeing power or institution in the pure nation state system that controls whether the international legal obligations are observed. Let alone enforced. The only supervision is done by the nation states among themselves. See Diagram 3.2 for the basic character of international public law.

3.1.3 Treaty making

In the law on making treaties, important issues are how to determine when the moment has arrived that the negotiations have ended and the treaty text becomes final (signature); when a state is bound by the treaty (ratification); when the treaty starts to work (entry into force) so its binding force has become a reality; and finally who takes care of the documents related to the negotiation process (depositary). Part of the answers to these questions can be found in the excerpts in Law text box 3.1 from the treaty that was made about how to make a treaty,

---

[33] For example: the 1966 United Nations' Covenants on Human Rights took twelve years of negotiation to adopt a final text in 1966, and then another ten years to collect enough ratifications to enter into force in 1976.

[34] Acceptation as a Member State of the United Nations is currently the best-established yardstick for recognition by the international community as an independent state. At the moment (2008) the UN has 192 members and since a fiercely neutral state like Switzerland accepted UN membership (in 2002 as the 190th) this criterion has gained in weight.

Diagram 3.2. Basic character of international public law.
One multilateral treaty between 6 states generates 15 bilateral relations. Each state has to maintain these relations for a particular subject matter with every other state. If all 192 states of the present international system were related by a multilateral treaty there would be 18,145 bilateral relations to maintain for that one treaty only. Many countries have hundreds of treaties to maintain. Not all of them are binding to all other states, but the total number of treaty relations remains staggering.

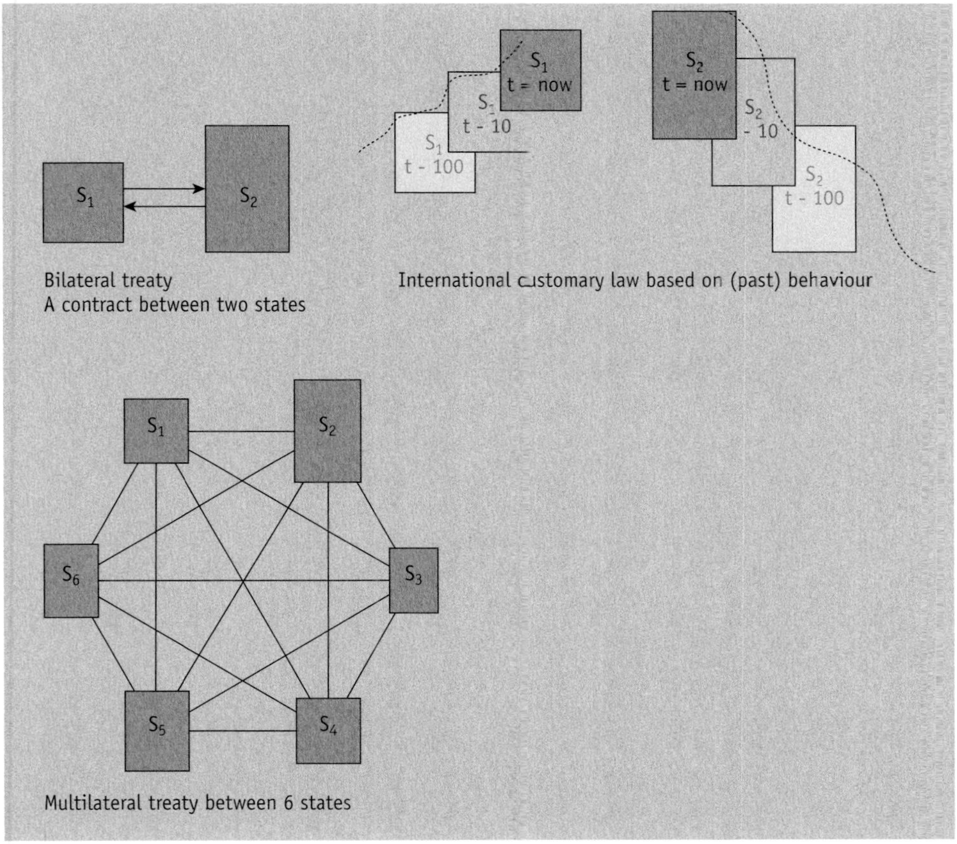

replacing prior customary law on this subject. The Charter of the United Nations serves as an example of the steps from signing a treaty to ratification and entry into force. See Law text box 3.2.

Law text box 3.1. Some excerpts from the 1969 Vienna Convention on the Law of Treaties (signed in 1969, entered into force eleven years later. See Abstract at the end of this Law text box). Source: United Nations Treaty Series (UNTS) 1155, p. 331 (See Reference for hyperlink).

Vienna Convention on the Law of Treaties

The States Parties to the present Convention,

Considering the fundamental role of treaties in the history of international relations,

Recognizing the ever-increasing importance of treaties as a source of international law and as a means of developing peaceful co-operation among nations, whatever their constitutional and social systems,

Noting that the principles of free consent and of good faith and the *pacta sunt servanda* rule[1] are universally recognized,

...

Affirming that the rules of customary international law will continue to govern questions not regulated by the provisions of the present Convention,

Have agreed as follows:

PART I. INTRODUCTION

Article 1

Scope of the present Convention

The present Convention applies to treaties between States.

...

Article 2

Use of terms

1. For the purposes of the present Convention:
   (a) 'treaty' means an international agreement concluded between States in written form and governed by international law, whether embodied in a single instrument or in two or more related instruments and whatever its particular designation;
   (b) 'ratification', 'acceptance', 'approval' and 'accession' mean in each case the international act so named whereby a State establishes on the international plane its consent to be bound by a treaty;
   (c) 'full powers' means a document emanating from the competent authority of a State ...

...

PART II. CONCLUSION AND ENTRY INTO FORCE OF TREATIES

SECTION 1. CONCLUSION OF TREATIES

Article 6

Capacity of States to conclude treaties

Every State possesses capacity to conclude treaties. ...

Article 9

Adoption of the text

1. The adoption of the text of a treaty takes place by the consent of all the States participating in its drawing up except as provided in paragraph 2.
2. The adoption of the text of a treaty at an international conference takes place by the vote of two-thirds of the States present and voting, unless by the same majority they shall decide to apply a different rule.

Article 10

Authentication of the text

The text of a treaty is established as authentic and definitive:

(a) by such procedure as may be provided for in the text or agreed upon by the States participating in its drawing up; or

(b) failing such procedure, by the signature, signature *ad referendum* or initialling by the representatives of those States of the text of the treaty or of the Final Act of a conference incorporating the text.

Article 11

Means of expressing consent to be bound by a treaty

The consent of a State to be bound by a treaty may be expressed by signature, exchange of instruments constituting a treaty, ratification, acceptance, approval or accession, or by any other means if so agreed.

...

Article 84

Entry into force

1. The present Convention shall enter into force on the thirtieth day following the date of deposit of the thirty-fifth instrument of ratification or accession.
2. For each State ratifying or acceding to the Convention after the deposit of the thirty-fifth instrument of ratification or accession, the Convention shall enter into force on the thirtieth day after deposit by such State of its instrument of ratification or accession.

Article 85

Authentic texts

The original of the present Convention, of which the Chinese, English, French, Russian and Spanish texts are equally authentic, shall be deposited with the Secretary-General of the United Nations.

IN WITNESS WHEREOF the undersigned Plenipotentiaries, being duly authorized thereto by their respective Governments, have signed the present Convention.

DONE at Vienna, this twenty-third day of May, one thousand nine hundred and sixty-nine.

Abstract:-

The Convention was adopted on 22 May 1969 and opened for signature on 23 May 1969 by the *United Nations Conference on the Law of Treaties*. The Conference was convened pursuant to General Assembly resolutions 2166 (XXI) of 5 December 1966 and 2287 (XXII) of 6 December 1967. The Conference held two sessions, both at the Neue Hofburg in Vienna, the first session from 26 March to 24 May 1968 and the second session from 9 April to 22 May 1969. In addition to the Convention, the Conference adopted the Final Act and certain declarations and resolutions, which are annexed to that Act. By unanimous decision of the Conference, the original of the Final Act was deposited in the archives of the Federal Ministry for Foreign Affairs of Austria. Entry into force on 27 January 1980, in accordance with article 84(1).

[1] This means: agreements are binding (footnote added to original text).

Law text box 3.2. Signature, ratification and entry into force. *Example: The Charter of the United Nations. Source: Article 110 Charter.*

The Charter of the United Nations was signed on 26 June 1945, in San Francisco, at the conclusion of the United Nations Conference on International Organization, and came into force on 24 October 1945. The Statute of the International Court of Justice is an integral part of the Charter.	
Five authentic language texts Depository	The present Charter, of which the Chinese, French, Russian, English, and Spanish texts are equally authentic, shall remain deposited in the archives of the Government of the United States of America. Duly certified copies thereof shall be transmitted by that Government to the Governments of the other signatory states.
Signature	IN FAITH WHEREOF the representatives of the Governments of the United Nations have signed the present Charter.
Place and Time	DONE at the city of San Francisco the twenty-sixth day of June, one thousand nine hundred and forty-five. The present Charter shall be ratified by the signatory states in accordance with their respective constitutional processes.
The ratifications depository	The ratifications shall be deposited with the Government of the United States of America, which shall notify all the signatory states of each deposit as well as the Secretary-General of the Organization when he has been appointed.
Entry into force Deposit of ratifications A protocol of deposited ratifications	The present Charter shall come into force upon the deposit of ratifications by the Republic of China, France, the Union of Soviet Socialist Republics, the United Kingdom of Great Britain and Northern Ireland, and the United States of America, and by a majority of the other signatory states. A protocol of the ratifications deposited shall thereupon be drawn up by the Government of the United States of America which shall communicate copies thereof to all the signatory states.
	The states signatory to the present Charter which ratify it after it has come into force will become original Members of the United Nations on the date of the deposit of their respective ratifications.

3.1.4 Multilateral treaties

Multilateral treaties form a complicated network because all the participating states are bound to each other on a bilateral basis. Even with a small number of participants it is difficult to visualise this network (see Diagram 3.2). If the states were to create an organisation instead of their contractual constructions the rules would be different, as each state becomes a member of the organisation and the relations between the individual states are governed by the rules of the organisation. These rules deal with membership, general meetings, and meetings of a governing board that has to look after the interests of the organisation and its members in the periods between the meetings of all participating states. The rules will also have to specify the powers of the different organs of the organisation. That would be a difficult issue in a pure nation state system. Compare Diagrams 3.2, 3.3 and 3.9 for the differences between treaties and two types of international organisations.

3.2 International organisations

In the twentieth century the national state system was transformed in certain aspects. First of all, many international organisations came into existence to perform tasks that are necessary in an interacting complex world.[35] The establishment of international organisations began in the second half of the eighteenth century for mail and telegraph. The large wave of international organisations came in the twentieth century.[36] These organisations are subjects of international public law,[37] breaking the monopoly of the nation state on participation in that law. Most of these organisations are still the instruments of the nation states. They are intergovernmental organisations: only the representatives of governments can participate in these organisations, each decision requires the consent of each member nation state, or in other words, no state can be bound against its will. Almost all decisions are mere advice: they do not create an obligation. Once a decision has been made, only the governments of the nation states can apply them in their territory and in their international behaviour. There is no supervising agency in an intergovernmental system. The faithful execution of international obligations can only be guaranteed by mutual surveillance among the participating states.

International organisations are the regular meeting place for many governments; the organisations seek to improve the effectiveness of their work by fostering negotiations to formulate and accept treaties, which bind the states. In that way they try to compensate for their inherent weakness by combining the strong elements of organisation and treaty. The organisation provides a stable meeting place with regulated procedures and permanent availability; the treaties provide their binding legal force. Increasingly, treaties contain a conciliation procedure to improve implementation of the treaty by the states by means of external surveys and help.

---

[35] Schermers, Henry G. and Niels M. Blokker, International Institutional Law. Unity within Diversity, 4th ed., The Hague, 2004.

[36] The General Postal Union was established in 1864, the International Telegraphic Union in 1865 and the International Meteorological Union in 1878.

[37] The position of non-governmental organisations (NGOs) in international law is debated, but by no means unimportant nor a novelty, like examples such as the International Red Cross show. Some international public organisations give observer status to NGOs, allowing them to participate and to have informal influence. The Statutes of the Codex Alimentarious Commission allow NGOs to attend meetings of the Commission as observers. Several subcommittees of the Codex Commission started as committees of NGOs that were taken over later on by public authorities. The position of transnational corporations merits attention as an influential special type of non-governmental organisation.

Diagram 3.3. A model of an intergovernmental international organisation. All participating states keep full sovereignty. All decisions are made by unanimity. All decisions do not bind the states: they formulate declarations, wishes or advice. Sometimes some purely procedural matters can be decided by majority vote.

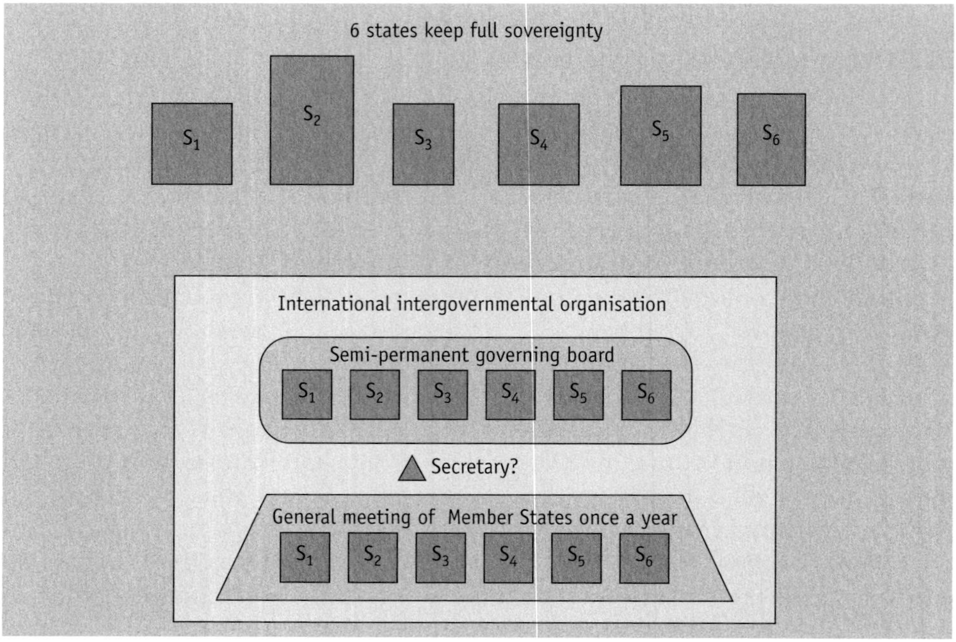

3.3 The United Nations

The UN is founded by the United Nations, the Allies in the Second World War, to be the central worldwide international organisation of all peace loving nations. It was made to succeed where the League of Nations had failed. It was made differently and different because of that. The UN was meant to be the guarantee for peace and the promoter of worldwide economic and social cooperation. The tasks and the powers to deal with them were laid down in its founding treaty, the Charter of the United Nations. See Diagram 3.4 for the Preamble (the solemn opening statement) beginning with the words: 'We the Peoples of the United Nations, determined ...'. The structure of the UN Charter is presented in law text box 3.3. Notice the sequences of the articles about purposes and tasks placed before the articles on the organisation that is created to do the job. See Law text boxes 3.3 and 3.4.

Law text box 3.3. The structure of the UN Charter: tasks determine organisation.

Task	Before	Means
I. Purposes and Principles	III	Organs
	IV	The General Assembly
	V	The Security Council
VI Pacific Settlement of Disputes	VII	Action with respect to threats to the peace, …
IX International Economic, and Social Co-operation;	X	The Economic and Social Council
XI Declaration Regarding Non-	XII	International Trusteeship System
Self-Governing Territories	XIII	The Trusteeship Council
I-XIII Tasks from the UN	XIV	The International Court of Justice
organisation	XV	The Secretariat
I-XV Demands from the UN	XVIII	Amendments
practice	XIX	Ratification and Signature

Diagram 3.4. The Charter of the United Nations.

Preamble

We the peoples of the United Nations determined

- to save succeeding generations from the scourge of war, which twice in our lifetime has brought untold sorrow to mankind, and
- to reaffirm faith in fundamental human rights, in the dignity and worth of the human person, in the equal rights of men and women and of nations large and small, and
- to establish conditions under which justice and respect for the obligations arising from treaties and other sources of international law can be maintained, and
- to promote social progress and better standards of life in larger freedom,
- to practice tolerance and live together in peace with one another as good neighbours, and
- to unite our strength to maintain international peace and security, and
- to ensure, by the acceptance of principles and the institution of methods, that armed force shall not be used, save in the common interest, and
- to employ international machinery for the promotion of the economic and social advancement of all peoples,
- HAVE RESOLVED TO COMBINE OUR EFFORTS TO ACCOMPLISH THESE AIMS
- Accordingly, our respective Governments, through representatives assembled in the city of San Francisco, who have exhibited their full powers found to be in good and due form, have agreed to the present Charter of the United Nations and do hereby establish an international organization to be known as the United Nations.

Chapter	
I	Purposes and Principles
II	Membership
III	Organs
IV	The General Assembly
V	The Security Council
VI	Pacific Settlement of Disputes
VII	Action with respect to threats to the peace, breach of the peace, and acts of aggression
VIII	Regional arrangements
IX	International Economic, and Social Co-operation;
X	The Economic and Social Council
XI	Declaration Regarding Non-Self-Governing Territories
XII	International Trusteeship System
XIII	The Trusteeship Council
XIV	The International Court of Justice
XV	The Secretariat
XVI	Miscellaneous Provisions
XVII	Transitional Security Arrangements
XVIII	Amendments
XIX	Ratification and Signature

A basic element of the structure of the Charter is the sequence of articles that put the purposes and tasks in first place and the organisation in second place. The organisation is made to serve the tasks. See for the tasks Law text box 3.4 Purposes and principles of the United Nations.

Law text box 3.4. Purposes and principles of the United Nations, Articles 1 and 2 United Nations Charter.

We the peoples of the United Nations
... our respective governments ... do hereby establish an international organization to be known as the United Nations.

CHARTER OF THE UNITED NATIONS

CHAPTER I

PURPOSES AND PRINCIPLES

Article 1

The Purposes of the United Nations are:

1. To maintain international peace and security, and to that end: to take effective collective measures for the prevention and removal of threats to the peace, and for the suppression of acts of aggression or other breaches of the peace, and to bring about by peaceful means, and in conformity with the principles of justice and international law, adjustment or settlement of international disputes or situations which might lead to a breach of the peace;
2. To develop friendly relations among nations based on respect for the principle of equal rights and self-determination of peoples, and to take other appropriate measures to strengthen universal peace;
3. To achieve international co-operation in solving international problems of an economic, social, cultural, or humanitarian character, and in promoting and encouraging respect for human rights and for fundamental freedoms for all without distinction as to race, sex, language, or religion; and
4. To be a centre for harmonizing the actions of nations in the attainment of these common ends.

Article 2

The Organization and its Members, in pursuit of the Purposes stated in Article 1, shall act in accordance with the following Principles.

1. The Organization is based on the principle of the sovereign equality of all its Members.
2. All Members, in order to ensure to all of them the rights and benefits resulting from membership, shall fulfil in good faith the obligations assumed by them in accordance with the present Charter.
3. All Members shall settle their international disputes by peaceful means in such a manner that international peace and security, and justice, are not endangered.
4. All Members shall refrain in their international relations from the threat or use of force against the territorial integrity or political independence of any state, or in any other manner inconsistent with the Purposes of the United Nations.
5. All Members shall give the United Nations every assistance in any action it takes in accordance with the present Charter, and shall refrain from giving assistance to any state against which the United Nations is taking preventive or enforcement action.
6. The Organization shall ensure that states which are not Members of the United Nations act in accordance with these Principles so far as may be necessary for the maintenance of international peace and security.
7. Nothing contained in the present Charter shall authorize the United Nations to intervene in matters which are essentially within the domestic jurisdiction of any state or shall require the Members to submit such matters to settlement under the present Charter; but this principle shall not prejudice the application of enforcement measures under Chapter VII.

The overview of the Charter shows the large amount of attention for 'threats to the peace, breaches of the peace and acts of aggression'. Compare it with the attention given to the rights of people, their social and economic development. See Diagram 3.5 for the organisation chart of The United Nations System. It is a simplification of a complicated structure with councils, commissions, committees, funds, programmes, specialised agencies, related organisations subsidiary bodies

Diagram 3.5. The organisational chart of The United Nations System.

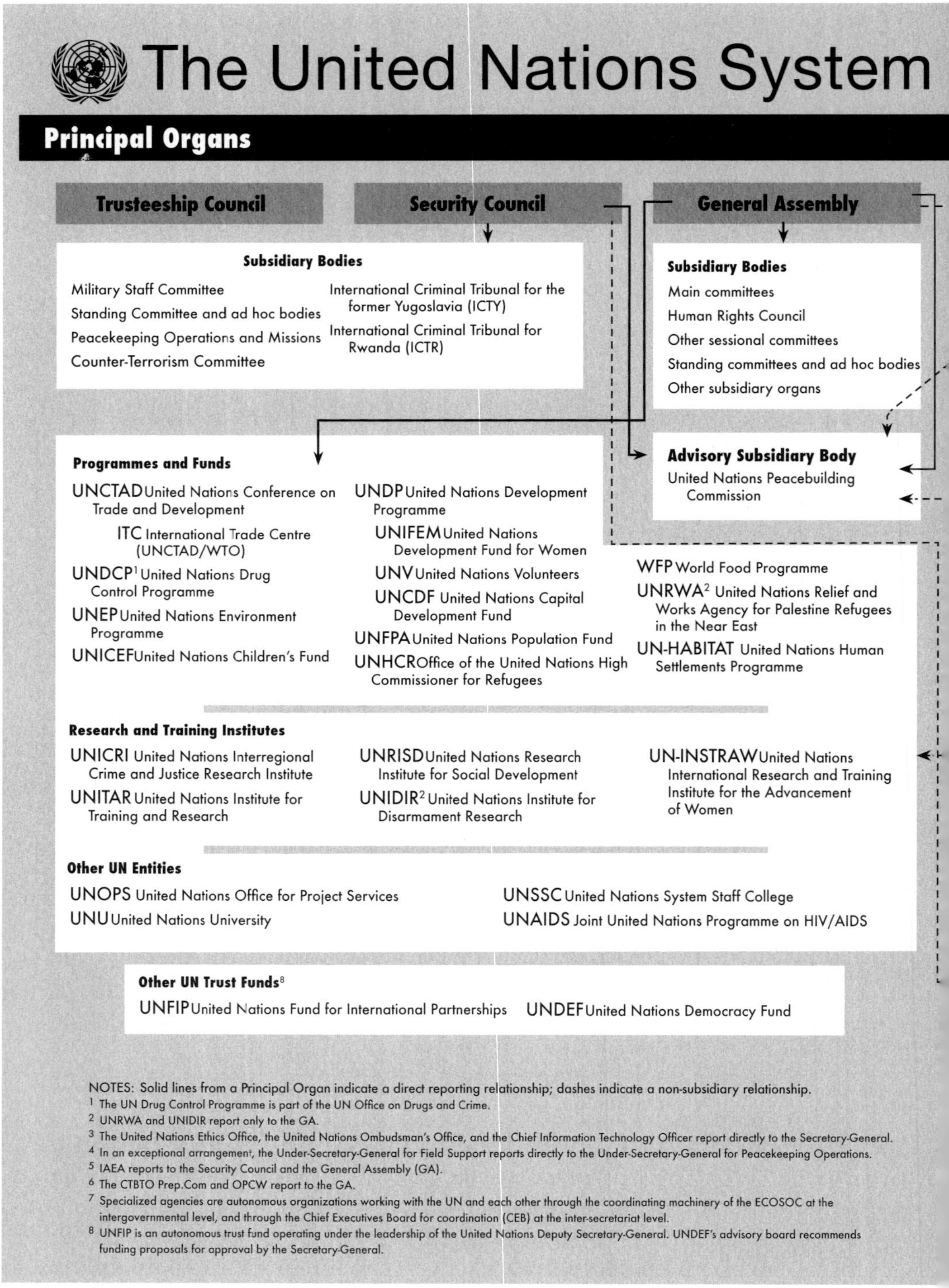

Economic and Social Council

Functional Commissions

Commissions on:
- Narcotic Drugs
- Crime Prevention and Criminal Justice
- Science and Technology for Development
- Sustainable Development
- Status of Women
- Population and Development

Commission for Social Development

Statistical Commission

Regional Commissions

Economic Commission for Africa (ECA)

Economic Commission for Europe (ECE)

Economic Commission for Latin America and the Caribbean (ECLAC)

Economic and Social Commission for Asia and the Pacific (ESCAP)

Economic and Social Commission for Western Asia (ESCWA)

Other Bodies

Permanent Forum on Indigenous Issues

United Nations Forum on Forests

Sessional and standing committees

Expert, ad hoc and related bodies

Related Organizations

WTO World Trade Organization

IAEA[5] International Atomic Energy Agency

CTBTO **Prep.Com**[6] PrepCom for the Nuclear-Test-Ban Treaty Organization

OPCW[6] Organization for the Prohibition of Chemical Weapons

International Court of Justice

Specialized Agencies[7]

ILO International Labour Organization

FAO Food and Agriculture Organization of the United Nations

UNESCO United Nations Educational, Scientific and Cultural Organization

WHO World Health Organization

World Bank Group

- IBRD International Bank for Reconstruction and Development
- IDA International Development Association
- IFC International Finance Corporation
- MIGA Multilateral Investment Guarantee Agency
- ICSID International Centre for Settlement of Investment Disputes

IMF International Monetary Fund

ICAO International Civil Aviation Organization

IMO International Maritime Organization

ITU International Telecommunication Union

UPU Universal Postal Union

WMO World Meteorological Organization

WIPO World Intellectual Property Organization

IFAD International Fund for Agricultural Development

UNIDO United Nations Industrial Development Organization

UNWTO World Tourism Organization

Secretariat

Departments and Offices

OSG[3] Office of the Secretary-General

OIOS Office of Internal Oversight Services

OLA Office of Legal Affairs

DPA Department of Political Affairs

UNODA Office for Disarmament Affairs

DPKO Department of Peacekeeping Operations

DFS[4] Department of Field Support

OCHA Office for the Coordination of Humanitarian Affairs

DESA Department of Economic and Social Affairs

DGACM Department for General Assembly and Conference Management

DPI Department of Public Information

DM Department of Management

UN-OHRLLS Office of the High Representative for the Least Developed Countries, Landlocked Developing Countries and Small Island Developing States

OHCHR Office of the United Nations High Commissioner for Human Rights

UNODC United Nations Office on Drugs and Crime

DSS Department of Safety and Security

UNOG UN Office at Geneva

UNOV UN Office at Vienna

UNON UN Office at Nairobi

Published by the United Nations Department of Public Information

DPI/2470–07-49950–December 2007–3M

and the six principal organs. See Diagram 3.6 for the principal organs of the United Nations: composition, functions, powers and place in the Charter.

Diagram 3.6. The principal organs of the United Nations: composition, functions, powers and place in the Charter. Source: UN Charter.

Composition Chapter III	UN Charter	Functions and powers
General Assembly 192 member states Session September-December Seat New York	Chapter IV 1. Article 10 2. 11(1) 3. 13 4. 14	Discussion and recommendations 1. Discuss any questions or any matters within the scope of the present Charter 2. Consider the general principles and cooperation to maintain international peace and security 3. Initiate studies and make recommendations to promote international co-operation. See Law text box 3.5 4. Recommend measures for the peaceful adjustment of any situation
Security Council 5 permanent members 10 chosen by UNGA from the regional groups	Chapter V	1. Primary responsibility for the maintenance of international peace and security 2. Acts on behalf of the member state 3. Plan system to regulate armaments to promote international peace and security with the least diversion for armaments of the world's human and economic resources
Economic and Social Council 54 members, 18 elected each year for three years	Chapter X Article 62(1) Article 62(2) 6. Article 62(3) 7. Article 62(4) 8. Article 63(1)	With respect to international economic, social, cultural, educational, health, and related matters: Make or initiate studies and reports Make recommendations to a. UNGA b. UN Members c. Specialised agencies concerned Promote respect for, and observance of, human rights and fundamental freedoms for all. Prepare draft conventions for submission to UNGA Call international conferences Make agreements to bring Specialised agencies in the UN system Coordinate of the specialised agencies through consultation

Composition Chapter III	UN Charter	Functions and powers
Specialised agencies	Chapter IX Article 57 Chapter X Article 63	19 Specialised agencies Food and Agriculture Organization of the United Nations World Health Organization. The World Trade Organisation is not a Specialised agency
International Court of Justice	Chapter XIV	The principal judicial organ Comply with ICJ decision Recourse to the Security Council Advisory opinion ICJ Statute determines the competence of the Court Only States can be parties in Court case Parties decide to put a dispute before the Court
Secretariat	Chapter XV	Secretary-General is the chief administrative officer Appointed by General Assembly after Security Council recommendation SG in all meetings of UNGA, Security Council, and ECOSOC

The activities of the Trusteeship Council ended in 1994 when Palau became independent. The Trusteeship Council had supervised the nation states that held former colonies in trust on behalf of the League of Nations. After the end of the First World War eleven colonies became international mandate areas entrusted to member states of the League of Nations. The UN took over after the Second World War. The eleven territories were administrated by independent states to guide these areas to independence.

The founders of the UN tried to separate the politics of security in terms of war and peace as far as possible from the politics of security in terms of basic needs and prosperity. The Security Council is responsible for the threats of violence, the Economic and Social Council (ECOSOC) is responsible for social and economic security. These two approaches to the common wealth are placed on either side of the General Assembly (UNGA), the weak main organ of the UN. See Law text box 3.5 on international cooperation in the economic and social aspects of society as a UN task.

Law text box 3.5. UN International Economic and Social Co-operation.

Charter of the United Nations
CHAPTER IX
INTERNATIONAL ECONOMIC AND SOCIAL CO-OPERATION
Article 55
With a view to the creation of conditions of stability and well-being which are necessary for peaceful and friendly relations among nations based on respect for the principle of equal rights and self-determination of peoples, the United Nations shall promote:
a. higher standards of living, full employment, and conditions of economic and social progress and development;
b. solutions of international economic, social, health, and related problems; and international cultural and educational co-operation; and
c. universal respect for, and observance of, human rights and fundamental freedoms for all without distinction as to race, sex, language, or religion.

Article 56
All Members pledge themselves to take joint and separate action in co-operation with the Organization for the achievement of the purposes set forth in Article 55.

Article 57
1. The various specialized agencies, established by intergovernmental agreement and having wide international responsibilities, as defined in their basic instruments, in economic, social, cultural, educational, health, and related fields, shall be brought into relationship with the United Nations in accordance with the provisions of Article 63.
2. Such agencies thus brought into relationship with the United Nations are hereinafter referred to as specialized agencies.

3.3.1 UN programmes, funds and conferences

The major difference between the programmes, funds and specialised agencies is that the programmes and funds are based on the authority of the UNGA to 'establish such subsidiary organs as it deems necessary for the performance of its functions'.[38] These entities report to the UNGA.

3.4 The specialised agencies of the United Nations

The United Nations (UN) family of organisations is a well-known grouping of intergovernmental organisations performing different kinds of services for the world. Some members of this family are specialised agencies like the Food and Agriculture Organisation (FAO) and the World Health Organisation (WHO). They have been active in the field of food law since their establishment in 1945 and 1948. Their work for the international community is in some ways comparable to the

[38] Article 22 UN Charter.

work of national ministries for their national community. Together they founded in 1963 the Codex Alimentarius Commission.[39] Membership of the Commission is open to Member States of FAO or WHO. One of the principal purposes of the Commission is the preparation of food standards and their publication in the Codex Alimentarius.

The specialised agencies have their own bases in the Charter and report directly to the Economic and Social Council (ECOSOC). The unity would come from ECOSOC's directions reinforced by the fact that each agency was admitted on the basis of a special agreement that stipulated the conditions of the recognition. Some of these conditions are that the agencies report to ECOSOC, accept the general guidance, exchange permanent liaison officers. Other fundamental aspects of the special relationship should have been the agencies' budgets that should be part of one central UN budget. The agencies' personnel would constitute one international civil service. Working for the same goals, with tasks that could be different but performed with, the same ethics and the same salaries and other conditions.

The budget unity came to nothing because that would require so much supervision by the UNGA that it would have to be in session most of the year. The UNGA's general session was planned to begin each year in September and finish in December. To drop the basic condition of one UN budget because the UNGA's sessions would be too long is like saying that you want the beginnings of a world government, except that you do not want a world government. The relations between the UN and the specialised agencies are much less intense than was intended.

The Charter has two conditions for international organisations that are brought into a special relationship with the UN. They have to be well-established international organisations with a set of purposes that are specified in their own basic document. See Law text box 3.6 with the essential excerpts from the Food and Agriculture Organisation of the United Nations. See Law text box 3.9 WHO on the same issue. See for the second element, the special agreement Law text box 3.7 with the first page of the special agreement between the FAO and the UN. The document has nine pages that are accessible at the UN web site.[40] The agreement itself did not establish the special relationship, it has to be recognised by UNGA. See Law text box 3.8 for the approval of the agreement.

[39] See the Codex Alimentarius Commission. Website: www.codexalimentarius.net.

[40] See the Reference, UN.

Law text box 3.6. Specialised agencies: FAO constitution.

Constitution of the Food and Agriculture Organization of the United Nations

- Preamble
- Article I Functions of the Organization
- Article XII Relations with the United Nations
- Article XVII Interpretation of the Constitution and Settlement of Legal Questions

Preamble

The Nations accepting this Constitution, being determined to promote the common welfare by furthering separate and collective action on their part for the purpose of:

- raising levels of nutrition and standards of living of the peoples under their respective jurisdictions;
- securing improvements in the efficiency of the production and distribution of all food and agricultural products;
- bettering the condition of rural populations;
- and thus contributing towards an expanding world economy and ensuring humanity's freedom from hunger;

hereby establish the Food and Agriculture Organization of the United Nations, hereinafter referred to as the 'Organization' through which the Members will report to one another on the measures taken and the progress achieved in the field of action set forth above.

Article I Functions of the Organization

1. The Organization shall collect, analyse, interpret and disseminate information relating to nutrition, food and agriculture. In this Constitution, the term 'agriculture' and its derivatives include fisheries, marine products, forestry and primary forestry products.
2. The Organization shall promote and, where appropriate, shall recommend national and international action with respect to:
   a. scientific, technological, social and economic research relating to nutrition, food and agriculture;
   b. the improvement of education and administration relating to nutrition, food and agriculture, and the spread of public knowledge of nutritional and agricultural science and practice;
   c. the conservation of natural resources and the adoption of improved methods of agricultural production;
   d. the improvement of the processing, marketing and distribution of food and agricultural products;
   e. the adoption of policies for the provision of adequate agricultural credit, national and international;
   f. the adoption of international policies with respect to agricultural commodity arrangements.
3. It shall also be the function of the Organization:
   a. to furnish such technical assistance as governments may request;

b. to organize, in cooperation with the governments concerned, such missions as may be needed to assist them to fulfil the obligation arising from their acceptance of the recommendations of the United Nations Conference on Food and Agriculture and of this Constitution; and
c. generally to take all necessary and appropriate action to implement the purposes of the Organization as set forth in the Preamble.

Article XII Relations with the United Nations

1. The Organization shall maintain relations with the United Nations as a specialized agency within the meaning of Article 57 of the Charter of the United Nations.
2. Agreements defining the relations between the Organization and the United Nations shall be subject to the approval of the Conference.

Article XVII Interpretation of the Constitution and Settlement of Legal Questions

1. Any question or dispute concerning the interpretation of this Constitution, if not settled by the Conference, shall be referred to the International Court of Justice in conformity with the Statute of the Court or to such other body as the Conference may determine.
2. Any request by the Organization to the International Court of Justice for an advisory opinion on legal questions arising within the scope of its activities shall be in accordance with any agreement between the Organization and the United Nations.
3. The reference of any question or dispute under this Article, or any request for an advisory opinion, shall be subject to procedures to be prescribed by the Conference.

Law text box 3.7. The first page of the specialised agency agreement between the UN and FAO, A/78, 30 September 1946, Item 24 of the provisional agenda for the second part of the first session of the General Assemble.

United Nations *Nations Unies*

GENERAL ASSEMBLY **ASSEMBLEE GENERALE**

Unrestricted
A/78
30 September 1946
Original: English, French

DRAFT AGREEMENT BETWEEN THE UNITED NATIONS AND THE FOOD AND AGRICULTURE ORGANIZATION OF THE UNITED NATIONS*

Item 24 of the provisional agenda for the second part of the first session of the General Assembly

Article 57 of the Charter of the United Nations provides that specialized agencies, established by inter-governmental agreement and having wide international responsibilities as defined in their basic instruments in economic, social, cultural, educational, health, and related fields, shall be brought into relationship with the United Nations.

Article XIII of the Constitution of the Food and Agriculture Organization of the United Nations provides that the Organization shall constitute a part of any general international organization to which may be entrusted the co-ordination of the activities of international organizations with specialized responsibilities.

Therefore, the United Nations and the Organization agree as follows:

ARTICLE I

The United Nations recognizes the Food and Agriculture Organization of the United Nations as a specialized agency and as being responsible for taking such action as may be appropriate under its basic instrument for the accomplishment of the purposes set forth therein.

ARTICLE II

Reciprocal representation

1. Representatives of the United Nations shall be invited to attend the meetings of the Conference of the Food and Agriculture Organization of the United Nations and its committees, the Executive Committee, and such general, regional or other special meetings as the Organization may convene, and to participate, without vote, in the deliberations of these bodies.

2. Representatives of the Food and Agriculture Organization of the United Nations shall be invited to attend meetings of the Economic and Social Council of the United Nations (hereinafter called the Council) and of its commissions and committees and to participate, without vote, in the deliberations of these bodies with respect to items on their agenda relating to matters within the scope of its activities.

3. Representatives of the Food and Agriculture Organization of the United Nations

* This agreement was recommended for approval by the General Assembly in a resolution adopted 21 June 1946 by the Economic and Social Council and amended by the addition of Article 9 on 3 October 1946, by the same Council.

PROJET D'ACCORD ENTRE LES NATIONS UNIES ET L'ORGANISATION DES NATIONS UNIES POUR L'ALIMENTATION ET L'AGRICULTURE*

Question No 24 de l'ordre du jour provisoire de la deuxième partie de la première session de l'Assemblée générale

L'Article 57 de la Charte des Nations Unies prévoit que les diverses institutions spécialisées, créées par accords inter-gouvernementaux et pourvues, aux termes de leurs statuts, d'attributions internationales étendues dans les domaines économique, social, de la culture intellectuelle et de l'éducation, de la santé publique et autres domaines connexes, seront reliées aux Nations Unies.

L'Article XIII de l'Acte constitutif de l'Organisation des Nations Unies pour l'Alimentation et l'Agriculture prévoit que cette Organisation s'intégrera dans toute organisation internationale générale qui pourra être chargée de coordonner l'activité des organismes internationaux à compétences spéciales.

En conséquence, les Nations Unies et l'Organisation conviennent de ce qui suit:

ARTICLE I

L'Organisation des Nations Unies pour l'Alimentation et l'Agriculture est reconnue par les Nations Unies en tant qu'institution spécialisée compétente pour prendre toutes les mesures conformes aux termes de son Acte Constitutif en vue d'atteindre les buts fixés par cet Acte.

ARTICLE II

Représentation réciproque

1. Des représentants des Nations Unies seront invités à assister aux réunions de la Conférence de l'Organisation des Nations Unies pour l'Alimentation et l'Agriculture et de ses commissions ainsi qu'à celles du Comité exécutif, et de toutes les conférences générales, régionales ou spéciales convoquées par l'Organisation, et à participer, sans droit de vote, aux délibérations de ces organes.

2. Des représentants de l'Organisation des Nations Unies pour l'Alimentation et l'Agriculture seront invités à assister aux réunions du Conseil économique et social des Nations Unies (désigné ci-dessous par le terme "Conseil"), de ses commissions et de ses comités et à participer, sans droit de vote, aux délibérations de ces organes, en ce qui concerne les questions figurant à leur ordre du jour et entrant dans le domaine de ses activités.

4. Des représentants de l'Organisation des Nations Unies pour l'Alimentation et l'Agri-

* Cet accord fut recommandé à l'approbation de l'Assemblée générale dans une résolution adoptée le 21 juin 1946 par le Conseil économique et social et amendée par l'addition de l'article 9, le 3 octobre 1946, par le même Conseil.

Law text box 3.8. The UN General Assembly Resolution 50 (I) approving the first four specialised agency agreements, among which FAO's, at the Sixty-fifth plenary meeting, 14 December 1946.

50 (I). Agreements with Specialized Agencies[1]

The General Assembly,

Whereas agreements entered into by the Economic and Social Council with certain specialized agencies are now before the General Assembly for approval:

Resolves to approve the agreements with the International Labour Organization,[2] the United Nations Educational, Scientific and Cultural Organization,[3] the Food and Agriculture Organization of the United Nations[4] and the International Civil Aviation Organization,[5] provided that, in the case of the agreement with the International Civil Aviation Organization, that Organization complies with any decision of the General Assembly regarding Franco Spain.

Furthermore, considering it essential that the policies and activities of the specialized agencies and of the organs of the United Nations should be co-ordinated:

Requests the Economic and Social Council to follow carefully the progress of such collaboration;

Instructs the Economic and Social Council to report on this question to the General Assembly within the space of three years, so as to keep the Assembly informed and in order that the Council and the General Assembly may, if necessary, and after consultation with the said agencies, formulate suitable proposals for improving such collaboration.

Sixty-fifth plenary meeting,
14 December 1946.

50 (I). Accords avec les institutions spécialisées[1]

L'Assemblée générale,

Considérant que les accords conclus par le Conseil économique et social avec certaines institutions spécialisées sont actuellement soumis à l'approbation de l'Assemblee,

Décide d'approuver les accords avec l'Organisation internationale du Travail[2], l'Organisation des Nations Unies pour l'éducation, la science et la culture[3], l'Organisation des Nations Unies pour l'alimentation et l'agriculture[4], et l'Organisation de l'aviation civile internationale[5], sous réserve, en ce qui touche l'accord avec l'Organisation de l'aviation civile internationale, que cette Organisation se conforme à toute décision de l'Assemblée générale concernant l'Espagne franquiste.

Considérant d'autre part que la coordination des programmes et des activités des institutions spécialisées et de ceux des organes des Nations Unies est essentielle,

Demande au Conseil économique et social de suivre attentivement le développement de cette collaboration;

Charge le Conseil économique et social de faire rapport sur cette question à l'Assemblée générale dans le délai de trois ans, afin d'informer l'Assemblée, et de façon que le Conseil et l'Assemblée puissent, s'il y a lieu, et après consultation avec ces institutions, formuler les propositions appropriées en vue d'améliorer cette collaboration.

Soixante-cinquième séance plénière,
le 14 décembre 1946.

Law text box 3.9. Specialised agency the World Health Organization.

CONSTITUTION OF THE WORLD HEALTH ORGANIZATION

THE STATES Parties to this Constitution declare, in conformity with the Charter of the United Nations, that the following principles are basic to the happiness, harmonious relations and security of all peoples:

Health is a state of complete physical, mental and social well-being and not merely the absence of disease or infirmity.

The enjoyment of the highest attainable standard of health is one of the fundamental rights of every human being without distinction of race, religion, political belief, economic or social condition.

The health of all peoples is fundamental to the attainment of peace and security and is dependent upon the fullest co-operation of individuals and States.

The achievement of any State in the promotion and protection of health

Governments have a responsibility for the health of their peoples which can be fulfilled only by the provision of adequate health and social measures.

ACCEPTING THESE PRINCIPLES, and for the purpose of co-operation among themselves and with others to promote and protect the health of all peoples, the Contracting Parties agree to the present Constitution and hereby establish the World Health Organization as a specialized agency within the terms of Article 57 of the Charter of the United Nations.

CHAPTER I – OBJECTIVE

Article 1

The objective of the World Health Organization (hereinafter called the Organization) shall be the attainment by all peoples of the highest possible level of health.

CHAPTER II – FUNCTIONS

Article 2

In order to achieve its objective, the functions of the Organization shall be:

(a) to act as the directing and co-ordinating authority on international health work;

(b) to establish and maintain effective collaboration with the United Nations, specialized agencies, governmental health administrations, professional groups and such other organizations as may be deemed appropriate;

(i) to promote ... the improvement of nutrition,

(u) to develop, establish and promote international standards with respect to food, biological, pharmaceutical and similar products;

Basic Documents, Forty-fifth edition, Supplement, October 2006
This text replaces that on pages 1-18 of the Forty-fifth edition of *Basic documents*, following the coming into force of amendments adopted by the Fifty-first World Health Assembly.

3.5 The World Trade Organization is a UN related organisation

The World Trade Organization is not a specialised agency. Its founding document, the Agreement establishing the World Trade Organization does not refer to the UN nor does it contain a clause like the FAO and WHO documents. There is no agreement about the specialised agency status. The articles of the WTO are about the organisation, its organs and the agreements between the member states to solve their trade differences. See Law text box 3.10. Compare these articles of the Agreement with the organigram in Diagram 3.7. See Chapter 16 for a selection of the results from the WTO practice.

Diagram 3.7. Organigram of the World Trade Organization.

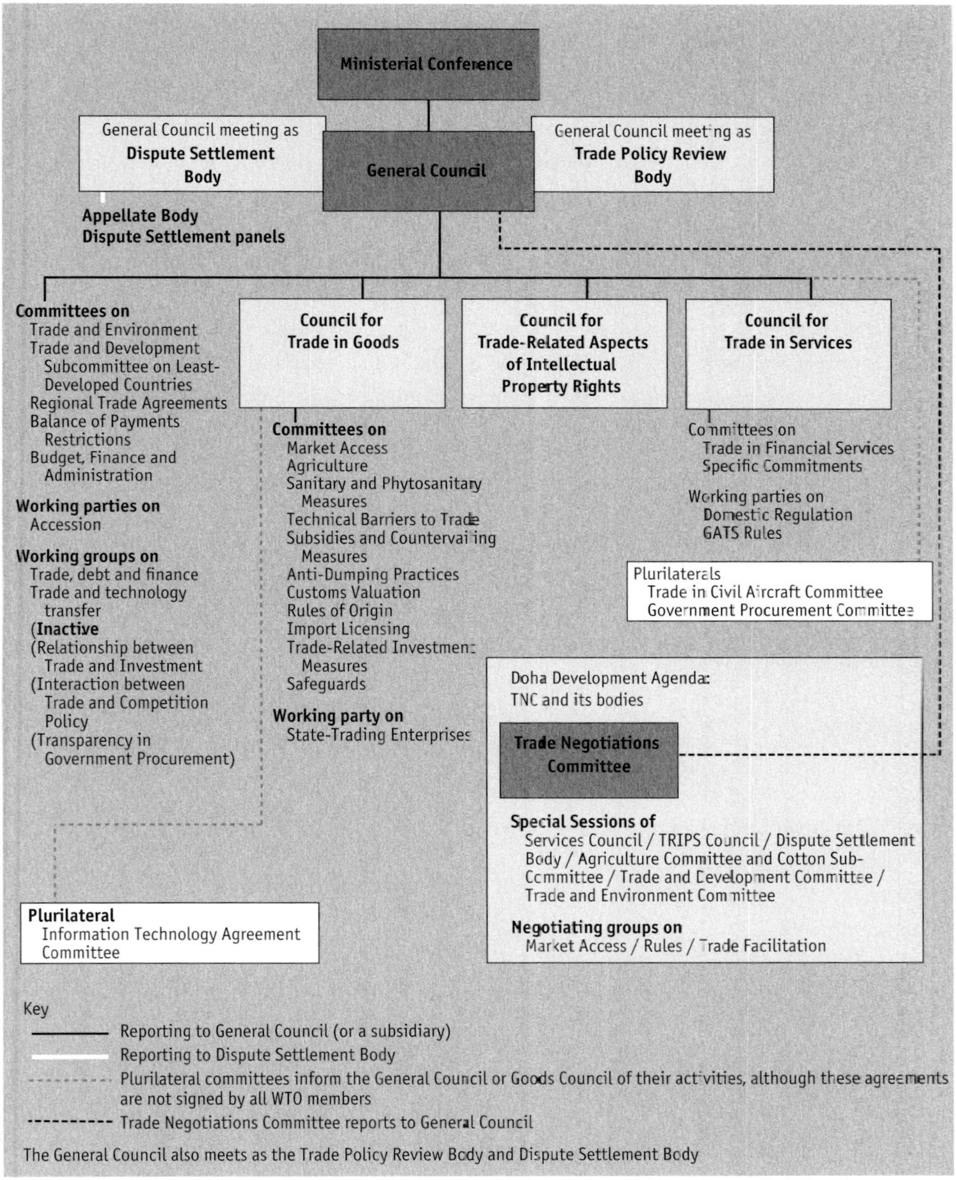

Law text box 3.10. The World Trade Organization is a UN related organisation.

AGREEMENT ESTABLISHING THE WORLD TRADE ORGANIZATION

The *Parties* to this Agreement,

Recognizing that their relations in the field of trade and economic endeavour should be conducted with a view to raising standards of living, ensuring full employment and a large and steadily growing volume of real income and effective demand, and expanding the production of and trade in goods and services, while allowing for the optimal use of the world's resources in accordance with the objective of sustainable development, seeking both to protect and preserve the environment and to enhance the means for doing so in a manner consistent with their respective needs and concerns at different levels of economic development,

Recognizing further that there is need for positive efforts designed to ensure that developing countries, and especially the least developed among them, secure a share in the growth in international trade commensurate with the needs of their economic development,

Being desirous of contributing to these objectives by entering into reciprocal and mutually advantageous arrangements directed to the substantial reduction of tariffs and other barriers to trade and to the elimination of discriminatory treatment in international trade relations,

Resolved, therefore, to develop an integrated, more viable and durable multilateral trading system encompassing the General Agreement on Tariffs and Trade, the results of past trade liberalization efforts, and all of the results of the Uruguay Round of Multilateral Trade Negotiations,

Determined to preserve the basic principles and to further the objectives underlying this multilateral trading system,

Agree as follows:

Article I

Establishment of the Organization

The World Trade Organization (hereinafter referred to as 'the WTO') is hereby established.

Article II

Scope of the WTO

1. The WTO shall provide the common institutional framework for the conduct of trade relations among its Members in matters related to the agreements and associated legal instruments included in the Annexes to this Agreement.
2. The agreements and associated legal instruments included in Annexes 1, 2 and 3 (hereinafter referred to as 'Multilateral Trade Agreements') are integral parts of this Agreement, binding on all Members.
3. The agreements and associated legal instruments included in Annex 4 (hereinafter referred to as 'Plurilateral Trade Agreements') are also part of this Agreement for those Members that have accepted them, and are binding on those Members. The Plurilateral Trade Agreements do not create either obligations or rights for Members that have not accepted them.

4. The General Agreement on Tariffs and Trade 1994 as specified in Annex 1A (hereinafter referred to as 'GATT 1994') is legally distinct from the General Agreement on Tariffs and Trade, dated 30 October 1947, annexed to the Final Act Adopted at the Conclusion of the Second Session of the Preparatory Committee of the United Nations Conference on Trade and Employment, as subsequently rectified, amended or modified (hereinafter referred to as 'GATT 1947').

Article III

Functions of the WTO

1. The WTO shall facilitate the implementation, administration and operation, and further the objectives, of this Agreement and of the Multilateral Trade Agreements, and shall also provide the framework for the implementation, administration and operation of the Plurilateral Trade Agreements.
2. The WTO shall provide the forum for negotiations among its Members concerning their multilateral trade relations in matters dealt with under the agreements in the Annexes to this Agreement. The WTO may also provide a forum for further negotiations among its Members concerning their multilateral trade relations, and a framework for the implementation of the results of such negotiations, as may be decided by the Ministerial Conference.
3. The WTO shall administer the Understanding on Rules and Procedures Governing the Settlement of Disputes (hereinafter referred to as the 'Dispute Settlement Understanding' or 'DSU') in Annex 2 to this Agreement.
4. The WTO shall administer the Trade Policy Review Mechanism (hereinafter referred to as the 'TPRM') provided for in Annex 3 to this Agreement.
5. With a view to achieving greater coherence in global economic policy-making, the WTO shall cooperate, as appropriate, with the International Monetary Fund and with the International Bank for Reconstruction and Development and its affiliated agencies.

Article IV

Structure of the WTO

1. There shall be a Ministerial Conference composed of representatives of all the Members, which shall meet at least once every two years. The Ministerial Conference shall carry out the functions of the WTO and take actions necessary to this effect. The Ministerial Conference shall have the authority to take decisions on all matters under any of the Multilateral Trade Agreements, if so requested by a Member, in accordance with the specific requirements for decision-making in this Agreement and in the relevant Multilateral Trade Agreement.
2. There shall be a General Council composed of representatives of all the Members, which shall meet as appropriate. In the intervals between meetings of the Ministerial Conference, its functions shall be conducted by the General Council. The General Council shall also carry out the functions assigned to it by this Agreement. The General Council shall establish its rules of procedure and approve the rules of procedure for the Committees provided for in paragraph 7.

3. The General Council shall convene as appropriate to discharge the responsibilities of the Dispute Settlement Body provided for in the Dispute Settlement Understanding. The Dispute Settlement Body may have its own chairman and shall establish such rules of procedure as it deems necessary for the fulfilment of those responsibilities.
4. The General Council shall convene as appropriate to discharge the responsibilities of the Trade Policy Review Body provided for in the TPRM. The Trade Policy Review Body may have its own chairman and shall establish such rules of procedure as it deems necessary for the fulfilment of those responsibilities.
5. There shall be a Council for Trade in Goods, a Council for Trade in Services and a Council for Trade-Related Aspects of Intellectual Property Rights (hereinafter referred to as the 'Council for TRIPS'), which shall operate under the general guidance of the General Council. The Council for Trade in Goods shall oversee the functioning of the Multilateral Trade Agreements in Annex 1A. The Council for Trade in Services shall oversee the functioning of the General Agreement on Trade in Services (hereinafter referred to as 'GATS'). The Council for TRIPS shall oversee the functioning of the Agreement on Trade-Related Aspects of Intellectual Property Rights (hereinafter referred to as the 'Agreement on TRIPS'). These Councils shall carry out the functions assigned to them by their respective agreements and by the General Council. They shall establish their respective rules of procedure subject to the approval of the General Council. Membership in these Councils shall be open to representatives of all Members. These Councils shall meet as necessary to carry out their functions.
6. The Council for Trade in Goods, the Council for Trade in Services and the Council for TRIPS shall establish subsidiary bodies as required. These subsidiary bodies shall establish their respective rules of procedure subject to the approval of their respective Councils.
7. The Ministerial Conference shall establish a Committee on Trade and Development, a Committee on Balance-of-Payments Restrictions and a Committee on Budget, Finance and Administration, which shall carry out the functions assigned to them by this Agreement and by the Multilateral Trade Agreements, and any additional functions assigned to them by the General Council, and may establish such additional Committees with such functions as it may deem appropriate. As part of its functions, the Committee on Trade and Development shall periodically review the special provisions in the Multilateral Trade Agreements in favour of the least-developed country Members and report to the General Council for appropriate action. Membership in these Committees shall be open to representatives of all Members.
8. The bodies provided for under the Plurilateral Trade Agreements shall carry out the functions assigned to them under those Agreements and shall operate within the institutional framework of the WTO. These bodies shall keep the General Council informed of their activities on a regular basis.

Article V

Relations with Other Organizations

1. The General Council shall make appropriate arrangements for effective cooperation with other intergovernmental organizations that have responsibilities related to those of the WTO.

2. The General Council may make appropriate arrangements for consultation and cooperation with non-governmental organizations concerned with matters related to those of the WTO.

Article VIII
Status of the WTO
1. The WTO shall have legal personality, and shall be accorded by each of its Members such legal capacity as may be necessary for the exercise of its functions.
2. The WTO shall be accorded by each of its Members such privileges and immunities as are necessary for the exercise of its functions.

3.6 Decision making in intergovernmental organisations

Decision making in the international organisations can be an arduous task for the representatives of the member states. Observers from other states and from other international organisations are usually present and have the opportunity to share their opinions but not their votes. The participation of representatives of non-governmental organisations opens new opportunities for discussion. And new questions about representation.

The UNECE Working Party on Agricultural Quality Standards has made international standards for fresh and fruit and vegetables, dry and dried produce, seed potatoes, meat, cut flowers, eggs and egg products. These standards are binding internal agreements for the states that accept them. Some of these standards are the subject of Chapter 15.

The UNECE Working Party fits in the organigram of the UN system as a working party of ECE, one of the regional organisations of ECOSOC. See Diagram 3.8.

3.6.1 The procedural aspects of international decision making

The following Draft Working Procedures of the UNECE Working Party on Agricultural Quality Standards contain a precise list of steps in the decision-making procedure. The steps are ranked in a descending order of preferences. When a consensus decision on a particular subject is not possible, the next best solution is to end the discussion with a conclusion that can be supported by as many participants as possible.

These conclusions vary from accepting the decision with registration of dissenting views in the report of the meeting to moving the decision to a subsequent meeting. Step V goes to the extreme of accepting as the final outcome of the negotiations a standard with footnotes mentioning the countries that do not agree.

Diagram 3.8. The UNECE Working Party on Agricultural Quality Standards.

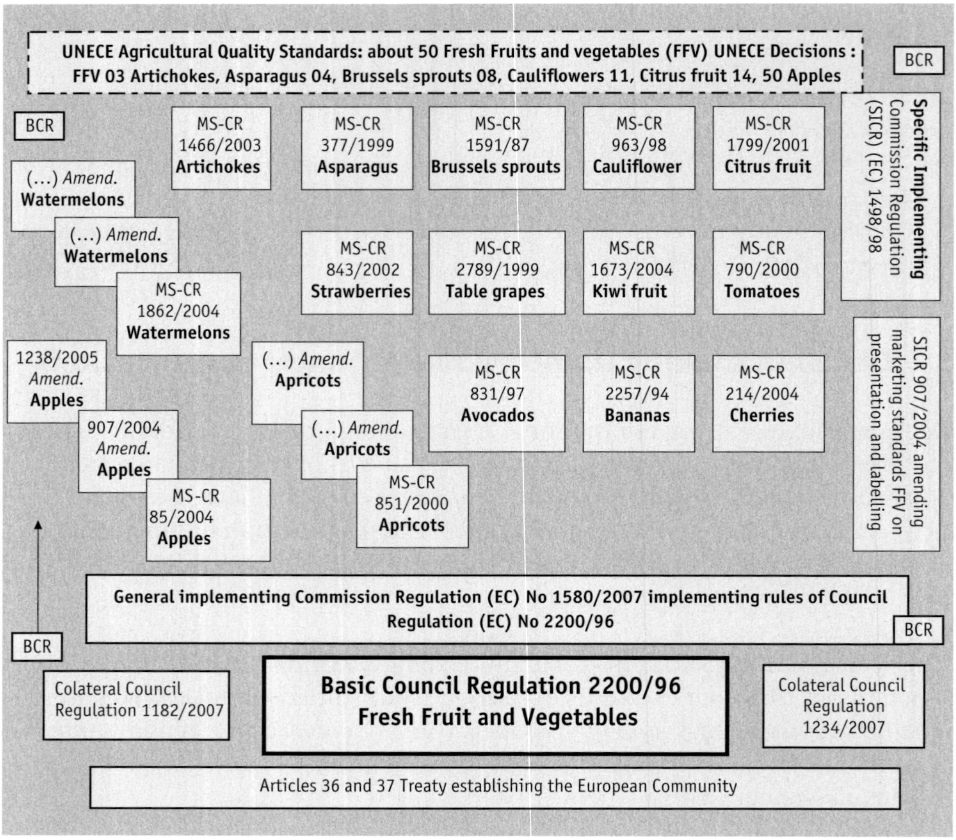

Take notice of the step in the succession of preferred outcomes where the non-governmental organisations are excluded from decision making. Up to that step all participants are asked to agree to a conclusion that will move decision making ahead with a special position for the dissenters. The non-governmental participants are not asked to step aside but they are set aside. The participants are separated into governmental and non-governmental and the governmental participants are asked to continue. See Law text box 3.11.

Law text box 3.11. Decision making in the UNECE Working Party on Agricultural Quality Standards. Source: ECOSOC, UNECE, Committee on Trade, ECE/TRADE/C/WP.7/2007/13, 16 August 2007.

Draft Working Procedures of the Working Party on Agricultural Quality Standards (Wp.7) and Its Specialized Sections

V. The development/revision process and decision-making procedure

17. The procedure for decision-making within the specialized sections and the Working Party is described below and has as its objective the widest possible acceptance of the standards and related material. Consensus is sought among all participants, and if that cannot be reached, between those representing national standard-setting authorities.

18. The following procedure shall be applied:

(i) The chairperson shall facilitate the discussion, striving to reach a consensus on the issue in question between all participants. The chairperson will summarize the discussion and will suggest the decision(s) to be taken by the meeting.
If there is consensus, a decision is taken and noted in the report of the session.

(ii) If no consensus is reached in accordance with (i), the chairperson shall ask the dissenting participants if they agree to let the decision stand and have their position noted in the report.
If there is agreement on this, a decision is taken and noted with the dissenting views in the report.

(iii) If the dissenting participants do not agree to the procedure under (ii), the chairperson shall ask all participants if they agree to delay a decision and continue to hold informal discussions during the intersessional period in a working group.
If there is consensus, the tasks for the working group are defined and the issue is put on the agenda for the next session.

(iv) If no consensus is reached in accordance with (iii) the chairperson shall ask the governmental representatives present if there is consensus among them on the issue in question.
If there is consensus among governmental representatives, a decision is taken and noted in the report with the dissenting views of other participants (private sector/associations).

(v) If there is no consensus in accordance with the procedure under (iv), the chairperson shall ask the dissenting countries if they agree to let the decision go forward and have their reservation noted in the report of the session and as a footnote to the standard, interpretative material or guideline in question[1].

(vi) If the dissenting countries do not agree to the procedure under (v), the chairperson shall ask the participants mentioned in (iv) if they agree to delay a decision and continue informal discussions in a working group in the intersessional period.
If several participants agree to this, the tasks for the working group are defined and the issue is put on the agenda for the next session.

(vii) If none of the dissenting countries agrees to the procedure under (vi) it is noted in the report that no decision could be reached on the issue in question. The item is considered as closed and the existing situation remains unchanged.

[1] Reservations should clearly indicate the reason. Preferably, an alternative wording/value should be suggested for inclusion in the text of the standard.

3.6.2 Examples of decision making

The following references to Law text boxes in Chapter 15 give some examples of international decision making with the rules of the UNECE Working Party on Agricultural Quality.

Law text box 15.12 UNECE Standard FFV-26 on the marketing and commercial quality control of peaches and nectarines. The European Community accepted this standard on the condition that they obtained a footnote on the Size Code D in part III of the standard, the Provisions concerning sizing. The footnote declares that marketing of size D is not allowed in the European Community from 1 July to 31 October.

In Law text box 15.14 there is a difference between the UNECE Standard DF-11 Dried grapes and the national legislations of Germany and Switzerland. The difference is about the tolerances for produce affected by mould, or the presence of dead or living insects. Tolerances are a part of a standard where exceptions to the quality criteria are allowed within an agreed range. Footnote 4 to the standard registers the dissenting positions of these two countries. Law text box 15.15 presents the definitions of the defects.

Law text box 15.16 shows the different effects of decision making in an international organisation where every state has to give its consent to every decision and the European Community also an international organisation, but one where decisions are taken by qualified majority decisions. Germany was able to maintain its zero tolerance legislation on the mould and insect defects in 1992 in the UNECE standard. Seven years later it had to accept the tolerances in Regulation 1666/1999 ... as regards the minimum marketing characteristics for certain varieties of dried grapes, made by the Commission of the European Communities.

See Law text box 15.10 for the comparable negotiations in the Codex Committee on Fresh Fruits and Vegetables about parameters to establish maturity requirements for table grapes. India and the US presented alternatives for what would become Codex Stan 255-2007 but could not convince the other members of the Codex Committee.

The other participants preferred Proposal A presented by the Working Group on Table Grapes. The US are members of the Codex Alimentarius Commission and the UNECE. Both organisations were negotiating their standards on table grapes. The US presented the same proposal in both organisations. With the same result. The UNECE standard registers the dissenting US position with the arguments. See the text of this footnote after Law text box 15.10.

3.6.3 Coordination between organisations

International organisations work in the same field quite regularly. Central coordination that would prevent duplication is weak. The organisations have to coordinate their efforts themselves.

The Codex Committee on Fresh Fruits and Vegetables (CX-731) works in the same field of standard-making for fresh fruits and vegetables. Their relations as UN organisations offer a structure to coordinate these activities. Several ways of coordination have been implemented over the course of time.

The UNECE Working Party has been active (under a different name) since 1961, when it published the first FFV-Standard, FFV 01 Apples and Pears. This took an incubation time of twelve years: UNECE started its activities on FFV Standards in 1949. In 2008 there are 53 standards and most have been revised several times.

The Codex Committee on Fresh Fruits and Vegetables (CX-731) was created in 1987 as the Codex Committee on Tropical Fresh Fruits and Vegetables.[41] At that point UNECE had a well-established record of FFV-Standard making. Coordination in that period followed directly from the difference in the terms of references. The Codex FFV group was making standards for papayas and mangoes, UNECE for cauliflower and cabbages.

The Codex Committee's name and Terms of Reference were amended by the 21st Session of the Commission in 1995. The term 'tropical' was deleted. This meant that more coordination became imperative because both UN organisations now worked to regulate the same fruits and vegetables. However, everyone felt confident that the Commission's decision to modify the Committee's terms of reference did not remove the long-standing procedures for cooperation between the two bodies.[42]

The potential areas and means of cooperation are explicit elements of the Terms of Reference of the Codex Committee on Fresh Fruits and Vegetables. The Terms of Reference are the basic documents that determine the tasks and means of the organisation. See Law text box 3.12.

[41] Established by the 17th Session of the Commission (1987) as the Codex Committee on Tropical Fresh Fruits and Vegetables. Its name and Terms of Reference were amended by the 21st Session of the Commission (1995). Host government: Mexico.

[42] Codex Alimentarius Procedural Manual, Ninth Edition, pages 150–151.

Law text box 3.12. Terms of Reference Codex Committee on Fresh Fruits and Vegetables (CX-731).

(a) to elaborate worldwide standards and codes of practice as may be appropriate for fresh fruits and vegetables;
(b) to consult with the UNECE Working Party on Agricultural Quality Standards in the elaboration of worldwide standards and codes of practice with particular regard to ensuring that there is no duplication of standards or codes of practice and that they follow the same broad format;
(c) to consult, as necessary, with other international organizations which are active in the area of standardization of fresh fruits and vegetables.
(b) carries a note 47 that is elaborated in Law text box 3.13.

Law text box 3.13. Cooperative relationship UNECE and Codex Committee FFV (CX-731).

Note 47 to Codex Committee FFV (CX-731)'s Terms of Reference
The Working Party on Agricultural Quality Standards of the United Nations Economic Commission for Europe:
1. may recommend that a worldwide Codex standard for fresh fruits and vegetables should be elaborated and submit its recommendation either to the Codex Committee on Fresh Fruits and Vegetables for consideration or to the Commission for approval;
2. may prepare 'proposed draft standards' for fresh fruits or vegetables at the request of the Codex Committee on Fresh Fruits and Vegetables or of the Commission for distribution by the Codex Secretariat at Step 3 of the Codex Procedure, and for further action by the Codex Committee on Fresh Fruits and Vegetables;
3. may wish to consider 'proposed draft standards' and 'draft standards' for fresh fruits and vegetables and transmit comments on them to the Codex Committee on Fresh Fruits and Vegetables at Steps 3 and 6 of the Codex Procedure; and
4. may perform specific tasks in relation to the elaboration of standards for fresh fruits and vegetables at the request of the Codex Committee on Fresh Fruits and Vegetables.

Codex 'proposed draft standards' and 'draft standards' for fresh fruits and vegetables at Steps 3 and 6 of the Codex Procedure should be submitted to the UN/ECE Secretariat to obtain comments.

So far coordination worked rather well. Of the 27 Codex standards on fresh fruit and vegetables only five overlap with the 53 UNECE standards. The overlap is on purpose to test the cooperation rules. The standard for grapes is one of these five.

The Secretary-General of the UN has several functions for the organisation. The Charter orders the UN Member States to deposit with the Secretary-General all the treaties they become party to.[43] The Secretary-General has to notify all Members of the UN of the existence of every treaty and its contents. In this way the Secretary-General has collected more than 40,000 treaties. They are published in the United Nations Treaty Series.[44]

3.7 Supranational international law

The limitation of state power has been more intensive on a regional scale. Noted examples are the European Community and the European Court of Human Rights[45] affiliated with the Council of Europe.[46]

International organisations that have real powers to limit their member states' sovereignty are called supranational. They are the opposite of intergovernmental organisations. Supranational international organisations often allow other representatives from interests inside the member state to participate in decision making, in addition to the representatives of the national government. Decisions can be taken by (qualified) majority vote. Many decisions are binding. Many decisions have direct effect: they work inside the member states without the intervention of the national government. Thus people can invoke the law of the supranational organisation when it influences their legal position. The organisation has institutions and a corps of civil servants who are empowered to carry out parts of its policies inside the member states. The national administrations have to co-operate with the supranational organisation and carry out the organisation's policies. Supranational organisations have independent institutions to supervise the execution of the organisations policies in the member states and to decide conflicts. Diagram 3.9 presents a model of an extremely supranational organisation where the influence of the member states is drastically reduced. Diagram 3.10 compares intergovernmental and supranational international organisations.

3.8 Human rights in international law

The third great change for classical international law, after the creation of international organisations and the endowment of supranational powers, was the reappearance of the individual human being. Old international law had exiled

[43] Article 102 UN Charter.

[44] The list of treaties and some 500 treaty texts are accessible with the internet http://untreaty.un.org.

[45] See its website: www.echr.coe.int.

[46] See its website: www.coe.int. The Council of Europe (COE) is easily confused with two bodies that belong to the European Union (EU), the European Council and the Council of the European Union. The Council of Europe, however, is another international organisation with a mainly intergovernmental character. It is both older and larger than the EU. It was founded in 1949 and currently has 45 Member States. Membership of the EU overlaps with membership of the COE, while the additional members of the COE are mainly Eastern European states. New EU members have always become COE members at an earlier date, as a testing and breeding place for their democratic qualities.

Diagram 3.9. A model of an extremely supranational international organisation. The Member States gave a part of their sovereignty to the supranational organisation. This organisation needs a state like organisation to fulfil its tasks, on which the Member States and their peoples depend: rule of law, human rights, minority rights, democratic government, checks and balances, separation of legislative, executive, and judiciary powers. Accolade 1 represents the sovereign powers that went from the national states to the supranational international organisation. Accolade 2 represents the remaining national powers. These create international law for the Member States outside the supranational organisation, and the need to co-ordinate the policies of the supranational organisation with those of the Member States.

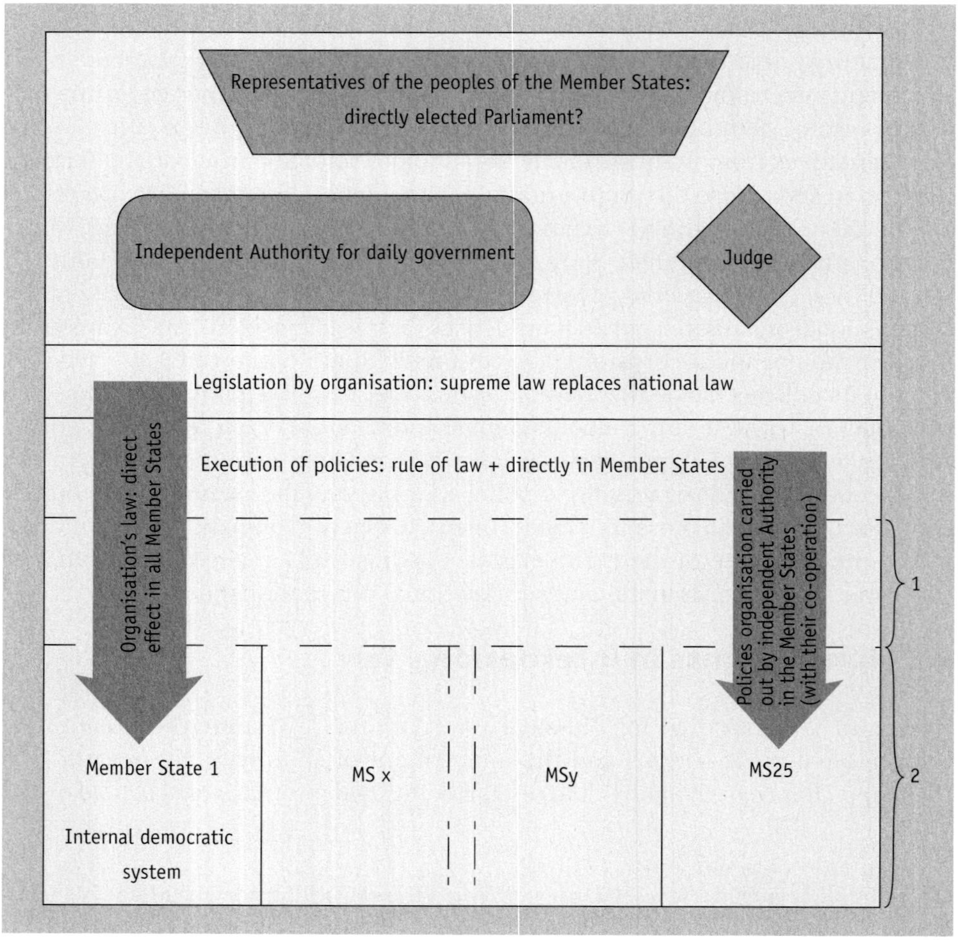

human beings to the inside of the nation state. In the twentieth century human beings became subjects of international law again through international treaties recognising human rights or individual criminal responsibility.

Diagram 3.10. Compare intergovernmental and supranational international organisations.
International organisations.

Aspects	Intergovernmental	Supranational
Actors	Between governments	Independent institutions
Who decides?	Unanimity decision	Majority vote
Power	Decision not binding	Decision binding
Who administers?	Administration independently by each national government	Administration independently by international organisation itself

The UN fostered treaties on human rights in 1966, and later, to complement the 1948 Universal Declaration of Human Rights and transform its content into binding treaty law. These treaties are important for food law because in addition to the classic freedoms from government oppression (freedom of religion, the press, association), they recognise entitlements to the essentials of life.[47] The 1966 treaties are the International Covenant on Civil and Political Rights, and the International Covenant on Economic, Social and Cultural Rights; both entered into force in 1976.

On a regional scale the European Convention for the Protection of Human Rights and Fundamental Freedoms, made in Rome in 1950, presented a powerful means of securing these rights. The treaty contains precise formulations of human rights and it established the international European Court of Human Rights. This court adjudicates complaints from individuals about failures of national states to secure their rights under the Convention. The notion that an individual could start an international court case against a sovereign state was so sensitive in the first decades that the individual had access only to the independent Commission of Human Rights. This Commission investigated the case and tried to find an amiable solution using the methods of silent diplomacy. However, if the Commission found indications of a serious breach of the Treaty, it could decide to start a court case. This could only be a case between the Commission and the accused state. The individual who complained was not a party in this conflict. In 1998 this was changed and the individual is now the claiming party in his own court case.

3.9 Food as a human right

The most fundamental dimension of international food law is the recognition by the United Nations and its member states of food as a human right. Article 11 of the International Covenant on Economic, Social and Cultural Rights (ICESCR) mentions the right to adequate food as part of the Right to an adequate standard of living. See Law text box 3.14.

[47] President Franklin D. Roosevelt formulated this as freedom from want in his 'Four Freedoms' Address to the USA Congress on January 6, 1941. Source: http://www.ourdocuments.gov.

Law text box 3.14. Article 11 ICESCR.

1. The States Parties to the present Covenant recognize the right of everyone to an adequate standard of living for himself and his family, including adequate food, clothing and housing, and to the continuous improvement of living conditions. The States Parties will take appropriate steps to ensure the realization of this right, recognizing to this effect the essential importance of international co-operation based on free consent.
2. The States Parties to the present Covenant, recognizing the fundamental right of everyone to be free from hunger, shall take, individually and through international co-operation, the measures, including specific programmes, which are needed:
   (a) To improve methods of production, conservation and distribution of food by making full use of technical and scientific knowledge, by disseminating knowledge of the principles of nutrition and by developing or reforming agrarian systems in such a way as to achieve the most efficient development and utilization of natural resources;
   (b) Taking into account the problems of both food-importing and food-exporting countries, to ensure an equitable distribution of world food supplies in relation to need.

The meaning of this article has been elaborated in general comments by the Committee on Economic, Social and Cultural Rights. According to General Comment nr. 12,[48] food is considered adequate if it is accessible in a quantity and quality sufficient to satisfy the dietary needs of individuals, free from adverse substances, and acceptable within a given culture.

With regard to the realisation of the human right to food, or *food security*, member states have three types of obligations: an obligation to respect – this is an obligation not to interfere with people's means to feed themselves; an obligation to protect – from interference by third parties; and an obligation to fulfil – provide food in situations like natural disasters where people are unable to take care of themselves.

These state obligations can be seen as the ultimate fundament of food law and agricultural law. Food law aims at ensuring the safety ('free from adverse substances') of available food and to a certain extent also its cultural acceptability (through labelling requirements with regard to ethical subjects like genetic modification and irradiation). The availability of food is a subject of agricultural policy and development cooperation. In 2005 FAO published 'Voluntary Guidelines to support the progressive realization of the right to adequate food in the context of national food security'.[49] So far the FAO member states have been unwilling to accept obligations under the right to food beyond the relation between states and their own population. If, however, the world is serious about the Millennium Development

[48] For hyperlinks see the reference list.
[49] For hyperlinks see the reference list.

Goals (in particular about halving world hunger by 2015) such limitations cannot be upheld.[50]

3.10 The relation between international and national law

Treaties and decisions of international organisations bind the participating states through their governments. If the treaty contains rules that can or have to operate for natural and legal persons inside the state, it is the national constitution – and not international law – which determines how this result is achieved. Some national constitutions are dualistic; they do not allow international law to operate inside the state. If this state becomes party to a treaty, which aims at creating rights or obligations for persons inside the state, only the national state can create these rights by transforming the international law into national law. After that there are legal obligations in two different spheres at the same time: the international and the national. The transformed rights and obligations have the force of national law and share the fate of this particular national law. If, at a later date, the national legislator creates national legislation with rules that are different from the legislation made to fulfil the treaty obligations, the later national legislative act overrules the earlier one. National judges have to apply the latest manifestation of the will of the national legislator. Even when they know, and the parties in the court case know, that their national state has an international obligation that, if honoured, would lead to a different judgment by the court. But in states with a dualistic system the breach of an international legal obligation caused by a wrong national law, is a matter only for the states participating in the treaty. Germany was a dualistic country but has now a monistic constitution. Great Britain is monistic for customary law and dualistic for treaty law. The common law favours a law of the land that includes international custom, whereas English constitutional law contains the rule that an Englishman can only be bound by written law that is accepted by Parliament according to certain procedures that are called the sovereignty of King in Parliament. See Diagram 3.11 Dualistic national law.

Other states, such as the Netherlands and the United States of America have a monistic system: it is based on the assumption that there is only one complex of law; international and national law are part of the same set of legal norms. The complete collection of law can be ordered into a coherent system without discrepancies. An apparent inconsistency can be solved by proper legal reasoning. The national constitution of monistic states allows international law to operate inside the state; it can or must be used by all persons, civil servants, higher and lower authorities and judges alike. This is called direct effect. The national law

[50] For further reading on the right to food see: B.M.J van der Meulen, The Right to Adequate Food. Food Law between the Market and Human Rights, Elsevier, The Hague, 2004; Wenche Barth Eide and Uwe Kracht (Eds.) Food and Human Rights in Development, Vol. I Legal and Institutional Dimensions and Selected topics, 2005; Vol II. Evolving Issues and Emerging Applications, 2007; George Kent, Freedom from Want. The Human Right to Adequate Food, 2005.

Diagram 3.11. Dualistic national law. Complete separation of two systems of law: one international for states and international organisations only, and one internal for national law only. Binding internal law can only be made by national authorities. They have to transform international obligations or rights into national law. Nobody inside the state can test whether this transformation was correct. The only test can be made by the treaty partners, but their decisions have no effect inside the national state.

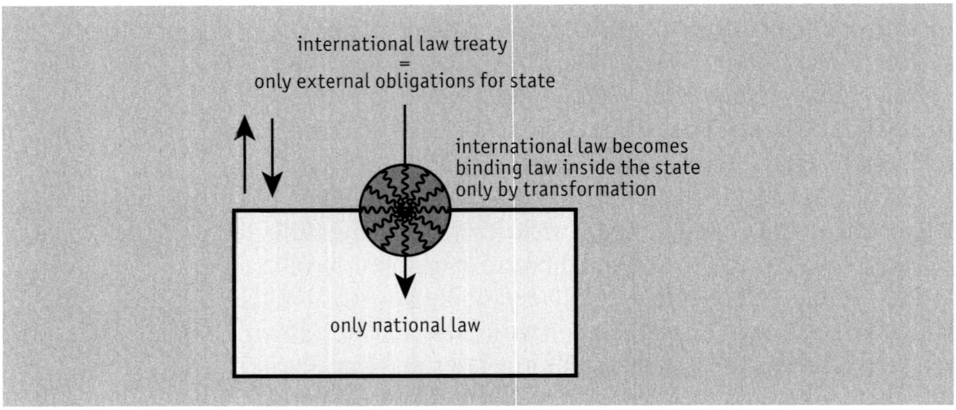

system also recognises the higher power of international law, its supremacy, accepting a hierarchy of norms. In this system the problems of duality do not arise. The higher international law is not affected by any change in national law. The monistic nation states do have problems of their own. It still has to be decided which part of international law is fit to be applied directly. Treaties that explicitly require additional national law clearly do not have direct effect. International laws operate inside the state only if they are self-executive. Law text boxes 3.15 and 3.16 give the Articles of the constitutions of the Netherlands and Germany that formulate their monistic position. Law text box 3.17 gives the dualistic Italian constitution. The English constitution is not written down, so its dualistic character cannot be presented in an authoritative text. The closely related topic of the supremacy of international law can be formulated in a monistic system, where it is combined with direct effect, and in a dualistic system, where it is an abstract declaration. See Law text boxes 3.18 and 3.19 for the situation in the Netherlands and Italy. Diagram 3.12 shows the hierarchy of legal norms and monistic national law.

Law text box 3.15. Relations between international and national law. Example of a monistic national legal system: the Netherlands (Source of translation: the Ministry of Interior and Kingdom Relations. For hyperlink see reference).

Article 93 Grondwet voor het Koninkrijk der Nederlanden 2002 (The Constitution for the Kingdom of The Netherlands 2002)
Provisions of treaties and of resolutions by international institutions which may be binding on all persons by virtue of their contents shall become binding after they have been published.

Law text box 3.16. Relations between international and national law. Examples of a monistic national legal system: Germany (For hyperlink see reference list.).

Artikel 25 Grundgesetz für die Bundesrepublik Deutschland (The Constitution for the Federal Republic of Germany)
[Völkerrecht und Bundesrecht]
Die allgemeinen Regeln des Völkerrechtes sind Bestandteil des Bundesrechtes. Sie gehen den Gesetzen vor und erzeugen Rechte und Pflichten unmittelbar für die Bewohner des Bundesgebietes.

Law text box 3.17. Relations international and national law. Example of a dualistic national legal system: Italy.

Costituzione della Repubblica Italiana (Constitution of the Italian Republic)
Sezione II La formazione delle leggi
Art. 80. Le Camere autorizzano con legge la ratifica dei trattati internazionali che sono di natura politica, o prevedono arbitrati o regolamenti giudiziari, o importano variazioni del territorio od oneri alle finanze o modificazioni di leggi.

Law text box 3.18. Relations international and national law. Example of the supremacy of international law in a monistic legal system: the Netherlands.

Article 94 Grondwet voor het Koninkrijk der Nederlanden 2002 (The Constitution for the Kingdom of the Netherlands 2002)
Statutory regulations in force within the Kingdom shall not be applicable if such application is in conflict with provisions of treaties that are binding on all persons or of resolutions by international institutions.

Law text box 3.19. Relations international and national law. Example of supremacy of international law in a dualistic national legal system: Italy.

Costituzione della Repubblica Italiana (Constitution of the Italian Republic)
Principi Fondamentali
Art. 10. L'ordinamento giuridico italiano si conforma alle norme del diritto internazionale generalmente riconosciute.

Diagram 3.12. Hierarchy of legal norms and monistic national law. In the monistic view of one system of law encompassing all law, the different levels of law of Diagram 3 get a hierarchical relationship.

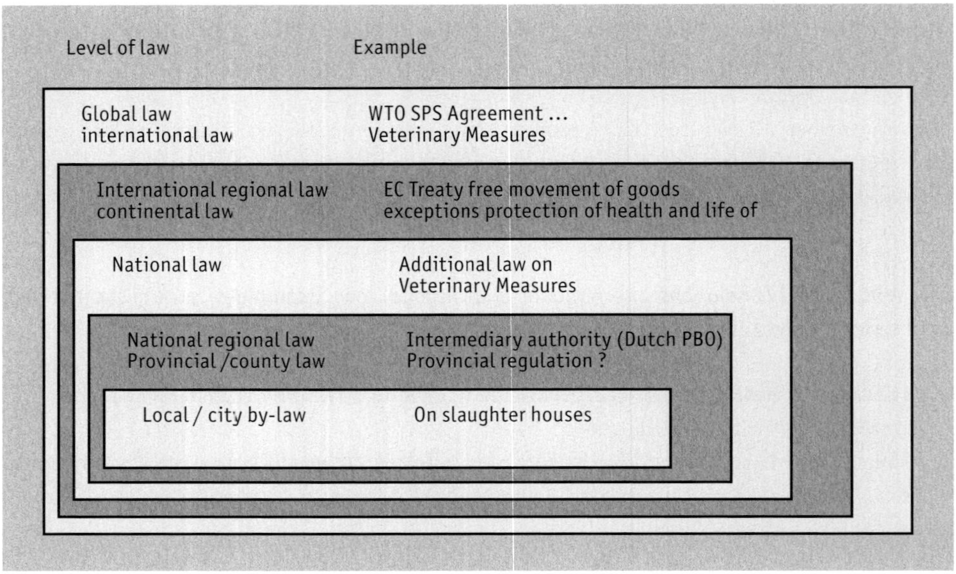

4. The European Union and food law

The European Union joins twenty-seven member states in a community of law.[51] This EU law plays a key role in food law, both when EU law deals expressly with food law, but also when EU law deals with other issues, like the internal market, which have a large structuring influence on food law. EU law has certain characteristics that make it a unique specimen of international law. EU law is the supreme law, regardless of what the national constitutions of the member states say on monism, dualism and supremacy. EU law makes contrary national law non-existent. So these characteristics structure what is possible and what is impossible in law, both on the level of the Union and on the level of the twenty-seven united European states. To understand food law it is therefore necessary to know the essentials of European Union law.

4.1 The reform between Union and Community

The Treaty establishing a Constitution for Europe failed to pass two referenda and the member states are trying to get back on track with the reforms through the Lisbon Treaty.[52] At the moment of writing these lines, nobody knows the outcome of the ratification process in the states where a referendum is part of the process. The changes that the Lisbon Treaty brings to the existing treaties are more on the organisation of the integration and less on the substance. This holds even more for food law.

The combined effect is that a large reorganisation is carried out to leave most things as they were before, except for some of the names and most of the article numbers. We have chosen to describe the main characteristics of the new treaties and to return to the elements that are the same in the existing law and the law as changed by the Lisbon Treaty. Appendix B provides a conversion table, where readers may find the equivalent article number in the new treaties for all the references.

[51] Official EU documents can be found on the internet: http://europa.eu. Choose from the twenty-three languages for instance the EN-Gateway to the European Union, then choose the tab Documents. The official source for EU documents is the Official Journal of the European Union, published every working day. It consists of two series, L (all binding legislation) and C (information, preparatory work, notices and recommendations), and a supplement S (tenders on EU scale for national public projects to enable all relevant companies in the EU to take part in the bidding to get the contract. Member states are not allowed to give preferential treatment to enterprises in their own country). For all practical purposes, the best entry to EU legislation and case law is Eur-Lex: http://eur-lex.europa.eu/.

[52] Treaty of Lisbon amending the Treaty on European Union and the Treaty establishing the European Community, signed at Lisbon, 13 December 2007. Official Journal C 306, 17 December 2007. Consolidated versions of the Treaty on European Union and the Treaty on the Functioning of the European Union. Official Journal C 115, 9 May 2008.

4.1.1 The TEU and the TFEU

The changes brought about by the Lisbon Treaty centre more than before on the division of powers. The multi-personality of the EU and EC will be terminated. When the 2007 Lisbon Treaty is ratified, the Communities, pillars and temple (represented in Diagram 4.1) will be replaced by a new basic structure that both remaining treaties indicate to: 'constitute the Treaties on which the Union is founded. These two Treaties, which have the same legal value, shall be referred to as "the Treaties" '.[53] Their individual names are Treaty on European Union TEU and the Treaty on the Functioning of the European Union (TFEU).

The original European Union was 'founded on the European Communities, supplemented by the policies and forms of cooperation established by this Treaty'.[54] The authors of the present treaty texts founded the Union not on its preceding Community because the former will take its place, a construct that appears to be more solid than written words.

The image of the Greek temple, used by many to characterise the EU and EC, is more vividly and more accurately replaced by the imago of The Two Towers, or, to compromise: The Two Treaty Towers.

The European Union steps down from its lofty position and assumes the identity, place and legal personality, in short all but the name of the European Community. The Communities, policies and pillars are redistributed among the two remaining treaties: the Treaty on European Union (TEU) and the Treaty on the Functioning of the European Union (TFEU).

The TEU remains the main seat of intergovernmental integration. The external and security policies, the middle pillar in Diagram 4.1 on the structure of the European Union, are transplanted to these outer reaches of the integration process. But in compensation, the TFEU tower continuous to have its own external actions in Part five of TFEU. See Diagram 4.2 about The Two Treaty Towers.

The EU cannot escape complete involvement in the community of European integration because it 'shall replace and succeed' the European Community.[55] The question is however what identity will result from this fusion. Will the new European Union be the European Community with another name? Or will the new European Union suppress not only the name but also the essential characteristics of the Community? It is not enough to refer to the different parts of both treaties

[53] Article 1(2) Treaty on the Functioning of the European Union, and Article 1, paragraph 3 Treaty on European Union.

[54] Article 1 TEU 1992.

[55] Article 1 TEU.

that continue to impress their contribution to the combination. The EEC went through twenty years of stand-still, followed by two decades of expansion on the basis of the same EEC Treaty.

The transfer of the main articles on tasks and policies from the former EC Treaty to the new EU Treaty pushes that treaty to the centre of the integration process. The TEU necessarily also introduces the institutions of the only remaining entity, the European Union. However, the TEU does little more than mentioning the existence of the institutions and the TFEU provides all the essentials for their existence and activities.

All the rules on the composition, tasks and powers of the institutions, and the instruments and procedures they need to exercise those powers, remain the substance of the Treaty that continues the former European Community Treaty, the Treaty on the Functioning of the European Union. Even the name is right: the EC was and remains about all that functions in the Union. If the Treaty of Lisbon is to become more than a clever expedient to pick up the pieces after the Constitution for Europe fell apart, it has to be that the Union has taken the place of the Community, and has become the Community.

The TFEU part of the new constellation remains the most supranational part although its intergovernmental metal is self evident. But the construction that places the Articles on the meagre citizenship of the Union in the TFEU, and not in the TEU, where logic and reason would expect it to be, can only be explained by the necessity to place what substance there is in this citizenship under the influence of the rights and remedies that are available for the people of the Union in their capacities in the Union as consumer, employer, worker and perhaps in the near future as voter too.[56]

The differences between The Two Towers are also exemplified by the arrangements for internal security, the remains of the third temple pillar of Diagram 4.1. Those remains have been transplanted to the TFEU. This reconstruction was already operative in the Treaty of Amsterdam. It is an inescapable construction as long as reality is meant to coincide with the basics of the rule of law. The recourse to independent judges is a basic element of the TFEU Tower.

These large-scale developments are the essence of the Lisbon Treaty that inherits the great statements agenda of the Constitution Treaty. The European Council, the meeting of the leaders of the governments of the member states, is getting

[56] The election of the members of the European Parliament is based on the national election legislation of the member states. That most remarkable contradiction between European aspirations and national practice is still on the agenda, Article 223 TFEU.

*Diagram 4.1. The structure of the European Union. The structure of the EU after the 1992 Maastricht Treaty. The European Community carries the weight and contains most policies. Policies directly relevant for food law are indicated by an asterisk *. The 1997 Amsterdam Treaty changed the European Union and the European Community Treaties, renaming the third pillar and transporting policies from the third to the first pillar, that is from the intergovernmental to the more supranational legal surroundings. An example is the objective to establish progressively an area of freedom, security and justice with free movement of persons and no internal borders as is required for the internal market.*
Freely adapted after The ABC of Community law by Dr Klaus-Dieter Borchardt, published by the European Communities.

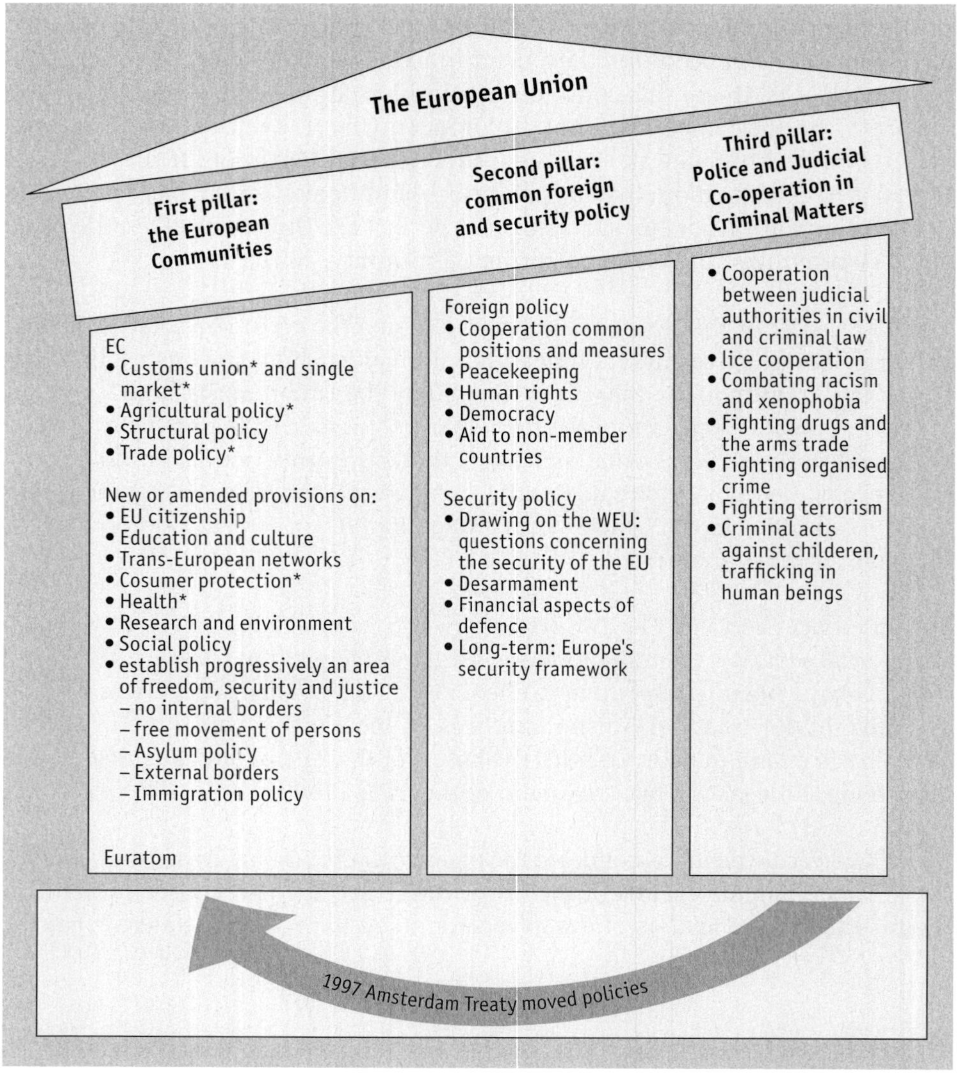

Diagram 4.2. The Two Treaty Towers.

Treaty on European Union

Preamble

Title I Common

Title II Democratic Principles

Title III Institutions

Title IV Enhanced Cooperation

Title V External Action Common Foreign and Security Policy from:

> Second pillar:
> common foreign
> and security policy

> Foreign policy
> - Cooperation common positions and measures
> - Peacekeeping
> - Human rights
> - Democracy
> - Aid to non-member countries

> Security policy
> - Drawing on the WEU: questions concerning the security of the EU
> - Desarmament
> - Financial aspects of defence
> - Long-term: Europe's security framework

Title VI Final Provisions

Treaty on the Functioning of the European Union

Preamble

Part one Principles

Title I Union Competence

> First pillar:
> the European
> Communities

Part two Non-discrimination and citizenship of the Union

> - EU citizenship

Part three Union policies and internal actions

Title I Internal market

Title II Free movement of goods

> EC
> - Customs union* and single market*
> - Agricultural policy*
> - Structural policy
> - Trade policy*

Title IV Free movement of persons, services and capital

Title V Area of Freedom, Security and Justice from:

> Third pillar:
> Police and Judicial
> Co-operation in
> Criminal Matters

> - Establish progressively an area of freedom, security and justice
>   - no internal borders
>   - free movement of persons
>   - asylum policy
>   - external borders
>   - immigration policy

its first president, a position that is not equal to the presidency of the European Union, but might be its beginning.[57]

The member states are still preoccupied with the extent of the powers of the Union. After all the spells that have ever been cast and repeated about supranationalism, intergovernmentalism, power attribution, implied powers, subsidiarity, proportionality, the still not satisfied urge to dwell upon the attribution of powers, instead of the goals these powers are supposed to attain, has led to a treaty text that spells the division of powers in five lengthy Articles.

The old statements are summarised by the Articles 4 and 5 TEU. As Law text box 4.1 shows, all that has changed is a new term for attribution of power: from now on it is conferral of power.

Law text box 4.1. Remaining competences, equality of member states and the principle of sincere cooperation. Source: Consolidated Version of the Treaty on European Union, Official Journal C 115, 9 May 2008, p. 18.

Treaty on European Union
Article 4

1. In accordance with Article 5, competences not conferred upon the Union in the Treaties remain with the Member States.
2. The Union shall respect the equality of Member States before the Treaties as well as their national identities, inherent in their fundamental structures, political and constitutional, inclusive of regional and local self-government. It shall respect their essential State functions, including ensuring the territorial integrity of the State, maintaining law and order and safeguarding national security. In particular, national security remains the sole responsibility of each Member State.
3. Pursuant to the principle of sincere cooperation, the Union and the Member States shall, in full mutual respect, assist each other in carrying out tasks which flow from the Treaties.
   The Member States shall take any appropriate measure, general or particular, to ensure fulfilment of the obligations arising out of the Treaties or resulting from the acts of the institutions of the Union.
   The Member States shall facilitate the achievement of the Union's tasks and refrain from any measure which could jeopardise the attainment of the Union's objectives.

4.1.2 Subsidiarity and proportionality

These two concepts have been part of EC treaty law to act as an assurance against the usurpation of too much power by the EU. Both principles prescribe an attitude for the EU institutions and the leaders of those institutions on how to use power.

[57] Article 15(5) and (6) TEU.

Both principles operate only in those situations where the EU has a power and a possibility to share that power with others. If the EU is the only entity that has powers, it cannot step down from its responsibility and give the power to another entity. It can delegate some of its powers as long as its responsibility is not made less. See Article 2 TFEU in Law text box 4.4 on the categories and areas of Union competence.

Law text box 4.2. Limits and use of Union competences: the principles of conferral, subsidiarity and proportionality. Source: Consolidated Version of the Treaty on European Union, Official Journal C 115, 9 May 2008, p. 18.

Treaty on European Union
Article 5
(ex Article 5 TEC)

1. The limits of Union competences are governed by the principle of conferral. The use of Union competences is governed by the principles of subsidiarity and proportionality.
2. Under the principle of conferral, the Union shall act only within the limits of the competences conferred upon it by the Member States in the Treaties to attain the objectives set out therein. Competences not conferred upon the Union in the Treaties remain with the Member States.
3. Under the principle of subsidiarity, in areas which do not fall within its exclusive competence, the Union shall act only if and in so far as the objectives of the proposed action cannot be sufficiently achieved by the Member States, either at central level or at regional and local level, but can rather, by reason of the scale or effects of the proposed action, be better achieved at Union level.
   The institutions of the Union shall apply the principle of subsidiarity as laid down in the Protocol on the application of the principles of subsidiarity and proportionality. National Parliaments ensure compliance with the principle of subsidiarity in accordance with the procedure set out in that Protocol.
4. Under the principle of proportionality, the content and form of Union action shall not exceed what is necessary to achieve the objectives of the Treaties.
   The institutions of the Union shall apply the principle of proportionality as laid down in the Protocol on the application of the principles of subsidiarity and proportionality.

Subsidiarity and proportionality do not question the existence of EU powers, they act as restraints. Subsidiarity asks the authority to reconsider whether the goals for which the power was given to the EU are not equally well served by the exercise of powers by institutions that are closer to the communities they serve. The EU could conclude that it would serve additional ends of society if it shared its power with national, regional or local authorities. The principle of subsidiarity was developed by Catholic social theories about the relations between society and state. These theories favoured the exercise of public power by authorities that are situated as closely as possible to the society they govern. Better still in their midst. It can be noted in passing that this theory shows how difficult it can be to practice what you preach.

The official interpretation of the principles of subsidiarity and proportionality is laid down in a special Protocol.[58] The implementation in practice demands an explicit statement by the institution that exercises its power that it has considered refraining from using it. When the test against the subsidiarity criterion does not lead to the conclusion to benefit decentralised authorities by not using the EU power, the next test is proportionality. The choices of policy and instruments must be commensurate with the policy objectives. Law text box 4.3 on the practice of subsidiarity and proportionality shows the public announcement about the weighing of these aspects and the consequences it had. The example is taken from a recent regulation that acts as the basis for the common market organisation for fruit and vegetables.

Law text box 4.3. The practise of subsidiarity and proportionality. Source: Official Journal L 273, 17 October 2007, p. 1.

Council Regulation (EC) No 1182/2007 of 26 September 2007 laying down specific rules as regards the fruit and vegetable sector, amending Directives 2001/112/EC and 2001/113/EC and Regulations (EEC) No 827/68, (EC) No 2200/96, (EC) No 2201/96, (EC) No 2826/2000, (EC) No 1782/2003 and (EC) No 318/2006 and repealing Regulation (EC) No 2202/96.
The Council of the European Union,
Having regard to the Treaty establishing the European Community, and in particular Articles 36 and 37 thereof,
...
Whereas:
(3) Since those objectives cannot be sufficiently achieved by the Member States due to the common nature of the market in fruit and vegetables and can therefore, by reason of the need for further common action, be better achieved at Community level, the Community may adopt measures, in accordance with the principle of subsidiarity, as set out in Article 5 of the Treaty. In accordance with the principle of proportionality, as set out in that Article, this Regulation does not go beyond what is necessary in order to achieve those objectives.

4.1.3 The division of powers between member states and the Union

The fine print of the division of powers can be found in the Treaty where the work is done: in the new Title I 'Categories and Areas of Union Competence', the Articles 2 to 6 of the TFEU. Although these articles are rather lengthy, they are reproduced in Law text box 4.4. They are likely to play a continuing part in

[58] Protocol on the application of the principles of subsidiarity and proportionality, Official Journal C 310, 16 December 2004, pp. 207-209.

the discussions about what the Union can do, may do, should do, ought to do, or not. Perhaps this codification of the present practice helps to focus on the issues instead of the power play. Then these articles will become one of the more tranquil trenches of The Two Towers Treaties.

It is worth noting the increasing weight of general statements and clauses about powers. This approach stands in opposition to the original main line of the treaties that refrained from sweeping statements and instead measured precisely the combination of institutions, voting requirements, instruments and procedures available for every separate policy. Now The Two Towers Treaties provide both: a general statement and a precise allocation.

Law text box 4.4. The categories and areas of Union competence. Source: Consolidated Version of the Treaty on the Functioning of the European Union (2008/C 115/01), Official Journal C 115, 9 May 2008, pp. 50-52.

The Treaty on the Functioning of the European Union
Title I. Categories and Areas of Union Competence
Article 2

1. When the Treaties confer on the Union exclusive competence in a specific area, only the Union may legislate and adopt legally binding acts, the Member States being able to do so themselves only if so empowered by the Union or for the implementation of Union acts.
2. When the Treaties confer on the Union a competence shared with the Member States in a specific area, the Union and the Member States may legislate and adopt legally binding acts in that area.
   The Member States shall exercise their competence to the extent that the Union has not exercised its competence. The Member States shall again exercise their competence to the extent that the Union has decided to cease exercising its competence.
3. The Member States shall coordinate their economic and employment policies within arrangements as determined by this Treaty, which the Union shall have competence to provide.
4. The Union shall have competence, in accordance with the provisions of the Treaty on European Union, to define and implement a common foreign and security policy, including the progressive framing of a common defence policy.
5. In certain areas and under the conditions laid down in the Treaties, the Union shall have competence to carry out actions to support, coordinate or supplement the actions of the Member States, without thereby superseding their competence in these areas.
   Legally binding acts of the Union adopted on the basis of the provisions of the Treaties relating to these areas shall not entail harmonisation of Member States' laws or regulations.
6. The scope of and arrangements for exercising the Union's competences shall be determined by the provisions of the Treaties relating to each area.

Article 3

1. The Union shall have exclusive competence in the following areas:
   (a) customs union;
   (b) the establishing of the competition rules necessary for the functioning of the internal market;
   (c) monetary policy for the Member States whose currency is the euro;
   (d) the conservation of marine biological resources under the common fisheries policy;
   (e) common commercial policy.
2. The Union shall also have exclusive competence for the conclusion of an international agreement when its conclusion is provided for in a legislative act of the Union or is necessary to enable the Union to exercise its internal competence, or in so far as its conclusion may affect common rules or alter their scope.

Article 4

1. The Union shall share competence with the Member States where the Treaties confer on it a competence which does not relate to the areas referred to in Articles 3 and 6.
2. Shared competence between the Union and the Member States applies in the following principal areas:
   (a) internal market;
   (b) social policy, for the aspects defined in this Treaty;
   (c) economic, social and territorial cohesion;
   (d) agriculture and fisheries, excluding the conservation of marine biological resources;
   (e) environment;
   (f) consumer protection;
   (g) transport;
   (h) trans-European networks;
   (i) energy;
   (j) area of freedom, security and justice;
   (k) common safety concerns in public health matters, for the aspects defined in this Treaty.
3. In the areas of research, technological development and space, the Union shall have competence to carry out activities, in particular to define and implement programmes; however, the exercise of that competence shall not result in Member States being prevented from exercising theirs.
4. In the areas of development cooperation and humanitarian aid, the Union shall have competence to carry out activities and conduct a common policy; however, the exercise of that competence shall not result in Member States being prevented from exercising theirs.

Article 5

1. The Member States shall coordinate their economic policies within the Union. To this end, the council shall adopt measures, in particular broad guidelines for these policies. Specific provisions shall apply to those Member States whose currency is the euro.
2. The Union shall take measures to ensure coordination of the employment policies of the Member States, in particular by defining guidelines for these policies.
3. The Union may take initiatives to ensure coordination of Member States' social policies.

Article 6

The Union shall have competence to carry out actions to support, coordinate or supplement the actions of the Member States. The areas of such action shall, at European level, be:

(a) protection and improvement of human health;
(b) industry;
(c) culture;
(d) tourism;
(e) education, vocational training, youth and sport;
(f) civil protection;
(g) administrative cooperation.

Articles 2 to 6 of the Treaty on the Functioning of the European Union are *proposed* law. They will enter into force when all member states have ratified the TEU and the TFEU. These Articles can be compared with the Articles of the Treaty establishing the European Community. See section 4.3. The Powers of the EU: attribution with Diagrams 4.4 and 4.5 and Law text boxes 4.6 Tasks of the European Community, Article 2 EC Treaty and 4.7 Activities of the European Community to fulfil her tasks, Article 3 EC Treaty.

4.1.4 Member state loyalty

Article 4 TEU raises the issue of the division of powers together with another subject, the loyalty to do everything possible to further the interests of the Union, and refrain from doing anything that might harm the interests of the Union. This double allegiance used to be the separate Article 10 of the EC Treaty. The Court of Justice has referred to it more and more to determine the obligations of the member states. It remains to be seen whether the new place of these principles in the powers section of the TEU will influence the Court's opinion.

4.2 The basic structure of the EU and its law

European integration led to the establishment of several international organisations, which are collectively known as the European Union.[59] In fact this is a conglomerate of organisations and political arrangements that is shaped by deliberate design but also by the day-to-day operations of this complicated machinery, the day-to-day work that not only carries out the tasks on the agenda, but by doing so in a particular way also changes the design of the machinery through practice. This combination of design and experience creates the EU as it actually is. This result is known as the '*acquis communautaire*'. It is the interlocking complex of the original treaties, the changes of the treaties, EU secondary legislation, the

[59] Literature: Gormley, Laurence W., Introduction to the Law of the European Communities, 3rd ed., London, 1998.

customs developed in practice and case law of the Court of Justice of the European Communities. It has to be accepted by all who want to join.[60] The European Union is founded on the European Communities,[61] supplemented by the policies and forms of co-operation established by the 1992 Maastricht Treaty on European Union (EU Treaty).[62] In this mix of international organisations with legal personality and policies without legal personality, the European Community (EC) is the most important ingredient. It has substantial supranational elements. Among the policies and forms of co-operation, the Common Foreign and Security Policy (CFSP) and Police and Judicial Co-operation in Criminal Matters are gradually deployed. Both are intergovernmental.

The ensemble is co-ordinated through the European Union, which is itself a political arrangement created by a treaty, but without legal personality. The European Community, created out of the European Economic Community (EEC), has the largest and most profound field of activities that touch upon most of the aspects of the daily life of the citizens in the Union. Central political guidance comes from the Union's European Council, because it is in this configuration that the prime ministers and the heads of state of the member states meet to chart the course and try to settle the differences that could not be overcome in the Council of the European Union. The concept of the Union rightly conveys that the EU is not a normal international organisation. It has characteristics which are not unique, because a few other international organisations have similar characteristics, but their intensity and their combination in the EU is unique and set the EU apart from other international organisations. The basic structure of the EU is often illustrated with a Greek temple front representing the building blocs of Communities and policies. Diagram 4.1 shows this scheme in an adapted version. The first pillar – the EC – is pictured as the thickest and the roof is slightly tilted to express that the whole structure rests mainly on the first pillar and much less on the other two.

To mention but a few of the characteristics: the EU conveys its own citizenship on all the citizens of the member states, who since then have dual citizenship.[63] The EU (mainly the EC) can create legislation, which is binding for its member states, all its citizens and all organisations within it spheres of authority. This

[60] Article 2, first sentence, fifth indent, and Article 3, first sentence EU Treaty.

[61] Originally there were three Communities: the European Coal and Steel Community (ECSC), founded in 1952, the European Economic Community and the European Atomic Energy Community, better known as Euratom, both founded in 1958. The ECSC ceased to exist when the fifty years duration of its founding Treaty lapsed. The two remaining Communities were founded for an indefinite period. The EC took over the functions of the ECSC in 2002.

[62] Article 1, third sentence, Treaty on European Union, as amended by the 1997 Treaty of Amsterdam, the 2001 Treaty of Nice and the 2003 Accession Treaties of the ten new Member States.

[63] Citizenship of the Union is regulated by Articles 17 – 22 European Community (!) Treaty. These rights will be come Articles 20 25 TFEU. Source for all EC Treaty articles: the English Consolidated version published 24 December 2002 in Official Journal C 325, p. 35.

EU law works directly inside the legal systems of the member states without any need for consent or interference by the national governments. It is supreme law in the sense that it puts aside as invalid any and every national law that is found to be contrary to EU law. Moreover, this is determined by independent judges who have to apply the law independently from the opinions and wishes of the national governments. This rule of EU law has to be carried out by both the specially created judiciaries of the EC and by all national judges. The EC can decide on many issues by majority vote, it has its own sources of income and determines its own budget. Conflicts between the institutions of the EC can be settled by the Court of Justice of the European Communities. The same goes for disputes between the member states and between the EC and the member states. An independent institution, the European Commission, supervises the faithful execution of Community obligations and EU law by the member states. If there are differences of opinion on these issues, the Commission can advise the member state to change its behaviour. If this state does not agree, it is up to the Commission to decide to bring this state before the Court of Justice. The Court decides the issue, and member states usually carry out this decision. Sometimes member states have to appear a second time before the Court, this time because they neglected to carry out the first verdict of the Court. Article 228(2) EC Treaty makes it possible to punish failing member states with a fine for having breached Community law. Diagram 4.3 represents the character of the European Community as a mix of supranational and intergovernmental elements. This mix is known as communautair, or, in English, in the words of the Draft Constitution for Europe: the Community way.

The decisive first step in the creation of this complex Union was set by a French Minister of Foreign Affairs, with a German name, Robert Schuman. On May 9, 1950 he read a declaration to the press which heralded a new approach of France's policies that sought a solution to the age-old problem of how to live peacefully with Germany. In dealing with EU law it is essential always to realise this highly political aspect of European Community law, even when you are buried by the oncoming avalanche of technical details of food law. European Union law always has an ingredient to push forward into the integration that must be achieved to pre-empt the issue of war and peace. Its nature and effects contribute to a larger structure that is designed never to raise that issue again. Law text box 4.5 presents the text of Schuman's offer to create a common future under a High Authority.

Diagram 4.3. The Community way: the European Community a mix of supranational and intergovernmental elements. The main institutions. The main Instruments. The relations between EC and Member States: supremacy and direct effect of EC law. The creation of legislation or policies through the codecision procedure: steps 1-6 linking Commission, Council and Parliament in a procedure where both Council and Parliament have the final say.

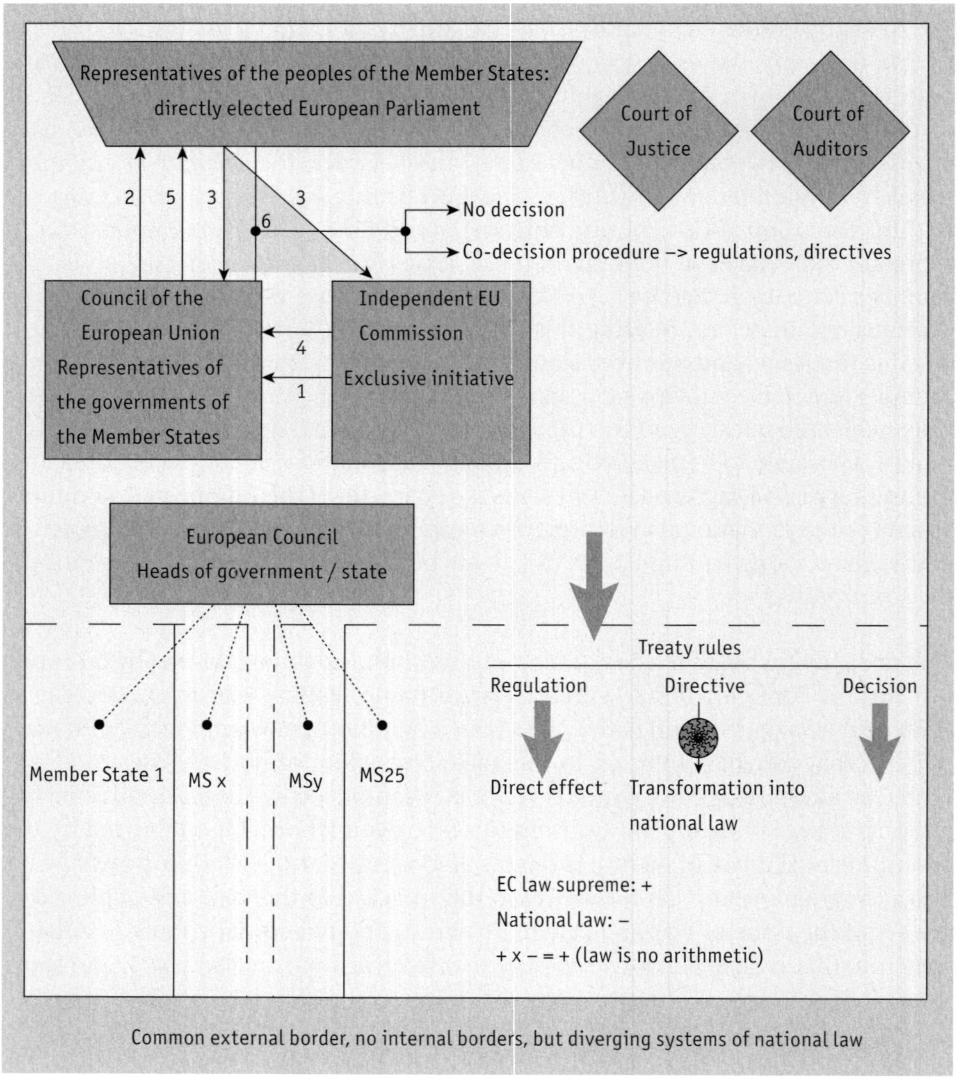

Law text box 4.5. The Schuman Declaration of 9 May 1950. (Source: Historical Archives of the European Union: http://europa.eu, choose tab Documents > Historical Archives of the European Union > Research by subject > Keywords).

'World peace cannot be safeguarded without the making of creative efforts proportionate to the dangers which threaten it. The contribution which an organised and living Europe can bring to civilisation is indispensable to the maintenance of peaceful relations. In taking upon herself for more than 20 years the role of champion of a united Europe, France has always had as her essential aim the service of peace. A united Europe was not achieved and we had war.

Europe will not be made all at once, or according to a single plan. It will be built through concrete achievements which first create a de facto solidarity. The coming together of the nations of Europe requires the elimination of the age-old opposition of France and Germany. Any action taken must in the first place concern these two countries.

With this aim in view, the French Government proposes that action be taken immediately on one limited but decisive point. It proposes that Franco-German production of coal and steel as a whole be placed under a common High Authority, within the framework of an organisation open to the participation of the other countries of Europe. The pooling of coal and steel production should immediately provide for the setting up of common foundations for economic development as a first step in the federation of Europe, and will change the destinies of those regions which have long been devoted to the manufacture of munitions of war, of which they have been the most constant victims.

The solidarity in production thus established will make it plain that any war between France and Germany becomes not merely unthinkable, but materially impossible. The setting up of this powerful productive unit, open to all countries willing to take part and bound ultimately to provide all the member countries with the basic elements of industrial production on the same terms, will lay a true foundation for their economic unification. This production will be offered to the world as a whole without distinction or exception, with the aim of contributing to raising living standards and to promoting peaceful achievements. [...]
In this way, there will be realised simply and speedily that fusion of interest which is indispensable to the establishment of a common economic system; it may be the leaver from which may grow a wider and deeper community between countries long opposed to one another by sanguinary divisions. By pooling basic production and by instituting a new High Authority, whose decisions will bind France, Germany and other member countries, this proposal will lead to the realisation of the first concrete foundation of a European federation indispensable to the preservation of peace.

To promote the realisation of the objectives defined, the French Government is ready to open negotiations on the following bases.

The task with which this common High Authority will be charged will be that of securing in the shortest possible time the modernisation of production and the improvement of its quality; the supply of coal and steel on identical terms to the French and German markets, as well as to the markets of other member countries; the development in common of exports to other countries; the equalisation and improvement of the living conditions of workers in these industries.

To achieve these objectives, starting from the very different conditions in which the production of member countries is at present situated, it is proposed that certain transitional measures should be instituted, such as the application of a production and investment plan, the establishment of compensating machinery for equating prices, and the creation of a restructuring fund to facilitate the rationalisation of production. The movement of coal and steel between member countries will immediately be freed from all customs duty, and will not be affected by differential transport rates. Conditions will gradually be created which will spontaneously provide for the more rational distribution of production at the highest level of productivity. In contrast to international cartels, which tend to impose restrictive practices on distribution and the exploitation of national markets, and to maintain high profits, the organisation will ensure the fusion of markets and the expansion of production.

The essential principles and undertakings defined above will be the subject of a treaty signed between the States and submitted for the ratification of their parliaments. The negotiations required to settle details of applications will be undertaken with the help of an arbitrator appointed by common agreement. He will be entrusted with the task of seeing that the agreements reached conform with the principles laid down, and, in the event of a deadlock, he will decide what solution is to be adopted.

The common High Authority entrusted with the management of the scheme will be composed of independent persons appointed by the governments, giving equal representation.

A chairman will be chosen by common agreement between the governments. The Authority's decisions will be enforceable in France, Germany and other member countries. Appropriate measures will be provided for means of appeal against the decisions of the Authority.

A representative of the United Nations will be accredited to the Authority, and will be instructed to make a public report to the United Nations twice yearly, giving an account of the working of the new organisation, particularly as concerns the safeguarding of its objectives.

The institution of the High Authority will in no way prejudge the methods of ownership of enterprises. In the exercise of its functions, the common High Authority will take into account the powers conferred upon the International Ruhr Authority and the obligations of all kinds imposed upon Germany, so long as these remain in force'.

4.3 The powers of the EU: attribution

4.3.1 Concept

When they founded the first organisations for integration in Europe, the European Coal and Steel Community in 1952 and the European Economic Community in 1958, the original six member states transferred a certain amount of their national sovereignty to the Communities, thus 'limiting their sovereignty and creating a Community based on law and binding them and their citizens, creating rights and obligations (...)' as stated by the Court of Justice in the Van Gend en Loos case[64] in 1962 and the Costa versus ENEL case in 1964.[65] The Court stated its fundamental position that 'the Community constitutes a new legal order, for the benefit of which the states have limited their sovereign rights, albeit within limited fields, and the subjects of which comprise not only the member states but also their nationals'.[66] These judgments by the Court of Justice have become corner stones of EC constitutional law. Individuals next to states as direct participants in this new legal order clearly set EU law apart from general international law, certainly at that time. However, the member states were determined to specify exactly which parts of their sovereignty, and to which extent, were transferred to the new organisations. The Communities have powers only if these are specified in the treaties and expressly transferred to them. In a national legal system the Constitution specifies the sovereignty assumed by the state and assigns specific parts of this national sovereignty to specific organs of the state, for example the legislature, the executive and the judiciary. They use their powers in a general way, subject to the conditions set by the Constitution. Usually emergency powers are also foreseen. The founders of the European Communities wrote into the treaties the system that the Communities have power only if a treaty article expressly gives this particular power. If the treaty is silent on a particular power, this power has remained in the hands of the member states. This basic principle is technically called the attribution of power.[67] Diagram 4.4 shows the attribution of power for agriculture policy. This attribution is rather simple, but carries major consequences for the regulatory and financial capacities of the EC, and leaves the European Parliament only the power of advice.

---

64 Case 26/62 NV Algemene Transport en Expeditie Onderneming Van Gend en Loos *versus (v.)* Nederlandse Administratie der belastingen [1963] European Court Reports (ECR) 1. The case law of the Court is published in the ECR that can be found in the EU Documentation Centres. They are also accessible on the website of the Court, curia.europa.eu and at Eur-Lex.

65 Case 6/64 Costa *v.* ENEL [1964] ECR 585.

66 Case 28/67 Firma Molkerei-Zentrale Westfalen Lippe GmbH *v.* Hauptzollamt Paderborn [1968] ECR 143 at 152.

67 See EC Treaty, Article 5, first sentence and Article 7, paragraph 1, second sentence, and (parts of) all articles in the Treaty's 'Part three Community Policies', attributing power for a specific policy.

Diagram 4.4. Attribution of powers: agriculture. The structure and the Articles of the European Community Treaty that establish the basic law for the common agricultural policy. The power clause indicates the attribution to the Council of the powers to legislate and decide on policy. The Council can create binding legal instruments only if the Commission has taken the initiative, and the European Parliament has given an advice. This is a real advice: it does not bind the Council.

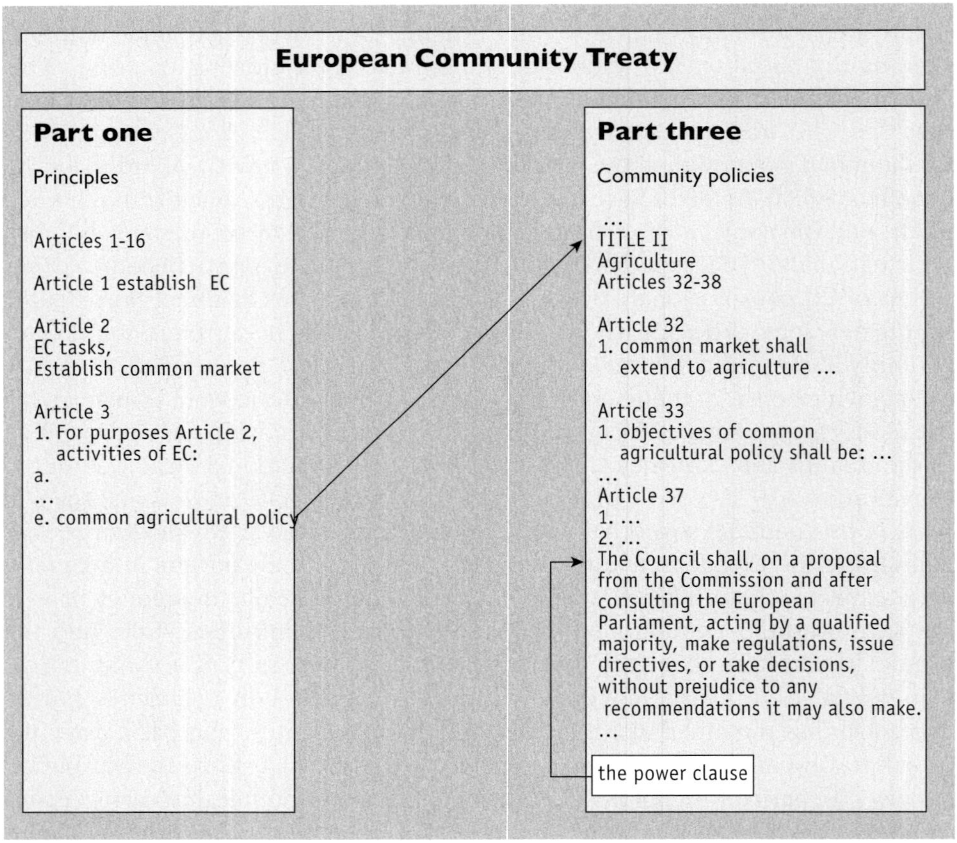

Right page:
Diagram 4.5. Attribution of powers: food policy and food law. Food policy and food law have several bases in the EC Treaty. Article 152 (4)(b) on public health is a remarkable derogation of the powers given for agriculture: since the 1997 Treaty of Amsterdam the agricultural treaty articles are overruled by Article 152 (4)(b). This is taking two steps at the same time: a rearrangement of priorities where agriculture tumbles from its costly pedestal, and a preference for legislation made by Parliament and Council acting together equally (human health protection) in stead of the Council deciding alone (agriculture).

European Community Treaty

Part one

Principles

Article 1 establish EC

Article 2
EC tasks,
Establish common market

Article 3
1. For purposes Article 2, activities of EC
timetable:
a. Customs Union
b. Common commercial policy
c. Internal market
...
e. Common agricultural policy
h. Approximation of laws
p. Public health
t. Consumer protection
...

Part three

Community policies

TITLE I Free movement of goods
Chapter 1 Customs Union
Article 25
Customs duties ... and charges having equivalent effect prohibited
Power clause: Article 26
Chapter 2 Prohibition of quantitative restrictions
Article 28 and 29
Quantitative restrictions and all measures having equivalent effect prohibited

TITLE II Agriculture
Article 32 (1) common market > agriculture
Article 34 (1)
Power clause: Article 37 ... (2)...

TITLE VI
Chapter 3 Approximation of laws
Power clause: Article 94 ... Council acting unanimously on a proposal from the Commission ... issue directives for approximation ... law Member States ... directly affect the establishment or functioning of the common market.
Power clause: Article 95 ... derogation from Article 94 ... Council ... procedure referred to in Article 251 ... measures for the approximation ... law Member States ...object establishment and functioning internal market

TITLE IX Common commercial policy
Power clause: Article 133 ... (2). Commission proposals to Council
Power clause: (3) agreements with States or international organisations ... Council authorise Commission to negotiations. Council and Commission responsible

TITLE XIII Public health
Article 152 (1) A high level of human health protection shall be ensured ...
Power clause: (4) The Council procedure Article 251 (b) **derogation from Article 37** measures in the veterinary and phytosanitary fields which have as their direct objective the protection of public health;

TITLE XIV Consumer protection
Article 153 (1) ... promote the interests of consumers and to ensure a high level of consumer protection. the Community shall contribute to protecting the health, safety and economic interests of consumers ...
Power clause: (4) Council, procedure Article 251 ... adopt the measures referred to in paragraph 3(b): (b) measures which support, supplement and monitor the policy pursued by the Member States.

The attribution of powers for food policy and food law is more complicated. This attribution has several bases in the EC Treaty, of which agriculture is only one, and today not the most important one. Diagram 4.5 indicates the different parts of the EC Treaty that attribute the powers needed to make food policy and food law.

The institutions of the Community have to prove that the necessary power resides with the Community each time they want to act. Therefore each authoritative act of the Communities starts by mentioning the specific treaty article(s) that give(s) the powers that are used: 'Having regard to Article (...)'. Diagram 4.6 shows the first and the last page of Regulation (EC) No 178/2002, usually called the General Food Law (GFL). It is a pivotal legislative instrument that lays the basis for further development of EU food law.[68] The Diagram indicates the traces of the various steps that are necessary to make legislation, in this example the EC Treaty bases needed to create food law. The Court of Justice verifies the existence of the powers used in each case it has to adjudicate. If the Court cannot establish the Treaty Article that gives this power to the Community, the action of the institution(s) is illegal by definition, because it is an exercise of power that transgresses the totality of powers that were given.[69]

4.3.2 The structure of the EC Treaty

The strict attribution of powers is further amplified by the distinction between two strands that run through the EC Treaty. In the institutional strand the new organisation founded in 1958 is set up. It has to be capable of running the EC policies, which contain essentials for the well being of the peoples in the member states, on a permanent basis. The EC can act because it has got legal personality. It has five institutions that carry out the different functions that are tied up with this new organisation.[70] The composition of each institution is prescribed along with the ways the functionaries are recruited who make these institutions work. Instruments are defined for legislation and for individual decisions. The budget is defined. Procedures are given that have to be followed when the particular instruments are used. Among these is the crucial capability to have decisions made by a majority vote. Institutions and member states are given access to an independent judge, one of the five institutions, to have differences of opinion settled. Natural and legal persons are protected by the rule of law, and by particular procedures to make this recourse to the law effective. Member states come under the surveillance of another independent institution, the Commission. In short, a new and complete organisation has been build, staffed and equipped.

---

[68] The complete GFL Regulation (consolidated version) is reproduced in Appendix A of this book.

[69] Article 230 EC Treaty lists four grounds for annulment of binding legal instruments: lack of competence is the first one.

[70] See Article 7 EC Treaty.

But at this point only an abstract toolkit has been created and entrusted to known functionaries, they cannot do anything with it yet. Because they do not have the powers they need.

For that the second strand, the policy strand, in the Treaty is needed. Article 2 lists the objectives and the means of the EC; Article 3 prescribes at least twenty-one activities that are necessary to reach the goals set in the preceding article. The third part of the Treaty unfolds the Article 3 activities into 31 Chapters, each a set of specifications attuned to the characteristics of its policy field. It is among this elaboration of each policy that the necessary powers are attributed. The EC Treaty provides a separate transfer of power for each separate policy. Each transfer takes from the abstract toolkit that which is deemed to fit the particular policy and assigns the institutions that have to carry out these tasks, in accordance with the procedures that are also given. The following Law text boxes 4.6 and 4.7, and Diagram 4.7 present the law that was made to create the structure of the treaty and its Community. The attribution of power for food policy that was traced earlier from the concrete example of the General Food Law, is now placed in the general pattern.

Law text box 4.6. Tasks of the European Community, Article 2 EC Treaty.

Article 2 EC Treaty

The Community shall have as its task, by establishing a common market and an economic and monetary union and by implementing common policies or activities referred to in Articles 3 and 4, to promote throughout the Community a harmonious, balanced and sustainable development of economic activities, a high level of employment and of social protection, equality between men and women, sustainable and non-inflationary growth, a high degree of competitiveness and convergence of economic performance, a high level of protection and improvement of the quality of the environment, the raising of the standard of living and quality of life, and economic and social cohesion and solidarity among Member States.

Following page:

Diagram 4.6. Attribution of powers for the General Food Law, Regulation 178/2002.

The first and last page of the General Food Law, Regulation 178/2002. Clauses indicating how the regulation was made, which powers attributed to whom that made the regulation possible, are highlighted. *(See next two pages)*

(first page)

L (legislation) series of Offical Journal for binding law

Number of the Official Journal

Pagenumber

I

(Acts whose publication is obligatory)

Regulation is based on EC Treaty

Co-decision procedure

REGULATION (EC) No 178/2002 OF THE EUROPEAN PARLIAMENT AND OF THE COUNCIL of 28 January 2002

laying down the general principles and requirements of food law, establishing the European Food Safety Authority and laying down procedures in matters of food safety

THE EUROPEAN PARLIAMENT AND THE COUNCIL OF THE EUROPEAN UNION,

Attribution: powers to make legislation are indicated

Having regard to the Treaty establishing the European Community, and in particular Articles 37, 95, 133 and Article 152(4)(b) thereof,

Exclusive right of initiative

Having regard to the proposal from the Commission [1],

Having regard to the opinion of the Economic and Social Committee [2],

Having regard to the opinion of the Committee of the Regions [3],

Co-decision procedure

Acting in accordance with the procedure laid down in Article 251 of the Treaty [4],

Whereas:

(1) The free movement of safe and wholesome food is an essential aspect of the internal market and contributes significantly to the health and well-being of citizens, and to their social and economic interests.

(2) A high level of protection of human life and health should be assured in the pursuit of Community policies.

(3) The free movement of food and feed within the Community can be achieved only if food and feed safety requirements do not differ significantly from Member State to Member State.

(4) There are important differences in relation to concepts, principles and procedures between the food laws of the Member States. When Member States adopt measures governing food, these differences may impede the free movement of food, create unequal conditions of competition, and may thereby directly affect the functioning of the internal market.

(5) Accordingly, it is necessary to approximate these concepts, principles and procedures so as to form a common basis for measures governing food and feed taken in the Member States and at Community level. It is however necessary to provide for sufficient time for the adaptation of any conflicting provisions in existing legislation, both at national and Community level, and to provide that, pending such adaptation, the relevant legislation be applied in the light of the principles set out in the present Regulation.

(6) Water is ingested directly or indirectly like other foods, thereby contributing to the overall exposure of a consumer to ingested substances, including chemical and microbiological contaminants. However, as the quality of water intended for human consumption is already controlled by Council Directives 80/778/EEC [5] and 98/83/EC [6], it suffices to consider water after the point of compliance referred to in Article 6 of Directive 98/83/EC.

(7) Within the context of food law it is appropriate to include requirements for feed, including its production and use where that feed is intended for food-producing animals. This is without prejudice to the similar requirements which have been applied so far and which will be applied in the future in feed legislation applicable to all animals, including pets.

(8) The Community has chosen a high level of health protection as appropriate in the development of food law, which it applies in a non-discriminatory manner whether food or feed is traded on the internal market or internationally.

(1) OJ C 96 E, 27.3.2001, p. 247.
(2) OJ C 155, 29.5.2001, p. 32.
(3) Opinion delivered on 14 June 2001 (not yet published in the Official Journal).
(4) Opinion of the European Parliament of 12 June 2001 (not yet published in the Official Journal), Council Common Position of 17 September 2001 (not yet published in the Official Journal) and Decision of the European Parliament of 11 December 2001 (not yet published in the Official Journal). Council Decision of 21 January 2002.

(5) OJ L 229, 30.8.1980, p. 11. Directive repealed by Directive 98/83/EC.
(6) OJ L 330, 5.12.1998, p. 32.

Necessary steps to create the regulation are registered in "Having regard to ..." and notes 1-4

(original page)

The Management Board of the Authority shall examine the conclusions of the evaluation and issue to the Commission such recommendations as may be necessary regarding changes in the Authority and its working practices. The evaluation and the recommendations shall be made public.

2. Before 1 January 2005, the Commission shall publish a report on the experience acquired from implementing Sections 1 and 2 of Chapter IV.

3. The reports and recommendations referred to in paragraphs 1 and 2 shall be forwarded to the Council and the European Parliament.

Article 62

References to the European Food Safety Authority and to the Standing Committee on the Food Chain and Animal Health

1. Every reference in Community legislation to the Scientific Committee on Food, the Scientific Committee on Animal Nutrition, the Scientific Veterinary Committee, the Scientific Committee on Pesticides, the Scientific Committee on Plants and the Scientific Steering Committee shall be replaced by a reference to the European Food Safety Authority.

2. Every reference in Community legislation to the Standing Committee on Foodstuffs, the Standing Committee for Feedingstuffs and the Standing Veterinary Committee shall be replaced by a reference to the Standing Committee on the Food Chain and Animal Health.

Every reference to the Standing Committee on Plant Health in Community legislation based upon and including Directives 76/895/EEC, 86/362/EEC, 86/363/EEC, 90/642/EEC and 91/414/EEC relating to plant protection products and the setting of maximum residue levels shall be replaced by a reference to the Standing Committee on the Food Chain and Animal Health.

3. For the purpose of paragraphs 1 and 2, 'Community legislation' shall mean all Community Regulations, Directives and Decisions.

4. Decisions 68/361/EEC, 69/414/EEC and 70/372/EEC are hereby repealed.

Article 63

Competence of the European Agency for the Evaluation of Medicinal Products

This Regulation shall be without prejudice to the competence conferred on the European Agency for the Evaluation of Medicinal Products by Regulation (EEC) No 2309/93, Regulation (EEC) No 2377/90, Council Directive 75/319/EEC [1] and Council Directive 81/851/EEC [2].

Article 64

Commencement of the Authority's operation

The Authority shall commence its operations on 1 January 2002.

Article 65

Entry into force ←

This Regulation shall enter into force on the 20th day following that of its publication in the *Official Journal of the European Communities*.

Articles 11 and 12 and Articles 14 to 20 shall apply from 1 January 2005.

Articles 29, 56, 57 and 60 and Article 62(1) shall apply as from the date of appointment of the members of the Scientific Committee and of the Scientific Panels which shall be announced by means of a notice in the 'C' series of the Official Journal.

This Regulation shall be binding in its entirety and directly applicable in all Member States.

→ Done at Brussels, 28 January 2002.

For the European Parliament	*For the Council*
The President	*The President*
P. COX	J. PIQUÉ I CAMPS

Co-decision procedure: consent of European Parliament and Council are necessary. So both presidents must sign.

Dates are necessary to get a valid working regulation
. date of formal decision
. date of publication see also top page 1 "Acts whose publication is obligatory"
. date of entry into force see Article 65

(1) OJ L 147, 9.6.1975, p. 13. Directive amended by Directive 2001/83/EC of the European Parliament and of the Council (OJ L 311, 28.11.2001, p. 67).
(2) OJ L 317, 6.11.1981, p. 1. Directive amended by Directive 2001/82/EC of the European Parliament and of the Council (OJ L 311, 28.11.2001, p. 1).

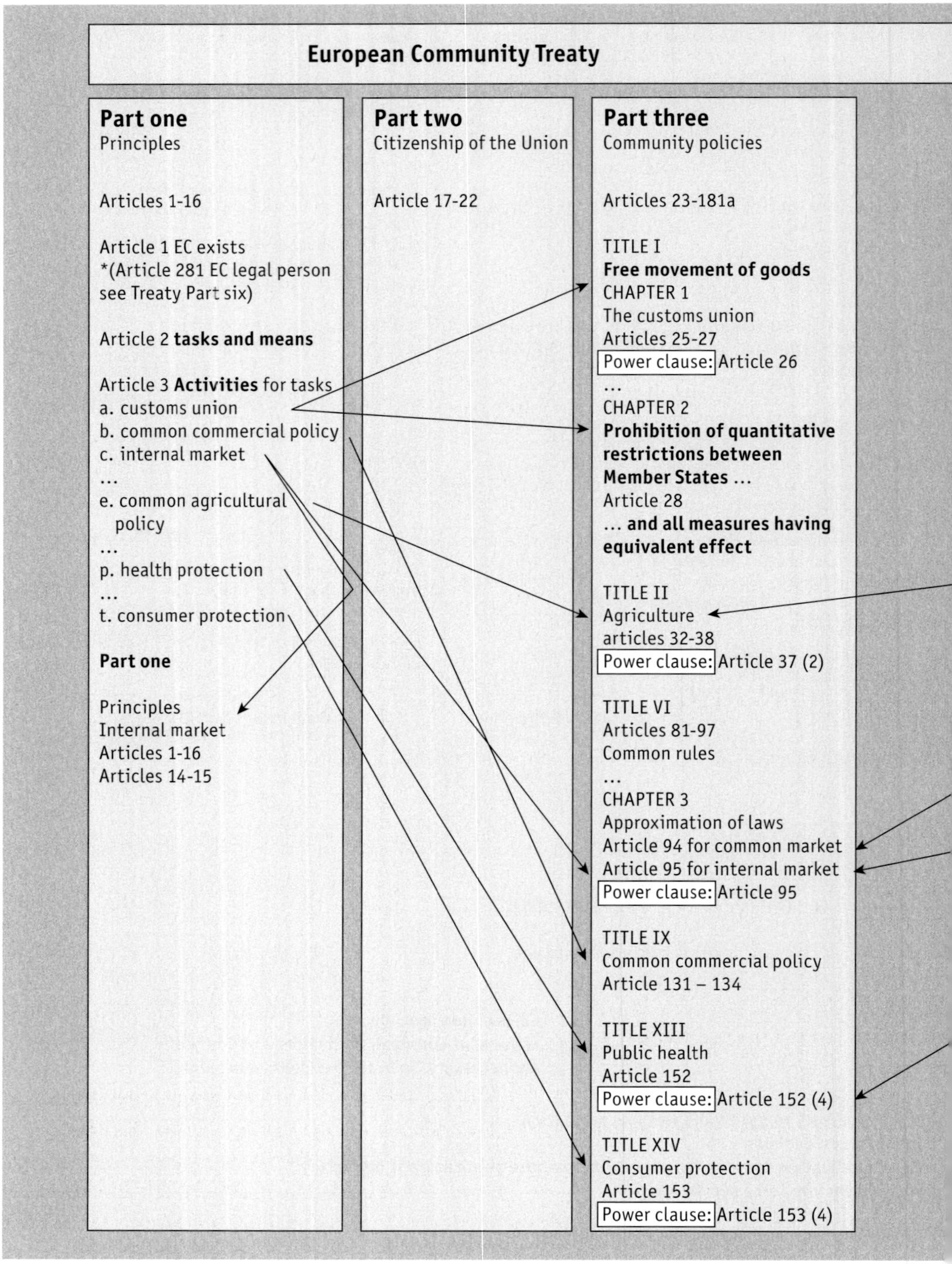
European Community Treaty
Part one
Principles
Articles 1-16
Article 1 EC exists
*(Article 281 EC legal person see Treaty Part six)
Article 2 tasks and means
Article 3 Activities for tasks
a. customs union
b. common commercial policy
c. internal market
...
e. common agricultural policy
...
p. health protection
...
t. consumer protection
Part one
Principles
Internal market
Articles 1-16
Articles 14-15
Part two
Citizenship of the Union
Article 17-22
Part three
Community policies
Articles 23-181a
TITLE I
Free movement of goods
CHAPTER 1
The customs union
Articles 25-27
Power clause: Article 26
...
CHAPTER 2
Prohibition of quantitative restrictions between Member States ...
Article 28
... and all measures having equivalent effect
TITLE II
Agriculture
articles 32-38
Power clause: Article 37 (2)
TITLE VI
Articles 81-97
Common rules
...
CHAPTER 3
Approximation of laws
Article 94 for common market
Article 95 for internal market
Power clause: Article 95
TITLE IX
Common commercial policy
Article 131 – 134
TITLE XIII
Public health
Article 152
Power clause: Article 152 (4)
TITLE XIV
Consumer protection
Article 153
Power clause: Article 153 (4)

European Community Treaty

Part four
Association overseas countries ...

Article 182-188

Part five
Institutions of the Community

Articles 189-280

TITLE I
Provisions governing the institutions
CHAPTER 1
The institutions
Articles 189-248
SECTION 1
The European Parliament
Article 189-201
Article 192
if other treaty Articles allow:
EP participates in decision
making ... with advice
...
CHAPTER 2
Provisions common
to several institutions
Articles 249-256
Article 249
definition of regulation
direcive decision ...
Article 251
co-decision procedure

Part six
General and final provisions

Article 281-314

*Article 281
The Community shall
have legal personality.

Annexes

Diagram 4.7. The structure of the European Community Treaty. Note that the common market, the first means to achieve integration, does not have its own distinct place in the Treaty. The reason: many (originally almost all) subjects listed in Article 3 after a-u and developed in Part three contribute to the creation and maintenance of the common market. The internal market was introduced in 1987 and has Articles 14-15 as its basis. The arrows from Part one to Part three indicate where the Activities of the EC are regulated. The arrows from Part five to Part three indicate which procedures are used to take decisions in Part three. All powers originate in Part three. Note that the Parliament has nothing to say on the customs union.

Law text box 4.7. Activities of the European Community to fulfil her tasks, Article 3 EC Treaty.

Article 3 EC Treaty

1. For the purposes set out in Article 2, the activities of the Community shall include, as provided in this Treaty and in accordance with the timetable set out therein:
   (a) the prohibition, as between Member States, of customs duties and quantitative restrictions on the import and export of goods, and of all other measures having equivalent effect;
   (b) a common commercial policy;
   (c) an internal market characterised by the abolition, as between Member States, of obstacles to the free movement of goods, persons, services and capital;
   (d) measures concerning the entry and movement of persons as provided for in Title IV;
   (e) a common policy in the sphere of agriculture and fisheries;
   (f) a common policy in the sphere of transport;
   (g) a system ensuring that competition in the internal market is not distorted;
   (h) the approximation of the laws of Member States to the extent required for the functioning of the common market;
   (i) the promotion of coordination between employment policies of the Member States with a view to enhancing their effectiveness by developing a coordinated strategy for employment;
   (j) a policy in the social sphere comprising a European Social Fund;
   (k) the strengthening of economic and social cohesion;
   (l) a policy in the sphere of the environment;
   (m) the strengthening of the competitiveness of Community industry;
   (n) the promotion of research and technological development;
   (o) encouragement for the establishment and development of trans-European networks;
   (p) a contribution to the attainment of a high level of health protection;
   (q) a contribution to education and training of quality and to the flowering of the cultures of the Member States;
   (r) a policy in the sphere of development cooperation;
   (s) the association of the overseas countries and territories in order to increase trade and promote jointly economic and social development;
   (t) a contribution to the strengthening of consumer protection;
   (u) measures in the spheres of energy, civil protection and tourism.
2. In all the activities referred to in this Article, the Community shall aim to eliminate inequalities, and to promote equality, between men and women.

4.3.3 Additional powers

Although the EC Treaty contains an extensive list of policies, it is not always clear under what heading a particular measure must be subsumed. In other words: which treaty articles have to be 'regarded'. Debates on the choice of the correct treaty article flare up every now and then. They are important when the choice makes a difference for the power of the institutions or for the type of instruments that can be used.

An example: during the preparation of the Regulation on Genetically Modified Food,[71] the question was debated as to whether the regulation should be based on article 95 EC Treaty (harmonisation) or on article 308 EC (creation of new Community powers). Article 95 – which was ultimately agreed upon – prescribes the co-decision procedure that gives the European Parliament as much influence as the Council. Article 308 prescribes a procedure that requires unanimity in the Council and thus gives the individual member states a lot of influence through a virtual veto right.[72]

Given the strict rules on the attribution of power, a problem could surface caused by the fact that on the one hand the EC has to achieve the goals specified in the Treaty while on the other hand it must have an explicit attribution of power for every step it takes. It might turn out that the EC is missing a power that is needed to carry out the task. The original treaty makers did not assume that they would be able to foresee all the necessities that might arise in the complicated process of integrating national societies. Nor did they pretend that all possible developments of the different national societies and their economies could be locked into the EC Treaty. They gave the treaty an escape clause to meet this type of emergency. Law text box 4.8 presents the escape clause.

Law text box 4.8. Safety valve for attribution of powers. Article 308 EC Treaty.

If action by the Community should prove necessary to attain, in the course of the operation of the common market, one of the objectives of the Community, and this Treaty has not provided the necessary powers, the Council shall, acting unanimously on a proposal from the Commission and after consulting the European Parliament, take the appropriate measures.

This Article (numbered 235 of the old EEC Treaty) served the Community with a way out that was used more than 120 times. It was used to integrate trade in processed agricultural products into the common agricultural policy and later to give the EEC a common regional policy, a social policy and an environmental policy. At that time the Treaty did not contain these policies.[73] The addition of these policies was later incorporated in the Single European Act, the 1986 Treaty changing the EEC Treaty.[74] That became a standard procedure: the development

[71] Regulation (EC) No 1829/2003 of the European Parliament and of the Council of 22 September 2003 on genetically modified food and feed (Text with EEA relevance). Official Journal L 268, 18 October 2003, pp. 1-23. See Chapter 9 for discussion of the GM-food regulation.

[72] See section 4.4 for discussion of the decision-making procedures. See also section 5.2 - 5.4

[73] See Gormley, page 239.

[74] 1986 Single European Act. Official Journal L 169, 29 June 1987.

made possible by Article 235/308 was later codified and enhanced in a revision of the EC Treaty. It can still be used for that purpose, although this is less likely because the EC Treaty now contains a greater array of policies and instruments.

4.3.4 Implied powers

To complete the picture of the powers of the EU, the 'implied powers' must be mentioned. These powers are not explicitly mentioned in the EC Treaty, but follow by necessity from the powers that can be found in that treaty. To give a historic case: if the EC Treaty gives powers to regulate fisheries in general, it follows from this internal authority that the Community also has the power to deal with international aspects of fisheries outside the EU. The Court of Justice of the European Communities has decided several times that the power to act within the EU includes the power to act outside the EU if the policy so requires.[75]

4.4 EU policy instruments

The EU has several instruments to carry out its tasks and policies.[76] These instruments are available for the institutions in different settings: for the European Parliament acting jointly with the Council on the basis of an initiative of the Commission; for the Council acting alone on the basis of an initiative of the Commission; and for the Commission acting on the basis of the powers given by the EC Treaty, and even more on the basis of the powers delegated to it by the Council.

Advice, recommendations, opinions are not binding policy statements. They may give guidance, rally support and lead to soft law. Soft law is a debated part of international law that prepares the way for customary law or treaty law. It enables states that do not want to bind themselves legally yet, to adopt and test certain rules and principles before they become law.[77]

The legally binding instruments are the regulation, the directive and the decision. They have quite different forms, and lead to different results. The regulation and the directive are legislative acts, the decision is an act made for one particular situation.

---

[75] Combined cases 3, 4 and 6/76, ECR 1976 1279 Kramer. Conservation of certain species of fish. EC party to a treaty to limit fishing in the North East Atlantic.

[76] Article 249 EC Treaty defines some important instruments.

[77] Malanczuk, Peter, Akehurst's Modern Introduction to International Law, 7th ed. London, 1997, pp. 54-55. Senden, Linda A.J., Soft Law in European Community Law, Oxford, 2004.

4.4.1 Legislation versus decision

Legislation creates rules that will be applied again and again to an unknown number of persons, each time that the situation occurs that is described in these rules. The rules are binding and they spell out the consequences for those persons who fulfil the conditions set in the rules.

A decision is essentially different, as it formulates the law for one specific situation and only for that particular situation. It is directed to a known person and defines a particular aspect of the legal situation for this particular person.[78] A decision constitutes not a rule, but the application of a rule in one particular event. The process to construct a decision and apply it to an isolated known individual is an exercise of public power that is regulated by administrative law. The question of the legality of legislation creating rules is essentially a constitutional law question. The legality of a general law is guarded by the representatives of the people who co-operated in parliament to make that law. In some countries the question of the legality of a general law can be brought before a constitutional court. Private persons cannot challenge the legality of a rule made by the legislator because that issue belongs to the public authorities. Private persons can challenge the legality of a decision made for them, or made for another individual but with significant influence on their legal position. They have the right to question this decision because the rule of law demands that individuals are treated according to rules and principles embodied in the law. To test whether the decision is made according to the law, the persons immediately concerned must have the opportunity to ask a judge to ascertain the legality of the decision.

And there the two distinct approaches, no challenge of rules, only of decisions, meet. The judge will test the decision against the legislation that gives the power to take decisions like this one. The judge will also verify whether this enabling legislation conforms to higher rules. The judge has to do the complete analysis of the relevant hierarchy of legal norms. If s/he finds a wrong, the rule cannot stand and the decision cannot be upheld. So the judge will disregard the wrong parts of the lower legislation and construct the decision as it legally has to be. The judge will declare a part of a rule, or the entire rule, to be invalid. It is up to the legislator to repair the rule by making new legislation. So the individual decision is in a sense the ticket that allows an individual to challenge legislation.

An unfortunate mix up of different meanings of the word 'decision' occurs because it is used in the strict sense described so far, but is also used more loosely for all kinds of determinations that do not have the legal consequences of the decision. They do not create rights or obligations for one particular individual. Government

[78] It is beyond the scope of this book to delve into the subtleties of decisions that address specific situations that cannot readily be connected to particular (legal) persons.

ministries and agencies take many decisions as steps in the process of preparation or administration, that have no legal effects for individuals outside the administration, because these are internal affairs for this particular branch of government. Perhaps more confusingly legislators decide to adopt a legislative act. That decision is a single unique one time only action to create a legal rule, so it is not a rule itself, but it is also not a decision in the sense of relevant administrative law.

4.4.2 The Treaty as primary law

Treaties, regulations, directives and decisions embody EU law. Treaties usually are a mix of legislation and decisions. The founding treaties are the primary law as they created the Communities. Primary law can only be changed by other primary law, such as new treaties or basic principles of international law (*ius cogens*). Because the founding treaties created a Community with sovereign powers taken over from the member states, the states can no longer change the EU Treaties among themselves: they have no say about the powers they have lost. The institutions of the Communities sharing in sovereignty have to participate in changing the primary law (Article 48 EU Treaty).

The EC Treaty has been changed twenty-one times since it came into force on January 1, 1958. A far higher frequency of changes than national constitutions have.[79] These amendments to the Treaty reflect the repeated accession of new states, the creation of new powers and the systematisation of all developments in the European Union. These repeated changes are now culminating in the Lisbon Treaty signed in 2007. It is to succeed where the Draft Treaty on the EU Constitution failed to get ratified.[80] To become part of the law, this Treaty must be accepted by all the member states according to the procedure prescribed by their national constitutions. The legislation based on the treaties carries out what was foreseen in the primary law, so in relation to the treaties all other instruments are secondary law. Of these, regulations are the instruments to create legislation that resemble most the legislative instruments used by the member states in their national systems. Directives are especially created for the peculiar EC combination of legislative activities of the EC in tandem with the member states. Decisions stand apart from the legislative acts; they are for individual cases and can be based on the treaties or on secondary legislation.

[79] Compare: the Constitution of the United States of America was made in 1787. Since then it has been changed eighteen times; giving an average of one change in twelve years. The average for the EC is two years.

[80] Official Journal C 169, 18 July 2003.

4.4.3 The regulation

Regulations are defined in the EC Treaty in this way: 'A regulation shall have general application. It shall be binding in its entirety and directly applicable in all Member States'.[81]

The elements 'general application', 'binding' and 'directly applicable', construct the character of the regulation: it is a legally binding rule, it is legislation binding all natural and legal persons, that fall under the jurisdiction of the EC, including the member states, the EC itself and hence its institutions, if they are in the situation defined in the rule. The jurisdiction of the EC extends itself over the combined territories of the member states and beyond when the EC takes legal action against persons or companies that influence the internal market from abroad. The regulation is binding as long as it is made in accordance with the EU Treaties, which prescribe the conditions, that have to be met if and when the EC institutions exercise their powers. Many conditions have to be met; they have been dealt with under the heading of the attribution of power. The EC Treaty prescribes four grounds for annulment, which the Court of Justice has to apply each time it uses a regulation to base a case on. One of these grounds is 'infringement of this Treaty or of any rule of law relating to its application'.[82] The regulation cuts the matter for which it is made as legislation right out of the national legislation of the member states. This matter is now legislated solely on the higher level of EU law. The regulation does not need national law to operate inside the member states. The regulation secures that its law is the same everywhere on the territory of the Union. Only when the regulation itself allows it, can different law be applied for certain regions or groups. Only when the regulation allows it, can national law make choices presented in the regulation or make more detailed rules.[83] Most EU regulations are carried out by the authorities of the member states.

These kinds of legal acts have to be made according to a strict procedure,[84] of which publication in the Official Journal of the European Union is one.[85] Under the rule of law legally binding instruments have to be known before they can be binding. The member states are not allowed to publish these EC regulations in their national law books or official journals. This is strictly prohibited to avoid confusion about the nature of this law. The regulation is binding because it is EC law, not because it is national law of the member states. To take it up in a

[81] Article 249 EC Treaty.

[82] Article 230 EC Treaty.

[83] At the moment of writing, a proposal is pending for a regulation on the provision of food information to the consumer (COM(2008) 40 final – discussed in Chapter 12). This proposed regulation devotes an entire chapter (VII articles 44-47) to national schemes.

[84] Articles 249-255 EC Treaty.

[85] Article 254 EC Treaty.

national law book could create the false impression that it is national law, or can be changed by a new national law made on a later date.[86]

The basic regulation

A distinction is made in practice between a basic regulation and other regulations. The basic regulation is based immediately on the relevant EC Treaty article(s). It contains the basic provisions for a particular EC policy. It sets the broad outlines and empowers the Council or the Commission to make more detailed regulations on certain issues. The EC Treaty and the basic regulation together determine the options for the more detailed legislation (*'Ah, ça, c'est une Idée, mais ce n'est pas dans la Régulation de Base…'.*). To give an example: all 21 different product sectors of the common agricultural policy each have their own basic regulation with the rules for their own common market organisation for cereals, for milk products, sugar, fresh fruit and vegetables. See Diagram 4.8 on the basic regulation of the sector fresh fruit and vegetables.

Diagram 4.8. The basic regulation between Treaty and implementing regulation.

Implementing regulation	Commission Regulation (EC) No 1580/2007 of 21 December 2007 laying down implementing rules of Council Regulations (EC) No 2200/96, (EC) No 2201/96 and (EC) No 1182/2007 in the fruit and vegetable sector. Official Journal L 350, 31 December 2007, pp. 1-98. and in particular Article 1(3) thereof Article 1(3)
Connecting Article	Article 1(3) Article 1(3) Regulation (EC) No 2200/96
Basic regulation	Council Regulation (EC) No 2200/96 of 28 October 1996 on the common organisation of the market in fruit and vegetables. Official Journal L 297, 21 November 1996, pp. 1-28. Refers to Article 37(2)(third paragraph) TEC
Power	Article 37(2)(third paragraph)
Treaty	Article 37(2)(third paragraph)
Text power clause *Treaty Article*	The Council shall, on a proposal from the Commission and after consulting the European Parliament, acting by a qualified majority, make regulations, issue directives, or take decisions, without prejudice to any recommendations it may also make.

The basic regulations empower the Council to make a price regulation each year to cover the market situation for the coming year. This issue is so important for the Council that it has reserved this power for itself. Other policy aspects or regulation

[86] This ban is on publication of EC legislation in official journals. Unofficial publication by private publishers is not forbidden.

can be delegated to the Commission. The dairy quota system was introduced by a Council regulation introducing a quota article into the basic regulation. At the same day a Council regulation was made, establishing the main provisions of the new quota system. This Council regulation was based on the new article in the basic regulation. Later the Commission made a regulation dealing with the details. The power to do this was contained in the Council regulation for the main provisions.

Regulation (EC) No 178/2002 of the European Parliament and of the Council of 28 January 2002 laying down the general principles and requirements of food law, establishing the European Food Safety Authority and laying down procedures in matters of food safety, known for short as the General Food Law, is in many ways the basic regulation for food policy and food law.[87]

The framework regulation is the instrument made by the legislator to determine the most important elements and formulate the conditions that have to guide the future legislator on how to fill in the framework. The framework regulation can also formulate the conditions that the more detailed regulations have to meet. The Council working together with the European Parliament will in many cases be the legislator of a framework regulation. However, there are still policies where the Council alone will be the framework legislator. The legislator who made the framework regulation can also make the legislation to fill in the framework. It can also be another legislator to whom this power is delegated, usually the Commission. In this book, for example, the discussions of food additives in Chapter 9 and of contaminants in Chapter 10 begin by introducing the framework directive and framework regulation respectively and then move on to discuss the legislation set in place to fill in the framework.

4.4.4 The directive

The directive was expressly designed as an additional instrument to facilitate the relationship between the law of the EC and the national law of the member states. The EC Treaty defines a directive as follows: 'A directive shall be binding, as to the result to be achieved, upon each member state to which it is addressed, but shall leave to the national authorities the choice of form and methods'.[88]

The directive can be addressed to one or more member states, but it is usually directed at all. It prescribes the objectives that have to be met, and the period in which this has to be achieved. It leaves to the member states the choice of the means to fulfil the obligation. The member states are the best experts on their own

[87] Official Journal L 31, 1 February 2002, p. 1. See the full text in Appendix A of this book.
[88] Article 249 EC Treaty.

system of national law. They are best suited to find the ways to fit their national legal system in the EC objectives and the rules prescribed by the directive.

The directive is used if the EC finds it necessary to harmonise the national laws of the member states: the laws in the member states do not have to be equal in all respects (in that case the regulation would be the required instrument), but must be sufficiently comparable to fit in with EC principles and policies. The European Economic Community (EEC) Treaty[89] foresaw the need especially for the common market to have large-scale harmonisation of national laws dealing with all aspects of goods that the Treaty prescribes to be in free movement. On the other hand nobody could foresee how many national laws had to be harmonised, nor to what extent. To solve this problem, the EEC Treaty offered in Article 100 (now 94 EC Treaty) the directive as a bridge between EC law and national law, and specified that unanimity was required for each harmonisation directive. In that way all member states could participate with confidence in the uncharted harmonisation effort, knowing they would be their own masters at all times.

In practice the difficulties arising from different national laws with an effect on the common market proved to be even tougher. To remedy a jammed decision-making process, the internal market program was launched in 1986 with the Treaty called Single European Act introducing the internal market and amending other articles of the EEC Treaty. One of these changes was the introduction of Article 100A (now Article 95 EC Treaty) allowing other instruments alongside directives, and prescribing decision making by majority vote. A quarter of a century of trying with unanimity had shown the impossibility of harmonising when every State has to agree with every detail. This was no surprise for the men who laid the foundations of the EEC Treaty. They wrote in the report commissioned by the governments of the six ECSC member states (the Spaak Report)[90] that the new Community had to have majority decision making if it was meant to work. A notorious example of the effects of not voting but aiming at unanimity is the Directive for fruit jams and marmalades that took eighteen years of negotiation; and after that landmark the negotiators moved to tackle the other products on the table.

The directive is EC law that is binding for the member states to which it is addressed. Usually it leads these states to change their national law, and then this national law is binding for those who live or work in this national law system.

In this case there are two sets of rules: the changed national law on the level of the member state and the directive on the EU level. The national rules have to

[89] The EEC Treaty is the founding document made in 1957 for the original European Economic Community, the precursor of the European Community.

[90] Spaak Report: Rapport des Chefs de Délégations aux Ministres des Affaires Etrangères. Secretariat of the Intergovernmental Conference, Brussels, 21 April 1956.

stay within the bounds specified in the directive. If the member state has fulfilled its obligation the national law will carry out the rules of the directive. However, opinions may differ. Then those who have to apply the national law (judges, government agencies, regional or local governments) are obliged to apply the national law as it is supposed to be, that is in the way the directive prescribes it. They have to examine the national law for compatibility with the EU directive. This is an important legal obligation that is one of the consequences of Article 10 EC Treaty, which instructs the member states on behaviour that is commensurate with their loyalty to the EU.

There are several ways that lead to a correct implementation of a directive.

Firstly, the Community legislator has to enact directives that are clearly formulated and leave little room for misinterpretation.

Secondly, the national legislator must transform the directive in the right way and in the period allowed by the EC.

Thirdly, if doubts arise as to the compatibility of a national law with a directive, the national judge has to interpret the relevant national law assuming that the national legislator did transform the directive to the best of his ability into national law. That is to say, the national judge must use the interpretation that brings national law closest to the content of the directive. This can eliminate a broad spectrum of possible doubt. But where forced interpretation would be stretching the national law into something it clearly is not, other methods are needed.

A clear-cut case is when the member state fails to make the required national law in the period of time specified in the directive, a situation that occurs frequently. In these circumstances with failing states, the question becomes urgent as to how the prescriptions of the directive can become binding law. EU law has to provide a solution for this problem. That solution is provided by the Court of Justice. It is called direct effect.

4.4.5 Direct effect

The Treaties contain many obligations for the member states and the institutions. In the first phase of the development of the European Economic Community, the member states thought that they were the sole concerned subjects of the rights and obligations spelled out for member states in the Treaty. The Van Gend en Loos case, mentioned earlier as one of the cornerstones of EC constitutional law, originated as a court case of this Dutch transport company against the Dutch tax authority. Van Gend en Loos refused to pay an increase of a customs duty levied for goods imported from Germany. In these early years of the EEC the old customs duties were abolished in three steps, with each step lasting four years. The EEC

Treaty contained a stand-still clause specifying that the member states would not increase existing duties while they were busy abolishing them.

Due to a commitment to the Benelux, based on a separate customs duties treaty, the Dutch government introduced a regrouping of existing duties. This included the increase of certain duties for goods that were brought into a different grouping. The transport company contested the increase it had to pay, basing its claim on the stand-still clause in the EEC Treaty. The Dutch government maintained that this obligation was a matter for the member states and the institutions only. This was a remarkable opinion for the government of a country that insists on the supremacy and direct effect of international law in general. The Dutch government maintained that natural and legal persons had nothing to do with this article, and can certainly not derive rights from this article written for the member states. The Court of Justice ruled that the stand-still clause was binding on the member states and at the same time created rights for their nationals. In this case the rule was easily applied: no increase meant that every national law that did increase duties is set aside by the EEC Treaty clause. Every person who is affected by this EEC law can base his claims directly on this treaty, national authorities are not needed to create rights derived from this part of the treaty. In other words, this article of the treaty has direct effect. Ultimately, the case law of the Court of Justice gave many articles of the EEC Treaty direct effect.

An article of a binding text can have direct effect if it meets the following criteria:

1. the obligation imposed on member states is clear and precise, and
2. unconditional and,
3. if implementing measures are provided for, the institutions or the member states are not allowed any margin of discretion.[91]

Basically, this means that the relevant part of the articles' text is clear enough on its own to be implemented (see for example Law text box 4.9).

Law text box 4.9. Some Articles of the European (Economic) Community Treaty with direct effect.

- Article 25 customs duties and charges having equivalent effect prohibited between member states.
- Article 28 quantitative restrictions on imports and all measures having equivalent effect prohibited between member states.
- Article 39 (1). Freedom of movement for workers secured within the Community.

[91] See Gormley, Laurence W., Introduction to the Law of the European Communities, 3rd ed., 1998 London, pp. 529-530.

- Article 43 Within the framework of the provisions set out below, restrictions on the freedom of establishment of nationals of a member state in the territory of another member state shall be prohibited.

  And so on al through the policies of the EC. One last example:
- Article 141 (1). Each member state shall ensure that the principle of equal pay for male and female workers for equal work or work of equal value is applied.

Note: the preference for direct effect of EC Treaty articles, giving private persons directly effective rights in the treaty, was so strong that even the principle of Article 141 got direct effect. It could be argued that especially a principle can not have direct effect because it needs additional legislation before it can be operative[1]

[1] But the Court preferred the right of persons, even when that had huge consequences for the economies of the Member States: retro-active payment of due equal payment? See: Defrenne v. SABENA case 43/75 1976 ECR 455.

In this way supervision of the treaties has become a concern for millions of natural and legal persons: each time one of their rights is involved, they can initiate a court case using the parts of the EU Treaties with direct effect. The constitutions of the member states can make no difference for direct effect of the treaties. The distinction between monism and dualism is irrelevant. The Court of Justice ruled that the European Communities and the internal market cannot be affected by national constitutions. The rules given by the national constitutions for the relations between international law and national law are valid only for the powers that remain with the member state. The sovereignty that the member states transferred to the EU, cannot be diminished by national constitutions or any other national law anymore.

4.4.6 Direct effect is not limited to Treaty articles

A regulation has direct effect (is directly applicable) by its definition. This instrument is made to rule all, without any interference of any other legislative authority. The regulation shall be applied to all situations that fall under its rules, and this application is immediate. The EU regulation has the same effects on national law as a fully self-executive treaty.[92]

Treaties got direct effect through case law, regulations by definition and directives by surprise. Over the decades, the experience with the directive as an instrument of EC law turned up two problems. Sometimes the national law made to implement the directive in national law contains phrases that (appear to) contradict the directive itself. Frequently member states are not capable of introducing the implementing national laws in time. This leads to a situation where some member states have

[92] See Chapter 3, section 3.4 on the relation between international and national law.

made the required law, while others have not. The result is a substantial difference in legal conditions across the EU.

Again EU law has to provide a solution for these problems. The Court of Justice has developed case law to enable EC law and the institutions to work as best as possible, given the difficulties of integration.[93] In this vein the Court ruled that if a national law contradicts the directive, the provisions of the directive will have direct effect if they meet the criteria. In this way the national judge will overrule national law. In the case of a directive that was not implemented in national law in the time set, the directive has itself as much direct effect as possible. The extent of this direct effect depends on how the directive is formulated. The criteria for direct effect have to be met. Public authorities of the failing member state have the legal obligation to apply the directive itself, as long as the required national law is not made. This is the way the directive, an instrument especially designed not to have direct effect, got direct effect anyway. See Law text box 4.10.

Law text box 4.10. Direct effect of directives, the Ratti case. Pubblico Ministero v. Ratti case 148/78 1979 ECR 1629.

Directive 73/173 required member states to introduce into their national law rules on the packaging and labelling of solvents. Italy failed to implement the directive and kept in force its national legislation. Ratti produced the solvents in accordance with Directive 73/173. In 1978 he was prosecuted in Milan for breaking the Italian law. In a preliminary procedure[1] the Court of Justice of the European Communities answered the questions of the Italian judge as follows:
'This question raises the general problem of the legal nature of the provisions of a directive adopted under Article 189 of the Treaty[2].
In this regard the settled case law of the Court, last reaffirmed by the judgment of 1 February 1977 in Case 51/76 Nederlandse Ondernemingen 1977 1 ECR 126, lays down that, whilst under Article 189 regulations are directly applicable and, consequently, by their nature capable of producing direct effects, that does not mean that other categories of acts covered by that article can never produce similar effects.
It would be incompatible with the binding effect which Article 189 ascribes to directives to exclude on principle the possibility of the obligations imposed by them being relied on by persons concerned.
Particularly in cases in which the Community authorities have, by means of directives, placed Member States under a duty to adopt a certain course of action, the effectiveness of such an act would be weakened if persons were prevented from relying on it in legal proceedings and national courts prevented from taking it into consideration as an element of Community law.
Consequently a Member State which has not adopted the implementing measures required by the directive in the prescribed periods, may not rely, as against individuals, on its own failure to perform the obligations which the directive entails.

[93] Pubblico Ministero v. Ratti case 148/78 1979 ECR 1629.

> It follows that a national court requested by a person who has complied with the provisions of a directive not to apply a national provision incompatible with the directive not incorporated into the national legal order of a defaulting Member State, must uphold that request if the obligation in question is unconditional and sufficiently precise.
>
> Therefore the answer to the first question must be that after the expiration of the period fixed for the implementation of a directive a Member State may not apply its internal law – even if it is provided with penal sanctions – which has not yet been adopted in compliance with the directive, to a person who has complied with the requirements of the directive'.
>
> [1] See Chapter 5, section 5.6.1.
>
> [2] Article 189 TEEC IS now Article 249 TEC.

Direct effect of a directive creates the situation that the parts of the directive with direct effect replace the faulty national legislation, and substitute the higher directly effective rules from the directive itself. The national judge then has to apply at the same time a national law and a higher EC directive with a different meaning, leaving him no choice but to disregard the national law and to apply the directly effective directive. Leaving it to the national legislator to repair the mistakes. However, directives were invented and joined to the Communities arsenal in order not to have direct effect. The Community already has a legislative instrument with direct effect, the regulation. Yet the Court of Justice decided that the fact that the treaties deliberately provided two legislative instruments one designed to have direct effect, and the other one designed not to have this effect, did not preclude the necessity to give the second instrument direct effect in cases where the member states failed to transform the directive into correct and fitting national law. The negligence or failure of the member state is not to be allowed to have a disruptive effect on Community law by cutting away in their jurisdiction the consequences of a legally made directive. Moreover, as the Court had decided earlier that the citizens of the member states were direct participants in the Communities' legal order, not to apply (a part of) a directive would rob them of their rights under EC law. So the directive is allowed to have direct effect as much as possible in the situation where the member state failed to implement the directive in the period prescribed, and as much as necessary to compensate for defective national legislation made to implement the directive. The Court continues to create as much room as possible for the efficient and correct working of Community law. It also continues to guard over the rights that natural and legal persons have under Community law, and to deal with failing member states as sternly as possible.

The direct effect of directives is not the same as the direct effect of regulations. The existence of the intermediate function of the member state makes the law more complicated. The fact that the applicable law is different from the national law may come as a surprise, at any rate it will come late, after a period in which the national law was applied. It is difficult to demand that private persons must have enough insight and knowledge of EC law, that they will know better than their government did what the correct application of EC law means in this particular case. The Court finds it impossible to confront private persons, companies large and small, with obligations stemming from a directive that their national government failed to implement properly. So the direct effect of directives can create rights, entitlements for natural and legal persons, but it cannot create obligations for them. The Court seeks on the other hand to find obligations for the member state as much as possible. The failing state is not allowed to reap profits from failure. Directives that create obligations are applied to public law authorities, they are also applied to legal persons where a public authority has a deciding power. To take an example from the case law, if a directive gives rights for workers, private employers cannot be forced to pay for these rights nor to allow them in cases where they have no direct monetary value. At the same time, public authorities who are employers do have to grant the directly effective directive rights to their employees. Even private law enterprises where a public authority has a deciding say (for instance, 51% of the shares) do have the obligation to grant the rights. The curious outcome of this case law is that a worker, who also cannot be required to have more EC legal expertise than his government, does obtain the rights from the directive if s/he happens to work for a organisation with public authority's dominance, while s/he will not have the same rights if s/he works for a private sector employer.

The basic norm of the Courts case law on the failure of the member states to implement directives, no obligations, only rights for private persons, does not have a solution for the situation where the right of one private person is the obligation of another. The Court has tried to remedy this situation with the decision in the Francovich case[94] that member states have to pay compensation for damages that are the result of the fact that the state did not make legislation to implement a directive.

The aim of stimulating the member states as much as possible to do their job properly and to apply EC law as it is meant to be, is a laudable objective, and is reflected in several other actions of the Court to further the rule of law in the European Union. The member state can not invoke or rely on a directive which it did not implement. In a criminal law case a Dutch prosecutor sought to punish the director of a restaurant where tap water was sold as high quality mineral water. This type of fraudulent handling of food with the use of the designation mineral water was not a criminal offence in Dutch law. However, it was an offence according to a Community directive meant to regulate the use of the designation mineral water. And in the usual way of operation of the combination of EC and national law, the national legal system has to provide for the prosecution of suspects and their punishment if found guilty. The public prosecutor in the Netherlands had no

[94] Francovich and Others *v.* Italian State cases C-6/90 and C-9/90 1991 ECR I-5357.

difficulty in providing evidence that the restaurant had indeed used the designation mineral water. So the prosecution based its case on the directive. However, the Dutch government had failed to implement that directive. The Court of Justice decided in a preliminary procedure that the directive can not be used by the State who failed to implement it. In addition to the firm case law of the Court not to reward states for their misbehaviour, there is also the criminal law requirement that an action can only be a crime if there is a law that has formulated exactly what behaviour is regarded as a crime. In addition to precise formulation, this law has to precede the behaviour of the accused. In other words one can only be accused of committing a crime, if it was defined as a crime before one acted. In the case of a directive that was valid and working in the EC law system at the time of the alleged actions, but still had to be transformed into national law, there is enough uncertainty to exclude any working of this directive to construct a crime of any kind.[95]

The principled difference between a regulation and a directive, which is the directive's reason for being, becomes more gradual in practice. Some regulations leave several choices to the member states, making additional national legislation necessary, while some directives cover so much detail as to leave no real choice to the member states. Yet even then the difference remains that the regulation produces law on the EU level, while even a detailed blueprint directive produces national law.[96]

In food law the Labelling directive 2000/13 discussed in Chapter 12 provides an excellent example of a directive so detailed that national legislators have little else to do than to copy and paste the provisions as set out in the directive. Regulation 178/2002 on the other hand contains examples of regulation provisions addressing the member states in a way similar to a directive.

4.4.7 The decision

The EC Treaty does not define the decision, but prescribes its consequences in Article 249. The Court of Justice defined the decision as 'a measure emanating from the competent authority, intended to produce legal effects and constituting the culmination of procedure within that authority, whereby the latter gives its final ruling in a form from which its nature can be identified'.[97] This definition lays great stress on the difference between a decision creating rights, and earlier communications during the preparation of the decision, such as a letter or a recommendation that does not create rights because it is not binding. Decisions

95 Officier van Justitie (Public Prosecutor) v. Kolpinghuis Nijmegen case 80/86 1987 ECR 3969.
96 See Diagram 6.1.
97 Case 54/65 1966 ECR 185 at 195.

binding natural and legal persons have to be based on rules, on legislation.[98] This is one of the consequences of the rule of law, the principle that government itself is bound by the law it has made. Arbitrary decisions are not allowed, especially when decisions in comparable cases turn out to be different without any argumentation that could explain the difference. Hence a prior law must spell out the conditions for each decision. This enables the executive to take the right decision, and gives the courts the yardstick to check the validity of the decision. The rule of law requires the possibility for every decision to be checked on its legality by a court of law.

Most decisions to carry out EU policies are taken by national authorities of the member states. Only a part of these EU policies' decisions are made at the EU level, and then in most cases by the European Commission. Appeals against a decision taken by an EC institution are brought directly before the Court of Justice of the European Communities or its Court of First Instance. The following is an example of a Commission decision that at the same time sheds light on the extent of the Community's jurisdiction even outside its territory. The Commission has repeatedly declared cartels involving companies outside the EC illegal and presented these 'foreign' companies with administrative sanctions of millions of ECU. They have to pay first, and only then they can start a case before the Court of First Instance of the European Communities. An example: the administrative sanctions applied by the Commission on the Swiss company Hoffmann – La Roche & Co. AG for misusing a dominant position in several markets for vitamins. Hoffmann – La Roche initiated a court case against the decision of the Commission, but the Court found for the Commission.[99]

Appeals against decisions on EU matters taken by national authorities must be submitted to the national courts. These must apply EU law. This law contains a mechanism called preliminary ruling to assist the national judges in their task to apply EU law (see the next Chapter). The national law systems of the member states must provide adequate means for a just procedure and for enforcement of the judgment.

[98] This separates decisions with effects outside the authority, from internal decisions, which do not have immediate effects for the outside world.

[99] Commission Decision 76/642/EEC of 9 June (IV/29.020 – Vitamins). Official Journal L223, 16 August 1976, pp. 27-38. Case 85/76 Hoffmann – La Roche & Co. AG *v*. Commission 1979 ECR 461).

5. The institutions of the European Community

The European Community has five institutions: the European Parliament, the Council, the Commission, the Court of Justice and the Court of Auditors.[100] The European Union borrows these bodies to perform certain tasks, but they remain institutions of the EC. The Union itself has but one body, the European Council.

5.1 The European Council

The European Council is the only body of the European Union that is regulated in the European Union Treaty.[101] It is not an institution. It originated from two sources, one outside and one inside EEC law. Outside: a summit meeting of the heads of state or government of the original six states that, from the perspective of the summit meeting, merely happen to be members of the EEC. Inside: an EEC Council meeting in a particular composition. As a summit conference, the heads of state or government met like any ordinary diplomatic conference, discussing issues that were retained in the national sovereignty. These matters outside of the EEC Treaty had to be co-ordinated with EEC policies on a more profound scale than the EEC Treaty prescribes as one of the tasks of the Council. So the heads of state or government debated the large topics, set out the course for the future and tried to settle differences from which the Council could not untangle itself.

Occasionally the heads of government constituted themselves as a meeting of the EEC Council to decide matters wholly inside the EEC powers. As the Council is composed of representatives of the member states on a ministerial level, they could very well exercise this power. The irregular meetings of the heads of state or government were re-organised into regular meetings in the European Council first three, later two times a year. The European Council is a strongly intergovernmental body that remains as far away from the EC methods of decision making as possible. Hence, the European Council no longer meets as Council of the European Community and usually leaves the measures to be decided to this Council to hammer out the details using its powers from the EC Treaty.

The European Council works now as a body of the European Union. It consists of the presidents of those states that have a politically active and responsible president, the prime ministers from the states with a ceremonial head of state, and the president of the European Commission. They are assisted by the Foreign Ministers and one additional member of the Commission. In this composition the European

100 Article 7 EC Treaty and Article 5 EU Treaty.

101 Article 4 EU Treaty.

Council now meets three times a year, in March, June and December to decide on the most important and politically controversial subjects. The European Council must present a report about each of its meetings to the European Parliament, and an annual report on the progress of the Union.[102] The European Council will become an institution of the European Union if or when the Lisbon Treaty is ratified.[103]

5.2 The Council of the European Union

For some politics is make-believe, if not belie. The Council of the European Communities is as much the Council of the European Union as it is Emperor of the Moon. Lunacy would add less to the general confusion than the pretence to be the Council of a Union that does not recognise this particular Council and already has a different council called European Council. The official name of the Council is 'Council' and that three times. Each of the founding treaties of the Coal and Steel Community, the Atomic Energy Community, and the European Economic Community instituted a Council. That is why the most straightforward institution calls itself the Court of the European Communities. The Commission does likewise. Mistaking the *pars pro toto* that becomes European Commission and European Parliament. But Council of the European Union is really over the edge. Nevertheless, the Council changed its letter-heading in an official document that has no legal base.[104] But perhaps reality is catching up: if the Lisbon Treaty is ratified by all, the European Community changes its name into European Union. However, while the Commission is officially named European Commission with permission to use the simple Commission, and the Court becomes the Court of the European Union, the Council is officially named 'Council'.

The Council is the most intergovernmental institution of the EC.[105] It consists of a representative of each of the member states, who can bind his government to the decisions made in Council. The representative has to be from a ministerial level. If general issues are on the agenda, it is usually the minister of Foreign Affairs. If more specialised subjects are to be debated, the Council will consist of the ministers with that specialisation: agriculture, Ecofin (economy and financial matters), social policies and so on. The presidency over the Council is held in turn by the member states for a period of six months. The order in which the member states take care of this office is determined until July 2020 by Council Decision 2007/5/EC, Euratom.

[102] Article 4 EU Treaty.
[103] Article 13 TEU.
[104] The Council changed its name into Council of the European Union when the European Union Treaty came into force. See Decision (93/591/EU, Euratom, ECSC, EC), Official Journal, L 281, 1993, p.18, rectified Official Journal L 285, 1993, p. 41. However the Treaties still use the name Council.
[105] Articles 202-210 EC Treaty.

The Council meets in the following nine different configurations:

- General Affairs and External Relations.
- Economic and Financial Affairs ('Ecofin')
- Justice and Home Affairs.
- Competitiveness (Internal Market, Industry and Research).
- Transport, Telecommunications and Energy.
- Environment.
- Education, Youth and Culture.
- Employment, Social Policy, Health and Consumer Affairs.
- Agriculture and Fisheries.

Food law can be on the agenda of the two last Councils. See Law text box 5.1 for the tasks of the Council.

Law text box 5.1. Tasks of the Council, Article 202 EC Treaty.

Article 202

To ensure that the objectives set out in this Treaty are attained the Council shall, in accordance with the provisions of this Treaty:

- ensure coordination of the general economic policies of the Member States,
- have power to take decisions,
- confer on the Commission, in the acts which the Council adopts, powers for the implementation of the rules which the Council lays down. The Council may impose certain requirements in respect of the exercise of these powers. The Council may also reserve the right, in specific cases, to exercise directly implementing powers itself. The procedures referred to above must be consonant with principles and rules to be laid down in advance by the Council, acting unanimously on a proposal from the Commission and after obtaining the opinion of the European Parliament.

It has an important role in creating legislation, although it needs an initiative proposal from the Commission before it can act. In an increasing number of policies it also needs the consent of the European Parliament. The EC Treaty leaves it to the Council to decide whether it will answer parliamentary questions. The Council decided to do so.

The Council empowers the Commission to negotiate treaties with other countries or international organisations. The Council decides on the purely intergovernmental policies such as the Common Foreign and Security Policy (CFSP) for external relations not covered by the European Community. The internal Police and Judicial Co-operation in Criminal Matters is also intergovernmental. The member states guard their monopoly on criminal justice meticulously. However, the human rights aspects and the often diffuse area between exclusive national and EC powers can lead to interference of the Court of Justice of the European Communities.

Work in the Council is prepared by COREPER,[106] a committee of national representatives (civil servants) at the level of ambassadors who are permanently present in Brussels, or by the Special Committee for Agriculture (CSA).

5.2.1 Voting in the Council of the European Union

Voting requirements in the Council vary with the Treaty articles that attribute the powers for each specific policy. Usually the Council can decide with a qualified majority.[107] For this each member state is given an amount of votes that reflects the population size only very roughly. In the EC with fifteen member states EC Commission proposals needed 62 votes of a total of 87. Proposals that are not based on a Commission initiative needed 62 votes coming from at least ten member states. The required number of states protects the smaller member states. It is assumed that the involvement of the independent Commission in decision making is a guarantee for al member states that their interests will be looked after objectively, the more so when a coalition of the powerful might short change the smaller member states. See Law text box 5.2 for the votes allotted to each member state.

Law text box 5.2. Voting to take decisions in the Council of 15 member states according to Article 205 of the European Community Treaty.

The votes of the member states in the Council were:

Germany, France, Italy and the United Kingdom	10
Spain	8
Belgium, Greece, the Netherlands and Portugal	5
Austria and Sweden	4
Denmark, Ireland and Finland	3
Luxembourg	2
Total	87

The condition whether or not a proposal from the Commission was necessary to take a decision determined two sets of necessary votes:

1. In (most) cases where the Treaties prescribed a proposal from the Commission the number of required votes was 62.
2. In cases where a decision could be taken without a proposal from the Commission, the number of the votes for a qualified majority was also 62, but those votes had to be cast by at least 10 members.

[106] Many of the acronyms and abbreviations commonly used in the EU are based on the French names (in this case: Comité de Représentants Permanent).

[107] Article 205 EC Treaty.

Voting requirements have been, and still are, an important issue for a number of member states. The question 'voting or consensus (not voting)' has played a major role in the development of the Communities and the voting system used by the Council is very important because it is copied in all committees that administer the policies of the Community.

Most policies require the formation of a committee composed of civil servants from the member states as their representatives, and a representative of the Commission as chairperson. For food law this is the Standing Committee on the Food Chain and Animal Health, established in Article 58 GFL.[108]

These are the so-called comitology committees that make hundreds of comitology regulations every year, especially about agriculture, food safety and consumer protection. The national civil servants participate in decision making with the same number of votes and the same voting rules as their ministers in the Council. The representative of the Commission has no vote, but is armed with some detailed procedural rules that can force the member states to take a decision. These precise comitology techniques are analysed in section 5.5. But the voting rules are explained here.

Each new treaty adds more policies to the list that are decided by a qualified majority instead of unanimity. The increase of the number of member states from fifteen to twenty-seven is seen as an unavoidable stimulant for decision making by a majority. The original six member states brought the Communities to a stand-still from 1966 until 1986, because they disregarded the EC Treaty articles that prescribe decision making by majority vote. The French boycotted the Communities' institutions for half a year in 1965. They did not accept the essential obligation written into the EEC Treaty that the third and last transition period of four years, which was to begin in 1966, would introduce majority voting. That would be unacceptable for the French Gaullist government. It could not allow that the vital interests of France would depend on a majority of other nation states. The other member states perceived only one way out to end the crises. They reverted to the classic diplomatic solution for a conflict between parties that refuse to come to terms: the agreement to disagree.

The member states agreed on the Luxembourg Accord.[109] They agreed that the French would return to the Council and the Communities could resume their normal business. The French remained convinced that no treaty could bring about a decision on vital French interests by a majority that did not include France herself. The other member states restated their position that the EEC Treaty enabled majority decisions. They declared themselves willing to seek a solution that would

---

108 See section 5.8.14.

109 Text of the Luxembourg Accord published in the EEC Bulletin no. 3, 1966, page 5.

be acceptable to all member states, if one or more of them would declare that their vital interests were at issue. This solution would have to be found within a reasonable period of time. This effort had to respect the interest of the states and of the Community. The French delegation re-iterated that the search for a solution acceptable for all would have to be continued until it was found. All six member states agreed that they disagreed on this last point. However, that did not impede the resumption of the Community activities according to the normal procedures (!). But after this statement was made and majority voting prescribed by the EEC Treaty started on 1 January 1966, all member states refrained from asking for a vote to determine the outcome of a discussion in the Council. Discussions went on indefinitely and the Community sank away in a quagmire of words. At the end of this period other member states began to invoke the vital national interest principle as well. Intergovernmentalism is a contagious affliction. In 1985 Germany blocked a decision on the price for wheat, because it did not agree with the outcome of the discussions. So the German minister invoked his country's vital national interests that were endangered by this proposed decision. The long periods of negotiations without decisions had a great effect on the functioning of the common market and most profoundly on food law.

The British, who joined the Communities in 1973, well after the Luxembourg Accord, were glad to seize the opportunity to use this hidden controversy in the *acquis communautaire* to further their cause to limit the powers of the Community as much as possible. This led to a new accord even after the creation of the European Union, the 1994 Ioannina Accord.[110] It declares that the member states have to take notice of the fact that the Council has to decide to continue discussions when a minority of 23-26 votes (the votes for each member state are weighted) declares that they are opposed to the decision that the majority is about to make in accord with the majority decision rule of the EEC Treaty. The Council will continue discussions to find a solution that is acceptable to at least 68 votes in a reasonable period of time while respecting (!) the EC Treaty articles. Where the Treaty prescribes that 62 votes are sufficient, the Council has raised the majority of 71.3% required by the Treaty to 78.2% required by the Council. Nothing gives the Council the power to change the EC Treaty single-handedly. To get a good perspective on this required majority: most states change their constitution with 66.7% of the votes and take other decisions by 50.1% when that is the available majority.

The 2001 Nice Treaty, that entered into force on 1 February 2003, has changed the requirements for majority decision making to prepare for the enlargement of the EU to twenty-five States in 2004 and twenty-seven in 2007. The enlargement was planned to parallel a profound change in the existing treaties that had carried the different European Communities from 1952 and 1958 into the next millennium.

110 Text of the Ioannina Accord published in the EEC Bulletin no. 3 1994, page 79.

The reform treaty was negotiated in the Intergovernmental Conference of the member states and signed in 2004 as the Treaty establishing a Constitution for Europe. It failed to get the required ratifications.

A new round of negotiations produced the Lisbon Treaty that was signed in December 2007. The Nice Treaty was made beforehand to be the reserve position in case one or more member states would not ratify the reform treaty. See Law text boxes 5.3 and 5.4 on voting (by qualified majority) in the Council according to the Nice Treaty and the successor to the failed reform treaty, the Lisbon Treaty signed in 2007.

Law text box 5.3. Voting to take decisions in the Council according to the 2001 Nice Treaty (in force).

From 1 November 2004 until the signed Constitution for Europe comes into force, the votes of the member states in the Council will be:

Germany, France, Italy and the United Kingdom	29
Spain and Poland	27
Romania	14
The Netherlands	13
Belgium, Czech Republic, Greece, Hungary and Portugal	12
Bulgaria, Austria and Sweden	10
Denmark, Ireland, Lithuania, Slovakia and Finland	7
Cyprus, Estonia, Latvia, Luxembourg and Slovenia	4
Malta	3
Total	345

To achieve a qualified majority three cumulative conditions have to be met:

1. a majority of member states approve
2. a specified minimum number of votes is cast in favour. The actual number will depend on how many new member states have joined at any particular time, but the percentage will remain approximately the same and cannot exceed 73.4%
3. a member state may ask for confirmation that the votes in favour represent at least 62% of the total population of the Union. If this is found not to be the case, the decision will not be adopted.

Law text box 5.4. Voting (by qualified majority) in the Council, Art. 16 TEU and 238 TFEU (proposed, signed in December 2007, to be ratified). Source: Consolidated versions of the Treaty on European Union and the Treaty on the Functioning of the European Union – Consolidated version of the Treaty on European Union – Consolidated version of the Treaty on the Functioning of the European Union – Protocols – Annexes – Declarations annexed to the Final Act of the Intergovernmental Conference which adopted the Treaty of Lisbon – Tables of equivalences. Official Journal C 115, 09 May 2008, pp. 1-388.

Article 16 Treaty on European Union

1. The Council shall, jointly with the European Parliament, exercise legislative and budgetary functions. It shall carry out policy-making and coordinating functions as laid down in the Treaties.
2. The Council shall consist of a representative of each Member State at ministerial level, who may commit the government of the Member State in question and cast its vote.
3. The Council shall act by a qualified majority except where the Treaties provide otherwise.
4. As from 1 November 2014, a qualified majority shall be defined as at least 55% of the members of the Council, comprising at least fifteen of them and representing Member States comprising at least 65% of the population of the Union.
   A blocking minority must include at least four Council members, failing which the qualified majority shall be deemed attained.
   The other arrangements governing the qualified majority are laid down in Article 238(2) of the Treaty on the Functioning of the European Union.
5. The transitional provisions relating to the definition of the qualified majority which shall be applicable until 31 October 2014 and those which shall be applicable from 1 November 2014 to 31 March 2017 are laid down in the Protocol on transitional provisions.

Article 238 Treaty on the Functioning of the European Union

(ex Article 205(1) and (2), TEC)

1. Where it is required to act by a simple majority, the Council shall act by a majority of its component members.
2. By way of derogation from Article 16(4) of the Treaty on European Union, as from 1 November 2014 and subject to the provisions laid down in the Protocol on transitional provisions, where the Council does not act on a proposal from the Commission or from the High Representative of the Union for Foreign Affairs and Security Policy, the qualified majority shall be defined as at least 72% of the members of the Council, representing Member States comprising at least 65% of the population of the Union.
3. As from 1 November 2014 and subject to the provisions laid down in the Protocol on transitional provisions, in cases where, under the Treaties, not all the members of the Council participate in voting, a qualified majority shall be defined as follows:
   (a) A qualified majority shall be defined as at least 55% of the members of the Council representing the participating Member States, comprising at least 65% of the population of these States.
   A blocking minority must include at least the minimum number of Council members representing more than 35% of the population of the participating Member States, plus one member, failing which the qualified majority shall be deemed attained;

(b) By way of derogation from point (a), where the Council does not act on a proposal from the Commission or from the High Representative of the Union for Foreign Affairs and Security Policy, the qualified majority shall be defined as at least 72% of the members of the Council representing the participating Member States, comprising at least 65% of the population of these States.

4. Abstentions by Members present in person or represented shall not prevent the adoption by the Council of acts which require unanimity.

5.3 The European Commission

The Commission (or European Commission)[111] consists of twenty-seven Commissioners, one from each member state. The Commissioners have to be independent. First, the chairperson is appointed by common accord of the governments of the member states, after s/he has received a vote of approval from the European Parliament. The other commissioners are selected by the member states in consultation with the chairperson. Then the whole procedure is repeated for the Commission collectively. The term of office is five years, and is renewable. It is synchronised with the five year term of the European Parliament, taking regard of the power the Parliament has to dismiss the Commission collectively.

The Commission is responsible for the day-by-day administration of the Union. See Law text box 5.5 for its tasks. Some of the administrative powers are given by the Treaties directly, most are given by the Council.[112] Comitology decision making is applied to the powers that the Council has delegated to the Commission. These powers are mentioned in Article 211 EC Treaty after the fourth dash.

Law text box 5.5. Tasks of the Commission, Article 211 EC Treaty.

Article 211

In order to ensure the proper functioning and development of the common market, the Commission shall:

- ensure that the provisions of this Treaty and the measures taken by the institutions pursuant thereto are applied,
- formulate recommendations or deliver opinions on matters dealt with in this Treaty, if it expressly so provides or if the Commission considers it necessary,
- have its own power of decision and participate in the shaping of measures taken by the Council and by the European Parliament in the manner provided for in this Treaty,
- exercise the powers conferred on it by the Council for the implementation of the rules laid down by the latter.

[111] Articles 211-219 EC Treaty.

[112] See Article 202 EC Treaty, law text box 5.1.

Each Commissioner has one or more specific policy fields as his primary responsibility. Decisions are taken by the Commission as a whole. The staff of civil servants for each policy field is organised in a Directorate General (DG). Food safety is the responsibility of DG Sanco (Health and Consumer Protection). The Commission has the exclusive right of initiative for EC legislation. This means that the Council and the European Parliament can make a law only if the Commission presents a proposal.

The Commission is the 'guardian of the Community Treaties'. It monitors the member states' implementation of EU law. It begins infringement proceedings in the event of any suspected violation of Community law by a member state.[113] The infringement procedure has two distinct phases. In the first phase the main aspect of the procedure is the clarification of the situation and the promotion of agreement between the parties. Therefore this phase is confidential. The Commission confronts the member state with its perception of a breach of Community law. The member state has ample opportunity to present its opinions on the issue. Information is shared. Perhaps the Commission is persuaded by the member state that there is no breach of Community law. Or the Commission remains convinced that the member state is acting wrongly. In that case the Commission can advise the member state on how to change its behaviour to end the breach. The state will reconsider and perhaps accept the Commission's point of view and correct the wrongdoing. Or the state remains convinced of its rightful position and rejects the advice. In that case it is for the Commission to decide to start phase two. The Commission is not obliged to proceed further with the infringement procedure. It can decide to accept the position of the member state. If the Commission is convinced that the wrong should be righted, it will start a public open court case by summoning the member state to appear before the Court of Justice of the European Communities to defend itself against the accusation that it has acted against specified articles of the Treaty. Lawyers of both parties will present their clients' views and evidence, the judges will ask their questions and finally the Court will give its judgement. The Court's decision is binding, the member state's position will be accepted or rejected, and country and Commission have to act accordingly.

The independent position of the European Commission, its power to supervise the member states, the power to administrate the Union's policies and take binding decisions underline that the Commission is a supranational element in the EU. However, the close surveillance by the Council of the Commission's activities render this supranational element rather weak. The comitology mechanism is more than an arrangement to co-ordinate EC policies with the policies of the member states, it is designed to serve the interests of the member states by giving the final say to these states themselves through their representatives in the committee and the Council. In the past the relationship of Council and Commission was

[113] Article 226 EC Treaty.

characterised by the fact that the Council was very unwilling to delegate some of its ample powers to the Commission. That attitude has changed.

5.4 The European Parliament

The European Parliament[114] located in Strasbourg and Brussels, and always on the move, represents the peoples of the member states. Every state has a fixed number of members of Parliament. They are chosen on the bases of twenty-seven national systems of direct general elections, which are held every five years. So far all efforts to create a uniform Union-wide European election system have been skilfully frustrated.

In the course of its fifty-six years of activities, the European Parliament has acquired more and more legislative powers. These range from advisory to co-decisive, depending on the procedure prescribed for the policy. When the Lisbon Treaty is ratified codecision becomes the normal way for legislation, and Parliament and Council are then on equal voting. The Parliament plays a major role in the budgetary procedure. It has supervisory powers over the Commission. These are exercised mainly through the fact that the Commission must answer parliamentary questions, and defend its proposals before Parliament. The Commission presents its annual report on the activities of the Communities. Parliament and Commission discuss it in a general policy debate. Parliament can, by a two-thirds majority of its members, pass a motion of censure and thereby compel the Commission to resign as a body. So far the Commission has been sent home only once. This was due to a case of corruption.

The 1992 Maastricht Treaty on the European Union substantially boosted Parliament's supervisory powers. It is empowered to set up special committees of inquiry[115] to look specifically at alleged cases of infringement of Community law or mismanagement. A committee of this kind was used, for example, to look into the Commission's responsibility for the delay in responding to the BSE crisis. In this context a motion of censure was introduced. Although it was not passed, it exercised considerable influence as will be elaborated on later.[116]

The work of the Parliament is prepared in committees. The committees that are most involved in matters related to food law are 'ENVI: Environment, public health and consumer policy' and 'AGRI: Agriculture and rural development'. The European Parliament has become a supranational element as an institution directly elected to represent the peoples of the Union, and equipped with real legislative powers.

114 Articles 189-201 EC Treaty.
115 Article 193 EC Treaty.
116 See Chapter 7, section 7.4.

5.5 Council and Commission: comitology

5.5.1 Introduction

Most EU policies are executed by the administrations of the member states, working in these cases under EU law. For this work the obligations contained in Article 10 EC Treaty are important: the member states have to take all appropriate measures, whether general or particular, to ensure fulfilment of the obligations which are based on the EC Treaty. The same rule applies to the work the states have to do as a result of actions taken by the institutions of the Community. The member states have to facilitate the achievement of the Community's tasks. They have to abstain from any measure which could jeopardise the attainment of the objectives of the EC Treaty.

Between the formulation of policy objectives and the regulations that serve these objectives at the EU level and the administration of these policies in the member states there are many implementing measures. These are made mainly at the Community level by the comitology committees using the comitology procedures.

Comitology committees
Comitology committees have already been introduced as committees where twenty-seven civil servants, one from each member state and representing that state, cooperate under the chairpersonship of a civil servant representing the Commission. The committee members have the votes and the chairperson has the procedures that the committee has to apply in its meetings. There are two levels of procedures here: the procedures that determine how the meetings of the committee are organised, how much time they have to cooperate, debate or negotiate before they have to take a decision. How decisions are made, how the votes are counted and how many votes are needed to take a decision. Most of these rules are recorded and the chairperson applies them, although the members can demand to have a vote about the procedures for their meetings too.

The second level of procedures is the set of rules that determine the powers that the committee has to decide. One type of committee can give the Commission advice, another type allows the Commission to take a decision but if the committee does not agree the Commission has to present that decision to the Council that can undo it. In a third type of procedure the Commission can not take a decision, but has to obtain a decision from the committee first.

Comitology measures
The committees can make different measures like regulations and decisions. When they make regulations, they can make more detailed rules or they have the power to replace rules from the basic regulation by rules that reflect scientific

or technical developments. When the measures are decisions the comitology committees apply EC rules to make EC decisions that have to be applied by the member states. Comitology has developed into a flexible way to make policies and law. A unique way in the literal sense that there are no other states or organisations with procedures and measures like this.

The list of examples of possible measures is endless. A comitology measure can contain the details that determine which substances are added to, or removed from, the list of substances that may not be added to food. The same goes for the list of substances that are allowed but only to specified maximum levels. It may be necessary to change this list not only for the substances but also for the levels. Rules about the registration of food businesses are changed to specify the units that have to be registered or the methods of registration and the access to this information. Some food businesses have to be approved before they begin their activities. The evaluation of the approval system can lead to changes that have to be decided at the Community level. The government organisations that have to inspect premises where food is prepared need detailed and up-to-date Community instructions to ensure effective inspections, the use of the best available techniques, the adoption of new methods or new standards.

EU food law is used to secure a high level of food safety for food and feed going through all the stages of primary production, preparation, processing, manufacturing, packaging, storing, transportation, distribution, handling and offering for sale or supply to the consumer. Food hygiene rules have to be applied at all these diverse stages. The movement of food and feed ingredients through all these stages must be retraceable in case something has gone wrong somewhere and it is imperative to find out how and where and who else might be at risk.

Who registers what and which records have to be kept? Which changes in the techniques of logistics and registration have consequences for food law that are too small to cause an essential change in legislation but large enough to make changes necessary?

If one would expect that the institution created by the treaties as the day-to-day authority, the Commission, would be the institution to look after these details one would be missing the strong opinions of the Council on this issue. The Council has held the key positions from the beginning of the EEC Treaty. The Council has made basic legislation with built-in mechanisms to exert its influence during the execution of Community policies. The EC Treaty supports the Council in this vision in a roundabout way in its article on the tasks of the Council. Law text box 5.6 combines the relevant parts of the articles about the tasks of the Council and the Commission, Articles 202 and 211.

Law text box 5.6. Delegation of powers from the Council to the Commission, Article 202 and 211 EC Treaty.

Article 202 EC Treaty

... To ensure that the objectives set out in this Treaty are attained the Council shall ...

- confer on the Commission, in the acts which the Council adopts, powers for the implementation of the rules which the Council lays down. The Council may impose certain requirements in respect of the exercise of these powers. The Council may also reserve the right, in specific cases, to exercise directly implementing powers itself. ...

And seen from the Commissions side:

Article 211 EC Treaty

'The Commission shall ... exercise the powers conferred on it by the Council for the implementation of the rules laid down by the latter',

The EC Treaty gives the Council the duty to pass on to the Commission the larger part of the executive powers it obtains from the treaty. These powers are specified in the basic regulations. The formulation of the third dash of Article 202 makes it clear that the Council can keep implementation powers only in exceptional cases. However, if the founding member states had wanted a more pronounced role for the Commission, they could easily have given these powers in the treaties directly to the Commission.

Even a Commission with increased powers to carry out Community policies would have to co-ordinate these with the policies of the member states. The division of powers between Community and member states makes co-ordination inevitable.

To serve the two goals of keeping the Commission in check, bridled, and to co-ordinate policies, the system of committees was developed to 'assist the Commission in the exercise of implementing powers', as the beautiful euphemism of Council Decision 1999/468/EC formulates it. The rules supporting this system have become known as comitology.[117]

This neologism covers the rules and traditions that have grown to regulate the working of several committees that were created to enable the Council to transfer powers to the Commission, and at the same time keep the final say for itself. The comitology rules are very important because they are used on a large scale in the day-to-day administration of EC policies. Basic regulations that contain the main rules for a policy prescribed by the EC Treaty also contain an article that creates

[117] See document 1999/468/EC: Council Decision of 28 June 1999 laying down the procedures for the exercise of implementing powers conferred on the Commission. Official Journal L 184, 17 July 1999, pp. 23-26.

a committee for the day-to-day management of that policy, or to make rules in certain situations and under certain conditions. The General Food Law does this in Articles 58 and 59 on the Standing Committee on the Food Chain and Animal Health (Law text box 5.7).

Law text box 5.7. The Standing Committee on the Food Chain and Animal Health, Articles 58 and 59 General Food Law, Regulation 178/2002.

Regulation 178/2002
Chapter v Procedures and final provisions
Section 1 Committee and mediation procedures
Article 58 Committee

1. The Commission shall be assisted by a Standing Committee on the Food Chain and Animal Health, hereinafter referred to as the 'Committee', composed of representatives of the Member States and chaired by the representative of the Commission. The Committee shall be organised in sections to deal with all relevant matters.
2. Where reference is made to this paragraph, the procedure laid down in Article 5 of Decision 1999/468/EC shall apply, in compliance with Articles 7 and 8 thereof.
3. The period provided for in Article 5(6) of Decision 1999/468/EC shall be three months.

Article 59 Functions assigned to the Committee

The Committee shall carry out the functions assigned to it by this Regulation and by other relevant Community provisions, in the cases and conditions provided for in those provisions. It may also examine any issue falling under those provisions, either at the initiative of the Chairman or at the written request of one of its members.

Article 58 refers to the Council Decision 1999/468/EC of 28 June 1999 laying down the procedures for the exercise of implementing powers conferred on the Commission. This Council Decision deals with the various committees that exist to keep the Council involved with the powers that it did delegate to the Commission. The Commission, the European Parliament and the Intergovernmental Conference that adopted the Treaty of Amsterdam to change the existing Treaties, all wanted the Council to change its former decision on the same subject, Decision 87/373/EEC. There were two major objections to the old Comitology Decision.

The first one was as old as the EC itself: the Council keeps the implementation of policies too much to itself and the Commission in shackles.

The second one was new and faced the consequences of the co-decision procedure where Council and European Parliament make legislation together. It is still only the Council that has a like minded committee to watch over and decide on transferring a part of the execution of this legislation to the Commission. It is only the Council that has the committee to give it a second chance to see whether the executive work of the Commission stays within the bounds of the law made by Parliament and Council. The co-decision procedure gives the Parliament an equal partnership, and so it is reasonable to give it an equal position in judging the executive policies of the Commission.

In time a third reason to modernise the Committee procedures became prominent: the need to keep the Parliament informed about the two to three thousand committee decisions a year. And beyond the Parliament its voters and the citizens of the Union, the general public. Tools for this objective are transparency and public access to Community documents (Article 255 EC Treaty).

5.5.2 Delegation of powers from the Council to the Commission

There are four elements in the comitology procedure that explain its special character:
1. The member states want to keep the power of the Community to an absolute minimum. They want to have control over every detail and they do not want the Commission to become a kind of Cabinet that rules the EU in close cooperation with the EP. If the Commission acquired that stature, the EU would be more democratic, but the member states would have lost control. Comitology is about giving someone a present and keeping it yourself.
2. The procedures have tight time schedules not because there is no time to lose, but because often the member states have to be forced to take a decision. A short period adds pressure, especially when different institutions get different time schedules.
3. It is important to mix the requirement to vote in support of or against a measure with the necessity to take a measure and the responsibilities of the Commission and the Council in such a way that when the fixed period goes by without a decision by the EP and, or, the Council, there is automatically a decision: the Commission's.
4. The fourth element is the empirical fact that a majority that opposes the Commission proposal is not necessarily the majority that supports another proposal. The fact that there will be a decision anyway will influence the negotiation position and tactics of the member states. A state may prefer to rely on that outcome as second best but good enough to try to negotiate a more preferred alternative by risky negotiations. It is worth a trial and the higher risk of failure is insured by the Commission proposal. On the other hand, one or more states may dislike the Commission proposal so much that they are more prepared to find a compromise.

The 1999 Comitology Decision distinguished four separate procedures:
1. the advisory procedure;
2. the management procedure;
3. the regulatory procedure; and
4. the safeguard procedure.

In 2006 a fifth procedure was added, the regulatory procedure with scrutiny.

The Comitology Decision tries to formulate criteria that can be used to determine which procedure fits best for the groups of basic regulations or directives that need a committee. The Council stresses the point that these criteria are by no means binding, so it can decide freely on the type of procedure each time it creates a basic document for a policy. The Council Decision does not discriminate between measures to implement a basic instrument that have themselves a regulatory, rule-making character and measures that are executive, implemented by executive decisions which apply rules to individual acts The choice of procedural methods for the adoption of implementing measures 'shall be guided by' (not decided by) the criteria that are part of the different procedures.

5.5.3 The advisory procedure and the Advisory Committee

The criteria for the advisory procedure are among the vaguest: it is to be used 'in any case in which it is considered to be the most appropriate', when the management and regulatory procedure are not used. The advisory procedure (Article 3 Decision) amounts to four steps.

One the representative of the Commission submits to the Committee a draft of the measures to be taken. The chairman decides on the time-limit within which the Committee has to decide, according to the urgency of the matter. If necessary by taking a vote.

Two the Committee gives its opinion on the draft.

Three the opinion is recorded in the minutes. Each member state has the right to ask to have its position recorded in the minutes.

Four the Commission *takes the utmost account* of the opinion delivered by the Committee. It informs the Advisory Committee of the manner in which the opinion has been taken into account.

5.5.4 The management procedure and the Management Committee

The management procedure will be used for management measures, such as those relating to the application of the common agricultural and common fisheries policies. Measures for the implementation of programmes with substantial budgetary implications are a second category. The measures can be executive or regulatory.

The management procedure (Article 4 Decision) starts with the same first two steps of the advisory procedure. But the procedure begins to introduce its characteristics in step two:

Two the opinion of the Committee is decided by the standard qualified majority.

Three the Commission can decide to take the measures it proposed and these measures work immediately.

Four the Commission has to send these measures to the Council immediately when they are not in accordance with the opinion of the Committee.

Five the Commission may, but does not have to, postpone application of the measures for a period to be laid down in each basic instrument. However, the period shall in no case exceed three months from the date when the Commission informed the Council.

Six the Council may take a different decision within the period mentioned in step Five. The Council too decides with the qualified majority of Article 205 (2) EC Treaty. If the Council is not able to take a decision in time, the measure of the Commission remains intact.

5.5.5 The regulatory procedure and the Regulatory Committee

The regulatory procedure is to be used for measures of general scope, designed to apply essential provisions of basic instruments. These basic regulations were described earlier.[118] The regulatory committee has to make decisions on measures concerning the protection of the health or safety of humans, animals or plants. It starts to work the same way, but the third step of the regulatory procedure (Article 5 Decision) is different:

Three the Commission can decide to implement its proposal only when it is in accordance with the opinion of the Committee.

Four the Commission has to submit, without delay, a proposal to the Council relating to the measures to be taken and has to inform the European Parliament if the measures proposed by the Commission are not in accordance with the opinion of the Committee, or if no opinion is delivered.

Five the European Parliament can decide for a basic instrument made with the co-decision procedure that the proposal of the Commission exceeds the implementing powers provided for in that basic instrument. In that case the Parliament shall inform the Council of its position.

Six a. the Council must adopt the Commission's proposal or indicate its opposition within the period laid down in each basic instrument. That period can not exceed three months from the date of referral to the Council. If on the expiry of that period the Council has not taken either one of these decisions (unable to find a majority saying 'Aye', and unable to find a majority saying 'Nay'), the proposed implementing act shall be adopted by the Commission.

Six b. if within that same period the Council has indicated by qualified majority that it opposes the proposal, the Commission has to re-examine it. The Commission may submit an amended proposal to the Council, re-submit

[118] See Chapter 4, section 4.4.3.

its original proposal or present a legislative proposal on the basis of the Treaty to change the basic regulation

The last option mentioned for the Commission, to return to the basic instrument and propose to amend it, is of course the solution that fits best when the European Parliament argues that the proposed implementing act transgresses the limits set by the enabling basic instrument. The discussion on a proposed change of the basic instrument can take away any doubts that may exist about the attributed powers.

If Council and Commission, or the Commission alone in cases where the Council can not find a majority to decide anything, go ahead, while the European Parliament is of the opinion that such a decision exceeds the limits set in the basic instrument, the Parliament has the instrument of Article 230 EC Treaty: it can ask the Court of Justice to destroy, to annul, the decision.

5.5.6 An example: management or regulatory procedure

In case C-122/04 Commission v. Council and Parliament, the institutions disagreed about the right comitology procedure to make implementing measures for the Forest Focus Regulation.

That regulation is the basis for a Union-wide scheme to monitor long-term developments in forests due to interactions with the environment, forest fires and other factors. The Commission asked the Court to annul Article 17(2) of that regulation because it prescribed the regulatory procedure for the adoption of implementing measures. In the Commission's opinion these implementing measures are management measures for an action programme.

The Court found that the basic regulation does not contain the essential elements that are necessary to direct the management of the scheme. The regulation is not detailed enough and the scheme contains some new policy instruments that are in development. Under these conditions the making of implementing rules or decisions can not be left to the management procedure. The essential elements are decided in the comitology committee. The regulatory procedure is the right choice based on Article 2(b) Comitology Decision. The Council has to keep the implementing measures under close supervision. The Commission's request was rejected.

The implication of this case law is that in the course of the development of a policy the basic regulation can be developed to such an extent that the application of the programme can be left to management measures. In other words, EU legislators who want to keep control of developing programmes have a choice: they can manage every detail themselves or make basic regulations that give them the tools to keep in touch.

5.5.7 The regulatory procedure with scrutiny and the regulatory procedure with Scrutiny Committee

The regulatory procedure with scrutiny gives the EP and the Council the power to test (to scrutinise) a comitology regulation made by the Committee against the basic codecision regulation made by EP and Council. The test has to establish that the Committee regulation respects the limits given by the basic regulation. The test has to prevent the undermining of the main rules by the comitology regulations. The regulatory procedure with scrutiny was added to the Council's Comitology Decision 1999/468/EC as Article 5a.

The scrutiny procedure is an obligation that the Council can not escape from. It is a permanent feature of regulations or other legal instruments made with the codecision procedure of Article 251 EC Treaty. The codecision procedure can be used to make several types of measures or instruments. It provides the boundaries for the implementing power given to the Committee.

Comitology and scrutiny in practice
The proposal for a Flavourings Regulation (PFlavR) will become the basic regulation for several types of comitology implementation regulations. The types that exist already and the new scrutiny type. Both will be explained with the comitology procedures that are built into the PFlavR[119]. This proposal has reached the phase where the Council has decided on its Common position on the amendments proposed by the EP in the first round of the codecision procedure.[120] In the second reading of the proposal EP and Council have to formulate a text that is accepted by both or there will be no regulation at all. That would postpone necessary improvements of the existing legislation. PFlavR is one of several proposals of the FIAP package. Each of these contain examples of how comitology procedures are used and what kind of substantive law are considered to need a particular comitology procedure. The Law text boxes 5.8 to 5.13 are used to demonstrate the

[119] Proposal for a Regulation of the European Parliament and of the Council on flavourings and certain food ingredients with flavouring properties for use in and on foods and amending Council Regulation (EEC) No 1576/89, Council Regulation (EEC) No 1601/91, Regulation (EC) No 2232/96 and Directive 2000/13/EC {SEC(2006)1042} {SEC(2006)1043} /* COM/2006/0427 final - COD 2006/0147.

[120] 52008AG0009 Common Position (EC) No 9/2008 of 10 March 2008 adopted by the Council, acting in accordance with the procedure referred to in Article 251 of the Treaty establishing the European Community, with a view to the adoption of a Regulation of the European Parliament and of the Council on flavourings and certain food ingredients with flavouring properties for use in and on foods and amending Council Regulations (EEC) No 1576/89 and (EEC) No 1601/91, Regulation (EC) No 2232/96 and Directive 2000/13/EC (Text with EEA relevance), Official Journal C 111E, 6 May 2008, pp. 46-67. The progress of the PFlavR from proposal to regulation can be followed with the EU Prelex search machine. See References.

essential issues. Law text box 5.13 contains an example of substantive law that plays a role in several examples in the Law text boxes 5.8 to 5.12. Refer back and forth between these boxes to see the combinations and what they mean.

Scrutiny procedure only for non-essential elements

The scrutiny procedure has to be used for non-essential elements of regulations made with the codecision procedure. The essential elements can only be changed by the full codecision procedure. The legislator indicates the parts of the PFlavR that are non-essential and may be amended with the Scrutiny Committee. The legislator can give another kind of comitology procedure to the new regulation too. EP and Council have to make clear and precise rules that can be used as a yardstick to establish whether the implementing regulation made by the Committee stays within the limits.[121]

To put the example in the right perspective three things are necessary:

- to have a clear presentation of the comitology options;
- to have a clear view on the substantive rules that are subjected to the comitology procedures;
- and to see the effects of the comitology procedures on the substantive rules.

First the comitology options in the PFlavR. Article 21 PFlavR mentions the Articles of the Comitology Decision 1999/468/EC that will be used by the PFlavR 'Where reference is made to this paragraph'. See Law text box 5.8 for the choices made for the proposed Flavourings regulation.

Law text box 5.8. The comitology procedures selected by Article 21 PflavR.

Article 21 Committee

1. The Commission shall be assisted by the Standing Committee on the Food Chain and Animal Health.
2. Where reference is made to this paragraph, Articles 5 and 7 of Decision 1999/468/EC shall apply, having regard to the provisions of Article 8 thereof. The period laid down in Article 5(6) of Decision 1999/468/EC shall be set at three months.
3. Where reference is made to this paragraph, Article 5a(1) to (4) and Article 7 of Decision 1999/468/EC shall apply, having regard to the provisions of Article 8 thereof.
4. Where reference is made to this paragraph, Article 5a(1), (2), (4) and (6), and Article 7 of Decision 1999/468/EC shall apply, having regard to the provisions of Article 8 thereof.

[121] The Commission uses the acronym 'PRAC' for the 'regulatory procedure with scrutiny'. This acronym comes from the French *procédure de réglementation avec contrôle*. Commission of the European Communities, Report from the Commission on the working of Committees during 2006 {SEC(2007) 1713}, COM/2007/0842 final, Brussels, 20 December 2007, p. 2.

Law text box 5.9. Article 6 PFlavR selects the regulatory comitology procedure in 3 steps.

3 steps:

I. Article 6(3) PFlavR Presence of certain substances
II. Article 21(2) PFlavR
III. Article 5 Decision 1999/468/EC

Step I.

Article 6 *Presence of certain substances*

1. Substances listed in Part A of Annex III shall not be added as such to food.
2. Without prejudice to Regulation (EC) No 1576/89, maximum levels of certain substances, naturally present in flavourings and/or food ingredients with flavouring properties, in the compound foods listed in Part B of Annex III shall not be exceeded as a result of the use of flavourings and/or food ingredients with flavouring properties in and on those foods. The maximum levels of the substances set out in Annex III shall apply to foods as marketed, unless otherwise stated. By way of derogation from this principle, for dried and/or concentrated foods which need to be reconstituted, the maximum levels shall apply to the food as reconstituted according to the instructions on the label, taking into account the minimum dilution factor.

Article 6(3) *PFlavR Presence of certain substances*

3. Detailed rules for the implementation of paragraph 2 may be adopted in accordance with **the regulatory procedure** referred to in Article 21(2), following the opinion of the European Food Safety Authority (hereinafter referred to as the 'Authority'), where necessary.

Step II. The regulatory procedure referred to in *Article 21(2) PFlavR*

Article 21(2)

Where reference is made to this paragraph, Articles 5 and 7 of Decision 1999/468/EC shall apply, having regard to the provisions of Article 8 thereof. The period laid down in Article 5(6) of Decision 1999/468/EC shall be set at three months.

Step III. *Decision 1999/468/EC*

Article 5: *the regulatory procedure with the regulatory committee.*

Article 7: *rules of procedure, public access to documents, list of all committees, annual report*

Article 8: *Options in case the EP makes a Resolution that the proposed draft implementing measures of the comitology committee exceed the implementing powers granted to the Committee in the basic codecision regulation.*

The Commission has three options:

1. change the proposed draft;
2. continue without changes;
3. stop the comitology procedure and start a codecision procedure with the view to make the (changed) draft measures part of the basic regulation itself.

Another example of substantive law subjected to comitology.

Law text box 5.10. Article 8 PFlavR selects the regulatory procedure with scrutiny to subject flavourings to evaluation and approval.

Article 8. *Flavourings and food ingredients with flavouring properties for which evaluation and approval are not required*

1. The following flavourings and food ingredients with flavouring properties may be used in or on foods without an evaluation and approval under this Regulation, provided that they comply with Article 4:
   (a) flavouring preparations referred to in Article 3(2)(d)(i);
   (b) thermal process flavourings referred to in Article 3(2)(e)(i) which comply with the conditions for the production of thermal process flavourings and maximum levels for certain substances in thermal process flavourings set out in Annex V;
   (c) flavour precursors referred to in Article 3(2)(g (i);
   (d) food ingredients with flavouring properties.
2. Notwithstanding paragraph 1, if the Commission, a Member State or the Authority expresses doubts concerning the safety of a flavouring or food ingredient with flavouring properties referred to in paragraph 1, a risk assessment of such flavouring or food ingredient with flavouring properties shall be carried out by the Authority.
   Articles 4 to 6 of Regulation (EC) No .../2008 [] shall then apply mutatis mutandis. If necessary, the Commission shall adopt measures, following the opinion of the Authority, which are designed to amend non-essential elements of this Regulation, inter alia by supplementing it, in accordance with **the regulatory procedure with scrutiny** referred to in Article 21(3). Such measures shall be laid down in Annexes III, IV and/or V where appropriate.

On imperative grounds of urgency, the Commission may use the **urgency procedure** referred to in Article 21(4) DFR.

The regulatory procedure with scrutiny referred to in Article 21(3)
- Article 21(3) Where reference is made to this paragraph, Article 5a(1) to (4), and Article 7 of Decision 1999/468/EC shall apply, having regard to the provisions of Article 8 there of.
- Decision 1999/468/EC:
- Article 5a(1) to (4) The regulatory procedure with scrutiny
- Article 5a(1): Scrutiny Committee and procedure
- Article 5a(2): The standard regulatory procedure

There are three possible outcomes:
1. Commission and Committee agree;
2. Commission and Committee do not agree;
3. the Committee can not decide on an opinion.

This Law text box continues with 1. The next Law text box continues with 2 and 3.

Article 5a(3): Commission and Committee agree
Article 5a(3)(a) Commission presents the draft implementing regulation to the Council and the EP

Article 5a(3)(b) Council and the EP test the draft implementing regulation on 5 grounds:

1. the draft exceeds the implementing powers provided for in the basic regulation;
2. the draft is not compatible with the aim of the basic regulation;
3. the draft is not compatible with the content of the basic regulation;
4. the draft regulation does not respect the principle of subsidiarity;
5. the draft regulation does not respect the principle of proportionality.

Article 5a(3)(c) if Council or EP or both oppose the draft within 3 months it cannot be adopted by the Commission. The Commission can:

1. submit to the Committee an amended draft
2. present a legislative proposal on the basis of the Treaty

Article 5a(3)(d) the Commission will adopt the draft implementing regulation when the Council and EP have not opposed the draft within 3 months

Articles7 and 8 pro memory

Law text box 5.11. The regulatory procedure with scrutiny: when the Commission and Committee do not agree.

2. Commission and Committee do not agree;
3. the Committee can not decide on an opinion.

Decision 1999/468/EC has a separate set of rules to deal with these alternatives:

Article 5a(4) no positive opinion from the representatives of the member states in the Committee

Article 5a(4)(a) Commission sends proposal to the Council and the EP

Note: the Commission needs the adoption of the proposal by both institutions. The procedure gives the Council the shortest period for a reaction. The EP cannot continue with discussions when the Council rejects the proposal. That would not make a difference in cases where the EP also rejects the proposal. If the EP wants to be the first to reject the proposal it is free to do so. But that is rational only in very limited circumstances. The procedure will be followed as indicated by Article 5a, but the final comment will review this aspect again

Article 5a(4)(b) The Council has 2 month to decide with the qualified majority

Article 5a(4)(c) The Commission can not adopt the proposal when the Council rejects it. The Commission can then:

1. submit an amended proposal to the *Council*, or:
2. present a legislative proposal on the basis of the Treaty = Article 251 EC codecision

Article 5a(4)(d) The Council sends the Commission proposal to the EP within the 2 month when the Council 'envisages' adoption

The Commission sends the proposal to the EP after the 2 month when the Council has not decided

Article 5a(4)(e) The EP can reject the proposal in the 4 months after receiving the Commission proposal conform Article 5a(4)(a).

Article 5a(4)(f) The Commission can not adopt the proposal when the EP rejects it. The Commission can then:

1. submit an amended proposal to the Committee, or

2. present a legislative proposal on the basis of the Treaty

Article 5a(4)(g) The Commission or the Council will adopt the proposal when the EP has not opposed the proposal within the 4 months

Law text box 5.12. Article 22 PFlavR on Amendments to Annexes II to V to reflect scientific and technical progress.

Article 22. Amendments to Annexes II to V

Amendments to Annexes II to V to this Regulation to reflect scientific and technical progress which are designed to amend non-essential elements of this Regulation shall be adopted in accordance with the regulatory procedure with scrutiny referred to in Article 21(3), following the opinion of the Authority, where necessary.

On imperative grounds of urgency, the Commission may use the urgency procedure referred to in Article 21(4).

Law text box 5.13. ANNEX III Regulation on flavourings.

Commission of the European Communities

Amended proposal for a Regulation of the European Parliament and of the Council on flavourings and certain food ingredients with flavouring properties for use in and on foods and amending Council Regulation (EEC) No 1576/89, Council Regulation (EEC) No 1601/91, Regulation (EC) No 2232/96 and Directive 2000/13/EC, COM(2007) 671 final, 2006/0147 (COD) Brussels, 24.10.2007.

(presented by the Commission pursuant to Article 250 (2) of the EC Treaty)

ANNEX III

Presence of certain substances

Part A: Substances which may not be added as such to food

- Agaric acid
- Capsaicin
- Hypericine
- Beta-asarone
- 1-Allyl-4-methoxybenzene
- Hydrocyanic acid
- Menthofuran
- 4-Allyl-1,2-dimethoxybenzene
- Pulegone
- Quassin
- 1-Allyl-3,4-methylene dioxy benzene, safrole

- Teucrin A
- Thujone (alpha and beta)

Part B: Maximum levels of certain substances, naturally present in flavourings and food ingredients with flavouring properties, in certain compound food to which flavourings and/or food ingredients with flavouring properties have been added

Name of the substance	Compound food in which the presence of the substance is restricted	Maximum level [mg/kg]
Beta-asarone	Alcoholic beverages	1.0
1-Allyl-4- methoxybenzene	Dairy products	50
	Processed fruits, vegetables (incl. mushrooms, fungi, roots, tubers, pulses and legumes), nuts and seeds	50
	Fish products	50
	Non-alcoholic beverages	10
Hydrocyanic acid	Nougat, marzipan or its substitutes or similar products	50
	Canned stone fruits	5
	Alcoholic beverages	35
Menthofuran	Mint/peppermint containing confectionery, except micro breath freshening confectionery	500
	Micro breath freshening confectionery[18]	3000
	Chewing gum	1000
	Mint/peppermint containing alcoholic beverages	200
4-Allyl-1,2-dimethoxybenzene,	Dairy products	20
	Meat and meat products, including poultry and game	15
	Fish and fish products	10
	Soups and sauces	60
	Ready-to-eat savouries	20
	Non-alcoholic beverages	1
Pulegone	Mint/peppermint containing confectionery, except micro breath freshening confectionery	250
	Micro breath freshening confectionery[18]	2000
	Chewing gum	350
	Mint/peppermint containing non-alcoholic beverages	20
	Mint/peppermint containing alcoholic beverages	100

[18] Candies with intensive taste; weight per candy not more than 1g (original footnote).

5.5.8 The safeguard procedure

The final procedure that is addressed by the 1999 Comitology Decision, is the safeguard procedure (Article 6 Decision). Several basic instruments contain rules for exceptional measures to be taken in exceptional circumstances. In these circumstances any delay can have grave consequences. Therefore, the day-to-day executive, the Commission, is empowered to take these measures. At the same time these measures can be of great consequence to the Community. The following procedure is prescribed:

One a. the Commission notifies the Council and the member states of any decision regarding safeguard measures.

One b. the basic instrument may stipulate that before adopting its decision, the Commission has to consult the member states in accordance with procedures to be determined in each case.

Two. any member state may refer the Commission's decision to the Council within a time-limit to be determined in the basic instrument in question.

Three a. the Council, acting with a qualified majority, may take a different decision within a time-limit to be determined in the basic instrument in question. In this case there are no lacunae: the measures applied by the Commission remain intact, while the Council deliberates. Once the Council has decided otherwise, the relevant power in the EC has determined that other measures, or no measures, are necessary.

Three b. alternatively, it may be stipulated in the basic instrument that the Council, acting by qualified majority, may confirm, amend or revoke the decision adopted by the Commission and that, if the Council has not taken a decision within the abovementioned time-limit, the decision of the Commission is deemed to be revoked.

Articles 53 and 54 of the General Food Law, Regulation 178/2002 introduce a safeguard procedure for food and feed that is likely to constitute a serious risk to human health, animal health or the environment.

5.5.9 The position of the European Parliament and the concerned citizen

The position of the European Parliament is made stronger for those measures that implement a basic instrument that was made by Council and Parliament acting together in the co-decision procedure. Article 8 of the Decision orders the Commission to re-examine its proposal if the European Parliament has passed a Resolution stating that the draft measures exceed the implementing powers provided for in the basic instrument. The Commission has to react in the time period prescribed for making implementing measures. The Commission has three options:

1. it can continue the procedure with its draft measures;
2. it can submit new draft measures to the Committee;
3. it can submit a proposal to the Parliament and the Council on the basis of the EC Treaty to change the basic instrument. The Commission has to inform both the Parliament and the Committee of the action it intends to take on the Parliament's Resolution and of its reasons for doing so.

The Council Decision gives Parliament more rights to get information in all Committee procedures. To enable the Parliament to exercise its rights, the Commission has to inform the Parliament on a regular basis. The Commission has to give three different types of information. The first type gives the opportunity to follow the work of the Committees. The Parliament will receive:
1. the agendas for the Committee meetings, together with the draft of the measures that will be discussed;
2. summary records of the meetings and the results of voting;
3. the list of the persons send by the Member States to represent them, indicating the authorities and organisations to which they belong.

This information must be given for those proposed implementing measures that are based on instruments that were created with the co-decision procedure. The Parliament has an interest to be informed about other proposals too. For these the Council Decision states that the Parliament will be kept informed whenever the Commission sends (proposals for) measures to the Council.

The second type of information is a survey of the activities of the Committees. The Commission has to publish from 2000 onwards an annual report on the working of the Committees.[122]

The third type of information gives the facts on what Committees there are and the documents that are produced. For the benefit of the Parliament and the Union citizen who wants to be kept informed, the Commission has to publish in the Official Journal a list of all Committees which assist the Commission in the exercise of implementing powers.[123] This list has to specify for each Committee the basic instrument(s) that created it. To complete the information, the Commission has to set up a public register with the references of all documents that are sent to the Parliament in the exercise of the duty of the Commission to keep the Parliament informed.[124] The Comitology Register was improved in April 2008 to give the

[122] Commission of the European Communities, Report from the Commission on the working of Committees during 2006 {SEC(2007) 1713}, COM/2007/0842 final, Brussels, 20 December 2007.
[123] Information from the Commission – List of committees which assist the Commission in the exercise of its implementing powers. Official Journal C 225, 08 August 2000, pp.2-18.
[124] Follow European Commission > Secretariat General > Transparency> Comitology Register. http://ec.europa.eu/transparency/regcomitology/index_en.htm

user the tools to find his way in all the different documents in all their different lay-outs and codes for every successive stage.

The Commission and the Parliament made an agreement on the procedures for implementation of the Comitology Decision.[125] They also agreed to give the Parliament information on those measures that are not based on basic instruments made with the co-decision procedure. Both parties agree that the Commission shall forward to the European Parliament, for information, at the request of the parliamentary committee responsible, specific draft measures for implementing basic instruments which, although not adopted under the co-decision procedure, are of particular importance to the European Parliament. Both parties underline cas law of the Court of First Instance that the European Parliament may request access to the minutes of committee meetings.[126]

5.6 The Court of Justice of the European Communities

The Court of Justice is the highest judicial authority in matters of Community law.[127] It derives its name from the two remaining Communities that attribute the power to judge.[128] In general terms, its task is to '... ensure that in the interpretation and application of this (EC) Treaty the law is observed'.[129] The Court of Justice has one judge per member state; the judges have to be independent from the member states and the institutions.[130] They are appointed for a period of six years by common accord of the governments of the member states. The period in office is renewable. The Court has jurisdiction in several quite different branches of law. The four most common types of cases are:

1. requests for a preliminary ruling;
2. proceedings for failure to fulfil an obligation, also called the infringement procedure;
3. proceedings for annulment;
4. proceedings for failure to act.

[125] Agreement between the European Parliament and the Commission on procedures for implementing Council Decision 1999/468/EC laying down the procedures for the exercise of implementing powers conferred on the Commission, as amended by Decision 2006/512/EC. Official Journal C 143, 10 June 2008, pp. 1-4. The original agreement is the Agreement between the European Parliament and the Commission on procedures for implementing Council Decision 1999/468/EC of 28 June 1999 laying down the procedures for the exercise of implementing powers conferred on the Commission. Official Journal L 256, 10 October 2000, pp. 19-20.

[126] Judgment of the Court of First Instance of the European Communities of 19 July 1999, Case T-188/97, Rothmans v Commission, 1999 ECR II-2463.

[127] Articles 220-245 EC Treaty.

[128] The European Union is too intergovernmental to give much room to the Court.

[129] Article 220 EC Treaty.

[130] Article 223 EC Treaty.

5.6.1 The preliminary ruling

European Community law contains a mechanism called preliminary ruling[131] to assist the national judges in their task to apply EU law. The same mechanism is designed to prevent national judges, who can be separated by almost a continent, from developing their own interpretations of EU law. That would break the unity of EU law and lead to different conditions on the internal market and in the execution of Community policies. Every national judge from the member states may ask the opinion of the Court of Justice on how to apply EU law in the case to be tried by the national judge. The Court of Justice does not take the case over from the national judge, nor does it pronounce statements on the national law applied in the proceedings. The Court of Justice answers the questions asked by the national judge on EU law to assist him as a colleague. These preliminary rulings guide all national judges in all member states who have to decide similar cases. The opinions expressed by the Court are binding. The importance of this preliminary ruling procedure is illustrated by the fact that several member states regularly use the opportunity given by EC law to intervene in the proceedings before the Court of Justice to present their opinions.

Whereas every national judge is allowed to ask the Court's opinion, every national judge who is the highest and therefore last national judge to sit on a case, is obliged to ask the advice of the Court of Justice if EU law is needed to come to a judgment. In this way EU law is likely to be applied in the same way everywhere. If not, the Commission can use its supervising power that can lead to a procedure against the member state for failure to fulfil an obligation. The persistent wrong interpretation of EC law by an independent national judge adds up to a failure of his state. The question as to whether the member state is wrong because its national judge is acting against EC law will be decided by the independent Court of Justice. However, the Commission has been reluctant in the past to open proceedings against a member state when the alleged failure was caused by a judge. A well-known case was the French Conseil d'Etat that had very strong, but wrong, ideas about how to apply EC law. The Commission answered on parliamentary questions that it would carefully consider the French position, taking note of the independence of the judiciary that needs special attention. In the course of a few years the Commission did nothing in public and the French high judge changed its way of applying EC law. In the Cassis de Dijon case, the Court of Justice formulated the principle of mutual acceptance of the food safety decisions of other EC member states. The Court did this in answering questions asked by a German judge using the preliminary ruling procedure.[132]

---

[131] Article 234 EC Treaty.

[132] See Chapter 7, sections 7.3.2 and 7.3.3 for an analysis of this case.

5.6.2 Proceedings for failure to fulfil an obligation, also called the infringement procedure

These proceedings[133] are described in the section on the work of the Commission as supervisor (Section 5.3). In case 178/84, the Commission v. Germany, the Commission asked the Court to forbid the German action of keeping foreign beers from the German market. The German government maintained that all drinks called 'beer' had to be made according to a centuries old recipe, called the *Reinheitsgebot*. The German government also wanted to ban those beers that were made with additives. The Commission charged that the German measures amounted to a measure with an effect equivalent to a quantitative restriction of imports of beer into Germany.[134]

The imported quantity in this case being zero, because no foreign beer was allowed. The EC Treaty does not allow such measures that hinder the free movement of goods. The German government countered by relying on the exception made in the EC Treaty. A member state is allowed to use an exception to free movement of goods if health risks are involved. The Court of Justice laughed the German health arguments away, and found for the Commission. By refusing access to the German market to foreign beers not made according to a German recipe, Germany failed to fulfil the obligation not to disturb the free movement of beers.

Experience has shown that several member states were very late to carry out a judgment of the Court. To remedy this situation a new procedure was introduced. The Commission can bring the failing state before the Court and demand execution of the judgment plus payment of a lump sum or penalty payment to be paid by the member state. The Court decides and can impose a lump sum or penalty payment. The Commission can use the judgment to force the member state to pay.[135]

5.6.3 Proceedings for annulment

If any of the member states, the Council, Commission or (under certain conditions) Parliament believes that a particular EU law is illegal they may ask the Court to annul it.[136] The Court reviews the legality of binding acts made by the institutions. There are four grounds to declare the act concerned void:

- lack of competence;
- infringement of an essential procedural requirement;
- infringement of the EC Treaty or of any rule of law relating to its application;
- misuse of powers.

---

133 Article 226 EC Treaty.

134 See Chapter 7, section 7.3.4 for an analysis of this concept.

135 Article 228 EC Treaty.

136 Article 230 EC Treaty.

The first ground, the lack of power has been explained above under 'The Powers of the EU: attribution'. An example of the second ground is a regulation on agriculture made by the Council, while the Council forgot to ask the advice of the European Parliament. Although this advice would not have bound the Council in any way, the Court found this omission to be an infringement of an essential procedural requirement, and declared the regulation to be void. The third ground is illustrated above under 'The regulation', at the end of the first paragraph. An example of the fourth ground is to use a regulation as an instrument to decide the legal position of one person only. The proceedings to obtain a review must be instituted within two months of the publication of the measure. However, everyone can at all times invoke the illegality of a regulation, on the same grounds for annulment, if that regulation is used to determine the outcome of a case.[137]

5.6.4 Proceedings for failure to act

The Treaty requires the European Parliament, the Council and the Commission to make certain decisions under certain circumstances. If they fail to do so, the member states and the other Community institutions can lodge a complaint with the Court to have this violation officially recorded. However, such an action may be brought only after the institution has been given the opportunity to remedy the situation. When the failure to act is held to be unlawful, it is for the institution concerned to put an end to the failure by appropriate measures.

5.6.5 The Court of First Instance

To cope with the tremendous workload of the Court of Justice, a Court of First Instance[138] was added later. It can have jurisdiction in the same subjects as the Court of Justice with the exception of those reserved in the Statute for the Court of Justice. Appeal to the Court of Justice against a decision given by the Court of First Instance can be based on points of law only. The facts of the case are determined only once by the first judiciary.

5.6.6 Proceedings initiated by natural or legal persons

The proceedings for annulment and for failure to act can be initiated by natural or legal persons. They can go to court only for acts or omissions that concern them personally, or as Article 230 puts it: '...may, under the same conditions, institute proceedings against a decision addressed to that person or against a decision which, although in the form of a regulation or a decision addressed to another person, is of direct and individual concern to the former'. The object of this formula is to prevent private persons from starting proceedings against legal rules, legislation contained in regulations or directives as such. That power is

[137] Article 241 EC Treaty.
[138] Article 225 EC Treaty.

reserved for the member states and the institutions. The cases initiated by natural or legal persons come before the Court of First Instance.

Both Courts are independent and have real powers to decide conflicts in a legal order where member states and persons have rights. The Court of Justice assists all national judges with the correct interpretation of the EU law they have to apply. It is clear that both courts are powerful supranational elements in the EC.

5.7 The European Court of Auditors

The European Court of Auditors[139] was added to the EC institutions by the 1992 Treaty on European Union. It consists of one national from each member state. The members of the Court of Auditors are appointed for a term of six years, which is renewable. The Council makes a list of candidates in accordance with the proposals made by each member state. The Council consults the European Parliament and decides by a qualified majority. The task of Court of Auditors is to examine the income and the expenditure of the Communities. It examines whether financial management has been sound and it will report on any irregularity found. The Court of Auditors reports annually, and this report is published in the Official Journal, together with the reactions of the institutions. The Court can publish special reports at any time. It has the power to carry out on-the-spot investigations in the offices of the institutions, and in the member states.

5.8 The European Food Safety Authority

The European Food Safety Authority (EFSA) is established in Article 22 of Regulation 178/2002 (the General Food Law, or: GFL) as an independent agency responsible for risk assessment and risk communication. The GFL gives EFSA (called 'the Authority') the following mission given in Law text box 5.14.

Law text box 5.14. Article 22(2) GFL on the mission of EFSA.

Article 22(2) GFL
The Authority shall provide scientific advice and scientific and technical support for the Community's legislation and policies in all fields which have a direct or indirect impact on food and feed safety. It shall provide independent information on all matters within these fields and communicate on risks.

The quality and accessibility of scientific advice is considered to be of paramount importance to ensure effective, timely and appropriate decision-making. EFSA must cover all parts of the food chain. Scientific matters are considered to be part

[139] Articles 246-248 EC Treaty.

of a continuum from primary production through the food production chain to the consumer. The operation of EFSA as an independent entity is intended to ensure that there is a functional separation of the scientific assessment of risk from risk management decisions. Scientific risk assessment should not be swayed by policy or other external considerations. The independent position is designed to guarantee impartiality and objectivity.

Risk management on the other hand, in its widest possible sense, remains within the domain of the Commission, the Parliament and the Council. Risk management decisions take into account all relevant aspects, not only science but also many other matters – for example economic, societal, traditional, ethical or environmental factors, as well as the feasibility of controls. Risk management is a function of accountable, political decision makers. Close collaboration between the independent EFSA and those charged with the responsibility of risk management can inform them with scientific risk assessment.

EFSA's Advisory Forum provides central co-ordination to the efforts and resources of the national food authorities and agencies in Europe. EFSA is also the centre for such networking.

5.8.1 The organisation of ESFA

An agency is a public law legal person, made to carry out a well-defined part of government policy, usually of a technical nature. The agency works outside the regular civil service management lines, although the statutes, charter or other documents made for the founding of the legal person can contain rules on the relations between the responsible public authority and the agency that can be quite close. It is often maintained by the Commission that letting agencies do a part of the job for the EC is a way to decentralise the power of the EC institutions involved, the Council and the Commission. However, whether there is in fact delegation of power depends on the charter given to each particular agency. Beyond that, there are good reasons why decentralisation cannot use agencies as a vehicle. The treaties determine the responsibilities of each institution, and this cannot be changed by creating an agency outside the 'normal' means. It is more relevant to describe the spreading of agencies across the combined territories of the Member States as deconcentration. Instead of centralisation of all supporting civil service units, the executive spreads its services all over the continent.

The EFSA has four bodies: the Management Board, the Executive Director (and her staff), the Advisory Forum with the member states and the Scientific Committee with the Scientific Panels.[140] The permanent staff supports the work of these bodies and contributes its own work to realise the tasks. See Diagram 5.1 for EFSA's organigram.

[140] Article 24 GFL.

Diagram 5.1. EFSA's organisational chart in 2008. Source: http://www.efsa.europa.eu/.

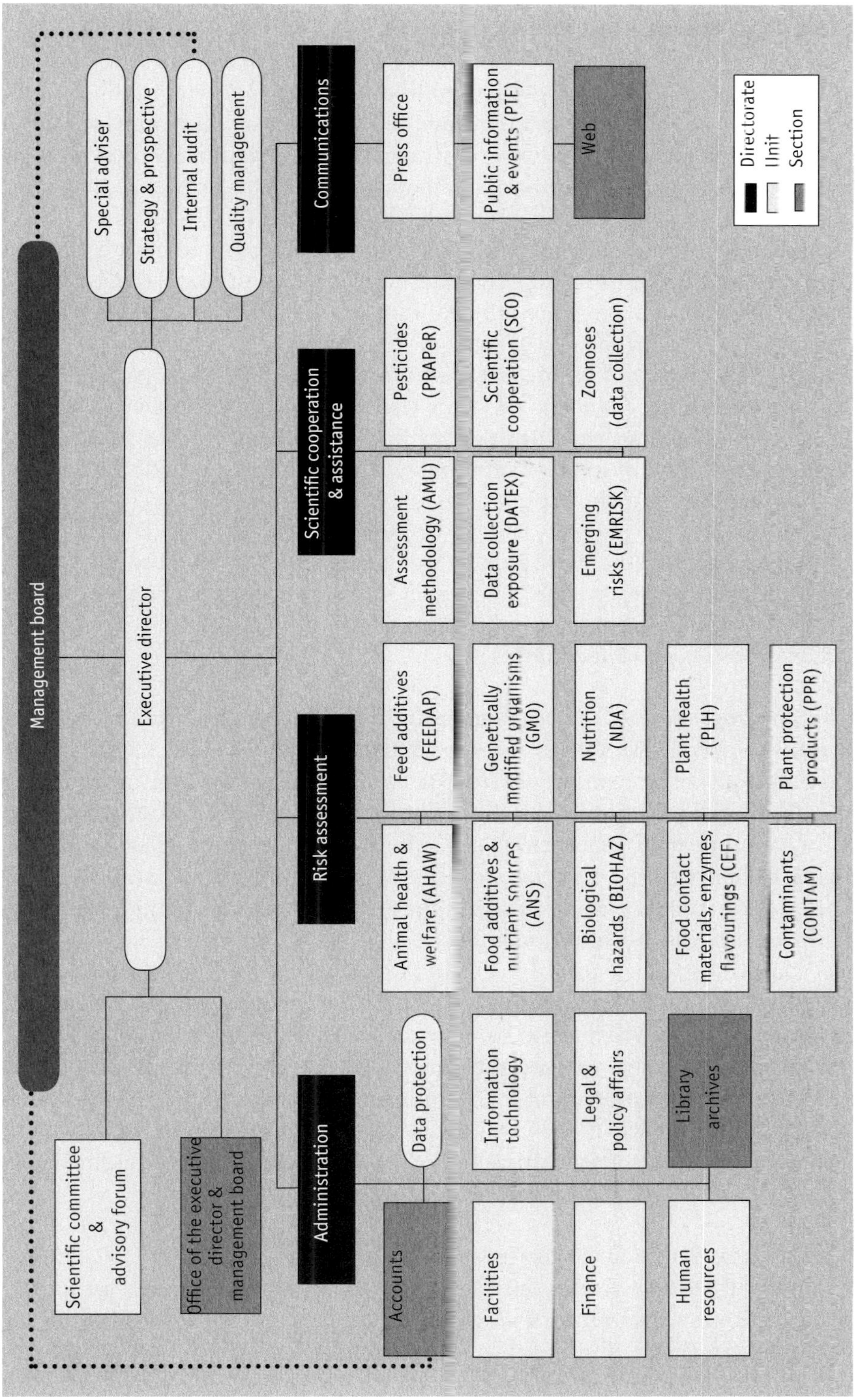

5.8.2 The Management Board

The Management Board is composed of one representative of the Commission and fourteen members who are appointed by the Council in consultation with the European Parliament from a list drawn up by the Commission. The fourteen members are selected on the basis of their competence and expertise. The principle of the broadest possible geographic distribution within the Union comes second to their excellent personal qualities. Four of the members must have a background in organisations representing consumers and other interests in the food chain.[141] The members have a term of office of four years that can be renewed once.

Half of the members of the original Management Board were appointed or reappointed with a mandate for the period 2006 to 2010. The new term of office of the remaining half runs from 1 July 2008 to 30 June 2012 to strike a balance between new appointments every four years and the experience and knowhow of the members already in office.

The open procedure for these appointments began in 2007 with the announcement of the requirements for the office and an invitation to participate, published in the Official Journal. The procedure was completed with Council Decision 2008/486/EC on 23 June 2008.

The four members of the Management Board who must have a background in organisations representing consumers and other interests in the food chain come from the following organisations: the Danish Agricultural Council, an independent organisation for farmers and their cooperatives (for the period 2006 to 2010), the UK consumer organisation 'Which?', the Federation of the German Food and Drink Industry (BVE), and the Finnish Consumers' Association (all three for the period 2008 to 2012). The Management Board adopts EFSA's internal rules, see Law text box 5.19 for some examples.

Decisions are made by a simple majority. The Board elects the Chair from its members for a renewable period of two years. Meetings will be held at the invitation of the Chair or at the request of at least a third of the members. The Executive Director has to be present at the meetings of the Management Board and take care of the Secretariat. The Chair of the Scientific Committee will be invited to attend the meetings. Both persons have no voting rights. See Diagram 5.1 for the Management Board's position in EFSA's organigram.

The Management Board tasks are to:
- ensure that EFSA carries out its mission and performs the tasks assigned to it;
- adopt EFSA's annual work programme;
- adopt a revisable multi-annual programme.

[141] Article 25 GFL.

Both must be consistent with the Community's legislative and policy priorities in the area of food safety. An annual general report on EFSA's activities has to be made before 30 March of the next year and published by 15 June.[142]

5.8.3 Regulation of EFSA

The creation of the European Food Safety Authority on 1 January 2002 and its expansion in 2008 beyond a staff of 310 civil servants, 200 experts in panels and work groups, 27 member states and 3 observer states in the Advisory Forum and similar developments over the whole range of tasks have their bases in legislation and are expressed in legal documents that create more rules or decisions about plans, programmes and the construction and maintenance of the organisation. To give an impression of the many documents that are part of the project, Diagrams 5.2 and 5.3, and Law text boxes 5.14 to 28 give the tasks and a selection of these documents. There are several types of documents: those directly related to the tasks of providing scientific opinions and risk communication, other indirectly related to the tasks as service documents shaping the facilities or conditions to enable the work on the tasks. Usually the content is indicated by the title. It is always accessible at EFSA's website.

Diagram 5.2. EFSA main tasks.

Article 33 GFL	Tasks described in Section 5.8.11	EFSA main tasks
29	1.	Scientific opinions
30	2.	Diverging scientific opinions
31	3	Scientific and technical assistance
32	4.	Scientific studies
33	5.	Data collection
33(5), 33(5)(a) 33(5)(b)	5.	Inventory of Data collecting systems at Community level before 1 March 2003
33(6)	5.	EFSA forwards results data collection to EF, Commission and member states
34	5.	Identification of emerging risks
35	6.	Rapid alert system
36	7.	Networking organisations
36	7.	Article 36 GFL financing of work group projects
22(2), 40	8.	EFSA communications in general and risk communication
	8.	The EFSA Register of Questions
41	8.	Access to documents
42	8.	Consumers, producers and other interested parties

142 Article 25(8)(second paragraph) in combination with 26(3)(b)(second paragraph) GFL.

Diagram 5.3. Six categories of EFSA's core management documents.

Policy and strategy papers	Law text box 5.15.
Operating rules	Law text box 5.17
Selection of experts	
Transparency and access to documents	Law text box 5.21
Administrative conduct and anti-corruption	Law text box 5.19
Finance	

Law text box 5.15. Examples of EFSA Core Management Documents: Policy and strategy papers.

Strategy for Cooperation and Networking with Member States	Articles 22(7), 23(g) and 36 GFL
Risk Communications strategy and plans	Articles 22(2), 23(j), 40 and 42 GFL

Law text box 5.16. Examples policy planning documents.

- Management Plan of the European Food Safety Authority for 2008, MB 13.12.07 – Adopted by written procedure on 21 December 2007. Done at Parma, on 21 December 2007, Dr Patrick Wall Chair
  Document providing the predicted work of the Authority during 2008 both in relation to its annual and multi-annual work programmes
- Annual Report 2007 Article 25(8)(second paragraph) GFL: before 30 March following year
- Annual work programme AWP Article 25(8) GFL: before 31 January each year
  Multi-annual work programme Article 25(8) GFL
- Finance Article 43 GFL
  Financial Regulation of the European Food Safety Authority
  Implementing Rules for the Financial Regulation

Law text box 5.17. Examples of EFSA Core Management Documents: Operating rules.

Decision of the Management Board of the European Food Safety Authority		
Subject	**MB Decision**	**Articles GFL**
• Rules of Procedure of the Management Board of the European Food Safety Authority, As last amended by the Management Board on 10 May 2006, Done at Parma, 10 May 2006, For the Management Board, Dr Stuart A. Slorach, The Chair.	10.05.2006.	25(3) 25(5)

• Decision concerning the establishment and operations of the Scientific Committee and Panels, The present Decision shall enter into force on the date of its adoption. The Management Board may return to these rules whenever deemed necessary and adopt any modifications needed, Bucharest, 11 September 2007, Dr Patrick G. Wall Chair	11.09.2007	25(3), 28(9)(a) to (g), 29(7)
• Decision concerning the operation of the Advisory Forum, These Rules and annexes shall enter into force immediately on their adoption by the Management Board. Done at Brussels, 21 January 2003, For the Management Board, Dr Stuart A. Slorach, The Chair.	21.01.2003.	25(3), 27(5)
• Decision on implementing rules concerning the tasks, duties and powers of the Data Protection Officer, Implementing rules, Article 7 This Decision shall enter into force on 1 February 2006 and shall be published on the Authority's website, Done at Parma, 24 January 2006, Stuart Slorach, The Chair.	24.1.2006	25(3), Chapter III

5.8.4 Integrity, independence and transparency

The integrity and independence of its staff and the members of its organisational bodies are of paramount importance to EFSA. The General Food Law gives clear instructions. The articles on independence and transparency are at the centre of EFSA's corporate identity and science generally. Transparency is about consistent and traceable conduct of the organisation and its functionaries and personnel. The openness of the organisation hinges partly on the crystal-clear commitments of the people involved, whose personal interests do not trouble the clear course of the organisation. Openness about potential relations between the job in the organisation, or one particular item on an agenda, and (the semblance of) personal interests connect the declarations of interests to transparency. See Law text box 5.18 for transparency, one of the central values for public law entities.

Law text box 5.18. EFSA transparency, Article 38 GFL.

Article 38 GFL

1. The Authority shall ensure that it carries out its activities with a high level of transparency. It shall in particular make public without delay:
   (a) agendas and minutes of the Scientific Committee and the Scientific Panels;
   (b) the opinions of the Scientific Committee and the Scientific Panels immediately after adoption, minority opinions always being included;
   (c) without prejudice to Articles 39 and 41, the information on which its opinions are based;

(d) the annual declarations of interest made by members of the Management Board, the Executive Director, members of the Advisory Forum and members of the Scientific Committee and Scientific Panels, as well as the declarations of interest made in relation to items on the agendas of meetings;
(e) the results of its scientific studies;
(f) the annual report of its activities;
(g) requests from the European Parliament, the Commission or a Member State for scientific opinions which have been refused or modified and the justifications for the refusal or modification.

2. The Management Board shall hold its meetings in public unless, acting on a proposal from the Executive Director, it decides otherwise for specific administrative points of its agenda, and may authorise consumer representatives or other interested parties to observe the proceedings of some of the Authority's activities.
3. The Authority shall lay down in its internal rules the practical arrangements for implementing the transparency rules referred to in paragraphs 1 and 2.

Article 38 GFL shows that the transparency principles are active on two different levels. All instructions are addressed to EFSA as an organisation and its activities, except Article 38(1)(d) that addresses individual persons. The content is different too: transparency as used in 38(1)(d) does not demand a contribution to the corporate transparency in the work attitude and activities; it demands integrity, the absence of personal interests and the prevention of every likelihood and appearance of personal graft and gain. EFSA has made internal guidance documents and forms to apply the GFL obligations (Law text box 5.19).

Law text box 5.19. Guidance Document on Declarations of Interests.

Guidance Documents	MB Decision number
• Guidance Document on Declarations of Interests, Annex 1 Declaration of Commitment	11.09.2007
• Guidance Document on Declarations of Interests, Annex 2, Annual Declaration of Interests.	11.09.2007
• Guidance Document on Declarations of Interests, Annex 3, Specific Declaration of Interests.	11.09.2007

The Declarations of Interests (DOI) of every person related to EFSA who has to make these declarations can be accessed at EFSA's web site on a first name basis. The Specific Declaration of Interests are required in addition to the general annual declaration for each separate occasion with regard to an agenda item where personal interests might (seem to) be present.

The personal transparency demands are linked to demands of independence and good administrative behaviour. See Law text box 5.20 on independence and Law text box 5.23 on the EFSA Code of good administrative behaviour. See Law text box 5.21 for aspects of transparency in relation to the organisation.

Law text box 5.20. Article 37 GFL on independence.

1. The members of the Management Board, the members of the Advisory Forum and the Executive Director shall undertake to act independently in the public interest.
   For this purpose, they shall make a declaration of commitment and a declaration of interests indicating either the absence of any interests which might be considered prejudicial to their independence or any direct or indirect interests which might be considered prejudicial to their independence. Those declarations shall be made annually in writing.
2. The members of the Scientific Committee and the Scientific Panels shall undertake to act independently of any external influence. For this purpose, they shall make a declaration of commitment and a declaration of interests indicating either the absence of any interests which might be considered prejudicial to their independence or any direct or indirect interests which might be considered prejudicial to their independence. Those declarations shall be made annually in writing.
3. The members of the Management Board, the Executive Director, the members of the Advisory Forum, the members of the Scientific Committee and the Scientific Panels, as well as external experts participating in their working groups shall declare at each meeting any interests which might be considered prejudicial to their independence in relation to the items on the agenda.

Law text box 5.21. Examples of EFSA Core Management Documents: Management Board decisions on transparency and access to documents

Subject	MB Decision number	Articles GFL
• Agreed Openness, transparency and confidentiality - general principles	16.09.2003 – 13	• 25(3), 37, 38, 38(3), 39 and 39(4) GFL.
• Implementing measures of transparency and confidentiality requirements	10.03.2005 – 10	
• Decision concerning access to documents	16.09.2003 – adopted	• 25(3), 41, 41(2)

5.8.5 EFSA Code of good administrative behaviour

EFSA's Management Board adopted the EFSA Code of good administrative behaviour in 2003.[143] It is a catalogue of the general principles of good governance described in Chapter 2 Introduction to law, section 2.5.6. Law text box 5.23 gives a concise impression of its content with an invitation to read the EFSA Code as a model for good administration and Courtesy. The Code invokes as one of its bases Article 41 of the Charter of Fundamental Rights, the European Union's surrogate Bill of Rights. It precedes highlights of the Code in Law text box 5.22.

Law text box 5.22. The Right to good administration, Article 41 Charter of Fundamental Rights of the European Union, 2000/C 364/01). Official Journal C 364, 18 December 2000.

Article 41 Right to good administration

1. Every person has the right to have his or her affairs handled impartially, fairly and within a reasonable time by the institutions and bodies of the Union.
2. This right includes: the right of every person to be heard, before any individual measure which would affect him or her adversely is taken;
   the right of every person to have access to his or her file, while respecting the legitimate interests of confidentiality and of professional and business secrecy;
   the obligation of the administration to give reasons for its decisions.
3. Every person has the right to have the Community make good any damage caused by its institutions or by its servants in the performance of their duties, in accordance with the general principles common to the laws of the Member States.
4. Every person may write to the institutions of the Union in one of the languages of the Treaties and must have an answer in the same language.

Law text box 5.23 gives from the EFSA Code of good administrative behaviour the considerations preceding the articles and the titles of the articles indicating their subject.

Law text box 5.23. EFSA Code of good administrative behaviour.

The management board

- Having regard to the Treaty of the European Union, and in particular Articles 21 and 195 thereof,
- Having regard to Article 41 of the Charter of Fundamental Rights, (...)(...)(...)

[143] MB Decision 16.09.2003-11-Adopted. Management Board of the European Food Safety Authority, EFSA Code of good administrative behaviour, Done at Brussels, 16 September 2003, Dr. Stuart Slorach, The Chair.

- WHEREAS the Amsterdam Treaty has explicitly introduced the concept of openness into the Treaty on European Union by stating that it marks a new stage in the process of creating an ever closer union in which decisions are taken as openly as possible and as closely as possible to the citizen,
- WHEREAS the Charter of fundamental rights proclaimed at the Nice Summit in December 2000 includes as fundamental rights of citizenship the right to good administration and the right to complain to the European Ombudsman against maladministration,
- WHEREAS, in order to bring the administration closer to the citizens and to guarantee a better quality of administration, a Code should be adopted which contains the basic principles of good administrative behaviour for agents and other servants of the Authority when dealing with the public,
- Considering it therefore desirable to establish a Code governing the principles of good administrative behaviour which the agents and other servants of the Authority should respect in their relations with the public, and to make this Code publicly available,

Has decided as follows:

Article	**Title**
1.	General provision
2	Personal scope of application
3.	Material scope of application
4.	Lawfulness
5.	Absence of discrimination
6.	Proportionality
7.	Absence of abuse of power
8.	Impartiality and independence
9.	Objectivity
10.	Legitimate expectations and consistency
11.	Fairness
12.	Courtesy
13.	Reply to letters in the language of the citizen
14.	Acknowledgement of receipt and indication of the competent agent or other servant
15.	Obligation to transfer to the competent service of the Authority
16.	Right to be heard and to make statements
17.	Reasonable time-limit for taking decisions
18.	Duty to state the grounds of decisions
19.	Indication of the possibilities of appeal
20.	Notification of the decision or recommendation
21	Data protection
22.	Requests for information
23.	Requests for public access to documents
24.	Keeping of adequate records
25.	Public access to the Code
26.	Right to complain to the European Ombudsman
27.	Revision

5.8.6 The Executive Director

The Executive Director is EFSA's legal representative.[144] She is responsible for:
a. the day-to-day administration of EFSA;
b. drawing up a proposal for EFSA's work programmes in consultation with the Commission;
c. implementing the work programmes and the decisions adopted by the Management Board;
d. ensuring the provision of appropriate scientific, technical and administrative support for the Scientific Committee and the Scientific Panels:
h. developing and maintaining contact with the European Parliament, and ensuring a regular dialogue with its relevant committees.

The Executive Director is responsible for the drafts of the programmes, reports and accounts that the Management Board has to decide on. The Executive Director takes care that the adopted programmes are sent to the European Parliament, the Council, the Commission and the Member States. The general report is sent to the European Parliament, the Council, the Commission the Court of Auditors, the European Economic and Social Committee and the Committee of the Regions. The work programmes and the general report are published. See Diagram 5.1 for the Executive Director's position in EFSA's organigram.

5.8.7 The Advisory Forum

The Advisory Forum is the link between EFSA and the member states.[145] It is composed of representatives from competent bodies in the member states which have tasks similar to those of EFSA. There will be one representative designated by each member state. Members of the Advisory Forum may not be members of the Management Board. The Executive Director convenes and chairs the Advisory Forum. A third of its members can also initiate a meeting. The Forum has to meet at least four times per year. Representatives of the Commission's departments can participate in the work of the Advisory Forum. The Executive Director can invite representatives of the European Parliament and from other relevant bodies to take part.

The Advisory Forum gives the Executive Director advice on all aspects of her tasks, and in particular on drawing up a proposal for EFSA's work programme. The Executive Director may also ask the Advisory Forum for advice on the prioritisation of requests for scientific opinions. The Advisory Forum is a mechanism for an exchange of information on potential risks and the pooling of knowledge. It ensures close cooperation between EFSA and the competent bodies in the member states.

144 Article 26 GFL.
145 Article 27GFL.

See Diagram 5.1 for the Advisory Forum's position in EFSA's organigram and the position of administrative support for the Advisory Forum under Scientific Committee and Advisory Forum.

5.8.8 Scientific opinions

Several scientific committees were attached to the EU Commission in the period preceding the GFL, now they are reorganised and have become part of EFSA. One Scientific Committee and ten permanent Scientific Panels are responsible for providing EFSA's scientific opinions, each within their own spheres of competence. The scientific panels have their legal base in Article 28(4) GFL. EFSA began with eight scientific panels each indicated by name in the GFL. The Commission has the authority to change the number and names of the panels. This authority can be used at the request of EFSA's managing board when changes are necessary 'in the light of technical and scientific development'. The Commission can exercise this authority only by using the procedure of Article 58 GFL, the comitology procedure with the representatives of the member states in the Standing Committee on the Food Chain and Animal Health.

5.8.9 The Scientific Panels

The procedure was used in 2006 when the Panel on plant health was split from the Panel on plant health, plant protection products and their residues.[146] Experience learned that the Panel on additives, flavourings, processing aids and materials in contact with food (AFC) had to deal with almost half of the requests for a scientific opinion. It is anticipated that this workload will become even heavier after the adoption of the Commission's food improvement agents package (FIAP) on food additives, food enzymes, flavourings and food ingredients. See Chapter 9, section 9.9 Developments.

It was decided to divide this panel in two: the Panel on food additives and nutrient sources added to food (ANS) and the Panel on food contact materials, enzymes, flavourings, and processing aids (CEF).[147] See Law text box 5.24 for an overview of EFSA's scientific panels.

---

[146] Commission Regulation (EC) No 575/2006 of 7 April 2006 amending Regulation (EC) No 178/2002 of the European Parliament and of the Council as regards the number and names of the permanent Scientific Panels of the European Food Safety Authority. Official Journal L 100, 08 April 2006, p. 3.

[147] MB 11.09.07 – 4.2 Proposal to divide the tasks of the AFC panel and Commission Regulation (EC) No 202/2008 of 4 March 2008 amending Regulation (EC) No 178/2002 of the European Parliament and of the Council as regards the number and names of the Scientific Panels of the European Food Safety Authority (Text with EEA relevance). Official Journal L 60, 5 March 2008, p. 17.

Law text box 5.24. EFSA's scientific panels, their acronyms, base in the GFL and mandates. The panels are presented in the sequence used at EFSA's website for easy access to the panel's sites.

Panel on food additives and nutrient sources added to food (ANS), based on Article 28(4)(a) GFL.
Mandate: the safety in use of:
- food additives;
- nutrient sources added to food and to food supplements; and
- associated subjects concerning the safety of other deliberately added substances including substances added for other than a technological purpose e.g. with functional properties but excluding flavourings and enzymes.

Panel on food contact materials, enzymes, flavourings, and processing aids (CEF), based on Article 28(4)(j) GFL.
Mandate: the safety in use of:
- food contact materials;
- flavourings and processing aids, including enzymes;
- associated subjects concerning the safety of other substances indirectly added to food; and
- questions related to the safety of new processes (e.g. irradiation).

Panel on animal health and welfare (AHAW) based on Article 28(4)(h) GFL.
Mandate: all aspects of animal health and animal welfare, primarily relating to food producing animals including fish.

Panel on biological hazards (BIOHAZ) based on Article 28(4)(f) GFL.
Mandate: biological hazards relating to food safety and food-borne disease, including food-borne zoonoses and transmissible spongiform encephalopathies, microbiology, food hygiene and associated waste management.

Panel on contaminants in the food chain (CONTAM) based on Article 28(4)(g) GFL.
Mandate: contaminants in food and feed, associated areas and undesirable substances such as natural toxicants, mycotoxins and residues of non authorised substances not covered by an other panel.

Panel on additives and products or substances used in animal feed (FEEDAP) based on Article 28(4)(b) GFL.
Mandate: safety for the animal, the user/worker, the consumer of products of animal origin, the environment and to the efficacy of biological and chemical products / substances intended for deliberate addition/use in animal feed.

Panel on Genetically Modified Organisms (GMO) based on Article 28(4)(d) GFL.
Mandate: genetically modified organisms, such as micro-organisms, plants and animals, relating to deliberate release into the environment and genetically modified food and feed, including products deriving from GMOs.

Panel on dietetic products, nutrition and allergies (NDA) based on Article 28(4)(e) GFL.
Mandate: dietetic products, human nutrition and food allergy, and other associated subjects such as novel foods.

Panel on plant protection products and their residues (PPR) based on Article 28(4)(c) GFL.
Mandate: safety of plant protection products for the user/worker, the consumer of treated products and the environment.

Panel on Plant health (PLH) based on Article 28(4)(i) GFL.
Mandate: plant health especially with regard to organisms that pose a risk to plant health. This panel was created to enlist a wide range of expertise in the various fields relevant to plant health, such as entomology, mycology, virology, bacteriology botany, agronomy, plant quarantine and epidemiology of plant diseases.

The procedures for the operation and cooperation of the Scientific Committee and the Scientific Panels have to be laid down in EFSA's internal rules. The Management Board used this delegation of power to make Decision concerning the establishment and operations of the Scientific Committee and Panels.[148] One of the Operating rules is given in Law text box 5.20. See Diagram 5.1 for the position of administrative support for the Scientific Panels in EFSA's organigram under Risk Assessment.

5.8.10 The Scientific Committee

The Scientific Committee is the institutionalised meeting of the Chairs of the Scientific Panels and six independent scientific experts who do not belong to any of the Scientific Panels. The six independent experts are appointed by the Management Board. The Scientific Panels are composed of independent scientific experts appointed by the Management Board. Ten panels have been established with a specified mandate so far.[149] Decisions are made with a simple majority vote, minority opinions are recorded with the name of the author and the argumentation. The representatives of the Commission's departments have a right to be present in the meetings of the Scientific Committee, the Scientific Panels and their working

[148] EFSA Management Board Decision concerning the establishment and operations of the Scientific Committee and Panels, 11 September 2007. See references for hyperlink.
[149] See for this list Article 28 GFL.

groups. They assist to clarify issues or give information. They are not allowed to influence discussions.

Both the Scientific Committee and the Scientific Panels can set up Working groups. Their expertise will be used to prepare draft scientific opinions. External experts, who possess particular and relevant scientific knowledge, can be invited to participate in a Working Group.[150] The Scientific Committee and permanent Scientific Panels can, where necessary, organise public hearings. Commission Regulation (EC) No 1304/2003 of 23 July 2003 prescribes the procedure that EFSA has to apply to requests for scientific opinions.[151]

The Scientific Committee is responsible for the general co-ordination necessary to ensure the consistency of the scientific opinion procedure, in particular with regard to the adoption of working procedures and harmonisation of working methods. It provides opinions on multi-sector issues falling within the competence of more than one Scientific Panel, and on issues which do not fall within the competence of any of the Scientific Panels. Where necessary, and particularly in the case of subjects which do not fall within the competence of any of the Scientific Panels, the Scientific Committee will set up Working Groups. In such cases, it shall draw on the expertise of those working groups when establishing scientific opinions. The GFL lays great stress on the openness and transparency of EFSA's activities, as far as confidential aspects of its work permit. See Diagram 5.1 for the position of administrative support for the Scientific Committee in EFSA's organigram under Scientific Committee and Advisory Forum.

5.8.11 Tasks of EFSA

The following eight tasks will be briefly described: presenting scientific opinions; finding a solution for diverging scientific opinions; providing scientific and technical assistance to the EU Commission; commissioning scientific studies; building a data collection; establishing monitoring procedures; promoting networking and (risk) communication. Finally EFSA has to process the information delivered by the rapid alert system:

Task 1. A main EFSA task is to prepare and present scientific opinions. This work is done by the Scientific Committee or the Scientific Panels. Requests for a scientific opinion are assigned by the Executive Director to one of the Scientific Panels according to its mandate, or to the Scientific Committee for questions on multi-sector issues falling within the competence of more than one Panel, and on issues which do not fall within the competence of

[150] Articles 5 and 6 MB Decision, 11.09.2007.

[151] Commission Regulation (EC) No 1304/2003 of 23 July 2003 on the procedure applied by the European Food Safety Authority to requests for scientific opinions referred to it. Official Journal L 185, 24 July 2003, p. 6, as corrected by Corrigendum, Official Journal L 186, 25 July 2003, p. 46, (1304/2003).

any of the Panels. Article 29 GFL specifies that opinions can be asked by the European Parliament, the member states and the Commission. EFSA can give opinions on its own initiative.

Regulation 1304/2003[152] on the procedure that EFSA has to apply to requests for scientific opinions explicitly orders EFSA in Article 3(1) to refuse to give an opinion to anyone else.

The Commission can ask EFSA to give opinions in addition to those based on the GFL in all specific cases where Community legislation grants this right.

ESFA has to operate a register of requested opinions and own initiative opinions. The register can be accessed by everyone and gives information on the progress of EFSA work.

Each scientific opinion has to contain the question, the background to the request, the information considered, the scientific reasoning and the opinion of the Scientific Committee or Panel. The full scientific opinion is published on EFSA's web site.

Task 2. In the case of diverging scientific opinions, the Advisory Forum has to contribute to find a solution when disagreement occurs between EFSA and an organisation working on the same topics in a member state. When both parties identify a substantive divergence of opinion over scientific issues, Article 30 (4) GFL orders them to tackle this problem. Their co-operation has to result in resolving the differences or a joint document clarifying the contentious scientific issues and identifying the relevant uncertainties in the data.

Task 3. Provide scientific and technical assistance to the EU Commission if requested. This assistance will be scientific or technical work involving the application of well-established scientific or technical principles. The scientific evaluation by EFSA is not needed. The assistance can be given without compromising the independent position of EFSA. The Commission will enlist this assistance especially for the establishment or evaluation of technical criteria and the development of technical guidelines.

Task 4. EFSA has to commission scientific studies necessary for the performance of its mission, using the best independent scientific resources available. EFSA has to avoid duplication with research programmes of the member states or the Community, and shall foster co-operation through appropriate co-ordination. The Advisory Forum has to assist EFSA in this respect, giving substance to its role to ensure pooling of knowledge and close co-operation between EFSA and the competent bodies in the member states.

Task 5. ESFA shall build up a collection of data in particular relating to:

a. food consumption and the exposure of individuals to risks related to the consumption of food;
b. incidence and prevalence of biological risk;

[152] Article 2 Regulation 1304/2003.

c. contaminants in food and feed;
d. residues.
EFSA will collect data in close co-operation with all organisations operating in the field of data collection, including those from applicant countries, third countries or international bodies.

Task 6. ESFA will establish monitoring procedures for the systematic collection of information to identify emerging risks in the fields within its mission. Where EFSA has information leading it to suspect a serious risk, the member states, other Community agencies and the Commission have to co-operate to find and deliver any relevant information to EFSA. To enable it to perform its task of monitoring the health and nutritional risks of foods as effectively as possible, EFSA shall receive all messages forwarded via the rapid alert system.[153] EFSA analyses this information and gives it to the Commission and the member states for risk analysis.

Task 7. EFSA has to promote networking between European organisations that work on the same fields as EFSA. The aim of such networking is, in particular, to facilitate a scientific co-operation framework by the coordination of activities, the exchange of information, the development and implementation of joint projects, and the exchange of expertise and best practices in the fields within EFSA's mission.[154]

Task 8. EFSA has to contribute to risk communication as an independent source of information with a solid reputation based on scientific excellence. EFSA's risk communication activities have to respect the Commission's risk communication about risk management decisions. Risk communication was one of the central issues in the evaluation of EFSA's first external evaluation.[155]

EFSA's Register of Questions is an example of the free flow of information on food relevant issues supported by the independent Authority. The register stood at 1811 questions on 1 July 2008. See Law text box 5.25 on the EFSA Register of Questions to get an impression of the information it provides. See the reference list for the access to the Register.

153 On the rapid alert system for food and feed see Chapter 13, section 13.4.

154 Article 36 GFL.

155 Article 61 GFL. The report: European Food Safety Authority, Evaluation of EFSA, Final Report, Contract FIN0105, Bureau van Dijk Ingénieurs Conseils with Arcadia International EEIG, Brussels, 5 December 2005. EFSA's reaction: Management Board of the European Food Safety Authority, Proposal for Management Board Conclusions of the External Evaluation of EFSA and Recommendations Arising from The Report, MB 20.06.2006-4.

Law text box 5.25. The EFSA Register of Questions.

Question number	Subject	Panel	Status	Details
EFSA-Q-2008-428	EU-wide collective scientific expertise on the possible causative factors of CCD affecting bee colonies.[1]	AMU	Registration not yet completed	

[1] CCD stands for Colony Collapse Disorder: the adult working bees leave the colony en masse for an unknown destination. The hive is left with a live queen, honey, immature brood, no dead bees and too few working bees. The cause or causes of this no-future scenario are not known. Vanishing bee populations are part of the human experience with bee keeping but reported cases have risen remarkably in the EU and the US since 2006. See the website of the Agricultural Research Service of the US Department of Agriculture for current research and estimates of $15 billion lost added value a year and the estimate that one third of the diet in the US depends directly and indirectly on bees. And for them these are only the pollinators from the old world. Google CCD bee or visit http://www.ars.usda.gov/News/docs.htm?docid=15572.

5.8.12 The organisation of the EFSA staff

The EFSA staff supports the work of the scientific panels, the workgroups, the advisory forum and takes care of the other ESFA tasks mentioned above. In 2007 the staff organisation was changed into four directorates: Administration to facilitate the work of the staff, Communication for EFSA's public information tasks and two scientific directorates. The Risk Assessment Directorate has ten groups that support the ten scientific panels to deliver risk assessments to Europe's risk managers. The Scientific Cooperation and Assistance Directorate has six units to support risk assessment work and to develop scientific cooperation. Two of these units cooperate directly with the member states on pesticides and transmissible animal diseases. See Law text box 5.26 for the six Units of ESFA's Scientific Cooperation and Assistance Directorate and Diagram 5.1 for the position of the Scientific Cooperation and Assistance Directorate in EFSA's organigram.

Law text box 5.26. The six Units of ESFA's Scientific Cooperation and Assistance Directorate and their tasks.

- Pesticide Risk Assessment Peer Review Unit (PRAPeR)
  This unit is responsible for EFSA's contribution to the EU peer review of active substances used in plant protection products
- Animal Diseases Transmissible to Humans (Zoonoses) Unit
  This unit analyses and reports data of zoonoses, antimicrobial resistance, microbiological contaminants and food-borne outbreaks. The data are submitted by the Member States and other reporting countries in accordance with Directive 2003/99/EC.

- Scientific Cooperation Unit

  The Scientific Co-operation unit supports other units within EFSA's and national food safety agencies. The objective is to foster scientific collaboration, projects and exchange of scientific information between EFSA and national food safety agencies in EU member states.
- Data Collection and Exposure unit (DATEX)
  The DATEX unit deals with the collection, collation and analysis of data on food consumption and chemical occurrence in food and feed for exposure assessments at European level.
- Emerging Risks Unit (EMRISK)
  The Emerging Risks unit (EMRISK) is responsible for establishing procedures to monitor, collect and analyse information and data in order to identify emerging risks in the field of food and feed safety with a view to their prevention.
- Assessment Methodology Unit (AMU)
  The Assessment Methodology Unit (AMU) provides technical support in the field of statistics, modelling, data management and risk assessment. It contributes in particular to the development and application of new or refined risk assessment approaches in the field of food and feed safety.

5.8.13 Legal protection

EFSA is not one of the institutions of the EU mentioned in the EC Treaty. For this reason, the provisions of legal protection in the Treaty do not apply to EFSA. However, article 47 GFL attributes jurisdiction to the European Court of Justice to decide on both contractual and non-contractual liability of EFSA.

5.9 The Standing Committee on the Food Chain and Animal Health

The Standing Committee on the Food Chain and Animal Health (SCFCAH) was established to ensure a more effective and comprehensive approach to the food chain aspects of food production.[156] It replaced the Standing Veterinary Committee, the Standing Committee for Foodstuffs, the Standing Committee for Feedingstuffs and the Standing Committee on Plant Health. The unified committee assists the Commission and the EFSA. The rules of the Council´s Decision on comitology make this Standing Committee a regulatory committee. See section 5.5 on comitology.

The Standing Committee on the Food Chain and Animal Health is organised in the following sections:
- General Food Law
- Biological Safety of the Food Chain
- Toxicological Safety of the Food Chain

[156] Article 58 GFL

- Controls and Import Conditions
- Animal Nutrition
- Genetically Modified Food and Environmental Risk
- Animal Health and Animal Welfare
- Phytopharmaceuticals

5.10 The Advisory group on the food chain and animal and plant health

In 2004 the EC Commission created an advisory group on the food chain and animal and plant health.[157] This group is attached directly to the Commission to give it advice on the following fields of the Commission's programme of work:
- food and feed safety;
- food and feed labelling and presentation;
- human nutrition, in relation to food legislation;
- animal health and welfare;
- matters relating to crop protection, plant protection products and its residues, and conditions for the marketing of seed and propagation material, including biodiversity, and including matters pertaining to industrial property.[158]

The group will bring together no more than 45 representatives of representative European organisations selected by the Commission. Each organisation has to coordinate consultation and information activities within its own organisation to present views that are as representative as possible. The selection criteria for membership of the advisory group are:
- the organisation's objective to protect interests in the fields of the Commission's work programme where the advisory group will be asked to advise;[159]
- the general nature of the protected interests;
- a representation covering all or most member states; and
- permanent existence at Community level; with
- direct access to members' expertise to permit swift and coordinated reactions.[160]

157 Commission Decision of 6 August 2004 concerning the creation of an advisory group on the food chain and animal and plant health (2004/613/EC). Official Journal L 275, 25 August 2004, pp. 17-19. Draft: Communication from the Commission, concerning the creation of an advisory group on the food chain and animal and plant health and the establishment of a consultation procedure on the food chain and animal and plant health through representative European bodies.

158 Article 2(1) Commission Decision 2004/613/EC.

159 Commission of the European Communities, Communication from the Commission to the European Parliament, the Council, the European Economic and Social Committee and the Committee of the Regions, Commission Legislative and Work Programme 2008, COM(2007) 640 final, Brussels, 23 October 2007.

160 Article 3(1) Commission Decision 2004/613/EC.

The list of the 36 organisations selected by the Commission is published in the Official Journal of the European Union.[161] See Law text box 15.27 for the interests represented by the selected organisations.

The advisory group is chaired by the Commission; it has two regular meetings each year at the premises of the Commission and whenever the Commission considers a meeting necessary.

The Commission takes care of the publicity for the work of the group.[162]

Law text box 15.27. List of members of the EU Commission's advisory group on the food chain and animal and plant health, Commission Decision (2005/C 97/02), Official Journal C 97, 21 April 2005, p. 2.

In accordance with Article 3(3) of Commission Decision 2004/613/EC of 6 August 2004, the Commission has drawn up the following list of members of the advisory group on the food chain and animal and plant health.	
Association des Industries de Poisson de la CE/Comité Import/Export Poissons	AIPCE-CEP
Animal Welfare Association	Animals Angels
Association of Poultry Processors and Poultry Import and Export Trade	AVEC
European Consumers' Organisation	BEUC
Chemical Industry Council Food Regulation Panel	CEFIC
Commerce Agro-Alimentaire	CELCAA
Confédération Européenne des Syndicats	CES/ETUC
Confédération des Industries Agro-Alimentaires	CIAA
Association of Meat Processing Industry	CLITRAVI
Association For Trade in Cereals, Oilseeds, Feedstuffs	COCERAL / EU
Agri-Cooperation	COPA-COGECA
European Crop Care Association	ECCA
Crop Protection Association	ECPA / EU
European Cold Storage and Logistics Association	ECSLA
European Dairy Association	EDA
European Federation of Food, Agriculture and Tourism Trade Unions	EFFAT
European Fat Processors and Renderers Association	EFPRA
European Modern Restaurants Association	EMRA
European Seed Association	ESA
Association of EU Chambers of Commerce and Industries	EUROCHAMBRES
Retail, Wholesale and International Trade Representation to the EU	EUROCOMMERCE
Community of Consumer Co-operatives	EUROCOOP / EU

[161] List of members of the advisory group on the food chain and animal and plant health. Official Journal C 97, 21 April 2005, p. 2.
[162] Article 4 Commission Decision 2004/613/EC.

Animal Welfare Organisation	EUROGROUP / EU
Association of Bioindustries	EUROPABIO / EU
Alimentation pour Animaux Familiers	FEDIAF
Fédération Européenne Fabricants Aliments Composés	FEFAC
Fédération Européenne de la Restauration Collective Concédée	FERCO
Fédération Européenne Santé Animale et Sécurité Sanitaire	FESASS
Forum for the Fresh Produce Industry	FRESHFEL
Federation Veterinarians of Europe	FVE
Hotels, restaurants and Cafés in Europe	HOTREC
Animal Health Industry	IFAH / EU
Federation of Organic Agriculture Movements	IFOAM / EU
Artisanat et Petites/Moyennes Entreprises	UEAPME
European Livestock and Meat Trading Union	UECBV
Union des Groupements de Détaillants Indépendants de l'Europe	UGAL

5.11 Stakeholders' participation

DG SANCO wants to reinforce stakeholders' participation in the preparation and evaluation of policies.[163] One of the activities is the Healthy Democracy process. Its aim is 'to improve stakeholder involvement and participation. In the long term, the aim is to establish a solid network of stakeholders and research bodies to improve its substantive performance.'[164]

A Peer Review Group was established in early 2006 to assist DG SANCO's efforts to improve stakeholder involvement. The Group selected a top ten of recommendations, see Law text box 5.28.[165]

Law text box 5.28. Stakeholder participation in SANCO's activities: Recommendations from the Peer Review Group.

I:	Establish a 'Stakeholder Dialogue Group' to get advice processes rather than on content
II:	Improve Transparency through better 'Forward Planning'
III:	More and Better Feedback

[163] European Commission, Health & Consumer Protection Directorate-General, Stakeholder Involvement Event, The Report, Brussels, 23 May 2007. European Commission, Health & Consumer Protection Directorate-General, 03 - Science and stakeholder relations, Joint meeting of the stakeholder dialogue group and the advisory group on the food chain and animal and plant health, summary record, Brussels, SANCO 03, 30 November 2007.

[164] European Commission, Health & Consumer Protection Directorate-General, Healthy democracy. Conclusions and Actions following the DG SANCO 2006 Peer Review Group on Stakeholder Involvement.

[165] The full report can be consulted at the following website: www.sanco-stakeholderinvolvement.eu.

IV: Engage the Un-engaged & Going Local
V: Driving Up Data Quality
VI: Definition of Representativeness
VII: Be Aware of Stakeholder Asymmetries
VIII: More Flexible and Longer Consultation Timeframe
IX: Improvement of Inter-DG Coordination
X: More Transparent Comitology

The fourth recommendation 'IV: Engage the Un-engaged & Going Local' addresses two major weaknesses of all international organisations, the remote or fragmented civil society. See Law text box 5.29.

Law text box 5.29. Stakeholder participation in SANCO's activities: Engage the Un-engaged & Going Local.

(Recommendation IV)
The Peer Review Group noted that the challenges of achieving representativeness and engaging hard-to-reach groups are exacerbated at the European level where there are few tangible connections between citizens and the Brussels institutions.
In order to ensure a better engagement, DG SANCO should
1. consider the use of Commission's delegations in Member States as platform for the debate
2. work together with existing stakeholders (in particular NGOs) to identify the 'unengaged'.

This recommendation led to an interesting proposal: that the Commission can use its permanent delegations in the member states as a platform for contacts with the civil societies of the member states to construct a European civil society.

The following observation is true for all international organisations: the challenges of all political entities to achieve representativeness and engage hard-to-reach groups 'are exacerbated at the European level where there are few tangible connections between citizens and the Brussels institutions.'

This is directly relevant for the stakeholder asymmetries of recommendation VII: those stakeholder groups that are connected with the EC have a disproportionate influence. The EC should be well aware of this phenomenon: agricultural stakeholders occupied half its budget and 60% of its legislation for decades.

6. The embedding of food law into substantive EU law

If there were no EU law, there certainly would be food law. If there were no food law, there certainly could not be EU law as we know it today. This is because food law is a necessity on its own and because food law is embedded in EU law that covers the essentials of the integration process. Without food law, the internal market could not be the same. The common market, set as a goal in 1958, and the internal market, set as a goal in 1986 were designed to be drivers of the integration process, as much, or even more than as motors of economic development. The hand in hand relationship between the internal market and food law made them both suffer the very low tides of European integration in the period of 1966 to 1986. The food law case law of the Court of Justice of the European Communities was a major factor in keeping integration alive in the ebb times and blooming in the renaissance that began in 1986. See Chapter 7, section 7.3 Advancement through case law in this book.

In addition to the formal structure of EU law, which determines what types of measures are possible, and what their effects are on the EU itself, on the EC institutions, the member states and private persons, and on the relations between these various actors, substantive EU laws determine to a considerable extent the conditions under which food law has to operate.

6.1 The Customs Union

Essential building blocks of the EEC Treaty were the customs union and the common market. The customs union required the abolition of customs duties and customs borders between the member states. This was linked with the creation of one external customs frontier that created the same conditions all along the common external border for entry of goods from the world outside the EEC. The customs union was allowed under the GATT[166] as an exception. During and after its creation the EC participated in several international negotiation rounds in GATT and its successor the World Trade Organisation (WTO).

On the inside the customs borders separating the member states had to be abolished over a transition period of twelve years, starting at the beginning of the EEC on 1 January 1958. This period was divided into three rounds each of four years. Decision making was to be by unanimous vote during the first two and by majority vote in the last period. So majority decision making was prescribed by the Treaty from 1966 onwards, and the customs union would be completed in 1970.

[166] General Agreement on Tariffs and Trade. See Chapter 16, section 16.2.2 in this book.

6.2 Ban on all customs levies and all measures with an equivalent effect

The prohibition of customs duties on imports and exports included charges having equivalent effect. To fulfil this obligation member states had to break down the legal instruments that they had developed in the course of preceding decades. Several legal instruments were used at the national borders on goods entering the state and sometimes on goods exported from the state. Persons transporting incoming goods were subjected to payment of a certain amount of money to obtain permission to cross the border with the goods. This generated income for the national government. It created at the same time an instrument to interfere in the market economies of the exporting and importing states. Allowing desired goods to enter without a customs levy did not increase their price on the internal market; subjecting the products of competing foreign producers to high customs levies protected the national producers. All kinds of levies were created with different names, different purposes, different ways of collection and with the common denominator that they all required a payment for entry of goods originating from abroad. The EEC Treaty ordered the removal of all customs levies and all measures with an effect equivalent to that of a customs levy.

6.3 Ban on quantitative restrictions

A second group of measures on customs borders had been created: quantitative restrictions. In a given year a certain amount of goods were allowed to be imported. When the last good under this quantity had crossed the border no additional goods were allowed during the remainder of the year. Anyone who still wanted such a good had to wait for the next year when a new quantity was opened, or not, depending on the policies of the national government. The quantitative restrictions have their own group of measures with equivalent effect. Although they did not have the form of a strait limitation of a quantity, practically speaking they had the same results. An example is the measure used by the Dutch government in the 1950's. Bakers had to bake bread with a certain percentage of Dutch grown wheat. This is another way to limit the amount of imported wheat. The EEC Treaty ordered the removal of quantitative restrictions and all measures with equivalent effect.

It is with these measures that food law can become involved. Many rules of food law are made to serve non-economic interests, like human health. The EC Treaty allows exceptions to free trade in these interests.[167] But even with these exceptions the question arises as to whether the food law measures are eligible to rank among the exceptions. A severe test has to be passed to determine the reality of the non-economic character of the measures. In other words, the question is whether the

[167] Article 30 EC Treaty.

measure in dispute is a trade barrier disguised as a food safety measure. If so, it is a measure having an effect equivalent to a quantitative restriction. In that case the exceptions on free movement of goods do not apply. The next question then raised is whether these food safety measures must be abolished because they interfere with the free movement of goods, or be allowed because the interests they serve are more important than free movement of goods. If the measures are indispensable, the final question is whether the combined interests of human health and the common market are better served with law made to protect human health on the level of the Community, or on the level of the member states. This raises the issues of harmonisation of the different national laws by a directive, or unification of the law by a regulation. The regulation gives the necessary rules on the level of the Community. When the Community has used its powers by making legislation on a topic, all member states lose their legislative powers on the same subject. All existing national (food) legislation on the same topics has to be terminated. If the member states fail to do this they may have to face a Court of Justice trial for infringement of EC obligations. Meanwhile their national legislation is overruled by the regulation. See Diagram 6.1 on the different effects of directives and regulations on national law

Diagram 6.1. Harmonisation of national law by an EC directive and unification into EC law by an EC regulation: no national laws left on the same subjects as covered by the EC regulation. The regulation can give the member states some legislative power on specific issues by delegation. The member states exercise this power on behalf of the Community.

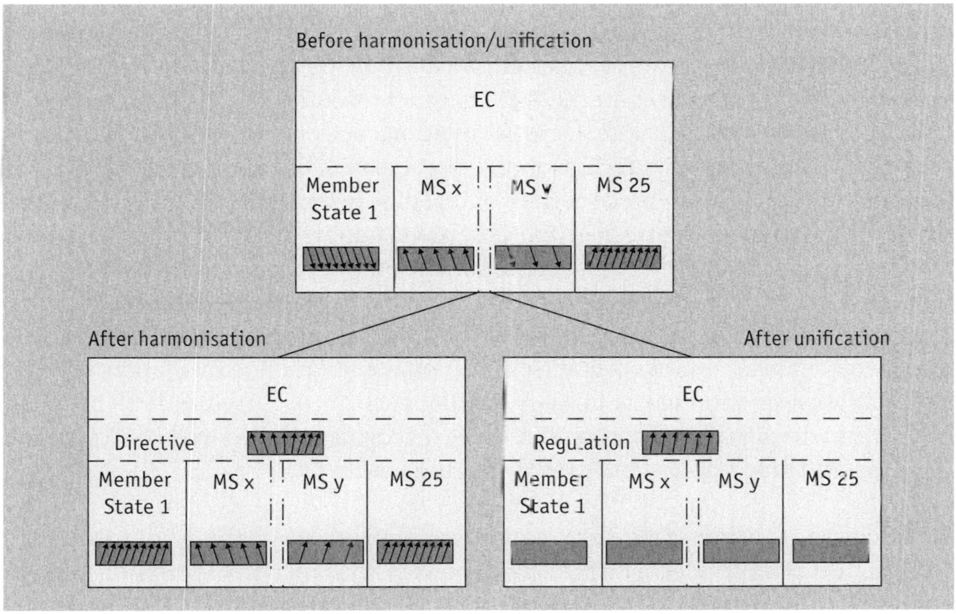

To get a good perspective on the problems connected to the question as to whether a particular legislative act is a measure of effect equivalent to a quantitative restriction, or an exception to free movement of goods that must be accepted, it is illuminating to look at the way situations may get out of hand when such rules do not function properly: e.g. a trade war.

6.4 Trade wars

The relations between the nation states and their economies can be characterised by a certain roughness, if there are no intermediate or reconciling structures like the EC or WTO. Take the relations between the United States and the European Union in recent years as an example. Even after decades of negotiating customs reduction treaties, and concluding them successfully, every now and then a trade war disrupts these relations. A disagreement about support given by the EU to the steel industry in the Community leads the US to install barriers for the import of cheese and flowers. First of all it is not quite clear why American aficionados of European cheeses should be punished by their government who increases the prices of these cheeses by putting a punitive levy on them when they are imported into the USA. The reason for the US government installing these extra charges is that years of complaining about EC subsidies for EC steel industries have not changed EC policies. And even if there is a reason why American cheese eaters must suffer for the loss of American steel companies, it is still unclear why European cheese makers have to suffer for the advantages given by their government to steel industries.

These imbalances are taken for granted, because the US government felt the need to do something, anything, in the steel conflict with the EU. It is an indication of basic characteristics of international relations acting outside of intermediate structures. There are many reasons why the steel dispute may be more the outcome of an escalation process, than of real differences in treatment of the steel market. To name but a few: the American government might be misinformed, it might be overstating the effects of EC policies, it might have neglected the fact that the European steel policy itself is a reaction to an earlier American policy to support their steel industry that is still in place, and so on. The basic issue is that no mechanism functions that would stimulate restraint, conciliation, or even impartial examination of the facts. A conflict like this occurred in 1998 between the US and the EU about steel with cheese as bargaining chip, and in 2002 when textiles and orange juice were drawn into the conflict.

Trade conflicts divided European nation states regularly in the past before they created the Communities. The transfer of powers, the creation of common policies and the common market make the recurrence of this type of conflict between the member states nearly impossible, simply because they do not have the instruments anymore that are necessary to be able to have a dispute like this. Even more important is the fact that when they do disagree, as they will, about the common policy, there are mechanisms that de-escalate the conflict instead of firing the blast furnace of dissent. The member states and the institutions are interlocked by the economic consequences of integration, and they are interlocked in the complicated web of competences, instruments, procedures and decisions of EC policy formation and execution. They are forced to negotiate. And if this turns out not to be enough to disband the conflict, they have recourse to an independent institution that will establish the facts of the case from a position outside of the conflict and with the prestige and deep roots of judges in the political and legal systems and rule of law in Europe. These impartial judges will not only assist the conflicting quarrelling states to see the facts as they are, they will also pronounce the outcome of the confrontation of these facts with the rules that were agreed on before. In short, a judge will decide an economic (political?) conflict on the basis of law.

Such is the past and the background for the law on the common market, the customs union and the common commercial policy for economic relations between the EU and countries outside of the Union. It is necessary to understand the problems that are connected with trade in food. Health issues that are raised for legitimate reasons have to face the suspicion created by a long history of appeals on health issues that actually were a front to hide a trade interest. This suspicion has even entered the EC Treaty where it grants in Article 30 exceptions to the rule of free movement of goods on the common market 'on grounds of public morality, public policy or public security; the protection of health and life of humans, animals or plants ...' and then expresses the need to shackle the exceptions for these meritorious causes with two chains. One that 'such prohibitions or restrictions shall not, however, constitute a means of arbitrary discrimination', and two 'nor a disguised restriction on trade between Member States'. The first limitation of the exceptions to the rule of free movement of goods is an expression of the need to ban any discrimination on grounds of nationality, Article 12 EC Treaty, a necessity if the EC is to build and maintain a common market out of former national markets. The second limitation of the exceptions is a reflection on the experience with customs law. Apparently experience had led to caution if not suspicion. On the level of the world wide international community, the same experiences have led to two WTO treaties: the Agreement on Technical Barriers to Trade (the TBT Agreement) and the Agreement on the Application of Sanitary and Phytosanitary Measures (the SPS Agreement). See Chapter 16 of this book.

6.5 The common market

The common market is next to the customs union another essential building block of integration. It prescribes free movement of goods across the whole territory of the Union, once they have been legally put on the market in any of the member states. This can be goods from countries outside the Union, or goods which were produced in one of the member states and have been put on the market. Free movement of goods is one of four fundamental free movement freedoms (the other three are free movement for persons, services and capital). These freedoms are crucial for the EC if it is to create one market, like the domestic market of a single state. The common market is not just free movement, but also an active government policy to keep the market functioning as a true market. Several policies support the common market, competition policy, private enterprises are not allowed to divide amongst themselves the market that the member states have unified. Public procurement policy, the governments of the states may not give preferential treatment to enterprises of their nationality when they are buying goods or investing in major projects. National governments have to follow EC rules on the support given to companies.

The central problem for the Community is that while the customs borders were dismantled, and later the borders checking the movement of persons were also abolished, this does not change the fact that the different national law systems of the member states still leave their imprint on the territory of the Community. Travelling from one member state to another one, is moving from one system of law to a different one. And these different legal systems have different rules for many aspects of the same goods, and especially so for food.

6.6 Technical barriers to trade

The creation of the common market had to face another barrier to free movement of goods, the technical barriers to trade. A classic example of a technical barrier to trade was the Belgian law that prescribed that butter being sold by retailers to consumers had to be packed as a cube. The reason for this requirement was to protect the consumer from confusing butter and margarine. Whatever the ideas behind this legislation were, the effect on producers outside Belgium was clear. If they wanted to export their butter to Belgium, they would have to install the machinery for packing that butter in a cube form. If they happened to be in a country where the traditional way to present butter is in rectangular blocs, this meant additional expenditure in machinery and space, and the logistics of a separate stream of products to Belgium. The Belgian national 'cubistic' legislation on butter is therefore a measure of equivalent effect as a quantitative restriction. The aim of preventing confusion between butter and margarine can be achieved with less drastic measures: for instance a label indicating the content.

There were two ways in which the Belgian law was enforced. Dismantling the customs borders had not removed customs' civil servants from the national borders. At that time the national borders still had controls on transport of goods across the border, to test whether the imported goods met the various technical requirements produced by national legislation, introduced to serve a wide variety of interests. Belgian civil servants patrolling the internal borders could intercept the rectangular butter transport before it became illegal because it brought the wrong butter form into Belgium. In this period it was a well-known complaint from transporters that while the customs barrier was removed, they still had to contend with all the different demands of the national law systems they crossed on their routes in integrating Europe. The transporter who had to take 72 different documents with him, that were required by the successive national authorities on his route, got almost legendary status. The effort to obtain all these documents from all these national administrations and the time lost by all the long delays at the internal borders between the EC Member states gave rise to calculations on how much economic capacity could be freed by a real common market.

The second way to enforce the Belgian cubical butter law is to have inspectors visit the retail shops regularly to check whether various food laws are obeyed. The cubic packaging requirement would be broken if the retailer offered imported rectangular blocs of butter for sale. The inspector then would confiscate these illegal packages and institute prosecution for offending the 'cubic-butter' law. Depending on the rules of the Belgian criminal enforcement law, this could be a penalty sum to be paid directly, or the duty to appear before a judge who would try the responsible retailer as a suspect of the crime of offering non-cubic butter for sale in a Belgian shop. If the judge would rest the case solely on Belgium law there could be no other outcome than to punish the offender with the sanctions provided by Belgium law. The consequence would be that no Belgium retailer would import butter in rectangular blocs. The Belgium territory of the common market would be effectively closed for these products. This effect is the same as a measure of effect equivalent to a quantitative import restriction. And that is forbidden by E(E)C law which is supreme to Belgian law. So the free movement of goods regulated in the E(E)C Treaty prescribed that the Belgian judge give no effect to the Belgian Cubic-Butter Law, and acquit the defendant retailer. To make sure that this was the correct thing to do, the Belgian judge, who had to decide this case, asked the advice of the Court of Justice of the European Communities.[168]

The Court ruled that the law demanding cubic butter was a technical barrier to trade, an unnecessary obstacle to free movement of goods. The consequence is that the Belgian law can not be applied to imports from other member states. So in the case of cubic butter, the Belgians would get the luxury of having both cubical and rectangular butter. Belgian producers will probably start to wonder why *they* are limited to production of cubes.

---

[168] Walter Rau *v.* De Smedt Case 261/81 1982 ECR 3961.

6.7 From common to internal market

In the 1985 White Paper Completing the Internal Market[169] the EU Commission took the consequences of the failure of the harmonisation effort for the common market. Although many directives had been made, there were still major obstacles on the road to one single market. The Commission's Internal Market White Paper gave an inventory of more than 300 legislative measures that were necessary to have a real common market with no internal borders. The program of the internal market was to achieve that objective by the last day of 1992. The Single European Act Treaty introduced the internal market in 1987 in the EEC Treaty and created a special harmonisation article for the effort to make the 300 measures before the target date. The new Article 100a (now 95) introduced the possibility of using other instruments for the effort to make common rules, and it opened majority decision-making for these measures. See Law text box 6.1.

Law text box 6.1. The two harmonisation articles of the EC Treaty: 94 for the common market and 95 for the internal market.

EC Treaty

TITLE VI Common rules on competition, taxation and approximation of laws

Chapter 3 Approximation of laws

Article 94

The Council shall, acting unanimously on a proposal from the Commission and after consulting the European Parliament and the Economic and Social Committee, issue directives for the approximation of such laws, regulations or administrative provisions of the Member States as directly affect the establishment or functioning of the common market.

Article 95

1. By way of derogation from Article 94 and save where otherwise provided in this Treaty, the following provisions shall apply for the achievement of the objectives set out in Article 14. The Council shall, acting in accordance with the procedure referred to in Article 251 and after consulting the Economic and Social Committee, adopt the measures for the approximation of the provisions laid down by law, regulation or administrative action in Member States which have as their object the establishment and functioning of the internal market.
2. Paragraph 1 shall not apply to fiscal provisions, to those relating to the free movement of persons nor to those relating to the rights and interests of employed persons.
3. The Commission, in its proposals envisaged in paragraph 1 concerning health, safety, environmental protection and consumer protection, will take as a base a high level of protection, taking account in particular of any new development based on scientific facts. Within their respective powers, the European Parliament and the Council will also seek to achieve this objective.

[169] COM(85) 310 Final, presented to the public by EC Commissioner Lord Cockfield on 15 June 1985.

4. If, after the adoption by the Council or by the Commission of a harmonisation measure, a Member State deems it necessary to maintain national provisions on grounds of major needs referred to in Article 30, or relating to the protection of the environment or the working environment, it shall notify the Commission of these provisions as well as the grounds for maintaining them.
5. Moreover, without prejudice to paragraph 4, if, after the adoption by the Council or by the Commission of a harmonisation measure, a Member State deems it necessary to introduce national provisions based on new scientific evidence relating to the protection of the environment or the working environment on grounds of a problem specific to that Member State arising after the adoption of the harmonisation measure, it shall notify the Commission of the envisaged provisions as well as the grounds for introducing them.
6. The Commission shall, within six months of the notifications as referred to in paragraphs 4 and 5, approve or reject the national provisions involved after having verified whether or not they are a means of arbitrary discrimination or a disguised restriction on trade between Member States and whether or not they shall constitute an obstacle to the functioning of the internal market. In the absence of a decision by the Commission within this period the national provisions referred to in paragraphs 4 and 5 shall be deemed to have been approved.
   When justified by the complexity of the matter and in the absence of danger for human health, the Commission may notify the Member State concerned that the period referred to in this paragraph may be extended for a further period of up to six months.
7. When, pursuant to paragraph 6, a Member State is authorised to maintain or introduce national provisions derogating from a harmonisation measure, the Commission shall immediately examine whether to propose an adaptation to that measure.
8. When a Member State raises a specific problem on public health in a field which has been the subject of prior harmonisation measures, it shall bring it to the attention of the Commission which shall immediately examine whether to propose appropriate measures to the Council.
9. By way of derogation from the procedure laid down in Articles 226 and 227, the Commission and any Member State may bring the matter directly before the Court of Justice if it considers that another Member State is making improper use of the powers provided for in this Article.
10. The harmonisation measures referred to above shall, in appropriate cases, include a safeguard clause authorising the Member States to take, for one or more of the non-economic reasons referred to in Article 30, provisional measures subject to a Community control procedure.

The Internal Market White Paper introduced a new approach to harmonisation. The case law of the Court of Justice prescribed mutual recognition of the laws of the member states if a good has been lawfully made and put on the market in a member state. This case law is discussed in Chapter 7, section 7.3. The exceptions to this principle that are compatible with the internal market can be made in Community law only. So the Commission proposed to concentrate the harmonisation effort on the national measures that create barriers to trade allowed by EC law. The legislative effort in the internal market programme had to exchange the legitimate national trade barriers for EC law to safeguard the interests of safety and health. The approach to regulate these concerns was changed. It is still referred to as 'the new approach'. Instead of making detailed rules for all aspects of the matter, the technical provisions were no longer a part of the EC legislation. The directives or regulations simply refer to standards made by European standardisation organisations. Industry founded these private law legal persons to develop unified European product standards and to rationalise the market. CEN and CENELEC are private standardisation organisations for technical consumer products. These organisations keep track of technical progress to keep the European standards up to date. The EC legislation follows the same developments by referring to these standards, without the need to go through the process of law-making. The reference in the directive or regulation to the technical standards does not make these standards part of the binding law. They remain voluntary, industry is stimulated to apply the standards because then their products get free movement on the internal market. National authorities have to assume that goods made according to the standards meet the requirements of EC legislation. For goods that are not made according to the standards it is up to the manufacturer to prove that the product meets the requirements of the directive.

6.8 Strengthening of substantive EC law

The BSE food crisis echoed in the Intergovernmental Conference on the 1997 Treaty of Amsterdam. This treaty changed the 1992 European Union Treaty and the 1992 European Community Treaty. A number of articles were changed to ensure better policies on, among other issues, food. Article 95 EC Treaty, the special harmonisation article introduced by the Single European Act to help the creation of the internal market, had in its third paragraph already the commitment that the Commission will base its harmonisation proposals on a high level of protection of public health, safety, environmental protection and consumer protection. The Amsterdam Treaty added to this: 'taking account in particular of any new development based on scientific facts'. This reference to new developments based on scientific facts is of obvious importance to food law and the work of the European Food Safety Agency. See Law text box 6.1 for the context of the two harmonisation treaty articles that have been and still are of great importance for food law.

The Amsterdam Treaty also changed Article 152 EC Treaty paragraph (1) into: 'A high level of human health protection shall *be ensured* in the definition and implementation of all Community policies and activities. Community action, which shall complement national policies ...'

In the original article, EC policies and activities had to *contribute to* a high level of human health protection. Furthermore, the same article gives the Council and the Parliament acting together the power to overrule agricultural interests for the sake of public health: Article 152(4)(b) '*by way of derogation from Article 37*, measures in the veterinary and phytosanitary fields which have as their direct objective the protection of public health;'.

Finally, the Amsterdam Treaty added to the already existing Article 153 on consumer protection the clause '... the Community shall contribute to protecting the health, safety and economic interests of consumers, ...'. Within the context of these developments as a whole, specific developments took place in the area of law that is particularly concerned with food.

7. Food law: development, crisis and transition

7.1 History of European food law

European Food Law has developed in several stages. As with any subject area, current situations and reactions can best be understood if one understands how the situation has developed. Therefore, it is useful to take historical developments into account in order to gain a better understanding of what remains from past structures, of mistakes made, lessons learned and probable future developments.

From the beginnings of the European Community in 1958 until the eruption of the BSE crisis in the mid-1990s, European food law was principally directed at the creation of an internal market for food products in the EU.

This market-oriented phase can be divided into two stages. During the first, emphasis was on harmonisation through vertical directives. This stage ended with the 'Cassis de Dijon' case law. During the second stage emphasis shifted to harmonisation through horizontal directives.[170]

The BSE crisis, and other food scares that followed soon after, brought to light many serious shortcomings in the existing body of European food law. It became evident that fundamental reforms would be needed. In January 2000, the Commission announced its vision for the future development of European food law in a 'White Paper on Food Safety'.[171]

The 'White Paper on Food Safety' emphasised the Commission's intent to change its focus in the area of food law from the development of a common market to assuring high levels of food safety. In the years since its publication, a great deal of important legislation has been passed, and further proposals are in development or under consideration. As this book looks toward the future, we will focus principally on food law as it has developed since the White Paper, and on proposals for continuing reform in coming years. See Diagram 7.1 on the development of European food law.

[170] The distinction between horizontal and vertical directives will be discussed hereafter.

[171] COM(1999) 719 def. Commission White Papers traditionally contain numerous proposals for Community action in specific areas, and are developed in order to launch consultation processes at the European level. If White Papers are favourably received by the Council, they often form the basis of later 'Action Programs' to implement their recommendations.

Diagram 7.1. Development of European food law.

Phase	Turning point	Orientation	Main instruments
first	Cassis de Dijon (1979)	market	Vertical directives
second	BSE crisis (1997)	market	Horizontal directives
third		safety (and market)	Regulations

7.2 Creating an internal market for food in Europe

When the six original members of what is today the European Union signed the Treaty of Rome in 1957, they created a community with an economic character. This was reflected not only in its original name – the European Economic Community – but also in the original goal to create a common market.

At the heart of the instruments to achieve this goal are the famous four freedoms of the European Union: the free movement of labour, the free movement of services, the free movement of capital and the free movement of goods. The free movement of goods (Article 3 (1)(c) EC Treaty) has been vital to the development of food law.

Although all member states agreed generally about the desirability of a free market unimpeded by national borders, in practice the tendency remained for each state to protect its own markets and enterprises wherever and however possible, and to trust the judgements of its own institutions before those of the Community or other members. Consequently, the member states preferred to trust their own laws and standards before those of the Community or other member states.

This limitation in objective and the struggle for its fulfilment left a clear mark on the initial development of European food law. Irrespective of how attractive the idea of a free market seemed, there still existed countless national provisions setting different standards for products and thus impeding the free movement of goods. As we have already seen on the example of the Belgian standard for margarine (Chapter 6, section 6.6), different standards mean additional costs and create de facto obstacles to the free movement of goods for producers who want to export their products.

During the first years of implementing of the ambitious idea of trade without frontiers, Community legislation aimed primarily at facilitating the internal market through the harmonisation of national standards. Agreement about the quality and identity of food products was considered necessary. To reach such agreement directives were issued on the composition of certain specific food products. This is called vertical (recipe, compositional or technical standards) legislation. This creation of similar standards in all the member states is called positive harmonisation.

Example of vertical legislation

A well-known example of recipe-legislation is the discussion about how much cocoa a food product should contain to be called chocolate, and whether vegetable fats other than cocoa butter may be used. The Directive relating to Cocoa and Chocolate products Intended for Human Consumption[1] set the cocoa percentage at 35 for the entire European Union. Since 3 August 2003[2] up to a maximum of 5% of the total weight may be added in other vegetable fats to certain chocolate products.

[1] Directive 73/241, meanwhile replaced by Directive 2000/36.

[2] The date on which the term of implementation of Directive 2000/36 expired. Since then this rule from the Directive has direct effect if it is not yet transformed into national law.

Early attempts to establish a common market for food products in Europe by prescribing harmonised product compositions along such lines faced two substantial obstacles. Firstly, at that time all legislation required unanimity in the Council, which gave each member state a virtual right of veto over new legislation.[172] Secondly, there was the sheer scale of the task. Browse through a supermarket in any EU member state and consider the variety of products on the shelves. There are, as the Community institutions soon realised, simply too many food products to deal with. Creating compositional standards for each product would have been a mission impossible, and the Commission wisely chose to seek alternatives. Nevertheless quite a few products remain subject to European rules on compositional standards.[173] These compositional standards form the legacy of the first phase of EU food law. They are being updated or replaced when necessary but no new products are being added. Compositional standards are outside the scope of this book. For some examples see diagram 7.2.

7.3 Advancement through case law

It was the Court of Justice of the European Communities that 'restarted the engine' of European co-operation in the area of food law, in this case through new, broad, interpretations of Article 28 of the EC Treaty.[174] Article 28 is a key provision for the free movement of goods on the common market. It prohibits

[172] See Chapter 5.

[173] E.g. sugar, honey, fruit juices, milk, spreadable fats, jams, jellies, marmalade, chestnut puree, coffee, chocolate, natural mineral waters, minced meat, eggs, fish. Wine legislation is a body of law in itself. For legislation on fresh fruit and vegetables, see Chapter 15.

[174] At that time numbered Article 30.

Diagram 7.2. Vertical legislation: examples of compositional standards.

Directive 2001/114	partly or wholly dehydrated preserved milk for human consumption
Directive 2001/113	fruit jams, jellies and marmalades and sweetened chestnut purée intended for human consumption
Directive 2001/112	fruit juices and certain similar products intended for human consumption
Directive 2001/111	certain sugars intended for human consumption
Directive 2001/110	honey
Directive 2000/36	cocoa and chocolate products intended for human consumption
Directive 1999/4	coffee extracts and chicory extracts
Regulation 122/94 / Regulation 1601/91	definition, description and presentation of aromatized wines, aromatized wine-based drinks, and aromatized wine-product cocktails
Directive 93/45	the manufacture of nectars without the addition of sugars or honey

quantitative restrictions on imports and all measures having equivalent effect.[175] See Law text box 7.1.

This article should be read in connection with Article 30 of the EC Treaty which lists possible exceptions to the free movement of goods. These exceptions are: public morality, public policy or public security; the protection of health and life of humans, animals or plants; the protection of national treasures possessing artistic, historic or archaeological value; or the protection of industrial or commercial property. Of particular relevance to food safety law will be, of course, exceptions justified on grounds of the protection of health and life of humans, animals or plants.

Law text box 7.1. Article 28 EC Treaty.

Article 28 EC Treaty
Quantitative restrictions on imports and all measures having equivalent effect shall be prohibited between Member States.

7.3.1 Dassonville

In the 1974 Dassonville-case[176], the European Court of Justice gave a broad definition of the concept of 'measures having equivalent effect'. The case concerned parallel imports of Scotch whisky into Belgium. Belgian law required that a certificate

[175] On the relevance of Article 25 EC Treaty banning customs duties and charges having equivalent effect, see Morten P. Broberg, Transforming the European Community's Regulation of Food Safety, SIEPS 2008:5, sections 2.3 and 2.4. For hyperlink see reference list.
[176] EC Court of Justice 11 July 1974, Case 8/74 (Dassonville), ECR 1974, page 837.

of origin from the British authorities accompany such products. Mr. Dassonville bought Scotch whisky in France for re-importation into Belgium. It was cheaper there, as Scottish exporters had been trying to gain a share in the French market with reduced prices. As Mr. Dassonville could not obtain British certificates of origin in France, he created his own and was subsequently charged with fraud by the Belgian authorities. The Belgian criminal court needed to determine whether convicting Mr. Dassonville for fraud was compatible with European Law. To settle this issue, the Belgian court submitted questions of interpretation to the European Court of Justice in Luxemburg. The European Court of Justice found that the Belgian law could not be applied as it constituted a restriction on trade and was thus prohibited under Article 28. The Court held 'that all trading rules enacted by Member States which are capable of hindering, directly or indirectly, actually or potentially, intra-Community trade are to be considered as measures having an effect equivalent to quantitative restrictions' and are thus prohibited in the absence of a specific allowable justification. Such justifications could only be the protection of human, animal or plant health. From this ruling follows that mere disparities between national laws can be held against an importing country as measures having equivalent effect to quantitative restrictions. In later rulings the Court detailed how such situations should be handled in practice.[177]

7.3.2 Cassis de Dijon

The Cassis de Dijon[178] ruling was seminal in this respect. A German chain of supermarkets – price fighter Rewe – sought to import Cassis de Dijon, a fruit liqueur, from France. The German authorities, however, refused to authorise the import because the alcohol content was lower than allowed by German national law, which stipulated that such liqueurs should contain at least 25% alcohol. Cassis de Dijon contained just 20% alcohol.

The German authorities acknowledged that this was a restriction on trade, but sought to justify it on the basis that beverages with too little alcohol pose several risks. The German authorities argued that alcoholic beverages with low alcohol content could induce people to develop tolerances for alcohol more quickly than beverages with higher alcohol content, and that consumers trusting the (German) law might feel cheated if they purchased such products with the expectation of higher alcohol content. Finally, Germany submitted that in the absence of such a law, beverages with low alcohol content would benefit from an unfair competitive advantage because taxes on alcohol are high, and beverages with lower alcoholic content would be saleable at significantly lower prices than products produced in Germany according to German law.

177 Some of the relevant cases not further discussed here, are cases; 407/53, 53/80, 132/80, 124/81, 249/81, 261/81, 177-178/82, 202/82, 222/82, 21/84, 90/86, 274/87, 277-318-319/91, 292/92 123/00.
178 EC Court of Justice 20 February 1979, Case 120/78 (Cassis de Dijon), ECR 1979, page 649.

The Court held that the *type* of arguments presented by the German authorities would be relevant, even where they did not come under the specific exceptions contained in the EC Treaty, provided that those arguments met an urgent need. This is known as the rule of reason. The Court's broad interpretation of the prohibition against trade restrictions should be applied within reason.

The Court found that Germany's public health argument did not meet this standard of reasonableness. The Court specifically cited the availability of a wide range of alcoholic beverages on the German market with alcohol content of less than 25%. As to the risk of consumers feeling cheated by lower than expected alcohol content, the Court suggested that such a risk could be eliminated with less effect on the common market by displaying the alcohol content on the beverages label.

For cases such as this one, in which there are no specific justifications for restrictions on the trade between member states, the Court introduced a general rule: products that have been lawfully produced and marketed in one of the member states, may not be kept out of other member states on the grounds that they do not comply with the national rules. This is called the principle of mutual recognition (Law text box 7.2).[179]

Law text box 7.2. ECJ in Cassis de Dijon on mutual recognition.

There is (...) no valid reason why, provided that they have been lawfully produced and marketed in one of the member states, alcoholic beverages should not be introduced into any other member state; the sale of such products may not be subject to a legal prohibition on the marketing of beverages with an alcohol content lower than the limit set by the national rules.
(...) The concept of 'measures having an effect equivalent to quantitative restrictions on imports' contained in article 30 of the EEC treaty is to be understood to mean that the fixing of a minimum alcohol content for alcoholic beverages intended for human consumption by the legislation of a Member State also falls within the prohibition laid down in that provision where the importation of alcoholic beverages lawfully produced and marketed in another member state is concerned.

7.3.3 Mutual recognition

In essence, the Court's ruling was that, within the context of the common market, what is good enough for consumers in one member state is good enough for consumers across the Community. This ruling broke the deadlock in the development of a free market resulting from the existence of different national laws. The principle of mutual recognition signalled a giant leap forwards in European law, and 'Cassis de Dijon' has become a symbol of this stage in the development of the European understanding of free movement of goods.

---

[179] Some other relevant cases in this line not discussed in this book are: 216/84, 17/93, 267-268/91, 391/92, 425-427/97, 405/98, 443/98, 37/99, 416/00, 497/03.

With its ruling the Court in Luxemburg laid the legal foundation for a well-functioning common market. Food products that comply with the statutory (safety) requirements of the member state where they are brought on the market must, in principle,[180] be admitted to the markets of all other member states. This form of harmonisation, where products are legal regardless of which national legal system they comply with, is known as negative harmonisation, as opposed to positive harmonisation which is ensuring that national legislation is similar.

Several commentators expressed concern that the Cassis de Dijon decision would lead to product standards based on the lowest common denominator. It is clear that manufacturers established in member states with the most lenient safety or technical requirements or legal procedures do gain a competitive advantage.

The limitations and drawbacks of the principle of mutual recognition highlighted the need for further harmonisation of product requirements at the European level. For member states with more stringent national standards, European-level legislation became the best hope for raising neighbours' standards. The Cassis de Dijon ruling marked a significant change in the perception of the benefits of harmonisation. Before Cassis, harmonisation was seen merely as a condition for the functioning of the common internal market. Afterwards, emphasis shifted to the need to alleviate the consequences of the common internal market. In legal terms, too, the wave of harmonisation that followed Cassis differed from earlier efforts. Emphasis shifted from product-specific, vertical (recipe) legislation, to horizontal legislation, meaning general rules addressing common aspects for all foodstuffs, or at least for as many foodstuffs as possible.

Example horizontal legislation.

A prime example of this development is the Labelling Directive,[1] which includes[2] a prohibition on misleading statements on foodstuff packaging[3] and a requirement to display specific indications, including a list of ingredients. Another example is the Hygiene Directive,[4] which requires manufacturers of foodstuffs to identify the critical points in the production process and to draw up procedures to ensure safety.[5]

[1] Directive 2000/13.

[2] Meaning: requires member states to implement such prohibition.

[3] Article 2(a).

[4] Directive 93/43. Late 2002 the European Commission announced that the Hygiene directive 93/43 and 17 other Directives will be joined and harmonised with other directives containing rules on hygiene for different products (such as fresh meat, milk and fish) and be simplified. A change of instrument was also foreseen. The Community exchanged the directives for one regulation. On 30 April 2004 Regulation 853/2004 was published, which entered into force on 1 January 2006. This regulation is discussed in Chapter 11.

[5] The so-called HACCP system, 'Hazard analysis and critical control points'.

[180] Exceptions can be based only on Article 30 of the EC Treaty or the rule of reason.

Mutual recognition remains the rule up to this day. The consequence bears repeating; foodstuffs that have legally come to the market in any member state, may in principle be sold without restrictions across the whole territory of the European Union.[181]

7.3.4 Reinheitsgebot

In line with 'Cassis de Dijon' is a later ruling, also concerning Germany. Germany had – and still has – special legislation on beer. A famous provision is the so-called 'Reinheitsgebot'. This German law on 'purity' of beer, is a historic law on taxes levied on beer. It dates back to 1516 when it was enacted by Duke William of Bavaria. Going back almost 500 years, it is probably the oldest piece of food legislation in force today. In short it says that beer may only be produced using four ingredients: barley, hops, yeast and water. In the early 1980s, this provision was applied in such a way that imported products not complying with it could not be brought to the market under the name of 'Bier'.

The European Commission took the view that those provisions were contrary to the ban on measures having an effect equivalent to quantitative restrictions on imports and brought infringement proceedings against the Federal Republic of Germany on two grounds, namely the prohibition on marketing under the designation '*Bier*' (beer) beers lawfully manufactured by different methods in other member states and the prohibition on importing beers containing additives. With the judgment of 12 March 1987 in Case 178/84 Commission vs. Germany,[182] the Court held that the prohibition on marketing beers imported from other member states which did not comply with the provisions in question was incompatible with Article 28[183] of the EC Treaty.

This case is one of many examples in which the Court applied its 'Cassis de Dijon' principles. It stands out from the other examples, however, mainly due to the follow up it enjoyed in the case discussed here below.

[181] The European Commission still grapples with the consequences of this case law. Immediately after the ruling, the Commission gave its interpretation: Communication from the Commission concerning the consequences of the judgment given by the Court of Justice on 20 February 1979 in case 120/78 ('Cassis de Dijon') (Official Journal C 256, 3 October 1980, pp. 2-3). Currently a proposal is pending for a Regulation on mutual recognition COM(2007) 36 final.
[182] [1987] ECR 1227, commonly known as 'Reinheitsgebot' or 'German beer'.
[183] At that time Article 30.

7.3.5 Brasserie du Pêcheur

After the Reinheitsgebot-ruling Brasserie du Pêcheur, a French company based at Schiltigheim (Alsace),[184] brought an action against the Federal Republic of Germany for reparation of the loss suffered by it as a result of that import restriction between 1981 and 1987, seeking damages to the sum of DM 1,800,000,[185] representing a fraction of the loss actually incurred. Before the German national court, Brasserie du Pêcheur claims that it was forced to discontinue exports of beer to Germany in late 1981 because the competent German authorities considered that the beer it produced did not comply with the Reinheitsgebot. The German Court sitting on the case (the Bundesgerichtshof) asked the EC Court of Justice for a preliminary ruling on the question as to whether indeed Germany could be held liable for this type of damages on the grounds that its national legislation infringed the principle of mutual recognition as enshrined in Article 28 of the EC Treaty.

The Court of Justice answered (as quoted in Law text box 7.3)[186] that member states are liable when their legislation infringes EC law if three conditions are met:

- the EC law infringed confers rights on the individuals (that is to say the claimants citizens as well as businesses);
- the breach of EC law is sufficiently serious, and
- there is a direct causal link between the breach and the damage sustained.

Law text box 7.3. ECJ 5 March 1996 Brasserie du Pêcheur.

ECJ on member state liability

'where a breach of Community law by a Member State is attributable to the national legislature acting in a field in which it has a wide discretion to make legislative choices, individuals suffering loss or injury thereby are entitled to reparation where the rule of Community law breached is intended to confer rights upon them, the breach is sufficiently serious and there is a direct causal link between the breach and the damage sustained by the individuals'.

Subsequently the Bundesgerichtshof made itself a laughing-stock in circles of EU law professionals by judging that in this case Brasserie du Pêcheur had not proven the required causal relation.

While it did not help Brasserie du Pêcheur in this case, the ruling of the ECJ is very important as it shows that EU member states can be held liable for infringements on EU (food) law, even if they occur in their legislation.

184 Well known among the brands Brasserie du Pêcheur holds is Kronenbourg beer.

185 About one million Euro.

186 ECJ 5 March 1996, Brasserie du Pêcheur SA v Bundesrepublik Deutschland and The Queen v Secretary of State for Transport, ex parte: Factortame Ltd and others, Joined cases C-46/93 and C-48/93, ECR 1996 p. I-01029.

Diagram 7.3. Case law on free movement of goods.

Case	Type of procedure	National procedure	Content
C-8/74 Dassonville	Preliminary ruling	Criminal	All trading rules potentially hindering intra-Community trade are measured having equivalent effect
C-120/78 Cassis de Dijon	Preliminary ruling	Administrative (tax) law	Mutual recognition
C-178/84 Reinheitsgebot	Infringement procedure	-	Mutual recognition
C-46/93 and C-48/93 Brasserie du Pêcheur	Preliminary ruling	Civil (tort) law	Member state is liable for damages if national legislation infringes on EC law

The legacy of the second phase of development of EU food law is the principle of mutual recognition and the horizontal approach to food legislation.

7.4 Breakdown

The heyday of market-oriented food law based on mutual recognition ended in tears. The food and agricultural sectors in the European Union emerged deeply traumatised from the 1990s. A series of crises resulted in a breakdown of consumer confidence in public authorities, industry and science. The third phase of EU food law can only be truly fathomed if the trauma to which it responds is understood.

Although the bovine spongiform encephalopathy (BSE) crisis was not the first and, in terms of death toll, not the worst[187] food safety crisis in the EU it caused an earthquake in the legal and regulatory landscape of Europe (see Diagram 7.4

187 Abaitua Borda I *et al.*, Toxic Oil Syndrome Mortality: The First Thirteen Years, 27 Int. J. Epidemiology 1057 (1998); Emilio Gelpí *et al.*, The Spanish Toxic Oil Syndrome Twenty Years After Its Onset: A Multidisciplinary Review of Scientific Knowledge, 110 Env. Health Persp. 457 (2002) (finding that the toxic oil syndrome (TOS) epidemic that occurred in Spain in the spring of 1981 caused approximately 20,000 cases of a new illness. Researchers identified 1,663 deaths between 1 May 1981 and 31 December 1994 among 19,754 TOS cohort members. Mortality was highest during 1981). The poisoning was caused by fraud consisting of mixing vehicle oil with consumption oil. Hyperlinks are available in the reference list.

for background information on BSE). Subsequent food safety scares,[188] outbreaks of animal diseases[189] and scandals over fraudulent practices, added to a sense of urgency to take protective measures. These fraudulent practices included the discharge of waste in animal feed[190] and the underworld involvement in the supply and employment of growth hormones[191] mounting to the murder of the veterinarian who brought the use of these illegal substances to the attention of the authorities and the public.[192]

[188] One example is the Belgian dioxin crises. It was caused by industry oil that had found its way into animal feed and subsequently into the food chain. Craig Whitney, Brussels Journal, Food Scandal Adds to Belgium's Image of Disarray, N.Y. Times, June 9, 1999. Another example is the introduction of merroxyprogesterone acetate (MPA) into pig feed in 2002. James Graff, One Sweet Mess, Time July 21, 2002. Sugar discharges from this production of MPA, a hormone used in contraceptive and hormone replacement pills, were used in pigs feed and by that route MPA entered the food chain. In 2004 a dioxin crisis broke out in the Netherlands. For hyperlinks see reference list.

[189] Like Food and Mouth Disease, SARS and lately Avian Influenza.

[190] Probably the cause of the first dioxin crisis. See Whitney supra note 24.

[191] Community and national legislatures in the EU have been battling the use of artificial hormones – DES (diethylstilbestrol) in particular – for years. When it turned out to be impossible to separate their use from body-proper hormones and to get them under control, finally all hormones were banned. The legislation on the use and application of hormones started with Directive 81/602 (prohibiting certain matters with hormonal effects and of stuffs with thyrostatic effects). Directive 81/602 has been supplemented by Directive 85/358/EEC and replaced by Directive 88/146/EEC (prohibition of applications of certain stuffs with hormonal effect in the cattle breeding sector). A next one, Directive 88/299 is aiming at the trade in animals and meat treated with stuffs with hormonal effect referred to in Directive 88/146.

[192] See Katherine Butler, Why the Mafia is into Your Beef: The EU Ban on Growth Hormones for Cows has Created a Lucrative Black Market, Independent (London), Mar. 19, 1996, for hyperlink see reference list.

On Monday evening 20 February 1995 close to his home in Wechelderzande (Belgium) Karel van Noppen, a Belgian veterinarian and inspector, was shot after exposing cattle breeders who illegally used hormones, their suppliers and civil servants who turned a blind eye to these practices. He had received several threats to discourage him from going after the 'hormones-mafia'. One of the inspectors accused by Van Noppen of corruption committed suicide in March 1996. In 2002 four people were found guilty by a jury, two of them cattle breeders. Katherine Butler, Four Men Found Guilty of Contract Hit on Vet, Independent (London), June 5, 2002, p. 11. The instigator of the assassination received a life sentence, the others 25 years each. Belgian Hormone Killers Jailed, EEC News, June 5, 2002, for a hyperlink see the reference list.

Diagram 7.4. Background on BSE[193]

Bovine spongiform encephalopathy (BSE) is a transmissible, slowly progressive degenerative disease of the central nervous system of adult cattle. This disease has a prolonged incubation period in cattle following oral exposure (2 to 8 years) and is always fatal. BSE is a type of transmissible spongiform encephalopathy (TSE), a fatal progressively degenerative disease of the central nervous system. TSEs occur in several animal species, like BSE in cattle, scrapie in sheep and goats, and some other. Consumption of contaminated feed transmits BSE. Infectious products include rendered animal proteins and compound animal feed containing meat-and-bone meal. Only a small amount of infectious material, perhaps as little as a gram of brain tissue, can transmit BSE.
BSE was first identified as neurological disease in cattle in the United Kingdom in 1986. BSE has been reported in a large number of countries, but the majority of confirmed cases have occurred in the UK.
Variant Creutzfeldt-Jakob disease (vCJD) is a rare and invariably fatal disease in humans first described in the United Kingdom in March 1996. Most victims of the disease are from the UK or have lived there for significant periods of time. The UK Department of Health indicated that 156 deaths from confirmed or probable vCJD had occurred between 1995 and 1 September 2006. vCJD, like BSE, is a TSE, characterised by a spongy degeneration of the brain and its ability to be transmitted. Clinical signs of the disease include psychiatric symptoms (e.g. depression), followed by neurological signs that include unsteadiness, difficulty walking and involuntary movements, ending with immobility and muteness. Victims of vCJD succumb to the disease at an average age of 29, after an illness with a median duration of 14 months.
Epidemiologists in the UK first reported the link between BSE and vCJD in 1996. After some initial uncertainty, the World Health Organization recognised the connection: 'Considerable epidemiological, neuropathological, and experimental data are consistent with the hypothesis that the agent that causes BSE in cattle also causes vCJD in humans. The most plausible route of human exposure is through the consumption of food contaminated with the BSE agent, although this has not been conclusively proven'. Tissue from the central nervous system of infected cattle is the most likely food contaminant.

Public awareness of the BSE-epidemic, and the time it had taken British and European authorities to address it, presented a major challenge to European co-operation in the area of food safety. When the extent of the crisis became public, the European Union issued a blanket ban on British beef exports. In response, Britain adopted a policy of non-co-operation with the European institutions, and sought to deny the extent and seriousness of the BSE problem.[194]

[193] Taken from Margaret Rosso Grossman, Animal Identification and Traceability under the US National Animal Identification System. Journal of Food Law & Policy, 2/2/2006, pp. 231-315. See this publication for sources.

[194] Symbolic became the TV footage where the responsible Secretary of State, John Gummer is shown feeding his little daughter a hamburger, to convince the public that nothing was wrong with British beef (16 may 1990 BBC). Text, picture and video available at: http://news.bbc.co.uk/onthisday/hi/dates/stories/may/16/newsid_2913000/2913807.stm

The European Parliament played a crucial role in defusing this crisis. Although often accused of being a debating society of little consequence, during the BSE crisis Parliament proved itself capable of political decisiveness and effective democratic oversight. A temporary Enquiry Committee was instituted to investigate the actions of the national and European agencies involved in the crisis.[195] The Enquiry Committee presented its report in early 1997 (See Diagram 7.5).[196] The report strongly criticised the British government as well as the European Commission. The Commission was accused of wrongly putting industry interests ahead of public health and consumer safety, science had been biased and transparency had been lacking.

Diagram 7.5. Highlights from the Ortega Medina enquiry report on BSE.

> Report on alleged contraventions or maladministration in the implementation of Community law in relation to BSE, 7 February 1997 A4-0020/97/A
>
> The preponderance of UK scientists and officials meant that the Scientific Veterinary Committee tended to reflect current thinking at the British Ministry of Agriculture, Fisheries and Food.
>
> It made a partial and biased reading of the advice and warnings of the scientists. The views of certain scientists who could be considered as more critical were not taken into account. Some members of the Southwood Committee have said publicly that the minutes of its meetings were drawn up by a UK Ministry of Agriculture official and contain omissions and discrepancies.
>
> In the BSE affair there has been, at the very least, a lack of transparency. This should appear clearer if one recalls that BSE has been the subject of an ongoing analysis by the BSE Subgroup of the Scientific Veterinary Committee. This subgroup has, almost throughout, been chaired by a UK national (first Mr Plowright and then Mr Bradley), and has included a substantial number of British scientists. Mr Bradley, who from 1969 to 1991 was head of the UK's Central Veterinary Laboratory and was subsequently an adviser to the British Ministry of Agriculture, has acted as rapporteur on BSE at the full meetings of the Scientific Veterinary Committee; it emerges, furthermore, from some of the minutes of the committee meetings that a number of members have suggested that Mr Bradley may have withheld information.
>
> The Commission has failed to guarantee the proper functioning of veterinary controls within the internal market, thus breaching Directive 89/662, under which the Commission is empowered and obliged to carry out on-the-spot inspections to ensure the effectiveness of veterinary controls. Under Article 16 of this directive, the Commission has, in general terms, to monitor and oversee the national authorities' control programmes. The failure of the Commission to undertake initiatives in this field vis-à-vis the British Government could be interpreted as implying an unacceptable lack of vigilance ('culpa in vigilando') on its part and a deliberate resolve to leave

195 Offical Journal C 261, 1996, p. 132.

196 Report of the Temporary Committee of Inquiry into BSE, set up by the Parliament in July 1996, on the alleged contraventions or maladministration in the implementation of Community law in relation to BSE, without prejudice to the jurisdiction of the Community and the national courts of 7 February 1997, A4-0020/97/A, PE 220.544/fin/A. The report is often referred to by the name of the chairman of the Enquiry Committee, namely the Ortega Medina report. For hyperlinks see reference list.

management of this issue in the hands of the British, all the more so since, at that time, they were the only ones affected by the disease.

The Commission's actions may be characterised as follows:
It has given priority to the management of the market, as opposed to the possible human health risks existing in the light of the numerous scientific uncertainties concerning the possible effects of BSE on humans, and has neglected the principle of preventive action. There is a considerable body of material confirming this attitude.
The testimonies of present and former Commissioners and senior Commission officials have made it obvious that BSE has consistently had major political implications; this may be explained in view of the huge economic interests at stake in the meat, feeding stuff and animal residue processing industries, but, in terms of principles, it cannot justify the management of the BSE crisis.
By virtue of the opaqueness, complexity and anti-democratic nature of its workings, the existing system of comitology seems to be totally exempt from any supervision, thereby enabling national and/or industrial interests to infiltrate the Community decision-making process. This phenomenon is particularly serious where public health protection is at stake.
The Commission has to date failed to submit any convincing proposals by which it could regain credibility and begin genuinely to exercise its responsibilities in the field of health and consumer protection.
On the other hand, transparency in connection with BSE policy is closely bound up with the conditions of functioning, transparency and facilities for expression characterising the work of the scientists attached to the advisory scientific committees, at both Commission and Member State level.
Equally, in the interests of the transparency of anti-BSE measures, provision should be made to change the criteria for recruiting scientific staff to the European institutions.
Also at issue here is the degree of transparency required for the state of scientific knowledge on a subject to be determined, as well as the political use made of that knowledge by national governments or Commissioners, in relation to the perceived level of risk at a given moment.
On these points, the committee proposes:
The rules governing the work of the scientific committees which advise the Commission should be reformed in such a way as to professionalise their organisation. The appointment of their members should in future be strictly based on objective professional qualifications. There should be improved guarantees concerning their independence, the recording of dissenting views and the funding available to them. The administrative procedures for reimbursing participants' expenses should be revised, to make it easier for independent scientists to attend. When animal health matters are discussed, doctors of human medicine should also be present, so as to improve the assessment of possible public health risks.

The Enquiry Committee did not confine itself to an analysis and critical comments. The report went on to make concrete recommendations for improvements to the structure of European food law. Paradoxically, this reproachful report followed by a motion of censure proposed to the European Parliament provided the Commission with the impetus it had hitherto lacked, indeed with a window of opportunity, to take the initiative for restructuring European food law in a way that considerably strengthened its own powers. The Commission's then President, Jacques Santer, undertook far-reaching commitments to implement the Committee's recommendations.

Progress was made along institutional lines as well as policy lines. The Directorate General (DG) XXIV 'Consumer Policy' created two years earlier, was reinforced and renamed 'Consumer and Health Protection Policy' and included the scientific advisory committees from the Directorate Generals for Industry and Agriculture.[197] A Scientific Steering Committee was created to bring wider scientific experience and overview to consumer health questions. The internal market 'product warning system' was also transferred from DGIII (Agriculture) to DGXXIV. As of 1997, the centre of gravity in food legislation moved from DG Agriculture to DGXXIV, now called 'SANCO'.

As early as May 1997, the Commission[198] published a Green Paper on the general principles of food law in the EU.[199] It set out the structure of a legal system capable of getting a firm grip on food production. Consumer protection was made the main priority. The Commission committed to strengthening its food safety control function. This led directly to the establishment of the Food and Veterinary Office (FVO) in Dublin in 1997.[200] The FVO was charged with carrying out the Commission's control responsibilities in the food safety sector, to include controlling animal health and welfare. Furthermore, the Commission announced the establishment of an independent[201] food safety authority.[202] At the European summit in Luxemburg at the end of the same year, the European Council adopted a statement on food safety.[203]

The Commission kept the pressure on beyond 1997, eventually gaining the support of the European Court of Justice for the measures that had been taken against

197 Grete Knudsen and Marjo Matikainen-Kallström, Joint Parliamentary Committee Report on food safety in the EEA, 1999 (for hyperlink see reference list); European Parliament Fact Sheets 4.10.1. Consumer Policy: principles and instruments, chapter 3 Reform in the wake of the BSE crisis (for hyperlink see reference list), Green Paper on general principles of food law – see next footnote.

198 Interestingly, DG Industry was the instigator.

199 Commission Green Paper on the General Principles of Food Law in the European Union, COM (1997) 176, for hyperlink see reference list.

200 See generally European Commission's Health and Consumer Protection DG, FVO at Home and Away, 7 Consumer Voice September 2002 and Health & Consumer Voice November 2007, Safer Food for Europe – over a decade of achievement for the FVO. For hyperlinks see the reference list.

201 It seems that right now more faith is placed in autonomous technocratic agencies than in politically responsible administrative bodies.

202 Communication of the European Commission, Consumer Health and Food Safety COM(97) 183 fin. of 30 April 1997. See also: Philip James, Fritz Kemper and Gerard Pascal, A European Food and Public Health Authority. The future of scientific advice in the EU, 1999, for hyperlinks see reference list.

203 Conclusions of Luxembourg Summit 1997, 13 December 1997, nr. 57, for hyperlink see reference list.

Great Britain at the climax of the crisis.[204] Meanwhile, public attention had turned to a new food safety scare: the Belgian dioxin crisis. The Commission proved it had learned valuable lessons from its experience with BSE, and moved quickly and efficiently to protect consumers from the dioxin crisis. Nonetheless, this second crisis brought to light further shortcomings in European food law.

Despite the resignation of Santer's Commission (which was succeeded by the Commission led by Romano Prodi), food safety remained a priority issue. On 12, January 2000 the Commission published its famous White Paper on Food Safety.[205]

7.5 The White Paper: a new vision on food law

The Commission's vision on the future shape of EU food law, its blueprint so to speak, was laid down in the White Paper on Food Safety. Before the BSE crisis, European food safety law was subordinated to the development of the internal market. The shortcomings in the handling of the crisis clearly revealed a need for a new, integrated approach to food safety.

The Commission aimed to restore and maintain consumer confidence. While the White Paper nowhere mentions it in so many words, this includes restoring the trustworthiness of the institutions concerned. To achieve this the Commission proposed an ambitious legislative programme. Eighty-four legislation and policy initiatives[206] were scheduled for the near future, and implementation commenced with unprecedented drive.

The White Paper focused on a review of food legislation in order to make it more coherent, comprehensive and up-to-date, and to strengthen enforcement.

Furthermore, the Commission backed the establishment of a new European Food Safety[207] Authority, to serve as the scientific point of reference for the whole Union, and thereby contribute to a high level of consumer health protection.

[204] See Case C-157/96, The Queen v. Ministry of Agric., Fisheries and Food, 1998 ECR I-02211; Case C-180/96, U.K. Gr. Brit and N. Ir. v. Commission, 1996 ECR I-03903; Case C-209/96 U.K. Gr. Brit and N. Ir. v. Commission, ECR 1998 I-05655.

[205] COM(1999) 719 def. Unlike a Green Paper that is intended mostly as a basis for public discussion, a White Paper contains concrete policy intentions. For hyperlink see reference list.

[206] Listed in the Annex to the White Paper. This Annex bears the title Action Plan on Food Safety.

[207] In the White Paper the Commission speaks of a European Food Authority. The word 'safety' was inserted later in the General Food Law. See hereafter.

7.5.1 Planning a European Food Safety Authority

The establishment of an independent European Food (Safety) Authority was considered by the Commission to be the most appropriate response to the need to guarantee a high level of food safety. According to the White Paper, this Authority should be entrusted with a number of key tasks embracing independent scientific advice on all aspects relating to food safety, operation of rapid alert systems, communication and dialogue with consumers on food safety and health issues as well as networking with national agencies and scientific bodies. The European Food (Safety) Authority ought to provide the Commission with the necessary scientific evaluation of risks associated with a product or technology, but it would remain the Commission's responsibility to decide on the appropriate response to that scientific evaluation.[208]

7.5.2 Planning new food safety legislation

Besides setting up the independent Authority, the White Paper called for a wide range of other measures to improve and bring coherence to the corpus of legislation covering all aspects of food products from 'farm to fork'.

The Commission identified measures necessary to improve food safety standards. Considering the developments described above, it is clear that, in a number of areas, existing European legislation had to be brought up to date. A new legal framework was proposed to cover the whole of the food chain, including animal feed production, the establishment of a high level of consumer health protection and clearly attributed primary responsibility for safe food to industry, producers and suppliers, including appropriate official controls at both national and European level. The ability to trace products through the whole food chain was considered a key issue.

The use of scientific advice should underpin food safety policy, whilst the precautionary principle[209] shall be used where appropriate. The ability to take rapid, effective, safeguard measures in response to health emergencies throughout the food chain was recognised as an important element.

Proposals for the animal feed sector were to ensure that only suitable materials would be used in its manufacture, and that the use of additives would be more effectively controlled. Certain food quality issues, including food additives and

[208] As we have seen in Chapter 5, the European Food Safety Authority was called in to being in Regulation 178/2002.

[209] This principle indicates caution in the face of scientific uncertainty. See hereafter.

flavourings and health claims, should be addressed, and controls over novel foods improved.[210]

7.5.3 Planning improvement of food safety controls

The experience of the Food and Veterinary Office, the Commission's own inspection service, which visits member states on a regular basis, has shown that there are wide variations in the manner in which Community legislation is implemented and enforced. According to the White Paper, this means that consumers cannot be sure of receiving the same level of protection across the Community, which makes it difficult to evaluate the effectiveness of national measures. The White Paper proposed to develop a Community framework for the development and operation of national control systems, in co-operation with the Member States. This would take account of existing best practices, and the experience of the FVO, and be based on agreed criteria for the performance of these systems, leading to clear guidelines on their operation.

In support of Community level controls, more rapid, easier-to-use, enforcement procedures in addition to existing infringement actions were to be developed. Controls on imports at the external borders of the Community should be extended to cover all feed and foodstuffs, and action taken to improve co-ordination between inspection posts.[211]

In the White Paper national authorities are held responsible for ensuring that food safety standards are respected by food and feed business operators. They need to establish control systems to ensure that Community rules are being respected and, where necessary, enforced. In the opinion of the Commission these systems should be developed at a Community level, so that a harmonised approach is followed. To ensure that national control systems are effective, the Commission, through the FVO, carries out a programme of audits and inspections to evaluate the performance of national authorities against their ability to deliver and operate effective control systems, and are supported by visits to individual premises to verify that acceptable standards are actually being met. The Commission envisioned a Community framework consisting of three core elements:

1. *Operational criteria set up at Community level*, which national authorities would be expected to meet. These criteria would form the key reference points against which the competent authorities would be audited by the FVO, thereby allowing it to develop a consistent, complete, approach to the audit of national systems.

[210] Two years after the publication of the White Paper new pieces of legislation started to appear in the Official Journal. The flow continues to this day.

[211] In Chapter 13 the new regime on enforcement will be discussed.

2. *The development of Community control guidelines.* These would promote coherent national strategies, and identify risk-based priorities and the most effective control procedures. A Community strategy would take a comprehensive, integrated, approach to the operation of controls. These guidelines would also provide advice on the development of systems to record the performance and results of control actions, as well as setting Community indicators of performance.
3. The enhancement of *administrative cooperation* in the development and operation of control systems. There would be a reinforced Community dimension to the exchange of best practice between national authorities. This would also include promoting mutual assistance between the member states by integrating and completing the existing legal framework.

Furthermore, this would cover issues such as training, information exchange and longer term strategic thinking at Community level.[212]

7.5.4 Planning improvement of consumer information

If consumers are to be satisfied that the actions proposed in the White Paper will lead to a genuine improvement in food safety standards, they must be kept well informed. The Commission, together with the new European Food Safety Authority, will promote a dialogue with consumers to encourage their involvement in the new food safety policy. At the same time, consumers need to be kept better informed of emerging food safety concerns, and of risks to certain groups from particular foods.

Consumers have the right to expect information on food quality and constituents that is helpful and clearly presented, so that informed choices can be made. Proposals on the labelling of foods, building on existing rules, have been brought forward in line with the White Paper proposals.[213] The importance of a balanced diet, and its impact on health, should also be presented to consumers.

7.5.5 International dimension

The Community is the world's largest importer and exporter of food products. The actions proposed in the White Paper will need to be effectively presented and explained to the EU's trading partners. An active role for the Community in international bodies will be an important element in explaining European developments in food safety.

212 White Paper, p. 30.

213 The principle of informed choice will be discussed in Chapter 12.

7.6 Intermezzo: documents

In this chapter we encountered a horde of different types of documents, with different legal relevance. For clarification Diagram 7.6 gives as overview.

Diagram 7.6. Types of documents within the Community.

Policy documents preceding legislation	**Legal acts mentioned in Article 249 of the EC Treaty**				**Policy documents following legislation**
Green paper *Discussion oriented*			Proposal *Usually from the Commission to the Parliament and the Council*	Proposal *Usually from the Commission to the Parliament and the Council*	Guideline *Interpretation of specific acts*
White Paper *Decision oriented*	Recommendation / opinion *Not binding*	Decision *Individually binding*	Directive *Binding on Member States*	Regulation *Generally binding on all addressees*	

Legal acts are defined in Article 249 of the EC Treaty:

- A *regulation* shall have general application. It shall be binding in its entirety and directly applicable in all Member States.
- A *directive* shall be binding, as to the result to be achieved, upon each Member State to which it is addressed, but shall leave to the national authorities the choice of form and methods.
- A *decision* shall be binding in its entirety upon those to whom it is addressed.
- *Recommendations* and *opinions* shall have no binding force.
- Policy documents come under various names. No formal definitions apply. The Glossary on the EU website describes Green and White Papers.
- *Green Papers* are documents published by the European Commission to stimulate discussion on given topics at European level. They invite the relevant parties (bodies or individuals) to participate in a consultation process and debate on the basis of the proposals they put forward. Green Papers may give rise to legislative developments that are then outlined in White Papers.
- Commission *White Papers* are documents containing proposals for Community action in a specific area. In some cases they follow a Green Paper published to launch a consultation process at European level. When a White Paper is

favourably received by the Council, it can lead to an action programme for the Union in the area concerned.
- After a piece of legislation has entered into force, sometimes the Commission publishes *Guidelines* to explain how this legislation is understood by the Commission and to help other stakeholders to deal with it.
- *Communication* is a name used for a wide variety of policy documents both preceding and following legislation.

The Green Paper and the White Paper discussed above are not *law*. They are *not binding* on anyone, but they do contain the intention to create a lot of legislation.

7.7 Follow up

The Annex to the aforementioned White Paper is the Action Plan on Food Safety, a list of 84 legislative steps that the Commission deemed necessary to create a regulatory framework capable of ensuring a high level of protection of consumers and public health.

The turn of the millennium saw the beginning of the planned overhaul of European food law. The first new regulation took effect in 2002 and in the few years that have since passed most of the 84 steps have been taken.[214] The new regulatory framework is based on regulations rather than directives.

Only two years after the White Paper was published, the cornerstone of new European food law was laid: Regulation 178/2002 of the European Parliament and of the Council of 28 January 2002 laying down the general principles and requirements of food law, establishing the European Food Safety Authority and laying down procedures in matters of food safety'.[215] This regulation is often referred to in English as the 'General Food Law'. The Germans speak of it as a 'Basisverordnung' – perhaps a more precise phrase given that the regulation is in fact the basis upon which European and national food laws are now being re-constructed.[216] The notion of a basic regulation has been discussed in Chapter 4, section 4.4.3. The main objective of the General Food Law is to secure a high level of protection of public health and consumer interests with regard to food

[214] See: Klaus Knipschild, Lebensmittelsicherheit als Aufgabe des Veterinär- und Lebensmittelrechts (diss.) Nomos Verlagsgesellschaft Baden-Baden, Germany 2003; Ulrich Nöhle, Risikokommunication und Risikomanagement in der erweiterten EU, ZLR 3/2005, p. 297-305 and Gijs Berends and Ignacio Carreno, Safeguards in food law – ensuring food scares are scarce, E.L. rev. 30/2005, p. 386-405.

[215] Official Journal L 31, 1 February 2002, p. 1.

[216] New European food law displays several characteristics in which it is different from its predecessor: more emphasis on horizontal regulations (than on vertical legislation) more emphasis on regulations that formulate the goals that have to be achieved, so-called objective regulations, than on means regulations, increased use of regulations (rather than directives) and thus increasing centralisation.

products. It does so by stating general principles, establishing the European Food Safety Authority and giving procedures to deal with emergencies.

The General Food Law will be discussed in more detail in the next chapter. After the General Food Law, whole packages of new legislation followed. See Diagram 7.7 for an overview.

Diagram 7.7. Highlights in the overhaul of EU food law.

2002	Regulation 178/2002 (GFL)	Chapter 8
2003	GMO package	Chapter 9
2004/2005	Regulations 852-854/2004 Hygiene package Regulation 882/2004 Official controls Regulation 1935/2004 Food contact materials	Chapters 11 and 13
2006/2007	Regulation 1924/2006 nutrition & health claims	Chapter 12
2007	White Paper A Strategy for Europe on Nutrition, Overweight and Obesity related health issues	
Ongoing	Obesity policy Modernisation pesticides legislation Modernisation legislation on additives and novel foods Modernisation of labelling legislation	

7.8 Future

It is next to impossible to predict how long we will remain in the third phase of EU food law and what will come afterwards.

The window of opportunity for large-scale legislative projects on food that opened after the animal health and food safety scares of the 1990s seems to be closing. Some finalising proposals are underway. If no major crisis sparks new action, it seems unlikely that more legislation of fundamental nature will be undertaken in the near future. The EU legislator will probably feel prompted to make an attempt at simplification and reduction of burdens for the food sector.

The most pressing issue on the agenda for the years to come is probably overweight and obesity. So far the EU legislator has not found suitable instruments to deal with this problem. Measures are currently limited to providing consumers with information directly and on food product labels.

7.9 An analytical approach to food law

The development of European food law, sketched in this chapter, has resulted in a vast body of heterogeneous legislative measures. Its development was driven by incident rather then by planning and – as pointed out in the White Paper – reflects little in the way of a coherent design. Nevertheless, in our opinion, it is possible to approach food law analytically. See Diagram 7.8 on the structure of food law we propose as the basis for further analysis in this book.

First a distinction can be made between substantive and procedural food law. Substantive law focuses on the content of legal relations. Procedural law focuses on how to realise this content. This includes procedures for pre-market approval of food products, legal protection against measures of the authorities and, most of all, inspection, monitoring and enforcement - including provisions that attribute the necessary powers to public authorities.

Next a distinction can be made between provisions addressing public authorities and provisions addressing food businesses. The former give powers and/or responsibilities to implement, enforce and to deal with incidents.

Diagram 7.8. The structure of food law.

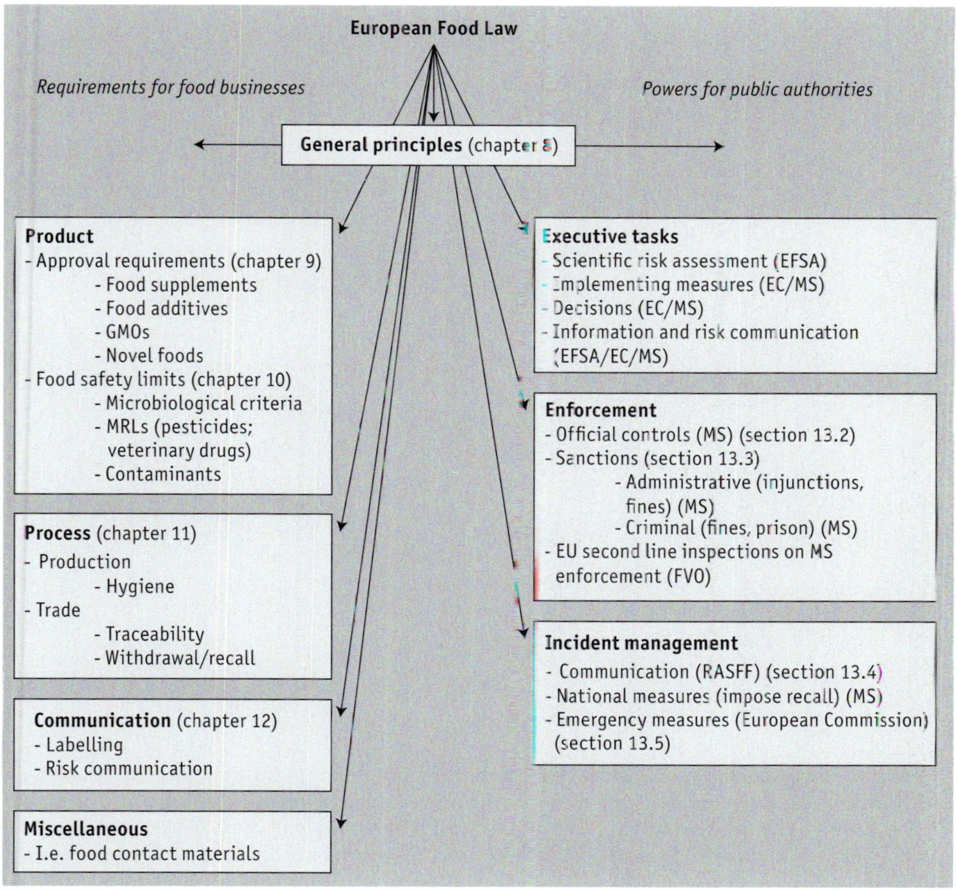

It appears that most of the substantive rules and regulations addressing food businesses can be categorised in a limited number of ways. These categories can be compared to 'atoms', which when combined in different ways form a huge variety of 'molecules'. Students and scholars who grasp the 'atoms' will find it easier to cope with the 'molecules'. Three[217] atoms are easily distinguished: (1) rules concerning the product (the substance of food as such), (2) rules concerning the process (the handling of food in production and trade), and (3) rules concerning communication about food. The distinction between these three types is not watertight. Often one can argue whether a certain rule is of one type or another[218] but that does not diminish the usefulness of the distinction. The account in the Chapters 9 up to 15 will be based on this distinction, but first we will to turn to the General Food Law. The General Food Law is intended to introduce the overall design that had previously been lacking in European food law. The General Food Law gives a context to the 'molecules' by assigning responsibilities and formulating goals and principles.

[217] In its definition of food law, German literature distinguishes some more different types: extraction, production, composition, quality, labelling, packaging and designation.

[218] For instance, the rule that a product must comprise of at least 35% of cacao to be called chocolate can be considered a rule on content (35%) or a rule on communication, 'if you want to call it chocolate...'.

8. The General Food Law: general provisions of food law

8.1 The General Food Law

The first step in the realisation of the reform of food law as planned in the White Paper on Food Safety, was the passage of 'Regulation (EC) No 178/2002 of the European Parliament and of the Council of 28 January 2002 laying down the general principles and requirements of food law, establishing the European Food Safety Authority and laying down procedures in matters of food safety'.[219] The popular name of this regulation is: the General Food Law (GFL). As is apparent from the regulation's official title, the General Food Law seeks to accomplish three objectives:[220]

1. To lay down the principles on which modern food legislation should be based in the European Union as well as in the member states.
2. To establish the European Food Safety Authority.
3. To establish procedures for food safety crises including the so-called Rapid Alert System.

To avoid confusion it should be noted that the General Food Law is not a code encompassing all food legislation. It is the fundament to a general part of food law.[221] Next to it many (hundreds) of other European and national rules and regulations continue to play their role.

This chapter treats the general provisions, laid down in the first two chapters of the GFL. The rest of the GFL, the institutional aspects, are covered in Chapters 5 and 13.

8.2 Aim and scope

The General Food Law provides a general framework for both national and community food law in the European Union. In Article 5 – discussed here below – the GFL gives the objectives of these national and European provisions of food law. In article 1 the GFL gives its own aim and scope (Law text box 8.1).

[219] Official Journal L 31, 1 February 2002, p. 1.

[220] These are the first three of the eighty-four legislative initiatives mentioned in the Action Plan on Food Safety, the Annex to the White Paper on Food Safety.

[221] The role the General Food Law plays with regard to food law is comparable to the role a constitution plays in a legal order. It must be stressed, however, that, technically speaking, the General Food Law is a regulation, and it is not given a higher status than other EU regulations or directives. Only by its purpose and wide scope of application does the General Food Law acquire its specific position in the food law system.

Law text box 8.1. Article 1 GFL on aim and scope of the GFL.

Article 1 GFL
Aim and scope

1. This Regulation provides the basis for the assurance of a high level of protection of human health and consumers' interest in relation to food, taking into account in particular the diversity in the supply of food including traditional products, whilst ensuring the effective functioning of the internal market.
   It establishes common principles and responsibilities, the means to provide a strong science base, efficient organisational arrangements and procedures to underpin decision-making in matters of food and feed safety.
2. For the purposes of paragraph 1, this Regulation lays down the general principles governing food and feed in general, and food and feed safety in particular, at Community and national level.
   It establishes the European Food Safety Authority.
   It lays down procedures for matters with a direct or indirect impact on food and feed safety.
3. This Regulation shall apply to all stages of production, processing and distribution of food and feed. It shall not apply to primary production for private domestic use or to the domestic preparation, handling or storage of food for private domestic consumption.

There are some basic notions in this article that have already been mentioned before:

- the principles and responsibilities are common to all food law in the EU;
- the principles and responsibilities are common to all stages of food and feed production and distribution ('from farm to fork').[222] This is sometimes called the 'holistic' approach to food law. Only primary production for private domestic use or the domestic preparation, handling or storage of food for private domestic consumption are exempted from the scope of application of the General Food Law.

8.3 Definitions

The first step that the GFL takes in integrating the whole body of national and community food law in the EU, is the development of a common 'language', by providing definitions for the most important notions. It is important to note that the definitions are given 'for the purpose of this Regulation'. By consequence the GFL definitions do not apply automatically in the legislation of the member states – although the GFL is a regulation – nor in other pieces of community legislation. The legislators will have to ensure that the GFL-definitions are introduced in all

[222] This farm to fork continuum is also referred to as a 'stable to table' or 'plough to plate' approach.

relevant legislative acts. An example can be found in the Hygiene Regulation for food of animal origin (853/2004) (Law text box 8.2).

Law text box 8.2. Inclusion of GFL definitions in Regulation 853/2004.

Article 2
Definitions
The following definitions shall apply for the purposes of this Regulation:
1. the definitions laid down in Regulation (EC) No 178/2002;
2. the definitions laid down in Regulation (EC) No 852/2004;
3. the definitions laid down in Annex I;
4. any technical definitions contained in Annexes II and III.

8.3.1 Food

The definition of 'food' provided in the second article of the General Food Law is essential (Law text box 8.3).[223] Its fulfilment is a precondition for the applicability of the GFL. If a product meets this definition it is a food in the sense of the GFL and the GFL applies to it. The same holds true for all the other laws and regulations that use this definition. In due course that should be the whole body of food law in the European Union and its member states.

Law text box 8.3. Definition of 'food' in Article 2 General Food Law.

Article 2
Definition of 'food'
For the purposes of this Regulation, 'food' (or 'foodstuff') means any substance or product, whether processed, partially processed or unprocessed, intended to be, or reasonably expected to be ingested by humans.
'Food' includes drink, chewing gum and any substance, including water, intentionally incorporated into the food during its manufacture, preparation or treatment. It includes water after the point of compliance as defined in Article 6 of Directive 98/83/EC and without prejudice to the requirements of Directives 80/778/EEC and 98/83/EC.
'Food' shall not include:
(a) feed;
(b) live animals unless they are prepared for placing on the market for human consumption;
(c) plants prior to harvesting;

[223] Surprisingly, although the European legislator had been very active in the field of food law, the term 'food' was for the first time defined in the 2002 General Food Law. The GFL does not distinguish between food and food ingredients as some older legislation does. Ingredients fulfil the definition of food and are (therefore) subject to the same safety rules. Only in labelling legislation does the distinction still have significance. See Chapter 12.

(d) medicinal products within the meaning of Council Directives 65/65/EEC and 92/73/EEC;
(e) cosmetics within the meaning of Council Directive 76/768/EEC;
(f) tobacco and tobacco products within the meaning of Council Directive 89/622/EEC;
(g) narcotic or psychotropic substances within the meaning of the United Nations Single Convention on Narcotic Drugs, 1961, and the United Nations Convention on Psychotropic Substances, 1971;
(h) residues and contaminants.

A product that may be used as a foodstuff, like e.g. palm oil, has to meet the food law requirements, until it is made clear that it will be used for other purposes. This category of substances is included in the definition as a substance that is 'reasonably expected' to be digested by humans.

Live animals included in the definition of food, are – in the European culture – mainly oysters. All other animals are generally slaughtered (killed) before they are eaten.

Case law that has evolved so far mainly focuses on the delineation of food and pharmaceuticals (medicinal products). The directive applicable to medicinal products is now 2001/83.[224] This directive gives two definitions of medicinal product, one 'by presentation' and one 'by function'. Under the first subparagraph of Article 1(2) of Directive 2001/83, a medicinal product is '[a]ny substance or combination of substances presented for treating or preventing disease in human beings', and according to the second subparagraph thereof, '[a]ny substance or combination of substances which may be administered to human beings with a view to making a medical diagnosis or to restoring, correcting or modifying physiological functions in human beings' is likewise to be considered a medicinal product.

A product is a medicinal product if it falls within either of those definitions. If it is a medicinal products it drops out of the definition of food. Unfortunately, in a case concerning the import into Germany of a product sold as food supplement in the member state of origin but classified as medicine in Germany, the Court had to decide that harmonisation of pharmaceutical law is not sufficiently complete to avoid the existence of differences in the classification of products as medicinal products or foodstuffs between member states. Thus, the fact that a product is classified as a foodstuff in another member state cannot prevent it from being classified as a medicinal product in the member state of importation, if it displays the characteristics of such a product.[225] For food law this has the unfortunate consequence that notwithstanding the common definition of food, it remains possible that a product is considered a food in one member state and a medicine in another.

224 It is unfortunate that the text of the GFL has not been updated in this regard.

225 Joined Cases C and-211/03, C-299/03 and C-316/03 to C-318/03 HLH Warenvertrieb and Orthica [2005] ECR I-5141, paragraph 56.

In the second case, also concerning Germany, the Court took the view that the German government has overstepped its margin of discretion by classifying garlic concentrates as medicines on the grounds that garlic has beneficial effects on health. The Court held that the product concerned, whose effect on physiological functions is no more than the effects a foodstuff consumed in a reasonable quantity may have on those functions, does not have a significant effect on the metabolism and cannot, therefore, be classified as a product capable of restoring, correcting or modifying physiological functions within the meaning of the second subparagraph of Article 1(2) of Directive 2001/83.[226] According to the Court, this qualification of a food as a medicine requiring pre-market approval constituted an infringement of the free movement of goods as protected in Article 28 of the EC Treaty.

Food businesses have it within their own power to present their product as having properties to cure (*etcetera*) bringing it within the ambit of pharmaceutical law. As regards the actual properties of the product, member states enjoy some discretion in classifying products as medicines. However, the beneficial effects of the products must be above the threshold of the effects a normal food can generate (Diagram 8.1). While the yardstick the Court applies is not very precise, at least it becomes clear that there is a yardstick and that the interpretation of the concepts of medicine and food may not vary too much between the member states.

Diagram 8.1. Medicine.

Medicine	By presentation	By function
	Business decides	MS has discretion. Effect should be above normal food consumed in reasonable quantity

8.3.2 Food law

The General Food Law defines 'food law'. With this definition it sets the scope for the general principles it contains (Law text box 8.4).[227]

[226] ECJ 15 November 2007, Case C-319/05 Commission v. Federal Republic of Germany, paragraph 68.

[227] The wording 'food law' is not the same in all language versions of the GFL. The French and the Dutch texts apply expressions best translated into English as 'food legislation' (*législation alimentaire* and *levensmiddelenwetgeving*, respectively). The German version (*Lebensmittelrecht*) is similar to the English text. The difference in meaning is if the word covers the entire system of law, including for example case law or only prescriptive texts. What follows in the GFL definition of food law is an enumeration of such texts. It is a broad enumeration including provisions originating from the legislature and from the executive, from the Community and from the member states. This may indicate that the French and Dutch wording are closer to the mark than the English and German wording. This book, however, and the underlying academic activity are not bound to any legal interpretation of a definition of food law. It includes case law and administrative practices in its area of interest.

Law text box 8.4. Definition of 'food law' Article 3(1) GFL.

Article 3(1) GFL
Definition of food law
'food law' means the laws, regulations and administrative provisions governing food in general, and food safety in particular, whether at Community or national level; it covers any stage of production, processing and distribution of food, and also of feed produced for, or fed to, food producing animals;

8.3.3 Food business

Other important definitions are those of 'food business' and 'food business operator'. These definitions are important because many provisions address these businesses (operators). If someone meets the definition, s/he has to comply with food law. The definitions are given in Law text box 8.5.

Law text box 8.5. Definitions of 'food business' and 'food business operator', Article 3(2/3) General Food Law.

Article 3(2/3) GFL
Definitions of food business and food business operator.
'food business' means any undertaking, whether for profit or not and whether public or private, carrying out any of the activities related to any stage of production, processing and distribution of food;
'food business operator' means the natural or legal persons responsible for ensuring that the requirements of food law are met within the food business under their control;

The definition of food business is very broad. In the European Parliament the question[228] has been raised as to whether the requirements of traceability (Article 18 GFL) apply to charities that collect and distribute food. From the response of the European Commission[229] it follows that such charities are indeed food businesses to which the requirements of food law apply (national agencies can however be lenient in the enforcement of compliance by charities).

Unfortunately the definition of food business operator is imprecise. The main function of this definition is to identify the natural or legal person who is responsible for complying with food law. To this effect see Article 17(1) GFL. By including in the definition that the operator is the one who is responsible, we end up with

[228] E-2704/04.
[229] E-2704/04DE.

a perfect circle where the GFL says that responsibility for compliance with food law rests with the one who is responsible.

Fortunately, the intention of the legislator is not as enigmatic as the words. Food business operator is the one who is in charge of the business, usually that would be the owner. This is the one who has the power to take the decisions that are decisive for compliance or non-compliance.

The Hygiene package – in particular Article 6 of Regulation 852/2004 – imposes a general obligation on food business operators to notify the national competent authorities and to register each establishment under its control that carries out any of the stages of production, processing and distribution of food.[230] See Law text box 8.6.

Law text box 8.6. Registration and approval of food businesses.

Article 6 Regulation 852/2004
Official controls, registration and approval

1. Food business operators shall cooperate with the competent authorities in accordance with other applicable Community legislation or, if it does not exist, with national law.
2. In particular, every food business operator shall notify the appropriate competent authority, in the manner that the latter requires, of each establishment under its control that carries out any of the stages of production, processing and distribution of food, with a view to the registration of each such establishment.
   Food business operators shall also ensure that the competent authority always has up-to-date information on establishments, including by notifying any significant change in activities and any closure of an existing establishment.
3. However, food business operators shall ensure that establishments are approved by the competent authority, following at least one on-site visit, when approval is required:
   (a) under the national law of the Member State in which the establishment is located;
   (b) under Regulation (EC) No 853/2004; or
   (c) by a decision adopted in accordance with the procedure referred to in Article 14(2).
   Any Member State requiring the approval of certain establishments located on its territory under national law, as provided for in subparagraph (a), shall inform the Commission and other Member States of the relevant national rules.

On top of the registration requirement, establishments of food businesses to which Regulation 853/2004 applies (and some others), that are establishments working with food of animal origin, need an approval after an on site inspection (Diagram 8.2).

[230] See also Article 31 Regulation 882/2004. See in more detail on this subject Chapter 11, section 11.1.5.

Diagram 8.2. Registration obligations of food business operators.

Notify	Each establishment for registration
Notify	Significant changes
Ensure approval following on-site visit	Establishments handling food of animal origin

8.3.4 Placing on the market

Many provision of food law apply to the 'placing on the market' of food by the food business operator. This concept is used in a rather wide meaning defined in Article 3(8) of the General Food Law (Law text box 8.7).

Law text box 8.7. Definition of 'placing on the market' in Article 3(8) GFL.

Article 3(8) GFL
Definition of placing on the market
'placing on the market' means the holding of food or feed for the purpose of sale, including offering for sale or any other form of transfer, whether free of charge or not, and the sale, distribution, and other forms of transfer themselves;

8.3.5 Competent Authority

Part of the sovereignty of the member states is the so-called 'principle of institutional autonomy'. EU law has little to say about the organisation of the public sector in the member states. Usually, obligations are conferred to the national 'competent authority'. It is for the national legislature to decide which state organ is its 'competent authority' in any given matter and to endow it with the powers necessary to fulfil its obligations under EU law. In most member states, food law is in the domain of either the Minister of Agriculture or the Minister of Public Health. Most member states also have a more-or-less independent food safety authority.

Next to the European Commission, the competent authority in the member states is the prime addressee of food law at the side of the public authorities. The concept has not been defined in the General Food Law. Regulation 852/2004 does give a definition that is suitable to applied in food law in general. See Law text box 8.8.

Law text box 8.8. Definition of 'competent authority' in Article 2(1)(d) Regulation 852/2004.

> **Article 2(1)(d) Regulation 852/2004**
> **Definition of competent authority**
> 'competent authority' means the central authority of a Member State competent to ensure compliance with the requirements of this Regulation or any other authority to which that central authority has delegated that competence; it shall also include, where appropriate, the corresponding authority of a third country;

In the General Food Law the word 'authority' refers to the European Food Safety Authority. In general this word is used in a broader meaning.

8.3.6 Food safety

Even though food safety is the main objective of food law, the GFL does not give a definition of food safety. As we will see here below it does provide for a ban on unsafe food and explains *in that context* when food is deemed to be unsafe. This does not mean, however, that we can simply strike the negatives to come to a definition of food safety – as some authors do.[231] Legal texts often apply double negations. This indicates that the legislator does not have a bipolar situation in mind, but a continuum with a grey area between the opposites. In this line of thinking 'not black' does not equal 'white', but leaves space for all kind of shades of grey, red, yellow and blue. All are ok, as long as it is not black. The GFL does not define food safety. It only says that food must *not* be *un*safe.

In contrast to the General Food Law, the Codex Alimentarius[232] does define the concept of food safety (Law text box 8.9).[233] It refers to not causing harm. There is no reason to presume that the notion of food safety is understood differently in EU food law.

Law text box 8.9. Definition of 'food safety' in Codex Alimentarius.

> Food safety - assurance that food will not cause harm to the consumer when it is prepared and/or eaten according to its intended use.

What the GFL does define, are the concepts of 'risk' and 'hazard' (Law text box 8.10).

---

[231] See for example Robert Riedl and Christina Riedl, Shortcomings of the New European Food Hygiene Legislation from the Viewpoint of a Competent Authority, EFFL, 3/2/2008, p. 64-83.
[232] On the Codex Alimentarius see Chapter 16.
[233] Recommended International Code of Practice General Principles of Food Hygiene, CAC/RCP 1-1969, rev. 4 (2003), p. 7. For a hyperlink see the list of references.

Law text box 8.10. Definition of 'risk' and 'hazard' Article 3(9) and 3(14) GFL.

Article 3(9) and 3(14) GFL
Definitions of risk and hazard
'risk' means a function of the probability of an adverse health effect and the severity of that effect, consequential to a hazard;
'hazard' means a biological, chemical or physical agent in, or condition of, food or feed with the potential to cause an adverse health effect;

These concepts help to identify in which situations a food may cause harm and thus is no longer safe. What can go wrong in food is probably in all situations of either a biological, a chemical or a physical nature.

8.4 General principles

The General Food Law is not entirely clear on the meaning it attaches to the word 'principle'.

In its second chapter, the General Food Law identifies six 'principles' of food law; four of these address food law as such and two address transparency. These principles are followed by three 'general obligations' of food trade. The second chapter ends with eight Articles containing 'general requirements' of food law.

The main distinction between the principles and the general requirements, is that the principles mainly address the legislator and the requirements mainly the businesses. The general obligations of food trade address all actors engaged in international trade, busineses and authorities.

In our view the 'general obligations' and the 'general requirements' are of the same basic nature as the 'principles'. For this reason we will call them all 'principles'.[234] These principles are presented in Diagram 8.3. We will discuss some of these principles briefly and elaborate a little bit more on the objectives of food law, risk analysis, the precautionary principle and the food safety principle (or duty of care) because it is the most important for food business operators. The principle on presentation (labelling) will be discussed in Chapter 12, section 12.1.1. The responsibilities of food business operators for traceability, withdrawal and recall will be discussed in Chapter 11, section 11.3.

[234] In the initial Commission proposal they were included in one section called 'Principles and requirements of food law'.

Diagram 8.3. Principles of food law (Chapter II GFL).

Principle	Content Details
General principles (section 1)	
General objectives (or: Focus) (art. 5)	Protection of • human life & health; • consumers interests; • fair trade; • animal health & welfare, plant health, environment; • free movement of feed & food products; • application of international standards.
Science based (art. 6)	Based on risk analysis Risk assessment based on all scientific evidence, independent, objective, transparent Risk management takes into account results of risk assessment, other legitimate factors, precautionary principle
Precautionary principle (art. 7)	If the possibility of harmful effects on health are identified, but scientific uncertainty persists; • provisional risk management measures may be taken; • pending further research; • proportionate; • no more restrictive to trade than required; • with regard to technical and economic feasibility and other legitimate factors; • measures shall be reviewed within a reasonable time.
Consumer protection (art. 8)	• Provide a basis for informed choice • Prevent fraudulent or deceptive practices; • Prevent adulteration of food; • Prevent other misleading practices
Principles of transparency (section 2)	
Public consultation (art. 9)	• the public shall be consulted in food legislation
Public information (art. 10)	• Risk communication • The general public shall be informed of suspected risks and of measures taken
General obligations of food trade (section 3)	
Import (art. 11)	• imports shall comply with EU food law
Export (art. 12)	• exports shall comply with EU food law
International standards (art. 13)	• Contribute to development • Promote international organisations • Contribute to agreements • Special attention to needs of developing countries • Promote consistency

Principle	Content	Details
General requirements (section 4)		
Food safety (art. 14)	• No placing unsafe food on the market • Applies to entire batch unless proven safe	Food is unsafe: • injurious to health • unfit for consumption (contamination, putrefaction, deterioration, decay) Regarding • normal use • information Regarding • long-term effects; including future generations; • cumulative toxic effects • sensitive category of consumers Food complying with food law is deemed safe for the aspects covered • compliance does not bar authorities from taking measures
Feed safety (art. 15)	• No placing unsafe feed on the market • No feeding unsafe feed to food producing animal	
Presentation (art. 16)	• No misleading consumers	
Responsibilities (art. 17)	• Business operators from farm to fork for following food law • Member States for enforcement from farm to fork (controls, communication & penalties)	
Traceability (art. 18)	• From farm to fork • One step up, one step down • Operators have systems in place • Information available for authorities • Adequate identification & labelling	
Responsibilities for food (art. 19)	• Operator, who has reason to doubt safety, must withdraw food • If food has reached consumer: inform consumer and if necessary recall • Inform and co-operate with competent authorities	
Responsibilities for feed (art. 20)	• Operator who has reason to doubt safety, must withdraw feed • Inform and co-operate with competent authorities	
Liability (art. 21)	• General provisions on product liability apply	

8.5 Focussed objectives

The GFL provides a limited set of objectives for food legislation.[235] In other words a principle of focus applies.

Food law shall pursue one or more of the general objectives of a high level of protection of human life and health and the protection of consumers' interests, including fair practices in food trade, taking account of, where appropriate, the protection of animal health and welfare, plant health and the environment.[236]

Next the free movement of food products is mentioned, as is adherence to international standards.

If we take a closer look at the words connected to the objectives mentioned, we notice subtle differences. The first two are to be pursued, the next to be taken account of, then aim to be achieved and finally to be taken into consideration. See Diagram 8.4. These differences have meaning, they are not just poetic variations on the same theme.

Diagram 8.4. General objectives of food law.

Pursue general objectives (paragraph 1)	Take account of (where appropriate)	Aim to achieve (paragraph 2)	Take into consideration (paragraph 3)
High level of protection of human life and health (elaborated in Arts. 6 and 7)	Animal health Animal welfare Plant health Environment	Free movement of compliant food and feed	International standards existing or imminent (except ...)
Protection of consumers' interests, including fair practices in food trade (elaborated in Art. 8)			

Article 5 GFL drastically limits the freedom of the legislator. Food law may only pursue the given objectives and no other objectives. The effect of this limitation is greatest for food law in the member states. National law may not depart from EU law. The EU legislator himself has the option to take other decisions in later

235 Article 5 GFL.

236 Consumer protection is considered a human right in the EU. Article 38 of the Charter of Fundamental Rights of the European Union reads: Union policies shall ensure a high level of consumer protection.

legislation. Two objectives are given: protection of human life and health and protection of (other) consumers' interests. The other principles elaborate on these objectives. From Articles 6 and 7 GFL it follows that pursuing protection of human health is seen as a matter in which science should be involved. Article 8 GFL focuses on the protection of other consumers' interests, for instance, protection from different types of unfair trading practices.

The objective of food (and feed!) law is to protect humans. If alternative ways to protect humans present themselves to the legislator, the interests of animals, plants and the environment can be taken into account. The method that is the most protective or least damaging to animals, plants or the environment can be chosen from different ways of protecting humans. All this should result in food and feed that can be freely traded all over the European Community. Where does the legislator find the alternatives suitable to pursue the objectives of food law? Probably in international standards like the Codex Alimentarius that have already been agreed upon or still are in the process. In making food law the legislator must confront himself with the question as to whether the solutions presented are suitable and then either follow them, or have good reasons to depart from them.

What about interests not mentioned in Article 5 as objectives to be pursued, achieved, taken into account or taken into consideration? The most striking example of such interests are the interests of food businesses. Even though food businesses are the addressees of most provisions of food law and thus the parties most affected by these provisions, their interests are not to be pursued! The absence of food businesses as subjects to be considered in food legislation, can probably be explained as an effect of the BSE crisis which prompted the new approach to food law as laid down in the GFL. As discussed in Chapter 7, section 7.4 the European Commission was criticised for being excessively influenced by commercial interests. In drafting Article 5, the Commission seems to have gone to the other extreme.

Not mentioned interests are protected by the principle of proportionality.[237] They may not be harmed more than is necessary to achieve the objective pursued.

[237] Recognised in Protocol (30) on the application of the principles of subsidiarity and proportionality (1997) to the EC Treaty.

8.6 Risk analysis, risk management and risk communication

8.6.1 Concepts

Food law is science based or, in the words of the GFL, 'food law shall be based on risk analysis except where this is not appropriate to the circumstances or the nature of the measure'.[238]

This principle is at the core of the new European approach to food law as 'food safety law'. The GFL regards risk analysis as a process consisting of three interconnected components: risk assessment, risk management and risk communication.[239] See Diagram 8.5.

Diagram 8.5. Components of risk analysis.

Activity	Elements	Product
Risk assessment	• hazard identification • hazard characterisation • exposure assessment • risk characterisation	Advice
Risk communication	• interactive exchange of information and opinions	Information
Risk management	• considering risk assessment and other legitimate factors • including precautionary principle • consultation with interested parties • weighing policy alternatives • selecting appropriate prevention and control options	Decision

The first of these three components, *risk assessment*, is seen as a scientifically based process consisting of four steps: hazard identification, hazard characterisation, exposure assessment and risk characterisation.[240] The European Food Safety Authority is the key player in risk assessment. Risk assessors provide information for decision makers (public authorities) to decide whether the risks deriving from a given product or activity are acceptable, and – if need be – to take appropriate measures to mitigate these risks.

The second, '*risk management*', is a broad concept. It means the process, distinct from risk assessment, of weighing policy alternatives in consultation with

[238] Article 6 GFL. There are some areas of food regulation that do not deal with hazards of a biological, chemical or physical nature and they do not require prior scientific risk assessment. An example of such measures are provisions relating to food labelling.
[239] Article 3 (10) GFL.
[240] Article 3 (11) GFL.

interested parties, considering risk assessment and other legitimate factors, and, if need be, selecting appropriate prevention and control options.[241] The options available to risk management encompass legislation, enforcement and everything in between. To a large extent risk management is the domain of the European Commission and the national authorities. To a lesser extent, the same is true for risk communication. Risk management takes into account the results of risk assessment, however in some cases other factors relevant to the matter under consideration should also be taken into account. These so-called 'other legitimate factors' (OLFs) include societal, economic, traditional, ethical and environmental factors and the feasibility of controls. In some cases, where – after the assessment of the available information – scientific uncertainty persists, the precautionary principle may be invoked where the conditions laid down in Article 7 are met (see hereafter section 8.7.2).

Choosing the level of protection is also an element of risk management. It is stated repeatedly that the EC chooses a high level of protection[242] and is thus likely to choose stringent measures to deal with identified risks.

The third element of risk analysis is risk communication. '*Risk communication*' means the interactive exchange of information and opinions throughout the risk analysis process. This includes hazards and risks in themselves, as well as risk-related factors and perceptions of risk among assessors, managers, consumers, feed and food businesses, the academic community and other interested parties. It also includes the explanation of risk assessment findings and the basis of risk management decisions.[243] Risk communication provides the explanation of risk assessment findings and the basis of risk management decisions, closes the gaps between experts, policy makers and other stakeholders. The BSE crisis in the UK taught a very important lesson about the importance of risk communication, its transparency and openness. Now EFSA can communicate risks on its own initiative in all fields within its mission, except for communicating risk management decisions, which falls within the competence of the Commission. Close cooperation between EFSA, the Commission and the member states is therefore necessary to ensure coherence of the risk communication process.

While in the ideal situation risk assessment comes before risk management,[244] risk communication plays a role in all the stages. Communication is crucial both for risk assessment and risk management to reach their intended results and then

[241] Article 3(12) GFL.

[242] For example Article 1 and 5 GFL.

[243] Article 3(13) GFL.

[244] Many publications represent the three activities in a circular way indicating that risk management decisions give rise to new risk assessment. While this may be true in many cases, risk management is not a legal precondition for risk assessment, while risk assessment is a condition for risk management.

to disseminate these. Risk communication in the guise of warning can even be a form of risk management.

8.6.2 Scope

The wording of Article 6 GFL might lead an unsuspecting reader to believe that all legislation on food or at least all legislation aiming to protect human life and health is preceded by scientific risk assessment. In so far as it gives rise to this expectation, Article 6 is a gross overstatement. In fact not one single example can be found of a regulation or directive of a general nature referring to an opinion of EFSA or another form of risk assessment that has been taken into account.

In other words: food law is not *based* on risk analysis. Risk analysis is an *instrument* of food law in so far as decisions are taken relating to specific foods. If we take a look at opinions issued by EFSA, they all relate to applications for approval (as discussed in Chapter 9), to the setting of food safety targets (as discussed in Chapter 10) or to the measures to be taken regarding certain risks. Such measures may be taken in the *form* of legislation (regulation or directive), they are however of a specific nature and thus in essence are administrative decisions.

This need not be surprising if we take another look at the definition of risk assessment. Hazard identification, hazard characterisation, exposure assessment in particular, and risk characterisation, by their very nature focus on specific products, substances or life forms.

8.7 Precautionary principle[245]

The precautionary principle adds subtlety to the risk-analysis principle. In specific circumstances where, following an assessment of available information, the possibility of harmful effects on health is identified but scientific uncertainty persists, provisional risk management measures necessary to ensure the high level of health protection chosen in the Community may be adopted, pending further scientific information for a more comprehensive risk assessment.[246]

8.7.1 Background

The precautionary principle deals with decision making in the face of scientific uncertainty. In Community law, the principle appeared for the first time in 1992 in the environmental title of the EC Treaty. However, its scope was not limited to environmental issues. The precautionary principle applied to other Community policies, including human, animal and plant health. A famous application of the

[245] Many thanks to Anna Szajkowska, who wrote this section.

[246] Article 7 GFL.

precautionary measures can be found in the judgements on the validity of the Community measure imposing a worldwide embargo on British beef exports, linked to the outbreak of BSE. In the BSE judgements, the European Court of justice stated: 'Where there is uncertainty as to the existence or extent of risks to human health, the institutions may take protective measures without having to wait until the reality and seriousness of those risks become fully apparent'. This formulation was repeated in subsequent rulings.

Recourse to the principle in the area of food safety has been a subject of controversy at the international level. This is because, under the strict scientific regime of the WTO Agreement on Sanitary and Phytosanitary Measures, such a principle - allowing for the adoption of a measure in case of insufficiency of scientific evidence - becomes a very powerful instrument, which can be used as a disguised form of protectionism.

Regardless of the status of the precautionary principle in international law, the European Community has consequently advocated its application to the new EU food safety policy. In 2000 the Commission published the Communication on the use of the precautionary principle, in order to inform all interested parties of a manner in which the principle was implemented in Community policies.[247]

The principle is now – for the first time in Community law - defined in Article 7 GFL. The definition also determines conditions for the application of the principle.

The GFL's preamble states that in some cases, scientific risk assessment alone can not provide all the necessary information on which the risk management should be based. The GFL invokes the precautionary principle to ensure health protection in the Community and to set a uniform basis for the use of precautionary measures within the Community, in order to avoid arbitrary decisions giving rise to unjustified barriers to the free movement of food and feed. The preamble states that in circumstances where 'a risk to life or health exists but scientific uncertainty persists, the precautionary principle provides a mechanism for determining risk management measures or other actions in order to ensure the high level of health protection chosen in the Community'.[248]

8.7.2 Conditions

Article 7(1) GFL sets out three pre-requisite conditions that have to be met if the precautionary principle is to be invoked in the Community or national policy:
1. There must be an assessment of available scientific data before a decision is made;

[247] Brussels 2.2.2000 COM(2000) 1 final. For a hyperlink see the reference list.
[248] See recitals 20 and 21.

2. The possibility of harmful effects on health is identified;
3. The risk assessment is inconclusive or inconsistent and the risk cannot be determined – scientific uncertainty persists.

8.7.3 Precaution and risk analysis

Article 6(3) mentions the precautionary principle among the elements that risk managers should take into account when taking decisions in the area of food safety. Thus, the precautionary principle is a risk management tool and it can only be used within the framework of the risk analysis methodology. Recourse to the principle presupposes a scientific risk evaluation which – due to the insufficient inconclusive or imprecise information – cannot assess the risk with sufficient certainty. The insufficiency of available information makes it impossible to base a risk management decision on risk assessment. However, the risk evaluation may identify potential risks, which, although not fully scientifically proven, are not acceptable to society and not consistent with the high level of protection of human health chosen in the Community. In these circumstances, the precautionary principle enables public authorities to act without having to wait until the reality and seriousness of those risk become fully apparent.

8.7.4 Provisional and proportional measures

Measures taken on the basis of the precautionary principle are provisional, 'pending further scientific information for a more comprehensive risk assessment'. The measures based on the precautionary principle should be maintained as long as the scientific data are inadequate, imprecise or inconclusive and as long as the risk is considered too high to be imposed on society. The provisional character is not linked to a time factor, but to the development of scientific knowledge. They shall 'be reviewed within a reasonable period of time, depending on the nature of the risk to life or health identified and the type of scientific information needed to clarify the scientific uncertainty and to conduct a more comprehensive risk assessment'.

According to the Commission's Communication, measures resulting from the precautionary principle may take various forms (Diagram 8.6). Besides the adoption of legal measures, there are other possibilities of action that can be inspired by the precautionary principle, such as funding a research program, informing the public about the adverse effects, etc. Precautionary measures must be proportional to the desired level of protection and no more restrictive of trade than it is required to achieve the high level of protection.

The definition of the precautionary principle includes a notion of 'cost-effectiveness': in considering precautionary measures regard must be had for technical and economic feasibility and other factors regarded as legitimate. However, according to

Diagram 8.6. Application of the precautionary principle.

Conditions	Measures
Risk assessment	Proportionate
Potential hazard	Provisional
Scientific uncertainty regarding risk	Reviewed after improved risk assessment

the case law of the ECJ, the protection of health takes precedence over economic considerations.

8.8 Food law and science

Norm and science can become interrelated in different ways; static and dynamic (Diagram 8.7). A norm is static if the specific outcomes of risk assessment in a specific moment in time, determine the norm, for example, when a maximum residue limit (or level) (MRL) is set. This MRL stays the same as long as the norm is not changed regardless of developments in scientific knowledge. A norm is dynamic if it relates to state of the art of scientific knowledge at the moment of application of the norm. Article 14 GFL to be discussed hereafter is an example of a dynamic norm. It sets a ban on bringing unsafe food to the market. As knowledge on food safety risks develops the exact meaning of the ban on unsafe food develops along with it. The disadvantage of static norms is that they easily get outdated, and thus lose relevance from a scientific point of view. The advantage is legal certainty. The norm can be understood at face value. The advantage of a dynamic norm is that scientifically it is always up to date. The disadvantage is a lack of legal certainty. Legislation is disclosed in a specific way at a specific place.[249] This makes it possible to inform oneself of changes in the text of the law. Scientific knowledge is disseminated in defuse ways. The state of the art cannot be established with the same certitude. Food business operators can never be entirely sure if their scientific knowledge is up to date. If it is not, they are not compliant with food law.

Diagram 8.7. Food law & science.

	Static	Dynamic	Zero tolerance
Norm	represents scientific opinion at the time of drafting	meaning evolves with scientific progress	meaning evolves with technological progress
Legal certainty	+	-	-
Scientific relevance	-	+	-

[249] For European legislation, this specific place is the Official Journal.

An especially intriguing norm is the contamination limit of zero. While this norm is static in its appearance, the meaning of zero (detection limit) evolves not with scientific opinion but with technological capacity. The smaller the quantities that can be measured, the more strict the norm 'zero' becomes. However, it may also become scientifically meaningless if the traces measured are no longer relevant from a food safety point of view.[250] Current technology can measure contamination in ppbs (parts per billion). The consequence is that if the sample is large enough anything can be found.

8.9 Other consumer interests

Article 8 GFL further details the other interests of consumers indicated in Article 5. It states that food law shall aim at the protection of the interests of consumers and shall provide a basis for consumers to make informed choices in relation to the foods they consume. It shall aim to prevent:

a. fraudulent or deceptive practices;
b. the adulteration of food; and
c. any other practices which may mislead the consumer.

Diagram 8.8 graphically represents this interpretation of consumer protection.

Diagram 8.8. Consumer protection.

Protect consumer interests	
Provide	**Prevent**
Basis for informed choice	a. fraudulent or deceptive practices b. the adulteration of food c. any other misleading practices

8.10 Transparency

8.10.1 Public consultation

Two principles fall under the heading 'transparency'. The first of them is that the public must be consulted in the development of food law.[251] The European Commission publishes proposals for new legislation on the Internet and invites comments from the public. This principle is in line with the reforms in European governance, launched by the Commission in the White Paper on European

[250] See for this opinion: Huub Lelieveld and Larry Keener, Global harmonization of food regulations and legislation - the Global Harmonization Initiative, Trends in Food Science & Technology 18 (2007): S15-S19.

[251] Article 9 GFL.

Governance in 2001.[252] The White Paper highlighted the need for opening up the policy-making process and getting citizens involved in shaping EU policies, under five guiding principles of EU governance: openness, participation, accountability, effectiveness and coherence.

8.10.2 Public information

The authorities have a duty to inform the public of food-borne health risks and the measures that are taken to counteract them.[253] This is part of the concept of 'risk communication'.

8.11 International trade

8.11.1 Import

European food safety requirements apply to imported food.[254] As we will see hereafter, these requirements on food safety not only address the condition of the product when it arrives at the European border, but also the way it has been handled in processing and trade and even in the choice of raw materials. This principle therefore implies considerable extra-territorial ambitions of EU food law.

8.11.2 Export

Exported food must also comply with the European food safety standards.[255] This principle on the one hand makes the European origin of a food product a quality guarantee. On the other hand it facilitates controls and enforcement as all production in the EU in principle has to meet the same safety standards, regardless of the market for which they are producing.

An exception applies if the authorities or the legislation in the country of destination request differently. In other circumstances food not complying with EU food law may only be (re)exported if the competent authorities in the country of destination have been informed of this non-compliance with EU law and have expressly agreed. Food that is injurious to health may never be (re)exported, regardless of the opinion of the authorities in the country of destination.

252 COM(2001) 428 final.
253 Article 10 GFL.
254 Article 11 GFL.
255 Article 12 GFL.

8.11.3 International standards

The EU and the Member States contribute to the development and application of international standards.[256] As discussed above, these standards in turn must be taken into account when developing food law in the EU (Article 5(3) GFL). We will return to this principle in Chapter 16.

8.12 Food safety: a duty of care

8.12.1 Responsibility

The most important *notion* in the General Food Law is the central place it accords to safety. The GFL imposes on food business operators the responsibility for the safety of the food they bring to the market. Article 17, which bears the title 'Responsibilities', states in its first paragraph that food business operators must ensure compliance with food law (Law text box 8.11).

Law text box 8.11. Article 17 (1) GFL on compliance with food law.

Article 17 (1) GFL
Food and feed business operators at all stages of production, processing and distribution within the businesses under their control shall ensure that foods or feeds satisfy the requirements of food law which are relevant to their activities and shall verify that such requirements are met.

This sounds like stating the obvious: 'one should comply with the law', but there is more to it than this. Article 14 GFL forbids bringing food to the market if it is unsafe. Food is deemed to be unsafe if it is injurious to health or unfit for human consumption. This imposes a general responsibility to ensure the safety of any food brought to the market. Furthermore, this implies a general risk for the food business operator in case a food that has been brought to the market turns out to have been injurious to health. Even the effects on the health of subsequent generations are taken into consideration. In other words adverse effects of food may constitute an offence committed by the food business operator.

Article 17(1) GFL is also of relevance for the legislator. If food business operators are to be responsible, food legislation should be drafted in such a way that they can indeed take responsibility. In the explanatory memorandum to the initial proposal[257] for what became the General Food Law, the European Commission put it this way:

256 Article 13 GFL.

257 Proposal for a Regulation of the European Parliament and of the Council laying down the general principles and requirements of food law, establishing the European Food Authority, and laying down procedures in matters of food, 8.11.2000, COM(2000) 716 final, pp. 10-11.

Responsibilities
In some areas of European food law, notably in hygiene legislation, the primary responsibility for ensuring compliance with food law, and in particular the safety of the food, rests with the food business. To complement and support this principle there must be adequate and effective controls organised by the competent authorities of the Member States. In other areas of food law this principle is not so widely applicable. This proposal will extend this principle to all food law, and lead to a general review of food law to establish if this principle is respected or whether there are rules where Community legislation has unnecessarily taken responsibility away from the feed or food business by prescribing how a given objective has to be achieved instead of fixing the objective.

In other words, given the choice the legislator should formulate norms in terms of results to achieve rather than in terms of ways to behave.

8.12.2 Ban on unsafe food

Undoubtedly the single most important *provision* in EU food law is Article 14 GFL (Law text box 8.12).

Law text box 8.12. Article 14 GFL ban on unsafe food.

Article 14
Food safety requirements

1. Food shall not be placed on the market if it is unsafe.
2. Food shall be deemed to be unsafe if it is considered to be:
   (a) injurious to health;
   (b) unfit for human consumption.
3. In determining whether any food is unsafe, regard shall be had:
   (a) to the normal conditions of use of the food by the consumer and at each stage of production, processing and distribution, and
   (b) to the information provided to the consumer, including information on the label, or other information generally available to the consumer concerning the avoidance of specific adverse health effects from a particular food or category of foods.
4. In determining whether any food is injurious to health, regard shall be had:
   (a) not only to the probable immediate and/or short-term and/or long-term effects of that food on the health of a person consuming it, but also on subsequent generations;
   (b) to the probable cumulative toxic effects;
   (c) to the particular health sensitivities of a specific category of consumers where the food is intended for that category of consumers.
5. In determining whether any food is unfit for human consumption, regard shall be had to whether the food is unacceptable for human consumption according to its intended use, for reasons of contamination, whether by extraneous matter or otherwise, or through putrefaction, deterioration or decay.

6. Where any food which is unsafe is part of a batch, lot or consignment of food of the same class or description, it shall be presumed that all the food in that batch, lot or consignment is also unsafe, unless following a detailed assessment there is no evidence that the rest of the batch, lot or consignment is unsafe.
7. Food that complies with specific Community provisions governing food safety shall be deemed to be safe insofar as the aspects covered by the specific Community provisions are concerned.
8. Conformity of a food with specific provisions applicable to that food shall not bar the competent authorities from taking appropriate measures to impose restrictions on it being placed on the market or to require its withdrawal from the market where there are reasons to suspect that, despite such conformity, the food is unsafe.
9. Where there are no specific Community provisions, food shall be deemed to be safe when it conforms to the specific provisions of national food law of the Member State in whose territory the food is marketed, such provisions being drawn up and applied without prejudice to the Treaty, in particular Articles 28 and 30 thereof.

Article 14(1) GFL puts a general ban on marketing unsafe food. The remainder of Article 14 GFL elaborates when and how food is deemed unsafe for the application of this ban. It brings together substantive and formal approaches. That is to say, first it addresses the factual effects of the food and then the conformity with legal requirements is taken into account.

In addressing the issue of unsafety normal conditions of use are taken as a starting point including the information provided to the consumer. In other words, the presence or absence of proper instructions of use or warnings (allergen labelling!) may determine the safety or unsafety of a food.

8.12.3 Health effects

Food is deemed unsafe if it is injurious to health.[258] In other words, the unsafety of food is based first and foremost on the effects that its consumption may have on the health of the consumer (patient). According to paragraph 4 of Article 14 this includes immediate, short-term and long-term effects and even effects on subsequent generations. As for this last category: experience in pharmacy has shown that consumption of the artificial hormone DES (diethylstilbestrol) is harmless to the consumer (patient) but does great damage to the child of which the consumer is pregnant at the time of consumption. DES once was the most notorious illegal hormone used in cattle rearing. It would therefore be conceivable that it is present in a food. If this is the case, it renders the food unsafe under this provision.

[258] Article 14(2)(a) GFL.

In determining the unsafety of the food, regard shall be had for cumulative toxic effects, e.g. probable negative effects of consumption in combination with other foods.

In determining whether a food is unsafe, an *ex-ante* position is taken. Regard is taken of the *probable* effects. For an effect to be probable, the relevant knowledge must exist at the time of placing on the market.

Finally, regard shall be had for the particular health sensitivities of a specific category of consumers where the food is intended for that category of consumers. For example, baby food should be free from adverse effects on babies. Food intended for the general public is not unsafe solely because of the fact that it may have adverse effects on babies. If, however, a specific category is part of the general public as is the case with people suffering from certain food allergies, food presented to the general public must be considered to be intended for this category as well and thus needs the appropriate warnings to be considered safe.

8.12.4 Unfit for consumption

Food is also deemed unsafe if it is unfit for human consumption (Article 14(2)(b) GFL). In determining whether any food is unfit for human consumption, regard shall be had for whether the food is unacceptable for human consumption according to its intended use, for reasons of contamination, whether by extraneous matter or otherwise, or through putrefaction, deterioration or decay (Article 14(5) GFL). Some scholars criticise this provision. They understand it to mean that it applies to foods that are *not* injurious to health but that are nevertheless labelled 'unsafe'. We prefer another reading. It is mainly a matter of burden of proof. If a food is deteriorated to such an extent that it is unfit for human consumption, no separate information is required regarding its probable effects on health in case of consumption. The nature of the microbes responsible for the deterioration (pathogenic or not) does not need to be established. If the food is unfit for consumption it is considered unsafe without further ado and should be treated as such.

8.12.5 Conclusions from sampling

Paragraph 6 of Article 14 addresses the consequences of the finding of an unsafe food. Where any food which is unsafe is part of a batch, lot or consignment of food of the same class or description, it shall be presumed that all the food in that batch, lot or consignment is also unsafe, unless following a detailed assessment there is no evidence that the rest of the batch, lot or consignment is unsafe.

Findings regarding unsafety apply to all foods regarded as 'the same' under this provision until counter proof has been provided.

8.12.6 Foods complying with food safety requirements

What level of contamination with toxins or pathogens renders a food unsafe? In general it has been left to science to answer this question. In many situations however, a generic answer has been laid down in legislation setting levels. Paragraphs 7 (Community provisions) and 9 (member state provisions) address this issue. A food in compliance with legal requirements is considered safe insofar as the aspects covered by these requirements are concerned. In other aspects they may still be unsafe. For example, a food is not unsafe due to pesticide residues if these residues are below the statutory maximum residue limit (MRL). If the same food is however contaminated by other toxins or pathogens it is still unsafe. New scientific data may even indicate that the food in compliance is unsafe because the MRL has been set too high.

To deal with such situations, paragraph 8 indicates that the presumption of safety based on compliance is open to counterproof. Competent authorities may still take measures if they have reason to suspect that despite the conformity, the food is unsafe.

8.12.7 Foods not complying with food safety requirements

Article 14 GFL basically takes a substantive approach to unsafety. Unsafety is determined on the basis of the probable effect. As we have seen above, this substantive approach is somewhat limited by formal statements of safety. Article 14 does *not* however take its consideration with legal provisions so far as to define foods *unsafe* on the basis that they are *not in conformity* with food safety requirements. Article 14 does not say that a food is unsafe if it surpasses an MRL or if it has not passed a required pre-market approval procedure! The ban of Article 14(1) to bring an unsafe food to the market does not apply to such 'illegal' foods if no adverse effect on health is probable.[259] To remain with the example of MRLs, usually in setting these such a wide safety margin is taken into account that indeed a food slightly surpassing the limit can still be safe in the sense that no adverse health effects are probable.

The fact that the ban *of Article 14(1) GFL* does not apply, does not mean however that food businesses are free to bring noncompliant foods to the market. Usually the specific legal framework applying to specific food safety requirements, includes a provision banning noncompliant products from the market. Indeed Article 19 GFL on withdrawal and recall applies to *all* foods not in compliance with food safety requirements. So unlike Article 14 GFL, Article 19 GFL takes a formal rather than a substantive approach to food safety. As a consequence the scope of

[259] Unless one argues that the mere fact of surpassing an MRL constitutes a contamination rendering the food unfit for human consumption in the sense of Article 14(2)(b) GFL.

Article 19 GFL includes all foods not in compliance with Article 14 GFL and all foods not in compliance with other food safety requirements.

Diagram 8.9 sums up the above. The diagram can be read like a decision tree if the aspects in the left-hand column are seen as questions. An affirmative answer takes the reader to the right, a negative answer takes the reader the next step down.

Note that foods qualified as unsafe have not been marked in the column representing Article 14(8) GFL. Member states need to have enforcement powers to demand withdrawal or recall of unsafe products.[260] Article 14 only addresses the fact that compliance with specific food safety requirements in itself does not provide full protection against the exercise of such powers. It does not grant those powers.

8.12.8 Unsafety and risk assessment

Article 14 does not distinguish between products that are inherently unsafe and products that are categorically not unsafe but have been rendered so by their specific condition. Many aspects of unsafety are known. The presence of pathogens, toxins or foreign objects can be established by visual inspection or by testing. Such inspection and testing is done by businesses as part of food hygiene (see Chapter 11) and by inspectors as part of official controls (see Chapter 13). Also with regard to safety, scientific questions may arise requiring risk assessment. If this risk assessment reveals scientific uncertainty as to the safety of a product, authorities can base safeguard measures on the precautionary principle.

8.13 Implementation of the General Food Law

The General Food Law was adopted on 28 January 2002. It was published in the Official Journal on 1 February 2002. Article 62 GFL states that it shall enter into force on the 20th day following that of its publication, therefore on 21 February 2002.

However, some transitory measures have been taken. In its second sentence Article 65 GFL states that the Articles 11, 12, and 14-20 apply from 1 January 2005. These articles are the ones that impose direct obligations on industry.

Article 4 GFL states in its third paragraph that existing food law principles and procedures shall be adapted as soon as possible and by 1 January 2007 at the latest in order to comply with Articles 5 to 10.

No timeframe is given for other legislation that might be necessary to implement the GFL, like the adoption of the definitions. However, it seems reasonable to include these measures in the legislation that has to be in place after 1 January 2007.

[260] See Article 54 Regulation 882/2004.

Diagram 8.9. Categories of unsafe food.

Condition	Qualification		Consequence of Article GFL 14(3)(b) remedy by information	14(8) authority measures	14(1) ban	19 withdrawal recall
Compliance with specific Community food safety requirements						
• Yes	Compliant			X		
• No	Non-compliant					X
• No, not applicable and other aspects				X		
Compliance with specific national food safety requirements						
• Yes	Compliant			X		
• No	Non-compliant					X
• No, not applicable and other aspects				X		
Contamination	Unfit for human consumption	Unsafe (distinguish all consumers and specific category in particular in applying information remedy)				
• Yes					X	X
Putrefaction						
• Yes					X	X
Deterioration						
• Yes					X	X
Decay						
• Yes					X	X
• No						
Immediate adverse health effects	Injurious to health					
• Yes			X		X	X
Short term adverse health effects						
• Yes			X		X	X
Long term adverse health effects						
• Yes			X		X	X
Adverse effects on subsequent generations						
• Yes			X		X	X
Cumulative toxic effects						
• Yes			X		X	X

It is not very common for a regulation to address the legislators in the member states the way the GFL does in Article 4. The form of EU legislation usually used to harmonise national legislation in the member states is the directive. For this reason one can say that a directive lays hidden within the General Food Law. If one looks again at the Action Plan on Food Safety,[261] at action 3 it can be noticed that the initial plan was to propose a General Food Law *Directive*. At the moment of publication of this Action Plan a proposal for this directive must already have been under construction. This proposal for a directive was then turned into a proposal for a regulation retaining much of its directive kind of content.

For some member states this has been confusing. By general theory, the obligations of member states with regard to regulations are to abolish conflicting national legislation, and to create the necessary structures for compliance and enforcement. Transposition of the regulation into national law is deemed forbidden.[262] In case of the General Food Law, this general theory has been overruled by the explicit command in Article 4 to the legislators to implement. A regulation is binding on all addressees including, if they are addressed, legislators.

Also by general theory, European law can impose obligations on national authorities, but whether these authorities acquire the powers needed to fulfil these obligations remains a matter of national law. The preliminary question has been raised with the European Court of Justice as to whether under circumstances national authorities can derive powers directly from an European regulation. The Court ruled on 13 March 2008.[263] Strictly speaking, the Court did not answer the question. It does however strongly reiterate the obligation of member states to comply with EU law, regardless of attribution of the power under national law. The message seems to be: better to *act ultra vires* (beyond the limit of legal powers) infringing national law than to infringe European law by not acting. The question as to whether an obligation implies a power probably remains a matter of national constitutional law.

In food law this issue may be of particular relevance in situations where action is due under Article 7 of the General Food Law (the precautionary principle) but conditions to act under national law are not met.[264]

---

[261] Annex to the White Paper on Food Safety.

[262] This understanding is based on the definition of regulation and on case law such as ECJ 7 February 1972, case 39/72 Commission v. Italy, ECR 1973, p. 101.

[263] ECJ 13 March 2008, cases 383/06-385/06.

[264] For example, in many cases enforcement measures rely on the existence of an infringement of the law, or at least a serious suspicion that one has been committed. This is distinct from scientific uncertainty relating to the safety of a food.

9. Product I: Authorisation requirements

9.1 Introduction

9.1.1 Legislation addressing the product

As indicated in Chapter 7, the major instruments addressing food businesses, are rules regarding the food (product) as such, rules regarding the process (the handling of the product) and rules regarding communication about food. This chapter and the next address the first category: rules regarding the product.

As discussed in Chapter 8, food may only be brought to the market if it is not unsafe. This principle applies *in concreto*. Apart from this legislation exists addressing food *in abstracto*. On a generic basis certain ingredients, organisms or other materials are judged to be marketable or not – mainly for reasons of unsafety.

German scholars distinguish two approaches to food law which they call the 'principle of abuse' and the 'prohibition principle with reservation of permission'.[265] If the former principle applies, food businesses are free in their actions but will be held responsible if they infringe the general norm of food safety. In other words the food is considered not to be categorically unsafe. If the latter principle applies, putting the food on the market is forbidden unless an express permission has been obtained. The food is considered categorically unsafe (until authorities decide otherwise).[266]

If the law does not explicitly state otherwise, the former principle applies. In other words in the absence of a prohibition freedom of choice applies. The number of prohibitions is however continuously increasing.

While we do not oppose the German approach, in this book we distinguish not two but four legislative approaches to food as such. The use and/or presence of ingredients, organisms or other materials in food can be free, conditional restricted or banned (Diagram 9.1). Food businesses are free to use any conventional ingredients having a history of safe use, for several innovative foods a requirement applies that their safety has to be approved before they may be brought to the market; for many substances or organisms known to pose food safety risks safety limits apply like the maximum residue limits of pesticides and veterinary drugs.

---

[265] Translation by Margret Will and Doris Guenther, Food Quality and Safety Standards, 2nd edition GTZ 2007, p. 16. For a hyperlink to this e-book see the reference list.

[266] In the USA scholars call this approach 'precautionary'. In the transatlantic debate this leads to some confusion. The precautionary principle as defined in Article 7 GFL deals with scientific uncertainty (which may warrant banning a product from the market). This precautionary approach requires scientific certainty (before the product may come to the market).

Finally, for some materials the food safety risk is judged to be such that they may not be used for and/or be present in food products at all.

Diagram 9.1. Product legislation.

Legislative approach	Example
Free	conventional ingredients with a history of safe use in the EU
Conditional	• additives • sweeteners • supplements • genetically modified foods • (other) novel foods
Restricted	• residues of pesticides • residues of veterinary drugs • (other) contaminants
Banned	• BSE risk material • zero tolerance residues / contaminants

This chapter addresses the first two categories indicated in Diagram 9.1 with an emphasis on the second. The next chapter addresses the last two categories indicated in Diagram 9.1 with an emphasis on the third.

9.1.2 Pre-market approval

The European legislator seems to work from the presumption that conventional foods, that is to say foods that have a tradition of use in the EU, can be considered safe unless new scientific findings indicate otherwise. In that case it is up to the legislator or in urgent situations to the executive to take action to protect safety. For other products, that is products that are in some way artificial or new, the safety must be proven before they may come to the market. The proof of safety is a matter of *science*. The presumption of safety of conventional foods may be understood as a mixture of *experience* as a knowledge base and of political realism. If a product has been consumed by many people for a significant period of time, apparently without doing them harm this may be a reasonable basis to consider them safe. On the other hand the legislator would probably overstep the limits of his democratic legitimacy if he would try to take off the market products known to create food safety risks but that many consumers are unwilling to give up (like alcohol and coffee). In this situation authorities have no alternative but to provide the consumer with the relevant information and leave it to the consumer to decide about consumption.

9.1.3 Positive lists

Among the earliest EEC legislation on food, is legislation on colourants. 'EEC Council Directive on the approximation of the rules of the Member States concerning the colouring matters authorised for use in foodstuffs intended for human consumption',[267] set out to establish a single list of colouring matters whose use is authorised for colouring foodstuffs and to lay down criteria of purity which those colouring matters must satisfy. Thus the first list was created of food products of a certain type that could be used, while products not on the list could not be used. This is a so-called positive list. The law does not say what is forbidden leaving the rest free as it usually does, but says what is allowed making the rest forbidden. The list is a part of the law (in this case an annex to the directive). To later include a product in the list (delete a product from the list or adapt the list in some other way) the law must be changed by the applicable procedure.

While the details differ greatly, this system of positive lists set by the law is still the core mechanism of pre-market approval schemes in EU food law. Below we discuss the major schemes: additives (section 9.2), food supplements (section 9.3), novel foods (section 9.4), genetically modified foods (section 9.5), functional foods as far as relevant are also discussed (section 9.6). A few other approval schemes are mentioned but not discussed (section 9.7). The chapter ends with some general observations on pre-market approval schemes (section 9.8) and an overview of developments regarding proposals for new legislation (section 9.9).

9.2 Additives[268]

9.2.1 The Additives Framework Directive: definition and general principles

At present, the basic provision setting the rules and procedures on additives is the Additives Framework Directive (89/107) on the approximation of the laws of the Member States concerning food additives authorised for use in foodstuffs intended for human consumption. There the definition of additives is given (Law text box 9.1).

[267] The uniform numbering system of European legislation did not yet exist. The directive was published in Official Journal 115, 11 November1962, pp. 2645-2654.

[268] Many thanks to Mr. Ronald Verbruggen (director Orbyte bvba; consultant Food regulatory and scientific affairs), who wrote the section on additives in the previous edition of this book. The authors updated and amended his text.

Law Text Box 9.1. Definition of 'additive'.

Article 2 Framework Directive 89/107
Definition of additive
any substance not normally consumed as a food in itself and not normally used as a characteristic ingredient of food whether or not it has nutritive value, the intentional addition of which to food for a technological purpose in the manufacture, processing, preparation, treatment, packaging, transport or storage of such food results, or may be reasonably expected to result, in it or its by-products becoming directly or indirectly a component of such foods.[1]

[1] This definition can be criticised; particularly when compared with the definition of processing aids in the same directive (see Law text box 9.2). These two definitions have clearly been modelled on the pre-existing definitions of Codex Alimentarius, although there are slight differences. One of the main problems with these definitions is that additives and processing aids are not clearly distinguished. This leads the authorities to classify certain processing aids as additives. Yet, there is considerable resistance to changing basic definitions, even in the face of their flawed logic.

Paraphrasing the definition one could call an additive a substance added to food for a technological purpose. In its Annex I the Additives Framework Directive sets out a comprehensive list of 24 categories of food additives.[269]

Some examples of coined names of additives categories are:
- anti-oxidants;
- preservatives;
- colours;
- sweeteners;
- emulsifiers;
- gelling agents; and
- anti-caking agents.

The food additives category descriptors refer to the technological function that the members of that category generally exert in food.

The legislation on additives is built on positive lists. As explained above, these are exhaustive lists that indicate which additives may be used in which food product and – many times – at which maximum level.[270] Any material not listed as authorised in the Food Additive Directives is prohibited as a food additive.

An amendment to the Additives Framework Directive (94/34) authorises member states to maintain a prohibition of certain additives in the production of certain

[269] It shall be noted that the concept of '*additive*' is being used for other products, e.g. for feed. Yet, for feed, the meaning of '*additive*' is quite different, and – at variance with food additives – includes a great many enzymes, micro-organisms, and coccidiostats.
[270] See however hereafter the concept of QS.

foodstuffs considered *traditional*. Such an exception was requested by Germany with a view to prevent the use of intense sweeteners in beers brewed according to the *Reinheitsgebot*.[271] Vigorous opposition from many sides led finally to the permission for all member states to make exemptions for 'traditional' foodstuffs from the horizontal legislation on additives in general; not just on sweeteners. In order to cope with the problem that EU law did not define *'traditional'*, the Commission published a Decision (292/97) listing for once and for all which foodstuffs can claim the exception *'traditional'* from the additive rules.[272]

9.2.2 Authorisation of additives

Authorisation of a new additive requires the EU legislator (Commission, Parliament and Council working together) to amend the directive holding the applicable positive list.

Before a substance is added to the list of additives it is subject to a safety assessment by EFSA. It must be demonstrated that there is a technological need, that there is no safety hazard for the consumer, and that the consumer is not misled when an additive is being used (Diagram 9.2). If a substance is approved it is assigned an E number. A food additive acquires its E number by being mentioned with an E number in an additives directive.[273] The E number can be used to draw up the ingredient list for the label on food products that contain the additive. However, the full name may be used as well instead of the E number.[274]

Diagram 9.2. Criteria for the authorisation of food additives.

Authorisation criteria	
Presence	Technological need
Absence	Safety hazard Misleading

Authorisations are generic. This means that food legislation does not limit the use of approved additives to the business that applied for approval.[275] All food businesses may use approved additives under the same conditions.

271 See Chapter 7.

272 A consolidated version of the Additives Framework Directive can be found in Eur-Lex. For the hyperlink see the reference list. The Decision with the list of 'traditional' foodstuffs however (292/97) is NOT part of that file.

273 The E numbers therefore are neither granted by a separate legislative act, nor by a scientific advisory committee (such as EFSA, the former SCF, etc.).

274 See also Chapter 12 on labelling.

275 If the additive is also patented the owner may bar other businesses from using the additive on the basis of patent law.

9.2.3 The additive authorising directives

Historically, additives authorisation directives, after the framework directive, were drawn up in three packs; first came sweeteners. They were followed by colours. And finally all the others were issued under the common name of 'miscellaneous additives' (*'food additives other than colours and sweeteners'*). The *'Miscellaneous Additives'* Directives comprise many functions. The two former groups each hold only one function. Some materials can occur in more than one function. For example, the polyols (such as sorbitol and xylitol) are listed both as sweeteners, and as humectants in the *'Miscellaneous Additives'* Directives.

9.2.4 Sweeteners directives

The Sweeteners Directive (94/35) has been amended four times. The first amendment (96/83) essentially filled gaps left in the first directive, and clarified some of the concepts. In 2003 an amendment was issued (2003/115), essentially in order to introduce two new sweetener compounds: sucralose, and the acesulfame-aspartame salt.[276]

9.2.5 Colours directive

The Colours Directive (94/36) has never been updated. It is not expected that new colours will be added in the near future.

9.2.6 'Miscellaneous Additives' directives

The *'Miscellaneous Additives'* holds many more additives than the two other directives. Where 15 sweeteners are authorised for use, and some 32 colours, *'Miscellaneous Additives'* authorises the use of close to 300 additives. The original Directive (95/2) has been amended seven times by 96/85 – 98/72 – 2000/5 – 2003/52 – 1882/2003 – 2003/114 – 2006/52[277]. The first three were the usual type of amendments, granting additional authorisations.

Directive 2003/52 is a bit unusual in that it prohibits one specific additive – E 425 konjac – in jelly confectionery, in order to prevent a risk of choking, due to the strong swelling of konjac when it absorbs water.

One of the novelties in the update 2003/114 is that it introduces the additives necessary for preparation, storage, and use of flavourings into the system. This

[276] A consolidated version of the Sweeteners Directives can be found in Eur-Lex. For the hyperlink see the reference list.

[277] A consolidated version of the *'Miscellaneous Additives'* Directive can be found in Eur-Lex. For the hyperlink see the reference list.

satisfies a longstanding request from the flavourings industry, in order to avoid problems occurring earlier. For years the flavourings industry has felt handicapped by the fact that, in flavourings, a number of additives were used for which no formal EU authorisations were ever given. Consequently this became a grey area for their labelling in the ingredient list.

9.2.7 Specifications: criteria of purity and identity

The EU has issued specifications (criteria of purity) for most additives authorised, in a set of several directives with amendments.

9.2.8 Additional general issues, safety, and principles

For the practitioner, the tables annexed to the directives, holding the lists of authorisations, are the main part. The Additives Framework Directive is the overarching text and is therefore the right place to establish the principles and give explanations of the concepts. Nevertheless, as the authorising directives were written, complements on concepts were added to these directives as well.

Two concepts clarified in that way are:

- '*Carry over*' which means that an additive may lawfully occur in a compound foodstuff to the extent that it is permitted in one of its ingredients. Under '*reverse carry over*' an additive may not occur in a food for direct consumption, or not occur at the level under consideration, but will be lawfully accepted if it is used in a raw material or in an intermediate, used solely in the preparation of a compound foodstuff, and to the extent that the resulting compound foodstuff conforms to the authorisations given in the directives. Those two carry over notions are expressed in the Colours Directive (Art. 3), as well as in the '*Miscellaneous Additives' Directive* (Art. 3(1)). Note though that the term '*carry over*' itself is not even mentioned in those Articles. The term appears however in the tables, for specific additives.
- '*Quantum satis*' (QS): The legislators have accepted this concept from Belgian law for a number of authorisations. It means that '*...no maximum level is specified. However additives shall be used in accordance with Good Manufacturing Practice (GMP), i.e. at a level not higher than is necessary to achieve the intended purpose and provided that they do not mislead the consumer*'. The notion is defined in Article 2(8) of the '*Miscellaneous Additives*' Directive and identically in Art. 2(7) of the Colours Directive. Remarkably, QS is also used, but not defined, in the Sweeteners Directive. There is no doubt, however, that the same interpretation is to be applied there.

9.2.9 Processing aids

As indicated above processing aids are outside the scope of the directives on additives. As we shall see below they are also outside the scope of the GM-package. We shall see in chapter 12 that to a large extent they are outside the scope of labelling legislation as well. See law text box 9.2 for a definition of processing aid.[278]

Law text box 9.2. Definition of 'processing aid' in Directive 89/107 (footnote to Article 1).

Article 1 Directive 89/107 footnote
Definition of processing aid
For the purpose of this Directive, 'processing aid' means any substance not consumed as a food ingredient by itself, intentionally used in the processing of raw materials, foods or their ingredients, to fulfil a certain technological purpose during treatment or processing and which may result in the unintentional but technically unavoidable presence of residues of the substance or its derivatives in the final product, provided that these residues do not present any health risk and do not have any technological effect on the finished product.

Processing aids are somewhat of an enigma in food law. It is not even entirely certain if they come within the definition of food. On the one hand processing aids may be reasonably expected to be ingested by humans but on the other hand if they are, maybe they must be seen as residues or contaminants that are outside the definition of food.[279] In any case their presence may not render a food unsafe.

For one type of processing aid an approval regime exists that we will however not discuss in this book: extraction solvents are regulated by Council Directive of 13 June 1988 on the approximation of the laws of the Member States on extraction solvents used in the production of foodstuffs and food ingredients (88/344).[280]

---

[278] The European Commission has proposed a new definition: 'processing aid' shall mean any substance which: (1) is not consumed as a food by itself; (2) is intentionally used in the processing of raw materials, foods or their ingredients, to fulfil a certain technological purpose during treatment or processing; and (3) may result in the unintentional but technically unavoidable presence in the final product of residues of the substance or its derivatives provided they do not present any health risk and do not have any technological effect on the final product'. Amended proposal for a Regulation of the European Parliament and of the Council on food additives 24.10.2007 COM(2007) 673 final.
[279] See: Article 2(h) GFL.
[280] Official Journal L 157, 24 June 1988, p. 28. For the hyperlink to a consolidated version see the reference list.

9.3 Food supplements

9.3.1 General

Another category to which a system of positive lists applies are food supplements. Food supplements are governed by Directive 2002/46 of the European Parliament and of the Council of 10 June 2002 on the approximation of the laws of the Member States relating to food supplements,[281] or more precisely by the national legislation implementing this directive.[282] In Article 2 the directive defines food supplements. See Law text box 9.3.

Law text box 9.3. Definitions in Article 2 Directive 2002/46/EC.

Article 2 Directive 2002/46

For the purposes of this Directive:

(a) 'food supplements' means foodstuffs the purpose of which is to supplement the normal diet and which are concentrated sources of nutrients or other substances with a nutritional or physiological effect, alone or in combination, marketed in dose form, namely forms such as capsules, pastilles, tablets, pills and other similar forms, sachets of powder, ampoules of liquids, drop dispensing bottles, and other similar forms of liquids and powders designed to be taken in measured small unit quantities.

(b) 'nutrients' means the following substances:

(i) vitamins,

(ii) minerals.

In short, food supplements are additional doses of vitamins, minerals and other substances. The directive has two annexes. One listing the vitamins and minerals that may be used in the production of food supplements and one giving the form in which they may be used.

The lists are generic. If a vitamin or mineral is included in the lists everyone is entitled to include them in food supplements. On the basis of Article 4(8) of the directive, the Commission can propose expanding its scope beyond vitamins and minerals.

9.3.2 Authorisation

The procedure for including other vitamins or minerals in the list is easier than the one that applies to additives. According to Article 5(5) of the directive, the

281 Official Journal L 183, 12 July 2002, p.51.

282 The country reports in EFFL/1/2006 are dedicated to the implementation of this directive in the member states. For a hyperlink to EFFL's homepage see the reference list.

lists can be modified through comitology. Also applying this procedure minimum and maximum amounts can be set per daily portion as recommended by the manufacturer.[283] The directive does not give any *criteria* for authorisation of vitamins or minerals.

9.3.3 Monitoring

To facilitate efficient monitoring of food supplements, member states may require food businesses to notify the competent authorities of the placing on the market by forwarding it a model of the label used for the product.[284]

9.4 Novel foods

9.4.1 Concept

Food products and ingredients[285] that have not been used to a significant degree for human consumption within the EU prior to passage of the Novel Foods Regulation 258/97[286] (15 May 1997), are so-called novel foods. They have to pass a safety assessment before they may be brought to the market.

The Novel Foods Regulation signifies an important step in the development of pre-market approval schemes in EU food law. The scheme is not limited to foods with a certain function but potentially covers a wide spectrum of products. Article 1 of the Novel Foods Regulation specifies four categories of novel foods, see Law text box 9.4 for the specifications.

Law text box 9.4. Definition of 'novel foods', Article 1(2) Novel Foods Regulation 258/97.

Article 1(2) Novel Foods Regulation 258/97
This Regulation shall apply to the placing on the market within the Community of foods and food ingredients which have not hitherto been used for human consumption to a significant degree within the Community and which fall under the following categories:
(c) foods and food ingredients with a new or intentionally modified primary molecular structure;
(d) foods and food ingredients consisting of or isolated from micro-organisms, fungi or algae;

[283] Article 5 Directive 2002/46.
[284] Article 10 Directive 2002/46.
[285] In the Novel Foods Regulation ingredients are separately mentioned. This is explained by the fact that this regulation pre-dates the General Food Law and its definition of food. An ingredient meets the definition of food and therefore would no longer need to be mentioned separately.
[286] Regulation (EC) No 258/97 of the European Parliament and of the Council of 27 January 1997 concerning novel foods and novel food ingredients, Official Journal L 43, 14 February1997, p. 1. Article 15: entry into force 90 days following its publication in the Official Journal.

(e) foods and food ingredients consisting of or isolated from plants and food ingredients isolated from animals, except for foods and food ingredients obtained by traditional propagating or breeding practices and having a history of safe food use;

(f) foods and food ingredients to which has been applied a production process not currently used, where that process gives rise to significant changes in the composition or structure of the foods or food ingredients which affect their nutritional value, metabolism or level of undesirable substances.

Until 18 April 2004, genetically modified foods were mentioned as (a) and (b). As from this date the lemmas (a) and (b) are deleted and a separate regime applies for GM foods.

This definitions seems to have aimed initially to cover *all* new food *products*, whether originating from animals, plants or micro-organisms, but only those new *processing* methods that have the effects mentioned sub c and f.

Foods can be considered new in two different ways. They may be the result of technical innovation and may not have existed before anywhere in the world or they may be known as food elsewhere in the world and be new only to the EU. The latter novel foods are often referred to as 'exotic'.

New breeds of plants or animals are exempt if they are propagated/bred in a normal way from 'conventional' parents. Innovations consisting of new combinations of conventional (or approved) ingredients are outside the scope of the regulation.

Article 2(1) of the Novel Foods Regulation further exempts from its scope additives, flavourings and extraction solvents. These products have their own regulatory framework as discussed above.

As from 2004 genetically modified organisms are also outside the scope of the Novel Foods Regulation. Even though one could argue that after the deletion of lemmas (a) and (b) in Article 1 of the Novel Foods Regulation, they still fall within the scope of the other lemmas, the specific regulations on GM food take precedence over the more general Novel Foods Regulation.[287]

For foods that existed before 15 May 1997, it is crucial to establish if they have been consumed within the Community (including the member states that acceded after this date) to a significant degree before that date. The criterion as worded in the regulation is however rather vague.

In a case where among other things the novelty of a food was at issue, the ECJ has been asked to clarify the concept. On 3 February 2005, the Advocate-General

[287] In legalese: *lex specialis derogat legi generali*. In English: the specific law takes precedence over the general law.

delivered an interesting opinion on the condition set in Article 1(2) of the Novel Foods Regulation:

> *'This condition consists of two elements: a time element and a quantitative element. As regards the time element, the parties in the main proceedings, the Member States that have made observations and the Commission all agree that it refers to the date of entry into force of the regulation, that is, 15 May 1997. I share this view. As regards the quantitative element 'not ... used ... to a significant degree within the Community', opinions differ somewhat. In my view, in order to interpret this element reference should be made to the purpose of Article 1(2) of the regulation. This provision is aimed at restricting the substantive scope of the regulation to 'novel' products. In fact, a product which, when the regulation entered into force, was already being marketed in one or more Member States and thus was available to the consumer was being used for human consumption to a significant degree and thus could not be novel. It therefore seems to me that the test should be the product's being on the market, a requirement which has the additional advantage of being simple and objectively verifiable. This leads me to the following answer:*
>
> *Foods, within the meaning of Article 1(2) of Regulation No 258/97, are not used to a significant degree within the Community, if upon the entry into force of that regulation they were not on the market in one or more Member States. The reference date for determining the degree of significance of human consumption of the food in question is 15 May 1997'.*

This interpretation clarifies an important concept in the definition of novel food. Unfortunately, the Court in its ruling did not, at least not explicitly, adopt the interpretation the Advocate General proposed. Instead it gave a more ambiguous interpretation.

The Court ruled:[288]

> *'Article 1(2) of Regulation (EC) No 258/97 of the European Parliament and of the Council of 27 January 1997 concerning novel foods and novel food ingredients is to be interpreted as meaning that a food or a food ingredient has not been used for human consumption to a significant degree within the Community if, when all the circumstances of the case are taken into account, it is established that that food or that food ingredient has not been consumed in a significant quantity by humans in any of the Member States before the reference date. 15 May 1997 is the reference date for the purpose of determining the extent of human consumption of that food or food ingredient'.*

[288] ECJ 9 June 2005, Joined Cases C-211/03, C-299/03, C-316/03, C-317/03 and C-318/03. HLH Warenvertriebs GmbH and Orthica BV v. Bundesrepublik Deutschland. Official Journal C193, 6 August 2005, p. 4.

The Court explains the vague term 'significant degree' by substituting it for another vague term 'significant quantity'. This interpretation is closer to the text than the one proposed by the Advocate General, but less clarifying.

9.4.2 Authorisation

Before being placed on the market, novel foods must undergo a safety assessment after which an authorisation decision may be taken.[289]

The criteria to judge the marketability of novel foods are laid down in Article 3(1) of the Novel Foods Regulation (Diagram 9.3):

Foods and food ingredients falling within the scope of this Regulation must not:
- present a danger for the consumer;
- mislead the consumer;
- differ from foods or food ingredients which they are intended to replace to such an extent that their normal consumption would be nutritionally disadvantageous for the consumer.

Diagram 9.3. Criteria for the authorisation of novel foods.

Authorisation criteria	
Absence	Danger for consumer Misleading Nutritional disadvantage

The assessment procedure is divided into two stages. An initial stage at member state level, in most cases followed by an additional stage at Community level.

Under the assessment procedure, the competent body of the member state, which receives an application for pre-market approval, must make an initial assessment and determine whether an additional assessment is required. If it is found that no additional assessment is required, and neither the Commission nor a member state raises an objection, the applicant will be informed that s/he may place the product on the market. In other cases[290] the Commission must take an authorisation decision with the assistance of the Standing Committee on the Food Chain and Animal Health.

[289] Guidance for the submission of an application is given in: Commission Recommendation 97/618/EC of 29 July 1997 concerning the scientific aspects and the presentation of information necessary to support applications for the placing on the market of novel foods and novel food ingredients and the preparation of initial assessment reports under Regulation (EC) No 258/97 of the European Parliament and of the Council. Official Journal L 253, 16 September 1997, pp. 1-36.
[290] Experience shows that this constitutes virtually all cases.

The authorisation decision defines the scope of the authorisation and specifies, as appropriate, the conditions of use, the designation of the food or food ingredient, its specification and the specific labelling requirements.

The authorisation is specific. It only gives the applicant the right to market the novel food concerned. If another business wants to market the same food it also has to apply for an authorisation. In this situation a simplified procedure applies. An example of a novel food that has been approved repeatedly is noni juice. Noni juice is an exotic fruit juice originating in Southeast Asia and new to the EU market.[291]

The regulation lays down specific requirements concerning the labelling of these foodstuffs. The following must be mentioned:

- any characteristics such as composition, nutritional value or the intended use of the new foodstuff which renders it no longer equivalent to an existing food;
- the presence of materials which may have implications for the health of some individuals;
- the presence of materials which give rise to ethical concerns.

This is in addition to the general requirements on labelling discussed in Chapter 12.

Example

A well-known example of an approved novel food is Becel Pro Activ; a spreadable fat with a blood cholesterol lowering[1] effect. See Commission Decision 2000/500 of 24 July 2000.

[1] Hence bcl, the abbreviation that turned into a name.

9.5 Genetically modified foods

9.5.1 Introduction

A special category of novel foods, which since 2004 is subject to a separate regulatory framework, are genetically modified organisms (GMOs) (including micro organisms) used for human consumption (GM food). GM foods need an authorisation on the basis of a double safety assessment before they may be brought to the market. They need an authorisation for the deliberate release into the environment, under the criteria laid down in Directive 2001/18 and an authorisation for use in food and/or feed under the criteria laid down in Regulation 1829/2003.

[291] The applications and the list of approved (or rejected) novel foods are available on the Internet. For the hyperlink see the reference list.

GM food represents a highly contested area in food law. It has fairly recently been modernised and as no further proposals for modifications are on the table, it is likely to keep its present shape for the years to come. For these reasons we will devote a little more attention to GM food than we have to the other food categories discussed in this chapter, thus treating GM as the most important example of the EU system of pre-market approval schemes.[292]

9.5.2 The GM package

On 18 April 2004 the core provisions of the current EU regulatory framework for genetically modified food products came into force. They supplemented some existing provisions and were fleshed out by some further texts. At present the framework is more or less finalised and the first experiences with it have been undergone.

The EU regulatory framework on GM-food now consists of several regulations of the Council and the European Parliament, regulations of the Commission and directives (Diagram 9.4).

Diagram 9.4. The GM package.

EU legislation on GM food

- The most important text surviving from the situation prior to 2004, is *Directive 2001/18* on the deliberate release into the environment of genetically modified organisms (OJ 2001 L 106/1). It regulates experimental releases and the placing on the market of genetically modified organisms. This directive has been amended by Decision 2002/623; Regulation 1829/2003 and Regulation 1830/2003.
- The core of the regulatory framework is *Regulation 1829/2003* on GM food and feed (OJ 2003 L 268/1). It regulates the placing on the market of food and feed products containing or consisting of GMOs and provides for the labelling of such products to the final consumer.
- *Regulation 1830/2003* on traceability and labelling of GMOs and the traceability of food and feed products from GMOs (OJ 2003 L 268/24) further elaborates the standards set in *Regulation 1829/2003* on labelling and adds a specific regime on traceability for GMOs, departing from the general traceability regime in the GFL.[1]

[292] In writing this section use has been made of previous publications, in particular: B M.J. van der Meulen, The new EU regulatory framework for GM food (Part I) Procedural aspects: safety assessment, authorisation and administrative review, Journal of International Biotechnology Law (JIBL) Vol. 02, 1, 2005, pp. 117-122; The new EU regulatory framework for GM food (Part II) Traceability, labelling & enforcement, JIBL Vol. 02, 1, 2005, pp. 158-162 (for the website of JIBL see the reference list); B.M.J. van der Meulen, Regulating GM food: three levels, three issues, in: Han Somsen (ed.) The Regulatory Challenge of Biotechnology. Human Genetics, Food and Patents, Biotechnology Regulation Series, Edward Elgar, Cheltenham UK/Northampton, MA, USA, 2007, pp. 139-155; and Bernd van der Meulen, The EU Regulatory Approach to GM Foods, The Kansas Journal of Law & Public Policy, Volume XVI Nr. 3, pp. 286-323.

- Commission *Regulation 65/2004* establishes a system for the development and assignment of unique identifiers for genetically modified organisms (OJ 2004, L 10/5). This system is used in the traceability regime introduced in Regulation 1830/2003.
- Commission *Regulation 641/2004* (OJ 2004, L 102/14) on the detailed rules for the implementation of Regulation 1829/2003, elaborates the authorisation procedure.
- For the sake of completeness one more directive, one more regulation and one recommendation have to be mentioned that are relevant for GMOs, but fall outside the scope of this book. Directive 90/219/EEC, as amended by Directive 98/81/EC, on the contained use of genetically modified micro-organisms (GMMs). This Directive regulates research and industrial work activities involving GMMs (such as genetically modified viruses or bacteria) under conditions of containment, i.e. in a closed environment in which contact with the population and the environment is avoided. This includes work activities in laboratories. Regulation 1946/2003 on transboundary movements of genetically modified organisms, implements the Cartagena Protocol on Biosafety.
- Commission Recommendation C (2003) 2624 (OJ 2003 L 189/36) on guidelines for national strategies and best practices to ensure coexistence provides Member States with policy options to protect conventional agriculture from GM admixture.

[1] See Chapter 8.

9.5.3 Novel Foods and GMOs

The legislation discussed in this section takes GM foods outside the scope of the Novel Foods Regulation and provides them with their own regulatory framework. This legislation is *lex specialis*, so, as far as it applies, the Novel Foods Regulation no longer applies unless this Regulation applies for another reason.[293] To this effect, recital 11 of Regulation 1829/2003 states, *inter alia*:

> *(F)oods covered by an authorisation granted under this Regulation will be exempted from the requirements of Regulation (EC) No 258/97 concerning novel foods and novel food ingredients, except where they fall under one or more of the categories referred to in Article 1(2)(a*[294]*) of Regulation (EC) No 258/97 in respect of a characteristic which has not been considered for the purpose of the authorisation granted under this Regulation.*

9.5.4 Environmental approval

History has shown that the balance in the natural environment from co-evolution is vulnerable to alien species. When man started to roam the globe, in his wake he wrought environmental disaster by accidental or intentional introduction of

[293] For example, if an exotic food (i.e. a food having a history of use only outside the EU) would be genetically modified, or if a novel technical process (e.g. high pressure processing the foodstuff) would be applied to a GMO, then both sets of rules would apply simultaneously.

[294] The reference to lemma (a) in Article 1(2) is obviously a mistake and should be read as (c)-(f).

foreign plants and animals into each new environment. Today, protective (sanitary and phytosanitary) measures try to avoid further damage.

It is conceivable that genetic engineering results in new species to which the environment proves vulnerable.[295] Protective measures have been agreed upon at the global level (na protocol[296]) and have also been taken in the EU. On 8 May 1990 Directive of 23 April 1990 on the deliberate release into the environment of genetically modified organisms (90/220) was published in its Official Journal.[297] This Directive was replaced by the current Directive 2001/18.[298]

This, the latter Directive is subdivided in four parts, A through D. Part A contains general provisions. Part B addresses the deliberate release of GMOs for any other purpose than for placing on the market. Part C deals with placing GMOs as such or in products on the market. Part D contains final provisions. The Directive takes a 'no unless' approach to GMOs. Releases into the environment are prohibited unless specifically approved, under procedures outlined in Part B (commonly used with a view to field trials). Part C of the Directive is the most important part with regard to GM foods.

The regular procedure first requires notification of the competent authority in the member state where the GMO is to be placed on the market for the first time.[299] This authority informs the Commission and the other member states. The competent authority assesses the notification.[300] At this point, the subsequent procedure depends upon whether the assessment report is favourable or not and whether other member states file objections or not. If the competent authority concludes that the GMO must not be placed on the market, the notification is rejected. If the report is favourable and no objections are made, the competent authority gives consent for a renewable maximum period of ten years.

---

295 It would be conceivable, for example, that resistance to certain natural enemies ('pests') or herbicides provides GMOs with an edge over natural species or human attempts to redress an unwanted situation.

296 Official Journal L 201, 2002, p. 50.

297 Council Directive of 23 April 1990 on the deliberate release into the environment of genetically modified organisms (90/220/EEC). Official Journal L 117, 1990, p. 15.

298 Directive 2001/18/EC of the European Parliament and of the Council of March 12, 2001 on the deliberate release into the environment of genetically modified organisms and repealing Council Directive 90/220/EEC. Official Journal L 106, 2001, p. 1; see also Daniel Lawrence, *et al.*, New Controls on the Deliberate Release of GMOs, European Environmental Law Review, pp. 51-56 (Feb. 2002).

299 Article 13 Directive 2001/18.

300 Article 14 Directive 2001/18.

In case of objections, the decision shall be taken in comitology.[301] Member states may not prohibit, restrict, or impede placement of GMOs on the market – as or in products – which comply with the requirements of Directive 2001/18.[302]

9.5.5 Food approval

Article 4(2) of Regulation 1829/2003 gives a general prohibition on GMOs on the market for food use unless the particular GMO is covered by an authorisation and the conditions to this authorisation are satisfied. The whole regulatory framework for pre-market approval for GM-food is built as a set of exceptions to this prohibition.

Scope
The authorisation requirements of Regulation 1829/2003 apply to: a) GMOs for food use; b) food containing or consisting of GMOs; and c) food produced from or containing ingredients produced from GMOs.[303]

The first two are straightforward; however, the concept 'produced *from*' may raise some questions. This concept can be understood to mean highly refined food (ingredients) made from GMOs, but no longer containing proteins or DNA (like soy oil or maize oil).[304] In theory, processing aids fall outside the scope of the Regulation. The Regulation does not apply to food produced *with* GM enzymes. Recital 16 of Regulation 1829/2003 reads:

> *This Regulation should cover food and feed produced 'from' a GMO but not food and feed [produced] 'with' a GMO. The determining criterion is whether or not material derived from the genetically modified source material is present in the food or in the feed. Processing aids which are only used during the food or feed production process are not covered by the definition[305] of food or feed and, therefore, are not included in the scope of this Regulation. Nor are food and feed which are manufactured with the help of a genetically modified processing aid included in the scope of this Regulation. Thus, products obtained from animals fed with genetically modified feed or treated with genetically modified medicinal*

[301] Articles 18 and 30 Directive 2001/18.
[302] Article 22 Directive 2001/18.
[303] Article 3 Regulation 1829/2003.
[304] This requirement raises some discussion on the question of what a GMO is and whether processing can remove this quality from a product. In particular in the USA it seems to have been argued that a GMO is no longer a GMO if the modified genes are no longer present.
[305] This assumption is debatable. Remember the definition of food in Article 2 of the GFL discussed in Chapter 2: 'For the purposes of this Regulation, "food" (or "foodstuff") means any substance or product, whether processed, partially processed or unprocessed, intended to be, or reasonably expected to be ingested by humans'. Processing aids are not intended to be ingested by humans, but depending upon the specific processing aid in question traces or residues may be expected to be ingested. This does not, however, alter the scope of Regulation 1829/2003.

products will be subject neither to the authorisation requirements nor to the labelling requirements referred to in this Regulation.

9.5.6 Application procedure

According to Article 5 of Regulation 1829/2003, an authorisation is granted exclusively on the basis of an application. Regulation 1829/2003 gives some requirements for the application procedure, which have been further elaborated in Commission Regulation 641/2004.

Criteria

The Regulation stipulates that GM food/feed must not: 'have adverse effects on human health, animal health, or the environment; mislead the consumer; or differ from the food/feed it is intended to replace to such an extent that its normal consumption would be nutritionally disadvantageous for the consumer/animals'[306] (Diagram 9.5). The burden of proof is on the applicant.

Diagram 9.5. Criteria for the authorisation of GM foods.

Authorisation criteria	
Absence	Adverse effects on health
	Adverse effects on the environment
	Misleading
	Nutritional disadvantage

The applicant

The applicant must define the scope of the application, indicate which parts are confidential,[307] and must include a monitoring plan, a labelling proposal and a detection method for the new GM food or feed.[308] S/he must present copies of available studies that have been carried out and any other available material demonstrating that the GM food complies with the mentioned criteria.[309] Applications are to be submitted to the competent authority of the member state where the GM food product will be marketed first.[310]

'One door one key'

The GM regulatory framework is based on the 'one door one key' principle. This phrase contains several elements. First, authorisation for GM foods is valid throughout the Community. Unlike, for instance, pharmaceutical products, there

306 Article 4 Regulation 1829/2003.
307 Article 30 Regulation 1829/2003.
308 Articles 2 and 3 Commission Regulation 641/2004.
309 Article 5(3) Regulation 1829/2003.
310 Article 5 Regulation 1829/2003.

is no need to acquire authorisation from each member state where the product is brought to market. Second, Regulation 1829/2003 makes it possible to file a single application for obtaining both the authorisation under Directive 2001/18 for release into the environment and the authorisation under Regulation 1829/2003 for placement on the market as a food or feed.[311] However, the applicant may also choose to follow two separate procedures. S/he may, for instance, want to perform field tests long before an authorisation for food use is relevant. Third, this single application is followed by a single risk *assessment* process, for which EFSA is responsible, and a single risk *management* process, involving both the Commission and the member states through a regulatory committee procedure.[312]

Finally, if a product is likely to be used as both a food and a feed, it must be authorised for both or not at all.[313] A single application shall be submitted and shall give rise to a single opinion from EFSA and a single Community decision.[314] A single authorisation is given for a GMO and all its possible uses, thus insuring against a repeat of the US experience with Starlink maize.[315]

The national competent authority

Compared to the Novel Foods Regulation, the role of the national authorities with regard to these applications is very limited. It does not go far beyond that of a post box. They receive applications[316] and must both acknowledge receipt of applications in writing within fourteen days and inform EFSA.[317] The application, and any supplementary information supplied by the applicant, must be made available to EFSA, which is responsible for a scientific risk assessment covering both environmental risks and a human and animal health safety assessment.

EFSA may ask national authorities to carry out risk assessments.[318] EFSA may also ask 'a competent authority designated in accordance with Article 4 of Directive 2001/18/EC' to carry out an environmental risk assessment. EFSA is even under an obligation to do so 'if the application concerns GMOs to be used as seeds or other plant-propagating material.

Opinion of EFSA

EFSA receives the application and any supplementary information supplied by the applicant from the national authorities. EFSA is responsible for a scientific risk assessment, covering both environmental risks and a human and animal

[311] Articles 5 and 7 Regulation 1829/2003.

[312] On the concepts risk assessment and risk management, see Chapter 8, section 8.6.

[313] Articles 15-26 Regulation 1829/2003. This book does not go into the details of the prescriptions that apply to feed in particular.

[314] Article 27 Regulation 1829/2003.

[315] 'Starlink' maize (corn) was a GM maize which was only authorised for feed but turned up in food.

[316] Article 5(2) Regulation 1829/2003.

[317] Idem; see also Article 5(2)(a) Commission Regulation 641/2004.

[318] Article 6 Regulation 1829/2003.

health safety assessment. EFSA can conduct the risk assessment itself, or it can ask a national food assessment body to perform this task. EFSA's assessments are subject to a six month time limit, although this may be extended if EFSA requests further information from the applicant.

Community Reference Laboratory
In Article 6(3)(d) of Regulation 1829/2003, EFSA is required to forward to the 'Community Reference Laboratory'[319] the particulars necessary to test and validate the method of detection and identification of the GMO proposed by the applicant.[320] It is assisted by a consortium of national reference Laboratories – the 'European Network of GMO laboratories'.

The Community reference laboratory is responsible for:

- reception, preparation, storage, maintenance and distribution to national reference laboratories of the appropriate positive and negative control samples;
- testing and validation of the method for detection, including sampling and identification of the transformation event and, where applicable, for the detection and identification of the transformation event in the food or feed;
- evaluating the data provided by the applicant for authorisation for placing the food or feed on the market, for the purpose of testing and validation of the method for sampling and detection;
- submitting full evaluation reports to EFSA.[321]

Publication
EFSA makes a public version[322] of its opinion available to the public. The public will be allowed to make comments to the Commission within thirty days from the publication.[323]

Commission
Within three months of receiving EFSA's opinion, the Commission will draft a proposal for granting or refusing authorisation on the basis of that opinion.[324] The proposal must be approved by a qualified majority[325] of the member states

[319] The Community Reference Laboratory is also referred to as the Community's 'Joint Research Centre'.
[320] Regulation 1829/2003 institutes the 'Community Reference Laboratory' in Article 32 and in its Annex.
[321] Annex of Regulation 1829/2003.
[322] That is to say, EFSA provides the public a text from which confidential information has been deleted.
[323] Articles 2; 5(2)(b), 6(7), 29-31 Regulation 1829/2003. Article 38(1) GFL. See also Article 38(1) Commission Regulation 65/2004. The comments received by EFSA are published on the Internet. For the hyperlink see the reference list.
[324] Article 7(1) Regulation 1829/2003.
[325] See Chapter 5.

within the Standing Committee on the Food Chain and Animal Health,[326] which is composed of representatives of the member states. If the Committee gives a favourable opinion, the Commission adopts the Decision. If not, the draft Decision is submitted to the Council of Ministers for adoption or rejection by qualified majority. If the Council does not act within three months, the Commission shall adopt the decision.[327]

Time involved

From the above it is obvious that the authorisation procedure for GM food is lengthy. Diagram 9.6 gives the official timescale. There is no mechanism, however, to ensure that deadlines are actually respected.

Diagram 9.6. Timeline GM food authorisation procedure.

14 days	MS to acknowledge and notify EFSA
6 months	EFSA risk assessment
PM	EFSA extension additional info
3 months	Commission draft proposal
PM	SCFCAH opinion
3 months	Council if SCFCAH unfavourable
PM	Commission if Council misses deadline
54 weeks + PM	Total

9.5.7 Authorisation

Scope

The authorisation lifts the prohibition against bringing a GM food into the market. The decision is addressed to the applicant. As a result, the applicant receives a *de facto* monopoly to bring the authorised GM product to the market until other applicants acquire authorisation as well.

Once granted, market authorisations for GM foods are valid for ten years throughout the Community.[328] Conditions and restrictions may be connected to authorisations, and the applicant may be obliged to implement a monitoring plan.[329]

[326] Article 58 GFL; Article 35 Regulation 1829/2003.

[327] These shifts in competence, depending upon the content of the decision and the amount of consent, seem deplorable from an accountability point of view.

[328] Article 7(5) Regulation 1829/2003. National legislation seeking to impose on supermarkets an obligation to place genetically modified foods in a place specially designated for them on separate shelves from non-genetically modified goods, is declared non-admissible by the Commission: Commission Decision (2006/255) of 14 March 2006 concerning national provisions imposing on supermarkets an obligation to place genetically modified foods on separate shelves from non-genetically modified foods, notified by Cyprus pursuant to Article 95(5) of the EC Treaty. Official Journal L 92, 30 March 2006, p. 12.

[329] Articles 5(3)(k), 5(5)(b), 9(1) Regulation 1829/2003.

Publication and registration
The applicant is informed without delay of a decision by the Commission. The details of the decision are published in the Official Journal of the European Union.[330] Products authorised shall be entered into a public register of GM food and feed.[331]

9.5.8 Identification

In Regulation 65/2004,[332] the Commission devised a system of unique identifiers that are to be assigned to each GMO. The Annex to this regulation gives the format. The Commission follows the formats for unique identifiers that have been established by the Organization for Economic Cooperation and Development (OECD) for use both in the context of its BioTrack product database and in the context of the Biosafety Clearing-House,[333] established by the Cartagena Protocol on Biosafety to the Convention on Biological Diversity.[334]

The applicant for an authorisation must develop the unique identifier for each GMO concerned.[335] The Commission specifies the identifier in the authorisation decision,[336] records it in the relevant registers[337] and ensures that it is communicated to the Biosafety Clearing-House as soon as possible.[338]

The unique identifiers consist of 9 alphanumeric digits. The first three indicate the business concerned. On 19 May 2004 for example, Syngenta Seeds BV received authorisation for Sweet maize (fresh or canned) with Unique ID: SYN-BT Ø 11-1 The transformation event (Bt11) is recognisable in the ID.

9.5.9 Liability

Article 7 (7) Regulation 1829/2003 states, 'The granting of authorisation shall not lessen the general civil and criminal liability of any food operator in respect of the food concerned'. Notwithstanding this provision, an authorisation certainly has influence on liability. Part of general civil liability law is product liability, as harmonised by Directive 85/374 and Directive 1999/34.[339] An important defence

---

330 Article 7(4) Regulation 1829/2003.
331 Article 28 Regulation 1829/2003; Community Register of GM Food and Feed, for a hyperlink see the reference list.
332 Official Journal L 10, 2004, p. 65.
333 See Biosafety Clearing House for a hyperlink see the reference list.
334 Recital 6 of Regulation 65/2004.
335 Article 2 Regulation 65/2004.
336 Article 3(a) Regulation 65/2004.
337 Articles 3(c) and 5(3) Regulation 65/2004.
338 Article 5(4) Regulation 65/2004.
339 See Chapter 14 and Nicole Coutrelis, Product Liability in the Food Sector, for a hyperlink see the reference list.

in European product liability law is the 'development risk' defence: the producer can disclaim liability if he proves that the state of scientific and technological knowledge at the time the product was put into circulation did not allow the existence of the defect to be discovered.[340] A favourable assessment by EFSA followed by an authorisation would seem to constitute considerable proof that this defence would sustain.

9.5.10 Modification and renewal

The authorisation-holder can propose to modify the terms of the authorisation, by application *mutatis mutandis* of the procedure to the proposal.[341] Authorisations are renewable for ten year periods.[342] Applications must be sent to the Commission one year before the expiration date of the authorisation at the latest.

This system of authorisations limited in time and renewals requiring application, seems to imply that the use of specific GM foods is phased out when a business is no longer willing to support it through application for renewal.[343]

9.5.11 Suspension and revocation

An authorisation, once granted, is not untouchable during its ten year period of validity. EFSA may, on its own initiative or on request, issue an opinion as to whether an authorisation for a product still meets the conditions. The Commission may then decide whether the authorisation shall be modified, suspended or revoked.

9.6 Functional foods

Functional foods is not a legal category. According to Nutriwatch,[344] the term functional foods was first introduced in Japan in the mid-1980s and refers to processed foods containing ingredients that aid specific bodily functions in addition to being nutritious.

According to the International Food Information Council (IFIC) Functional Foods are foods or dietary components that may provide a health benefit beyond basic nutrition.[345]

---

[340] Article 7(e) Directive 85/374.

[341] Article 9(2) Regulation 1829/2003.

[342] Article 11(1) Regulation 1829/2003.

[343] See for example: Commission Decision of 25 April 2007 on the withdrawal from the market of products derived from GA21xMON810 (MON-ØØØ21-9xMON-ØØ81Ø-6) maize (notified under document number C(2007) 1810) (2007/308/EC). Official Journal L 117, 5 May 2007, p. 25.

[344] For a hyperlink see the reference list.

[345] For a hyperlink see the reference list.

As functional foods is not as such a legal category, no pre-market approval requirement exists. If these foods are safe and if they do not fall within another category for which approval is required, they can be brought to the market.

From the food law point of view the most important aspect of functional foods arises if the beneficial properties of functional foods are communicated to consumers. Such communication will constitute a nutrition or health claim that may only be used if it is in accordance with Regulation 1924/2006. This regulation is treated in Chapter 12 on labelling.

The authorisation is different from the safety assessment of the products discussed in this chapter (Diagram 9.7). Central in safety assessment is what the product does not do (cause harm), central in the assessment of health claims is what the food does do (provide the promised health effects).

Diagram 9.7. Criteria for the authorisation of health claims.

Authorisation criteria	
Presence	Scientific substantiation of claimed effect
Absence	Misleading Raise doubt about other foods Encourage excessive consumption

9.7 Other approval schemes

Outside the domain of food law approval schemes apply that may be of relevance for the food sector like pharmaceuticals, veterinary drugs, pesticides and chemicals (REACH) that cannot be discussed here.[346]

Also within the domain of food law further approval procedures exist for example for extraction solvents,[347] some flavourings,[348] infant formulae,[349] some other foods for particular nutritional uses,[350] novel feed and novel food contact materials,[351]

[346] For sources on veterinary drugs and pesticides see Chapter 10. For REACH see Regulation 1907/2006.

[347] Council Directive of 13 June 1988 on the approximation of the laws of the Member States on extraction solvents used in the production of foodstuffs and food ingredients (88/344/EEC).

[348] Framework Directive 88/388; Council Decision 88/389; Directive 89/1007; Regulation 2232/96; Commission Decision 1999/217 adopting a register of flavouring substances; Regulation 2065/2003 on smoke flavourings;

[349] Directive 91/321 on infant formulae and follow-on formulae.

[350] Directive 89/398; Directive 2001/15 on substances that may be added for specific nutritional purposes in foods for particular nutritional uses.

[351] See Regulation 1935/2004, Official Journal L 338, 13 November 2004.

decontaminants.[352] In addition the use of certain messages must be approved in advance: protected designations of origin, protected geographical indications[353] and traditional specialties.[354] Even voluntary labelling of beef and veal must be approved.[355]

9.8 Pre-market approval schemes

9.8.1 Precautionary approach

In this chapter we have encountered an expanding EU policy of requiring safety assessment of certain types of foods before they may enter the market. This policy applies positive lists holding the products that may be brought to the market and banning those that have not been included in the list. This policy is sometimes referred to as 'precautionary'. Scientific certainty about safety is required upfront. The burden of proof to provide this certainty is on the businesses that wish to bring a product to the market. Risk assessment (by EFSA) consists mainly of checking the homework done by the applicant. Risk management takes the form of deciding whether or not to grant approval.

The European Commission sees this approach as an application of the precautionary principle. In its Communication on the precautionary principle,[356] the Commission states:

> *'Community rules and those of many third countries enshrine the principle of prior approval (positive list) before the placing on the market of certain products, such as drugs, pesticides or food additives. This is one way of applying the precautionary principle, by shifting responsibility for producing scientific evidence. This applies in particular to substances deemed 'a priori' hazardous or which are potentially hazardous at a certain level of absorption. In this case the legislator, by way of precaution, has clearly reversed the burden of proof by requiring that the substances be deemed hazardous until proven otherwise. Hence it is up to the business community to carry out the scientific work needed to evaluate the risk. As long as the human health risk cannot be evaluated with sufficient certainty, the legislator is not legally entitled to authorise use of the substance, unless exceptionally for test purposes'.*

[352] Article 3(2) first sentence Regulation 853/2004: Food business operators shall not use any substance other than potable water – or, when Regulation (EC) No 852/2004 or this Regulation permits its use, clean water – to remove surface contamination from products of animal origin, unless use of the substance has been approved in accordance with the procedure referred to in Article 12(2).

[353] See Regulation 510/2006, Official Journal L 93, 31 March 2006.

[354] See Regulation 509/2006, Official Journal L 93, 31 March 2006, p.3.

[355] See Regulation 1760/2000, Official Journal L 204, 2000, pp. 1-10.

[356] Brussels 2.2.2000 COM(2000) 1 final. For a hyperlink see the reference list.

This interpretation of the precautionary principle goes beyond Article 7 GFL. This Article limits the scope of the precautionary principle to the situation where a risk assessment has already taken place and scientific uncertainty persists. It is not about shifting the burden of proof of risk assessment. Generally speaking, in pre-market approval schemes there will be little room left for applying the precautionary principle as defined in Article 7 GFL. If the dossier provided by the applicant leaves scientific uncertainty as to the safety of the product, the standard of proof for authorisation has not been met and authorisation will be denied.[357]

So far no firm structure for per-market approval has established itself. In each instance where a new requirement is introduced, a new procedure has been developed. If one does not want to call the result a mess, at least it shows an interesting diversity.

9.8.2 Criteria

The criteria applied in pre-market approval schemes are not identical but similar usually comprising safety, misleading and nutritional disadvantage.

Diagram 9.8 gives an overview of the criteria as worded in the different provisions. If we assume that the legislator has similar notions in mind when referring to safety hazards, danger for the consumer and adverse effects on health, the core issues are protecting the consumer from products that pose a risk to health, that appear to be something which they are not and that are nutritionally of lower quality than their conventional counterparts. An additional justification is only required for additives (technological need).

The three major criteria are all negative, e.g. they are about what the food must *not* do. The text of the law seems to leave little leeway for balancing risks and benefits. Possible benefits are not mentioned as criteria, therefore it seems unlikely that benefits can outweigh disadvantages. For example, a calorie free sweetener with beneficial effects for diabetics may not find its way to the EU market if it is likely to be allergenic to some other consumers.

9.8.3 Competences

The competences to deal with and decide on an application for pre-market approval varies significantly from scheme to scheme. The competence to receive an application is either with the national competent authority or the Commission, but never with EFSA who in many cases will be the first actually to work on the

[357] This can only be different if authorities see reasons to bring forward counter-proof against the favourable outcome of the risk assessment or if they want to impose conditions along with the approval.

Diagram 9.8. Criteria for market authorisation.

	Additives (including sweeteners and colourants)	Food supplements	Novel foods	GM food	Functional foods
Presence					
Technological need	X				
Scientific substantiation of claimed effect					X
Absence					
Safety hazard	X				
Danger for consumer			X		
Adverse effects on health		?		X	
Adverse effects on the environment				X	
Misleading consumer	X	?	X	X	X
Nutritional disadvantage			X	X	
Raise doubt about other foods					X
Encourage excessive consumption					X

case. Risk assessment is the competence of either EFSA or a national body. As discussed above, if EFSA is competent it may pass on the task to a colleague at national level. The biggest diversity, however, concerns the competence to actually decide on the application, this may even vary within one scheme. Diagram 9.9 gives an overview of the various competences.

9.8.4 Authorisations

EU pre-market approval schemes on food differ in the legal effect of authorisation, e.g. of inclusion of a product in the positive list or register. Sometimes the authorisation is generic sometimes it is exclusively for the applicant. Generic authorisations address the product. It acquires the status 'fit for the EU market'. Exclusive authorisations address the applicant. S/he acquires the privilege to bring the product to the market. Diagram 9.10 gives an overview.

As will be discussed in Chapter 12 on labelling, to different types of nutrition and health claims different authorisation schemes apply.

From the point of view of consumers generic authorisations have the advantage that once a product is approved it can come to the market easily. For some businesses

Diagram 9.9. Competences in pre-market approval schemes.

	Receive application	**Risk assessment**	**Decision**		
Additives (including sweeteners and colourants)	Commission	EFSA	Commission, Parliament, Council		
Food supplements	Commission	EFSA	Commission & SCFCAH		
Novel foods initial assessment	National competent authority	National risk assessment body	National competent authority		
Novel foods additional assessment		EFSA	Commission & SCFCAH		
GM environmental approval	National competent authority	National risk assessment body	Assessment is negative: National competent authority	Assessment favourable no objections: National competent authority	Assessment favourable objections: Commission & SCFCAH
GM food approval	National competent authority	EFSA	SCFCAH favourable: Commission	SCFCAH not favourable: Council	SCFCAH not favourable, but Council misses 3 month deadline: Commission

Diagram 9.10. Characteristics of authorisations.

	Generic	**Exclusive**
Additives (including sweeteners and colourants)	X	
Food supplements	X	
Novel foods		X
GM food		X
Functional foods	X	X
Protected designations	X	

generic authorisations have the advantage that once the safety of a product has been established no more resources have to be invested to acquire the right to access the market. Exclusive authorisations provide a temporary advantage to businesses who invest resources in fulfilling the procedure. As a reward they receive a monopoly in marketing the product concerned. This monopoly is somewhat comparable to a patent. The major difference between a patent and a market authorisation, however, is that enforcement of a patent is a private law matter of which the patent holder has to take care. Keeping unauthorised foods from the market is a public law food safety issue for which the enforcement authorities of the member states are responsible.

In practical terms, exclusive authorisation is to the advantage of businesses that are first to go through the procedure, while generic authorisations are to the advantage of businesses that follow after another has dealt with the procedure.

9.8.5 Road map

Because the procedures differ it is all the more important for businesses in need of market clearance to find the right procedure. To this end the decision tree set out in Diagram 9.11 may be helpful. The value of this decision tree should not be over-estimated, however. In practice the decision as to the applicable procedure

Diagram 9.11. Decision tree on pre-market approval schemes.

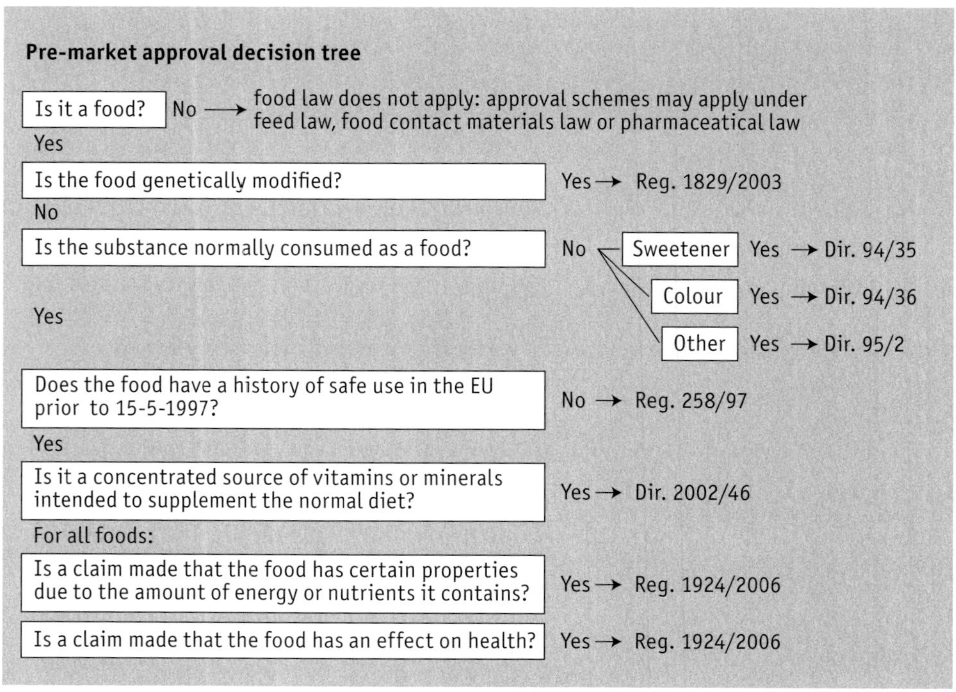

is not always taken on the basis of interpretation of the law, but on the basis of a compromise between member state representatives involved in comitology. Also, there is a certain tendency to simply follow the road the applicant has chosen.

9.8.6 Patentability

Pre-market approval schemes are the domain par excellence of the innovative players in the food industry. A food not yet approved for the EU market suggests a discovery either in science or in some other geographical part of the world or an invention either regarding a product or a process.

As discussed in Chapter 2 inventions that exhibit an inventive step which is of practical use and have not been disclosed before, may be eligible for protection by a patent. While 'newness' is not understood the same way in patent law as in pre-market approval schemes, there is considerable overlap.

It has been debated if innovations in the field of biotechnology can be protected by patents.[358] Some argued that living and self-reproducing matter cannot be subject of inventions as understood in patent law. For the EU this issue has been resolved by Directive 98/44 on the legal protection of biotechnological inventions,[359] extending patent protection to such inventions.

9.9 Developments

9.9.1 Introduction

On 28 July 2006, the European Commission submitted a package of four proposals on food improvement agents to the Council and the European Parliament.[360] This package aims to harmonise some of the procedures for pre-market approval, to recast the legislation on additives and to introduce a pre-market approval requirement for flavourings[361] and enzymes.[362] A little later a proposal was published to recast

[358] On this debate see: Han Somsen (ed.) The Regulatory Challenge of Biotechnology. Human Genetics, Food and Patents, Biotechnology Regulation Series, Edward Elgar, Cheltenham UK/ Northampton, MA, USA, 2007.

[359] Directive 98/44/EC of the European Parliament and of the Council of 6 July 1998 on the legal protection of biotechnological inventions, Official Journal L 213, 30 July 1998, p. 13.

[360] For a hyperlink see the reference list.

[361] Currently for flavourings the inverse applies. 'Council Directive of 22 June 1988 on the approximation of the laws of the Member States relating to flavourings for use in foodstuffs and to source materials for their Production' (Directive 88/383/EEC) addresses contaminants It applies negative lists holding substances and quantities that should not be present in the final food product.

[362] At the end of 2007 updated versions of these proposals were published including amendments proposed by the European Parliament. The remarks in this section refer to these versions.

the Novel Foods Regulation.[363] In these proposals a separation is made between procedural matters governed by a common procedures regulation and substantive matters governed by what is called sectoral food laws. From each sectoral food law follows a (positive) list of products approved through the common procedure.

All proposals concern regulations. For food additives and flavourings this would mean that harmonised national law of the member states is replaced by uniform EU law. This development is in line with the general trend in EU food law to move from directives to regulations.[364]

9.9.2 Common procedure

The Commission proposed a Regulation establishing a common authorisation procedure for food additives, food enzymes, food flavouring and novel foods.[365] In this proposal, the positive lists are updated through regulations set by the Commission applying the comitology procedure with scrutiny.[366] In practice this means that the Commission needs the approval of the SCFCAH and that the European Parliament has the power to decide if it also wants to have a say in the matter. EFSA is responsible for risk assessment, e.g. scientific advice.

9.9.3 Additives

The 'Proposal for a Regulation of the European Parliament and of the Council on food additives'[367] merges and updates the '*Miscellaneous Additives*' Directive, the Sweetener directive and the Colours directive discussed in sections 9.2.6, 9.2.4 and 9.2.5. It also holds some provisions regarding genetically modified additives.

9.9.4 Flavourings

The 'Proposal for a Regulation of the European Parliament and of the Council on flavourings and certain food ingredients with flavouring properties for use in and on foods and amending Council Regulation (EEC) No 1576/89, Council Regulation (EEC) No 1601/91, Regulation (EC) No 2232/96 and Directive 2000/13/EC',[368] provides for a Community list of flavourings and source materials approved for use in and on foods; for conditions of use of flavourings and food ingredients with flavouring properties in and on foods, and; rules on labelling of flavourings.

---

[363] COM(2007) 872 Proposal for a Regulation of the European Parliament and of the Council on novel foods and amending Regulation (EC) No XXX/XXXX [common procedure].
[364] As set out in Chapter 7.
[365] COM(2007) 672 final.
[366] See Chapter 5.
[367] COM(2007) 673 final.
[368] COM(2007) 671 final.

9.9.5 Enzymes

The 'Proposal for a Regulation of the European Parliament and of the Council on food enzymes and amending Council Directive 83/417/EEC, Council Regulation (EC) No 1493/1999, Directive 2000/13/EC of the European Parliament and of the Council, and Council Directive 2001/112/EC and Regulation (EC) No 258/97 of the European Parliament and of the Council',[369] provides for (a) a Community list of approved food enzymes; conditions of use of food enzymes in foods; rules on labelling of food enzymes sold as such.

9.9.6 Novel Foods

From the application of the Common Procedures Regulation to the new Novel Foods Regulation it follows that a two-level procedure will no longer apply (at member state level and Community level) but only a procedure at Community level.

The authorisation will be generic and no longer exclusive unless the application is based on new knowledge. In that case a system of data protection also applies.

Some of the concepts have been clarified. A special procedure is included to determine if a product has a history of safe use in the EU. The Commission can require the member states to provide information in this regard.

A simplified procedure is foreseen for exotic novel foods. If they have a history of safe use outside the EU a notification is sufficient, no application procedure is required.

9.9.7 Implementation

Will the new legislation come into force any time soon? This is difficult to predict. The urgency to improve food legislation that was felt after the BSE crisis is waning. The European Parliament and the member states seem to take a more critical position towards Commission proposals to change food legislation. It remains to be seen whether the European Parliament is willing to agree to a limitation of its influence on the approval of food additives.

The authors of this book are of the opinion that political decisions should focus on formulating the general requirements for the approval of food products. With regard to specific applications the decision should be limited to applying these requirements in a legal technical manner on the basis of scientific advice. Political discussion and compromise should concern the principles, not the specific products. From this point of view, involvement of the European Parliament is not recommendable, nor even of the member states through the SCFCAH.

[369] COM(2007) 670 final.

10. Product 2: food safety criteria: contaminants and restricted substances

10.1 Introduction

In the previous chapter we introduced four legislative approaches to food as such. These approaches were summarised in a diagram that is repeated here below (Diagram 10.1). In the previous chapter we discussed the first two approaches, in this chapter we will address the second two, with an emphasis on the first of these.

Diagram 10.1. Product legislation.

Legislative approach	**Example**
Free	conventional ingredients with a history of safe use in the EU
Conditional	• additives • sweeteners • supplements • genetically modified foods • (other) novel foods
Restricted	residues of pesticides residues of veterinary drugs (other) contaminants
Banned	• BSE risk material • zero tolerance residues / contaminants

The instrument of choice to deal with undesirable substances is to set limits to their presence. Such limits go by different names. In the title of this chapter we have followed the wording of Regulation 2073/2005 on microbiological criteria on foodstuffs (Law text box 10.1).

Law text box 10.1. Article 2(c) Regulation 2073/2005 defining 'food safety criterion'.

Article 2(c)
Defining food safety criterion
'food safety criterion' means a criterion defining the acceptability of a product or a batch of foodstuff applicable to products placed on the market

The phrase 'food safety criterion' nicely expresses that we are dealing with limits to be respected with a view to food safety. The Codex Alimentarius also applies some similarly expressive phrases (Law text box 10.2).[370]

Law text box 10.2. Codex Procedural Manual definitions.

Food Safety Objective (FSO): The maximum frequency and/or concentration of a hazard in a food at the time of consumption that provides or contributes to the appropriate level of protection (ALOP).
Performance Criterion (PC): The effect in frequency and/or concentration of a hazard in a food that must be achieved by the application of one or more control measures to provide or contribute to a PO or an FSO.
Performance Objective (PO): The maximum frequency and/or concentration of a hazard in a food at a specified step in the food chain before the time of consumption that provides or contributes to an FSO or ALOP, as applicable.

10.2 Contaminants: general principles

Beside raw materials that the producer intentionally includes in a food product, all kinds of chemicals or (micro) organisms may find their way into the final product unintentionally before it reaches the consumer.

This situation is covered to a certain extent by the general rules on food safety, which insist that no dangers to the consumer be present. However, there are also more specific rules. First among these is the Framework Regulation 315/93.[371] This regulation opens the possibility of establishing maximum tolerances (content levels) for certain substances in food. If these levels are surpassed, the food may not be brought to the market. The regulation opens in the first paragraph of Article 1 with a definition of 'contaminant' (Law text box 10.3).

Law text box 10.3. Definition of 'a contaminant'.

Article 1(1) Framework Regulation 315/93
Definition of a contaminant
Contaminant means any substance not intentionally added to food which is present in such food as a result of the production (including operations carried out in crop husbandry, animal husbandry and veterinary medicine), manufacture, processing, preparation, treatment, packing, packaging, transport or holding of such food, or as a result of environmental contamination. Extraneous matter, such as, for example, insect fragments, animal hair, etc, is not covered by this definition.

---

[370] Codex Alimentarius Commission, Procedural Manual, 17th edition, Rome 2007, Definition of Risk Analysis Terms Related to Food Safety, p. 45. For a hyperlink see the reference list.
[371] Council regulation 315/93 of 8 February 1993 laying down Community procedures for contaminants in food. Official Journal L 37, 13 February 1993, p.1.

The application of this definition shows that the concept of contaminant covers two of the three hazards usually distinguished in food law:[372] chemical and biological hazards. Physical hazards are not included in the definition of contaminants.

The regulation adheres to the principle of food business responsibility.[373] It states generally that food containing a contaminant in an amount which is unacceptable from the public health viewpoint and in particular at a toxicological level shall not be placed on the market.[374] The relation of the Framework regulation to other legislation is subtle. On the one hand it states that it shall not apply to contaminants which are subject to more specific Community rules,[375] on the other hand (other) provisions shall be adopted in accordance with this regulation.[376]

These latter provisions are to be adopted by the Commission through comitology,[377] after consultation with EFSA.[378] The most important requirement for these provisions is that contaminant levels shall be kept as low as can reasonably be achieved by following good practices at all the stages referred to in Article 1 (see Law text box 10.3).[379] The tolerances shall be adopted in the form of a non-exhaustive[380] Community list and may include:

- limits for the same contaminant in different foods;
- analytical detection limits;
- a reference to the sampling and analysis methods to be used.[381]

As a consequence of the principle defined in the framework regulation, in setting specific contaminant levels in legislation, two parameters are applied; *necessity* and *safety*. The level of necessity is based on what is unavoidable when applying good practices. What *is* avoidable, should be avoided and is not accepted on the market. Safety on the other hand is based on risk assessment in which toxicology plays an important role. The lowest of the two defines acceptability.

Commission Regulation 1881/2006 (replacing Regulation 466/2001) implements the framework regulation, by setting maximum levels. It further elaborates on the principles. In the case of contaminants which are considered to be genotoxic carcinogens or in cases where current exposure of the population or of vulnerable

---

372 See Article 3(14) GFL.

373 Now codified in Article 17(1) GFL.

374 Article 2(1) Regulation 315/93.

375 Article 1(2) Regulation 315/93; these more specific rules are listed by the Commission.

376 Article 1(3) Regulation 315/93.

377 Articles 2(3) and 8 Regulation 315/93.

378 Article 3 Regulation 315/93.

379 Article 2(2) Regulation 315/93.

380 This means that the list has no effect for situations not included in the list, that is to say not mentioned contaminant-food combinations. For these the general safety requirement applies (Article 14 GFL and Article 2(1) Regulation 315/93.)

381 Article 2(3) Regulation 315/93.

groups in the population is close to or exceeds the tolerable intake, maximum levels should be set at a level which is as low as reasonably achievable (ALARA).[382]

Further it holds a prohibition on decontamination through mixing contaminated foods with less or non-contaminated ones[383] (to acquire a product that no longer surpasses the limits). Foods contaminated with mycotoxins shall not be decontaminated by chemical treatments.[384] However, sorting as a method to separate contaminated from non-contaminated foods is acceptable for groundnuts, nuts, dried fruit and maize.[385]

10.3 Mycotoxins and chemicals

The annex to Regulation 1881/2006 sets limits for nitrates in spinach, lettuce and cereal based baby foods; for mycotoxins (in particular aflatoxin, ochratoxin A, patulin, deoxynivalenol, zearalenone, fumonisins, T-2 and Ht-2 toxin), heavy metals (lead, cadmium, mercury, tin), 3-MCPDs, dioxins and PCBs, PAHs (benzo(a)pyrene). Diagram 10.2 shows the format of this annex.

Diagram 10.2. Format of the annex to Regulation 1881/2006.

ANNEX **Maximum levels for certain contaminants in foodstuffs** *Section 1: Nitrate*			
	Foodstuffs	Maximum levels (mg NO_3/kg)	
1.1	Fresh spinach (*Spinacia oleracea*)	Harvested 1 October to 31 March Harvested 1 April to 30 September 2	3 000 500
1.2	Preserved, deep-frozen or frozen spinach		2 000
1.3	Fresh Lettuce (*Lactuca sativa* L.) (protected and open-grown lettuce) excluding lettuce listed in point 1.4	Harvested 1 October to 31 March: • lettuce grown under cover • lettuce grown in the open air Harvested 1 April to 30 September: • lettuce grown under cover • lettuce grown in the open air	 4 500 4 000 3 500 2 500
1.4	Iceberg-type lettuce	• Lettuce grown under cover • Lettuce grown in the open air	2 500 2 000
1.5	Processed cereal-based foods and baby foods for infants and young children		200

382 Recital 4 Regulation 1881/2006.
383 Article 3(3) Regulation 1881/2006.
384 Article 3(4) Regulation 1881/2006.
385 Article 4 Regulation 1881/2006.

10.4 Acrylamide

Acrylamide is a specific case in the approach to contaminants. No safety targets have been set in legislation, only guidance is given on how to reduce its prevalence. Acrylamide forms in certain food as a result of cooking practices and is commonly found in starchy foods, such as potato and cereal products which have been deep-fried, roasted or baked at temperatures above 120 °C.

This substance is known to have potential carcinogenic effects. Research is being undertaken to better understand the process of its formation and to find ways to reduce its presence in food. A careful selection of raw material as well as certain cooking practices are known to help limit the formation of acrylamide in potato products and bread.

10.5 Biological hazards

10.5.1 Introduction

Biological hazards in food mainly originate from viruses (like Noroviruses and Hepatitis A), from bacteria (like *Salmonella*, *Campylobacter*, *E. coli*, *Listeria monocytogenes*), from other protozoans (such as amoebas), from parasites or from prions.

EU legislation takes a multi-step approach to these hazards. Food hygiene (discussed in Chapter 11) aims at prevention. Protozoic and parasitic hazards are controlled at the slaughter-line. For viruses (so far) no specific legislation exists. Bacteria are discussed in section 10.5.2 and prions in section 10.10.

10.5.2 Microbiological criteria

Bacterial hazards are the subject of Commission regulation 2073/2005 of 15 November 2005 on microbiological criteria for foodstuffs.[386] This regulation is based on Article 4 of Regulation 852/2004 (also known as Hygiene 1)[387] stating that food business operators are to comply with microbiological criteria set by the Commission.

The most important part of Regulation 2073/2005 is its 'Annex I microbiological criteria for foodstuffs'. This annex consists of three chapters (I Food safety criteria, II Process hygiene criteria, and III Rules for sampling and preparation of test samples).

Diagram 10.3 shows the format of food safety criteria in Annex I chapter I of Regulation 2073/2005. This chapter of the annex comprises a table subdivided into

[386] Official Journal L 338, 22 December 2005, p. 1. Ammended by Commission Regulation 1441/2007.
[387] Discussed hereafter in Chapter 11.

Diagram 10.3. Format of food safety criteria in Regulation 2073/2005.

	Food category	Micro-organisms/ their toxins, metabolites	Sampling-plan		Limits		Analytical reference method	Stage where the criterion applies
			n	c	m	M		
1.1.	Ready-to-eat foods intended for infants and ready-to-eat foods for special medical purposes	*Listeria monocytogenes*	10	0	Absence in 25 g		EN/ISO 11290-1	Products placed on the market during their shelf-life
1.2.	Ready-to-eat foods able to support the growth of L. monocytogenes, other than those intended for infants and for special medical purposes	*Listeria monocytogenes*	5	0	100 cfu/g+		EN/ISO 11290-2	Products placed on the market during their shelf-life
			5	0	Absence in 25 g		EN/ISO 11290-1	Before the food has left the immediate control of the food business operator, who has produced it

six columns giving: the food category, the micro-organism, sampling plan, the limits, the analytical reference method and the stage where the criterion applies.

The process hygiene criteria in Chapter II follow a similar format, adding a seventh column indicating the action to be taken in case of unsatisfactory results.

Chapter I gives microbiological criteria for: *Listeria monocytogenes*, *Salmonella*, *Staphylococcal* enterotoxins, *Enterobacter sakazakii*, *E. coli* and histamine.

A 'microbiological criterion' means a criterion defining the acceptability of a product, a batch of foodstuffs or a process, based on the absence, presence or number of micro-organisms, and/or on the quantity of their toxins/metabolites, per unit(s) of mass, volume, area or batch.[388]

Food business operators are under the obligation to ensure that foodstuffs comply with the relevant criteria set out in Annex I.[389] This obligation applies in all stages of the food chain and should be fulfilled in the context of the HACCP plan.[390] See Law text box 10.4.

Law text box 10.4. Regulation 2073/2005 on compliance with microbiological criteria.

Article 3
General requirements

1. Food business operators shall ensure that foodstuffs comply with the relevant microbiological criteria set out in Annex I. To this end the food business operators at each stage of food production, processing and distribution, including retail, shall take measures, as part of their procedures based on HACCP principles together with the implementation of good hygiene practice, to ensure the following:
   (a) that the supply, handling and processing of raw materials and foodstuffs under their control are carried out in such a way that the process hygiene criteria are met,
   (b) that the food safety criteria applicable throughout the shelf-life of the products can be met under reasonably foreseeable conditions of distribution, storage and use.
2. As necessary, the food business operators responsible for the manufacture of the product shall conduct studies in accordance with Annex II in order to investigate compliance with the criteria throughout the shelf-life. In particular, this applies to ready-to-eat foods that are able to support the growth of Listeria monocytogenes and that may pose a Listeria monocytogenes risk for public health.

Food businesses may collaborate in conducting those studies.
Guidelines for conducting those studies may be included in the guides to good practice referred to in Article 7 of Regulation (EC) No 852/2004.

[388] Article 2(b) Regulation 2073/2005.
[389] Article 3(1) Regulation 2073/2005.
[390] As discussed in Chapter 11.

When testing against food safety criteria set out in Chapter 1 of Annex I provides unsatisfactory results, the product or batch of foodstuffs shall be withdrawn or recalled in accordance with Article 19 of the General Food Law.[391]

10.6 Residues

A particular kind of contaminant is residue from veterinary medicine, additives in feeding stuffs (in animal products like meat, milk or eggs), or crop protection products (in plants). Residues are substances that can occur in foodstuffs as a side effect of using veterinary medicines or phytosanitary products. They are unwanted traces of medicines or plant protection products (pesticides or fungicides) or derivatives thereof which remain in the final product. For these products maximum residue levels (MRLs) can be established. If these levels are surpassed, the food may not be brought to the market.

10.7 Pesticide residues

The legislation on pesticide residues is a good example of the EU approach to the presence of undesired substances in food. The regulatory framework on pesticides consists of two parts: the pre-market approval of pesticides for use in agriculture and the establishment of maximum residue limits in food commodities.

10.7.1 Pre-market approval of pesticides

In 1991, the Council adopted Directive 91/414 concerning the placing of plant protection products on the market. This Directive provides for the Commission to examine pesticide active substances under all their safety aspects (consumer protection, worker protection, fate and behaviour in the environment, ecotoxicology). Active substances that have been approved, are included in Annex I to this directive. With regard to active substances that where on the market when the directive entered into force, a work program has been set up to re-evaluate them to decide on inclusion in Annex I. As long as no decision is taken at EU level, member states decide on the status of the substance.

New active substances – that is substances not on the market before 25 July 1993 – may not be brought to the EU market before they have been included in Annex I.

The approval of products (as opposed to active substances) is left to the member states. Member states may only approve products based on active substances on Annex I (or enjoying transitory measures). Member states may also temporarily

391 Article 7(2) Regulation 2073/2005. Article 19 GFL on recall is discussed in Chapters 8 and 11.

approve products based on substances that await inclusion in Annex I. Some substances are excluded from authorisation (like DDT, Aldrin, HCH).[392]

The setting of MRLs is very closely coordinated with the parallel activities on this evaluation of pesticides active ingredients.

10.7.2 Pesticide MRLs

The setting of MRLs has been codified in Regulation 396/2005.[393] The entry into force of this regulation has been postponed several times, lately until 2 September 2008.[394] MRLs are not maximum toxicological limits. They are based on good agricultural practice and they represent the maximum amount of residue that might be expected on a commodity if good agricultural practice was adhered to during the use of a pesticide. Nonetheless, when MRLs are set, care is taken to ensure that the maximum levels do not give rise to toxicological concerns.

In principle, MRLs are set on the basis of the following:

a. Supervised agricultural residue trials establish the residue level in or on an agricultural crop treated with a pesticide under specified use conditions (Good Agricultural Practice = GAP). This results in the Supervised Trial Median Residue Level (STMR) and the Highest Residue Level (HR).
b. Using appropriate consumer intake models, the daily residue intake under normal and worst case conditions can be estimated for the European population and for national populations and sub-populations (e.g. infants).
c. Data from toxicological tests on the pesticide allow for the fixing of an 'acceptable daily intake' (ADI). Usually this involves finding the highest dose that would produce no adverse effects over a lifetime (chronic) exposure period and then applying appropriate safety factors. From animal testing the NOAEL is derived; the 'No observed adverse effects level'. The quantity of pesticide residue represented by the NOAEL is two times divided by 10; once to account for the difference in sensitivity between species and once to account for the difference in sensitivity between individuals. By consequence the ADI generally is 1/100 of the NOAEL. The ADI is based on an average diet.
d. In addition with a view to an extreme diet the Acute Reference Dose (ARfD) is fixed for substances that may be acute toxic.

---

392 Directive 79/117.

393 Regulation 396/2005 of the European Parliament and of the Council of 23 February 2005 on maximum residue levels of pesticides in products of plant and animal origin. Official Journal L 70, 16 March 2005, p. 1.

394 Previous pesticide MRL legislation was derived from/based on four Council Directives: Directive 76/895 establishing MRLs for selected fruits and vegetables; Directive 86/362 establishing MRLs for cereals and cereal products; Directive 86/363 establishing MRLs in products of animal origin; and Directive 90/642 establishing MRLs in products of plant origin, including fruits and vegetables. Until the entry into force, Chapters II, III and V to the Regulation are not applicable; and the national MRL of each Member State for each pesticide/crop combination remains in force.

e. If the estimated daily consumer intake for all commodities calculated under (b) is lower than the ADI calculated under (c) and the HR for extreme daily intake lower then the ARfD calculated under (d), then the STMR under (a) is set as the MRL. In cases where the calculated intake is higher, the use conditions described in (a) need to be modified to reduce the residue level in the commodity. If this is not possible the use of that pesticide on that crop cannot be tolerated and the MRL is set at the limit of determination (LOD; effectively zero). This zero level does not express that even minute traces of the substance are unsafe, but that the substance may not be used.

MRLs for processed products and composite foodstuffs are normally calculated on the basis of the MRL set for the agricultural commodity by application of an appropriate dilution or concentration factor. For composite foodstuffs MRLs are calculated taking into account the relative concentrations of the ingredients in the composite foodstuff. Only exceptionally may specific MRLs be determined for certain processed products or certain composite foodstuffs.

10.7.3 Default MRL

Regulation 396/2005 sets a general maximum pesticide residue level in foodstuffs of 0.01 mg/kg. This general level is applicable 'by default', i.e. in all cases where an MRL has not been specifically set for a product or product type. In this way now all foods intended for human (or animal) consumption in the European Union are subject to a maximum residue level of pesticides in their composition.

If a specific MRL has been set (for a food/pesticide combination), this takes precedence over the general MRL. The products to which MRLs apply are listed in Annex I of Regulation 396/2005.[395] Specific MRLs are listed in Annex II. Annex III (part A and part B) holds temporary MRLs.[396] These are national MRLs still to be harmonised at EU level. In Annex IV active substances shall be listed that need no MRL because they do not pose a health risk.

10.8 Residues of veterinary drugs

The framework regulation for veterinary drugs, is Regulation 2377/90.[397] This Regulation lays down a Community procedure for the establishment of maximum residue limits of veterinary medicinal products in foodstuffs of animal origin.

[395] This annex has been drawn up by Regulation 178/2006.

[396] See Regulation 149/2008 for the latest update of these annexes. Official Journal L 58, 1 March 2008.

[397] Regulation 2377/90 of 26 June 1990 laying down a Community procedure for the establishment of maximum residue limits of veterinary medicinal products in foodstuffs of animal origin. Official Journal L 224, 18 August 1990.

To a certain extent the structure is comparable to the one that applies to pesticides. A double procedure has to be followed. One for approval as veterinary drug based on the effectiveness and safety of the product for the animal concerned,[398] and one setting the maximum residue limit of the product in the food of animal origin (mainly meat and dairy). The operative part of the regulation is in its annexes. The annexes are updated by comitology.[399]

Annex I contains a list of pharmacologically active substances used in veterinary medicinal products in respect of which maximum residue limits have been established.[400] Substances for which it is not necessary for the protection of public health to establish an MRL are listed in Annex II.[401] Annex III is for provisional MRLs.[402]Where it appears from risk assessment that a maximum residue limit cannot be established in respect of a pharmacologically active substance used in veterinary medicinal products because residues of the substances concerned, at whatever limit, in foodstuffs of animal origin constitute a hazard to the health of the consumer, that substance shall be included in a list in Annex IV. The administration of the substances listed in Annex IV to food-producing animals is prohibited throughout the Community.[403] A zero tolerance applies to substances not listed in Annex I, II or III.

Annex IV holds substances like *Aristolochia* spp. and preparations thereof, e.g. chloramphenicol, chloroform, chlorpromazine, colchicine, dapsone, dimetridazole, metronidazole, nitrofurans (including furazolidone) and ronidazole. The European Court of Justice has ruled that if in controls an Annex-IV substance is found (in that case furazolidone and chloramphenicol) seizure and destruction of the food in question is imperative – no matter how minute the trace.[404] A default level as described for pesticides does not apply. However some reference points for action have been set. See Commision Decision 2002/657, 2003/181, 2004/25 and 2005/3.

10.9 Hormones

Directive 96/22[405] prohibits the use in stock farming of certain substances having a hormonal or thyrostatic action and of ß-agonists. Or, to put it more precisely, it imposes upon the member states to prohibit the placing on the market of these

398 On the basis of Directive 2001/82.
399 Article 8 Regulation 2377/90.
400 Article 2 Regulation 2377/90.
401 Article 3 Regulation 2377/90.
402 Article 4 Regulation 2377/90.
403 Article 5 Regulation 2377/90.
404 ECJ 28 September 2006 cases C-129/05 and C-130/05, NV Raverco (C-129/05), Coxon & Chatterton Ltd (C-130/05) v. Minister van Landbouw, Natuur en Voedselkwaliteit (NL).
405 Council Directive 96/22 of 29 April 1996 concerning the prohibition on the use in stockfarming of certain substances having a hormonal or thyrostatic action and of ß-agonists. Official Journal L 125, 23 May 1996.

products[406] and their administration to farm or aquaculture animals.[407] Some exceptions can be made for therapeutic purposes.[408]

The placing on the market[409] for human consumption and the import[410] of aquaculture animals to which such substances have been administered and of processed products derived from such animals shall also be prohibited, even if the exception for therapeutic purposes applies.[411]

10.10 TSE risk material

Materials that by the current state of scientific knowledge are believed to transmit TSE-causing prions, are placed under several restrictions and banned from use in food. Commission decision 2000/418[412] regulates the use of material presenting risks as regards transmissible spongiform encephalopathies and provides for the removal and destruction of specified risk materials listed in its Annex I. This annex includes:
1. The skull including the brains and eyes, the tonsils, the spinal cord of bovine animals aged over 12 months, and the intestines from the duodenum to the rectum of bovine animals of all ages;
2. The skull including the brains and eyes, the tonsils and the spinal cord of ovine and caprine animals aged over 12 months or that have a permanent incisor erupted through the gum, and the spleen of ovine and caprine animals of all ages.

10.11 Animal by-products[413]

In connection with the measures to ensure that no TSE risk material enters the food chain, Regulation 1774/2002 on animal by-products[414] ensures the further safe disposal of these materials. The regulation aims to integrate the animal by-products sector into the 'farm to fork' approach of food law. It introduces stringent conditions throughout the food and feed chains requiring safe collection, transport, storage, handling, processing, uses and disposal of animal by-products.

Animal by-products are the parts of a slaughtered animal that are not directly consumed by humans, including dead on farm animals and catering waste (i.e.

406 Article 2 Directive 96/22.
407 Article 3 Directive 96/22.
408 Article 4 Directive 96/22.
409 Article 3(c)(d0 and (e) Directive 96/22.
410 Article 11(2) Directive 96/22.
411 Article 7(2) Directive 96/22.
412 Commission decision 2000/418 regulating the use of material presenting risks as regards transmissible spongiform encephalopathies. Official Journal L 158, 30 June 2000, p. 76.
413 This section is based on MEMO/04/107 of the European Commission.
414 Regulation 1774/2002 laying down health rules concerning animal by-products not intended for human consumption. Official Journal L 273, 10 October 2002, p. 1.

waste food originating from restaurants, catering facilities and kitchens) that contains or has been in contact with meat products, whether cooked or uncooked. Some of these products are used in animal proteins like meat-and-bone-meal, fats, gelatine, collagen, pet food and other technical products, such as glue, leathers, soaps, fertilisers, etc. The alternative is their destruction, most often by incineration.

In the past, raw material of a lower health standard than the one used for human food were permitted for use in animal feeds. For example, animals that died on farm and were unfit for human consumption could enter the animal feed chain. This practice of recycling cadavers and material unfit for human consumption into the feed chain is seen as the main factor in the spreading of the BSE epidemic, but also of other food safety and animal health emergencies, such as the dioxin crises and foot and mouth disease. This practice is now prohibited.

The Regulation classifies animal by-products into three categories based on their potential risk to animals, the public or to the environment, and sets out how each category must or may be disposed of.

Category 1 materials (i.e. animal by-products presenting highest risk such as TSEs or scrapie, residues of prohibited substance e.g. hormone used for growth promotion or environmental contaminants e.g. dioxins, PCBs) must be completely disposed of as waste by incineration or landfill after appropriate heat treatment.[415]

Category 2 materials include animal by-products presenting a risk of contamination with other animal diseases (e.g. animals which die on farm or are killed in the context of disease control measures on farm or at risk of residues of veterinary drugs), and may be recycled for uses other than feeds after appropriate treatment (e.g. biogas, composting, oleo-chemical products, etc).[416]

Only category 3 materials (i.e. by-products derived from healthy animals slaughtered for human consumption) may be used in the production of feeds following appropriate treatment in approved processing plants.[417]

The Regulation also requires reliable traceability and identification systems or marking for certain materials intended for specific disposal options (e.g. incineration of meat and bone meal) to avoid possible frauds or risk of diversion of unauthorised products into food and feed. It is prohibited to use animal by-products to feed the same species or as fertiliser.[418]

---

415 Article 4 Regulation 1774/2002.

416 Article 5 Regulation 1774/2002.

417 Article 6 Regulation 1774/2002.

418 Article 22 Regulation 1774/2002.

10.12 Overview

The legislative approach to undesired substances in food adds to the general ban on unsafe food specific limits for certain food/substance combinations. Often sampling methods are regulated as well. While these have not been discussed in this chapter, they have been included in Diagram 10.4. Diagram 10.4 gives an overview of substances discussed in this chapter and the legislation that applies to their presence. In addition to this legislation, some examples are given of legislation dealing with sampling and analysis and some guidance documents available on the EU website to help businesses and inspectors deal with their legal obligations.

Diagram 10.4. Overview of contaminants legislation.

Substance	Limit	Sampling method	Guidance
Chemicals	Reg. 1881/2006	Reg. 1881/2006	
• lead, cadmium, mercury, inorganic tin, 3-MCPD, benzo(a)pyrene	Reg. 1881/2006	Reg. 333/2007	
• Methyl mercury	Reg. 1881/2006		D/530286
• Dioxin	Reg. 1881/2006	Reg. 1883/2006	Guidelines; Rec. 2006/88; COM(2001) 593
• PCBs	Reg. 1881/2006	Reg. 1883/2006	Rec. 2006/88
• PAHs	Reg. 1881/2006		Rec. 2005/108
• Furans	Reg. 1881/2006		Rec. 2006/88; COM(2001) 593
• Polychlorinated Biphenyls			COM(2001) 593
Mycotoxins	Reg. 1881/2006	Reg. 401/2006	
• Patulin	Reg. 1881/2006		Rec. 2003/598
• Aflatoxin	Reg. 1881/2006		Guidance document for Competent Authorities for the control of compliance with EU legislation on aflatoxins (no n°)
Pesticides	Reg. 396/2005	Reg. 396/2005	
Veterinary drugs	Reg. 2377/90		Notice to applicants F2/AW D(2003)
Hormones	Dir. 96/22 (ban)		
Microbes	Reg. 2073/2005	Reg. 2073/2005	
TSE risk material	Dec. 2000/418 (ban)		

11. Process: food handling, hygiene, traceability and recall

Without a doubt the rules on the process represent the hard core of food safety law addressing food business operators. In this chapter the subject matter is subdivided into three parts. Requirements aimed at preventing food safety problems, requirements to be prepared for food safety problems and requirements to deal with food safety problems. The latter two issues are the subject of – essentially – one article each. To the former a whole package of regulations and directives applies. This difference in complexity is reflected in the attention given in this chapter. See Diagram 11.1 on food handling.

Diagram 11.1. Food handling.

	Production	**Trade**
Preventing problems (section 11.1)	HACCP (section 11.1.7)	(Tracking & tracing)
Preparing for problems (section 11.2)	(HACCP) (section 11.2.1)	Tracking & tracing (sections 11.2.2-11.2.5)
Dealing with problems (section 11.3)	(HACCP)	Withdrawal & recall (sections 11.3.1-11.3.4)

When a food business operator starts a new production process, or engages in new trade relations, s/he has to ascertain that both the handling of the food by the company and between companies is in agreement with the applicable provisions of food law. According to Article 17 of the General Food Law, food business operators are responsible for meeting the relevant (food safety) requirements at all stages of production, processing and distribution of food. Under the Hygiene Regulation 852/2004 they are even held responsible for formulating these requirements.

11.1 Preventing problems: food hygiene

11.1.1 Introduction

In Greek mythology, *Hygieia* – from who's name the word hygiene has been derived – daughter to Asclepius the god of medicine and healing (Aesculapius in Latin) and sister to Panacea who represented cure from sickness, was the goddess for maintenance of good health and prevention of disease. Safe food is probably the first prerequisite to maintain good health. It is fitting therefore that the word hygiene is used for measures to ensure food safety even though in common speech the word has the more narrow meaning of cleanliness.

The safety of food products on a consumer's plate depends largely on the way they have been produced. For this reason rules have been made to ensure that safe methods of production are used. The legislation on the safe production of food is distributed over four EU regulations, 852/2004, 853/2004, 854/2004 and 882/2004, that came into force in 2006. They replaced the national food hygiene laws of the member states that had been harmonised on the basis of one general EU Directive (93/43), and 17 vertical (product specific) directives for food products of animal origin (meat, fish, eggs, etc.).

The new uniform EU legislation introduces a different organisation of food hygiene law, sharpens some of the instruments of the old legislation and extents its rule for the first time over primary production (the food produced by collecting the fruits of fields and forests, hunting, fisheries, and all the different types of agriculture). The word 'hygiene' is taken in a broad sense. See Law text box 11.1 for the definition of food hygiene in EU law.

Law text box 11.1. The definition of 'food hygiene' in Regulation 852/2004.

Article 2 Definitions

1. For the purposes of this Regulation:
   (a) 'food hygiene', hereinafter called 'hygiene', means the measures and conditions necessary to control hazards and to ensure fitness for human consumption of a foodstuff taking into account its intended use;

11.2.2 EU food hygiene legislation

Regulation 852/2004 on the hygiene of foodstuffs is the centre of the new EC food hygiene legislation. This regulation provides the principles, rules, requirements and instruments for food hygiene law, and addresses the food business operators of all foodstuffs of every stage of the food production chain. The scope of this regulation is the collection of activities and situations where the food hygiene legislation of the EU applies.

The scope of the EU hygiene legislation

The scope of a regulation is the collection of activities and situations to which the rules and determinations of the regulation must be applied. Article 1 of Regulation 852/2004 is written to state the scope, at least that is what the title of that article suggests.[419] Article 1 comes closest to the description of its scope, the

[419] However, it is mainly a list of policy preferences that the legislator wants to achieve and his leading principles. Article 1 is the list of objectives of the regulation in the area and for the activities that fall under its sway. That is not the same as the extent of the area where the powers can or have to be exercised.

activities that the hygiene regulation is made to regulate, in the second sentence of its first paragraph:

> *'This Regulation shall apply to all stages of production, processing and distribution of food and to exports, and without prejudice to more specific requirements relating to food hygiene'.*

In this scope we recognise the holistic approach to food law discussed in Chapter 8. This description of the scope is somewhat more at a distance from the food production chain than the immediate predecessor of Regulation 852/2004, Directive 93/43, in its description of its objective. Article 3(1) of that directive prescribed:

> *'The preparation, processing, manufacturing, packaging, storing, transportation, distribution, handling and offering for sale or supply of foodstuffs shall be carried out in a hygienic way'.*[420]

Legislation is often more to the point when it excludes particular activities or situations from its scope. The four categories of matters that remain outside the rules of Regulation 852/2004 are:

1. primary production for private domestic use;
2. domestic preparation, handling or storage of food for private domestic consumption;
3. direct supply, by the producer, of small quantities of primary products to the final consumer or to local retail establishments directly supplying the final consumer;
4. collection centres and tanneries which fall within the definition of food business only because they handle raw material for the production of gelatine or collagen.[421]

The first two exclusions deal with two types of food production where the produce is not put on the market. In category 1 the food business operator, who is active in the primary stage of the food production chain, consumes the produce privately.

In category 2 a person who is not a food business operator at all, performs a series of actions that belong to the core activities of a group of food business operators but are in this case part of self provision outside the commercial food chain.[422]

The third category excludes direct local supply from the scope of Regulation 852/2004. This exclusion aims to prevent the full weight of EC food hygiene law applying to small local direct supply of primary products to the consumer, and local

[420] Article 3 Directive 93/43.

[421] Article 1(2) Regulation 852/2004.

[422] Article 1(2)(a) and (b) Regulation 852/2004.

supply of local retailers that stay away from the internal market by keeping their transactions with primary producers and local consumers close to home.[423]

The hygiene package

The scope of Regulation 852/2004 (this regulation is sometimes referred to as 'Hygiene 1') determines the outer reaches of the scopes of the other hygiene regulations because all add more specific legislation to the basic rules of Regulation 852/2004 and therefore remain within its bounds.

Regulation 853/2004 (sometimes referred to as 'Hygiene 2') lays down rules on the hygiene of food of animal origin. These rules supplement those laid down by Regulation 852/2004.[424]

Regulation 854/2004 (sometimes referred to as 'Hygiene 3') adds the rules that are necessary to organise official controls on compliance with Regulation 853/2004.[425]

The rules of Regulation 853/2004 and Regulation 854/2004 often deal with the same situation from opposite perspectives. Where, for example, Regulation 853/2004 commands the food business operator to cooperate with the competent authorities, Regulation 854/2004 directs the member states to see to it that food business operators offer all assistance needed to ensure that official controls carried out by the competent authority can be performed effectively.[426]

Regulation 882/2004 adds controls to prevent, eliminate or handle risks to humans and animals and guarantee fair practices in feed and food trade to protect consumer interests.[427]

The four regulations form a stack of rules addressed mainly to food business operators, but also to the Commission, to the Standing Committee on the Food Chain and Animal Health (SCFCAH), and to the member states. The rules are

[423] Article 1(2)(c) Regulation 852/2004. The member states get the assignment in Article 1(3) to make national law to rule over this situation. The freedom of the member states to make the rules that fit local-regional situations best is circumscribed by the condition that this national law must 'ensure the achievement of the objectives of this Regulation'. In effect this is a mini-directive surfacing in the midst of a regulation. This additional legislative task is akin to, but not mentioned in, Article 13 where the member states get other assignments or freedoms to legislate to safeguard traditional methods or to assist food business operators in areas with geographic constraints (Article 13(4)(a) Regulation 852/2004). The construction that allows national deviations from EC food hygiene law, provided they are so small and local that they do not disturb the internal market resembles the *'de minimis'* or bagatelle rule in EC competition law.

[424] Article 1 Regulation 853/2004.

[425] Article 1(2) Regulation 854/2004.

[426] Article 4(1) Regulation 854/2004.

[427] On official controls see also Chapter 13.

organised according to the definitions, principles and rules on food safety of the General Food Law and on the hygiene of foodstuffs of Regulation 852/2004. They become more specialised with Regulation 853/2004 that deals first with food of animal origin in general, and then with food of specific animal origins like fish, game, meat and milk, and continues with subdivisions that address food business operators responsible for ever more specialised foodstuffs of animal origin.

Who follows the trail encounters rules like:

> *'the temperature of the meat of lagomorphs is maintained at not more than 4 °C during cutting, boning, trimming, slicing, dicing, wrapping and packaging'.*[428]

Regulations 854/2004 and 882/2004 cover the rules on how food hygiene is controlled and enforced. The combination of rules on hygiene and rules on control creates new rules that are directly relevant for the food business operators.

The four regulations call for implementing regulations, made by the Commission in cooperation with the representatives of the member states in the Standing Committee on the Food Chain and Animal Health. To this category belong the regulations 2073/2005 on microbiological criteria for foodstuffs,[429] 2074/2005 implementing certain rules on food of animal origin, 2075/2005 on official controls for *Trichinella* in meat, and 2076/2005 with transitional arrangements. They entered into force together with the four hygiene regulations. Amidst the regulations one Directive 2004/41 was made to repeal most of the old hygiene directives and provide for transitory measures.

The stack of rules contains not only regulations but also explanations of the regulations in guidance documents usually written by civil servants from the Commission's Directorate-General Health & Consumer Protection. One of these guidance documents is presented by the SCFCAH. These documents offer a cautious type of interpretation: on the one hand they present the opinions of the public servants who are more involved with these matters and command greater expertise than anyone else, and present these opinions to the stakeholders in the light of transparency, while on the other hand they caution every reader that these opinions carry no weight and are used by each at his own peril, because only the Court of Justice has the power to present the final interpretation. While it is proper that the ultimate power of interpretation of the Court of Justice is respected, the non-binding character of the guidance documents does not go so far that the Commission can hold it against food businesses if they act as suggested in the guidelines.

[428] Regulation 853/2004, Annex III Specific requirements, Section II: Meat from poultry and lagomorphs, Chapter V: Hygiene during and after cutting and boning.

[429] On this regulation see also Chapter 10.

Law text box 11.2 presents a simplified[430] overview of the regulations, directive, and guidance documents of the EU food hygiene legislation. Diagram 11.2 gives a schematic representation of the relations between the regulations. The guidance documents are attachments to the regulations that they explain.

Law text box 11.2. A simplified overview of the regulations, directive, and guidance documents of the EU food hygiene legislation: the 'hygiene package'.

0. Regulation (EC) No 178/2002 of the European Parliament and of the Council of 28 January 2002 laying down the general principles and requirements of food law, establishing the European Food Safety Authority and laying down procedures in matters of food safety (Official Journal L 31, 1 February 2002, pp. 1-24).
   0a. Standing Committee on the Food Chain and Animal Health, Guidance on the Implementation of Articles 11, 12, 16, 17, 18, 19 and 20 of Regulation (EC) N° 178/2002 on General Food Law, Conclusions of the Standing Committee on the Food Chain and Animal Health, 20 December 2004.
1. Regulation (EC) No 852/2004 of the European Parliament and of the Council of 29 April 2004 on the hygiene of foodstuffs (Corrigendum: Official Journal L 226, 25 June 2004, pp. 3-21).
   1a. European Commission, Health & Consumer Protection Directorate-General, Guidance document on the implementation of certain provisions of Regulation (EC) No 852/2004 On the hygiene of foodstuffs, Brussels, 21 December 2005, pp. 1-17.
   1b. European Commission, Health & Consumer Protection Directorate-General, Guidance document on the implementation of procedures based on the HACCP principles, and on the facilitation of the implementation of the HACCP principles in certain food businesses, Brussels, 16 November 2005, pp. 1-26.
   1c. European Commission, Health & Consumer Protection Directorate-General, Directorate E – Safety of the food chain, E2 – Hygiene and control measures. Technical Specifications in Relation to the Master List and the Lists of EU Approved Food Establishments, SANCO/2179/2005 Revision 5. Presented at the meeting of the Standing Committee on the Food Chain and Animal Health on 22-23 November 2005.
   1d. European Commission, Health & Consumer Protection Directorate-General, Guidance document on certain key questions related to import requirements and the new rules on food hygiene and on official food controls, Brussels, 5.1.2006, pp. 1-28.

[430] One could argue that also part of the Hygiene package are: Directive 2002/99 laying down the animal health rules governing the production, processing, distribution and introduction of products of animal origin for human consumption (Official Journal L 18, 23 january 2003, p.11); with the connected General guidance on EU import and transit rules for live animals and animal products from third countries, DG Sanco Directorate D - Animal health and welfare 30 April 2006; Regulation (EC) No 183/2005 laying down requirements for feed hygiene (Official Journal L 35, 8 February 2005, pp.1-22) and the Opinion of the European Economic and Social Committee on 'Hygiene rules and artisanal food processors' (2006/C 65/25; Official Journal C 65, 17 March 2006, 141-148).

2. Regulation (EC) No 853/2004 of the European Parliament and of the Council of 29 April 2004 laying down specific hygiene rules for food of animal origin (Corrigendum: Official Journal L 226, 25 June 2004, pp. 22-82).
   2a. European Commission, Health & Consumer Protection Directorate-General, Guidance document on the implementation of certain provisions of Regulation (EC) No 853/2004 on the hygiene of food of animal origin, Brussels, 21 December 2005, pp. 1-21.
3. Directive 2004/41/EC of the European Parliament and of the Council of 21 April 2004 Repealing Certain Directives Concerning Food Hygiene and Health Conditions for the Production and Placing on the Market of Certain Products of Animal Origin Intended for Human Consumption and Amending Council Directives 89/662/EEC and 92/118/EEC and Council Decision 95/408/EC (Official Journal L 157, 30 April 2004, pp. 33-44).
4. Regulation (EC) No 854/2004 of the European Parliament and of the Council of 29 April 2004 laying down specific rules for the organisation of official controls on products of animal origin intended for human consumption (Corrigendum: Official Journal L 226, 25 June 2004, pp. 83-127).
5. Regulation (EC) No 882/2004 of the European Parliament and of the Council of 29 April 2004 on official controls performed to ensure the verification of compliance with feed and food law, animal health and animal welfare rules (Corrigendum: Official Journal L 191, 28 May 2004, pp. 1-52).
6. Commission Regulation (EC) No 2073/2005 of 15 November 2005 on microbiological criteria for foodstuffs (Official Journal L 338, 22 December 2005, pp. 1-26).
7. Commission Regulation (EC) No 2074/2005 of 5 December 2005 laying down implementing measures for certain products under Regulation (EC) No 853/2004 of the European Parliament and of the Council and for the organisation of official controls under Regulation (EC) No 854/2004 of the European Parliament and of the Council and Regulation (EC) No 882/2004 of the European Parliament and of the Council, derogating from Regulation (EC) No 852/2004 of the European Parliament and of the Council and amending Regulations (EC) No 853/2004 and (EC) No 854/2004 (Official Journal L 338, 22 December 2005, pp. 27-59).
8. Commission Regulation (EC) No 2075/2005 of 5 December 2005 laying down specific rules on official controls for Trichinella in meat (Official Journal L 338, 22 December 2005, pp. 60-82).
9. Commission Regulation (EC) No 2076/2005 of 5 December 2005 laying down transitional arrangements for the implementation of Regulation (EC) No 853/2004, (EC) No 854/2004 and (EC) No 882/2004 of the European Parliament and of the Council and amending Regulations (EC) No 853/2004 and (EC) No 854/2004 (Official Journal L 338, 22 December 2005, pp. 83-88).

Diagram 11.2. The hygiene package and related texts.

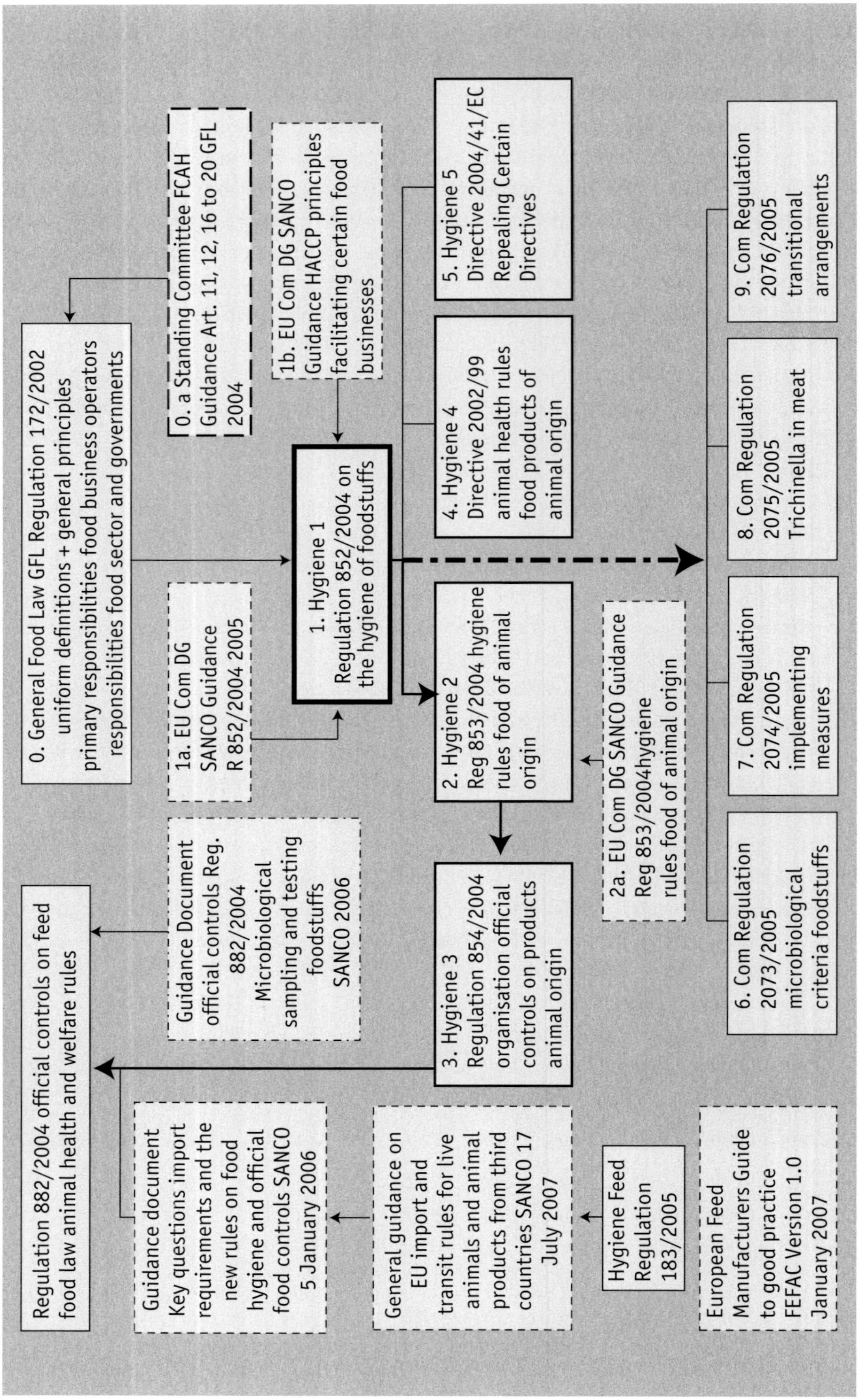

11.1.3 Instruments of food hygiene law

Regulation 852/2004 uses mainly three types of instruments to regulate the hygiene of foodstuffs: prescriptive rules, procedures based on the Hazard Analysis and Critical Control Point (HACCP) system and guides to good hygiene practice. EU regulations often contain a mix of rules and decisions addressed to a mix of EU institutions, the member states, the citizens and their organisations. Regulation 852/2004 is directed mainly at the food business operators, but also at the food business sectors, consumer organisations and authorities on the national level[431] and on the Union level,[432] to the Commission,[433] to the SCFCAH[434] and to the member states.[435]

The ultimate aim of all these rules, invitations, exceptions, delegations of power and assignment of duties is to influence the activities and positions of the people who are involved with the hygiene aspects of food to secure a high level of food safety.

Rules as an instrument for food hygiene
Among the rules directed at the different persons and organisations mentioned above, one group addresses the food business operators directly. To distinguish these rules from the other instruments, we will call them 'direct legislation'. These are the examples of legislation in the classic sense of rules laid down for persons and situations outside the organisation of government to be applied time and again, as long as the conditions set by the legislation for its application are fulfilled. The direct legislation can be found in a few articles of the main body of Regulation 852/2004, in its two Annexes and in many articles of Regulation 853/2004

431 For example in Article 8(1) Regulation 852/2004 where the national food sector organisations are asked to make guides to good hygiene practices.
432 In Article 9(2)(a) where the Commission has to consult them on European guides to good practice.
433 In Article 15 where the Commission is charged to consult with EFSA on hygiene matters that could have a significant impact on public health.
434 In its Comitology Article 14.
435 In Article 13(3) and 13(4)(a)(i) where member states get the power to take national measures to enable the continued use of traditional methods, at any of the stages of production, processing or distribution of food. The special position of the EU as a half-way house between an international organisation and a (federal) state gives its rules and decisions a hybrid character. Rules directed to the authorities of the member states are applied by them to take decisions that are necessary to give effect to EU law. When a system of EU hygiene law is introduced replacing directives by regulations it operates directly for the persons or organisations that are addressed by the articles. That does not mean that the rules and decisions of the regulation take care of themselves, that the authorities of the member states have to wait and see what happens. When the regulations mention a duty to approve establishments where food of animal origin is processed, arrangements have to be made that some authority will issue approvals. In most cases the EU institutions do not set up an EU system. Authorities of the member states will then create national systems of approval that will issue national approvals based on EU criteria.

The second and most important type of instrument is the creation of the obligation for food business operators to apply a procedure based on the HACCP system. This system of food safety management was developed in the US and has been promoted for almost four decades by the Codex Alimentarius Commission.

The third type is the creation of guides to good hygiene practice, developed by food business sectors, accepted voluntarily by food business operators, promoted and approved by the member states and registered by the Commission.

All these instruments were already in use in the old food hygiene legislation of the EU, but less complete or under different conditions.

The layout of the Regulations 852/2004 and 853/2004
The food hygiene legislation of the EU is made as a system of stacked regulations where each regulation has a systematic exposition of its contents. This layout is presented in Diagrams 11.3 and 11.4 for Regulation 852/2004 and Regulation 853/2004.

11.1.4 Direct legislation

Article 3 of Regulation 852/2004 reiterates the responsibility of food business operators expressed in Article 17(1) GFL. Food business operators shall ensure that all stages of production, processing and distribution food under their control satisfy the relevant hygiene requirements of this regulation.

Regulation 852/2004 deals in Article 4 with the complexity of EU hygiene legislation. This article elaborates which provisions apply to whom:
- businesses in primary production apply Annex I A of Regulation 852/2004 and any specific requirements of Regulation 853/2004;
- other businesses apply Annex II of Regulation 852/2004 and any specific requirements of Regulation 853/2004;
- all food businesses shall comply with hygiene measures set by the European Commission (on microbiology, temperature control and the like);
- all food business may use guides to Good hygiene Practice to comply with their obligations.

Article 4 connects the rules of Regulation 852/2004 with the rules of Regulation 853/2004 explicitly. It underlines the binding force and the unity of the articles in the main body of Regulation 852/2004 with its two Annexes and the corresponding parts of Regulation 853/2004. This is especially important for the unity of the direct legislation directed to the food business operators.

Diagram 11.3. The internal organisation of Regulation 852/2004 on the hygiene of foodstuffs.

Chapter I General provisions	**Chapter II Food business operators' obligations**	**Chapter III Guides to Good Practice**	**Chapter IV Imports and Exports**	**Chapter V Final provisions**	**Annex I Primary Production**	**Annex II General hygiene requirements for all food business operators (Except when Annex I applies) Chapter I-XII**
				Art. 12 Implementing measures and transitional arrangements	Part A: General Hygiene Provisions for Primary Production and Associated Operations	I General requirements for food premises (other than those specified in Chapter III) II Specific requirements in rooms where foodstuffs are prepared, treated or processed (excluding dining areas and those premises specified in Chapter III) III Requirements for movable and/or temporary premises (such as marquees, market stalls, mobile sales vehicles), premises used primarily as a private dwelling-house but where foods are regularly prepared for placing on the market and vending machines
				Art. 13 Amendment and adaptation of Annexes I and II		
	Art. 3 General obligation					
Art. 1 Scope	Art. 4 General and specific hygiene requirements	Art. 7 Development, dissemination and use of guides	Art. 10 Imports	Art. 14 Committee procedure		IV Transport
Art. 2 Definitions	Art. 5 Hazard analysis and critical control points	Art. 8 National guides	Art. 11 Exports	Art. 15 Consultation of the European Food Safety Authority		V Equipment requirements VI Food waste VII Water supply VIII Personal hygiene
	Art. 6 Official controls, registration and approval	Art. 9 Community guides		Art. 16 Report to the European Parliament and to the Council	Part B: Recommendations for Guides to Good Hygiene Practice	IX Provisions applicable to foodstuffs X Provisions applicable to the wrapping and packaging of foodstuffs XI Heat treatment XII Training
				Art. 17 Repeals		
				Art. 18 Entry into force		
What is this regulation about?	*Introduction of obligations, direct legislation, and alternative system of hazard management*	*Instrument for voluntary cooperation and preparation*	*Art. 3-6 < Art. 11 and 12 GFL*	*Internal maintenance of legislation*	*A: direct legislation, B: advise*	*Detailed direct legislation for food business operators active after primary production and dealing with food of vegetal origin, animal origin or both.*

Diagram 11.4. The internal organisation of Regulation 853/2004 laying down specific hygiene rules for food of animal origin.

Chapter I General provisions	Chapter II Food business operators' obligations	Chapter III Trade	Chapter IV Final provisions	Annex I Definitions	Annex II Requirements concerning several products of animal origin	Annex III Specific requirements
				1. Meat		I: Meat of domestic ungulates
			Art. 9 Implementing measures and transitional measures			II: Meat from poultry and lagomorphs III: Meat of farmed game IV: Wild game meat
			Art. 10 Amendment and adaptation of Annexes II and III		Section I Identification marking A. Application of the identification mark B. Form of the identification mark C. Method of marking Section II: Objectives of HACCP-based procedures	V: Minced meat, meat preparations and mechanically separated meat (msm) VI: Meat products
	Art. 3 General obligations		Art. 11 Specific decisions			
Art. 1 Scope	Art. 4 Registration and approval of establishments	Art. 7 Documents	Art. 12 Committee procedure	2. Live bivalve molluscs		VII: Live bivalve molluscs
Art. 2 Definitions	Art. 5 Health and identification marking	Art. 8 Special guarantees on negative outcome of microbiological tests and elimination of salmonella for meat and eggs	Art. 13 Consultation of the European Food Safety Authority	3. Fishery products		VIII: Fishery products
	Art. 6 Products of animal origin from outside the Community		Art. 14 Report to the European Parliament and to the Council	4. Milk 5. Eggs 6. Frogs' legs and snails 7. Processed products	Section III: Food chain information	IX: Raw milk and dairy products X: Eggs and egg products XI: Frogs' legs and snails XII: Rendered animal fats and greaves XIII: Treated stomachs, bladders and intestines XIV: Gelatine XV: Collagen
			Art. 15 Entry into force			
				8. Other definitions		Appendix to Annex III
What is this regulation about?	Introduction of general obligation, announcement of instruments	Special guarantees for Sweden and Finland	Internal provisions for the application and maintenance of the regulation	Concepts determining application of regulation	Direct legislation for identification of products	Direct legislation for foodstuff indicated by Section headings

The fact that the most detailed rules that prescribe directly what behaviour is expected from the food business operators is part of the annexes does not mean that these rules have a lower rank than the rules in the main body of the regulations. They are an integral part of the regulations, as Article 4 shows for Regulation 852/2004.

These rules of a technical nature are placed in the annexes because the annexes can be changed by the comitology procedure. Normally, the co-decision procedure where the full power of the European Parliament is brought to bear, applies to changes (in the main body) in the regulation. In comitology the representatives of the member states take decisions with the weighted votes of the member states, under the chairmanship of a representative of the Commission.[436] The European Parliament agreed to give up some of its power to facilitate changes needed to keep up with technical developments.

11.1.5 Registration and approval

As has been mentioned in Chapter 8, section 8.3.3 establishments used for any stage in the food chain must be registered and in many cases approved. This requirement is one of the examples where the complexity of the hygiene package is felt. Provisions dealing with this issue are: Article 6 of Regulation 852/2004, Article 4 of Regulation 853/2004, Article 3 of Regulation 854/2004 and Article 31 of Regulation 882/2004.

Registration of establishments where food is handled

Article 6 of Regulation 852/2004 has the heading 'Official controls, registration and approval'. It addresses food business operators. It is the basis of the obligation to have each food establishment registered, but not the basis of the EU approval system.

Every food business operator has to apply for registration of each establishment under his control where any of the stages of production, processing and distribution of food is carried out. The registration has to contain the essential data on the address, and the food hygiene related activities at that address.[437] The address of each premises has to be registered when the establishment has different premises.[438]

The food business operator has to see to it that the competent authority has up-to-date information on establishments at all times. Significant changes in activities and closure of an existing establishment have to be reported to the authorities.

436 On comitology see Chapter 5, section 5.5.

437 Article 6 Regulation 852/2004.

438 Article 6 in combination with Chapter I of Annex II Regulation 852/2004.

The authorities in the member states have to make the procedures on how to obtain registration.[439]

Approval of establishments

Every establishment in the EU where food of animal origin is produced or handled has to be approved by the authorities of the member states applying EU legislation. What is the basis of this approval system? It takes some close reading to find that basis in Regulation 854/2004, the regulation on hygiene controls.[440]

In fact, four regulations deal with the subject of approval of establishments. Article 6 of Regulation 852/2004 prepares the approval systems by making the food business operator responsible for the approval by the competent authorities and even for the fact that this approval is given only after the authority has paid at least one on-site visit. This is clearly more than an obligation to cooperate with the authorities.

However, these responsibilities of the food business operator do not create the approval system. Article 6(3) merely prepares the food business operator in case an approval system is part of national law, Regulation 853/2004 or one of the comitology decisions.

Regulation 853/2004 and the consequences

Article 4 of Regulation 853/2004 has the heading 'registration and approval'. It supports the requirements of registration and approval by dealing with its consequences. Food business operators are not allowed to place their products on the market if they have been made in or otherwise related to an establishment that has not been approved.[441] Likewise operators have to stop with every food hygiene related activity when the approval of their establishment has been withdrawn.[442]

The granting and cancelling of approvals are based on the next food hygiene regulation.[443]

Regulation 854/2004 approval and approval number

Article 3(5) of Regulation 854/2004 creates the EU approval system for establishments that begin placing products of animal origin on the market. It prescribes that the competent authority has to make an on-site visit and will approve an establishment only if the food business operator has demonstrated that he meets the relevant

[439] Article 31(1)(a) Regulation 882/2004.
[440] It is unclear why registration and approval are based on different regulations.
[441] Article 4(2) of Regulation 853/2004.
[442] Article 4(4) of Regulation 853/2004.
[443] Article 4(3) of Regulation 853/2004.

requirements of Regulations 852/2004 and 853/2004 and other of food law.[444] The competent authority gives each approved establishment an approval number with a code that indicates the type of product of animal origin that is manufactured in that establishment.[445]

Regulation 882/2004 and the list of all approved establishments in the EU
Regulation 882/2004, finally, is involved because it orders the member states to make the procedures that food business operators have to follow when they apply for approval of their establishment.[446] The member states have to maintain up-to-date lists of approved establishments, with their respective approval numbers and other relevant information, and make them available to other member states and to the public.[447]

The Commission has created a website that provides access to the national lists of the EU member states, the other EEA countries and other countries with special agreements (Switzerland, Føroyar, San Marino).[448]

11.1.6 Prerequisites

The annexes to Regulation 852/2004 contain direct legislation of a technical and detailed nature. Annex I is made for the primary sector. The special position of primary production is discussed at the end of this section.

Annex II is called General Hygiene Requirements for All Food Business Operators (Except When Annex I Applies). It contains direct legislation addressed to all food business operators outside primary production and its associated activities. The rules in this annex are often referred to as the 'prerequisites'. This term expresses that it only makes sense to apply HACCP (discussed hereafter) if basic requirements are fulfilled. The rules are organised into twelve chapters by applying two principles. First the locality where the activities of the food business take place (Chapters I-III). Then the aspects of hygiene that are relevant in all stages of the production chain. These aspects are the production inputs, equipment, clean working circumstances and water supply (Chapters V-VII), the human factor in personal hygiene and training (Chapters VIII and XII) and the protection, wrapping and packaging of the cause of it all, the product food (Chapters IX and

444 Article 3(1)(a) Regulation 854/2004.
445 Article 3(3) Regulation 854/2004.
446 Article 31(2)(a) Regulation 882/2004.
447 Article 3(6) Regulation 854/2004 and Article 31(2)(a) Regulation 882/2004. That even the Commission's civil servants occasionally get lost in the forest of seemingly redundant articles of the hygiene complex, is shown on the website of the list of approved food establishments where the obligation to approve establishments is attributed to Regulation 882/2004 in general. It is however very particularly Article 3(5) of Regulation 854/2004, Regulation 882/2004 that provides the procedures.
448 See the reference list for a hyperlink to the Community Register of approved food establishments.

X). Transport holds the position between the localised factors and the mobilised factors in Chapter IV.

Food premises

Annex II opens with a puzzle on the location where food hygiene legislation is to be applied. The convolutions of the sequence of the first three chapters give the distinct impression that the legislator is trying to get a grip on the many possible establishments, places, rooms, tents and other things that have to be captured under the law that is laid down for the operator who is active in them. The legislator uses the term 'premises' to differentiate the relevant places. There is no definition here and no use of the term 'establishment' that is used to register or approve a food business. Regulation 852/2004 does give the definition of the term establishment: 'any unit of a food business', but does not use it when localisation is the subject of the legislation.[449] The combination with the GFL definition of food business makes clear that an establishment is a unit of a concerted activity where both place and activity are at issue but the activity dominates the concept. One thing seems clear however: when food business operators have to provide information on the whereabouts of their business units they have to be specific about the premises level.[450] The presentation of the direct legislation in Annex II is organised according to premises that are immovable and a recognisable part of the means used in the food production chain dedicated to food or movable and equally dedicated such as fishing ships in Chapter I. They become detailed at the room level and in close contact with spaces used for other activities from which they have to be separated in Chapter II, and pass into the impermanent, temporarily built structures in Chapter III to become fully mobile in Chapter IV, but then they are no longer business units, they have become means of transport only.

Rules addressed to a food business operator deal with an operator who is either stationary or on the move. When he is stationary he has a location that is temporarily or more or less permanent.[451]

The function of direct legislation in the annexes is to provide a guaranteed minimum.

449 Article 2(1)(c) Regulation 852/2004.

450 The legislation made to assist the implementation of the EU food hygiene regulations in the part of the UK after devolution called England provides the following definition of premises: 'premises' includes any establishment, any place, vehicle, stall or moveable structure and any ship or aircraft. Article 2(1) Interpretation, Statutory Instruments 2005 No. 2059 Food, England. The Food Hygiene (England) Regulations 2005, Made 21st July 2005, Laid before Parliament 10th August 2005, Coming into force 1st January 2006.

451 Reality is a flux. Persons are even more flexible as no one would imagine a person to be permanently located on some spot. It is not the position of the food business operator as such that is of interest here, we are not looking for the operator in or after business hours, but the position of the relevant activity or inactivity.

Article 4 performs a core function for the larger set of direct rules on food hygiene. Two of the legislator's instruments, HACCP procedures and voluntary guides, are based on a high degree of autonomy for the food business operators. They will use these instruments according to their experience and knowledge.

But to leave it at that would make the objective of secured food hygiene dependent on the uncertain success of 'procedures based on' HACCP, something that is a set of procedures by itself, and on the voluntary adoption of good practices. A degree of dependence and uncertainty that is unacceptable for a legislator who wants to maintain a high level of food safety, after earlier failures. So, for short, the direct legislation in the annexes acts as the available reserve legislation that is made to guarantee the objective of a high level of food hygiene as best as legislation can. The other two instruments can improve that result or compensate the weaknesses of direct regulation.

The direct legislation represents the old style food hygiene legislation: the legislator prescribes the rules that have to be applied by all those involved with food hygiene. A control system is set up to guard over the implementation of the legislation and enforcement measures are available. In relation to the other elements of Regulation 852/2004 it can be said that the rules provide the clearest information for food business operators on what they have to do to meet the requirements of the law.

Set against these other approaches, the binding rules set the stage for the other instruments of Regulation 852/2004 by providing the floor on which they have to perform their part. If that floor is set high enough it can spur a dynamic mix of instruments to compensate each other's weak points. Recital 12 of Regulation 852/2004 wishes just that:

> *'Food safety is a result of several factors: legislation should lay down minimum hygiene requirements; ...';*

Law text box 11.3 gives the chapter headings each with one article to illustrate the contents and organisation of Annex II to Regulation 852/2004. It gives an impression of the direct legislation in Annex II as it is not possible to discuss these very detailed rules at this point. The examples are representative for the rules in Annex II of Regulation 852/2004. They also indicate the character of the annexes with direct legislation of the other three major food hygiene regulations.

Law text box 11.3. Annex II to Regulation 852/2004: chapter headings with one representative article per chapter.

Annex II General Hygiene Requirements for All Food Business Operators (Except When Annex I Applies)

I Food premises

2. The layout, design, construction, siting and size of food premises are to: (a) permit adequate maintenance, cleaning and/or disinfection, avoid or minimise air-borne contamination, and provide adequate working space to allow for the hygienic performance of all operations;

II Rooms

1. In rooms where food is prepared, treated or processed (excluding dining areas and those premises specified in Chapter III, but including rooms contained in means of transport) the design and layout are to permit good food hygiene practices, including protection against contamination between and during operations. In particular:

(b) wall surfaces are to be maintained in a sound condition and be easy to clean and, where necessary, to disinfect. This will require the use of impervious, non-absorbent, washable and non-toxic materials and require a smooth surface up to a height appropriate for the operations unless food business operators can satisfy the competent authority that other materials used are appropriate;

III Special types of food premises: not permanent, not fixed, nor exclusive

Requirements for movable and/or temporary premises (such as marquees, market stalls, mobile sales vehicles), premises used primarily as a private dwelling-house but where foods are regularly prepared for placing on the market and vending machines

1. Premises and vending machines are, so far as is reasonably practicable, to be so sited, designed, constructed and kept clean and maintained in good repair and condition as to avoid the risk of contamination, in particular by animals and pests.
2. In particular, where necessary:

(a) appropriate facilities are to be available to maintain adequate personal hygiene (including facilities for the hygienic washing and drying of hands, hygienic sanitary arrangements and changing facilities);

IV Transport

1. Conveyances and/or containers used for transporting foodstuffs are to be kept clean and maintained in good repair and condition to protect foodstuffs from contamination and are, where necessary, to be designed and constructed to permit adequate cleaning and/or disinfection.
5. Where conveyances and/or containers have been used for transporting anything other than foodstuffs or for transporting different foodstuffs, there is to be effective cleaning between loads to avoid the risk of contamination.

V Equipment

1. All articles, fittings and equipment with which food comes into contact are to:

(a) be effectively cleaned and, where necessary, disinfected. Cleaning and disinfection are to take place at a frequency sufficient to avoid any risk of contamination;

VI Food waste

1. Food waste, non-edible by-products and other refuse are to be removed from rooms where food is present as quickly as possible, so as to avoid their accumulation.

VII Water supply

1. (a) There is to be an adequate supply of potable water, which is to be used whenever necessary to ensure that foodstuffs are not contaminated;

(b) Clean water may be used with whole fishery products. Clean seawater may be used with live bivalve molluscs, echinoderms, tunicates and marine gastropods; clean water may also be used for external washing. When such water is used, adequate facilities are to be available for its supply.

VIII Personal hygiene

1. Every person working in a food-handling area is to maintain a high degree of personal cleanliness and is to wear suitable, clean and, where necessary, protective clothing.
2. No person suffering from, or being a carrier of a disease likely to be transmitted through food or afflicted, for example, with infected wounds, skin infections, sores or diarrhoea is to be permitted to handle food or enter any food-handling area in any capacity if there is any likelihood of direct or indirect contamination. Any person so affected and employed in a food business and who is likely to come into contact with food is to report immediately the illness or symptoms, and if possible their causes, to the food business operator.

IX Foodstuffs

3. At all stages of production, processing and distribution, food is to be protected against any contamination likely to render the food unfit for human consumption, injurious to health or contaminated in such a way that it would be unreasonable to expect it to be consumed in that state.

X Provisions applicable to the wrapping and packaging of foodstuffs

3. Wrapping and packaging operations are to be carried out so as to avoid contamination of the products. Where appropriate and in particular in the case of cans and glass jars, the integrity of the container's construction and its cleanliness is to be assured.

XI Heat treatment

XII Training

Food business operators are to ensure:

1. that food handlers are supervised and instructed and/or trained in food hygiene matters commensurate with their work activity;
2. that those responsible for the development and maintenance of the procedure referred to in Article 5(1) of this Regulation or for the operation of relevant guides have received adequate training in the application of the HACCP principles;

11.1.7 HACCP

Space age experience has shown that the testing of food products does not provide sufficient certainty that similar products in the same lot are safe. To ensure that astronauts will not suffer from diarrhoea or food poisoning during their stay in space, in 1959 the US space agency NASA developed a method of food production aimed at eliminating all possible hazards from the production process. This is the so-called HACCP-system (Hazard Analysis and Critical Control Points).[452] Within this system the production process is analysed to establish what kind of hazards may enter the product in which part of the process. Procedures have been developed to prevent hazards or to deal with the consequences. Meticulous application of such a system in combination with testing of products achieves the highest possible level of food safety. The World Health Organisation (WHO) and the Food and Agricultural Organisation (FAO) have recommended the world wide use of HACCP-based systems to ensure safe production of food (e.g. food hygiene).[453] This recommendation has been implemented in EU legislation. The application of HACCP is obligatory for virtually[454] all food businesses in the EU. As a consequence food businesses have to analyse their processes, to establish procedures to ensure hygiene and to exercise self control on the functioning of these systems. In other words: the businesses have to formulate and uphold the rules that apply to their processes.

The 'Hazard analysis and critical control point', system is the second type of instrument of Regulation 852/2004. It holds a prominent place in EU food hygiene law. According to Article 5(1) Regulation 852/2004, food business operators shall put in place, implement and maintain a permanent procedure based on the HACCP principles. The EU definition of the HACCP principles is in line with the international standard for the first time. The HACCP system is well established. It has been adopted by the Codex Alimentarius Commission in 1969. The present Codex version is the fourth revision from 2003. See Law text box 11.4 for the position of the HACCP system in EU hygiene law.

Law text box 11.4. Definition of HACCP principles in Article 5, Regulation 852/2004.

Article 5
Hazard analysis and critical control points

1. Food business operators shall put in place, implement and maintain a permanent procedure or procedures based on the HACCP principles.
2. The HACCP principles referred to in paragraph 1 consist of the following:

---

452 See on HACCP and other quality assurance systems: M. Fogden, Hygiene, in: Kaarin Goodburn (ed.) EU food law, Woodhead Publishing Cambridge UK, 2001; P.A. Luning, W.J. Marcelis and W.M.F. Jongen, Food quality management. a techno-managerial approach, Wageningen Academic Publishers The Netherlands 2002; and M. van der Spiegel, Measuring effectiveness of food quality management (diss.) Wageningen University, the Netherlands 2004.

453 See: for instance CAC/RCP 1-1969, rev. 4 (2003) Recommended International Code of Practice General Principles of Food Hygiene; CAC/GL 21 - 1997; Principles for the Establishment and Application of Microbiological Criteria for Foods; CAC/GL-30 (1999) Principles and Guidelines for the Conduct of Microbiological Risk Assessment. These texts have been published in: Codex Alimentarius, Basis texts on Food Hygiene, 3rd edition Rome, 2003. for a hyperlink see the reference list.

454 There are some exceptions. E.g. a somewhat less stringent regime of food hygiene applies to primary production.

(a) dentifying any hazards that must be prevented, eliminated or reduced to acceptable levels;
(b) identifying the critical control points at the step or steps at which control is essential to prevent or eliminate a hazard or to reduce it to acceptable levels;
(c) establishing critical limits at critical control points which separate acceptability from unacceptability for the prevention, elimination or reduction of identified hazards;
(d) establishing and implementing effective monitoring procedures at critical control points;
(e) establishing corrective actions when monitoring indicates that a critical control point is not under control;
(f) establishing procedures, which shall be carried out regularly, to verify that the measures outlined in subparagraphs (a) to (e) are working effectively; and
(g) establishing documents and records commensurate with the nature and size of the food business to demonstrate the effective application of the measures outlined in subparagraphs (a) to (f).

When any modification is made in the product, process, or any step, food business operators shall review the procedure and make the necessary changes to it.

3. Paragraph 1 shall apply only to food business operators carrying out any stage of production, processing and distribution of food after primary production [...].
4. Food business operators shall:
(a) provide the competent authority with evidence of their compliance with paragraph 1 in the manner that the competent authority requires, taking account of the nature and size of the food business;
(b) ensure that any documents describing the procedures developed in accordance with this Article are up-to-date at all times;
(c) retain any other documents and records for an appropriate period.
5. Detailed arrangements for the implementation of this Article may be laid down in accordance with the procedure referred to in Article 14(2). Such arrangements may facilitate the implementation of this Article by certain food business operators, in particular by providing for the use of procedures set out in guides for the application of HACCP principles, in order to comply with paragraph 1. Such arrangements may also specify the period during which food business operators shall retain documents and records in accordance with paragraph 4(c).

The HACCP system

With regard to the HACCP approach, the food business operator is set on a course that will give him more control over the processes he is responsible for, more information on what goes on and what goes wrong in his business and hence the tools to guarantee food hygiene and to improve on standards already achieved. The application of HACCP is a continuing process that is founded on the efforts already made, on changes in the food business internally, and in the outside world. The responsible food business operator is approached in a way that is very different from a set of rules specified in advance and applied to situations that must be isolated to determine whether a certain rule has been applied correctly.

The HACCP approach offers not a specified set of rules on what is allowed but a method to achieve what is allowed, and an incentive to do even better.

The food business operators applying HACCP has to analyse his or her own processes; has to identify the hazards and has to decide on the measures to deal with them. For this reason HACCP is often referred to as enforced (or imposed) self-regulation. 'Self-regulation' because ultimately the rules applying to the production process have to be formulated by the food business operator. 'Imposed' because unlike other types of self-regulation to do so is not a free choice.

The EU applications of the HACCP system

The EU has had a haphazard relationship with HACCP. Parts and pieces of the system were introduced by the EC in the past. Directive 93/43 ordered food business operators to apply principles such as the HACCP principles to identify the critical points in the food production under their command. The directive did prescribe the use of a system based on HACCP that more or less resembled the first six steps of the present Article 5(2)(a-f) of regulation 852/2004, but in different words and a different 5 steps sequence.[455] It did not include the present Article 5(2)(g), the document and record system to demonstrate the effective application of the steps a-f. Documentation and record keeping are essential to be able to evaluate and compare the developments over a period of time.

The introduction of documents and record keeping, the obligation to keep them up-to-date at all time and to retain them for an appropriate period have the added effect that official controls have extensive inside information.

Micro enterprises and HACCP guidance

An academic study in the UK in 2003 suggested that 62 percent of small food business proprietors do not understand which food safety regulations are relevant to them, and 42 per cent do not understand hazard analysis.[456]

The position of food business operators active in small firms has been debated extensively. The argument that the formulation of the HACCP obligations in Regulation 852/2004 is made to allow different applications, especially for small firms and the explicit statement in Article 5(5) that arrangements for the implementation may facilitate the implementation of HACCP by certain food business operators, was not reassuring. The repeated attempts to explain the flexibility of the system in stakeholder meetings did not reassure either. Nor did

[455] Article 3(2-5) Directive 93/43.

[456] Hampton, Philip, Reducing administrative burdens: effective inspection and enforcement, HM Treasury, March 2005, point 12 on page 5. For a hyperlink see the reference list.

the authoritative interpretation of the new hygiene legislation in the guidance document.[457]

The concerns for small businesses resulted in the introduction of a proposal to change Article 5. See Law text box 11.5 for the text of the proposal and its current position in the decision making procedures.

Law text box 11.5. Proposal: no HACCP obligations for micro-enterprises.

Article 2
In Article 5(3) of Regulation (EC) No 852/2004, the following sentence is added:
Without prejudice to the other requirements of this Regulation, paragraph 1 shall not apply to businesses which are micro-enterprises within the meaning of Commission Recommendation 2003/361/EC of 6 May 2003[11] and the activities of which consist predominantly in the direct sale of food to the final consumer.

Proposal for a Regulation of the European Parliament and of the Council amending Regulation No 11 concerning the abolition of discrimination in transport rates and conditions, in implementation of Article 79 (3) of the Treaty establishing the European Economic Community and Regulation (EC) No 852/2004 of the European Parliament and the Council on the hygiene of foodstuffs {SEC(2007) 301} {SEC(2007) 302} {SEC(2007) 303} {SEC(2007) 304}, COM/2007/0090 final - COD 2007/0037. Date of document: 06/03/2007, date of transmission: 07/03/2007; Forwarded to the Council for first reading.
Current status: Approval with amendments by European Parliament on 5 June 2008 in first reading. Formal adoption by Council on 12 June 2008.

11.1.8 Guides to Good Hygiene Practice

The third type of instrument of Regulation 852/2004 for food hygiene, the guides to good hygiene practice, provides an alternative to the individual application of HACCP. See Law text box 11.6.

Law text box 11.6. Article 4(6) Regulation 852/2004 on Guides to Good Hygiene Practice.

Article 4(6) Regulation 852/2004
Food business operators may use the guides provided for in Articles 7, 8 and 9 as an aid to compliance with their obligations under this Regulation.

457 Guidance document 2b in Law text box 11.2 and Diagram 11.2; Guidance document on the implementation of procedures based on the HACCP principles, and on the facilitation of the implementation of the HACCP, principles in certain food businesses, Brussels, 2005. A handicap may have been the standard statement in every guidance document that the Commission takes no responsibility for the interpretation, and the further cautioning of every reader not to rely on the guidance document.

The national guides are made by the food business sectors on their own initiative. The legislation for the European guides makes it possible for the Commission to take the initiative on the EU level, if the member states allow it. But it can hardly be more than a spark that ignites a burning desire by food producers to make a European guide, there is no sense in forcing voluntary participation.

Chapter III of Regulation 852/2004 gives rules that have to be applied when a Guide is made, that instruct the member states to assess the national guides and to forward the approved guides to the Commission. Guides can also be made on the EU level.

National guides

The national guides will be developed by the food business sectors themselves.

The persons or organisations in the food business sectors who take the initiative to develop a guide have to meet three conditions:

- They have to consult representatives of the persons and organisations whose interest may be substantially affected. The regulation mentions competent authorities and consumer groups explicitly;[458]
- The drafters have to use the relevant codes of practice of the Codex Alimentarius;
- They have to use the recommendations set out in Annex I Part B of Regulation 852/2004 when primary production is involved.[459]

The legislator recommends each initiative to seek the support of their national standards institute to benefit from its authority.

Approval by the member state

The member states have to assess the national guides to ensure that the three conditions set for their development have been observed.[460]

In addition the member states have to test the guides on two other aspects, their practicality and potential to help the food business operator to fulfil a part of his food hygiene obligations. Regulation 852/2004 specifies the parts where good hygiene practices can be most effective: the general obligation of Article 3, the rules and the two Annexes based on Article 4, the permanent procedures based on the HACCP principles of Article 5 and the specific obligations under Regulation 853/2004.

The member states have to send the guides that have passed the test to the Commission who will place them in a register without further testing.

458 Article 8(1)(a) Regulation 852/2004.
459 Article 8(1)(a) - (c) Regulation 852/2004.
460 Article 8(3)(a) Regulation 852/2004.

EC register of national guides

The Commission has to set up a register of national guides and make that available to all member states.[461] The Commission made the EC 'Register of national guides to good hygiene practice' publicly available on a webpage of DG Sanco.[462] The Register began with a list of 415 national guides and gives for each one the following information: title in the original language, title in English, country, language, author, edition, and ISBN or ISSN. It presents a list of keywords on good hygiene practices with an internet address or other contact in the member states. Many of these guides where made under the old Council Directive 93/43/EEC on the hygiene of foodstuffs. The new legislation contains the standard rule that these guides continue to apply when they are compatible with its objectives.[463]

European Guides

The Commission takes a more active part in the creation of guides at the EU level than the governments do at the member state level. The Commission has to use the Comitology procedure to decide with the member states whether European guides will be made, and what scope and subject matter they will have. Article 9 of regulation 852/2004 mentions explicitly European Community guides to good hygiene practice and guides for the application of the HACCP principles.

When the member states have decided to make a European guide, it is for the Commission to ensure that they will be made. The Commission will perform tasks that are comparable with the tasks of the member states in the development process of the national guides, but markedly more active. European guides are published in the Official Journal of the EU. The Commission has published guidelines for the development of community guides to good practice for hygiene and for the application of the HACCP principles.[464]

National and European guides

When the law for EU voluntary guides to good hygiene practice is compared with the law on the national guides there are a number of marked differences. Two main points are the dominance of the EU in the procedure to develop European guides, and the position of the member states. Subsidiarity explains part of the elaborate testing that has to be done before guides on the EU level are even contemplated.

---

461 Article 8(4) Regulation 852/2004.

462 The Register's internet address can be found in the reference list.

463 Article 8(5) Regulation 852/2004.

464 Guidelines for the development of community guides to good practice for hygiene and for the application of the HACCP principles, in accordance with Article 9 of Regulation (EC) No 852/2004 on the hygiene of foodstuffs and Article 22 of Regulation (EC) No 183/2005 laying down requirements for feed hygiene.

On the other hand the more active position of the Commission can be explained by a shortage of representative partners over the full range of affected interests due to the weaker civil society on the EU level when compared with the national level. The Commission is more active on the EU level to compensate for the missing parts of the civil society. Law text box 11.7 on the role of governments in the promotion of guides to good hygiene practice compares the different rules for the development of these guides on the national and EU levels.

Law text box 11.7. The role of governments in the promotion of guides to good hygiene practice.

Task in the development of guides to good hygiene practice	**Performed by the government of the member states for national guides Art. 8 Reg. 852/2004**	**Performed by the Commission for Community guides. Art. 9 Reg. 852/2004**
Initiative:	No government decisions on desirability or necessity and contents	
Functions of public law authorities	National governments encourage national guide. Art. 7	Member states decide first in Comitology procedure whether European guides are made, their scope and subject matter: Art. 9(1).
	National governments make information available on how to make guides (No Article)	
Development and dissemination	By food business sectors: Art. 8(1)	'By' appropriate representatives of European food business sectors, including SMEs and other interested parties like consumer groups: Art. 9(2)(a) 'by'.
Public law authorities do more than encouraging and take the initiative	No	'or in' *consultation with* same groups: Art. 9(2)(a)
	Commission can take the initiative. Art. 9(2)(a) 'or in'	
Parties whose interests may be substantially affected	such as competent authorities and consumer groups; Art. 8(1)(a)	including competent authorities: Article 9(2)(b)

Task in the development of guides to good hygiene practice	**Performed by the government of the member states for national guides Art. 8 Reg. 852/2004**	**Performed by the Commission for Community guides. Art. 9 Reg. 852/2004**
Contribution of parties with substantially affected interests to the development of guides	In consultation with their representatives Art. 8(1)(a)	Collaboration of those parties: Article 9(2)(b)
Relevant codes of practice of the Codex Alimentarius	Having regard to Codex Art. 8(1)(b)	Having regard to Codex Art. 9(2)(c)
Guides for primary production and those associated operations listed in Annex I, having regard to the recommendations set out in Part B of Annex I.	Yes, Art. 8(1)(c)	Yes, Art. 9(2)(d)
Role for standards institute in development of guides	Developed under the aegis of a national standards institute explicitly mentioned. Refer to institutes in Annex I to Directive 98/34/EC Art. 8(2)	Existing European institutes not mentioned
Who makes assessment?	National government of the member states Art. 8(3)	Member states in SCFCAH. The Committee referred to in Article 14). Art. 9(3)(a).
Standards	Developed	
Assessment object	National guides	*Draft* Community guides
Developed in accordance with demands of Regulation 852/2004	Art. 8(3)(a)	paragraph 2; Art. 9(3)(a).
Practicable for the sectors to which they refer throughout the Community;	Art. 8(3)(b)	Art. 9(3)(b).
Suitable as guides to compliance with Articles 3, 4 and 5, Regulation 852/2004	Art. 8(3)(c)	Art. 9(3)(c).
Who reviews?	No review	Commission shall invite the SCFCAH of Article 14. Art. 9(4)
Review	No review	Periodically to review Community guides prepared in accordance with this Article, in cooperation with the bodies mentioned in paragraph 2. Art. 9(4)

Task in the development of guides to good hygiene practice	Performed by the government of the member states for national guides Art. 8 Reg. 852/2004	Performed by the Commission for Community guides. Art. 9 Reg. 852/2004
Aim of the review	No review	To ensure that the guides remain practicable and to take account of technological and scientific developments. Art. 9(4)(par. 2)
Central collection of guides	Forward national guides that comply with Art. 8(3)(a-c) to the Commission. Art. 8(4)	
Public information on guides	Commission runs a register with the titles and references of the national guides and makes it available for the member states. Art. 8(4)	The titles and references of Community guides prepared in accordance with this Article shall be published in the C series of the Official Journal of the European Union. Art. 9(5).
Guides made according to preceding Directive 93/43/EEC	Continue to apply when compatible with Regulation 852/2004 Art. 8(5)	No mention of European guides to good hygiene practice made according to preceding Directive 93/43/EEC

11.1.9 Primary production

Primary production holds a special position in the food hygiene regulations. It has its own Annex I in Regulation 852/2004 with direct legislation in Part A and forceful advice on how to make guides to good hygiene practice in Part B.[465] It is exempted from the HACCP obligation,[466] but encouraged to experiment with it.[467] It is cautioned that it may be subjected to the HACCP system in the near future. The evaluation report that the Commission has to present to the European Parliament and the Council before 21 May 2009 is to consider whether it is desirable and practicable to extent HACCP to primary production.[468]

[465] Articles 8(1)(c) and 9(2)(d) Regulation 852/2004.

[466] Recital 11 and Article 5(3) Regulation 852/2004.

[467] Recital 14 Regulation 852/2004. As discussed in Chapter 17, private standards like GlobalGAP included obligations to apply HACCP at the farm level.

[468] Article 16 Regulation 852/2004.

This announcement fits in a more general pattern to reduce the special treatment of primary production in EU law. The inclusion of primary production in the mainstream of food hygiene legislation, with its own channel in that stream, has been a fact only since 2006 when the present food hygiene regulations came into force. The old food hygiene legislation placed primary production outside its scope by using the definition of food hygiene presented in Law text box 11.8.

Law text box 11.8. The exclusion of primary production from the old hygiene legislation.

Article 2 Directive 93/43.
For the purposes of this Directive:
- food hygiene, hereinafter called 'hygiene' shall mean all measures necessary to ensure the safety and wholesomeness of foodstuffs. The measures shall cover all stages after primary production (the latter including, for example, harvesting, slaughter and milking), during preparation, processing, manufacturing, packaging, storing, transportation, distribution, handling and offering for sale or supply to the consumer.

Compare with recital (11) and Article 1(1)(b) of Regulation 852/2004 for the inclusion of primary production in the present food hygiene legislation.

The borderline between primary production and the next production stages
The article of Annex I called Scope is of special importance because it determines the dividing line between primary production and the next stages of the food production chain. Article I of Annex I defines the associated operations, the operations so closely connected to primary production that they are categorised with primary production for legislative purposes. The GFL and Regulation 852/2004 do not present a definition of primary production itself. Primary production is to be known by its fruits because Article 2 of Regulation 852/2004 gives the following definition: "primary products" means products of primary production including products of the soil, of stock farming, of hunting and fishing'.[469] Therefore primary production is the combination of this definition and the associated operations. Diagram 11.5 presents these operations.

The article on hygiene provisions contains two general duties that can be found in paragraphs 2 and 6 and a repetition of already existing obligations based on other legislation in paragraph 3. These paragraphs for all operators are separated by paragraph 4 that addresses operators dealing with products of animal origin, and paragraph 5 written for operators dealing with plant products. This pattern of a common paragraph for the vegetal and animal branches of food production, followed by a separate paragraph for each of them is also applied in Article A (III) on record-keeping.

469 Article 2(1)(b) Regulation 852/2004.

Diagram 11.5. The operations associated with primary production in Annex I to Regulation 852/2004 (Source: Annex I to Regulation 852/2004).

Number	Title and Contents
Part A	General hygiene provisions for primary production and associated operations = *binding rules*
A.(I). Scope	
A(I)(1)	Primary production and following associated operations:
A(I)(1)(a)	transport, storage and handling of primary products at the place of production
A(I)(1)(c)*	the transport of live animals when necessary
A(I)(1)(c)(c)**	For products of plant origin, fishery products and wild game, transport to an establishment
A (II) Hygiene provisions	
A (III) Record-keeping	

* (b) is missing in the original.
** Double(c) is in the original.

11.2 Preparing for problems: traceability

11.2.1 HACCP

The HACCP system discussed above is not only relevant for the prevention of food safety problems. The principle mentioned in Article 5(1)(e) of Regulation 852/2004 requires that the HACCP-plan includes corrective action to be taken in case of problems. The legislator leaves it largely to the food business operator to deal with problems that occur within the business. However for problems that may effect other stages in the food chain, some mandatory requirements are in place.

11.2.2 Tracking and tracing

The General Food Law requires that food and food ingredients be traceable. Recitals 28 and 29 to the General Food Law read:

> *'Experience has shown that the functioning of the internal market in food or feed can be jeopardised where it is impossible to trace food and feed. It is therefore necessary to establish a comprehensive system of traceability within food and feed businesses so that targeted and accurate withdrawals can be undertaken or information given to consumers or control officials, thereby avoiding the potential for unnecessary wider disruption in the event of food safety problems'.*
>
> *'It is necessary to ensure that a food or feed business including an importer can identify at least the business from which the food, feed, animal or*

substance that may be incorporated into a food or feed has been supplied, to ensure that on investigation, traceability can be assured at all stages'.

The intention of the traceability system is therefore to enable food safety problems to be identified at the source, and across the food chain. To this end food business operators must keep comprehensive records of exactly where their food material originated and where it went.

For food products of animal origin traceability is nothing new. The General Food Law, however, broadens the scope of traceability to all foods. In this section we will discuss the general provisions in the General Food Law, requirements for traceability of food producing animals and traceability requirements for genetically modified foods. The concept of traceability is defined in Article 3(15) GFL. See Law text box 11.9

Law text box 11.9. Article 3(15) GFL on traceability.

Article 3(15) Regulation 178/2002
'traceability' means the ability to trace and follow a food, feed, food-producing animal or substance intended to be, or expected to be incorporated into a food or feed, through all stages of production, processing and distribution.

The main aim of traceability is to be able to quickly identify the source of a food safety problem and to conduct well aimed recalls to take affected products from the market. In practice, traceability schemes are used for other purposes as well. They play a role, for example, in assuring consumers that products possess certain invisible qualities relating to their origin and the way they have been handled (kosher, hallal, organic, etc.). A new regulation regarding food contact materials has a similar traceability scheme.[470] This regulation expresses what had been suspected all along: traceability is also meant to facilitate attribution of responsibility (e.g. liability).[471] There is no reason to suppose that this notion applies to food contact materials exclusively.

Whether the possibility of using traceability to establish liability is considered an advantage or a disadvantage depends upon one's point of view. For businesses at the end of the food chain, it seems advantageous for liability to be passed to the companies where the problem originated. Businesses in the latter position would probably see this as a disadvantage.

470 Regulation 1935/2004 on materials and articles intended to come into contact with food
471 Article 17 Regulation 1935/2004.

If no other, more specific requirements apply based on the General Food Law, businesses must be able to trace their inputs and outputs one step up and one step down.[472] For the majority of farm animals more specific requirements do apply.[473]

11.2.3 General Food Law

The General Food Law requires in Article 18 that food, feed, food-producing animals, and any other substance intended or expected to be incorporated into a food or feed shall be traceable at all stages of production, processing and distribution. See Law text box 11.10.

Law text box 11.10. Article 18 GFL on traceability.

Article 18 regulation 178/2002
Traceability

1. The traceability of food, feed, food-producing animals, and any other substance intended to be, or expected to be, incorporated into a food or feed shall be established at all stages of production, processing and distribution.
2. Food and feed business operators shall be able to identify any person from whom they have been supplied with a food, a feed, a food-producing animal, or any substance intended to be, or expected to be, incorporated into a food or feed.
   To this end, such operators shall have in place systems and procedures which allow for this information to be made available to the competent authorities on demand.
3. Food and feed business operators shall have in place systems and procedures to identify the other businesses to which their products have been supplied. This information shall be made available to the competent authorities on demand.
4. Food or feed which is placed on the market or is likely to be placed on the market in the Community shall be adequately labelled or identified to facilitate its traceability, through relevant documentation or information in accordance with the relevant requirements of more specific provisions.
5. Provisions for the purpose of applying the requirements of this Article in respect of specific sectors may be adopted in accordance with the procedure laid down in Article 58(2).

To this end, food and feed business operators must be able to identify any person who has supplied them with a food, feed, food-producing animal, or any substance intended or expected to be incorporated into a food or feed. They must also be able to identify all businesses to which their products have been supplied.

---

472 Recital 29 GFL.

473 See also: S. Ammendrup & A. E. Füssell, Legislative Requirements for the Identification and Traceability of Farm Animals within the European Union, Revue scientifique et technique (International Office of Epizootics), 2001, p. 437.

Business operators shall have in place systems and procedures that allow this information to be made available to competent authorities on demand. The law has little to say on the makeup of the traceability system. This is left to the discretion of the businesses concerned. An important decision they have to make is on the batch size they apply in their system. Does it cover for example one hour of production, a day, a week? The bigger the batch, the easier to manage the system. The smaller the batch, the smaller the damage if a product recall has to be undertaken.

Food or feed which is or is likely to be placed on the market in the European Community must be adequately labelled or identified to facilitate its traceability through relevant documentation or information in accordance with the relevant requirements of more specific provisions.[474] Often the date marking is used for this purpose.[475]

The requirement includes only *businesses*, it does not extend to the consumer. In practice this means that traceability terminates at the retail end. It begins before primary production as it includes the inputs of the primary sector. In a guidance document that provides an interpretation to the most important provisions in the GFL,[476] the Standing Committee on the Food Chain and Animal Health took the position that traceability requirements apply only from entry past the EU border onwards; that is to say, authorities will not demand information regarding the origin of the product in a third country from which it was imported. It is unclear what the basis is for this limited interpretation – the text of the GFL does not provide a foothold.[477]

This same document also concludes that businesses are not obligated to ensure internal traceability. In other words, they have to know where the ingredients came from and where the products went but not necessarily which ingredients went into which products. This interpretation seems to expose a major flaw in the system. In cases where internal traceability is not assured, it seems highly problematic to reconstruct the entire chain to trace the origins and consequences of a food safety problem.[478]

474 See also Chapter 12, section 12.15 on labelling.

475 This explains why sometimes on the label the durability of a product is not only expressed in a date but in hours and minutes as well.

476 Guidance on the Implementation of Articles 11, 12, 16, 17, 18, 19 and 20 of Regulation (EC) n° 178/2002 on General Food Law, Conclusions of the Standing Committee on the Food Chain and Animal Health (2004). For hyperlink see reference list.

477 Article 11 GFL rather suggests the contrary.

478 As is discussed in Chapter 17, this flow is remedied in several private standards that explicitly do require internal traceability.

The burden to reconstruct the whole food chain when an incident occurs is on the authorities and to that end traceability information has to be made available to those authorities on demand.

11.2.4 Traceability of food producing animals

Traceability legislation on living animals goes well beyond the general requirements of food law as it includes veterinary purposes into their framework.[479] That is to say that infectious diseases are not only being controlled for food safety reasons in a strict sense, but also for economic reasons including preventing residues of veterinary products entering the food chain, the protection of healthy animals and the protection of the reputation of the EU and its member states of safe agricultural products of high quality. Identification of animals also plays a role in the common agricultural policy – in particular, for the supervision of premiums.

An identification system must be regarded as a prerequisite for effective traceability. When discussing traceability of animals and animal products it is important to note that although of primary importance, identification is only one of the issues at stake. The basic requirements in European legislation to provide for an adequate system of identification of animals predate the General Food Law. They are laid down in two Directives. Article 3(1)(c) of Directive 90/425 states that animals for intra-Community trade must be identified in accordance with the requirements of Community rules and be registered in such a way that the original or transit holding, centre or organisation can be traced. These identification and registration systems are to be extended to the movements of animals within the territory of each member state.[480] In addition, Article 14 of Directive 91/496[481] states that the identification and registration as provided for in Article 3(1)(c) of Directive 90/425 of imported animals must be carried out before area-specific checks have been made, except in the case of animals for slaughter and registered equidae (donkeys and horses).[482]

The member states must collect all information in a database. Originally the implementing rules concerning the identification and registration of animals in aforementioned Directives were laid down in Directive 92/102 on the identification and registration of animals. Following several crises (discussed in Chapter 7), specific requirements were drafted for bovine, ovine, and caprine animals. However,

[479] For a detailed account see: B.M.J. van der Meulen and A.A. Freriks, 'Beastly Bureaucracy' Animal Traceability, Identification and Labeling in EU Law, Journal of Food Law & Policy, Vol. 2/2006/2, pp. 317-359.

[480] Article 3(1)(c) Directive 90/425. See also Directive 2002/33 (amending directive 90/425).

[481] See also Directive 96/43 (amending Directive 91/496).

[482] Directive 91/496 laying down the principles governing the organization of veterinary checks on animals entering the Community from third countries and amending Directives 89/662/EEC, 90/425/EEC and 90/675/EEC.

the original Directive from 1992 is still in force for porcine animals (pigs). On the basis of Directive 92/102 member states must have in place systems for the identification and registration of groups of pigs, including ear tags, registers per holding and a computerised database at national level.[483]

Before the BSE crisis, the rules concerning the identification and the registration of bovine animals (cattle and buffaloes) were also laid down in Directive 92/102. In order to re-establish market stability after the BSE-crisis, the European legislature held that the transparency of the conditions for the production and marketing of the products concerned, particularly in regard to traceability, had to be improved. This led to the establishment of, on the one hand, a more efficient system for the identification and registration of bovine animals at the production stage and, on the other hand, a specific Community labelling system in the beef sector. The new system was laid down in Regulation 820/97 establishing a system for the identification and registration of bovine animals and regarding the labelling of beef and beef products. Apart from identification requirements, the Regulation introduced a labelling system that was optional for operators and organisations marketing beef until 1 January 2000 in the sense that operators and organisations wishing to label their beef had to do so in accordance with the Regulation. A compulsory beef-labelling system for all the member states had to be introduced after 1 January 2000.

The improvements in the regulatory system brought about by this Regulation, exerted a positive influence on consumption of beef. 'In order to maintain and strengthen the confidence of consumers in beef and to avoid misleading them, it was deemed necessary to further develop the framework in which the information was made available to consumers by sufficient and clear labelling of the product'. This led to a mandatory labelling system that is laid down in Regulation 1760/2000 that replaces the former Regulation entirely. Since 2000, both the identification and labelling requirements are therefore set out in Regulation 1760/2000. Although the system has been set out in a *regulation*, to a large extent, it addresses the national legislatures in the member states. Member states must set up a cattle identification and registration system. The system for the identification and registration of bovine animals must be comprised of ear tags to identify animals individually, computerised databases, animal passports, and individual registers on each holding.[484]

The basic objectives of the requirements set out in Regulation 1760/2000 are:

483 See also Commission Decision 2000/678.

484 Specific requirements on ear tags, passports and holding registers are laid down in Commission Regulation 911/2004 implementing Regulation 1760/2000 of the European Parliament and of the Council as regards ear tags, passports ad holding registers; and Commission Regulation 887/2004.

- the localisation and tracing of animals for veterinary purposes, which is of crucial importance for the control of infectious diseases;
- the traceability of beef for public health reasons, and
- the management and supervision of livestock premiums as part of the reform of management of the common agricultural policy.[485]

Ovine and caprine animals (sheep and goats) were excluded from the scope of Directive 92/102 in 2004. Based upon Article 3(1) of Regulation 21/2004 the system for the identification and registration of animals comprises the means of identification to identify each animal, up-to-date registers kept on each holding, movement documents and a central register or a computer database. For traceability requirements regarding fish see Regulation 2065/2001.

11.2.5 GM traceability

Aim of GM Traceability
Article 1 of Regulation 1830/2003 states that traceability of GM foods has as its objectives:
- facilitating accurate labelling;
- monitoring the effects on the environment and, where appropriate, on health; and
- implementing appropriate risk management measures including, if necessary, withdrawal of products.[486]

Content of GM Traceability
Regulation 1830/2003 defines traceability as 'the ability to trace GMOs and products produced from GMOs at all stages of their placing on the market through the production and distribution chains'. Unlike the GFL, Regulation 1830/2003 requires a paper trail to accompany GM food. This paper trail ensures internal traceability. The flaw indicated above, which may exist in the general system of traceability, therefore does not occur with regard to GM food.

At the first stage of placing a product consisting of or containing GMOs on the market, including bulk quantities, operators must ensure that information: (a) that the product contains or consists of GMOs and (b) providing the unique

485 See Report from the European Commission to the Council and the European Parliament on the Possibility of Introduction of Electronic Identification for Bovine Animals, COM(2005) 9 final, 25 January 2005, p. 5.

486 Regulation 1830/2003 concerning the traceability and labelling of genetically modified organisms and the traceability of food and feed products produced from genetically modified organisms and amending Directive 2001/18/EC. On GM traceability see: Margaret Rossc Grossman, Traceability and Labeling of Genetically Modified Crops, Food and Feed in the European Union, Journal of Food Law & Policy, Vol. 1/2005/1, pp. 43-85.

identifier(s) assigned to those GMOs[487] is transmitted in writing to the operator receiving the product. At every following stage, the same information must be passed on for each ingredient or additive that it concerns.[488]

This seems easy on paper, but in practice, it is next to impossible to preserve the identity of each raw material through to the end-products in which they are used. Identity preservation[489] is hard to realise, for example, in bulk storage, in continuous production processes, and in cases where failed products re-enter the production chain as raw materials.[490] Additionally, all information must be kept for five years.[491] Small traces – no more than 0.9% – are exempted from the traceability requirements if they are adventitious and unavoidable.[492]

11.3 Dealing with problems: recall

11.3.1 Withdrawal and recall

As elaborated in Chapter 8, food business operators may not bring food to the market if it is unsafe (Article 14 GFL). The product must be withdrawn from downstream businesses or recalled from the consumer if unsafe food nonetheless is discovered to have made it to market. The General Food Law deals with this situation in article 19 shown in Law text box 11.11.

Law text box 11.11. Responsibilities for food: food business operators, Article 19 General Food Law Regulation 178/2002.

> ***Regulation 178/2002***
> Article 19
> Responsibilities for food: food business operators
> 1 If a food business operator considers or has reason to believe that a food which it has imported, produced, processed, manufactured or distributed is not in compliance with the food safety requirements, it shall immediately initiate procedures to withdraw the food in question from the market where the food has left the immediate control of that initial food business operator and inform the competent authorities thereof. Where the product may have reached the consumer, the operator shall effectively and accurately inform the consumers of the reason for its withdrawal, and if necessary, recall from consumers products already supplied to them when other measures are not sufficient to achieve a high level of health protection.

[487] On these identifiers, see Chapter 9, section 9.5.8.
[488] Article 4(1) and (2) Regulation 1830/2003.
[489] Also called internal traceability.
[490] Also called 'rework'.
[491] Articles 4(5) and 5(2) Regulation 1830/2003.
[492] Article 7 Regulation 1830/2003.

2. A food business operator responsible for retail or distribution activities which do not affect the packaging, labelling, safety or integrity of the food shall, within the limits of its respective activities, initiate procedures to withdraw from the market products not in compliance with the food-safety requirements and shall participate in contributing to the safety of the food by passing on relevant information necessary to trace a food, cooperating in the action taken by producers, processors, manufacturers and/or the competent authorities.
3. A food business operator shall immediately inform the competent authorities if it considers or has reason to believe that a food which it has placed on the market may be injurious to human health. Operators shall inform the competent authorities of the action taken to prevent risks to the final consumer and shall not prevent or discourage any person from cooperating, in accordance with national law and legal practice, with the competent authorities, where this may prevent, reduce or eliminate a risk arising from a food.
4. Food business operators shall collaborate with the competent authorities on action taken to avoid or reduce risks posed by a food which they supply or have supplied.

The food business operator who considers or has reason to believe that a food s/he has imported, produced, processed, manufactured or distributed, is not in compliance with the food safety requirements, has at least four duties:

First, there is the duty to immediately initiate procedures to *withdraw* the food in question from the market.

Second, the operator must immediately *inform* the authorities that s/he has reason to believe that an unsafe food has been placed on the market. The operator must also inform the authorities of all actions taken to deal with the problem.

Third, in case the product may have already reached consumers, the operator shall effectively and accurately inform those consumers of the reason for its withdrawal, and *recall* products already supplied when other measures are deemed insufficient to achieve a high level of health protection.

Finally, the food business operator has a duty to *collaborate* with the competent authorities on actions taken to avoid or reduce risks posed by foods, which s/he supplied.

If the concerned food business operator has an adequate traceability system in place, withdrawal should not be too much of a problem. All the information on which product to withdraw from which customer should be present in the system. However, it is not required that traceability systems encompass the consumer. Therefore in most cases the business operator will not have in his possession information on the identity of the concerned consumers. For this reason recall-actions need to resort to publicity in the media.

11.3.2 Responsible food business operator

Who is responsible for withdrawal and recall? In its first paragraph Article 19 GFL mentions all possible types of food business that may have handled the food at issue. The only condition setting Article 19 in operation is that the business operator has reason to believe that the food is not in compliance with food safety requirements. Article 19 is not limited to the business that may have caused this non-compliance. Each player in the chain bears full responsibility. A business may not excuse itself by stating that it is not at fault. Naturally it may prompt the business that was at fault to take the required action or hold that business liable for costs incurred. Once a business starts adequate actions, other businesses can limit themselves to supporting this action.

The responsibility is somewhat limited in section 2 for food businesses that by their very nature are unlikely to have caused the problem.

11.3.3 Non-compliance

The condition set in article 19(1) GFL is not that the food is unsafe, but that it is not in compliance with the food safety requirements. The food safety requirements are all legal requirements set on the food with a view to ensuring food safety, including for example the food safety targets discussed in Chapter 10. As is explained in that chapter, these targets often apply safety margins. The ADI for pesticide residues for example is usually set at 1/100 of the NOAEL. As a consequence of this margin a non-compliant food need not be unsafe within the meaning of article 14 GFL (injurious to health). In paragraph 3 of Article 19 GFL, the obligation to immediately inform the competent authorities is limited to the situation where the food may be injurious to health (thus unsafe).

11.3.4 Measures

Article 19 GFL explicitly mentions withdrawal (from other businesses) and recall (from consumers) as measures to be taken. Slightly hidden at the end of paragraph 1 is the sentence: 'when other measures are not sufficient to achieve a high level of health protection'. This sentence implies that the food business operator is empowered to take other measures than withdrawal or recall if these other measures are sufficient to achieve a high level of health protection. In practice we see, for example, that businesses that omitted to mention allergens on the label of a product issue a public warning without calling the product back.

The exception that 'other measures' may be taken if they are effective, does not apply to the obligation to inform the authorities.

Discussion on the obligation to co-operate and the rights of the defence

It is likely that in several member states discussion will arise as to what extent the information that business operators are obliged to provide under Article 18 or 19 GFL, may be used by the authorities when imposing sanctions on the operator for infringing on Article 14 GFL.

The German application of this provision – § 44(4) of the Lebensmittel-, Bedarfsgegenstände- und Futtermittelgesetzbuch (the Code on food, food contact materials and feed) – explicitly states that the information provided by the food business operator may not be used against him in criminal proceedings. This provision will undoubtedly stimulate operators to come forward with problems they discover within their organisation. However, there is also the risk that such a provision will be misused to escape punishment for intentional neglect.

11.4 Food safety law for businesses

EU food hygiene legislation with the central place its gives to the HACCP principles, traceability and recall requirements are tell-tale implementations of the principle underlying Article 17(1) GFL. Food business operators are responsible. EU legislation imposes upon them to achieve food safety. To a large extent is has been left to the business operators to decide how best to meet this responsibility in the specific case.

12. Informed choice: presentation of food products

12.1 Introduction

12.1.1 Principles

It is important for food businesses to communicate with their customers and consumers. Probably the most important means of communication are the words and pictures attached to the food product on the label. From the point of view of the business, the most important messages will usually be the identity of the brand under which the product is sold. This brand can be protected from other businesses by registering it as a trade mark. This option is discussed in Chapter 2.

The freedom of expression[493] that food business operators can exercise on the label, is limited in food law. Certain information is mandatory, other information is prohibited. The General Food Law lays down the principles on consumer information in Articles 8 and 16 (See Law text boxes 12.1 and 12.2). Their function is to give consumers the opportunity to make informed choices and to protect them from misleading practices.

Law text box 12.1. Protection of consumers' interests, Article 8 General Food Law Regulation 178/2002.

Article 8
Protection of consumers' interests
Food law shall aim at the protection of the interests of consumers and shall provide a basis for consumers to make informed choices in relation to the foods they consume. It shall aim at the prevention of:
(a) fraudulent or deceptive practices;
(b) the adulteration of food; and
(c) any other practices which may mislead the consumer.

[493] Article 11(1) of the Charter of Fundamental Rights of the European Union reads: 'Everyone has the right to freedom of expression. This right shall include freedom to hold opinions and to receive and impart information and ideas without interference by public authority and regardless of frontiers'. In Article 52 the Charter sets the conditions for limiting the exercise of fundamental rights: 'Any limitation on the exercise of the rights and freedoms recognised by this Charter must be provided for by law and respect the essence of those rights and freedoms. Subject to the principle of proportionality, limitations may be made only if they are necessary and genuinely meet objectives of general interest recognised by the Union or the need to protect the rights and freedoms of others'. It is unfortunate that nowhere in food labelling law does the EU legislator make the effort to actually demonstrate that these conditions have been considered and that they are met.

Law text box 12.2. Presentation, Article 16 General Food Law Regulation 178/2002.

Article 16
Presentation
Without prejudice to more specific provisions of food law, the labelling, advertising and presentation of food or feed, including their shape, appearance or packaging, the packaging materials used, the manner in which they are arranged and the setting in which they are displayed, and the information which is made available about them through whatever medium, shall not mislead consumers.

Article 8 GFL addresses the legislator. Article 16 GFL addresses the businesses. This principle has been elaborated in the (horizontal) Labelling directive. Several other pieces of legislation give additional standards on consumer information (Law text box 12.3.)

Law text box 12.3. Labelling directive on misleading.

Article 2 (1)
1. The labelling and methods used must not:
   (a) be such as could mislead the purchaser to a material degree, particularly:
      (i) as to the characteristics of the foodstuff and, in particular, as to its nature, identity, properties, composition, quantity, durability, origin or provenance, method of manufacture or production;
      (ii) by attributing to the foodstuff effects or properties which it does not possess;
      (iii) by suggesting that the foodstuff possesses special characteristics when in fact all similar foodstuffs possess such characteristics;
   (b) subject to Community provisions applicable to natural mineral waters and foodstuffs for particular nutritional uses, attribute to any foodstuff the property of preventing, treating or curing a human disease, or refer to such properties.

12.1.2 Marketing

With regard to sales of food and other products, economists distinguish a marketing mix of four 'P's: product, price, promotion, and place. Appealing products need to be presented at affordable prices and in accessible places and the customer has to be informed about this.

Businesses give themselves and their products identity through branding. Brands are made recognisable with the help of trademarks, trade names, shapes, colours and by other measures. Their content, however, goes beyond these visible aspects and may include an entire image of quality, reliability, style, etcetera. Traditionally branding has been the domain of producers. In recent decades, however, retail businesses have increasingly applied brands of their own. These retail brands are often referred to as 'private labels'. Initially they were understood to represent low quality and low price as compared to premium brands, but nowadays retail chains bring high quality private labels as well.

It should be noted that in economic literature the expression 'labelling' covers a concept of image building. As we will see below, in food law the expressions 'label' and labelling' are much more mundane in meaning. They do not go far beyond the piece of paper actually stuck to a food product and the message it contains.

12.1.3 Food labelling legislation

From the beginning of the development of EU food law, most pieces of legislation contained provisions on labelling, indeed many still do. A first step to codify food labelling law in horizontal legislation was Directive 79/112 relating to the labelling, presentation and advertising of foodstuffs. This directive has been frequently and substantially amended. After twenty years a recast was due. The directive has been replaced by 'Directive 2000/13 on the approximation of the laws of the Member States relating to the labelling, presentation and advertising of foodstuffs'. This directive is known as 'the Labelling directive' or 'the General labelling directive'. This directive is at the heart of this chapter.

The European Commission has issued a proposal to once again recast food labelling legislation, this time no longer in the form of a directive, but of a regulation. On 30 January 2008 the Commission published a 'Proposal for a Regulation of the European Parliament and of the Council on the provision of food information to consumers' (hereafter: the 'food information proposal').[494] Here below, in discussing the different aspects of current food labelling law reference will be made to the changes envisaged in this proposal.

12.1.4 Overview

In this chapter we will first address the mandatory labelling requirements from the Labelling directive. In particular the name of the food; the list of ingredients including additives and allergens; the quantity and the durability of the food. Then we will turn to labelling requirements in other legislation: nutrition labelling; protected designations and organics; GM-labelling and health claims. At the end of the chapter we will indicate some further provisions not discussed in this book.

[494] COM(2008)40 final.

12.2 Labelling

An important issue in consumer protection is to ensure that the consumer is aware of what he or she consumes. Many rules exist concerning the obligation of food business operators to provide the consumer with adequate information by labelling.[495] As stated above, currently the most important codification of these rules is to be found in Directive 2000/13 of the European Parliament and of the Council of 20 March 2000 on the approximation of the laws of the Member States relating to the labelling, presentation and advertising of foodstuffs: hereafter called 'Labelling directive'.[496]

Labelling means 'any words, particulars, trade marks, brand name, pictorial matter or symbol relating to a foodstuff and placed on any packaging, document, notice, label, ring or collar accompanying or referring to such foodstuff'.[497] Labelling may not be misleading.

Food labelling law identifies mandatory information, information that is restricted or forbidden (because it is deemed to be misleading or for another reason). The broad definition of labelling is in particular important with regard to the restrictions made on information. These restrictions apply to documents or notices referring to a food. As far as the mandatory information is concerned, 'labelling' should be understood in a more narrow sense. The information should actually accompany the food. The food information proposal is helpful in this regard by providing an additional definition of 'label': 'label' means any tag, brand, mark, pictorial or other descriptive matter written, printed, stencilled, marked, embossed or impressed on, or attached to, a container of food.[498]

The general principle that food business operators are responsible across the entire food chain (Article 17(1) GFL), applies to labelling. In case C-315/05 a supermarket was charged for selling liquors with a lower alcohol content than indicated on the label. It argued that the labelling requirements apply to the producer, not to the retailer. The Court of Justice gave the preliminary ruling that Directive 2000/13 must be interpreted as not precluding legislation of a member state 'which makes it possible for an operator, established in that Member State, which distributes a pre-packaged alcoholic beverage to be delivered as such within the meaning of Article 1 of that directive, produced by an operator established in another Member State, to be held liable for an infringement of that provision, established by a public authority, resulting from the producer's inaccurate statement on the product label of the alcoholic strength by volume of the product and, consequently,

495 See also the rules on additives and novel foods mentioned above.
496 Official Journal L 109, 6 May 2000, p. 29.
497 Article 1(2)(a) of the Labelling directive. The food information proposal applies an almost identical definition substituting the word 'foodstuff' by 'food' (Article 2(2)(j)).
498 Article 2(2)(i).

to be penalised by an administrative fine, even where, as the mere distributor it simply markets the product as delivered to it by the producer'.[499]

12.3 Mandatory information

All pre-packaged foodstuffs must be labelled in a language that is easily understood by consumers.[500] Usually this means in the national language of the member state. The Labelling directive gives a list of ten required (mandatory) pieces of information (Law text box 12.4).

Law text box 12.4. Article 3(1) Labelling directive on mandatory labelling.

In accordance with Articles 4 to 17 and subject to the exceptions contained therein, indication of the following particulars alone shall be compulsory on the labelling of foodstuffs:

1. the name under which the product is sold;
2. the list of ingredients;
3. the quantity of certain ingredients or categories of ingredients (...);
4. in the case of pre-packaged foodstuffs, the net quantity;
5. the date of minimum durability or, in the case of foodstuffs which, from the microbiological point of view, are highly perishable, the 'use by' date;
6. any special storage conditions or conditions of use;
7. the name or business name and address of the manufacturer or packager, or of a seller established within the Community. (...)
8. particulars of the place of origin or provenance where failure to give such particulars might mislead the consumer to a material degree as to the true origin or provenance of the foodstuff;
9. instructions for use when it would be impossible to make appropriate use of the foodstuff in the absence of such instructions;
10. with respect to beverages containing more than 1.2% by volume of alcohol, the actual alcoholic strength by volume.[1]

[1] See also Commission Directive 87/250/EEC of 15 April 1987 on the indication of alcoholic strength by volume in the labelling of alcoholic beverages for sale to the ultimate consumer.

Each item is elaborated in one or more of the subsequent articles. Most of these requirements are self-evident. We will therefore discuss only the most important.

The food information proposal adds two items to the list. Indication of ingredients causing allergies or intolerances and a nutrition declaration.[501] The former is

[499] ECJ 23 November 2006 case C-315/05, Lidl Italia Srl v. Comune di Arcole (VR).

[500] Article 16 Labelling directive; Article 16 Food information proposal.

[501] Article 9(1)(c) and (l).

already present in the Labelling directive as part of the obligation to list the ingredients, the latter is not mandatory at present.

The proposal requires all these twelve mandatory particulars to be printed on the package or on the label in characters of a font size of at least 3 mm and to be presented in a way so as to ensure a significant contrast between the print and background.[502] An exception applies if the largest surface is less than 10 cm^2.

12.4 Name

The name-requirement has been elaborated in Article 5 of the Labelling directive.[503] The use of the word 'name' in the English language version of the Labelling directive is a little confusing. Other language versions use words that may be translated as 'designation' or 'indication'.[504]

The name that must appear on the label is not what in common speech is understood by 'name': the brand name under which the product is marketed (like 'Twix'), but the generic name ('subtitle') which describes the nature of the product ('milk chocolate covered caramel and biscuit'). If Community law or national law establishes a protected name (like 'milk chocolate'), it must be used for products that meet that prescription. Conversely, if the requirements connected to a protected name are not met, it may not be used. If no such protected name applies, the customary name may be used (i.e. goulash soup) and in the absence of that a description of the foodstuff and its use that is clear enough to let the purchaser know its true nature and distinguish it from other products with which it might be confused.

In this provision the impact is felt of vertical food legislation. This type of legislation connects compositional standards to legal names. For some examples from EU law, see Chapter 7.2. From this section the following diagram (12.1) is repeated with examples of vertical legislation.

---

502 Article 14 of the proposal. This requirement has sparked significant opposition from food businesses claiming that on small packages it is next to impossible to fulfil.

503 Article 18 of the food information proposal in conjunction with the definitions of legal name (Article 2(2)(l) 'legal name' means the name of a food prescribed in the Community provisions applicable to it or, in the absence of such Community provisions, the name provided for in the laws, regulations and administrative provisions applicable in the Member State in which the food is sold to the final consumer or to mass caterers), customary name (Article 2(2)(m) 'customary name' means a name which is accepted as the name of the food without it needing further explanation by consumers in the Member State in which it is sold), descriptive name (Article 2(2)(n) 'descriptive name' means a name providing a description of the food, and if necessary of its use, which is sufficiently clear to enable the consumers to know its true nature and distinguish it from other products with which it might be confused) and Annex V.

504 In German: *Verkehrsbezeichnung*, in Dutch: *aanduiding*, in French: dénomination de vente.

Diagram 12.1. Verticals.

Directive 2001/114	partly or wholly dehydrated preserved milk for human consumption
Directive 2001/113	fruit jams, jellies and marmalades and sweetened chestnut purée intended for human consumption
Directive 2001/112	fruit juices and certain similar products intended for human consumption
Directive 2001/111	certain sugars intended for human consumption
Directive 2001/110	honey
Directive 2000/36	cocoa and chocolate products intended for human consumption
Directive 1999/4	coffee extracts and chicory extracts
Regulation 122/94 / Regulation 1601/91	definition, description and presentation of aromatized wines, aromatized wine-based drinks, and aromatized wine-product cocktails
Directive 93/45	the manufacture of nectars without the addition of sugars or honey

Some EU member states have extensive provisions on food names.[505] Surprisingly, no reference is made to the Codex Alimentarius. The Codex contains a great many vertical standards. Given the commitment the EU professes regarding the development of international food standards,[506] it would have been fitting to include the names set in Codex in this provision. As the situation now stands the names provided by Codex may exercise some influence through adoption in vertical legislation at EU or member state level, by becoming customary or through case law. In deciding if vertical provisions in member state law constitute barriers to trade, the ECJ sometimes takes the codex Alimentarius into consideration.[507]

Protected designation of origin are treated here below in section 12.10.

The name under which the product is sold shall include or be accompanied by particulars as to the physical condition of the foodstuff or the specific treatment which it has undergone (e.g. powdered, freeze-dried, deep-frozen, concentrated, smoked) in all cases where omission of such information could create confusion in the mind of the purchaser.[508]

Any foodstuff which has been treated with ionising radiation must bear an indication to that effect. Article 5(3) here gives a list of applicable expressions in all official languages of the EU. This is a little surprising as all languages have their own official version of the directive with the appropriate expressions.[509]

---

505 Germany and Austria, for example, have their 'Lebensmittelbuch'. These books can be compared to official encyclopaedias of food.

506 As expressed in Articles 5(3) and 13 of the General Food Law.

507 See for example the Emmenthal cheese case discussed in Chapter 16, section 16.4 (ECJ judgment 5 December 2000, case C-448/98).

508 Article 5(3) Labelling directive.

509 In the food information proposal this curiosity has not been repeated.

12.5 List of ingredients

12.5.1 Ingredients

The obligation to provide the list of ingredients has been elaborated on in Article 6 of the Labelling directive. The list of ingredients shall include any substances, including additives, used in the manufacture or preparation of a foodstuff and still present, even if in altered form, in the finished product.[510] The structure discussed in the previous section regarding the name of a food applies to ingredients as well.

Ingredients that themselves consist of several ingredients (so-called compound ingredients) may be mentioned as single ingredient provided they are no more then 2% of the finished product. Otherwise the ingredients of which they consist must be mentioned separately.[511]

Several exceptions apply to the obligation to list ingredients (for example, for fresh fruit, vinegar, cheese, butter, products consisting of one single ingredient recognisable from the name, and beverages containing more than 1.2% of alcohol). The most important exception to the obligation to mention substances used in the manufacture applies to additives or other substances used as processing aids. The labelling directive gives no definition of processing aids. The food information proposal[512] refers to the definition given in footnote 1 to Directive 89/107. In practice this definition is already being used in this context: for the purpose of this Directive, 'processing aid' means any substance not consumed as a food ingredient by itself, intentionally used in the processing of raw materials, foods or their ingredients, to fulfil a certain technological purpose during treatment or processing and which may result in the unintentional but technically unavoidable presence of residues of the substance or its derivatives in the final product, provided that these residues do not present any health risk and do not have any technological effect on the finished product.

12.5.2 Quantity

The ingredients must be listed in descending order of weight. The quantity of an ingredient (as a percentage) must be mentioned[513] only:

- where the ingredient or category of ingredients concerned appears in the name under which the foodstuff is sold;

[510] Article 6(4)(a) Labelling directive.
[511] Article 6(8) Labelling directive.
[512] Article 2(1)(c).
[513] This is known as quantitative ingredients declaration, or; QUID. On this subject see: General guidelines for implementing the principle of Quantitative Ingredients Declaration (QUID) – Article 7 of Directive 79/112/EEC as amended by Directive 97/4/EC. For a hyperlink see the reference list.

- where it is usually associated with that name by the consumer;
- where the ingredient or category of ingredients concerned is emphasised on the labelling in words, pictures or graphics, or
- where the ingredient or category of ingredients concerned is essential to characterise the foodstuff and distinguish it from products with which it might otherwise be confused due to its name[514] or appearance.

12.5.3 Labelling of food additives[515]

Labelling of food additives is an issue of prime importance, to the consumer as well as to the user industry. Additives are ingredients. Article 6 of the Labelling directive makes labelling of their use compulsory in the ingredient list. There are however some exemptions; the most notable one being drinks with an alcohol content of more than 1.2%. So far, these need not carry ingredient labelling. Consequently alcohol-free beers routinely carry a list of ingredients. Alcoholic drinks often do not show an ingredients list, except in countries where national law requires it, such as in Germany.[516]

Additives whose presence in a foodstuff is merely due to carry over[517] and that have no technological function in the final foodstuff need not be indicated in the ingredient list. 'Solvents' or 'media' for additives or for flavouring need not be labelled either.[518] Additives in the ingredient list must be preceded by the name of their additive labelling category (i.e. their function[519]), as laid down in Annex II of Directive 2000/13. If a substance exerts more than one function, it is the principal function that should be indicated.

There are additional special labelling requirements for certain categories of additives for sweeteners and colours. Agents causing severe adverse reactions have to be indicated by a warning on the label. The only additives to which this requirement applies are the sulphites. Irrespective whether it is for the purpose of intolerance warnings or for ingredient listing, sulphites are considered not present when their total quantity from all sources does not reach 10 mg/kg of

[514] Here to be understood both in its legal meaning discussed above and in the meaning it has in common speech.

[515] Many thanks to Mr. Ronald Verbruggen (director Orbyte bvba; consultant Food regulatory and scientific affairs), who wrote this section.

[516] It is the author's perception that enactment of a measure to generalise the labelling of ingredients to all alcoholic drinks in all member states of the EU is several years late due to the political and procedural problems involved.

[517] For the notion of carry over, see: Chapter 9, section 9.2.8.

[518] Article 6(4)(c)(ii) of Directive 2000/13.

[519] See Chapter 9, section 9.2.1.

product. The additives must be designated by their specific name or by their E number. The E number is a number officially assigned by the EU.[520]

As to the specific name to be used, it seems reasonable to assume that, in addition to the names used in the directives, generally accepted synonyms can also be used. No doubt synonyms listed in the official specifications of the EU and of JECFA[521] are to be considered 'generally accepted' and understood. They could hardly be considered misleading. Still, it remains to be seen whether all these synonyms rather than only the exact directive designations for the additives are to be used. It is clear however that commercial trade names are not acceptable for use in ingredient lists.

In addition to the rules on the labelling for additives on 'pre-packaged food', there are also rules for the labelling of '*food additives sold as such*', to manufacturers (additives as ingredient raw materials by themselves), as well as to the ultimate consumer (in baking powder, or in table-top sweeteners).[522] Note that table-top sweeteners are a specific type of foodstuffs mainly consisting of (mixtures of) additives. The latter general rules can be found in the Additives Framework Directive (98/107).

12.5.4 Allergens

In 2003 the Labelling directive 2000/13 has been changed to ensure that the presence of substances known for their ability to spark allergic reactions is always included in the list of ingredients, even in case of minute quantities.[523]

The presentation of this requirement in the Labelling directive is not very easy to understand. The structure is as follows. Article 6(1) states: Ingredients shall be listed in accordance with this Article and Annexes I, II, III and IIIa. The Annex last mentioned, Annex IIIa, provides a list of (currently) fourteen substances (and their derivates) considered allergenic. Therefore from Article 6(1) in connection

[520] Complementary lower case specifiers sometimes have to be added to distinguish very similar substances with specifications somewhat different from the ones of the main parent compounds. These specifiers can be of two kinds. Specifiers 'i, ii, iii, etc.' indicate that the ADI is not different and therefore different conditions of use do not have to be established. And, in ingredient labelling, E-i numbers can be put together with the parent substance (i.e. neither a separate item nor a 'i, ii, iii ...' specifier is required in the ingredient list). Specifiers 'a, b, c ... etc.', on the other hand, indicate that a separate risk evaluation was carried out, which resulted in an independent ADI. Consequently such substances are assigned independent conditions of use, and should therefore be labelled separately – with their specifier – as different ingredients. Examples of the first kind are the diphosphates: E 450 i through vii. Examples of the second kind are E 407 (carrageenan) (10) and E 407a (alternatively refined carrageenan).

[521] Joint FAO/WHO Expert Committee on Food Additives

[522] See in article 4 Directive 94/35.

[523] Directive 2003/89, amending Directive 2000/13.

with this list follows the obligation to included these substances in the list of ingredients on the label. Furthermore, Article 6(3a) of the Labelling directives lifts the exception for alcoholic beverages. In other words, if an allergen listed in Annex IIIa is used as an ingredient for an alcoholic beverage, it must be mentioned on the label. The exception on the labelling requirement longer applies. Article 6(10) lifts most other exceptions including the one for processing aids.

Annex IIIa can be updated by comitology on the basis of an opinion issued by EFSA.[524] In this way it will gradually include more substances. The allergens mentioned in Annex IIIa must be mentioned with a clear reference to their name. The Labelling directive does not provide for an obligation to use any form of the word 'allergy'. The European Commission has published guidelines[525] for the implementation of these provisions (Diagram 12.2).

Diagram 12.2. Allergenic ingredients listed in Annex IIIa of the Labelling directive.

Category	**Exceptions[1]**
Cereals containing gluten	+
Crustaceans and products thereof	-
Eggs and products thereof	-
Fish and products thereof	+
Peanuts and products thereof	-
Soybeans and products thereof	+
Milk and products thereof (including lactose)	+
Nuts (almonds, hazelnuts, walnuts, cashews, pecan nuts, Brazil nuts, pistachio nuts, macadamia nuts and Queensland nuts) and products thereof	+
Celery and products thereof	-
Mustard and products thereof	-
Sesame seeds and products thereof	-
Sulphur dioxide and sulphites at concentrations of more than 10 mg/kg or 10 mg/litre expressed as SO2	-
Lupin and products thereof	-
Molluscs and products thereof	-
[1] In case certain exceptions apply to the obligation to label (derivates of) these substances, this is indicated with a '+' in the diagram. For details see the Annex IIIa to Regulation 2000/13.	

[524] Article 6(11) Labelling directive.

[525] Guidelines regarding/relating to Article 6, paragraph 10 of Directive 2000/13/EC as amended by Directive 2003/89/EC. See also: Guidelines from the Commission' services for the contents of the notifications requested by new paragraph 11 of Directive 2000/13/EC, as amended by Directive 2003/89/EC and Second administrative guidance from the Commission' services for the application of Article 6 paragraph 11 of Directive 2000/13/EC. For hyperlinks see the reference list.

The food information proposal[526] applies a more accessible system for the labelling of allergens consisting of one Article (22) and one annex (Annex II), thus presenting basically the same rules in a much clearer way.

The allergen labelling requirement applies to ingredients used not to the hypothetical possibility of presence.[527] It seems likely, however, that consumers will attach more meaning to allergen labelling. At the current stage of development of food hygiene they will expect that nothing will be present in food products that has not knowingly been added or accepted by the manufacturer. From this point of view the allergen is either mentioned on the label, or it is not present. In reaction to this expectation a practice has developed among manufacturers with limited control on food hygiene to apply the so-called 'may contain' labelling. This practice seems to aim at limiting the manufacturers' liability in case of cross contamination by informing the consumer that traces of allergens can be present in the product. In this context, one encounters phrases like: 'produced in a factory also processing nuts'.

12.6 Net quantity

On the label of pre-packaged foods, the net quantity must be indicated. It should be expressed in metric units of mass or, for liquid foods, volume. The net quantity is often followed by the symbol 'e' (Diagram 12.3). This indicates that the manufacturer has carried out a statistical control according to an EU-approved method, with the guarantee that the net weight is not below the declared value. This e-symbol

Diagram 12.3. EEC mark as established by Directives 75/106 and 76/211.

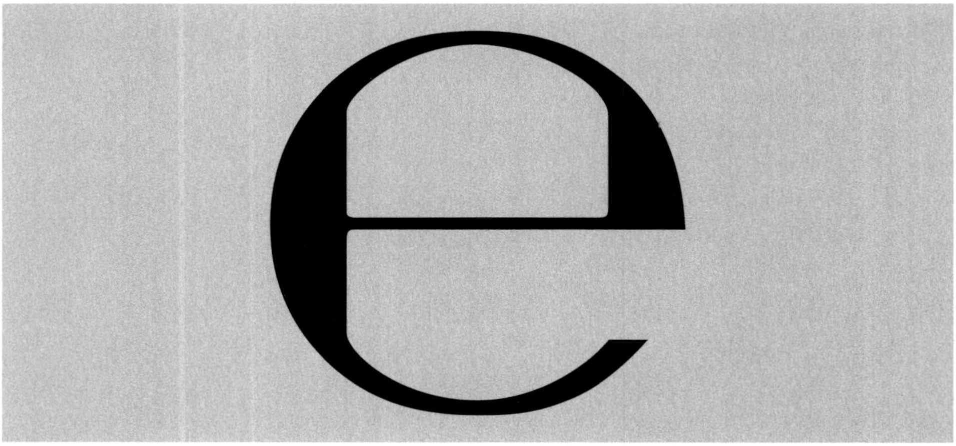

526 See section 12.1.3.

527 For example as a consequence of cross contamination.

has been regulated by Directive 75/106[528] for liquids and in Directive 76/211[529] for other products.

When the pre-packaged item contains two or more individual pre-packaged items containing the same quantity of the same product, the net quantity in each individual package should be indicated, together with the total number of packages (unless this is clearly seen). For foods normally sold by number, the total number should be indicated rather than the net quantity. For solid foods sold in liquid media, the drained net weight must also be indicated.[530]

The indication of the net quantity is important for the consumer's informed choice regarding value for price. In this context Directive 93/6[531] is relevant. This directive requires indication of the selling price and the price per unit of measurement of products offered by traders to consumers.

12.7 Durability

The Labelling directive applies two dates: a date of minimum durability and a use by date. The first is dealt with in Article 9, the second in Article 10.

The food business operator is responsible for setting these dates. The business has the discretion to choose the date more or less conservatively. That is to say s/he is under no obligation to choose the latest possible date.

The directive gives formats and wordings for indicating the date on the label The date of minimum durability refers to the quality of the product. This is expressed in the phrase: 'Best before (end)...'. The mere fact that the best before date passes does not lead to the conclusion that the food is no longer safe or is unfit for human consumption. It is not banned from the market.

The 'use–by' date on the other hand is a food safety date that has to be applied in the case of foodstuffs which, from the microbiological point of view, are highly perishable and are therefore likely after a short period to constitute an immediate danger to human health.

[528] Council Directive of 19 December 1974 on the approximation of the laws of the Member States relating to the making-up by volume of certain prepackaged liquids (75/106/EEC). Official Journal L 42, 15 February 1975, p. 1.

[529] Council Directive of 20 January 1976 on the approximation of the laws of the Member States relating to the making-up by weight or by volume of certain prepackaged products (76/211/EEC). Official Journal L 46, 21 February 1976, p. 1.

[530] J. Claude Cheftel, Food and nutrition labelling in the European Union, Food Chemistry 93 (2005), pp. 531-550.

[531] Directive 98/6/EC of the European Parliament and of the Council of 16 February 1998 on consumer protection in the indication of the prices of products offered to consumers. Official Journal L 80, 18 March 1998, pp. 27-31.

12.8 Origin labelling

Some countries like the USA,[532] Australia and New Zealand[533] require the labelling of the country of origin of certain food products. In the EU, the Labelling directive[534] only requires particulars of the place of origin or provenance to be labelled where failure to give such particulars might mislead the consumer to a material degree[535] as to the true origin or provenance of the foodstuff.

This requirement elaborates on Article 2(1)(a)(i) stating that the labelling and the methods used must not be such as could mislead the purchaser to a material degree particularly as to (as far as relevant in the current context) the origin or provenance of the foodstuff.

The food information proposal[536] incorporates the definition of country of origin from the Community Customs Code. The proposal takes as a general principle that food information shall not be misleading as to the country of origin or place of provenance.[537] By consequence, indication of the country of origin or place of provenance is mandatory where failure to indicate this might mislead the consumer to a material degree as to the true country of origin or place of provenance of the food, in particular if the information accompanying the food or the label as a whole would otherwise imply that the food has a different country of origin or place of provenance.[538]

In the food information proposal, the chapter on voluntary food information explicitly deals with origin labelling in the situations where it is not mandatory. See Law text box 12.5.

---

532 The USA 2002 Farm Bill requires country of origin labeling (COOL) for beef, lamb, pork, fish, perishable agricultural commodities, and peanuts. The entry into force has – except for fish and shellfish – been delayed several times. Currently the date aimed at is 30 September 2008.

533 A new standard in the Australia New Zealand Food Standards Code requires packaged food to carry a separate statement identifying the country where the food was produced, made or packaged. The new country of origin labelling standard for packaged food has been phased in over a two-year period from 8 December 2005.

534 Article 3(1)(8).

535 This expression indicates that the issue must be more than a trifle.

536 Article 2(3) COM(2008) 40 final.

537 Article 7(1)(a).

538 Article 9(1)(i).

Law text box 12.5. Article 35 food information proposal on provenance.

Article 35 (2), (3) and (4)

2. Without prejudice to labelling in accordance with specific Community legislation, paragraphs 3 and 4 shall apply where the country of origin or the place of provenance of a food is voluntarily indicated to inform consumers that a food originates or comes from the European Community or a given country or place.
3. Where the country of origin or the place of provenance of the food is not the same as the one of its primary ingredient(s), the country of origin or place of provenance of those ingredient(s) shall also be given.
4. For meat, other than beef and veal, the indication on the country of origin or place of provenance may be given as a single place only where animals have been born, reared and slaughtered in the same country or place. In other cases information on each of the different places of birth, rearing and slaughter shall be given.

The Community Customs Code[539] defines the origin of goods among other things for the purpose of applying the Customs Tariff of the EC.

Goods originating in a country are:

- goods wholly obtained (including harvested) or produced in a country or on board a factory ship;
- goods that underwent their last, substantial, economically justified processing or working resulting in a new product or representing an important stage of manufacture.

Food businesses are free to label the origin of their products. Member states however are not at liberty to introduce mandatory or even voluntary schemes. Case law of the ECJ consistently holds origin labelling legislation to constitute trade barriers not compatible with Article 28 EC Treaty. The following two cases may stand as example.

The first case[540] deals with national legislation prohibiting the retail sale of certain products imported from other member states, unless they bear or are accompanied by an indication of origin. The Court is highly critical. For several reasons it concludes that the measure at issue is a barrier to trade for which no justification can be found in EC law. The court argues that such a requirement, to label the origin in an other member state, would necessarily increase the production costs of the imported article and make it more expensive. Further it has to be recognised that the purpose of indications of origin or origin-marking is to enable consumers to distinguish between domestic and imported products and that this enables them

[539] Article 22-27 Regulation 2913/92.

[540] ECJ 25 April 1985, Commission v. UK, case 207/83.

to assert any prejudices which they may have against foreign products. In short, provisions in question are liable to have the effect of increasing the production costs of imported goods and making it more difficult to sell them. The Court also notes that if the national origin of goods brings certain qualities to the minds of consumers, it is in manufacturers' interests to indicate it themselves on the goods or on their packaging and it is not necessary to compel them to do so. In that case, the protection of consumers is sufficiently guaranteed by rules which enable the use of false indications of origin to be prohibited. Such rules are not called into question by the EEC treaty.

The second case[541] is about an origin related quality label. By awarding the quality label 'Markenqualität aus deutschen Landen' (quality label for produce made in Germany) to finished products of a certain quality produced in Germany, the Federal Republic of Germany has failed to fulfil its obligations under (now) Article 28 of the EC Treaty.

The contested scheme has, at least potentially, restrictive effects on the free movement of goods between member states. Such a scheme, set up in order to promote the distribution of agricultural and food products made in Germany and for which the advertising message underlines the German origin of the relevant products, may encourage consumers to buy the products with the label to the exclusion of imported products.

The fact that the use of that quality label is optional does not mean that it ceases to be an unjustified obstacle to trade if the use of that designation promotes or is likely to promote the marketing of the product concerned as compared with products which do not benefit from its use.

The limits set to national legislation, do not apply to the EU legislator. At EU level currently a proposal is pending for a country of origin marking scheme.[542] This scheme only applies to a limited number of non-food products imported from outside the EU. As we will see in Chapter 15, the country of origin of fresh fruit and vegetables must be indicated. The same is true for beef.

12.9 Nutrition labelling

Currently, nutrition labelling is voluntary in the EU. It is governed by Directive 90/496. If a food business chooses to provide nutrition information, it has to comply with this directive. The provision of nutrition information becomes mandatory if a nutrition or health claim is being made.[543]

[541] ECJ 5 November 2002, Commission v. Germany, case C-325/00, ECR 2002, p. I-09977.
[542] Commission proposal for a 'Council Regulation on the indication of the country of origin of certain products imported from third countries' (COM(2005) 661 final).
[543] On nutrition and health claims see here after section 12.14.

'Nutrition labelling' means any information on the label that relates to energy value and to the following nutrients: protein, carbohydrate, fat, fibre, sodium, vitamins and minerals present in significant amounts.

Where nutrition labelling is provided, the information to be given should consist of either group 1 (the so-called 'big four') or group 2 (the so-called 'big eight') in the following order:

- Group 1
  - the energy value;
  - the amount of protein, carbohydrate and fat.
- Group 2
  - the energy value;
  - the amount of protein, carbohydrate, sugar, fat, saturates, fibre and sodium.

The energy value and the proportion of nutrients must be declared in specific units per 100 grams or per 100 millilitres. Information on vitamins and minerals must be expressed as a percentage of the recommended daily allowance (RDA). The information on the label must be presented in tabular form with the numbers aligned or if space does not permit, in linear form in a language easily understood by the consumer.

The food information proposal sets out to turn nutrition labelling mandatory. The system is slightly different from the current one. In stead of a 'big four' and 'big eight', a 'big five' applies:

- energy value;
- the amounts of fat, saturates, carbohydrates with specific reference to sugars, and salt.

To these five one or more of the following may be added:[544]

- trans fats;
- mono-unsaturates;
- polyunsaturates;
- polyols;
- starch;
- fibre;
- protein;
- any of the minerals or vitamins listed in an annex to the proposal, if present in significant amounts.

[544] Article 29.

The proposal holds provisions for the calculation of the energy content.[545] The quantities must be expressed on a portion basis in prescribed units of measurement and in a percentage of reference intakes listed in an annex. The nutrition information must be presented 'in the principal field of vision'; in the wording of the proposal;[546] or 'front of pack' as it is expressed by businesses (Diagram 12.4).[547] By rendering nutrition labelling mandatory, the food information proposal makes the first real contribution to aligning legislation to obesity policy.

Diagram 12.4. Annex XIII of the food information proposal on the order of presentation.

Part C - Order of presentation of energy and nutrients appearing in a nutrition declaration

The order of presentation of the information on the energy and nutrients, as appropriate, shall be the following:

energy	**kJ and kcal**
fat	g
of which	
• saturates	g
• trans fats	g
• mono-unsaturates	g
• polyunsaturates	g
carbohydrate	
of which	
• sugars	g
• polyols	g
• starch	g
fibre	g
protein	g
salt	g
vitamins and minerals	the units specified in point 1 of Part A of Annex XI

12.10 Protected designations

Regulation 2082/92 on agricultural indications, establishes rules for the protection of certain designations of origin (PDO) and geographical indications (PGI) on agricultural products. The regulation provides opportunities for small-scale producers to use these quality symbols as a means of promoting their products, without the long and costly process of obtaining a trademark for their product.[548]

---

545 Article 30.

546 Article 34.

547 Article 34.

548 See for trademarks Chapter 2.

To a certain extent they are comparable to collective trade marks in the sense that they can be used by a group of producers to distinguish their product.

Member states may not introduce additional schemes.[549]

12.10.1 Origin

A PDO, 'protected designation of origin' (e.g. 'Parma ham' or 'Camembert de Normandie'), is the name of a region or specific place that is used to describe an agricultural product or foodstuff originating in that region or place. The PDO should designate only those products that exhibit the quality or characteristics, which are essentially, or exclusively due to a particular geographical environment with its inherent natural and human factors, and the production, processing and preparation which take place in the defined geographical area.

12.10.2 Geography

A PGI, 'protected geographical indication' (e.g. 'Ardennen ham or Danablu cheese), is the name of a region or a specific place used to describe an agricultural product or foodstuff originating in that region or place which possesses a specific quality, reputation or other characteristics attributable to that geographical origin and the production and/or processing and/or preparation which take place in the defined geographical area.

To obtain a Protected Designation of Origin the area must be precisely defined, all stages of production, processing and preparation, from the raw materials to the finished product, must take place in the area that lends its name to the product. The characteristics of the product must be essentially or exclusively due to the place of origin. In contrast to the PDO the ties between area and product are much less strict for a PGI. The product must have been produced in the indicated geographical area. However, it is sufficient that only one of the stages of production has taken place in that area. Also, the characteristics of the product do not have to be essentially or exclusively due to the indicated area. For a PGI it is sufficient that only one characteristic of the product can be attributed to the area, for instance its reputation.

Producers can file an application for registration of a protected designation through their national authorities. The national authorities inform the public of the request made, and ensure that any interested party in the member state can

---

[549] ECJ 6 March 2003, Commission vs. Germany, Case C-6/02: protected designations of origin may not be introduced by national legislation but may only be afforded within the framework of Regulation (EC) 2081/92 (now Regulation (EC) 510/2006).

object if it wishes. Where the request is acceptable, the member state sends it to the Commission for registration; if not, it rejects it.

The Commission examines requests sent by member states, including the main elements of the specification gathered in each case in a 'single document', and assesses whether they meet the requirements under the relevant regulation. The Commission assesses any objections to the registration of a designation submitted by third parties. It can call on independent scientific advice. If an application satisfies the rules then the single document referring to that application for registration is published in the Official Journal.

12.10.3 Tradition

Regulation 509/2006[550] has introduced a register of recognised traditional specialties. To obtain the TSG (Traditional Speciality Guaranteed) designation a product must possess features that distinguish it from other products, and it must be traditional. The specific features required by the TSG system include:

- use of traditional raw materials in production of a foodstuff; or
- traditional composition; or
- mode of production and/or processing reflecting traditional methods.

'Traditional' in this context[551] means proven usage on the EU market for a time period showing transmission between generations; this usually means a minimum of 25 years.

An application for a TSG designation must be accompanied by specifications enabling compliance with registration conditions, including at least:

- The name to be registered, and an indication of whether the producer/group is applying for registration with or without reservation of the name and whether the name can be registered in one or more languages.
- A description of the characteristics of the product giving its main physical, chemical, microbiological and/or organoleptic characteristics which relate to the specific character.
- A description of the method of production, including the nature and characteristics of the raw material and/or ingredients used and/or the method of preparation of the product.
- Details allowing appraisal of traditional character – i.e. the key elements that define and prove the product's specific character.

[550] Council Regulation (EC) No 509/2006 of 20 March 2006 on agricultural products and foodstuffs as traditional specialities guaranteed. Official Journal L 93, 31 March 2006, p.1.

[551] Hygiene legislation applies its own definition of traditional.

The application for registration of a name in the register of TSGs can be done with or without reservation of the name. 'Without reservation of the name' means that the registered name may continue to be used on the labelling of products not corresponding to the registered specification, but the indication 'traditional speciality guaranteed', the abbreviation 'TSG' or the associated EU logo, may not be indicated thereon (Mozzarella cheese is an example of a TSG without reservation of the name). 'With reservation of the name' means that the name, even where unaccompanied by the indication 'traditional speciality guaranteed', the abbreviation 'TSG' or the associated EU logo, may no longer be used on the labelling of similar foodstuffs not satisfying the registered specification (an example of reservation of a name is Jamón Serrano).[552]

12.11 Organic

Regulation 834/2007[553] establishes conditions for the use of terms referring to the 'organic'[554] production method (such as 'eco' and 'bio'). Such terms may only be used in labelling, advertisement or in trade marks with regard to products which satisfy the requirements set out under or pursuant to that regulation. In case of processed food at least 95% of the ingredients (by weight) must be organic. Additional information has to be supplied as well, such as the number of the control authority. The regulation sets out the objectives and principles of organic production (Law text boxes 12.6 and 12.7).

Law text box 12.6. Objectives of organic production.

Article 3 Regulation 834/2007 on organic production and labelling of organic products

Organic production shall pursue the following general objectives:

(a) establish a sustainable management system for agriculture that:
   (i) respects nature's systems and cycles and sustains and enhances the health of soil, water, plants and animals and the balance between them;
   (ii) contributes to a high level of biological diversity

---

552 The wording of this section has been derived from the fact sheet 'European policy for quality agricultural products' Published by DG AGRI (2007).

553 Council Regulation (EC) No 834/2007 of 28 June 2007 on organic production and labelling of organic products and repealing Regulation (EEC) No 2092/91. Official Journal L 189, 20 July 2007, pp. 1-23.

554 The term 'organic', as originally conceived, derived from a belief in the farm as a self-sustaining, living organism. The English word was made popular by Lord Northbourn in his book Look to the Land (1940). Today, in its broader meaning, organic refers to the importance of the interactions between the living organisms that inhabit the farm. Many English speakers, having first come across the term in chemistry lessons where organic refers to anything derived from carbon-containing compounds, mistakenly assume that the word has a similar meaning when applied to farming and food; Rod MacRae, 'A history of sustainable agriculture', 1990. For a hyperlink see the reference list.

(iii) makes responsible use of energy and the natural resources, such as water, soil, organic matter and air;
(iv) respects high animal welfare standards and in particular meets animals' species-specific behavioural needs;

(b) aim at producing products of high quality;
(c) aim at producing a wide variety of foods and other agricultural products that respond to consumers' demand for goods produced by the use of processes that do not harm the environment, human health, plant health or animal health and welfare.

Law text box 12.7. Principles of organic production.

Article 4 Regulation 834/2007 on organic production and labelling of organic products

Organic production shall be based on the following principles:

(a) the appropriate design and management of biological processes based on ecological systems using natural resources which are internal to the system by methods that:
(i) use living organisms and mechanical production methods;
(ii) practice land-related crop cultivation and livestock production or practice aquaculture which complies with the principle of sustainable exploitation of fisheries;
(iii) exclude the use of GMOs and products produced from or by GMOs with the exception of veterinary medicinal products;
(iv) are based on risk assessment, and the use of precautionary and preventive measures, when appropriate;

(b) the restriction of the use of external inputs. Where external inputs are required or the appropriate management practices and methods referred to in paragraph (a) do not exist, these shall be limited to:
(i) inputs from organic production;
(ii) natural or naturally-derived substances;
(iii) low solubility mineral fertilisers;

(c) the strict limitation of the use of chemically synthesised inputs to exceptional cases these being:
(i) where the appropriate management practices do not exist; and
(ii) the external inputs referred to in paragraph (b) are not available on the market; or
(iii) where the use of external inputs referred to in paragraph (b) contributes to unacceptable environmental impacts;

(d) the adaptation, where necessary, and within the framework of this Regulation, of the rules of organic production taking account of sanitary status, regional differences in climate and local conditions, stages of development and specific husbandry practices.

12.12 GM-labelling

In relation to GM food, the principle of informed choice requires that consumers are informed of the use of gene technology in the process that ultimately leads to the food product they are about to buy or to consume. Therefore Regulation 1829/2003 (Article 13) requires that 'the words 'genetically modified' or 'produced from genetically modified [name of the ingredient]' shall appear in the list of ingredients'.[555] This requirement has been further elaborated in Article 4(6) of Regulation 1830/2003 reproduced in Law text box 12.8.

Law text box 12.8. Principle of informed choice: GM labelling. Labelling genetically modified organisms, Article 13 Regulation 1829/2003 and Article 4 (6) Regulation 1830/2003.

Article 13 Regulation 1829/2003

... 'the words "genetically modified" or "produced from genetically modified [name of the ingredient]" shall appear in the list of ingredients'.

Article 4 (6) of Regulation 1830/2003:

For products consisting of or containing GMOs, operators shall ensure that:

(a) for pre-packaged products consisting of, or containing GMOs, the words 'This product contains genetically modified organisms' or 'This product contains genetically modified (name of organism(s))' appear on a label;

(b) for non-pre-packaged products offered to the final consumer the words 'This product contains genetically modified organisms' or 'This product contains genetically modified (name of organism(s))' shall appear on, or in connection with, the display of the product.

These labelling requirements apply to all products derived from GMOs even highly refined products. An exception for products in which no protein or DNA is present that existed before 2004 is no longer made.

However, a few exceptions remain. The labelling requirement does not apply to foods containing material which contains, consists of or is produced from GMOs in a proportion no higher than 0.9%[556] of the food ingredients considered individually or food consisting of a single ingredient, provided that this presence is adventitious or technically unavoidable.

[555] It should be noted that the word 'genetically' must be in the labelling. It may cause some confusion that there are additives that must be labelled as 'modified starch'. Here the word 'modified' refers to conventional techniques of modification, not to gene technology.

[556] Art. 12(2) Regulation 1829/2003. In case the GMO has not yet been authorised, a presence of 0.5% maximum is considered not to constitute an infringement provided that this GMO has benefited from a favourable opinion from the Community Scientific Committee(s) or the Authority before the date of application of Regulation 1829/2003 (art. 47 Reg. 1829/2003).

The burden of proof is on industry: 'In order to establish that the presence of this material is adventitious or technically unavoidable, operators must be in a position to supply evidence to satisfy the competent authorities that they have taken appropriate steps to avoid the presence of such material'.[557]

To comply with this requirement food business operators must have detailed information at their disposal concerning the history of the raw materials they use.

For example, research has shown that it takes a distance of 24.5 metres between a field of GM maize and a field of non-GM maize for the non-GM field to remain below the 0.9% threshold. Other products need even greater distances. Labelling standards will require complete transparency and traceability in the food chain, and a strict segregation of the GM food chain from the conventional food chain for producers on the non-GM side to be able to live up to these standards.

12.13 Beef and veal

After the BSE crises discussed in Chapter 7, legislation on cattle and derived products (beef and veal) has become more strict. This also has its impact on food labelling law. In addition to the general labelling requirements, Regulation 1760/2000 contains some compulsory provisions and some voluntary measures.[558] This regulation, replacing earlier legislation, aims at maintaining and strengthening consumer confidence in beef and to avoid misleading them by ensuring that information is made available by sufficient and clear labelling.

12.13.1 Compulsory

Operators and organisations marketing beef in the Community are obliged to label beef in accordance with Article 13 of Regulation 1760/2000. The compulsory labelling system shall ensure a link between, on the one hand, the identification of the carcass, quarter or pieces of meat and, on the other hand, the individual animal or, where this is sufficient to enable the accuracy of the information on the label to be checked, the group of animals concerned.

Further, the label must show:
- in which country the animals were born;
- in which country the animals were fattened/bred;
- a code for the country and the slaughterhouse where the slaughter took place.

[557] Article 12(3) Regulation 1829/2003.
[558] Council Regulation (EC) 1760/2000. Official Journal L 204, 17 July 2000, pp. 1-10.

For minced meat some derogations apply.[559] For example, the three issues mentioned above may be replaced by an indication of the country (member state or third country) where the meat was prepared and 'origin' if this is not the same country. Beef imported from a third country may be labelled 'Origin: non-EC' and 'Slaughtered in: (name of third country)' if all the required information is not available.

12.13.2 Voluntary

If businesses want to include information on the label beyond the mandatory information on the label, they must send a specification for approval to the responsible authority in the member state where the product is sold. Member states must notify the labels they approve to the Commission (Article 16). Commission Regulation (EC) no. 1825/2000 gives more detailed rules.[560]

Voluntary labelling specifications must indicate:

- the information to be included on the label;
- the measures to be taken to ensure the accuracy of the information;
- the control system which will be applied at all stages of production and sale, including the controls to be carried out by an independent body recognised by the competent authority and designated by the business. These bodies shall comply with the criteria set out in European Standard EN/45011;
- in the case of an organisation of businesses, the measures to be taken in relation to any member which fails to comply with the specifications. Member states may decide that controls by an independent body may be replaced by controls by a competent authority. The competent authority shall in that case have at its disposal the qualified staff and resources necessary to carry out the requisite controls. The costs of controls shall be borne by the business(es) using the labelling system.[561]

12.14 Nutrition and health claims

Article 2(1)(b) of the Labelling directive states in general that labelling must not attribute to any foodstuff the property of preventing, treating or curing a human disease, or refer to such properties.

559 Article K1.

560 Commission Regulation (EC) No. 1825/2000 of 25 August 2000 laying down detailed rules for the application of Regulation (EC) No. 1760/2000 of the European Parliament and of the Council as regards the labelling of beef and beef products. Official Journal L 216, 26 August 2000, pp. 8-12.

561 Article 16.

Regulation 1924/2006[562] deals more specifically with messages about the relation between a certain food and consumers' health. This regulation covers claims about what a food *is* (contains): nutrition claims (e.g. 'rich in vitamin C' or 'low in fat') and about what a food *does:* health claims (i.e. claims of a positive relationship between a specific food and improved health). It sets rules for making such claims and also allows some health claims that were previously prohibited. Disease-related messages ('reduction of disease risk' claims), which until recently were totally prohibited, can now be allowed if they are scientifically substantiated. Claims authorised at the European level are entered in a register.

Nutrition and health claims are only allowed if they are substantiated by generally accepted scientific evidence.[563] The food business operator must justify any claims used. A 'claim' in this context[564] is any message or representation, which is not mandatory under Community or national legislation, including pictorial, graphic or symbolic representation, in any form, which states, suggests or implies that a food has particular characteristics.[565] A claim may only be made for a substance that is present in the food in a bio-available form and in a sufficient quantity for the claimed effect.[566] If a claim is made, nutrition labelling becomes mandatory.[567]

12.14.1 Nutrition claims

A 'Nutrition claim' is any claim, which states, suggests or implies that a food has particular beneficial nutrition properties due to:

a. the energy (calorific value) it
   (1) provides;
   (2) provides at a reduced or increased rate; or
   (3) does not provide; and/or
b. the nutrients or other substances it
   (1) contains;
   (2) contains in reduced or increased proportions; or
   (3) does not contain.[568]

[562] Regulation (EC) No 1924/2006 of the European Parliament and of the Council of 20 December 2006 on nutrition and health claims made on Foods. Official Journal L 12, 18 January 2007, p. 3 (corrigendum). Here after; NHCR.

[563] Article 6 NHCR.

[564] The reader be reminded that in legal literature one encounters the word 'claim' in different meanings. In litigations (mainly tort law) the 'claim' represents the compensation the initiator of the procedure demands the opponent to pay. In patent law the 'claim' relates to the property of an invention that makes it new and thus eligible for patent protection. In the context we are discussing now 'claim' is a statement a food business makes about a property of a food product. The product exhibiting the claimed property is often referred to as a functional food.

[565] Article 2(2)(1) NHCR.

[566] Article 5 NHCR.

[567] Article 7 NHCR.

[568] Article 2(2)(4) NHCR.

The regulation comes with an exhaustive annex listing nutrition claims that can be made (e.g. low energy, low fat, fat free, with no added sugars, high fibre, light, etc.) and the conditions applying to them. For instance, a claim stating that a product is 'light' or 'lite', and any claim likely to have the same meaning for the consumer, must meet the same conditions as those set for the term 'reduced'. That is, the claim shall be accompanied by an indication of the characteristic(s) which make the food 'light' or 'lite'. A claim that a food is energy-reduced, and any claim likely to have the same meaning for the consumer, may only be made where the energy value is reduced by at least 30%, with an indication of the characteristic(s), which make(s) the food reduced in its total energy value.

Nutrition claims that are not listed in the annex, are not permitted. The annex can be updated through comitology. The Commission can consult EFSA and interested parties.[569]

12.14.2 Health claims

'Health claim' means any claim that states, suggests or implies that a relationship exists between a food category, a food or one of its constituents, and health.[570] Health claims must be authorised by the Commission on the basis of an assessment carried out by EFSA. The applicant must provide a dossier containing scientific studies to substantiate the claim and a proposal for the wording of the claim.

The application must be sent to the national competent authority of a member state. This authority shall acknowledge receipt, and pass the application on to EFSA. EFSA in turn informs the other member states and the Commission.[571] EFSA gives its opinion within five months. The applicant and members of the public can make comments.[572] The Commission will send a draft decision to the SCFCAH. If SCFCAH agrees the Commission adopts the decision. In case of a favourable decision, the approved claim shall be included in Community Register of nutrition and health claims made on food.[573]

The regulation applies a system of data protection. For a period of five years the confidential scientific data supplied by the applicant, may not be used without the applicants consent for the benefit of a subsequent applicant.[574]

569 Article 8 NHCR.
570 Article 2(2)(5) NHCR. On health claims see Korver, Onno, Kühn, Martha Celcilia, Richardson, David, The Functional Foods Dossier: Building Solid Health Claims, Bennekom (The Netherlands), 2004. See also the special issue of European Food and Feed Law Review 2 (1) 2007.
571 Article 15 NHCR.
572 Article 16 NHCR.
573 Article 20 NHCR.
574 Article 21 NHCR.

A specific form of health claim is the 'reduction of disease risk claim'. This is any health claim that states, suggests or implies that the consumption of a food category, a food or one of its constituents significantly reduces a risk factor in the development of a human disease.[575] In addition to the requirements that apply to all health claims, in connection to the reduction of disease risk claim a statement must be made indicating that the disease to which the claim is referring has multiple risk factors and that altering one of these risk factors may or may not have a beneficial effect.[576]

12.14.3 General limitations

The regulation introduces limits on food business operators rights to communicate the nutritional or health benefits for certain food with undesirable 'nutritional profiles'. The commission is empowered to set these profiles through comitology and with advice of EFSA by 19 January 2009 at the latest.[577] The profiles will relate to foods that are high in fat or sugar and the like. According to the Commission, such foods can be consumed in moderation as part of a healthy diet, but to associate them with health and nutrition claims may lead consumers that are currently eating them in moderation to consume them in greater quantities. The Commission will not call them 'bad food' but prevents them from being marketed as 'good food' with positive messages about health and nutritional benefits. Health claims on beverages containing more than 1.2% alcohol are also not allowed since alcohol is known to entail other health and social problems. For such beverages, only claims referring to a reduction in alcohol or energy content are allowed.[578]

It follows from the regulation's new approach to health claims that any information about foods and their nutritional or health benefits used in labelling, marketing and advertising which is not clear, accurate and meaningful,[579] and which cannot be substantiated, will not be permitted. Furthermore, vague claims referring to general well-being (e.g. 'helps your body to resist stress', 'preserves youth') or claims making reference to psychological and behavioural functions (e.g. 'improves your memory' or 'reduces stress and adds optimism') are not allowed. Slimming or weight control claims are also forbidden.

Reference to and endorsement by individual doctors or health professionals is not permitted.[580]

---

575 Article 2(2)(6) NHCR.
576 Article 14(2) NHCR.
577 Article 4(1) NHCR.
578 Article 4(3) NHCR.
579 Article 5(2) NHCR: The use of nutrition and health claims shall only be permitted if the average consumer can be expected to understand the beneficial effects as expressed in the claim.
580 Article 12(c) NHCR.

12.15 Indications for other purposes than consumer information

The label is not only the appropriate place to provide the consumer with information, it is also the vehicle to transport information for other parties like public authorities and food chain partners.

According to Article 18(4) of the General Food Law, food placed on the market in the European Community must be adequately labelled or identified to facilitate its traceability. Directive 89/396 requires that foodstuffs carry a mark identifying the lot to which a foodstuff belongs. It defines 'lot' as a batch of sales units of a foodstuff produced, manufactured or packaged under practically the same conditions.

The indication to identify the lot should be determined by the producer, manufacturer or packager or by the first seller in the EU. The marking shall be preceded by the letter 'L' except in cases when it is clearly distinguishable from other indications on the label. The lot identification is not necessary if the date (day and month) of minimum durability or 'use by' date, appears in uncoded form on the label. As we have seen above, it is now mandatory that such date be present. On the basis of Regulations 253/2004 and 254/2004 meat products have to bear a health mark indicating the slaughterhouse where the animal has been slaughtered.

12.16 Further labelling provisions

We are under no illusion that in this chapter we can provide an exhaustive overview of all food legislation with provisions on labelling. However, for the benefit of readers active in a specific domain we will list a few more provisions:

- Veal: Regulation 700/2007 and Regulation 566/2008;
- Eggs: Regulation 1028/2006, Commission regulation 557/2007;
- Novel foods: Regulation 258/97;
- Quinine and caffeine: Commission Directive 2002/67;
- Thorough cooking of *Salmonella* risked meat: Commission Regulation 2073/2005 (Article 6);
- Miscellaneous Directive 2008/5 of 30 January 2008 concerning the compulsory indication on the labelling of certain foodstuffs of particulars other than those provided for in Directive 2000/13/EC of the European Parliament and of the Council Regulation 608/2004 lays down labelling requirements for foods and food ingredients with added phytosterols, phytosterol esters, phytostanols and phytostanol esters (used to reduce cholesterol levels). For labelling purposes, phytosterols, phytosterol esters, phytostanols and phytostanol esters must be designated respectively by the terms 'plant sterols', 'plant sterol esters', 'plant stanols' or 'plant stanol esters'.

Most of these provisions are included in the food information proposal.

12.17 In summary

Despite the work that has been invested in the codification of food labelling legislation, the situation is still very complex. Many different laws must be consulted in designing or checking a label. Diagram 12.5 gives a summary of the issues discussed in this chapter. It can be used as a starting point for devising a labelling checklist. The rows represent the type of information, the columns represent the kind of requirement that is made on this information.

Diagram 12.5. Elements for food labelling checklist.

	Mandatory 2000/13	Mandatory other	Approval required	Voluntary regulated	Voluntary	Banned	Food information proposal
Product identity	Name			Verticals	Trade mark or fantasy name	Misleading 16 GFL 2(1) 2000/13	Similar
	Ingredients	Quinine / caffeine phytosterols		E-numbers for additives	Processing aids		Codified
	Allergens in annex				Other allergens		Clarified
	Alcohol content		Nutrition claim	Nutrition information			Nutrition becomes mandatory
	Quantity						Similar
Product condition	Durability					Misleading 16 GFL 2(1) 2000/13	Similar
	Frozen, etc.						Similar
Process	Irradiated	GM	Traditional	Organic			Similar
Origin	Business	Health mark Beef / Veal	PDO / PGI			Misleading 16 GFL 2(1) 2000/13	Definition of concept
	Place or country to avoid misleading				Country (including EU)		Clarified
Effects						Misleading 16 GFL 2(1) 2000/13	Similar
		Health claim			Cure		Not included
					Claims on Foods with 'wrong' profile		Not included
					Endorsed by medical profession		Not included
Packaging		Lot					Not included
	Protective atmosphere 2008/5						Similar
Other		Price	Other aspects of beef / veal			Misleading 16 GFL 2(1) 2000/13	Not included
	Language				Additional languages		Similar

13. Public powers: official controls, enforcement and incident management

13.1 Introduction

A typical feature of law is that people can be forced to comply with it. Sanctions and coercive measures can be applied to those who do not.

It is the responsibility of the member states to enforce food law, and to monitor and verify that the relevant requirements of food law are fulfilled by food and feed business operators at all stages of production, processing and distribution. For that purpose, they have to maintain a system of official controls and other activities appropriate to the circumstances, including public communication on food and feed safety and risks, food and feed safety surveillance and other monitoring activities covering all stages of production, processing and distribution (Law text box 13.1).

Law text box 13.1. Article 17(2) GFL on the Member States' responsibility to enforce food law.

Article 17(2) Regulation 178/2002
Member States shall enforce food law, and monitor and verify that the relevant requirements of food law are fulfilled by food and feed business operators at all stages of production, processing and distribution.
For that purpose, they shall maintain a system of official controls and other activities as appropriate to the circumstances, including public communication on food and feed safety and risk, food and feed safety surveillance and other monitoring activities covering all stages of production, processing and distribution.
Member States shall also lay down the rules on measures and penalties applicable to infringements of food and feed law. The measures and penalties provided for shall be effective, proportionate and dissuasive.

Generally speaking enforcement encompasses both verification of compliance with legal obligations and application of sanctions in case of infringements. Although Article 17 of the General Food Law holds the member states responsible for the enforcement of food law, European food law increasingly sets standards for national enforcement and provides for supervision. On 30 April 2004 a Regulation was published in the Official Journal of the European Union: '*Regulation (EC) No 882/2004 of the European Parliament and of the Council of 29 April 2004 on official controls performed to ensure the verification of compliance with feed and food law, animal health and animal welfare rules*'.

This Regulation 882/2004 includes obligations for verification by the member states, measures to be taken in case of infringements, a framework for co-operation between national authorities and the Commission, and for the Commission to monitor the performance of national authorities in the member states and in third countries.

Infringements on food law may cause food safety incidents. Such incidents can however also occur for other reasons (accidents). Incident management and enforcement can be closely related, but they are not necessarily the same thing. For powers to deal with food safety incidents one has to turn to the General Food Law.

In this chapter we will discuss two enforcement issues (first official controls, then measures in case of non-compliance) and two incident management issues (rapid alert system and emergency measures).

13.2 Official controls

National inspectors supervise application of the requirements of food law. In several member states these inspectors work in the context of food safety authorities, which are often more or less autonomous agencies.

The national inspectors have powers under national law to inspect premises where food is handled and to report on irregularities. Such irregularities may result in sanctions. Some member states use administrative law sanctions, others use criminal law.

13.2.1 General controls

Since the food safety scares, EU food law has turned its attention increasingly to situations that at first sight seem to be internal matters of the member states.

Regulation 882/2004 is concerned with food-related controls in general.[581] It distinguishes a great variety of inspections types: 'official control', 'verification', 'audit', 'inspection', 'monitoring', 'surveillance', 'sampling for analysis', 'official certification', 'official detention', 'documentary check', 'identity check' and 'physical check'.[582] These distinctions seem rather subtle for a framework that is intended to be applied in all 27 member states.

Member states are responsible for ensuring that official controls are carried out regularly, with appropriate frequency, and on a risk basis.[583] What frequency is appropriate depends among other things on identified risks and past performance.

581 Not only in intra-Community trade.

582 Article 2 Regulation 882/2004, definitions.

583 Article 3(1) Regulation 882/2004.

Good past performance by a food business may lead to a reduced frequency in inspections.

Official controls must cover the whole food chain 'from farm to fork'. As a rule they must be carried out without prior warning.[584] Nevertheless, the national competent authority must ensure that they carry out their activities with a high level of transparency.[585] National legislation must ensure the staffs of the competent authorities have access to premises of and documentation kept by food business operators.[586]

The member states may collect fees or charges to cover the costs occasioned by official controls. For some activities they are even obliged to do so in order to avoid a distortion of intra-community trade by different practices.[587] If non-compliance leads to extra official controls then the operators responsible will be charged.[588]

The regulation requires member states to prepare integrated multi-annual national control plans, to report on the results yearly and also to prepare contingency plans for dealing with emergency situations.[589]

In addition to regulation 882/2004, Regulation 854/2004 holds specific measures to control compliance with Regulation 853/2004 (on hygiene of food of animal origin). The Regulation lays down requirements as regards for instance the approval of establishments, assistance in carrying out controls, presentation of documents, etc. The controls include audits of HACCP and good hygiene practices.

13.2.2 Obligations of food business operators

Food business operators are obliged to undergo any inspection and to assist the staff of the competent national authority in the accomplishment of their tasks. However, satisfactory results do not affect their duty to comply with food law, nor excuse them from future official controls. They are even under obligation to take the initiative to inform the authorities of food safety problems that occur in their businesses.[590]

---

584 Article 3(3) Regulation 882/2004.

585 Article 7 Regulation 882/2004.

586 Article 4 and 8 Regulation 882/2004.

587 Article 27 Regulation 882/2004.

588 Article 28 Regulation 882/2004.

589 Articles 41-43 Regulation 882/2004.

590 Article 19(3) GFL. On the staking of private and official controls see B.M.J. van der Meulen and A.A. Freriks, Millefeuille. The emergence of a multi-layered controls system in the European food sector, Utrecht Law Review, Vol. 2, No. 1, pp. 156-176, June 2006. For a hyperlink see the reference list.

13.2.3 International trade

To ensure official controls in international trade with third countries, member states may designate particular points of entry in their territory, which have access to appropriate control facilities.[591] Furthermore, they may require food business operators to give prior notification of imports from non-member states.

13.2.4 Intra-community trade

Two EU Directives concern controls of intra-community trade in live animals and products of animal origin.[592] The member states are under an obligation to ensure that products are accompanied by health certificates or other documents that European Community rules provide for. Products may only be intended for trade when they have been obtained, checked, marked and labelled in accordance with Community rules. Checks can be carried out on the place of dispatch and at the place of destination. The Directives require notification to other member states in case an animal disease occurs, and adequate measures must be taken.[593]

13.2.5 Intra-Community co-operation

For people and goods the European Union has created a common market without internal borders. The same is not true, however, for national authorities. The powers of national authorities are strictly limited to their national jurisdictions. This hampers effective surveillance of international food chains. The regulation provides some instruments to cope with this situation.[594]

Member states must establish powers and procedures for sharing information between relevant parties. The competent authorities must provide each other with administrative assistance, which may include participation in on-the-spot controls.

National authorities must provide each other with all necessary information and documents and they must arrange for the conduct of any administrative enquiries necessary to obtain such information and documents.

[591] Article 17 Regulation 882/2004.

[592] Council Directive 90/425/EEC of 26 June 1990 concerning veterinary and zootechnical checks applicable in intra-Community trade in certain live animals and products with a view to the completion of the internal market. Official Journal L 224, 18 August 1990, pp. 29; and Council Directive 89/662/EEC concerning veterinary checks in intra-Community trade with a view to the completion of the European market. Official Journal L 395, 30 December 1989, corrigendum Official Journal L 151, 15 June 1990.

[593] Regulation 882/2004 does not introduce any changes in specific rules on controls in the field of animal health and animal welfare.

[594] Articles 34-38 Regulation 882/2004.

In cases with ramifications in several member states or with a particular interest at Community level, the Commission is empowered to coordinate actions undertaken by the member states. The Commission may even send an inspection team to carry out an official control on the spot.[595]

13.2.6 Second line inspections

In 1997, the Food and Veterinary Office was instituted. It is not an independent agency like EFSA, but a part of DG Sanco. It has its headquarters in Ireland, however, at distance from the other parts of DG Sanco in Brussels. This indicates that at least a certain degree of independence is intended.

The FVO has two main tasks. It audits the performance of national agencies and it inspects the performance of industry and public authorities in third countries that wish to export food products to the European union. Although the FVO is not mentioned by name, Regulation 882/2004 provides a basis for its activities (Law text box 13.2). The Member States must give all necessary assistance and provide all documentation that the Commission experts – the FVO – request.

Law text box 13.2. Basis for audits in member states, Article 45(1) Regulation 882/2004.

Article 45(1) Regulation 882/2004
Commission experts shall carry out general and specific audits in Member States. The Commission may appoint experts from Member States to assist its own experts. General and specific audits shall be organised in cooperation with Member States' competent authorities. Audits shall be carried out on a regular basis. Their main purpose shall be to verify that, overall, official controls take place in Member States in accordance with the multi-annual national control plans referred to in Article 41 and in compliance with Community law. For this purpose, and in order to facilitate the efficiency and effectiveness of the audits, the Commission may, in advance of carrying out such audits, request that the Member States provide, as soon as possible, up to date copies of national control plans.

13.2.7 Controls in third countries

Although the FVO has no jurisdiction outside the EU, the regulation indicates in Article 46 that official controls may take place in third countries.

595 Article 40 Regulation 882/2004.

Law text box 13.3. Official controls in third countries, Article 46 Regulation 882/2004.

Article 46 Regulation 882/2004
Commission experts may carry out official controls in third countries in order to verify [...] the compliance or equivalence of third country legislation and systems with Community feed and food law and Community animal health legislation. The Commission may appoint experts from Member States to assist its own experts.

These controls in third countries may only be executed if the authorities in those countries agree to them. However as such controls may be a condition for export to the EU these authorities often have little alternative. The inverse situation also exists, third countries carrying out inspections in the EU, and the regulation requires the Commission to assist member states in dealing with such situations.[596]

13.3 Measures in case of non-compliance

Generally speaking, when confronted with non-compliance, enforcement authorities have one of two options at their disposition and often both. They can take measures to remedy the problem and to ensure future compliance, or they can take measures to punish the perpetrator to deter him or her as well as others from future infringements. Both lines of action are available in most member states.

13.3.1 Measures to remedy non-compliance

If a member state establishes the non-compliance of a food business operator, it shall take action to ensure that the operator remedies the situation. When deciding which action to take, the competent authority shall take account of the nature of the non-compliance and the operator's past record with regard to non-compliance.[597]

Such action can include the imposition of sanitation procedures or the recall of a food product, the restriction or prohibition of placing foods on the market, or a closure of all or a part of the business concerned. In case of imported products these measures may include: destruction, special treatment to solve the irregularity, and re-dispatch of the product to the state of origin. For the latter action a timeframe of no more than 60 days applies.

[596] Article 52 Regulation 882/2004.
[597] Article 54 Regulation 882/2004.

13.3.2 Legal protection

Article 54 (3)(b) of Regulation 882/2004 states that the competent authority must provide the operator concerned with information on rights of appeal against the decision taken and on the applicable procedure and time limits.

13.3.3 Measures to punish non-compliance

Member states shall lay down the rules on sanctions applicable to infringements of feed and food law and other Community provisions relating to the protection of animal health and welfare and shall take all measures necessary to ensure that they are implemented. The sanctions provided for must be effective, proportionate and dissuasive.[598]

The nature of the sanctions – administrative or criminal – is left entirely to the discretion of the member states. The Commission in its first draft[599] intended to impose the use of criminal law on the Member States, but this intention did not survive the legislative process.

13.3.4 Public communication

Increasingly food safety inspection agencies in the member states inform the general public about the results of their inspections.[600] The reasons for doing so seem to vary. In case a food safety issue is at hand, an obligation to issue a public warning follows from Article 10 GFL (Law text box 13.4).[601]

Law text box 13.4. Article 10 GFL Public information.

Article 10 Regulation 178/2002
Public information
Without prejudice to the applicable provisions of Community and national law on access to documents, where there are reasonable grounds to suspect that a food or feed may present a risk for human or animal health, then, depending on the nature, seriousness and extent of that risk, public authorities shall take appropriate steps to inform the general public of the nature of the risk to health, identifying to the fullest extent possible the food or feed, or type of food or feed, the risk that it may present, and the measures which are taken or about to be taken to prevent, reduce or eliminate that risk.

598 Article 55 Regulation 882/2004.
599 European Commission, Proposal for a Regulation of the European Parliament and of the Council on official feed and food controls 5.2.2003, COM(2003) 52 final, Article 55.
600 See on this subject the special issue of the European Food & Feed Law Review 5/2007.
601 See also Article 7 Regulation 882/2004.

Article 10 GFL belongs to the domain of risk communication. Warning the public about imminent risks is a form of remedying non-compliance. Some member states, however, inform the public of all inspection results or of all infringements. If this is done to deter the business from infringements by threatening their reputation (often called naming & shaming) this is more a sanction of a punitive (punishing) nature.

13.3.5 Measures in case of lax enforcement

Regulation 882/2004 closely relates enforcement to incident management. In case of serious failure of a member state's control system, the European Commission can deploy its emergency powers discussed in section 13.5. See Law text box 13.5.

Law text box 13.5. Article 56 Regulation 882/2004 on safeguard measures.

Article 56 Regulation 882/2004
Safeguard measures

1. Measures shall be taken under the procedures provided for in Article 53 of Regulation (EC) No 178/2002 if:
   (a) the Commission has evidence of a serious failure in a Member State's control systems; and
   (b) such failure may constitute a possible and widespread risk for human health, animal health or animal welfare, either directly or through the environment.
2. Such measures shall be adopted only after:
   (a) Community controls have shown and reported non-compliance with Community legislation; and
   (b) the Member State concerned has failed to correct the situation upon request and within the time limit set by the Commission.

13.4 Incident management[602]

The BSE crisis and other food safety incidents demonstrated the need for improved, more comprehensive, Community coordinated procedures for emergency and crisis management and for a system of rapid alert. The legal basis for the system and procedures is in Chapter IV of the General Food Law.

13.4.1 Rapid alert system

A system for rapid alert has existed in the field of food safety since 1979. However, the scope of the former system initially did not include feed. The Rapid Alert

[602] Many thanks to Anna Szajkowska for writing most of this section.

System for Food and Feed (RASFF) introduced by the General Food Law,[603] covers food and feed, in line with the 'farm to fork' approach.

The RASFF is a network for exchanging information about direct or indirect risks to human health deriving from food or feed. The system involves the member states, EFSA[604] and the Commission. Participation in the RASSF may be extended to third countries or international organisations, on the basis of agreements with the Community.[605]

13.4.2 Transmission of information

Where a member of the network has information about the existence of a serious direct or indirect risk relating to food or feed, it has to notify the Commission.[606] The Commission is responsible for managing the network. The Commission assesses the information received and categorises the notification under one of three categories. The information can also be rejected from transmission through the RASFF by the Commission, if the criteria for notification are not satisfied or if the information is insufficient. The notifying country is informed of this decision.

The notification is transmitted to RASFF contact points designated by all members of the network and to EFSA. Additionally, when the notification concerns an attempt to import banned products (border rejection), the information is sent to the EU Border Inspections Posts (BIPs) in order to increase the vigilance and to ensure that the rejected product does not re-enter the Community through another border post.[607] And when it is known that a product subject to a notification has been exported to a third country or when a notification concerns a product originating from a third country, the Commission also sends information to that third country.[608]

EFSA's role is to analyse the content of the notification and to supply scientific and technical information that will be helpful to member states.[609]

---

603 Article 50(1) GFL.

604 EFSA is included to enable it to perform its task of monitoring the health and nutritional risks; Article 35 GFL.

605 Article 50(6) GFL.

606 Article 50(2) GFL.

607 Article 50(3) GFL.

608 Article 50(4) GFL.

609 Article 50(2) GFL.

13.4.3 Notification categories

The notification are classified in the following categories:[610]

- alert – where there is an identified direct or indirect risk to health and immediate action is required;
- information notification – relating to a food or feed that was placed on the market but the risk does not require any immediate action, or the product has not reached or is no longer present on the markets of the other members of the network; or
- border rejections - concerning consignments that have been tested and rejected at the external borders of the EU (and at the borders of the European Economic Area - EEA).

13.4.4 Public information and confidentiality rules

The Commission publishes weekly overviews of the notifications transmitted through the RASFF.[611] The public has access to information on:

- product description (e.g. 'sliced steam-cooked chicken fillets from Belgium', 'ice-cream from the UK');
- the nature of the risk (e.g. 'glass fragments', 'too high content of sulphite'); and
- the measure taken ('product recalled from consumer', 'public warning-press release').

For the protection of commercial information, the trade names and the identity of individual companies are not made available to the public. The full information is only available to the members of the network. In the Commission's opinion, this should not influence the level of consumer protection, since a notification through the RASFF implies that all required measures have been or are in the process of being taken. However, in exceptional circumstances, where the protection of human health requires greater transparency, this information can also be made public.

13.4.5 Collateral damage

Swift action is at the heart of the RASFF. Rapidity, however, includes an inherent risk that mistakes are being made. On 10 March 2004 the Court of first instance ruled in a case initiated by Malagutti-Vezinhet SA versus the European Commission.[612] Malagutti applied for compensation for the damage it allegedly suffered after

[610] This classification was put in place on 1 January 2008 and differs from the classification used until then. Border rejections were included in the other two while another third category – news notifications – was applied. See for example RASFF annual report 2006.

[611] On transparency and confidentiality, see; Article 52 GFL.

[612] Case T-177/02.

the Commission issued a rapid alert message notifying the presence of pesticide residues in apples from France and giving Malagutti's name as the exporter of the goods in question. The Court dismissed the application. Non-contractual liability on the part of the Community is subject to a number of conditions: unlawfulness of the conduct alleged against the Community institutions, actual damage and the existence of a causal link between the conduct of the institution and the damage complained of (Law text box 13.6). According to the Court, if one of those conditions is not satisfied, the entire action must be dismissed and it is not necessary to consider the other conditions.

Law text box 13.6. Article 288 EC treaty on non-contractual liability.

Article 288 EC Treaty

(...)

In the case of non-contractual liability, the Community shall, in accordance with the general principles common to the laws of the Member States, make good any damage caused by its institutions or by its servants in the performance of their duties.

(...)

Conditions elaborated by the European Court of Justice:

- unlawfulness;
- actual damage, and
- causal link between the conduct and the damage

The Court has summarised it findings as follows. The Community rapid alert system for food and feed confers on the national authorities only, and not on the Commission, responsibility for establishing whether there is a serious and immediate risk to the health and safety of consumers. It is thus incumbent upon the national authorities, once they have detected a serious and immediate risk the effects of which extend or could extend beyond their territory, immediately to inform the Commission and provide it with information to identify the product and the supply chain. The Commission, for its own part, confines itself to checking whether the information falls, as such, within the scope of the RASFF and the accuracy of the findings and analyses that led the national authorities to send that information does not have to be checked. As regards the prevention of risks to the health of consumers, and if any doubt remains, under the precautionary principle prevailing in the matter of the protection of public health the competent authority may be obliged to take appropriate measures to prevent certain potential risks for public health without having to wait until the existence and seriousness of those risks has been fully demonstrated. If it was necessary to wait until all the research was completed before adopting such measures the precautionary principle would be rendered devoid of purpose. That reasoning also applies in the case of a rapid information procedure, and, consequently, an undertaking which is a victim of that alert system introduced in order to protect human health must accept its adverse economic consequences, since the protection of public health must take precedence over economic considerations.

In short, if mistakes are being made in applying the RASFF normally there is no liability on the part of the European Commission.[613]

13.4.6 INFOSAN

RASFF participates in the International Food Safety Authorities Network (INFOSAN). INFOSAN is a network for the dissemination of important information about global food safety issues at world level.

In response to recommendations from several international conferences, resolutions from the World Health Assembly and guidelines from the Codex Alimentarius Commission, the World Health Organization (WHO), in collaboration with the Food and Agriculture Organization of the United Nations (FAO) developed INFOSAN to promote the exchange of food safety information and to improve collaboration among food safety authorities at the national and international level. The INFOSAN network provides a mechanism for the exchange of information on both routine and emerging food safety issues.

INFOSAN Emergency is designed to provide rapid access to information during food safety emergencies. As of October 2006, 151 countries are members of the INFOSAN network. Each member country has designated one or several INFOSAN Focal Points. Each country also has one dedicated INFOSAN emergency contact point that will be activated specifically in major international emergencies involving disease from or contamination in food.[614]

The RASFF was nominated on 18 March 2005 as INFOSAN emergency contact point for the transmission of INFOSAN food safety information. At the meeting of 20 September 2005 of the standing committee for the safety of the food chain and animal health, all member states of the EU and the EFTA (European Free Trade Association) countries agreed that the RASFF would be the single point of information exchange for the INFOSAN network.

[613] This ruling is in conformity with the general case law on non-contractual liability of the European institutions. Nevertheless, another approach would not have been inconceivable. In some of the member states case law has developed that answers similar questions in a different way. The Dutch supreme court for instance judged with regard to police actions that were justified on the basis of knowledge available at the time of action, but later turned out to have been directed against an innocent person, that for reasons of fairness damages should not be borne by the innocent victim, but by society as a whole through the government.

[614] World Health Organisation in cooperation with the Food and Agricultural Organisation of the United Nations, The International Food Safety Authorities Network (INFOSAN) Users Guide, October 2006, for a hyperlink see the reference list.

More close cooperation and clear procedures should be established between both systems in order to avoid overlap and misunderstanding, particularly in relation to the information transmitted to third countries.[615]

13.5 Emergencies

In the event of a serious risk to human health, animal health or the environment, urgent measures have to be taken. When there is limited time available and important values are at stake, adequate procedures allowing for taking effective and coordinated action are of the utmost importance.

13.5.1 Role of food business operators

The primary responsibility for ensuring that foods or feeds satisfy the requirements of food law rests with the food business operators.[616] If the operators have reason to believe that their food or feed is unsafe, they shall immediately inform the competent authorities and withdraw the food or feed from the market and – if need be – recall it from the consumers. During these procedures, the operators are obliged to collaborate closely with the enforcement authorities.[617]

13.5.2 Role of national authorities

National authorities in the member states enforce food law, monitor and verify whether food and feed business operators comply with the requirements of food law. In some cases, problems will be notified to the national authorities by food or feed business operators, who will also initiate withdrawals and recalls. There will be other instances where a problem is identified by the authorities, through inspection, outbreaks of disease, the testing of food samples or complaints by either consumers or competitors. A food alert may also result from information received through the RASFF. The authorities are the contact point for information and communication about the food or feed incident, and they coordinate investigations relating to withdrawals and recalls on a larger scale.

When the national authority adopts measures aimed at restricting the placing on the market or forcing the withdrawal or recall of food or feed, it shall immediately notify the Commission under the RASFF. It shall also inform the Commission of rejections of consignments at its Border Inspection Post, and of recommendations or agreements with food/feed business operators preventing, limiting or imposing special conditions on the placing on the market or the use of food or feed on account of a serious risk to human health requiring rapid action.

615 RASFF annual report 2006.

616 Article 17(1) GFL.

617 See Chapter 11 for a more detailed description of the responsibility of food businesses.

13.5.3 Role of the European Commission

Apart from managing the RASFF and conducting the so-called second-line inspections auditing the performance of the enforcement authorities in the member states (see section 13.2.6), the Commission has special powers for taking emergency measures, through a single emergency procedure.

13.5.4 Powers of the European Commission

Before the General Food Law entered into force, the mechanisms for adopting emergency measures by the Commission were different in various areas of legislation. The scope of the emergency measure introduced in Article 53 GFL covers all types of food and feed, whether originating in one of the member states or in a third country, and therefore the emergency measure ensures consistency and adequate coordination of the risks applying to different categories of foods or feeds. Where a food or feed is likely to constitute a serious risk to human health, animal health or the environment, and that – given the gravity of the situation – the risk cannot be contained satisfactorily by means of measures taken by the member state(s)[618] concerned, the Commission shall:

- suspend the placing on the market of the food/feed in question;
- lay down special conditions for the food/feed in question;
- adopt any other appropriate interim measure.

The Commission can initiate such action at the request of a member state, but also on its own initiative. If the Commission, following information from a member state on the need to take emergency measures, does not initiate the procedure for the adoption of emergency measures at Community level, Article 54 GFL empowers the member state in question to adopt interim protective measures. The member state may maintain its national interim protective measures until a Community decision has been adopted concerning the extension, amendment or abrogation of the said measures.

In a guidance document,[619] the SCFCAH summarises the measures the European Commission can take in the scheme represented in Diagram 13.1.

[618] The subsidiarity principle applies. If action by the member state(s) can solve the problem, the Commission should not become involved.

[619] Standing Committee on the Food Chain and Animal health (section Toxicological Safety) Modus Operandi for the management of new food safety incidents with a potential for extension involving a chemical substance, January 2006.

Diagram 13.1. Binding measures on EU markets and/or imports.

Commission Decision	Special marketing conditions	Compulsory controls on the market
	Special import conditions	Analytical report attesting the absence of undue substance (exporters responsible)
		Official certificate with the analytical report
		Requirement of additional guarantees (sampling and analysis by the competent authorities before export)
		Import controls in the Member States
	Restrictions and listing	Establishment of a list of obligatory point of entry in the EU
		Listing of the exporters authorised to export on a positive list
		Listing of the third countries authorised to export on a positive list
	Suspension	Prohibition of the import of the product coming from certain countries
		Suspension on the placing on the market

Example
Article 53 GFL empowers the Commission to adopt measures in individual cases, which are normally in the competence of the national authorities. For example, in 2006, on the basis of Article 53 GFL, the Commission took an emergency measure prohibiting the placing on the market of all curd cheese manufactured by the British company Bowland Dairy Products Ltd. During an on-site visit the Commission's inspectors from the Food and Veterinary Office discovered that in the production process the company used milk that did not comply with the hygiene requirements, in particular milk which had been tested positive for the presence of antibiotic residues. According to the Commission, the UK authorities did not check that the operational conditions communicated to the company had been met and therefore failed to comply with their control obligation, and – in order to address the immediate risk to human health in the Community (the products were exported to virtually all member states) – introduced the ban on the company's products.

The relation between Articles 53 and 54 GFL is subtle (Diagram 13.2). Conditions for the application by the Commission of the powers granted in Article 53 GFL,

Diagram 13.2. Emergency measures.

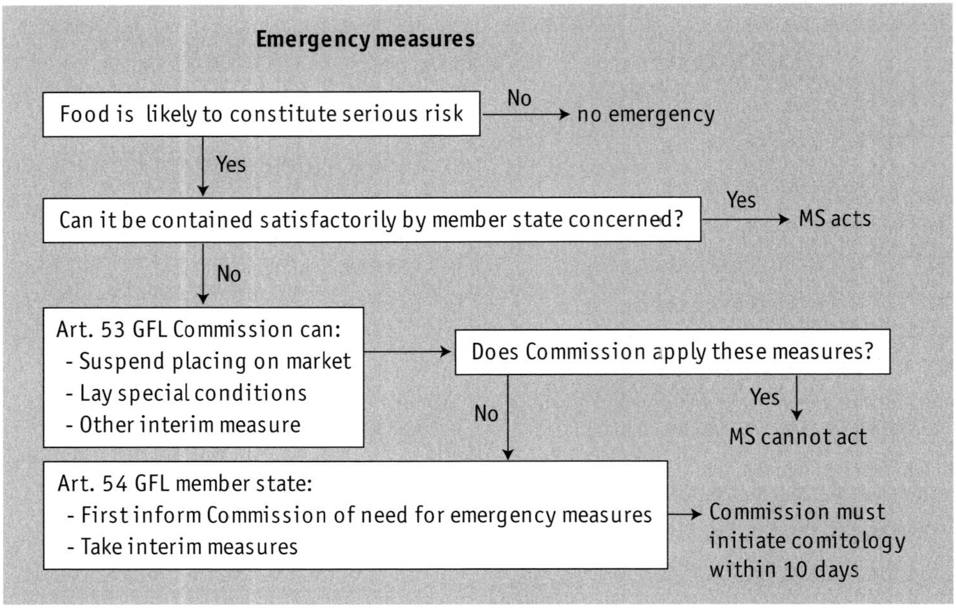

are that measures by the member state(s) cannot satisfactorily contain the risk.[620] The condition for action by member state(s) further to Article 54 GFL is that the Commission does not act on the basis of Article 53 GFL. At first sight these conditions seem contradictory. They make sense, however, if we presume that the member states in Article 53 GFL who take precedence over the Commission are not the same as the member states in Article 54 who follow after the Commission remains passive. It seems likely that in most cases the former will be the member states where the problem originates. They should act. If they cannot, it is up to the Commission and not to other member states to take measures that may create barriers to trade. If, however, the member state(s) where the problem originates nor the Commission take effective action, the threatened member state(s) may take matters into their own hands (by closing the border to certain products).

13.5.5 Crisis management

Some risks deriving from food and feed can be of such extreme danger or difficulty, that they will be unlikely to be prevented, eliminated or reduced to an acceptable level by provisions in place or managed solely by way of the application of Articles 53 and 54 GFL. In order to better manage these exceptional situations, the General

[620] According to Article 56 Regulation 882/2004 this situation may occur if the Commission has evidence of a serious failure in a Member State's control systems.

Food Law envisaged the adoption of a general plan for food/feed crisis management and the setting up of a crisis unit.[621]

13.5.6 General plan for crisis management

The general plan for food/feed crisis management was adopted by the Commission in 2004.[622] The plan specifies: the crisis situations, the procedure leading to the application of the general plan, the establishment of a network of crisis coordinators, the practical procedures for managing a crisis, the role of the crisis unit, the practical functioning of the crisis unit (composition, means of operation, actions), the link between the crisis unit and the decision-making process, the resolution of the crisis, the management procedures in the event of a potentially serious risk, the communication strategy and the principles for transparency.

The crisis situation is characterised in particular by the following critical factors:

- the situation involves a serious direct or indirect risk to human health and/or is perceived or publicised as such or can be perceived and/or publicised as such;
- the risk is spread or could be spread to a large part of the food chain; and
- it is highly likely that the risk will spread to several member states and/or non-Community countries.

13.5.7 Crisis unit

The crisis unit assists the European Commission in risk management, ensuring that crises are managed in a more effective, quicker and coordinated way. The crisis unit is responsible for collecting and assessing available information and identifying possible options to prevent, eliminate or reduce the risk as rapidly as possible.[623] An important task is to identify the best ways of informing the public of the risks and measures taken in a transparent way. The crisis unit consists of crisis coordinators designated by each member state, EFSA and the Commission.

However, the crisis unit is not vested with any power to adopt decisions on the management of risk or for implementing legislation. In consequence, crisis management will be adopted according to specific procedures already in place.

621 Articles 55 and 56 GFL. See also Article 13 Regulation 882/2004.

622 Commission Decision 2004/478.

623 Article 57 GFL.

14. Consumer

14.1 For you, about you, over you, without you

Even though the first and foremost objectives of EU food law are to protect consumers' health and other consumers' interests, no provision can be found actually granting the individual consumer a right s/he can uphold in a court of law.

Nevertheless, EU food law increasingly mentions 'consumers' rights'.[624] If we take a closer look at the way food law protects these rights, they turn out to be about empowerment in the marketplace, not in the courts of law. Actual legal rights for consumers have to be found outside the scope of food law.

14.2 The consumer in European case law

In case law defining the extent of member states' powers to limit the free movement of goods with a view to protecting consumers' interests, the European Court of Justice has elaborated a consumer concept.

In Community law, the concept of 'average consumer' has become a benchmark to assess the impact of trade practices and the responsibility of the public authorities in the field of consumer protection. A commercial practice is considered misleading if an average consumer would be misled by it. The General Food Law does not contain a definition of an 'average consumer', nor does any other piece of food legislation. The concept is interpreted in the case law of the ECJ as 'a consumer, who is reasonably well-informed and reasonably observant and circumspect, taking into account social, cultural and linguistic factors'. The average consumer test is not a statistical test, it defines a way in which Community and national authorities judge particular cases, by determining the reaction of the typical consumer in a given situation.

Food law also contains provisions aimed at the protection of particular groups of consumers, such as children, people with allergies, etc., who are more vulnerable to unfair trade practices. In this case, the impact of the commercial practice will be assessed from the perspective of the average consumer of that group.

In Chapter 7 we discussed the principle of mutual recognition as defined in the Cassis de Dijon ruling of the ECJ. From the point of view of the development of the concept of an 'average consumer', one consideration in the Cassis de Dijon case deserves further attention. The Court stated that consumers may be

---

624 See for the latest example (at the time of writing) the proposal for a consumer food information regulation (COM(2008) 40 final) discussed in Chapter 12

adequately protected if they are adequately informed.[625] The case is a preliminary ruling. Rewe supermarkets were denied by the German authorities the right to import Cassis de Dijon because due to its alcohol content of 20% this product did not conform to German product standards on fruit liquor demanding an alcohol content of at least 25%. One of the questions at issue was whether this standard was justified for reasons of consumer protection.

Law text box 14.1. The Court of Justice on the position of the consumer.

EC Court of Justice 20 February 1979, Case 120/78 (Cassis de Dijon)
'As the Commission rightly observed, the fixing of limits in relation to the alcohol content of beverages may lead to the standardisation of products placed on the market and of their designations, in the interests of a greater transparency of commercial transactions and offers for sale to the public.
However, this line of argument cannot be taken so far as to regard the mandatory fixing of minimum alcohol content as being an essential guarantee of the fairness of commercial transactions, since it is a simple matter to ensure that suitable information is conveyed to the purchaser by requiring the display of an indication of origin and of the alcohol content on the packaging of products'.

This passage illustrates the position of the consumer in European food law. Unlike under German law at that time (and under US law to this day), the Court will not treat European consumers as ignorant, highly vulnerable, or in need of protection by legislators who deem that they know what is best for the consumer. Rather, European food law presumes that consumers are reasonably intelligent, responsible and capable of making informed choices. As a consequence, the Court deems empowering the consumer by providing information to make informed choices, the preferable alternative to thinking on behalf of the consumer. If labelling requirements provide sufficient protection to the consumer, member states' measures like product bans are not acceptable.

This approach of the ECJ has undoubtedly influenced EC legislation. It has not, however, set limits to it. As EU law is common to all member states, it can hardly create trade distortions encroaching on Article 28 of the EC Treaty. The EU legislator therefore may well go further in consumer protection than the ECJ would accept from the member states.

14.3 Responsibility?

The consumer is often considered to be the weak spot in EU food law. DG Sanco's popular slogan has it that food law applies 'from farm to fork'. On closer inspection,

---

625 See also Law text box 16.8 (Emmenthal cheese case).

this does not entirely hold. Provisions of food law do not end at the moment of *consumption by* the final consumer, but at the moment of *delivery to* the final consumer. Food (safety) requirements do not reach into the private kitchen. If all businesses comply with food safety requirements the food will still be unsafe if it is mishandled in the kitchen. This risk however is outside the remit of food safety law. Article 17 of the General Food Law is exemplary in this respect. It attributes responsibilities to food business operators and to the member states, but not to consumers.

14.4 Collective rights

While the consumer is virtually absent in food law as an individual, food law does address the consumer as a species. In the Articles 9 and 10 of the General Food Law for example, food authorities are instructed to respect transparency regarding the consumer. Indeed, consumer representatives[626] are sometimes consulted in the preparation of food policy or legislation. Drafts of legislation and of certain decisions are published on DG Sanco's website to give consumers the opportunity to give their opinion.[627] What these authorities subsequently do with these opinions is, however, left to their discretion. The ECJ will not hear grievances.

14.5 Complaints

Consumers can complain to food safety inspectors if they believe they have been confronted with infringements of food law. It is a matter of national law if they hold any position in the subsequent procedure or if this procedure is considered a matter only regarding the authority and the accused business.

14.6 Individual consumers' rights?

While food law does not directly provide consumers with legal rights, it does influence the rights they have on other bases. By defining the legal requirements for food it gives substance to the contracts consumers conclude with food businesses. In general it can be considered fair to interpret consumer contracts as being about food in compliance with the law. If the food is not in compliance, it should not be too difficult for the consumer to get a refund. Infringements of food safety requirements may also easily constitute a basis for non-contractual (tort) liability. Consumer law has created an instrument meant to support the consumer in tort cases in their dealings with producers of defective products, called product liability law.

[626] In particular the European Consumers' Organisation BEUC (Bureau Européen des Unions de Consommateurs).

[627] See for example: Article 38(1) GFL; Articles 2; 5(2)(b), 6(7), 29-31 Regulation 1829/2003; and Article 38(1) Commission Regulation 65/2004. See also Article 16 Regulation 1924/2006.

14.7 Product liability law

Parties who suffer damage may take legal action against operators. One could call this private law enforcement. The food business operator, who by bringing unsafe food to the market causes a customer to suffer damages, can be held liable under tort law if it can be proven that he was at fault.

Besides tort law, a more specific regime concerning defective products also exists and covers food products as well. Product liability law is not food law in a strict sense, but as it is highly relevant for the food sector it is fitting that a short description be given here.[628]

14.7.1 Strict liability

The rules on product liability have been harmonised in the European Union by Directive 85/374.[629] Directive 85/374 lays down the principle of strict liability of the producer, which means that a producer may be held responsible for a damage caused by a defective product s/he has put on the market even in the absence of fault. Diagram 14.1 compares the requirements of tort law to product liability law.

Diagram 14.1. Requirements for liability under tort law and product liability law.

Tort	Product liability
Unlawfulness	Defective product
Fault	
Personal damage	Damage
Causality	Causality

14.7.2 Producer

The producer within the meaning of the directive is not only the manufacturer of the final product, but also any other person in the chain who has produced raw materials or a component of the product, or any person who, 'by putting his name, trade mark or other distinguishing feature on the product, presents himself as its producer'.[630] All these persons bear full liability,[631] and consequently the

[628] In writing this section, use has been made of Nicole Coutrelis, Product Liability in the Food Sector. For hyperlink see reference list.
[629] As amended by Directive 1999/34.
[630] Hence the relevance of Article 3(1)(7) of Regulation 2000/13 requiring indication of the name or business name and address of the manufacturer or packager, or of a seller established within the Community.
[631] In legalese: liability is jointly and severally. See Article 5 of Directive 85/374.

victim may make a claim against any of these persons for complete compensation. The *supplier* is not responsible, except in cases when s/he does not, or cannot,[632] inform the victim of the producer's identity.

Law text box 14.2 shows side by side Article 3 of the product liability directive on the concept of producer and Article 3(2) of the General Food Law on the concept of food business. Although phrased very differently, in practice they will often refer to the same addressee.

Law text box 14.2. Producer and food business.

Article 3 Directive 85/374	**Article 3(2) Regulation 178/2002**
1. 'Producer' means the manufacturer of a finished product, the producer of any raw material or the manufacturer of a component part and any person who, by putting his name, trade mark or other distinguishing feature on the product presents himself as its producer. 2. Without prejudice to the liability of the producer, any person who imports into the Community a product for sale, hire, leasing or any form of distribution in the course of his business shall be deemed to be a producer within the meaning of this Directive and shall be responsible as a producer. 3. Where the producer of the product cannot be identified, each supplier of the product shall be treated as its producer unless he informs the injured person, within a reasonable time, of the identity of the producer or of the person who supplied him with the product. The same shall apply, in the case of an imported product, if this product does not indicate the identity of the importer referred to in paragraph 2, even if the name of the producer is indicated.	'food business' means any undertaking, whether for profit or not and whether public or private, carrying out any of the activities related to any stage of production, processing and distribution of food;

[632] If traceability requirements have been complied with, the supplier should be able to identify the producer.

14.7.3 Damage

Product liability law covers damages caused by death or by personal injuries and to private property of a non-commercial nature. See Law text box 14.3. Damage to property is only covered if it is more than 500 Euro.[633] The text speaks of ECU. This former European Currency Unit has now been replaced by the Euro at an exchange rate of 1:1.

Law text box 14.3. Article 9 Directive 85/374 on damage.

Article 9
For the purpose of Article 1, 'damage' means:
(a) damage caused by death or by personal injuries;
(b) damage to, or destruction of, any item of property other than the defective product itself, with a lower threshold of 500 ECU, provided that the item of property:
(i) is of a type ordinarily intended for private use or consumption,
and
(ii) was used by the injured person mainly for his own private use or consumption.
This Article shall be without prejudice to national provisions relating to non-material damage.

14.7.4 Conditions

The plaintiff (victim) must prove three conditions:
1. A damage to the person (death or personal injury) or to the person's private property (damages to professional property are not covered by the directive – it is about consumer protection only). For the food sector, this implies that only the final consumer can invoke product liability. Operators within the food chain can only refer to the contract provisions that they have agreed upon, or – in the absence of those – to tort law.[634]
2. A defect of the product, which is established when the product does not provide the safety that one is entitled to expect, taking into account particularly its presentation, the use which could be reasonably expected and the time at which the product was put into circulation. A mere lack of conformity to specifications (stemming from regulations or from a contract) is not sufficient to declare a product defective if safety is not at stake (Law text box 14.4).

[633] According to the European Court of Justice, the consequence of the choice made by the Community legislature is that, in order to avoid an excessive number of actions, in the event of minor material damage the victims of defective products cannot rely on the rules of liability laid down in the Directive but must bring an action under the ordinary law of contractual or non-contractual liability. ECJ 25 April 2002, case C-154/00, ECR 2002, I-03879.
[634] See Chapter 2.

In the field of food, due to the number of food safety requirements, consumers are entitled to expect a high degree of safety. The producer can influence the expectations of the consumer by providing specific information, warnings, instructions on use and storage on the label. A food, for example, with allergens is not considered unsafe if the presence of these allergens is mentioned on the label.

3. A causal relationship between the defect and the damage. Consumers of unsafe food may experience some difficulty in proving the causal relationship between a specific food and the (health) damages that have been suffered. The food disappears by its very use and usually people use large varieties of food. This renders the cause of a food-borne damage difficult to determine.

Law text box 14.4. Article 6 Directive 85/374 on defective product.

Article 6

1. A product is defective when it does not provide the safety which a person is entitled to expect, taking all circumstances into account,
including:
(a) the presentation of the product;
(b) the use to which it could reasonably be expected that the product would be put
(c) the time when the product was put into circulation.
2. A product shall not be considered defective for the sole reason that a better product is subsequently put into circulation.

14.7.5 Defences

In order to disclaim liability, a producer has to prove the existence of one (or several) of the following circumstances:

- s/he did not put the product in circulation;
- the product was not defective when put into circulation;
- the product was not manufactured by the producer for sale or any form of distribution;
- the defect is due to compliance with mandatory regulations issued by public authorities;
- the state of scientific and technological knowledge at the time the product was put into circulation did not allow the existence of the defect to be discovered ('development risk');
- the defect of the final product (in case the manufacturer of a raw material or component is held liable) is attributable to the design of the final product or to the instructions of the manufacturer;
- the damage is caused, totally or in part, through the fault of the victim.

If the hygiene prescriptions have been followed and well documented, this may be of great help in building a defence that the product was not defective when put into circulation. In the case of a food that passed a pre-market approval (like novel foods and GMOs) the 'development risk' defence is worth considering, as an extensive scientific safety assessment is part of such authorisation procedure (see Chapter 9). If the assessment did not uncover the defect, it seems probable that this defect could at that moment not be discovered.

In practice few product liability cases occur in the food sector. On the one hand it is difficult for consumers to prove their case and often damages are too low to bother trying, on the other hand food business operators do not like the bad publicity that may be involved in a court case and go to some lengths to keep their consumers happy by dealing with complaints in a generous way.

14.8 Concluding remark

The individual consumer is not an addressee of EU food law. S/he is not held responsible for her or his contribution to food (un)safety and s/he is not endowed with legal powers under food law. Food law does, however, add to the level of protection under general consumer law by defining the level of safety a consumer may expect from food products.

15. Quality and marketing standards for fresh fruit and vegetables

15.1 Marketing and quality standards

The integration of the European states became involved with agriculture in 1958 when the EU began its second metamorphoses, the European Economic Community stadium. Additional metamorphoses added up to the EU. Agriculture became one of its most important policy areas on two accounts. The provision of food had been one of the major concerns of the national governments before integration began, and the economic depression and world war had increased that concern. The second account began to run when the creation of the common market led to the common agricultural policy. Integration of the agricultural and food policies of the member states was sought in the creation of a common market organisation for the major agricultural product sectors such as milk and milk products, cereals, sugar, beef and veal, ultimately twenty-one different organisations.

Each sector had its own policy goals and a set of instruments that was attuned to both the policies and the products. Many common market organisations relied on some kind of government intervention that would lessen the great fluctuation of market prices, a characteristic of agricultural products.

The EEC basic regulations for these products contained the right for every farmer to sell the products grown on the territories of the member states to the governments' intervention bureaux. These would pay the price that was fixed in each year's implementing regulation. That price was published in advance of the sowing season to enable each farmer to use that information to decide which crops would generate the highest returns, both in quantities and money.

Although the EEC had bound itself to buy every quantity of agrarian products, it had no obligation to buy everything no matter what quality. The minimum quality standards were also laid down in binding legal documents. The traders in agrarian products used the EEC standards as references in all trade.[635]

Many things have changed in the intervention system but the quality standards are still in force. They have become a central element of Regulation 1234/2007 that replaces the different market organisations by the Single Common Market Organisation.[636] For two examples from different product sectors, see Law text

[635] Simon Harris, Alan Swinbank, and Guy Wilkinson, The Food and Farm Policies of the European Community, Chichester 1983, p. 297.

[636] Council Regulation (EC) No 1234/2007 of 22 October 2007 establishing a common organisation of agricultural markets and on specific provisions for certain agricultural products (Single CMO Regulation). Official Journal L 299, 16 November 2007, pp. 1-149.

box 15.1 with the EU Standard quality for paddy rice and Law text box 15.2 with the standard quality for white sugar.

Law text box 15.1. The EU Standard quality for paddy rice in the season 2007-2008 (Source: Annex IV Standard quality of paddy rice and sugar, EU Regulation 1234/2007).

Annex IV Standard quality of paddy rice and sugar, EU Regulation 1234/2007).

Paddy rice of standard quality shall:

(a) be of a sound and fair marketable quality, free of odour;
(b) contain a moisture content of maximum 13%;
(c) have a yield of wholly milled rice 63% by weight in whole grains (with a tolerance of 3% of clipped grains) of which a percentage by weight of wholly milled rice grains which are not of unimpaired quality:

chalky grains of paddy rice under CN codes CN 10061027 and CN 10061098	1.5%
chalky grains of paddy rice under CN codes other than CN 10061027 and CN 10061098	2.0%
Grains striated with red	1.0%
spotted grains	0.50%
stained grains	0.25%
yellow grains	0.02%
amber grains	0.05%

Law text box 15.2. Standard quality for white sugar (Source: Annex IV Standard quality of paddy rice and sugar, EU Regulation 1234/2007).

B. Standard qualities for sugar
   I. Standard quality for sugar beet
   II. Standard quality for white sugar
   III. Standard quality for raw sugar

(...)

II. Standard quality for white sugar

1. White sugar of the standard quality shall have the following characteristics:
   (a) be of sound, genuine and merchantable quality; dry, in homogeneous granulated crystals, free-flowing;
   (b) minimum polarisation: 99.7;
   (c) maximum moisture content: 0.06%;
   (d) maximum invert sugar content: 0.04%;
   (e) the number of points determined under paragraph 2 shall not exceed a total of 22, nor:
      - 15 for the ash content;
      - 9 for the colour type, determined using the method of the Brunswick Institute of Agricultural Technology (hereinafter referred to as the Brunswick method);

- 6 for the colouring of the solution, determined using the method of the International Commission for Uniform Methods of Sugar Analysis (hereinafter referred to as the ICUMSA method).

2. One point shall correspond to:
   (a) 0.0018% of ash content determined using the ICUMSA[1] method at 28o Brix;
   (b) 0.5 units of colour type determined using the Brunswick method;
   (c) 7.5 units of colouring of the solution determined using the ICUMSA method.
3. The methods for determining the factors referred to in paragraph 1 shall be those used for determining those factors under the intervention measures.

[1] International Commission for Uniform Methods of Sugar Analysis (ICUMSA) is a world-wide body which brings together the activities of the National Committees for Sugar Analysis in more than thirty member countries. ICUMSA's analytical methods are recognised by the sugar industry and authorities such as the Codex Alimentarius Commission, the OIML, the EU, and the US Food Chemicals Codex.
OIML Organisation internationale de métrologie légale Convention establishing an International Organisation of Legal Metrology, done at Paris - France, the 12th of October 1955. Modified in 1968 by amendment of Article XIII (In conformity with the provisions of Article XXXIX). Official translation in English made by the British Government and published under Treaty series No 60 of 1962. The official international text is in French.

Commercial requirements and developments in technical analysis can make it necessary for the Commission to take swift action to amend the specifications of the standard sugar qualities in the relevant Annex.[637] Regulation 1234/2007 takes fifty years of experience with marketing standards into the Single common market organisation with the following statement:

> *'The application of standards for the marketing of agricultural products can contribute to improving the economic conditions for the production and marketing as well as the quality of such products. The application of such standards is therefore in the interest of producers, traders and consumers. Accordingly, within the CMOs for bananas, olive oil and table olives, live plants, eggs and poultrymeat, marketing standards were put in place which relate, in particular, to quality, grading, weight, sizing, packaging, wrapping, storage, transport, presentation, origin and labelling. It is appropriate to maintain that approach under this Regulation.'*[638]

In addition to the marketing standards mentioned in the quote several other standards were or are taken into Regulation 1234/2007. It is replacing the individual common market organisations one by one, as their seasonal agricultural year expires in the period 2007-2008. The sector fruit and vegetables stands for two sectors: fresh fruit and vegetables and processed fruit and vegetables. The fresh fruit and

[637] Recital (13) Regulation 1234/2007.
[638] Recital (49) Regulation 1234/2007.

vegetables were absorbed into the Single common market organisation on 1 July 2008.[639] The processed fruit and vegetables will enter the Single common market organisation on 1 October 2008, after a detour through the sugar sector.[640]

15.2 The fresh fruit and vegetables FFV standard

Almost all fresh fruit and vegetables that are important for European diets have passed a quality standard test before they are allowed to be on the European markets. The EU maintains a system of 34 regulations that define the required properties of 39 fruit and vegetables. See Law text box 15.3. Diagram 15.1 shows how the quality standards fit into the EU legislation.

Law text box 15.3. The Fresh Fruit and Vegetables subjected to a quality or marketing regulation of the European Union. Situation on 1 June 2008.

Every regulation contains articles that provide the obligation to apply the standard and an Annex with the text of the standard.

	39 different fruit or vegetables and 1 mixed bag	34 regulations
1.	Apples	(EC) Regulation 85/2004
2.	Apricots	(EC) Regulation 851/2000
3.	Artichokes	(EC) Regulation 1466/2003
4.	Asparagus	(EC) Regulation 2377/1999
5.	Aubergines	(EEC) Regulation 1292/81
6.	Avocados	(EC) Regulation 831/97
7.	Beans	(EC) Regulation 912/2001
8.	Cabbages, Brussels sprouts, Ribbed celery, Spinach	(EEC) Regulation 591/87
9.	Carrots	(EC) Regulation 730/1999
10.	Cauliflower	(EC) Regulation 963/98
11.	Cherries	(EC) Regulation 214/2004
12.	Citrus fruit	(EC) Regulation 1799/2001
13.	Courgettes	(EC) Regulation 1757/2003
14	Cucumbers	(EEC) Regulation 1677/88
15.	Cultivated mushrooms	(EC) Regulation 1863/2004

[639] Article 3 Council Regulation (EC) No 361/2008 of 14 April 2008 amending Regulation (EC) No 1234/2007 establishing a common organisation of agricultural markets and on specific provisions for certain agricultural products (Single CMO Regulation). Official Journal L 121, 7 May 2008, pp. 1-31.

[640] Article 54 Regulation 1182/2007 repealed Regulation 2202/96. Council Regulation (EC) No 1182/2007 of 26 September 2007 laying down specific rules as regards the fruit and vegetable sector, amending Directives 2001/112/EC and 2001/113/EC and Regulations (EEC) No 827/68, (EC) No 2200/96, (EC) No 2201/96, (EC) No 2826/2000, (EC) No 1782/2003 and (EC) No 318/2006 and repealing Regulation (EC) No 2202/96. Official Journal L 273, 17 October 2007, pp. 1-30. Regulation 2202/96's product scope, the processed fruit and vegetables, was transferred to Council Regulation (EC) No 318/2006 of 20 February 2006 on the common organisation of the markets in the sugar sector. Official Journal L 58, 28 February 2006, pp. 1-31. The sugar common market organisation will cease to exist on 30 September 2008.

16. Garlic	(EC) Regulation 2288/97
17. Hazelnuts in shell	(EC) Regulation 1284/2002
18. Kiwifruit	(EC) Regulation 1673/2004
19. Leeks	(EC) Regulation 2396/2001
20. Lettuces, curled-leaved and broad-leaved endives	(EC) Regulation 1543/2001
21. Melons	(EC) Regulation 1615/2001
22. Onions	(EC) Regulation 1508/2001
23. Peaches and Nectarines	(EC) Regulation 1861/2004
24. Pears	(EC) Regulation 86/2004
25. Peas	(EC) Regulation 2561/1999
26. Plums	(EC) Regulation 1168/1999
27. Strawberries	(EC) Regulation 843/2002
28. Sweet peppers	(EC) Regulation 1455/1999
29. Table grapes	(EC) Regulation 2789/1999
30. Tomatoes	(EC) Regulation 790/2000
31. Walnuts in shell	(EC) Regulation 175/2001
32. Watermelons	(EC) Regulation 1862/2004
33. Witloof chicory	(EEC) Regulation 2213/83
34. Mixed packages	(EC) Regulation 48/2003

The EU has used the standard system since 1962 as an instrument to promote and increase the quality of agricultural production. The development of the standards began in 1949 on the initiative of the United Nations Economic Commission for Europe (UNECE) one of the five world regional subsidiaries created by the UN Economic and Social Council.

The quality standard system is created to facilitate international trade in agricultural products. The central idea of the standard was and is to establish a control system operated by the government of the exporting state that will allow export of agricultural products only when they fulfil the conditions of the standard. The government of the importing state can rely on these controls because both governments have accepted the standard and have given each other assurances about the control measures. Trust in the standard is also founded on periodic double checks made by the importing state.

The quality standard replaced the system where every national government organised its own control system on imported food, each with its own norms. The standard unifies the rules on the export-import system when both states accept the same standard. That is an additional bounty: it makes trade far less complicated.

Diagram 15.1. UNECE Agricultural Quality Standards.

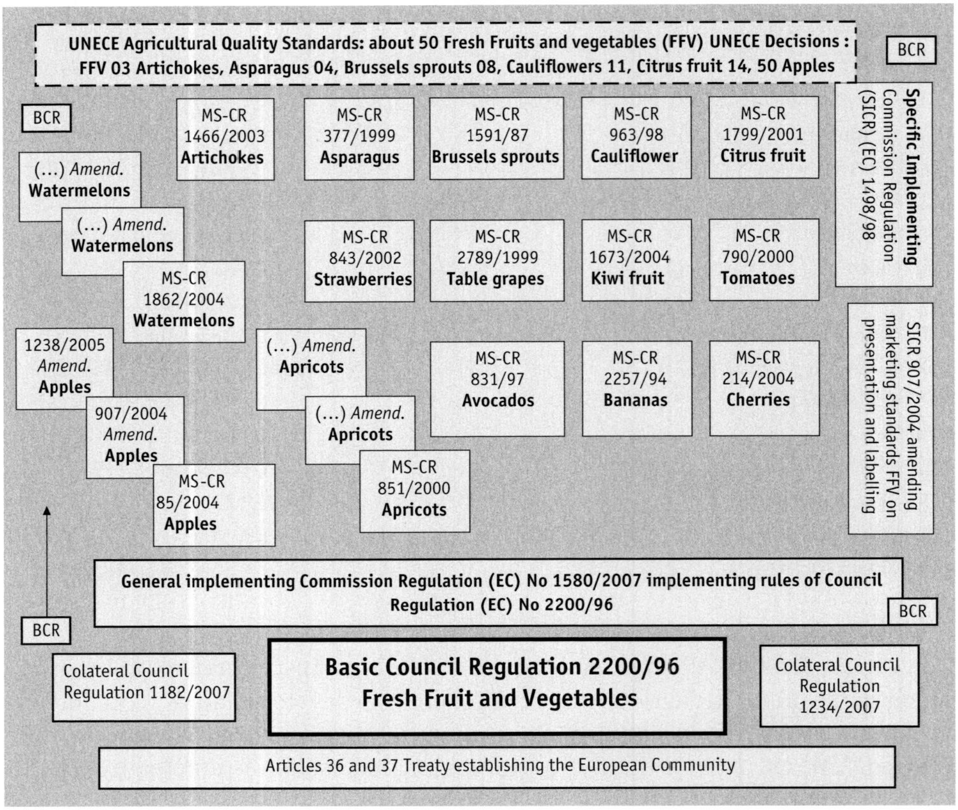

15.2.1 The essence of the FFV quality standard

Quality standards for fresh fruit or vegetables are special because they test the produce on the biological properties it must have at the moment when the consumer will eat it. After separation from the plant, or soil, fresh fruit and vegetables are developing to an optimum of ripeness or other coveted qualities and then start to decline into less appreciated quantities. Producers, traders, transporters and retailers will apply logistics and a range of product related measures to have the fruit or vegetable for sale at the moment just before it is most attractive. This dynamic development and the time squeeze of freshness dictate the contents of the standard.

15.3 The UNECE model for the FFV standard

15.3.1 Common structure and formal recognition

All marketing standards for fresh fruit and vegetables follow the same design in the structure of the text and have a common wording as far as possible, given the differences between individual fruits and vegetables. This common structure is explained by the functions of the standard that prompted the selection and the sequence of the criteria. The UNECE Working Group 7 has made the Standard layout as a practical model for UNECE standards.[641]

The same model standard is the core subject of the UNECE Geneva Protocol on Standardization, published in 1958, and revised in 1985.[642] This Protocol introduced the standard and still determines the way standards are made, the subjects of the standards, the type of the rules, the stages of the production process they regulate and the territorial areas where they are applied. It did so before the first Standards were published, and the revision after twenty-five years confirms the consensus on the necessary text of the standard. Experience did not call for major changes. The Protocol presents the subjects for the standards in words, reasoning and contents that together form the model that the FFV-Standards follow closely. The collection of standards with the same structure confirms the usefulness of the model.

The governments that accept the Protocol send a message to that effect to the UNECE. They have the obligation to put the rules into effect within one year after their message.

15.3.2 The legal force of the Geneva Protocol

The legal force of the Geneva Protocol has been described by an anonymous UNECE lawyer as soft law 'because it has the wording of a treaty but has not been signed and ratified as a treaty'. This interpretation finds support in Article X of the Protocol, presented in Law text box 15.4. Article X opens the perspective of a treaty that will give the European system of standardisation of fruit and vegetables a definite status.

---

641 In full: Standard layout for UNECE standards concerning the marketing and commercial quality control of Fresh Fruit and Vegetables. The 2003 version is based on document TRADE/WP.7/2002/9/Add.13 of 23 January 2003. The Standard Layout 2007 will replace the 2003 version after the completion of the recommendation phase in November 2008 if all agree. Both versions can be found at http://www.unece.org/trade/agr/standard/fresh/fresh_e.htm.

642 In full: Revised Geneva Protocol on Standardization of Fresh Fruit and Vegetables and Dry and Dried Fruit, published 1958 and revised 1985. At: http://www.unece.org/trade/agr/info/gevprot/gevprot.htm.

Law text box 15.4. The prospect of a treaty for the UNECE standardisation of fruit and vegetables (Source: Revised Geneva Protocol on Standardization of Fresh Fruit and Vegetables and Dry and Dried Fruit, published 1958 and revised 1985).

Article X. Geneva Protocol.
The Working Party shall also be responsible for drawing up, whenever it thinks best, the clauses of an international agreement calculated to confer a definite status on the European system of standardisation of fruit and vegetables.

Nine years of preparation of the standards had already accumulated at the time the Protocol was made. All this work continued for six decades without the need to apply Article X of the Protocol.

The binding effect of the never ratified Geneva Protocol can also be considered in the light of the continuing cooperation and the programme to create binding standards that the state parties will implement. In that light the conclusion will be that the states are bound by an international agreement that has the force of a treaty. What it lacks in formal attributes, a register of ratification statements, it makes up for with the notification to the Secretary of the UNECE, which a ratification, and the tradition established by practice.

Law text box 15.5 presents Protocol Article VII that determines the strength of the obligations that the states accept. Note that the assumption is that every state has or will make its national commodity standard. The state will adapt its national standards to the text of the Protocol that is similar to the text of the model FFV-standard.

Law text box 15.5. The legal force of the Agricultural Quality Standards made according to the Geneva Protocol on Standardization of Fresh Fruit and Vegetables.

Article VII Geneva Protocol.
Each government accepting this Protocol undertakes to take the necessary steps under its domestic law *to adapt its commodity standards* to the general provisions set forth above in the Protocol. In so doing *it also undertakes to refer to the individual standards* to be prepared by the Working Party on Standardization of Perishable Produce and Quality Development on the basis of the foregoing general provisions, and *shall have regard as far as possible to the particular provisions thereof.*

The co-existence of the Protocol and the national standards reflects a dualist concept of international law. In a monist concept a national standard is not necessary. The acceptance of the Protocol as a model text will lead to a certain degree of harmonisation of the standards of the different national states.

Note that the obligation in the case of an individual standard for a specific commodity is weak: the states accept the obligation to refer to the specific standard. When they make a national standard they will mention the existence of the international UNECE standard on the same commodity. But they are not bound to copy the contents of the international standard. They '*shall have regard as far as possible to the particular provisions thereof*', which means that they are free to decide to give their national standard a different content.

The thorough preparations of the standards, the time invested and the consensus sought do not always succeed in producing a text that everyone accepts. International law recognises the reservation as a solution for the state that does not want to reject the complete text on one minor subject, but does not want to accept that minor subject either. The registration of the reservation secures the freedom of that state to refuse application of that rule and to follow a different rule. Experience can change the opinions and the text to accept the opinion of the dissenting state. See Law text boxes 15.10 and 15.12 for examples of reservations made by the US and the EU.

15.4 Integration of the quality standard in EU law

15.4.1 Introduction

The latest EU legislation on the marketing standard can be found in Regulation 1234/2007 in its Title II Rules concerning marketing and production, Chapter I Marketing standards and conditions for the production, Section I Marketing standards. However, these articles have entered into force only recently, and incompletely. The body of applicable rules still rests on the former basic regulations. Law text box 15.6. presents a part of the newest EU legislation on marketing standard. Law text box 15.7 presents the EU legislation on marketing standards that will be analysed in this chapter.

Law text box 15.6. The newest EU legislation on marketing standard.

1. Provision may be made by the Commission for marketing standards for one or more of the products of the following sectors: (...)
2. The standards referred to in paragraph 1:
   (a) shall be established taking into account, in particular:
      (i) the specificities of the products concerned
      (ii) the need to ensure the conditions for a smooth disposal of those products on the market;
      (iii) the interest of consumers to receive adequate and transparent product information;
      (iv) (...);
   (b) may in particular relate to quality, grading, weight, sizing, packaging, wrapping, storage, transport, presentation, origin and labelling.

3. Save as otherwise provided for by the Commission in accordance with the criteria referred to in point (a) of paragraph 2, the products for which marketing standards have been laid down may be marketed in the Community only in accordance with such standards.
   Without prejudice to any specific provisions which may be adopted by the Commission in accordance with Article 194, Member States shall check whether those products conform to those standards and shall apply penalties as appropriate.

Law text box 15.7. Regulation (EC) No 1182/2007 on marketing standards.

Title II
Classification of products
Article 2
Marketing standards

1. The products listed in Article 1(2) of Regulation (EC) No 2200/96 which are intended to be sold fresh to the consumer, may only be marketed if they are sound, fair and of marketable quality and if the country of origin is indicated.
2. Provision may be made by the Commission for marketing standards for one or more of the products listed in Article 1(2) of Regulation (EC) No 2200/96 and in Article 1(2) of Regulation (EC) No 2201/96.
3. In so doing, the Commission shall take account of the Standard recommendations adopted by the United Nations Economic Commission for Europe (UNECE).
4. The marketing standards referred to in paragraphs 1 and 2:
   (a) shall apply at all marketing stages including import and export unless otherwise provided for by the Commission;
   (b) shall be established taking into account, in particular, the specificities of the products concerned, the need to ensure the conditions for a smooth disposal of those products on the market and the interest of consumers in receiving adequate and transparent product information as regards in particular the country of origin, the class and, where appropriate, the variety (or the commercial type) of the product;
   (c) may in particular relate to quality, grading into classes, sizing, packaging, wrapping, storage, transport, presentation, marketing and labelling.
5. The holder of products covered by the adopted marketing standards may not display such products or offer them for sale or deliver or market them in any manner within the Community other than in conformity with those standards. The holder shall be responsible for ensuring such conformity.
6. Without prejudice to any specific provisions which may be adopted by the Commission in accordance with Article 42, Member States shall check selectively, based on a risk analysis, whether those products conform to those marketing standards. These checks shall be focused on the stage prior to dispatch from the production areas when the products are being packed or loaded. For products from third countries, checks shall be done prior to release for free circulation.
7. Until new marketing standards are adopted, the marketing standards drawn up pursuant to Regulation (EC) No 2200/96 and Regulation (EC) No 2201/96 shall continue to apply.

15.4.2 The main points of EU law on marketing standards

Eligible products and general minimum standard

All basic regulations for the market organisation of fruit and vegetables contain a list of fruit and vegetables that the Commission can subject to a standard. These foodstuffs are identified by their number in the Common Customs Nomenclature. The Commission may make a standard but does not have to.

The products that the Commission has to apply a standard to are listed in an Annex to the regulation. It is not yet clear whether the two lists system, one voluntary for the Commission and the other one mandatory, will be continued in the new marketing standard regime announced by Regulation 1234/2007.

The fruit and vegetables for which the Commission has not made a standard are not left unprotected. Article 2(1) gives the rules that protect the consumer of those out of standard fruit and vegetables.

The member states are not allowed to make standards when the EU has not made them, nor to make different standards. Case law of the Court of Justice established that the fresh fruit and vegetable regulations constitute a complete EU power. The member states are not allowed to interfere with it, even when the Commission has not used its power.[643]

The consequences of a marketing standard

Article 2(1) is written to safeguard the minimum qualities for a part of the fresh fruit and vegetables. This follows from the combination of Article 2(1) and Article 2(2). The products listed in Regulation 2200/96 establish a group of fresh fruit and vegetables.[644] Article 2(2) gives the Commission the power to make marketing standards for this group. It is a power without the obligation to use it ('Provision *may* be made ...'). Article 2(1) therefore gives the minimum conditions that apply to all the products in the list. They 'may only be marketed if they are sound, fair and of marketable quality and if the country of origin is indicated'. The public authorities have to organise inspections to enforce the law on marketing requirements for fresh fruit and vegetables. That law is the collection of the law made on and by marketing standards plus the rule of Article 2(1). The inspectors,

643 Case 255/86, Commission of the European Communities v Kingdom of Belgium, Failure of a State to fulfil its obligations, ECR 1988, p. 693.

644 Regulation 2200/96 is written for fruit and vegetables. The not necessary implication that this is the group of fresh fruit and vegetables follows from the combination of this regulation with Regulation 2201/96 on processed fruit and vegetables. If Regulation 2201/96 takes out all the rules for the processed produce, it still does not bar Regulation 2200/96 from presenting the rules for all fruit and vegetables and those specific for the fresh produce. Occasionally Regulation 2200/96 presents rules for processed fruit and vegetables. The sequence of both regulations is another indication for that relation. International law on fruit and vegetables makes a clear distinction between fresh and processed.

and, ultimately, the judges will have to establish the meaning of the words 'sound, fair and of marketable quality'. They will do that on the basis of established practise and experts' opinions on what conduct becomes the holder of unregulated fresh fruits and vegetables.

Commission power

Article 2(2) gives the Commission the power to make marketing standards for both fresh and processed fruit and vegetables. The wish to make marketing standards for processed produce too has been included in earlier basic regulations without anything like the collection of EU FFV standards. The EU does not follow international collections of standards for processed produce like the Dry and Dried Produce Standard of UNECE. The many types of processing have inspired the EU so far to some haphazard measures.

Take account of the UNECE Standard

The EU generally follows the UNECE standard. The Commission gives various reasons: for simplicity, transparency, fair marketing conditions. The EU reserves the right to determine the conditions on which each standard will be accepted. The Geneva Protocol allows this. Each accepted standard is imported in EU law as 'annexed cargo'. The standard is annexed to a regulation, the standard becomes binding EU law because the regulation has that power. Although the standards are very detailed and carefully constructed to function as a complete set of rules there is no hint whatsoever of a possible direct effect of the accepted standard on its own force.

The checkpoint(s)

The EU demands on what a standard is supposed to do are summarised in paragraph 4. Article 2(4)(a) is the outspoken preference of the EU and one of the few differences between the UNECE and the EU interpretation.

The EU marketing standards apply at all marketing stages, the UNECE only at the moment of establishing conformity just before export. See Law text box 15.8 for the different ideas on the admissibility or necessity of more than one checkpoint.

Law text box 15.8. The checkpoints.

FFV-46: Kiwifruit 2008

The purpose of the Standard is to define the quality requirements of kiwifruit, at the export control stage, after preparation and packaging.

FFV-50: Apples 2007

The purpose of the standard is to define the quality requirements of apples at the export-control stage after preparation and packaging.

Commission Regulation 85/2004/ EC

The purpose of the standard is to define the quality requirements of apples, after preparation and packaging.

Codex Stan

'This Standard applies to commercial varieties of oranges grown from *Citrus sinensis* (L.) Osbeck, of the Rutaceae *family*, to be supplied fresh to the consumer, after preparation and packaging. Oranges for industrial processing are excluded.

UNECE FFV-19 Table grapes, 1961, revised 2007

The purpose of the standard is to define the quality requirements of table grapes at the export-control stage after preparation and packaging.

EU Regulation 843/2002

The purpose of the standard is to define the quality requirements for strawberries at the dispatching stage, after preparation and packaging.

EU 1999

The standard shall apply at all stages of marketing under the conditions laid down in Regulation (EC) No 2200/96.

The different descriptions of the purpose of the standard in EU and UNECE law reveal the different ideas about the checkpoint where the produce is tested against the standard. Both standards use the same words to describe the purpose: it is to define the quality requirements of a particular fruit or vegetable. The descriptions become different where they indicate when the criteria of the standard define the product. That moment is indicated in the EU legislation as 'after preparation and packaging'. In the UNECE standards it is 'at the export-control stage after preparation and packaging'. The Codex standards describe the point where the definitions of the standard are valid as the point where the standard applies 'after preparation and packaging'.

The difference between the EU and UNECE is more explicit in the EU legislation on the standards. Article 2(4) leaves no doubt: 'the marketing standards referred to in paragraphs 1 and 2: (a) shall apply at all marketing stages including import and export unless otherwise provided for by the Commission'. It follows that the EU legislation applies the set of rules 'after preparation and packaging' to all marketing stages including import and export.

The checklist

The checklist of elements in Article 2(4)(b) that the EU considers to be necessary is directed to the marketing side of the standard, both in functions and in priorities. Among the functions appears 'a smooth disposal of those products on the market' for the first time, while the priorities stand out by the 'shall be established taking into account' of subparagraph (b) versus the 'may in particular relate to' of (c).

That paragraph refers to the characteristic elements of the original quality standards. The difference between the two sets of conditions is partly explained by the wish to extend the use of the standard to a wider set of situations where the essentials may be incompatible with the biologic logic of the fruit or vegetables' development to an optimal quality. The preference given to marketability in general squares with the established internal market.

The holder held responsible and punishable
Article 2(5) determines the punishment and the perpetrator in one sentence. The condition is that only standard conform products can be on the market. It makes no difference whether the produce is actually offered for sale, every action related to a market and a product held by a person is sufficient to establish a (beginning of) marketing.

These actions or situations are unlawful. Sanctions are applied: the produce may not be sold and is bound to lose much or all of its value. The member states have to organise efficient controls to prevent the marketing of sub-standard produce, to confiscate the wanting produce and to prosecute the responsible persons.

One of them is easily identified. To avoid the almost limitless ingenuity to devise and deploy constructions that serve to disguise or obscure who is responsible to whom and for what, Article 2(5) introduces the simple rule that the person who is found with the merchandise is the person who is responsible, accountable, and punishable. Proof of property rights is not relevant.

15.5 The UNECE model for the FFV quality standard

The quality standard is made to select, prescribe and promote the quality of the product and to introduce different grades of quality. A higher quality is expected to get a higher price on the markets and different quality grades can open a greater section of the market with lower graded quality for a lower price.

The model for the FFV quality standard has a structure that is made to express the primary importance of quality and the elements that support quality by their contents and by the sequence in which they become an activated part of the standard. Diagram 15.2 is used to analyse the contents of the model. The columns on the left side of Diagram 15.2 present interpretations to support the discussion. The right-hand column presents the elements following under:

I. Definition of produce:
- The elements II-V secure the quality content.
- V and VI serve to protect that quality, to provide a positive and representative image and accurate information about the essential aspects of the product.

- VI A to D identify the characteristic properties that II – IV developed as selection criteria. The two items of VI D indicate the expectations of the most likely profit generating factors.
- The identification of the packer and dispatcher serve to secure the information needed to connect product and production circumstances. They operate at points in the food chain where the harvest of several producers is collected and the final packaging into larger transport unities take place. It is the ideal bottleneck for inspection and registration of shipments. The place to anchor the control system that has to trace the produce across the continents.

The model presented with the sections I-VI plus the Annex List of Varieties are used, with small adaptations, in every standard developed for fresh fruit and vegetables by the UNECE. From the first FFV-01 Apples and Pears published in 1962 to the most recent one, FFV-46 Kiwifruit published in 2008.

The EU regulations for fresh fruit and vegetables are based on the UNECE standards. The standards are also used by the Organisation for Economic Cooperation and Development (OECD) for the extensive brochures they make to explain the standards.

The model used by the Codex Alimentarius Commission is the same with an extension. Codex FFV standards have added a section 7 on Contaminants and 8 on Hygiene. In addition Codex standards always refer to collections of rules on the subjects hygiene and contaminants.

Element I the legal definition of fresh fruit or vegetable
The analysis of the elements of the model begins with the definition that determines which fruit or vegetable is subject to the standard. Its legal function is to establish, as clearly and sharply as possible, the borderline between situations for which the standard is made, where it applies, and the situations on the other side of the borderline that are beyond its reach. The situations that fit the definition fall under the scope[645] of that part of the law. The function of the definition is that of the key to the subject matter of the standard, the rights it creates, the prescriptions the prohibitions. The range of the columns at the left-hand side of Diagram 15.2 gives an indication of these relations.

The definition of the fresh fruit and vegetables standard has two elements (Law text box 15.9). The first element is the determination of the biologic species, variety or cultivar that is defined by a Linnaean taxonomic formula with the general

[645] Scope, definition and subject matter: see Guide 13 1 in the Joint Practical Guide of the European Parliament, the Council and the Commission, for persons involved in the drafting of legislation within the Community institutions, Brussels 16 March 2000.

Diagram 15.2. The model for the fresh fruit and vegetables standards.

<table>
<tr><th colspan="5">Interpretation of the model</th><th>The model organised in Sections I-VI
This model is developed and used by the UNECE, the EU and the OECD</th></tr>
<tr><td rowspan="6">The indication of the power to make the standard is not present in the document. See references at the base of the table</td><td rowspan="4">The key that makes the connection between the scope and the subject matter
The scope refers to the categories of situations of fact or of law and the persons to which the act applies</td><td colspan="3">Definition determines the scope of the standard: the situations that are ruled by it</td><td>I. Definition of produce</td></tr>
<tr><td rowspan="3">The subject matter: the contents of the standard norms
Subject matter is what the act deals with</td><td rowspan="2">The properties of the product: the fresh fruit as it is marketed</td><td>The prescribed properties of the fruit or vegetable that are close to the intrinsic qualities</td><td>II. Provisions concerning quality
A. Minimum requirements
B. Maturity requirements
C. Classification
(i) 'Extra' Class
(ii) Class I
(iii) Class II
III. Provisions concerning sizing</td></tr>
<tr><td>The correction to the attributed qualities: exceptions allowed by the standard to the rule that established the qualities</td><td>IV. Provisions concerning tolerances
A. Quality tolerances
(i) 'Extra' Class
(ii) Class I
(iii) Class II
B. Size tolerances</td></tr>
<tr><td>The conditions in which the fruit or vegetable is transported and inspected</td><td></td><td>V. Provisions concerning presentation
A. Uniformity
B. Packaging
C. Presentation
VI. Provisions concerning marking
A. Identification
• Packer
• Dispatcher
B. Nature of produce
C. Origin of produce
D. Commercial specifications
• Class
• Size (if sized)
E. Official control mark (optional)
Annex List of Varieties</td></tr>
<tr><td colspan="4"></td><td>Codex FFV Standards continue with
7. Contaminants
8. Hygiene</td></tr>
<tr><td colspan="4"></td><td>Codex refers to Regulations WHO</td></tr>
</table>

structure of 'Family, species, L.'. The second element restricts the application of the standard to the defined fruit or vegetable that is not processed.

Law text box 15.9. Definitions of produce: the definitions of table grapes and kiwi in FFV standards made by Codex, EU and UNECE.

Codex

1. Definition of produce

This Standard applies to commercial varieties (cultivars) of table grapes grown from *Vitis vinifera* L., of the *Vitaceae* family, to be supplied fresh to the consumer, after preparation and packaging. Grapes for industrial processing are excluded.

EU

The marketing standard for table grapes falling within CN code 0806 10 10 shall be as set out in the Annex.

This standard applies to table grapes of varieties (cultivars) grown from *Vitis vinifera* L. to be supplied fresh to the consumer, table grapes for industrial processing being excluded.

UNECE

This standard applies to table grapes of varieties (cultivars) grown from *Vitis vinifera* L. to be supplied fresh to the consumer, table grapes for industrial processing being excluded.

UNECE

This Standard applies to kiwifruit (also known as *actinidia* or *kiwis*) of varieties (cultivars) grown from *Actinidia chinensis Planch* and *Actinidia deliciosa* (A. Chev., C.F. Liang and A.R. Ferguson[1]) to be supplied fresh to the consumer, kiwifruit for industrial processing being excluded.

[1] On this reference, see Liang Chou-Fen and A.R. Ferguson, The botanical nomenclature of the kiwifruit and related taxa, New Zealand Journal of Botany, 1986, Vol. 24, pp. 183-184. For hyperlink see reference list.

Element II. Provisions concerning quality

Quality figures prominently in the subject matter of the standards, with four different entries: minimum quality, maturity requirements, the introduction of different quality classes and the quality tolerances. The criteria selected to test quality aspects begin with the definition of minimum requirements that separates the unacceptable from the barely acceptable and continues to divide the acceptable into two or three classes descending from extra class to first class into second class. Every quality class is defined by the characteristic properties of the fruit or vegetable and compared with the other class(es) on the extent of the expression of these qualities and the presence of defects

The tolerances are the next step in the evaluation scheme. They introduce a systematic correction on the grading into classes. The variability of circumstances and individual properties of grown produce is still far greater than production control allows for manufactured or machine-made products. The tolerances permit the presence of lower graded produce in the higher class.

Element IIA: The minimum quality requirements
The standards describe the properties of the fruit or vegetable, and the conditions it is in, to establish criteria to determine the access of that produce to the market as fresh fruit and vegetable with an indicated set of qualities. The standard operates as a part of the legislation that is made to determine what is accepted as food and as food with particular properties. The standards are made to provide the conditions that make it possible to export fresh fruit and vegetables to a country that accepts the inspection results of the exporting country. This function determines the contents of the standards and the way they are applied. The transformation of unilateral national decisions to allow or refuse the import into cooperation between import and export country requires agreement on two issues. The grounds that determine the acceptability of the products and the way these grounds are applied.

The following Diagrams show the criteria that were developed to make it possible to inspect produce before export takes place and guarantee its condition in the period up to consumption. Diagram 15.3 compares the minimum requirements for two different fruits by different organisations. The 2.1.1 section of the Codex Standard contains the dynamic quality elements that formulate criteria to be used at the moment of inspection that will predict the qualities at the moment of consumption

Diagram 15.4 compares the minimum quality requirements set by the present EU Regulation 2789/1999 for Table grapes with the first EEC standard in 1962 and the UNECE and Codex standards of 2007. The diagram shows the stability in the criteria used by the EU in four and a half decades. It also shows the degree of consensus between three different organisations that continue to make their own standards.

Element IIB: Maturity requirements
The maturity requirement is a check on ripeness. The *minimum* maturity requirements applied to table grapes demand that the grapes are sufficiently developed and ripened. Several techniques have been developed, such as the measurement of the sugar/acid ratio or the determination of the Brix value by using the different refractions of light to measure the soluble solids content. Standards are based on specialised knowledge and techniques that are used to develop criteria and tests to establish when products meet the requirements. That information is expressed in statements such as those in Law text box 15.10 on the discussion about the maturity requirement for table grapes. The discussion can be followed in the agenda documents.

The technical expertise does not have to lead to outcomes that are shared by all. Differences of opinion can continue on questions like the range of the chosen values and their suitability for particular varieties. Agreement on the desirability

Diagram 15.3. The minimum requirements for quality grading in UNECE FFV Apples compared with the Codex Standard for Papaya (CODEX STAN 183-1993, Rev. 1-2001, Amd. 1-2005).

2. Provisions concerning quality ***2.1 Minimum requirements***	
Apples	*Papaya*
In all classes, subject to the special provisions for each class and the tolerances allowed, apples must be:	In all classes, subject to the special provisions for each class and the tolerances allowed, the papayas must be:
• intact	• whole
• sound, produce affected by rotting or deterioration such as to make it unfit for consumption is excluded	• sound, produce affected by rotting or deterioration such as to make it unfit for consumption is excluded
• clean, practically free of any visible foreign matter	• clean, practically free of any visible foreign matter
• practically free from pests	• practically free of damage caused by pests
• practically free from damage caused by pests	• practically free of pests affecting the general appearance of the produce
• free of abnormal external moisture	• free of abnormal external moisture, excluding condensation following removal from cold storage
• free of any foreign smell and/or taste	• free of any foreign smell and/or taste
In addition, they must have been carefully picked.	• firm
	• fresh in appearance
	• free of damage caused by low and/or high temperatures
	The peduncle, if present, should not exceed a length of 1 cm
Codex only: 2.1.1 The papayas must have been carefully picked and have reached an appropriate degree of development and ripeness account being taken of the characteristics of the variety and/or commercial type and the area in which they are grown. The development and condition of the papayas must be such as to enable them: – to withstand transport and handling; and – to arrive in satisfactory condition at the place of destination. This provision allows for smell caused by conservation agents used in compliance with corresponding regulations.	

of different values for different varieties or circumstances leads often to an Annex in a legal document collecting all the particulars that defy a rule.

Diagram 15.4. Minimum quality requirements for table grapes in 4 Fresh Fruit Standards.

EC Regulation No 2789/1999	EEC Regulation 58 Annex I/7 1962	UNECE FFV-19, revised in 2007	Codex Stan 255-2007
In all classes, subject to the special provisions for each class and the tolerances allowed, bunches and berries must be:	(i) Bunches and berries must be:	In all classes, subject to the special provisions for each class and the tolerances allowed, bunches and berries must be:	In all classes, subject to the special provisions for each class and the tolerances allowed, the bunches and berries must be:
• sound	• sound	• sound	• sound
produce affected by rotting or deterioration such as to make it unfit for consumption is excluded		produce affected by rotting or deterioration such as to make it unfit for consumption is excluded	produce affected by rotting or deterioration such as to make it unfit for consumption is excluded;
• clean, practically free of any visible foreign matter	• clean, and *in particular* free from all visible *traces of chemicals*	• clean, practically free of any visible foreign matter	• clean, practically free of any visible foreign matter;
• practically free from pests		• practically free from pests	• practically free of pests and
• practically free from damage caused by pests	• free from damage *by insects or disease*	• free from damage caused by pests *affecting the flesh*	damage caused by them *affecting the general appearance of the produce*
	• free from all visible traces of mould		
• free of abnormal external moisture	• free from abnormal external moisture	• free of abnormal external moisture	• free of abnormal external moisture, *excluding condensation following removal from cold storage*
• free of any foreign smell and/or taste	• free from foreign smell or taste	• free of any foreign smell and/or taste	• free of any foreign smell and/or taste
			• *practically free of damage caused by low and/or high temperatures*

In addition, berries must be:	(ii) In addition, berries must be:	In addition, berries must be:	In addition, the berries must be:
• intact		• intact	• *whole*
• well formed	• well-formed	• well formed	• well formed
• normally developed	• normally developed	• normally developed	• normally developed
	• firmly attached to the stalk.		
Pigmentation due to sun is not a defect	Pigmentation due to sun is not a defect. (Burst or damaged berries must be cut out, without unduly depleting the bunches)	Pigmentation due to sun is not a defect	Pigmentation due to sun is not a defect *so long as this only affects the skin of the berries*
Bunches must have been carefully picked	(iii) Bunches must have been carefully picked		2.1.1 The bunches must have been carefully picked
The table grapes must be sufficiently developed and display satisfactory ripeness			
The development and condition of the table grapes must be such as to enable them:	The state of ripeness must be such as to allow the produce:	The development and condition of the table grapes must be such as to enable them:	The development and condition of the table grapes must be such as to enable them:
• to withstand transport and handling, and	• to withstand transport and handling	• to withstand transportation and handling	• to withstand transport and handling; and
• to arrive in satisfactory condition at the place of destination	• and to meet market requirements at the place of destination	• to arrive in satisfactory condition at the place of destination	• to arrive in satisfactory condition at the place of destination

Law text box 15.10. Negotiations about parameters to establish maturity requirements for table grapes. Item 2.1.2 of what would become Codex Stan 255-2007.

Agenda Item 4(a) CX/FFV 06/13/7 April 2006

joint FAO/WHO food standards programme codex committee on fresh fruits and vegetables

13th Session, Mexico City, Mexico, 25 - 29 September 2006

Proposed draft section 2.1.2 - Maturity requirements and section 3.1 - minimum bunch weight (draft Codex Standard for Table Grapes)

(at step 3)

Background

Maturity Requirements

8. The working group based its discussions on the proposal contained in ALINORM 05/28/35-Appendix V and the comments3 submitted through CL 2005/25-FFV as well as relevant UN/ECE documents including the UN/ECE Standard/Recommendation for Table Grapes. Following an extensive discussion, the working group agreed on a proposal as contained in Part A of Annex I. The delegations of the USA and India expressed their reservation to this proposal.
9. The delegation of the USA indicated that some parts of the proposal did not account for the differences in maturity levels and special attributes on individual table grapes varieties and production zones. Both delegations requested that the proposal should indicate exemptions for some grape varieties which were not supported by the other delegations. Consequently, the delegations of the USA and India made an additional proposal as contained in Part B of Annex I.

Annex I

Proposed draft section 2.1.2 - maturity requirements and section 3.1 - minimum bunch weight (draft codex standard for table grapes)

(at step 3)

Proposal A (working group on table grapes) ***Section 2.1.2 - Maturity Requirements***	**Proposal B (United States of America and India)** ***Section 2.1.2 - Maturity Requirements***
The table grapes must be sufficiently developed and display satisfactory ripeness. In order to satisfy this requirement, the fruit must have obtained a refractometric index of at least 16° Brix.	The table grapes must be sufficiently developed and display satisfactory ripeness. In order to satisfy this requirement, the fruit must have obtained a refractometric index of at least 16° Brix.
Fruit with a lower refractometric index are accepted provided the sugar/acid ratio is at least equal to: (a) 20:1 if the Brix level is greater than or equal to 12.5° and less than 14° Brix, (b) 18:1 if the Brix level is greater than or equal to 14° and less than 16° Brix.	Fruit with a lower refractometric index (less than 16° Brix) are accepted provided the sugar/acid ratio is at least equal to 20:1.

	Exceptions: (a) **T. Seedless and mutants**: • 17.0° Brix; Ratio not applicable or • 15.0°-16.9° Brix; Ratio 20:1 or • Not acceptable below 15° Brix. (b) **Perlette & Sugraone** • 15.5° Brix; Ratio not applicable or • 14.0°-15.4° Brix; Ratio 20:1 or • Not acceptable below 14° Brix.

The new Codex and UNECE standards on table grapes follow the text on maturity requirements of proposal A in Annex I.[646] The UNECE standard has a footnote with the following text:

'Reservation by the United States of America: "The uniform approach applied to the minimum maturity requirements in the UNECE Standard for Table Grapes does not correctly reflect minimum maturity requirements for all table grape varieties from all geographical production regions, and the practices of the table grape industry"'.

Element IIC: Classification

The creation of different grades of quality introduces the possibility to market the fruit or vegetable at different prices which can enlarge demand by attracting additional buyers and buyers who will pay a higher price for a higher quality product. It is also an incentive to improve craftsmanship and production circumstances.

The qualifications that create the different quality classes are in general formulated to establish three classes (Law text box 15.11):

Extra Class - The fresh fruit and vegetables produce in this class must be of superior quality. They must be characteristic of the variety and/or commercial type. They must be free of defects, with the exception of very slight superficial defects, provided these do not affect the general appearance of the produce, the quality, the keeping quality and presentation in the package.

Class I - The products in this class must be of good quality. They must be characteristic of the variety and/or commercial type. The following slight defects, however, may be allowed, provided these do not affect the general appearance of the produce, the quality, the keeping quality and presentation in the package:

[646] Codex Stan 255-2007 Table Grapes, and UNECE FFV-19 Table Grapes, 2007. Commission Regulation 2789/1999, the EU marketing standard for table grapes does not have a maturity requirement criterion.

- slight defects in shape;
- slight skin defects (i.e. mechanical bruising, sun spots and/or latex burns). The total area affected shall not exceed 10% of the total surface.

The defects must not, in any case, affect the pulp of the fruit.

Class II - This class includes FFV produce that does not qualify for inclusion in the higher classes, but satisfy the minimum requirements specified above. The following defects, however, may be allowed, provided the FFV produce retain their essential characteristics as regards the quality, the keeping quality and presentation:
- defects in shape;
- defects in colouring;
- skin defects (i.e. mechanical bruising, sun spots and latex burns). The total area affected should not exceed 15% of the total surface;
- slight marks caused by pests.

The defects must not, in any case, affect the pulp of the fruit.

Law text box 15.11. Classification of apples (Source: Commission Regulation (EC) No 85/2004 of 15 January 2004 laying down the marketing standard for apples).

B. Classification: Apples are classified in three classes defined below.

(i) 'Extra' class

Apples in this class must be of superior quality. In shape, size and colouring, they must be characteristic of the variety and with the stalk which must be intact.

The flesh must be perfectly sound.

They must be free from defects with the exception of very slight superficial defects provided these do not affect the general appearance of the produce, the quality, the keeping quality and presentation in the package.

(ii) Class I

Apples in this class must be of good quality. In shape, size and colouring, they must be characteristic of the variety.

The flesh must be perfectly sound.

The following slight defects, however, may be allowed provided these do not affect the general appearance of the produce, the quality, the keeping quality and presentation in the package:
- a slight defect in shape,
- a slight defect in development,
- a slight defect in colouring,
- slight skin defects which must not extend over more than:
  - 2 cm in length for defects of elongated shape;
  - 1 cm^2 of total surface area for other defects, with the exception of scab (*Venturia inaequalis*), which must not extend over more than 0.25 cm^2 of total surface area;

- slight bruising not exceeding 1 cm^2 of total surface area and not discoloured.

The stalk may be missing, provided the break is clean and the adjacent skin is not damaged.

(iii) Class II

This class includes apples which do not qualify for inclusion in the higher classes but satisfy the minimum requirements specified above.

The flesh must be free from major defects.

The following defects are allowed provided the fruit retains its essential characteristics as regards the quality, the keeping quality and presentation:

- defects in shape,
- defects in development,
- defects in colouring,
- skin defects which must not extend over more than
  - 4 cm in length for defects of elongated shape;
  - 2,5 cm^2 of total surface area for other defects, with the exception of scab (*Venturia inaequalis*), which must not extend over more than 1 cm^2 of total surface area;
  - slight bruising not exceeding 1.5 cm^2 of total surface area which may be slightly discoloured.

Element III: Provisions concerning sizing

Sizing is an independent aspect of the standard. It is illustrated in Law box 15.12. Note the special reservation made by the EU

Law text box 15.12. Sizing provisions for peaches and nectarines.

PART I: Revised standard – UNECE standard FFV-26

concerning the marketing and commercial quality control of **peaches and nectarines**

Published 1961 – Revised 1994, 2003, 2004

III. Provisions concerning sizing

Size is determined by:
- circumference, or
- maximum diameter of the equatorial section.

Peaches and nectarines must be graded according to the following scale:

Diameter	Size Code	Circumference
90 mm and over	AAAA	28 cm and over
80 mm and over but under 90 mm	AAA	25 cm and over but under 28 cm
73 mm and over but under 80 mm	AA	23 cm and over but under 25 cm
67 mm and over but under 73 mm	A	21 cm and over but under 23 cm
61 mm and over but under 67 mm	B	19 cm and over but under 21 cm
56 mm and over but under 61 mm	C	17.5 cm and over but under 19 cm
51 mm and over but under 56 mm	D [1]	16 cm and over but under 17.5 cm

The minimum size allowed for the 'Extra' Class is 17.5 cm (circumference) and 56 mm (diameter).

Sizing is compulsory for all classes.

[1] In the European Community the marketing of size D is not allowed from 1 July to 31 October.

Element IV Provisions concerning tolerances

Tolerances are exceptions to the classification of qualities or sizes that are accepted by the standard within the margins specified. Quality tolerances have general structure as presented in Element IVA and illustrated by Law boxes 15.13 and 15.14. Law box 15.13 shows that a rule laid down in a standard can be interpreted by someone in the food production chain to his advantage but against the words and the intention of the standard.

Law text box 15.13. An interpretation of the tolerances that are a part of the Agricultural Quality Standards (Source: Found in an interpretative footnote to Article IV A. of the Geneva Protocol, Revised Geneva Protocol on Standardization of Fresh Fruit and Vegetables and Dry and Dried Fruit, published 1958 and revised 1985).

Article IV. Provisions concerning tolerances

A. Quality tolerances

A certain percentage, by number of weight, of product not fulfilling the quality requirements of the class concerned may be allowed in each package, but in general this tolerance shall not exceed 5 per cent in the 'Extra' class or 10 per cent in classes I and II.

Footnote 1 in the original

The packer/exporter should do everything possible to ensure that the produce arrives at its destination in good condition. He should therefore refrain from deliberately exploiting the full tolerances indicated above as they are only to allow for material or human errors which may occur in packing, handling or transport.

The example presented in the Law boxes 15.14 to 15.16 is also about interpretation of standards and the position taken by some governments to make certain that there cannot be room for unwanted interpretations. The example of Law box 15.14 is taken from the group of processed fruit and vegetables. This group is not as well developed as the FFV group but is made by the same organisation using the same procedures and techniques. Note in Law text boxes 15.14 and 15.15 the specific technical know-how needed to appreciate the finesses. Note too the reservations made by Germany and Switzerland. Compare these Law text boxes with Law text box 15.16 for the effects of an EU regulation on the German position with regard to the aspects 'mould' and 'insect damage'.

Law text box 15.14. Conflict between the UNECE Standard DF-11 Dried grapes and the national legislations of Germany and of Switzerland on tolerances for produce affected by mould, or the presence of dead or living insects (Source: UNECE Standard DF-11 concerning the marketing and commercial quality control of dried grapes moving in international trade between and to UNECE member countries).

UNECE Standard DF-11 Dried grapes adopted 1992

IV. Provisions concerning tolerances

Tolerances in respect of quality shall be allowed in each package for produce not satisfying the requirements of the class indicated, are given in the following tables:

A. Quality tolerances

Seedless

Tolerances for defective fruit

Permitted defects 3 Class Extra Class Class	**Percent by weight**			**By count**		
	Extra Class	**Class I**	**Class II**	**Extra Class**	**Class I**	**Class II**
Pieces of stem (per kg)	-	-	-	1	2	2
Capstem (per cent)	-	-	-	4	5	5
Immature and/or undeveloped berries	2	3	4	-	-	-
Berries having seeds in seedless types (per cent)	-	-	-	0.1	0.5	0 1
Mouldy [4]	2	3	4	-	-	-
Insect damaged [4]	0.5	0.5	1	-	-	-
Damaged	3	4	5	-	-	-
Sugared	8	12	15	-	-	-
Extraneous vegetable material	0.01	0.03	0.04	-	-	-
Mineral impurities	0.01	0.01	0.01	-	-	-

[4] (Original footnote 4): The national legislations of Germany and of Switzerland do not permit tolerances for produce affected by mould, or the presence of dead or living insects.

Law text box 15.15. Definitions of defects: Mouldy and Insect damage in UNECE Standard DF-11 Dried grapes (Source: Annex II Definitions of defects of UNECE Standard DF-11 concerning the marketing and commercial quality control of dried grapes moving in international trade between and to UNECE member countries).

UNECE Standard DF-11 Dried grapes adopted 1992	
Piece of Stem	Any portion of branch or main stem of the vine which that is not a capstem
Capstem	Small woody stem exceeding 3 mm in length which attached the grape to the branch of the bunch and whether or not attached to a dried grape
Mouldy	Mould filaments visible to the naked eye
Insect damage	Visible damage caused by insects and animal parasites, or the presence of dead insects or insect debris

Law text box 15.16. EU Quality tolerances for Seedless grapes on Mould and Insect damage (Source: Annex Commission Regulation (EC) 1666/1999 … as regards the minimum marketing characteristics for certain varieties of dried grapes).

Annex Commission Regulation 1666/1999

4. Tolerances

The tolerances in respect of quality allowed in each package for produce not satisfying the requirements for the class indicated are as follows:

Seedless

Permitted defects	**Tolerances for defective fruit**	
	Percent by weight	**By number**
Pieces of stem (per kg)	-	2.00
Pedicels (%)	-	5.00
Immature and/or undeveloped berries	4.00	
Berries having seeds in seedless types		1.00
Mouldy	4.00	-
Insect damaged	1.00	-
Damaged	5.00	-
Sugared	15.00	-
Extraneous vegetable material	0.03	-
Mineral impurities	0.03	-

Element IVA: Quality tolerances

1. Extra Class defined as five percent by number or weight not satisfying the requirements of the class, but meeting fully the requirements of Class I or, exceptionally, its tolerances.
2. Class I defined by ten percent by number or weight not satisfying the requirements of the class, but meeting those of Class II or, exceptionally, coming within the tolerances of that class.
3. Class II defined by the presence of ten percent by number or weight satisfying neither the requirements of the class nor the minimum requirements, with the exception of produce affected by rotting or any other deterioration rendering it unfit for consumption.

UNECE Standard DF-11 concerning the marketing and commercial quality control of dried grapes moving in international trade between and to UNECE member countries led to the differences between the consensus of all UNECE members except Germany and Switzerland (see Law text boxes 15.14-15.16).

Element IVB: Size tolerances

Tolerances in respect of quality and size are allowed in each package (or in each lot for produce presented in bulk) for produce not satisfying the requirements of the class indicated, on condition. For all classes, 10% by number or weight corresponding to the size immediately above and/or below that indicated on the package, with a minimum of 190 g in the smallest size range.

Element VA: Provisions concerning presentation - uniformity
The contents of each package must be uniform and contain only products of the same origin, variety and/or commercial type, quality and size. For Extra Class, colour and ripeness should be uniform. The visible part of the contents of the package must be representative of the entire contents.

Element VB: Provisions concerning presentation - packaging
Packaging must protect the produce properly. The materials used inside the package must be new, clean, and of a quality such as to avoid causing any external or internal damage to the produce. The use of materials, particularly of paper or stamps bearing trade specifications is allowed, provided the printing or labelling has been done with non-toxic ink or glue.

Element V: Presentation
The function of presentation is illustrated by the change of Regulation 782/2007 in Law box 15.17.

Law text box 15.17. Abolishing compulsory indication of the number of units on the package label (Source: Official Journal of the European Union).

Commission Regulation (EC) No 782/2007 of 3 July 2007 amending Regulation (EC) No 634/2006 laying down the marketing standard applicable to headed cabbages, Official Journal L 174, 4 July 2007, p. 7.

The commission of the European Communities,

Having regard to the Treaty establishing the European Community,

Having regard to Council Regulation (EC) No 2200/96 of 28 October 1996 on the common organisation of the market in fruit and vegetables [1], and in particular Article 2(2) thereof,

Whereas:

1. The provisions on labelling in the marketing standard for headed cabbages laid down in Commission Regulation (EC) No 634/2006 [2] provide for the compulsory indication of the number of units on the package.
2. To facilitate trade and given the fact that headed cabbages are generally sold by weight and not by number of units, that requirement should be abolished.
3. Regulation (EC) No 634/2006 should therefore be amended accordingly.
4. The measures provided for in this Regulation are in accordance with the opinion of the Management Committee for Fresh Fruit and Vegetables,

has adopted this regulation:

Article 1

The second indent of point 6.1.D of the Annex to Regulation (EC) No 634/2006 is hereby deleted.

Article 2

This Regulation shall enter into force on the 20th day following its publication in the Official Journal of the European Union.

This Regulation shall be binding in its entirety and directly applicable in all Member States.

Done at Brussels, 3 July 2007.

For the Commission
Mariann Fischer Boel
Member of the Commission

[1] OJ L 297, 21.11.1996, p. 1. Regulation as last amended by Commission Regulation (EC) No 47/2003 (OJ L 7, 11.1.2003, p. 64).

[2] OJ L 112, 26.4.2006, p. 3

Element VI: Provisions concerning marking

A compilation of some of these rules in Law text box 15.18 makes the meaning of this part of the model standard clear. It also shows the differences made between the stages in the food production chain and the differences in national legislation on the identification of the persons involved with packing or dispatching the produce.

Law text box 15.18. Provisions concerning marking.

VI. Provisions concerning marking

Each package[1] must bear the following particulars, in letters grouped on the same side, legibly and indelibly marked, and visible from the outside:

A. Identification

Packer	)	Name and address or
and/or	)	officially issued or
Dispatcher	)	accepted code mark.[2]

B. Nature of produce
- 'Peaches' or 'Nectarines', if the contents are not visible from the outside
- Colour of the flesh
- Name of the variety (optional).

C. Origin of produce
- Country of origin and, optionally, district where grown, or national, regional or local place name.

D. Commercial specifications
- Class
- Size expressed in minimum and maximum diameters or minimum and maximum circumference, or according to the code size out in section III 'Provisions Concerning Sizing'
- Number of units (optional).

E. Official control mark (optional)

Published 1961 – Revised 1994, 2003, 2004

[1] (Original Footnote): Package units of produce prepacked for direct sale to the consumer shall not be subject to these marking provisions but shall conform to the national requirements. However, the markings referred to shall in any event be shown on the transport packaging containing such package units.

[2] (Original Footnote): The national legislation of a number of countries requires the explicit declaration of the name and address. However, in the case where a code mark is used, the reference 'packer and/or dispatcher (or equivalent abbreviations)' has to be indicated in close connection with the code mark, and the code mark should be preceded by the ISO 3166 (alpha) country/area code of the recognising country, if not the country of origin.

15.6 Control

15.6.1 International aspects

International agreement on the need for and contents of agricultural quality standards is expressed by the Geneva Protocol. It is confirmed by each accepted product standard. International cooperation involves the United Nations system through the Economic Commission for Europe and the Codex Alimentarius Commission. On the world regional scale two other international organisations have been actively involved in the creation, dissemination, explanation and revision of the standards. The Organisation for Economic Cooperation and Development OECD will probably leave this field of activities but the EU has laid the foundation in Regulation 1234/2007 for more standards than before.

At this junction it will be fitting to review briefly the control mechanisms that form the backbone of rules and standards. At the end the standard will be back at the beginning.

15.6.2 International commitment

The activities in the four international organisations underline the commitments of the participating states and the EU. Commitment without control is of little use. Standards have a certain built in control as everything that does not fit the standard cannot participate in the standardised activity. Standards are made to give rewards. EU standards go further: they do not limit participation, they exclude legal existence. Control is needed to square the facts with legal non-existence. The FFV standards are even more control dependent because they are made to replace one type of border control by another more convenient form. For the EU controls extend to the whole market. Substandard fruit and vegetables is not allowed to be on the road.

To make control feasible two general measures set the stage on which control has to be applied. First of all rules have been made to limit the scope of the standard to the regional collecting centres and further on along the food production chain. Primary producers moving products to the regional collecting and dispatch centres move outside the standard. Secondly, for all the movements from the regional centres and further, everyone caught with the produce is presumed to be the knowing and responsible person, the holder.

The EU-based checks follow the food production chain except the last stage, the sale at the retail point to the consumer. The member states have the responsibility to provide fitting inspections at that point.[647] The EU applies the same standard to products on the internal market, for export and for import.

15.6.3 Inspection

The inspection methods prescribed in Regulation 1580/2007 Annex VI are a combination of document inspections, inspection of the goods and matching of document and product. Document inspections follow the paper trail of certificates that are transported with the goods, registers and the digital food prints that supply or supplant the paper part of the trail.

Inspection of the goods is performed by taking samples and by physical inspection of the fruit or vegetable and the presentation, marking and packaging. The samples will be taken at random from different points in the quantity of the produce. For packed produce the number of packages determines the number of the packages that must be taken for inspection, running from 5 out of a hundred to minimal 15 out of more than a thousand. It is based on statistics and the standard's rule that the produce is presented in a way that secures that the visible part of the produce represents the complete quantity.[648]

The physical check of the packaging and presentation tests the packaging and the material used in the package for suitability, cleanness and other specifications of the standard. The marking is tested against the prescripts of the standard and the accuracy with which it is performed. Packaging and marking are interdependent and require a definition of the pre-packed foodstuff.

15.6.4 Finding of non-conformity and self-checks

When the inspector finds fresh fruit or vegetables that do not meet the obligations specified in the marketing standard, a finding of non-conformity will be sent to the trader. Several actions and reactions will follow upon that finding. The

[647] Article 20(1)(2nd paragraph), Regulation 1580/2007.

[648] Annex VI point 2, Regulation 1580/2007.

wanting produce may not be moved without the authorisation of the inspection. The trader can decide to bring the shipment into conformity. The inspection will investigate the produce to establish that the failures have been repaired. The produce may not be marketed as long as the inspection body is verifying the facts.[649] When the trader wants to bring the products to another member state to 'bring them into conformity' there, the inspector can allow that but will see to it that the member states will cooperate to ensure that all goods will enter the EU in conformity with the standard.

The inspector can allow alternative uses for the sub-standard products such as animal feed, industrial processing, other non-food uses, but when every alternative has been tried and has failed, the inspector can order the trader to take adequate measures to ensure that the products can not be used as food.[650]

Traders who meet the conditions set by the EU on facilities, trained personnel and an excellent record of conformity can get a self-control certificate. The EU assumes that the products handled by these traders conform to regulations. Double checks by the EU serve to keep the EU informed and the trader on track.

15.6.5 Checks by exporting country

The EU conformity checks can be transferred to exporting third countries. National governments have to present a request to the EU. The EU and the requesting country negotiate the terms of this special relationship.

The Commission has to approve the conformity checking operations of the third country. Commission Regulation 1580/2007 contains the essential conditions that must be met. The third country government has to appoint the official authority that will be responsible for the checking operations and for the contacts with the EU.[651] Its inspection bodies must provide satisfactory guarantees, and they must have the necessary personnel, equipment and facilities to carry out the checks according to the methods described in Annex VI.[652]

The EU decision to accept self checking of the exporting country is made through the Comitology procedure laid down in Article 46 of Regulation (EC) No 2200/96. The exporting country must apply the Community marketing standards, or at least equivalent standards for products exported to the Community.

649 Article 20(3)(2nd paragraph), Regulation 1580/2007.

650 Article 20(3)(4th paragraph), Regulation 1580/2007.

651 Article 13(2)(2nd paragraph), Regulation 1580/2007.

652 Regulation (EC) No 1580/2007 Chapter II Checks on conformity to marketing standards Section 3 Checks performed by third countries, Article 13(1) Approval of checking operations performed by third countries prior to import into the Community.

The list of countries whose checks on conformity have been approved by the EU can be found in Part A of Annex IV. Details of their official authorities and inspection bodies are set out in Part B and the models for the certificates in Part C. Law text box 15.19 presents the nine states that have attained this special position.[653]

Law text box 15.19. The EU accepts the checks on quality standard conformity of 9 countries (Source: Commission Regulation 1580/2007/EC Annex IV).

The countries whose Checks on Conformity Have Been Approved Under Article 13 Part A: List of Countries and Products Concerned	
Country	**Products**
Switzerland	Fresh fruit and vegetables other than citrus fruit
Morocco	Fresh fruit and vegetables
South Africa	Fresh fruit and vegetables
Israel	Fresh fruit and vegetables
India	Fresh fruit and vegetables
New Zealand	Apples, pears and kiwi fruit
Senegal	Fresh fruit and vegetables
Kenya	Fresh fruit and vegetables
Turkey	Fresh fruit and vegetables
Regulation (EC) No 1580/2007 Chapter II Checks on conformity to marketing standards Section 3 Checks performed by third countries, Article 13(1) Approval of checking operations performed by third countries prior to import into the Community.	

15.6.6 Certificates

The inspection bodies of the approved states have to draw up a certificate of conformity for each lot that they check before it enters the Community customs territory. The specifics of this certificate are prescribed by Regulation 1580/2007. The standard is set out in Annex III.[654] See Law text box 15.20 for a part of the requirements.

[653] Article 13(4) and Annex IV, Regulation 1580/2007.

[654] Article 14(1) and Annex III Regulation 1580/2007.

Law text box 15.20. The certificate of conformity (Source: Article 14(2) Certificates Regulation (EC) No 1580/2007).

Article 14(2) Certificates Regulation (EC) No 1580/2007
2. The certificate shall bear the word 'original'.
Where additional copies are required, they should be stamped with the word 'copy'. The competent authorities in the Community shall accept as valid only the original of the certificate.
The form shall measure 210 × 297 mm; a tolerance of up to plus 8 mm or minus 5 mm in the length may be allowed. The paper used shall be white, not containing mechanical pulp, sized for writing and shall weigh not less than 40 g/m^2. The forms shall be printed and completed in one of the official languages of the Community.

The standard forms of the certificates are established by Comitology decisions.[655] The Commission and the third country can decide to apply a different lay out. Article 14(2) prescribes: The certificate shall bear the word 'original'. This use of the quality standard is also its original, tolerance included.

15.6.7 Concluding remarks

The essential aspect of the quality and marketing standards is that they close the market for produce that does not match the requirements. Terminology on standards in EU documents has changed over the years from common quality standard via quality standard to marketing standard. Is this a change of words or a change of instrument? Comparing the standards over the entire period for the fresh fruit and vegetables group shows clearly that the instrument has not changed. But the use of the instrument did change in two ways.

The first could hardly have surprised the EEC member states but they had to see it happen first. The standards were introduced during the transition period when the common market was being made. Their use then is similar to their use now on a larger scale with perhaps a different perspective. The uncertainty between the member states at that time was probably greater than the uncertainty between WTO member states today. The EEC member states applied before and during the transition period the same type of international trade instruments to each other's trade as were used between WTO member states only recently or are used still today. But the EEC countries had no precedent of a successful economic integration of national economies in peace time. The experiences of the German states before 1870 with economic integration were an example, but one that carried Bismarck's mark of wars of aggression against Denmark to increase Prussian influence with German territory, and a war against a fellow great power

[655] Article 13(1) Regulation 1580/2007.

to create the German empire with a Prussian emperor. Not the framework one would wish to establish a menu of safe quality fruit and vegetables, let alone the integration of entire economies.

As a matter of fact, the fruit and vegetable standards were used by the EEC to relax national restrictions on trade between the member states to create the common market. Customs duties and quantitative restrictions on imports between member states were abolished with a special status for products graded under the common quality standards. The reduction of restrictive measures was linked by a time table to the increased use of the quality standards. Removal of protection would be applied to the produce in the sequence from produce of the highest grades first to lower grades later.[656] The same rules were applied to measures having an effect equivalent to quantitative restrictions on import.

Member states could reinstate protective measures in the reverse order when the market suffered a crisis. They were not allowed to apply these emergency measures to produce of the 'extra' class, but they could ask the Commission to authorise it.[657] Member states had to notify the Commission and each other of the measures they had taken at the latest on the day they were applied. The Commission would consult the Comitology management committee and issue an emergency measure with detailed instructions to the member states. Any member state could ask the Council to reconsider the Commission decision. That request had to be made within three working days. The Council would meet without delay.[658]

Member states had to reduce the inevitable damages caused by the closing of the border by keeping the border open for goods in transit that is not destined for the importing country. They had to take special measures to limit the damage for traders whose products were stranded at the border.

The principle of community preference meant that every protective measure that would have consequences for the trade between the member states had to be applied first to third countries.[659] The imports from these countries could be suspended but also be charged by a countervailing duty. A member state could apply these measures and they would be taken over by the institutions of the EEC.[660]

---

[656] Article 8 and 9 EEC Council Regulation No 23 on the progressive establishment of a common organisation of the market in fruit and vegetables. Official Journal 30, 20 April 1962, pp. 965-988.
[657] Article 10(1)(second paragraph), 10(4) and 9(2)(a) Regulation 23 of 1962.
[658] Article 10(2) and 10(3) Regulation 23 of 1962.
[659] Article 10(5) Regulation 23 of 1962.
[660] Article 11 Regulation 23 of 1962.

The regulation made these measures available when the serious disturbances on the market were caused by imports from third countries. A complex situation with different views about cause and effect could raise the same disputes on fact and rules that in the past divided the member states of the EU and nowadays the WTO.

The second change in the use of the standards is related to the changed environment created by the common market and the quality standards. It explains a preference for the marketing aspect.

The standards were used in the process described above with effects for member states and third countries that have consequences for the meaning of the words export and import. The EU has to differentiate between countries that are external foreign countries outside the common customs border and the internal foreign countries. These terms are used to stress the point that with the EU things are different now than they were before the EEC. The words export and import have two meanings nowadays, although strictly speaking only exports and imports across the common customs border take place under conditions that are expressed by these words. Exports from Italy to the Netherlands are as little and as much exports as exports from Rotterdam to Amsterdam.

As the EEC created its common market and common external customs border it would create a paradox. The standards used between the member states to create the common market would disappear with its growing presence. According to the original design the standards could only remain in trade across the customs border. Moving this border outward to include a larger part of the surface of the earth made the EU no different from countries with a large population living on a large territory. Europeans just needed some time to get used to the idea.

There is no plan to lay down a law that creates the obligation to use an instrument only according to its original design. For many UNECE members and many more Codex Commission members standards remain export related instruments that guarantee export quality. And production for export quality does not necessarily mean that the same standard applies to the produce sold in the country. For the EU the quality standard is applied to all trade everywhere.

The preferred use of the name marketing standard indicates a willingness to apply the instrument in a wider field than the one used by the FFV team. Such wider use has a track record of its own, but not as extensive, yet. A wider use also means more distance from the typical quality aspects of fresh fruit and vegetables. Where does one encounter a quality test like this:

Law text box 15.21. Common quality standard for garlic in EEC Regulation 10/1965.

C. Classification

(i) 'Extra' Class

Garlic of this class must be of superlative quality and of a colour typical of the commercial type.

(...)

(ii) Class I

Garlic of this class must be of good quality.

The bulbs must be:

- whole
- of fairly regular shape and of a colour typical of the commercial type to which they belong.

They may have: (...)

- small tears in the outer skin of the bulb.

(...)

(iii) Class II

Garlic in this class must be of marketable quality. It must satisfy the minimum requirements but may display the following blemishes:

- tears in the outer skin of the bulb

16. International food law[661]

16.1 Introduction

The European Union is not an island. The EU engages on a large scale in trade with third countries. Food is one of the largest product sectors of trade, both in tonnes and in turnover.[662] On the global level the World Trade Organisation[663] (WTO) tries to remove barriers to trade not unlike the way the EU has tried to remove these kinds of barriers from the internal market.

To achieve this, several measures have been taken. Tariff barriers were reduced and to the extent that this was successful non-tariff barriers became more of a concern. The basic treaty addressing trade in goods is the General Agreement on Tariffs and Trade (GATT). The GATT recognises that certain exceptions to free trade can be necessary to protect higher values like health and (food) safety.

In the food trade differences in technical standards like packaging requirements may cause problems, but it is mostly concerns about food safety, human health, animal and plant health that induce national authorities to take measures which may frustrate the free flow of trade. To address these concerns two WTO treaties were concluded: the Agreement on Technical Barriers to Trade (the TBT Agreement) and the Agreement on the Application of Sanitary and Phytosanitary Measures (the SPS Agreement).

The SPS Agreement was drawn up to ensure that countries only apply measures to protect human and animal health (sanitary measures) and plant health (phytosanitary measures) based on the assessment of risk, or in other words, based

---

661 Many thanks to Isabel Cachapa Rodrigues for her suggestions regarding this chapter.

662 According to the WTO International Trade Statistics 2007 (p. 38) as from 2005 the EU is the world's leading exporter of agricultural products (80% of which is food). For a hyperlink see the reference list.

The White Paper on Food Safety has the following to say on the agro-food sector in the EU (COM (1999) 719 final, p, 5): 'The agro-food sector is of major importance for the European economy as a whole. The food and drink industry is a leading industrial sector in the EU, with an annual production worth almost 600 billion €, or about 15% of total manufacturing output. An international comparison shows the EU as the world's largest producer of food and drink products. The food and drink industry is the third largest industrial employer of the EU with over 2.6 million employees, of which 30% are in small and medium enterprises. On the other hand, the agricultural sector has an annual production of about 220 billion € and provides the equivalent of 7.5 million full-time jobs. Exports of agricultural and food and drink products are worth about 50 billion € a year. The economic importance and the ubiquity of food in our life suggest that there must be a prime interest in food safety in society as a whole, and in particular by public authorities and producers'. Note that these figures do not include the 12 new Member States who joined the EU since 1 May 2004.

663 Established 1 January 1995 by the Agreement Establishing the World Trade Organization as the result of the so-called Uruguay round of trade negotiations and signed in Marrakesh on 15 April 1994 (WTO Agreement). The WTO is the institutional continuation of the General Agreement on Tariffs and Trade 1947 (GATT).

on science. The SPS Agreement incorporates, therefore, safety aspects of foods in trade. The TBT Agreement covers all technical requirements and standards (applied to all commodities), such as labelling, that are not covered by the SPS Agreement. Therefore, the SPS and TBT Agreements can be seen as complementing each other. In this chapter we will limit our attention to the SPS Agreement.

16.2 The World Trade Organisation

16.2.1 Structure

The WTO is different things at different times. It is a platform for negotiation on world trade, but it is also a system of law. This system of law comprises a so-called 'single undertaking'. This means that once accord has been reached on certain agreements, states have to accept the whole package or nothing at all. They cannot pick and choose. There are three major domains: trade in goods, governed by the General Agreement on Tariffs and Trade (GATT), trade in services, governed by the General Agreement on Trade in Services (GATS) and intellectual property rights, governed by the Agreement on Trade Related Aspects of Intellectual Property Rights (TRIPs). For food law GATT is the most important of these agreements.

To a certain extent the WTO is a supranational organisation. The treaties concluded between its members are binding. There is the Dispute Settlement Understanding, providing an arbitration procedure to resolve conflicts.[664] If a party wants to present a conflict, a Dispute Settlement Body (DSB) is formed to arbitrate on the basis of WTO law. If a party does not agree with the decision of the DSB, it can take the case to an Appellate Body (AB). The WTO does not have powers to enforce decisions taken in this arbitration procedure. It can condone however that if the decision reached is not implemented by the party found at fault,[665] the winning party may implement economic sanctions. These sanctions usually take the form of additional import levies on goods from the state found at fault. If the levies are condoned by the DSB (or the AB), setting them does not in itself constitute an infringement of WTO obligations. Diagram 16.1 represents the structure of the WTO. The WTO is not a large international organisation with institutions like the EU. It only has a permanent secretariat in Geneva.

[664] See the Understanding on Rules and Procedures Governing the Settlement of Disputes. For a hyperlink see reference list.

[665] An important case involving the EU is the so-called EU Biotech case. The de facto moratorium on GM food in several EU Member States was found to constitute an infringement. For hyperlinks on this case see reference list. See on this case: Dario Bevilacqua, the EC-Biotech Case, EFFL 1/6/2006, pp. 331-347.

Diagram 16.1. Structure of the WTO.

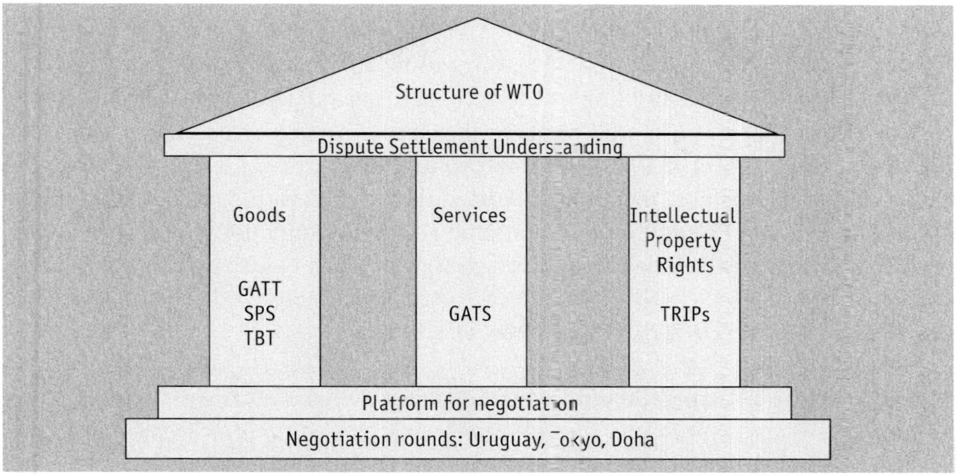

16.2.2 GATT

The GATT predates the WTO. It entered into force in 1947. By means of the GATT 1994, the GATT 1947 was included as an annex in the WTO Agreement.[666] GATT aims to liberalise international trade by setting equal treatment of all trading partners as the norm.[667] The GATT recognises, however, the necessity to make exceptions. The most important exceptions can be found in Article XX (general exceptions) and Article XXI (security exceptions). Food law, as we have seen previously, aims to protect consumer health. As a consequence the most important exception to international free trade from a food law point of view is the protection of health. This exception can be found in Article XX(b) of the GATT. See Law text box 16.1. The exception given for the protection of human, animal or plant life or health has been further elaborated in the SPS Agreement.

Law text box 16.1. Article XX(b) GATT on (phyto)sanitary measures.

Article XX: General Exceptions

Subject to the requirement that such measures are not applied in a manner which would constitute a means of arbitrary or unjustifiable discrimination between countries where the same conditions prevail, or a disguised restriction on international trade, nothing in this Agreement shall be construed to prevent the adoption or enforcement by any contracting party of measures:

(a) (...);

(b) necessary to protect human, animal or plant life or health;

(...)

[666] WTO Agreement, Annex 1A: Multilateral Agreements on Trade in Goods.

[667] Most favoured nation clause (Article I GATT).

16.2.3 The Agreement on the Application of Sanitary and Phytosanitary Measures

As follows from the above, the SPS Agreement is very important from a food safety point of view. The SPS Agreement recognises and further elaborates on the right of the parties to this agreement to take sanitary and phytosanitary measures necessary for the protection of human, animal or plant life or health, provided that such measures are not inconsistent with the provisions of this agreement. The measures must be scientifically justified and they may not be discriminating, nor constitute disguised barriers to international trade (Law text box 16.2).

Law text box 16.2. Article 2(2) SPS agreement on science.

Agreement on the application of sanitary and phytosanitary measures

Members,

Reaffirming that no Member should be prevented from adopting or enforcing measures necessary to protect human, animal or plant life or health, subject to the requirement that these measures are not applied in a manner which would constitute a means of arbitrary or unjustifiable discrimination between Members where the same conditions prevail or a disguised restriction on international trade;

...

Article 2

Basic Rights and Obligations

1. Members have the right to take sanitary and phytosanitary measures necessary for the protection of human, animal or plant life or health, provided that such measures are not inconsistent with the provisions of this Agreement.
2. Members shall ensure that any sanitary or phytosanitary measure is applied only to the extent necessary to protect human, animal or plant life or health, is based on scientific principles and is not maintained without sufficient scientific evidence, except as provided for in paragraph 7 of Article 5.[1]

(...)

[1] This provision probably stood as a model for the wording of the precautionary principle in Article 7 of the General Food Law. Article 5(7) SPS Agreement: In cases where relevant scientific evidence is insufficient, a Member may provisionally adopt sanitary or phytosanitary measures on the basis of available pertinent information, including that from the relevant international organisations as well as from sanitary or phytosanitary measures applied by other Members. In such circumstances, Members shall seek to obtain the additional information necessary for a more objective assessment of risk and review the sanitary or phytosanitary measure accordingly within a reasonable period of time.

If the measures are in conformity with international standards, no scientific proof of their necessity is required. These measures are by definition considered to be necessary (Law text box 16.3).

Law text box 16.3. Article 3(2) SPS Agreement on international standards.

Article 3
Harmonisation

1. To harmonise sanitary and phytosanitary measures on as wide a basis as possible, Members shall base their sanitary or phytosanitary measures on international standards, guidelines or recommendations, where they exist, except as otherwise provided for in this Agreement (...).
2. Sanitary or phytosanitary measures which conform to international standards, guidelines or recommendations shall be deemed to be necessary to protect human, animal or plant life or health, and presumed to be consistent with the relevant provisions of this Agreement and of GATT 1994.

(...)

The most important international standards regarding SPS are set by the so-called three sisters of the SPS Agreement (Law text box 16.4). The Codex Alimentarius Commission (CAC), the International Office of Epizootics (OIE)[668] and the Secretariat of the International Plant Protection Convention (IPPC). The standards on food and on food safety are mainly to be found in the so-called Codex Alimentarius.[669] In this book we will not discuss the other two sisters.

Law text box 16.4. The SPS's 'three sisters'.

SPS Agreement Annex A(3) Definitions

International standards, guidelines and recommendations

(a) for food safety, the standards, guidelines and recommendations established by the Codex Alimentarius Commission relating to food additives, veterinary drug and pesticide residues, contaminants, methods of analysis and sampling, and codes and guidelines of hygienic practice;

[668] The abbreviation follows the French spelling.

[669] The Agreement on Technical Barriers To Trade, (TBT Agreement) has similar articles. Article 2. on 'Preparation, Adoption and Application of Technical Regulations by Central Government Bodies' rules:
With respect to their central government bodies:
2.1 Members shall ensure that in respect of technical regulations, products imported from the territory of any Member shall be accorded treatment no less favourable than that accorded to like products of national origin and to like products originating in any other country.
2.2 Members shall ensure that technical regulations are not prepared, adopted or applied with a view to or with the effect of creating unnecessary obstacles to international trade (...)
(...)
2.6 With a view to harmonising technical regulations on as wide a basis as possible, Members shall play a full part, within the limits of their resources, in the preparation by appropriate international standardising bodies of international standards for products for which they either have adopted or expect to adopt, technical regulations.

(b) for animal health and zoonoses, the standards, guidelines and recommendations developed under the auspices of the International Office of Epizootics;
(c) for plant health, the international standards, guidelines and recommendations developed under the auspices of the Secretariat of the International Plant Protection Convention in cooperation with regional organisations operating within the framework of the International Plant Protection Convention; and
(d) for matters not covered by the above organisations, appropriate standards, guidelines and recommendations promulgated by other relevant international organisations open for membership to all Members, as identified by the Committee.

If no international standards apply or if measures are chosen that are stricter than the applicable international standards, the burden of proof is on the authority taking the measure. Scientific research will have to provide the proof required.

The European Union was confronted with this requirement in a dispute about meat from American cattle that had been treated with hormones. The Union refused to admit this meat to its market. The United States filed a complaint under the WTO, and was found to be in the right.[670] The Codex Alimentarius allows the use of a limited number of hormones under certain restrictions in cattle. The EU could not proof that their concern was science based.

16.3 Codex Alimentarius

16.3.1 General

What is this Codex Alimentarius that provides such important standards for international trade in food? In 1961 the Food and Agricultural Organisation (FAO) and the World Health Organisation (WHO)[671] established the Codex Alimentarius Commission (CAC). Over the years the CAC established specialised committees. These committees are hosted by member states all over the world. Some 175 countries, representing about 98% of the world's population, participate in the work of Codex Alimentarius.

Food standards are established through an elaborate procedure of international negotiations. Currently it comprises eight steps. A proposal is in the pipeline to reduce the number of steps to five (the first five indicated in Diagram 16.2).

[670] The WTO's appellate body ruled on 16 January 1998 (WT/DS48/AB/R). For a hyperlink see reference list. On this case see Dario Bevilacqua, The Codex Alimentarius Commission and its Influence on European and National Food Policy. EFFL 1/1/2006, pp. 3-16.
[671] On the contribution of the WHO to international food law, see also section 13.4.6 on the global alert system of the International Food Safety Network INFOSAN.

Diagram 16.2. Codex procedure for adopting standards and codes.

Steps	Procedures at each step
Step 1	Member government proposal submitted to a Codex committee
Step 2	Draft elaborated by a member government within the committee
Step 3	Draft circulated to members and international organisations for comments
Step 4	Draft with comments back to the committee
Step 5	Draft revised and submitted to the CAC for consideration
Step 6	Revised draft circulated to members and international organisations for comments
Step 7	Draft with comments considered by committee. CAC either adopts the code or sends it back to committee for revision
Step 8	CAC adopts the standard or code of practice, which is circulated to member countries and international organisations

All standards taken together are called '*Codex Alimentarius*'. In Latin this means 'food code'. It can be seen as a virtual book filled with food standards. The food standards represent models for national legislation on food.

Beside the food standards, Codex Alimentarius includes advisory provisions called codes of practice or guidelines. These codes of practice and guidelines mainly address food businesses.

At present the Codex comprises more than 200 standards, close to 50 food hygiene and technological codes of practice, some 60 guidelines, over 1,000 food additives and contaminants evaluations and over 3,200 maximum residue limits for pesticides and veterinary drugs. Finally, the Codex Alimentarius includes requirements of a horizontal nature on labelling and presentation and on methods of analysis and sampling.[672] The examples given here below show a certain familiarity from the point of view of EU food law.

16.3.2 Procedural Manual

The 'constitution' of the Codex Alimentarius is the Procedural Manual. The Procedural Manual not only gives the procedures and format for setting Codex Standards and Guidelines, but also some general principles and definitions (Law text

672 Susana Navarro and Richard Wood, Codex Deciphered, Leatherhead Surry UK, 2001, p. 1. On Codex Alimentarius, see also: FAO, Understanding The Codex Alimentarius, Rome 2005; Eddie Kimbrell, What is Codex Alimentarius, AgBioForum, Vol. 3 nr. 4, 2000, pp 197-202; FAO/WHO, Report of the Evaluation Of The Codex Alimentarius And Other FAO And WHO Food Standards Work. For hyperlinks see reference list. The most important book on the Codex Alimentarius, is probably the dissertation of: Marielle D. Masson-Matthee, The Codex Alimentarius Commission and Its Standards. An examination of the legal aspects of the Codex Alimentarius Commission. Asser Press, the Netherlands, 2007.

box 16.5). The principles relate among other things to the scientific substantiation of the work of Codex Alimentarius and the use of risk analysis for food safety (Law text box 16.6).

Law text box 16.5. Some definitions in the Codex Alimentarius Procedural Manual.

Food means any substance, whether processed, semi-processed or raw, which is intended for human consumption, and includes drink, chewing gum and any substance which has been used in the manufacture, preparation or treatment of 'food' but does not include cosmetics or tobacco or substances used only as drugs.
Food hygiene comprises conditions and measures necessary for the production, processing, storage and distribution of food designed to ensure a safe, sound, wholesome product fit for human consumption.
Food additive means any substance not normally consumed as a food by itself and not normally used as a typical ingredient of the food, whether or not it has nutritive value, the intentional addition of which to food for a technological (including organoleptic) purpose in the manufacture, processing, preparation, treatment, packing, packaging, transport or holding of such food results, or may be reasonably expected to result, (directly or indirectly) in it or its by-products becoming a component of or otherwise affecting the characteristics of such foods. The term does not include 'contaminants' or substances added to food for maintaining or improving nutritional qualities.

Law text box 16.6. Some principles in the Codex Alimentarius Procedural Manual.

Statements of Principle concerning the role of science in the Codex decision-making process and the extent to which other factors are taken into account

1. The food standards, guidelines and other recommendations of Codex Alimentarius shall be based on the principle of sound scientific analysis and evidence, involving a thorough review of all relevant information, in order that the standards assure the quality and safety of the food supply.
2. When elaborating and deciding upon food standards Codex Alimentarius will have regard, where appropriate, to other legitimate factors relevant for the health protection of consumers and for the promotion of fair practices in food trade.
3. In this regard it is noted that food labelling plays an important role in furthering both of these objectives.
4. When the situation arises that members of Codex agree on the necessary level of protection of public health but hold differing views about other considerations, members may abstain from acceptance of the relevant standard without necessarily preventing the decision by Codex.

16.3.3 Standards

The work of the CAC has resulted in a vast collection of internationally agreed food standards that are presented in a uniform format. Most of these standards are of a vertical nature. They address all principal foods, whether processed, semi-processed or raw. Standards of a horizontal nature are often called 'general standards', like the General Standard for the Labelling of Prepackaged Foods[673]

According to this general standard, the following information shall appear on the labelling of prepackaged foods:

- the name of the food; this name shall indicate the true nature of the food;
- list of ingredients (in particular if one of a list of 8 allergens is present);
- net contents;
- name and address of the business;
- country of origin where omission could mislead the consumer;
- lot identification;
- date marking and storage instructions;
- instructions for use.

16.3.4 Codes

In addition to the formally accepted standards the Codex includes recommended provisions called codes of practice or guidelines. There is, for example, a 'Code of Ethics for International Trade in Food',[674] and a set of hygiene codes like the 'Recommended International Code of Practice General Principles of Food Hygiene' and the 'Hazard Analysis and Critical Control Point (HACCP) System and Guidelines for its Application' (Law text box 16.7).

Law text box 16.7. The principles of HACCP according to Codex Alimentarius.

Principle 1	Conduct a hazard analysis.
Principle 2	Determine the Critical Control Points (CCPs).
Principle 3	Establish critical limit(s).
Principle 4	Establish a system to monitor control of the CCP.
Principle 5	Establish the corrective action to be taken when monitoring indicates that a particular CCP is not under control.
Principle 6	Establish procedures for verification to confirm that the HACCP system is working effectively.
Principle 7	Establish documentation concerning all procedures and records appropriate to these principles and their application.

673 CODEX STAN 1-1985 (Rev. 1-1991).
674 CAC/RCP 20-1979 (Rev. 1-1985).

16.3.5 Legal force

The Codex standards do not represent legally binding norms. They do slightly resemble the directives in European law in the sense that they present models for national legislation, however without the obligation to implement them. Member states undertake to transform the Codex standards into national legislation. However, no sanctions apply if they do not honour this undertaking.

One might ask what is the use of such non-binding standards. The answer comprises different elements. Generally nation states are reluctant to enter into internationally binding agreements because these limit their sovereignty. For this reason it turns out to be easier to agree on non-binding 'soft law' standards than on binding 'hard law'. By agreeing on non-binding standards, the participating states develop a common language. All states and other subjects of international law will mean the same thing when they meet to negotiate about food, they mean food as defined in the Codex. The same holds true for milk and honey and all the standards that have been agreed upon. The notion of HACCP has been developed – and is understood – within the framework of Codex Alimentarius.[675] In this way the Codex Alimentarius provides a common frame of reference, but there is more.

The mere fact that national specialists on food law enter into discussion on these standards will influence them in their work at home. A civil servant drafting a piece of legislation will look for examples. As regards food s/he will find examples in abundance in the Codex. In these subtle ways the Codex Alimentarius is likely to have a major impact on the development of food law in many countries even without a strict legal obligation to implement.

It turns out more than once that soft law has a tendency to solidify. Once agreements are reached parties tend to put more weight on them than was initially intended. In the following sections it will be shown that this is true for Codex standards as well. Due to several developments they are well on their way to acquiring at least a quasi-binding force.

16.3.6 WTO/SPS

As we have seen above, the inclusion of the Codex Alimentarius in the SPS Agreement, greatly enhances its significance. WTO members who follow Codex standards are liberated from the burden to prove the necessity of the sanitary and phytosanitary measures they take. If they cannot base their measures on Codex, they have to prove that their measures are science-based.

[675] Recommended International Code Of Practice General Principles Of Food Hygiene Cac/Rcp 1-1969, Rev. 3-1997, Amd. (1999).

For the food sector the practical result is that they have access to the majority of the world's markets if their products are up to Codex standard. It is much easier to apply Codex than to study and apply a whole range of differing national standards. The catch is that industry depends on their national governments to take action within WTO if they have to face trade barriers that do not comply with Codex. The EU provides the option for its businesses to call on the European Commission for support if they are confronted by trade barriers in third countries. See section 16.5.1.

16.4 European Union

Also in the context of European food law the Codex is increasing its legal impact. Again the European Court of Justice is the engine that propels progress. In its case law it uses Codex standards as an interpretation aid for open standards in European law. In the so-called Emmenthal cheese case, for instance, the Court was called upon to judge whether the definition of Emmenthal cheese in French legislation constituted a barrier to trade as interdicted in Article 28 of the EC Treaty.[676] The case concerned a French cheese trader who was prosecuted for attempting to sell a product as Emmenthal cheese that did not have a brown rind as required in the French standard for Emmenthal cheese. The Court decided that the French law was indeed in breach of Article 28 of the EC Treaty. In its reasoning the Court considered that the definition of Emmenthal in the Codex does not in all situations require a rind (Law text box 16.8). In other words: in cases like this, the Codex standard helps to define the limits that European law sets to national legislators.

Law text box 16.8. Codex Alimentarius used by the Court of Justice of the European Communities to define Emmenthal cheese, judgment 5 December 2000, case C-448/98.

32. In the case at issue in the main proceedings it should be noted that according to the Codex Alimentarius referred to in paragraph 10 of this judgment, which provides indications allowing the characteristics of the product concerned to be defined, a cheese manufactured without rind may be given the name Emmenthal since it is made from ingredients and in accordance with a method of manufacture identical to those used for Emmenthal with rind save for a difference in treatment at the maturing stage. Moreover it is undisputed that such an Emmenthal cheese variant is lawfully manufactured and marketed in Member States other than the French Republic.
33. Therefore even if the difference in the maturing method between Emmenthal with rind and Emmenthal without rind were capable of constituting a factor likely to mislead consumers it would be sufficient whilst maintaining the designation Emmenthal for that designation to be accompanied by appropriate information concerning that difference.

[676] At that time numbered 30.

34. In those circumstances the absence of rind cannot be regarded as a characteristic justifying refusal of the use of the Emmenthal designation for goods from other Member States where they are lawfully manufactured and marketed under that designation.
35. The answer to the question referred for a preliminary ruling must therefore be that Article 30 of the Treaty precludes a Member State from applying to products imported from another Member State where they are lawfully produced and marketed a national rule prohibiting the marketing of a cheese without rind under the designation Emmenthal in that Member State.

16.4.1 Codex in the General Food Law

The significance of the Codex Alimentarius is recognised in the General Food Law. In Article 13 the General Food Law lays emphasis on the importance of the development of international standards. More important however is Article 5, paragraph 3 of the General Food Law. Although this paragraph leaves a wide margin of appreciation for the national and EU legislators, it introduces an obligation to take international standards like Codex into account (Law text box 16.9).

Law text box 16.9. International standards for food law, Article 5(3) General Food Law.

Article 5(3) Regulation 178/2002
Where international standards exist or their completion is imminent, they shall be taken into consideration in the development or adaptation of food law, except where such standards or relevant parts would be an ineffective or inappropriate means for the fulfilment of the legitimate objectives of food law or where there is a scientific justification, or where they would result in a different level of protection from the one determined as appropriate in the Community.

This comes close to an obligation under European law for both the Union and the member states to include standards like the Codex in national and community food legislation. If this Article is indeed interpreted and applied in this way, this will mean a boost for the legal position of Codex standards in Europe. The General Food Law itself gives the proper example. The definition of food, which is the GFL's foundation, is based on the Codex Alimentarius (Law text box 16.10).

Law text box 16.10. Compare definition of 'food' in Codex Alimentarius Commission Procedural Manual with definition of 'food' in Article 2 General Food Law.

Codex Alimentarius - Procedural Manual, definitions for the Purposes of the Codex Alimentarius, page 49:

For the Purposes of the Codex Alimentarius:

Food means any substance, whether processed, semi-processed or raw, which is intended for human consumption, and includes drink, chewing gum and any substance which has been used in the manufacture, preparation or treatment of 'food' but does not include cosmetics or tobacco or substances used only as drugs.

Article 2 Regulation 178/2002

Definition of 'food'

For the purposes of this Regulation, 'food' (or 'foodstuff') means any substance or product, whether processed, partially processed or unprocessed, intended to be, or reasonably expected to be ingested by humans.

'Food' includes drink, chewing gum and any substance, including water, intentionally incorporated into the food during its manufacture, preparation or treatment. It includes water after the point of compliance as defined in Article 6 of Directive 98/83/EC and without prejudice to the requirements of Directives 80/778/EEC and 98/83/EC.

'Food' shall not include:

(a) feed;
(b) live animals unless they are prepared for placing on the market for human consumption;
(c) plants prior to harvesting;
(d) medicinal products within the meaning of Council Directives 65/65/EEC and 92/73/EEC;
(e) cosmetics within the meaning of Council Directive 76/768/EEC;
(f) tobacco and tobacco products within the meaning of Council Directive 89/622/EEC;
(g) narcotic or psychotropic substances within the meaning of the United Nations Single Convention on Narcotic Drugs, 1961, and the United Nations Convention on Psychotropic Substances, 1971;
(h) residues and contaminants.

This example is followed in later food legislation as well. The General hygiene regulation (852/2004), for example, states in its 15th consideration:

> *'The HACCP requirements should take account of the principles contained in the Codex Alimentarius'.*

Also the principle laid down in Article 6 GFL that food law shall be based on risk analysis can be understood in this context. If requirements of European food safety law are not in conformity with the Codex Alimentarius, sooner or later they will be contested under the SPS Agreement as barriers to international trade. They will only stand in the WTO forum if they are science based, that is, based on risk analysis.

16.4.2 The EU joins Codex

For over 40 years, the EU was not a member of the Codex Alimentarius Commission. It exercised its influence through its member states who were in Codex. On 17 November 2003[677] the logical next step was taken in the process of increasing recognition of Codex. The Council applied on behalf of the European Communities for membership of the Codex Alimentarius Commission. The EC is now a full member of the CAC.

16.5 Businesses and international trade disputes

16.5.1 The Trade Barriers Regulation

The WTO dispute settlement procedure is only accessible for the members of the WTO. Only states are members. The procedure is therefore not directly available for businesses. The EU, however, provides some relief.

On 1 January 1995 (the starting date of the WTO) Regulation 3286/94 the so-called Trade Barriers Regulation (TBR) came into force.[678] This regulation gives businesses,[679] their associations and EU member states the right to lodge a complaint with the European Commission against barriers to trade adopted or maintained by third countries. The complaint must show the existence of the measure, that it is contrary to international obligations and that it has adverse effects. If it is warranted by the Community interest, the Commission will investigate the case and – if the Commission agrees that an infringement of international (WTO) law has taken place – try to come to a solution either through negotiations or, if necessary, a dispute settlement procedure.

16.5.2 Damages

Economic sanctions in reaction to infringements of WTO-law usually take the form of punitive import duties on products from the country that was found at fault in the dispute settlement procedure. The products concerned are not necessarily those that profited from the trade barrier at issue. The businesses producing and exporting the products that are subject to these import duties are likely to

[677] Council decision 2003/822/EC. Official Journal L 309, 26 November 2003, p. 14. In this way point 83 in the Action Plan on Food Safety (Annex to the White Paper on Food Safety) has been implemented.

[678] Council Regulation (EC) No 3286/94 of 22 December 1994 laying down Community procedures in the field of the common commercial policy in order to ensure the exercise of the Community's rights under international trade rules, in particular those established under the auspices of the World Trade Organization. Official Journal L 349, 31 December 1994, p. 71). A brochure about the TBR is available on the internet. For a hyperlink see the reference list.

[679] Called 'community enterprise' if they complain about barriers to export and 'community industry' if they complain about barriers to import.

suffer damages. One could argue that these damages are caused by the actions of their authorities that constituted the illegal barrier to trade. The European Court of Justice has ruled that the EU is not liable for such damages caused by EU measures.[680] The possibility of being hit by such import duties is considered to be part of the normal risk of engaging in international trade.

16.6 Concluding remark

Unlike EU food law, international food law mostly exercises its influence on businesses (and consumers) in an indirect way. It sets requirements on states and provides procedures for states. Natural and legal persons depend on their states to comply and to take action.

680 See for example CFI 14 December 2005, case T-383/00, Beamglow Ltd vs. European Parliament, Council of the European Union and Commission of the European Communities, ECR 2005, II-05459.

17. Private food law[681]

17.1 Voluntary rules

In the course of this book we have encountered several types of rules on food with which there is no actual obligation to comply; they are in other words not binding or at least not made binding by legislation. This is true for example for the hygiene codes discussed in Chapter 11, for the codes of conduct discussed in Chapter 16 and also for quite a lot of other texts on food.

A food business may choose to apply such rules thinking this is a good way to comply with the mandatory requirements of the law (e.g. apply hygiene codes to comply with HACCP), that this may improve the safety or other quality aspects of the product or for many other reasons.

If the owner of a business decides to apply non-binding rules, this may establish an internal obligation: the premises owned by the concern and the people working there may come under the obligation to apply these rules. The legal mechanism behind such obligations may be found in property law (the owner has a say over his company), corporate law (the articles of association bind the partners in the company) or labour law (the labour contract gives the employer a certain power to impose duties upon the employee).

If a business communicates to its trading partners – its customers in particular – that it applies certain rules in the production of its products, this may become part of the offer it makes in the market: a guarantee that the product meets a certain level of quality as expressed in the rules applied to it(s production) If this feature is important to the customer it may become part of the contract between the producer and his customer. A contract is binding upon the parties to it. Therefore, if a set of rules not binding as such is included in a contract, it thus becomes binding for the parties to the contract.

Customers may require their suppliers to apply certain rules or to meet certain standards. If the suppliers agree, again this becomes part of the contract and thus a binding obligation. A contract requires mutual agreement. The specific content may be suggested by either party.

As long as there is no contract, there is no obligation to apply the non-binding rules. If most of the purchasers on the market (or a very powerful purchaser) make the application of certain rules a strict condition to enter into contractual relations, there still is no legal obligation for producers to apply these rules. They will know, however, that they can only acquire contracts if they are willing to

[681] Many thanks to Maria Litjens for ideas and inspiring discussion.

accept the obligation. In a way the obligation is in the air. It is hovering over the contracts yet to be concluded. Legally there is no obligation to apply the rules, but if you do not, you are out of business. In such a situation we may call the rules concerned 'de facto' binding. No obligation follows from the law (*de iure*) to comply with these rules, but such a necessity to do so follows from the facts in case (*de facto*) that in practice it feels like an obligation.

The combination of these elements – the power to create obligations by means of contracts and the power of certain players to dictate the terms of contract to such an extent that they have to be fulfilled even before the contract is concluded – forms the basis of a development where the private sector creates norms that apply to the food sector in addition to and even in competition with food law as discussed in the rest of this book. The legal foundation underlying the rest of this book is legislation e.g. public law. Contract is a part of private (civil) law.[682]

17.2 The legend of private standards

In Chapter 7 of this book, we have taken the position that many aspects of food law can only be understood if we take into account how it has developed historically. Also for private food law it helps to take its development into consideration. This development, however, is scattered and as yet largely unrecorded. For these reasons and for simplicity's sake, unlike Chapter 7 where we have elaborated history as it has actually occurred, in this chapter we will make a composition of developments that have taken place at diverse times and places or that could have taken place and weld this into a 'legend' of private food law that may help us to understand in the way history does.

One can imagine a development of contracts in the food chain from simple to complex. A simple contract states the identity, the quantity and price of the product to be sold by the vendor to the purchaser. The contract becomes more complex if it defines safety or other quality requirements like levels of contamination. Experience has shown that the safety of the product is influenced by the way it is handled (HACCP). The contract may therefore go beyond the product as such and include aspects of product handling, etc., etc.

[682] In this connection the expression 'self-regulation' is often applied. The interinstitutional agreement on better law-making of the European Parliament, Council and Commission (Official Journal C 321, 31 December 2003, p. 01), for example, defines self-regulation as: 'the possibility for economic operators, the social partners, non-governmental organisations or associations to adopt amongst themselves and for themselves common guidelines at European level (particularly codes of practice or sectoral agreements)'. While this definitions applies to most of the private schemes discussed in this chapter, we avoid the expression 'self-regulation'. In our opinion the word as well as the definition convey too much of an impression of harmony and mutual understanding while – as we will see – in practice the creation of private schemes may well be based on market power of some businesses and dependence of others. In such situations legal theory still recognises equality, but in common speech this word is likely to create an incorrect image.

Now one can imagine a second development. A company that has invested time and resources (maybe to pay for legal advice) in elaborating a complex contract and is happy with the results, will try to use the same provisions again. If this company has the bargaining power to impose the contractual provisions on its partners, it may start to use this contract as a model or even as general provisions to all the contracts it concludes.

It takes a lot of expertise to develop a good model. Consultants may come to the market or businesses may cooperate to develop model contracts of ever increasing quality. And isn't it much easier instead of exchanging huge stacks of paper every time a contract is concluded to simply indicate the model that applies? Today it is sufficient to indicate in the contract the identity, quantity and price of the product and to stipulate that it conforms to ISO 22.000, BRC or SQF.[683]

17.3 Chain orchestration

17.3.1 Contracts

The impact of the private scheme can go beyond the immediate contractual relation. A contract is a relation between two parties. The safety and quality of a food product supplied by one business to the next, may largely depend however on the way it has been dealt with earlier in the chain. So the customer depends on the agreements reached between his supplier and the previous supplier. S/he is however an outsider in this agreement. By demanding that in this relation a certain standard applies, a purchaser can exercise considerable influence on contractual relations upstream. A core issue, for example, in the fair trade scheme[684] is that the workers at the very beginning of the chain (employees and smallholders in third world countries) receive reasonable remuneration for their efforts. The businesses expressing this wish often are not the ones who have financial relations with these people. For this reason they demand their suppliers to provide proof (through certification) of applying fair conditions. In this way private standards can be used as an instrument for what is called 'chain orchestration'.

17.3.2 Vertical integration

Another approach to ensuring performance upstream in the chain – to which chain orchestration on the basis of contracts is the modern alternative – is through vertical integration. Businesses are vertically integrated if the different links of the chain are part of one concern. This can be achieved by setting up or acquiring businesses taking care of supply or to enter into a joint venture with a supplier. In

[683] The meaning of these abbreviations is explained hereafter.
[684] For hyperlink see reference list.

such situations, the legal instrument of governance is found in property and/or associations law.

17.4 Owning a scheme

The models described above represent a certain value. Sometimes the texts are available for free.[685] It can be in the interest of the businesses that apply it if they are easily accessible. It is also possible that access to the scheme is given only for payment.[686] The legal instrument that makes it possible to claim ownership of the text of the scheme is copyright. The copyright holder is entitled to decide on the conditions and price for circulation.

17.5 Enforcement

Generally speaking, legislation creates obligations towards the public authorities representing society as a whole. In case of non-compliance, sanctions may come as a consequence.

Contracts create obligations between parties and provide these parties with instruments to deal with non-compliance by the other parties. In case of non-compliance liability for damages arises, contractual relations may be ended and all kinds of consequences may arise that have been agreed upon in the contract (like contractual fines). The difference in consequence of non-conformity with public law and non-conformity with private law can make it sensible to create obligations by contract that are similar to or even the same as obligations that are also present in public law. We see for instance that all the major private food law schemes include the obligation to apply HACCP.

17.6 Audits

In the contractual relation it can be agreed that the customer has the right to visit the suppliers' premises to check if the agreed practices are being applied with the agreed results. Such inspection visits are generally known as 'audits'. It has been recorded that big production companies had special divisions where several people had full time jobs receiving auditors. In due course it was noted that all these auditors where checking for similar requirements. Along with the development described above where standard contracts were welded into harmonised and commonly used models, another development took place.

685 Like GlobalGAP.
686 Like ISO.

Instead of every customer of a certain producer auditing the producer it became accepted that one player would audit on behalf of all.[687] If the auditor considered the requirements of the applicable standard to be met, s/he would provide a certificate to the audited business to give it an instrument to communicate its compliance to its customers. In case the audit shows non-compliance, no certification is provided and/or the right to use the mark representing the certification is withdrawn. As a consequence the company can no longer do business with customers that demand certification.

In this way the formulation of norms, the inspection of their fulfilment and the proof of their fulfilment in the form of a certificate and the sanction on non-compliance in the form of withdrawal of certification developed into structures known as certification schemes. If the customers whom the certification communicates are other businesses, the certification scheme is called B-to-B (business to business). If the customers to are the final consumers, the certification scheme is called B-to-C (business to consumer).

17.7 Certification mark

Connected to a certification scheme is often a symbol that is owned by the owner(s) of the scheme. This ownership usually takes the form of a trademark. As we have seen in Chapter 2 the owner of a trademark has the right to allow or forbid its use by others. On this basis the owner has the legal power to impose compliance with the intended use as proof of fulfilment or sanction for non-compliance (Law text box 17.1).

Law text box 17.1. SQF on use of certification trade mark.

3 Conditions for using the SQF 2000 Certification Trade Mark

3.1 A producer shall, for the duration of its certification, prove to the satisfaction of SQFI[1] or the LCB[2] that its quality system satisfies the requirements set forth in the current edition of the SQF 2000 Code; and

3.2 A producer must only use the SQF 2000 Certification Trade Mark in accordance with its Certificate of Registration and these rules.

[1] SQF Institute (footnote added to the original text).

[2] Licensed Certification Body (footnote added to the original text).

[687] This player would be an independent third party trusted by all parties concerned. Three types of audits can be distinguished: one party audits (self-controls or internal audits), two party audits (audits by the customer) and third party audits (audits by auditors independent of both other parties).

17.8 Accreditation

It is considered of vital importance that certifying bodies can be trusted. To ensure this, schemes have been set up to certify the certifiers. Such schemes can be strictly private, but in many countries public authorities take an interest as well. In such countries, legislation is put in place setting standards for the recognition of certification.[688] On the basis of such standards, certifiers can ask for accreditation to prove to their customers that the product they deliver (e.g. proof of compliance with private standards) is up to standard.

Accreditation therefore is the official certification of certifiers often by or with the consent of public authorities.

17.9 Standard setting

In the legend described above the initiative to set up private schemes is placed with businesses holding a dominant position in the market. Initially these businesses were mainly the famous brand holders using certification to be able to ensure a constant product quality in order to uphold the reputation of the brand. Such brand-related quality schemes still play an important role. Of late, however, retailers' brands (the so-called private labels) have acquired a position on the market that has made them leaders in the creation of private food law. All the examples discussed below originate from retailer initiatives.

Private standards, however, are not always based on market power. They may also result from agreements reached with various stakeholders, for example in round tables. In particular, schemes dealing with general interests like protection of the environment and corporate social responsibility take account of opinions of third parties (third from the point of view of the parties to the contract to which the scheme applies) including NGOs.

17.10 Structure of private food law

The structure of private food law, as set out in the above, is summarised in Diagram 17.1. Rules have been agreed upon in the context of the standard setting organisation. This organisation is the owner (copyright holder) of these rules. The standard-setting organisation can consist of businesses using (or imposing) the standard, but it can also be independent. Connected to the rules can be a certification symbol protected as a trade mark. The standard-setting organisation

[688] On 14 February 2007, the European Commission published a proposal for a regulation on accreditation: Proposal for a Regulation of the European Parliament and of the Council setting out the requirements for accreditation and market surveillance relating to the marketing of products (COM(2007) 37 final). This proposal does not apply, however, to the food sector.

Diagram 17.1. The structure of private food law.

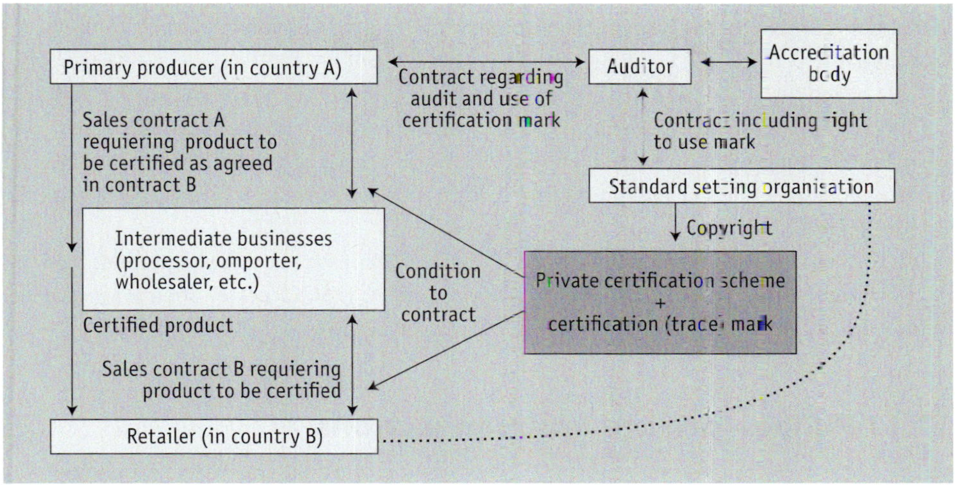

agrees (maybe through a licence contract or – as far as the rules are concerned – by putting them in the public domain) to the use of these rules and the trademark by auditors and food businesses. One of the actors in the chain decides on the applicability of the scheme. It includes the scheme in its contractual requirements and requires it to be included in contracts earlier in the chain as well. The auditor checks for compliance with the scheme, certifies (or refuses to certify) the audited business and decides to license (or withhold) the right to use the certification mark. The quality of the auditor in turn is assured through accreditation.[689]

17.11 Interconnected private schemes

Diagram 17.1 shows two contractual relations (representing a longer chain) where in each link the same private scheme applies. In practice also examples are found where the scheme applied in one link, requires another link to apply another scheme. In the Dutch dairy sector, for example, dairy producing businesses require dairy farmers to be certified (Law text box 17.2). The applicable certification scheme requires them to use as feed for milk-producing animals only products obtained from businesses certified for a certain feed quality scheme. In this way private food law obtains a web-like structure of interrelated schemes.

[689] Most private schemes require accreditation as laid down in the International Standard ISO/IEC Guide 65.

Law text box 17.2. Dutch HACCP on application of other schemes.

HACCP Certification Regulations 2006
Article 4
Where these regulations do not stipulate any other requirements with respect to the HACCP certification process, the certification bodies have to apply the procedures set in force for the certification of quality systems, that are accredited on the basis of EN 45012 or ISO/IEC Guide 62, excepting article 3.3. of ISO/IEC Guide 62. This article is replaced by article 5.3 of ISO/IEC Guide 66:1998.
With the information/application phase of the certification process, these regulations have to be submitted by the certification body to anyone requesting HACCP certification in accordance with clause 3.1.1.1 of EN 45012:1998 and ISO/IEC Guide 62:1996.

17.12 Public – private interconnections

Private schemes are not only interconnected among themselves, but also with public law. The vast majority of private certification schemes refers to public law requirements that have to be complied with. Less common but also existing is the inverse where public law provisions require compliance with private schemes. Legislation on community reference laboratories (see Chapter 11) or on methods of sampling (see Chapter 10) refer to private law technical standards. Yet another public law approach to private regulation is where legislation imposes upon stakeholders the duty to regulate for themselves. The most notorious example is the HACCP requirement in Regulation 852/2004. The very essence of HACCP is that a business sets up rules for its own processing. In the case of HACCP it is not a voluntary choice but a public law obligation that will be enforced by public authorities. Such situations are known as imposed self-regulation or enforced self-regulation.

17.13 Motives

What are the driving forces behind private food law? Probably they are too numerous to provide an exhaustive overview and motives may differ from stakeholder to stakeholder, but at least some points can be identified.

The motive mentioned in most private food schemes is food safety. Food safety is important for the protection of consumers, to comply with consumers wishes and also to comply with public law requirements.

Compliance with public law requirements can be a motive in itself. To comply with their own legal obligations, businesses depend on how the product has been dealt with upstream. Therefore they may want to ensure themselves with private law instruments that legal obligations are being complied with, or to impose these obligations on producers working in countries where different legal requirements apply, thus using private law to bridge the gap between different legal systems. Connected to compliance is liability. On the one hand businesses may try to pass on liability to other links in chain (some require insurance and guarantees from producers), on the other hand explicit agreements are a way to show that everything possible has been done to avoid non-compliance. In civil and criminal cases this may be used in what is called a due diligence defence.

Further private law is used to discourage the legislator from taking charge. If businesses solve problems there will be less urgency for the legislator to intervene. Businesses prefer private law to public law as it reflects their own wishes better and it is easier to change if the need arises. Also private law can be used to supplement or repair public law. As we have seen in Chapter 8, for example, public law on traceability is lacking in certainty as to whether internal traceability (within a business) is required. ISO 22.000 explicitly requires internal traceability. While EU legislation exempts the primary sector from HACCP, private schemes usually impose it on this sector as well.

As we have seen in Chapter 13, official controls are risk based and control intensity relates to compliance history. Certification may be an instrument to convince inspection agencies that the level of compliance is high and therefore the urgency for official controls low.[690]

Private standards that go beyond compliance, that is to say apply higher safety and/or quality standards than public law, may help a business to distinguish itself on the market and acquire a share of the (top end) market. Or, to phrase a similar thought differently, raising standards may be used to protect markets from competitors.

Finally, corporate social responsibility is a driving factor of private regulation. With a view to showing their commitment to contributing their part to sustainable development, businesses bind themselves to private schemes that elaborate on these interests.

17.14 Examples

Below are some examples of the private schemes that currently seem to be leading on the market.[691]

[690] On the stacking of private and official controls see: B.M.J. van der Meulen and A.A. Freriks, Millefeuille. The emergence of a multi-layered controls system in the European food sector, Utrecht Law Review, Vol. 2, No. 1, pp. 156-176, June 2006. For a hyperlink see the reference list.

[691] The overview is based on the information provided by the owners of these schemes. No critical comparison is intended at this stage of the research.

In our account of public food law in this book we have distinguished rules regarding the *product* (market approval and safety targets: Chapters 9 and 10), rules regarding the *process* (hygiene, traceability and risk management; Chapter 11), rules regarding the *communication* (mainly labelling: Chapter 12) and public powers (enforcement and incident management: Chapter 13). In private food law we find similar ingredients, but in a different mix. *Product* related rules mainly concern safety and quality targets. Rules on the *process* (hygiene, traceability and risk management) are the core. *Labelling* provisions will usually be limited to the use of the certification mark. The place public powers of inspection and enforcement hold in public food law, is taken in private food law by the powers granted by the businesses themselves to the auditors. The most important additions to the types of food rules we have encountered in public law, are provisions governing business organisation and management systems and provisions on information sharing within the food chain (so-called chain transparency).[692]

17.15 Good Agricultural Practices

17.15.1 GAP/GMP

Many private food safety systems are based on HACCP as described in Chapter 11 and some form of good practices, like good agricultural practices (GAP) or good manufacturing practices (GMP).

In the words of the UN Food and Agricultural Organisation FAO,[693] the concept of Good Agricultural Practices has evolved in recent years in the context of a rapidly changing and globalising food economy and as a result of the concerns and commitments of a wide range of stakeholders about food production and security, food safety and quality, and the environmental sustainability of agriculture. These stakeholders include governments, food processing and retailing industries, farmers, and consumers, who seek to meet specific objectives of food security, food quality, production efficiency, livelihoods and environmental benefits in both the medium and long term. GAP offers a means to help reach those objectives. Broadly defined, GAP applies available knowledge to addressing environmental, economic and social sustainability for on-farm production and post-production processes resulting in safe and healthy food (and non-food agricultural products). Many farmers

[692] On private schemes, see W. van Plaggenhoef, M. Batterink and J.H. Trienekens, International Trade and Food Safety. Overview of legislation and standards, Wageningen University 2003; Grace Chia-Hui Lee, Private Food Standards and their Impacts on Developing Countries, European Commission, DG Trade Unit G2; Margret Will and Doris Guenther, Food Quality and Safety Standards, as required by EU Law and the Private Industry With special reference to the MEDA countries' exports of fresh and processed fruits & vegetables, herbs & spices A Practitioners' Reference Book, 2nd edition GTZ 2007; Working Party on Agricultural Policies and Markets, Final Report on Private Standards and the Shaping of the Agro-Food System, OECD 2006; for hyperlinks see reference list.

[693] FAO Committee On Agriculture, Development of a Framework for Good Agricultural Practices, Seventeenth Session, Rome, 31 March-4 April 2003.

in developed and developing countries already apply GAP through sustainable agricultural methods such as integrated pest management, integrated nutrient management and conservation agriculture. These methods are applied in a range of farming systems and scales of production units, including as a contribution to food security, facilitated by supportive government policies and programmes.

GAP represents the state of the art in sustainable agriculture. Something similar is true for GMP. It is not law in itself,[694] but through private schemes it can acquire legal relevance.

17.15.2 HACCP

The version of HACCP described in Chapter 11, is the one codified in Regulation 852/2004 of the European Union. The version referred to in private schemes is often the one laid down in the Codex Alimentarius.[695] The former is based on the latter but it is not as elaborate. Through their inclusion in private schemes, the non-binding Codex acquires a measure of legal effect. Inclusion of HACCP in private schemes adds for European businesses applicability in sectors exempted from Regulation 852/2004 (the primary sector in particular), enforcement through private law instruments and visibility through certification.[696] For non-European businesses it brings an obligation that may not or not in the same way follow from their own public law system.

17.15.3 EurepGAP/GlobalGAP[697]

EurepGAP started in 1997 as an initiative by retailers belonging to the Euro-Retailer Produce Working Group (EUREP). British retailers in conjunction with supermarkets in continental Europe were the driving forces. They reacted to growing concerns of consumers regarding product safety, environmental and labour standards and decided to harmonise their own often very different standards for agricultural products.

[694] P.A. Luning, W.J. Marcelis and W.M.F. Jongen, Food Quality Management. A techno-managerial approach, Wageningen Academic, the Netherlands 2002, p. 225 refer to Good Practices as 'self-discipline'.

[695] The Codex Basic Text on hygiene, is a standard work comprising of: Recommended International Code of Practice General Principles of Food Hygiene CAC/RCP 1-1969, Rev. 4 (2003); Hazard Analysis and Critical Control Point (HACCP) System and Guidelines for its Application; Principles for the Establishment and Application of Microbiological Criteria for Foods CAC/GL 21 – 1997, and Principles and Guidelines for the Conduct of Microbiological Risk Assessment CAC/GL-30 (1999). For a hyperlink see the reference list.

[696] See for example the Dutch HACCP certification scheme (based in Apeldoorn, the Netherlands). See http://www.foodsafetymanagement.info.

[697] Information from the GlobalGAP website http://www.globalgap.org.

The development of common certification standards was also in the interest of producers. Those with contractual relations to several retailers explained that they had to undergo multiple audits against different criteria every year. With this in mind, EUREP started working on harmonised standards and procedures for the development of Good Agricultural Practices[698] in conventional agriculture including highlighting the importance of Integrated Crop Management and a responsible approach to worker welfare.

Over the next ten years a growing number of producers and retailers around the globe joined in with the idea as this matched the emerging pattern of globalised trading: EurepGAP began to gain in global significance. To align EurepGAP's name with the proposition as the pre-eminent international GAP standard and to prevent confusion with its growing range of public sector and civil society stakeholders, the Board decided to undertake the step to re-brand. It was considered a natural path and evolution that led EurepGAP to become GlobalGAP. The decision was announced in September 2007 at the 8th global conference in Bangkok.

GlobalGAP has established itself as a key reference for Good Agricultural Practices in the global market-place, by translating consumer requirements into agricultural production in a rapidly growing list of countries – currently more than 80 on every continent (Diagram 17.2).

GlobalGAP is a private sector body that sets voluntary standards for the certification of agricultural products around the globe. The aim is to establish one single standard for Good Agricultural Practice with different product applications capable of adapting to the whole of global agriculture. Governance is by a Board whose decisions are based on a structured consultation process. In the board retailers and suppliers are represented. Sector specific interests and multi-stakeholder input are consolidated to ensure global acceptance. Sector Committees discuss and decide upon product and sector specific issues. All committees have 50% retailer and 50% producer/supplier representation.

GlobalGAP is a pre-farm-gate standard, which means that the certificate covers the process of the certified product from farm inputs like feed or seedlings and all the farming activities until the product leaves the farm. GlobalGAP is a business-to-business label and is therefore not directly visible to consumers. Its certification is carried out by more than 100 independent and accredited certification bodies in more than 80 countries. It is open to all producers worldwide. GlobalGAP includes annual inspections of the producers and additional unannounced inspections.

[698] Hence the GAP part in the name.

Diagram 17.2. GlobalGAP structure. (Source: GlobalGAP Control Points and Compliance Criteria Plant Propagation Material March 2008.)

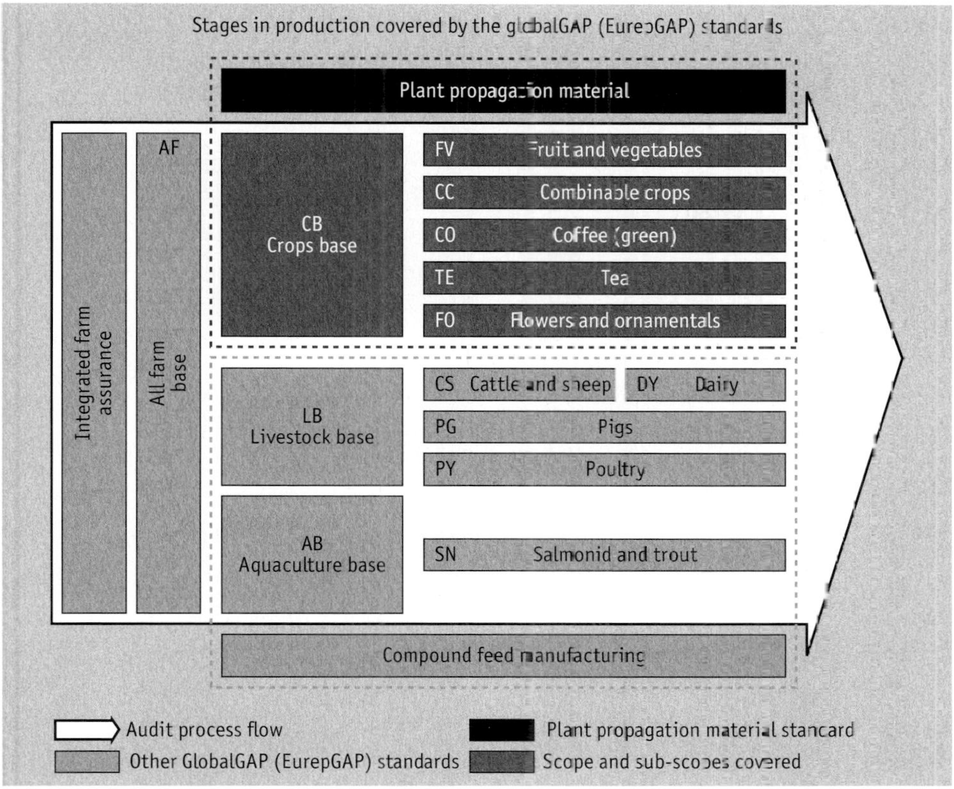

GlobalGAP consists of a set of normative documents. These documents cover the GlobalGAP General Regulations, the GlobalGAP Control Points and Compliance Criteria (from which Law text box 17.3 is taken) and the GlobalGAP Checklist.

Law text box 17.3. GlobalGAP on traceability and record keeping[699].

N° b	Control point	Compliance criteria	Level
PM 1	Traceability		
PM 1.1	Is GLOBALGAP (EUREPGAP) registered product traceable back to and trackable from the registered nursery (and other relevant registered areas) where it has been grown?	There is a documented identification and traceability system that allows GLOBALGAP (EUREPGAP) registered plants to be traced back by individual batch numbers which relate to customer orders, on a per batch basis to inputs (such as Seed Lot / Growing Media Batch / Growing or Germination Temperature Regimes / Crop protection materials applied / plant movements within the nursery) to the registered nursery, and tracked forward to the immediate customer. No N/A.	Major must
PM 1.2	Do all propagators have a documented procedure to manage the withdrawal of registered products from the market?	All propagators must have access to documented procedures which identify the type of event that may result in a withdrawal, persons responsible for taking decisions on the possible withdrawal of product, the mechanism for notifying customers and the GLOBALGAP (EUREPGAP) CB (if a sanction was not issued by the CB and the propagator or group recalled the products out of free will) and methods of reconciling stock. The procedures must be tested annually to ensure that it is sufficient. Procedure must be demonstrated.	Major must
PM 2	Record keeping and internal self-assessment		
PM 2.1	Are all records requested during the external inspection accessible and kept for a minimum period of time of two years, unless a longer requirement is stated in specific control points?	Propagators keep up to date records for a minimum of two years from the date of first inspection, unless legally required to do so for a longer period. No N/A.	Minor must
PM 2.2	Does the propagator take responsibility to undertake a minimum of one internal self-assessment per year against the GLOBALGAP (EUREPGAP) Standard?	There is documentary evidence that the GLOBALGAP (EUREPGAP) or benchmarked standard internal self-assessment under responsibility of the propagator has been carried out and are recorded annually. No N/A.	Major must
PM 2.3	Are effective corrective actions taken as a result of non-conformances detected during the internal self-assessment?	Effective corrective actions are documented and have been implemented. No N/A	Major must

[699] Source: GlobalGAP Control Points and Compliance Criteria Plant Propagation Material March 2008.

As many other on-farm assurance systems have been in place for some time prior to the existence of GlobalGAP, a way had to be found to encourage the development of regionally adjusted management systems and thus prevent farmers from having to undergo multiple audits. Existing national or regional farm assurance schemes can seek recognition as equivalent to GlobalGAP through independent benchmarking. The recognised schemes are represented in Diagram 17.2 as 'integrated farm assurance' (schemes).

The GlobalGAP standard is subject to a three year revision cycle of continuous improvement to take into account technological and market developments.

17.16 BRC[700]

In 1998 the British Retail Consortium (BRC based in London), responding to industry needs, developed and introduced the BRC Food Technical Standard to be used to evaluate manufacturers of retailers' own brand food products. In BRC the British supermarkets such as Tesco, Sainsbury, Safeway and Summerfield participate. In the early days each retailer inspected his own suppliers. These common efforts to inspect suppliers have huge cost advantages for retailers because a supplier fulfils the requirements of all British retailers once.

BRC is designed to be used as a pillar to help retailers and brand owners with their 'due diligence' defence, should they be subject to a prosecution by the enforcement authorities. Under EU food law, retailers and brand owners have a legal responsibility for their brands.

In a short space of time, the BRC Standard became invaluable to other organisations across the sector. It is regarded as a benchmark for best practice in the food industry. This and its use outside the UK has seen it evolve into a global standard used not just to assess retailer suppliers, but as a framework upon which many companies have based their supplier assessment programmes and manufacture of some branded products.

The majority of UK, and many European and global retailers, and brand owners will only consider business with suppliers who have gained certification to the appropriate BRC Global Standard (Law text box 17.4).

700 Information from BRC website http://www.brc.org.uk.

Law text box 17.4. BRC principle on management commitment[701].

2.1.1 Senior Management Commitment

Within a food business, food safety must be seen as a cross-functional responsibility, including activities that draw on many departments using different skills and levels of management expertise in the organisation. Effective food safety management extends beyond technical departments and must involve commitment from production operations, engineering, distribution management, procurement of raw materials, customer feed back and human resource activity such as training.

The starting point for an effective food safety plan is the commitment of senior management to the development of an all-encompassing policy as a means to guide the activities that collectively assure food safety. The Global Standard for Food Safety places a high priority on clear evidence of senior management commitment.

Following the success and widespread acceptance of the Global Standard – Food, the BRC published the first issue of the Packaging Standard in 2002, followed by Consumer Products Standard in August 2003, and finally by the BRC Global Standard – Storage and Distribution in August 2006. Each of these standards is regularly reviewed and each standard is fully revised and updated at least every 3 years after extensive consultation with a wide range of stakeholders.

17.17 IFS[702]

In 2002, in order to create a common food safety standard, German food retailers from the HDE (Hauptverband des Deutschen Einzelhandels) developed a common audit standard called International Food Standard or IFS. In 2003, French food retailers (and wholesalers) from the FCD (Fédération des entreprises du Commerce et de la Distribution) joined the IFS Working Group.

The aim of the IFS (now based in Paris) is to create a consistent evaluation system for all companies supplying retailer branded food products with uniform formulations, uniform audit procedures and mutual acceptance of audits, which will create a high level of transparency throughout the supply chain. The IFS defines requirements in content, procedure and evaluation of audits and a requirement profile for the certification bodies and auditors. The IFS standard (the so-called catalogue of requirements) consists of five parts called chapters:

- management of the quality system;
- management responsibility;

[701] From BRC Global Standard for Food Safety, issue 5 2008, section 2.1 Principles of the Global Standard for Food Safety.

[702] The information in this section has been taken from the IFS website http://www.food-care.info.

- resource management;
- product realisation;
- measurements, analyses, improvements.

The auditor will audit against the IFS standard which is divided into two levels plus recommendation on higher level. In the chapter 'Management of the quality system' requirements concerning the HACCP system, the HACCP team and the HACCP analysis are defined. It also contains rules for a quality manual to be applied and the obligation to keep reports and documents. The chapter 'Management responsibility' deals with the responsibility of the management, the management commitment, the management review and the customer focus. The chapter 'Resource management' addresses personnel issues (hygiene, medical screening) and staff facilities. Chapter 'Product realisation' is the most extensive one. It considers topics about e.g. specifications for products, factory environment, pest control, maintenance, traceability; GMOs and allergens. The last chapter, 'Measurements, analyses, improvements', deals with e.g. internal audit, all kind of controls during production steps, product analysis and corrective actions.

The requirements for auditors and the certification bodies are strictly regulated. All certification bodies shall have an accreditation against EN 45011 on IFS – International Food Standard. Only authorised auditors who have passed a written and oral examination can audit against the standard. The auditor shall have professional knowledge of the IFS. The auditors can only audit against their competence in a certain sector (at least 2 years professional experience in the specific sector or at least 10 audits in this sector). Finally, auditors who comply with these requirements shall only work for one IFS certification body accredited for auditing against the IFS.[703]

17.18 SQF[704]

Safe Quality Food (SQF; now based in Arlington USA) is an Australian initiative. Besides food safety, SQF focuses on product quality and stimulation of improvement strategies. The main goal of SQF is to control the whole chain. However SQF recognises that one standard does not work for all companies in the chain and that most present standards only work for big companies. Most procedures associated with the standards are too elaborate and laborious for small companies. So SQF developed two different norms, the SQF 1000 and the SQF 2000. The SQF 2000 Code was developed in consultation with the food industry and quality professionals. HACCP guidelines, as developed by the Codex Alimentarius Commission, form

[703] The question as to whether such requirement is compatible with competition law (Article 81 EC Treaty) is outside the scope of this book.

[704] The information for this section has been taken from the SQF 2000 Code 5th edition issued November 2005 and the SQF 2000 Certification Trade Mark rules for use 7th edition amended November 2005.

the basis of the Code. Unlike other well-recognised quality systems like BRC, HACCP and ISO 9000,[705] SQF combines a management quality system, like ISO 9000 and a food safety system (HACCP) with requirements for tracking and tracing. Besides the CCP, Critical Quality Points are also identified, which makes SQF an integrated system.

The SQF codes (in particular the 1000 and 2000 Code) provide the food sector (primary producers, food manufacturers, retailers, agents and exporters) with a food safety and quality management certification program that is tailored to its requirements and enables suppliers to meet regulatory, food safety and commercial quality criteria in a cost-effective manner. In 1994 the Code was developed and pilot programs implemented to ensure its applicability to the food sector. It was circulated in draft form for comment to experts in quality management, food safety, and food regulation, food processing, agriculture production systems, food retailing, food distribution and HACCP.

The Food Marketing Institute (FMI) acquired the rights to the SQF Program in August 2003 and has established the SQF Institute (SQFI) Division to manage the program. The SQF 2000 Code is recognised by the Global Food Safety Initiative[706] as a standard that meets its benchmark requirements.

The SQF 2000 Code can be used by all sectors of the food industry. The Code is an HACCP-based quality management system that encapsulates NACMCF[707] and CODEX HACCP Principles and Guidelines, proven methods used by the food industry to reduce the incidence of unsafe food reaching the marketplace (Law text box 17.5). It is designed to support industry or company branded product and to offer benefits to suppliers at all links in the food supply chain.

Law text box 17.5. SQF 2000 on HACCP (Edition 5 issued November 2005).

Appendix 2. Principles & Application of HACCP

(Adapted from Codex Alimentarius Commission – Recommended International Code of Practice General Principles of Food Hygiene, *CAC/RCP 1-1969, Rev. 4-2003*)

Preliminary Steps	1. Assemble HACCP team with expertise in product and processes 2. Describe product 3. Identify intended use 4. Construct flow diagram 5. Confirm flow diagram against process in operation (or planned process)

[705] On quality management in general. See section 17.19 for ISO 22.000 on food.
[706] Discussed in section 17.20.
[707] National Advisory Committee on Microbiological Criteria for Foods.

HACCP Principle	HACCP Application
1. Conduct a hazard analysis.	6 List all potential hazards associated with each step and consider any measures to control identified hazards.
2. Determine Critical Control Points (CCPs).	7. Determine CCPs.
3. Establish critical limit(s).	8. Establish critical limits and tolerance levels. Determine at what point critical limit is exceeded based on known limits or risk assessment if unknown.
4. Establish system to monitor control of CCP(s).	9. Establish a monitoring system for CCP that is able to detect loss of control i.e. when critical limits are exceeded. Consider continuous monitoring and/or periodic audit.
5. Establish corrective action to be taken when monitoring indicates CCP(s) are not under control.	10. Establish corrective actions that are able to deal with loss of control when it occurs and is capable of determining when CCP has been brought under control.
6. Establish procedures for verification to confirm that the HACCP system is working effectively.	11. Establish procedures for verification or audit that include review of HACCP system and records, records of deviations and actions taken in order to confirm that CCPs are kept under control.
7. Establish documentation covering all procedures and records appropriate to these principles and their application.	12. Documentation and record keeping should be appropriate to the nature and scale of the operation.

The SQF 2000 Code enables a supplier to demonstrate that they can supply food that is safe and that meets the quality specified by a customer. Certified SQF 2000 suppliers receiving raw materials from suppliers who have implemented the SQF 1000 Code can ensure that, through these complimentary systems product is traceable from the producer to the consumer.

The SQF 2000 Code also provides a mechanism for the food sectors of developing countries seeking to effectively enter the global food market to implement a management system that addresses their needs and the needs of their customers.

17.19 ISO 22.000[708]

The international organisation ISO (International Organization of Standardization) has decades of experience developing standards for many different types of applications. One of the most popular and most recognised is the Quality Management System standard ISO 9001. This standard was developed to provide a uniform standard worldwide for quality management. A buyer in one part of the world would have a degree of confidence in the quality practices of a registered company in another part of the world. This standard was used as the basis for other more specific standards for quality management in the automotive industry, the medical device industry, and the aerospace industry.

Now this approach has been taken for food safety management. ISO and its member countries used the Quality Management System approach, and tailored it to apply to food safety, incorporating the HACCP principles into the quality management system. The resulting standard is ISO 22.000.

ISO 22.000 requires that the business design and document a Food Safety Management System (FSMS). The standard contains the specific requirements to be addressed by the FSMS. Generally the standard addresses:

- Having an overall Food Safety Policy for the organisation, developed by top management.
- Setting objectives that will drive companies' efforts to comply with this policy.
- Planning and designing a management system and documenting the system.
- Maintaining records of the performance of the system.
- Establishing a group of qualified individuals to make up a Food Safety Team.
- Defining communication procedures to ensure effective communication with important contacts outside the company (regulatory, customers, suppliers and others) and for effective internal communication.
- Having an emergency plan.
- Holding management review meetings to evaluate the performance of the FSMS.
- Providing adequate resources for the effective operation of the FSMS including appropriately trained and qualified personnel, sufficient infrastructure and appropriate work environment to ensure food safety.
- Following HACCP principles.
- Establishing a traceability system for identification of product.
- Establishing a corrective action system and control of nonconforming product.
- Maintaining a documented procedure for handling withdrawal of product.

[708] www.22000-tools.com.

- Controlling monitoring and measuring devices.
- Establishing and maintaining an internal audit program.
- Continually updating and improving the FSFM.

17.20 GFSI[709]

The Global Food Safety Initiative (GFSI), co-ordinated by CIES (Comité International d'Entreprise à Succursales; The Food Business Forum), was launched in May 2000 as a reaction to the proliferation of private standards. Much of the advantages of private food law will be lost, if every important player in the marketplace defines a separate set of private standards.

GFSI started to benchmark private standards. This gives businesses the opportunity to send out the message in the market that for them it does not matter which particular standard is applied, as long as it is GFSI endorsed. In this way GFSI is developing into the standard of standards. The most powerful retailers in Europe, Asia and the USA have agreed to demand GFSI compliant certification for their own private label products. The GFSI mission is: continuous improvement in food safety management systems to ensure confidence in the delivery of safe food to consumers.

The GFSI objectives are to:
1. Converge food safety standards by maintaining a benchmarking process for food safety management schemes.
2. Improve cost efficiency throughout the food supply chain through the common acceptance of GFSI recognised standards by retailers around the world.
3. Provide a unique international stakeholder platform for networking, knowledge exchange and sharing of best food safety practices and information.

In the light of the plethora of food safety standards, the GFSI Task Force decided not to write a new standard. Instead, they compiled a set of 'Key Elements' to serve as the requirements against which existing food safety standards will be benchmarked. The 'Key Elements' as defined by the Task Force are:
1. Food Safety Management Systems.
2. Good Practices for Agriculture, Manufacturing and Distribution.
3. HACCP.

Under the umbrella of the Global Food Safety Initiative, seven major retailers have come to a common acceptance of four GFSI benchmarked food safety schemes. Retailers accept certificates based on standards in order to be able to make an assessment of their suppliers of private-label products and fresh products and

709 The information for this section has been taken from the GFSI pages on http://www.cies-net.com.

meat, to ensure that production is carried out in a safe manner. There are many of these standards and suppliers with many customers may be audited many times per year, at a high cost and with little added benefit.

The GFSI Guidance Document Version 5 (released September 2007) contains commonly agreed criteria for food safety standards, against which any food or farm assurance standard can be benchmarked. In addition to the 'key elements' the Guidance Document holds 'requirements for the delivery of food safety management systems' regarding certification and accreditation. GFSI does not undertake any accreditation or certification activities.

The benchmarking work undertaken by the standard owners and other key stakeholders on four food safety schemes (BRC, IFS, Dutch HACCP and SQF) has now reached a point of convergence. Each scheme has now aligned itself with common criteria defined by food safety experts from the food business, with the objective of making food manufacture as safe as possible. As a result, this will also drive cost efficiency in the supply chain and reduce the duplication of audits.

The GFSI vision of 'once certified, accepted everywhere' has now become a reality. Carrefour, Tesco, Metro, Migros, Ahold, Wal-Mart and Delhaize have agreed to reduce duplication in the supply chain through the common acceptance of any of the four GFSI benchmark schemes. The GFSI Foundation Board, a retailer-driven group, with manufacturer advisory members, provides the strategic direction and oversees the daily management. Membership of the Board is by invitation only.

The GFSI Technical Committee was formed in September 2006 and is composed of retailers, manufacturers, standard owners, certification bodies, accreditation bodies, industry associations and other technical experts. It provides technical expertise and advice for the GFSI Board and replaces a previous GFSI retailer-only Task Force. Membership of the Technical Committee is by invitation only.

A crucial moment in its development was the entry of Wal-Mart into the scheme (February 2008). Noteworthy is Wal-Mart's comment: 'GFSI Standards provide real time details on where suppliers fall short in food safety on a plant-by-plant basis and go beyond the current FDA[710] or USDA[711] required audit process'. Wal-Mart is the first US-based grocery chain to require GFSI, the company claims. The company has published a schedule to suppliers requiring completion of initial certification between July and December 2008, with full certification required by July 2009. Through GFSI benchmarking private food law seems to be achieving what public food law (through the Codex Alimentarius) never could: truly global harmonisation of food safety standards.

[710] Food and Drug Administration. The food regulatory agency in the USA.

[711] The US Department of Agriculture.

17.21 WTO

Private food law is rapidly replacing public law as the determining factor in international food chains. Within the WTO the question has been raised as to whether private standards constitute a new generation of trade barriers that member states of the WTO should take on.[712]

St. Vincent and the Grenadines, supported by Jamaica, Peru, Ecuador, and Argentina, complained that 'EurepGAP' SPS standards imposed by the Euro-Retailer Produce Working Group, composed primarily of food retailers, were more strict than EU governments' requirements. Referring to Article 13 of the SPS Agreement, which says that member governments 'shall take such reasonable measures as may be available to them to ensure that non-governmental entities within their territories (...) comply with the relevant provisions of this agreement,' these countries argue that only the public law EU rules should apply to the private sector (Law text box 17.6).[713]

Law text box 17.6. Article 13 SPS agreement.

Article 13
Implementation
Members are fully responsible under this Agreement for the observance of all obligations set forth herein. Members shall formulate and implement positive measures and mechanisms in support of the observance of the provisions of this Agreement by other than central government bodies. Members shall take such reasonable measures as may be available to them to ensure that non-governmental entities within their territories, as well as regional bodies in which relevant entities within their territories are members, comply with the relevant provisions of this Agreement. In addition, Members shall not take measures which have the effect of, directly or indirectly, requiring or encouraging such regional or non-governmental entities, or local governmental bodies, to act in a manner inconsistent with the provisions of this Agreement. Members shall ensure that they rely on the services of non-governmental entities for implementing sanitary or phytosanitary measures only if these entities comply with the provisions of this Agreement.

So far it is believed that Article 13 of the SPS Agreement aims at entities that in reality are governmental in a private law guise. The text, however, leaves room for the interpretation that it also applies to 'real' private actors. From a legal point of view there is a fundamental difference between the situation where a product may not be brought to the market (because it does not comply with public law requirements) and the situation where a product legally brought to the market

712 29-30 meeting of the Committee on Sanitary and Phytosanitary (SPS) Measures.

713 See ICTSD Bridges weekly news digest Volume 9 Number 24 6 July 2005 and Volume 7 Number 13, 6 July 2007.

is not bought by its intended customers (because it does not comply with these customers' private law requirements). From an economic point of view and for all practical purposes these two situations amount to the same thing where the customers concerned dominate the market.

This discussion pinpoints a weak aspect of private food law. It seems at present underdeveloped in checks and balances. It will be very interesting to follow the further developments!

18. Conclusion

Food law can not be understood in isolation of the general aspects of EU law. Nevertheless in several countries food law as a functional area of law has become an academic specialisation in its own right. From the 2000 White Paper on Food Safety onwards, a new body of food (safety) law has come to fruition in the EU. The (2002) General Food Law provides the general principles. The most important of these is a duty of care for food safety resting on food business operators. Food business operators have to address the legal limits to their liberty in the choice of raw materials, their obligations in organising their production processes and trade relations and the rules concerning their communication with consumers.

To study EU food law in further detail, it is helpful to distinguish substantive food law and procedural food law. The main part of substantive food law addressing food businesses consists of three types of rules: rules on the product, rules on the process and rules on the communication about food. Rules addressing public authorities grant them powers of enforcement and incident management.

Substantive rules have to function within the legal system that produces them. For food law and food safety law the legal environment has become increasingly international, which increases the complexity of the law. The actions of the Codex Alimentarius Commission and other United Nations' organisations have been sketched to indicate the many rules and actions on food law that originate at the international level outside the EU. These inputs have to be channelled through the complex of the Union and its member states. Their internal relations both in lawmaking and policy development and execution have been described and were found to be in perpetual change. The shift in legislative instruments from directives to regulations signals a centralisation of food law at the EU level with less room for national adaptation.

Substantive rules need procedures for their implementation. In this book some procedures have been discussed, mainly in the context of pre-market approval of food. Attention has been given to enforcement, both under public law and private liability law.

Scholars and practitioners in food law may want to keep their eyes wide open for developments in the private sector. It may well be that private food law, in particular at the global level, will make a bid for the dominant position currently held by public food law as a framework for food business relations.

On the following pages the reader will find some suggestions (websites and books) for further reading on the subjects discussed in this book.

Websites

Agricultural Research Service of the US Department of Agriculture – http://www.ars.usda.gov

Codex Alimentarius Commission – www.codexalimentarius.net

Commission of the European Communities – http://ec.europa.eu/

Comitology register – http://ec.europa.eu/transparency/regcomitology/registre.cfm?CL=en

Community Register of approved food establishments – http://ec.europa.eu/food/food/biosafety/establishments/list_en.htm

Council – http://www.consilium.europa.eu

Council of Europe – www.coe.int

Court of Auditors – http://eca.europa.eu/portal/page/portal/eca_main_pages/home

Court of Justice of the European Communities – http://curia.eu.int

DG Sanco – http://ec.europa.eu/food/

European Committee for Standardization – www.cen.eu

European Council – http://www.consilium.europa.eu

European Court of Human Rights – www.echr.coe.int

European Food Law Association – www.efla-aeda.org

European Food Safety Authority – www.efsa.europa.eu

European Institute for Food Law – www.food-law.nl

European Parliament – http://www.europarl.europa.eu/

European Parliament's legislative Observatory – http://www.europarl.europa.eu/oeil/index.jsp

European Union – http://europa.eu/

FAOLEX Legal Database – http://faolex.fao.org/

Food and Agricultural Import Regulations and Standards (FAIRS) Reports – http://useu.usmission.gov/agri/fairs.html

Food and Agriculture Organisation – www.fao.org

Foodlaw-Reading – www.rdg.ac.uk/foodlaw/

Forum of European Food Law Enforcement Practitioners – www.flep.org

Global Agriculture Information Network (GAIN) – http://www.fas.usda.gov/scriptsw/AttacheRep/default.asp

Institut für Angewandtes Lebensmittel- und Futtermittelrecht – www.ifal.eu

International Court of Justice – www.icj-cij.org

International Food Law Students Forum – http://moose.nimio.info/foodlaw/

International Food Policy Research Institute – www.ifpri.org

International Portal on Food Safety, Animal and Plant Health – www.ipfsaph.org

Joint FAO/WHO Expert Committee on Food Additives – http://jecfa.ilsi.org

Law and Governance Group Wageningen University – www.law.wur.nl

Nederlandse Vereniging voor Levensmiddelenrecht (Dutch Food Law Association) – www.nvlr.nl

Porte d'Europe, information on EU integration – www.portedeurope.org

SANCO Stakeholder Involvement – www.sanco-stakeholderinvolvement.eu.

Standing Committee on the Food Chain and Animal Health – http://ec.europa.eu/food/fs/rc/scfcah/index_en.html

Survey of EC food legislation – http://europa.eu/eur-lex/en/lif/reg/en_register_133014.html

Treaty Series, United Nations – http://untreaty.un.org

UNECE Working Party on Agricultural Quality Standards – http://www.unece.org/trade/agr/welcome.htm

United Nations – www.un.org

United Nations System (access to UN organisation) – http://www.unsystem.org/

United Nations Treaty Series – http://untreaty.un.org

USEU – http://useu.usmission.gov/agri/usda.html

World Health Organisation – www.who.int

World Intellectual Property Organization – www.wipo.int

World Trade Organisation – www.wto.org

Suggestions for further reading

Alemanno, A., Trade in Food: Regulatory and Judicial Approaches in the EC and the WTO, Cameron May 2007.

Broberg, M.P. Transforming the European Community's Regulation of Food Safety, Sieps Stockholm 2008 (hyperlink in reference list).

Codex Alimentarius Commission, Procedural Manual, 17th ed. Rome, 2007 (hyperlink in reference list).

Eide, W.B. and Kracht, U., Food and Human Rights in Development. Vol. I Legal and Institutional Dimensions and Selected Topics, Itersentia Antwerpen – Oxford, 2005.

Eide, W.B. and Kracht, U., Food and Human Rights in Development. Vol. II. Evolving Issues and Emerging Applications, Itersentia Antwerpen – Oxford, 2007.

European Food & Feed Law Review, Lexxion Berlin (hyperlink in reference list).

FAO/WHO, Understanding The Codex Alimentarius, Rome, 2005 (hyperlink in reference list).

Food and Agriculture Organization of the United Nations, 'Voluntary Guidelines to support the progressive realization of the right to adequate food in the context of national food security', Rome 2005. (hyperlink in reference list).

Goodburn, K. (ed.), EU food law. A practical guide Cambridge, 2001 (hyperlink in reference list).

Holland, D. and Pope, H., EU Food Law and Policy, The Hague, 2004.

Jongen, W.M.F. and Meulenberg, M.T.G., Innovation in Agri-Food systems. Product quality and consumer acceptance, Wageningen 2005.

Kent, G., Freedom from Want. The Human Right to Adequate Food, Georgetown University Press 2005.

Korver, O., Kühn, M.C. and Richardson, D., The Functional Foods Dossier: Building Solid Health Claims, Bennekom (The Netherlands), 2nd ed 2006.

Lugt, M., Enforcing European and National Food Law in the Netherlands and England Lelystad, 1999.

Luning, P.A., Devlieghere, F. and Verhé, R., Safety in the agri-food chain Wageningen Academic Publishers, 2006.

MacMaolain, C., EU Food Law. Protecting Consumers and Health in a Common Market, Hart Publishers 2007.

Masson-Matthee, M.D. The Codex Alimentarius Commission and Its Standards, Asser Press The Hague, 2007.

Malanczuk, P., Akehurst's Modern Introduction to International Law, 7th ed. London, 1997.

Navarro, S. and Wood, R., Codex Deciphered, Leatherhead Surry UK, 2001.

O'Rourke, R., European food Law, 3rd ed., Sweet & Maxwell, 2005.

Roosevelt, F.D. Four Freedoms Address to the USA Congress, January 6, 1941 (hyperlink in reference list).

Somsen, H., The Regulatory Challenge of Biotechnology. Human Genetics, Food and Patents, Cheltenham : Edward Elgar Publishing Limited, 2007 (Biotechnology Regulation Series).

Senden, L.A.J., Soft Law in European Community Law, Oxford, 2004.

United Nations Human Rights Committee on Economic, Social and Cultural Rights, General Comment nr. 12 (hyperlink in reference list)

Van den Bossche, P., Schrijver, N. and Faber, G., Unilateral Measures Addressing non-Trade Concerns, Ministry of Foreign Affairs, The Hague 2007 (hyperlink in reference list).

Van der Meulen, B.M.J., The Right to Adequate Food. Food Law between the Market and Human Rights, The Hague, 2004.

Verbruggen, R., The regulatory status of Additives, Processing Aids, and Enzymes in the EU and in Codex Alimentarius, In: World Food Regulation Review, 2003 pages 14-20.

Vos, E., EU Food Safety Regulation in the Aftermath of the BSE Crisis, Journal of Consumer Policy23, pages 227-255, Deventer, 2000.

Vos, E. and Wendler, F. (eds.) Food Safety Regulation in Europe. A comparative Institutional Analysis, Intersentia Antwerpen - oxford 2006

Weatherill, S., Cases & Materials on EU Law, 6th ed., Oxford, 2003.

Wijnands, J.H.M, van der Meulen, B.M.J., Poppe, K.J. and Bremmers, H.J. Competitiveness of the European Food Industry. An economic and legal assessment, Luxembourg, Office for Official Publications of the European Communities, 2007 (hyperlink in reference list).

References

As far as available we have included hyperlinks to the documents quoted. These were operational when we finalised the manuscript on 1 August 2008, but they are subject to many changes. For your convenience the list is available on the websites of Wageningen Academic Publishers (www.wageningenacademic.com/foodlaw) and the European Institute for food law with active hyperlinks.

EU law

Legislation and soft law

Treaties and related texts

Charter of Fundamental Rights of the European Union http://eur-lex.europa.eu/JOHtml.do?uri=OJ:C:2007:303:SOM:EN:HTML

EC Treaty. http://eur-lex.europa.eu/LexUriServ/LexUriServ.do?uri=OJ:C:2006:321E:0001:0331:EN:pdf

Ioannina Accord. EEC Bulletin no. 3 1994, page 79. http://europa.eu/scadplus/glossary/ioannina_compromise_en.htm

Luxembourg Accord. EEC Bulletin no. 3 1966, page 5. http://europa.eu/scadplus/glossary/luxembourg_compromise_en.htm

Single European Act. Official Journal L 169 of 29 June 1987

Treaty of Amsterdam. http://europa.eu.int/eur-lex/lex/en/treaties/dat/11997D/htm/11997D.html

Treaty of Maastricht Official Journal C 191 of 29 July 1992. http://eur-lex.europa.eu/en/treaties/dat/11992M/htm/11992M.html

Treaty on European Union (Lisbon) http://eur-lex.europa.eu/JOHtml.do?uri=OJ:C:2008:115:SOM:EN:HTML

Treaty on the Functioning of the European Union (Lisbon). http://eur-lex.europa.eu/JOHtml.do?uri=OJ:C:2008:115:SOM:EN:HTML

Protocol on the application of the principles of subsidiarity and proportionality. Official Journal C 310, 16 December 2004, pp. 207-209.

Directives

EEC Council Directive on the approximation of the rules of the member states concerning the colouring matters authorised for use in foodstuffs intended for human consumption. Official Journal 115, 11 November 1962, pp. 2645-2654. http://eur-lex.europa.eu/LexUriServ/LexUriServ.do?uri=CELEX:31962L2645:EN:HTML

Council Directive 73/241/EEC on the approximation of the laws of the Member States relating to cocoa and chocolate products intended for human consumption. Official Journal L 228, 16 August 1973, pp. 23-35. consolidated version: http://eur-lex.europa.eu/LexUriServ/LexUriServ.do?uri=CONSLEG:1973L0241:19880101:EN:PDF

Council Directive of 19 December 1974 on the approximation of the laws of the Member States relating to the making-up by volume of certain prepackaged liquids (75/106/EEC). Official Journal L 42, 15 February 1975, p. 1. consolidated version: http://eur-lex.europa.eu/LexUriServ/LexUriServ.do?uri=CONSLEG:1975L0106:20040501:EN:PDF

Council Directive of 20 January 1976 on the approximation of the laws of the Member States relating to the making-up by weight or by volume of certain prepackaged products (76/211/EEC). Official Journal L 46, 21 February 1976, p. 1. consolidated version: http://eur-lex.europa.eu/LexUriServ/LexUriServ.do?uri=CONSLEG:1976L0211:19780929:EN:PDF

Council Directive 76/895/EEC of 23 November 1976 relating to the fixing of maximum levels for pesticide residues in and on fruit and vegetables. Official Journal L 340, 9 December 1976, pp. 26-31. http://eur-lex.europa.eu/LexUriServ/LexUriServ.do?uri=CELEX:31976L0895:EN:HTML

Council Directive 79/117/EEC of 21 December 1978 prohibiting the placing on the market and use of plant protection products containing certain active substances. Official Journal L 33, 8 February 1979, pp. 36-40. http://eur-lex.europa.eu/LexUriServ/LexUriServ.do?uri=CELEX:31979L0117:EN:HTML

Council Directive 80/778/EEC of 15 July 1980 relating to the quality of water intended for human consumption. Official Journal L 229, 30 August 1980, pp. 11-29. consolidated version: http://eur-lex.europa.eu/LexUriServ/LexUriServ.do?uri=CONSLEG:1980L0778:19950101:EN:PDF

Council Directive 81/602/EEC of 31 July 1981 concerning the prohibition of certain substances having a hormonal action and of any substances having a thyrostatic action. Official Journal L 222, 7 August 1981, pp. 32-33. http://eur-lex.europa.eu/LexUriServ/LexUriServ.do?uri=CELEX:31981L0602:EN:HTML

Council Directive 83/417/EEC of 25 July 1983 on the approximation of the laws of the Member States relating to certain lactoproteins (caseins and caseinates) intended for human consumption. Official Journal L 237, 26 August 1983, pp. 25-31. http://eur-lex.europa.eu/LexUriServ/LexUriServ.do?uri=OJ:L:1983:237:0025:012:EN:HTML

Council Directive 85/358/EEC of 16 July 1985 supplementing Directive 81/602/EEC concerning the prohibition of certain substances having a hormonal action and of any substances having a thyrostatic action. Official Journal L 191, 23.7.1985, pp. 46-49 http://eur-lex.europa.eu/LexUriServ/LexUriServ.do?uri=CELEX:31985L0358:EN:HTML

Council Directive 85/374/EEC of 25 July 1985 on the approximation of the laws, regulations and administrative provisions of the Member States concerning liability for defective products. Official Journal L 210, 7 August 1985, pp. 29-33. http://eur-lex.europa.eu/LexUriServ/LexUriServ.do?uri=CELEX:31985L0374:EN:HTML

Council Directive 86/362/EEC of 24 July 1986 on the fixing of maximum levels for pesticide residues in and on cereals. Official Journal L 221, 7 August 1986, pp. 37-42. http://eur-lex.europa.eu/LexUriServ/LexUriServ.do?uri=CELEX:31986L0362:EN:HTML

Council Directive 86/363/EEC of 24 July 1986 on the fixing of maximum levels for pesticide residues in and on foodstuffs of animal origin. Official Journal L 221, 7 August 1986, pp. 43-47. http://eur-lex.europa.eu/LexUriServ/LexUriServ.do?uri=CELEX:31986L0363:EN:HTML

Council Directive 88/146/EEC of 7 March 1988 prohibiting the use in livestock farming of certain substances having a hormonal action. Official Journal L 70, 16 March 1988, pp. 16-18. http://eur-lex.europa.eu/LexUriServ/LexUriServ.do?uri=CELEX:31988L0146:EN:HTML

Council Directive 88/299/EEC of 17 May 1988 on trade in animals treated with certain substances having a hormonal action and their meat, as referred to in Article 7 of Directive 88/146/EEC. Official Journal L 128, 21 May 1988, pp. 36-38. http://eur-lex.europa.eu/LexUriServ/LexUriServ.do?uri=CELEX:31988L0299:EN:HTML

Council Directive 88/344/EEC of 13 June 1988 on the approximation of the laws of the Member States on extraction solvents used in the production of foodstuffs and food ingredients. Official Journal L 157, 24 June 1988, pp. 28-33. consolidated version: http://eur-lex.europa.eu/LexUriServ/LexUriServ.do?uri=CONSLEG:1988L0344:19971223:EN:PDF

Council Directive 88/388/EEC of 22 June 1988 on the approximation of the laws of the Member States relating to flavourings for use in foodstuffs and to source materials for their production. Official Journal L 184, 15 July 1988). Corrected version in Official Journal L 345, 14 December 1988, pp. 29-29. Consolidated version: http://eur-lex.europa.eu/LexUriServ/LexUriServ.do?uri=CONSLEG:1988L0388:20031120:EN:PDF

Council Directive 89/107/EEC of 21 December 1988 on the approximation of the laws of the Member States concerning food additives authorized for use in foodstuffs intended for human consumption. Official Journal L 40, 11 February 1989, pp. 27-33. consolidated version: http://eur-lex.europa.eu/LexUriServ/LexUriServ.do?uri=CONSLEG:1989L0107:20031120:EN:PDF.

Council Directive 89/398/EEC of 3 May 1989 on the approximation of the laws of the Member States relating to foodstuffs intended for particular nutritional uses. Official Journal L 186, 30 June 1989, pp. 27-32. corrigendum in Official Journal L 275, 5 October 1990, p. 42. consolidated version: http://eur-lex.europa.eu/LexUriServ/LexUriServ.do?uri=CONSLEG:1989L0398:20031120:EN:PDF

Council Directive 89/662/EEC concerning veterinary checks in intra-Community trade with a view to the completion of the European market. Official Journal L 395, 30 December 1989, corrigendum in Official Journal L 151, 15 June 1990. consolidated version: http://eur-lex.europa.eu/LexUriServ/LexUriServ.do?uri=CONSLEG:1989L0662:20040430:EN:PDF

Council Directive 90/219/EEC of 23 April 1990 on the contained use of genetically modified micro-organisms. Official Journal L 117, 8 May 1990, pp. 1-14. http://eur-lex.europa.eu/LexUriServ/LexUriServ.do?uri=CELEX:31990L0219:EN:HTML

Council Directive 90/220/EEC of 23 April 1990 on the deliberate release into the environment of genetically modified organisms. Official Journal L 117, 8 May 1990, pp. 15-27. consolidated version: http://eur-lex.europa.eu/LexUriServ/LexUriServ.do?uri=CONSLEG:1990L0220:19970628:EN:PDF

Council Directive 90/425/EEC of 26 June 1990 concerning veterinary and zootechnical checks applicable in intra-Community trade in certain live animals and products with a view to the completion of the internal market. Official Journal L 224, 18 August 1990, pp. 29. consolidated version; http://eur-lex.europa.eu/LexUriServ/LexUriServ.do?uri=CONSLEG:1990L0425:20021119:EN:PDF

Council Directive 90/496/EEC of 24 September 1990 on nutrition labelling for foodstuffs. Official Journal L 276, 6 October 1990, pp. 40-44. consolidated version: http://eur-lex.europa.eu/LexUriServ/LexUriServ.do?uri=CONSLEG:1990L0496:20040109:EN:PDF

Council Directive 90/642/EEC of 27 November 1990 on the fixing of maximum levels for pesticide residues in and on certain products of plant origin, including fruit and vegetables. Official Journal L 350, 14 December 1990, pp. 71-79. consolidated version: http://eur-lex.europa.eu/LexUriServ/LexUriServ.do?uri=CONSLEG:1990L0642:20060216:EN:PDF

Commission Directive 91/321/EEC of 14 May 1991 on infant formulae and follow-on formulae. Official Journal L 175, 4 July 1991, pp. 35-49. http://eur-lex.europa.eu/LexUriServ/LexUriServ.do?uri=CELEX:31991L0321:EN:HTML

Council Directive 91/496/EEC of 15 July 1991 laying down the principles governing the organization of veterinary checks on animals entering the Community from third countries and amending Directives 89/662/EEC, 90/425/EEC and 90/675/EEC. Official Journal L 268, 24 |September 1991, pp. 56. consolidated version; http://eur-lex.europa.eu/LexUriServ/LexUriServ.do?uri=CONSLEG:1991L0496:20070101:EN:PDF

Council Directive 92/102/EEC of 27 November 1992 on the identification and registration of animals. Official Journal L 355, 5 December 1992, pp. 32-36. consolidated version: http://eur-lex.europa.eu/LexUriServ/LexUriServ.do?uri=CONSLEG:1992L0102:20050709:EN:PDF

Council Directive 93/43/EEC of 14 June 1993 on the hygiene of foodstuffs. Official Journal L 175, 19 July 1993, pp. 1-11. consolidated version: http://eur-lex.europa.eu/LexUriServ/LexUriServ.do?uri=CONSLEG:1993L0043:20031120:EN:PDF

Commission Directive 93/45/EEC of 17 June 1993 concerning the manufacture of nectars without the addition of sugars or honey. Official Journal L 159, 1 July 1993, pp. 133-133. http://eur-lex.europa.eu/LexUriServ/LexUriServ.do?uri=CELEX:31993L0045:EN:HTML

European Parliament and Council Directive 94/34/EC of 30 June 1994 amending Directive 89/107/EEC on the approximation of the laws of Member States concerning food additives authorized for use in foodstuffs intended for human consumption. Official Journal L 237, 10 September 1994, pp. 1-2. http://eur-lex.europa.eu/LexUriServ/LexUriServ.do?uri=CELEX:31994L0034:EN:HTML

European Parliament and Council Directive 94/35/EC of 30 June 1994 on sweeteners for use in foodstuffs. Official Journal L 237, 10 September 1994, pp. 3-12. consolidated version: http://eur-lex.europa.eu/LexUriServ/LexUriServ.do?uri=CONSLEG:1994L0035:20060815:EN:PDF

European Parliament and Council Directive 94/36/EC of 30 June 1994 on colours for use in foodstuffs. Official Journal L 237, 10 September 1994, pp. 13-29, corrigendum in Official Journal L 259, 7 October 1994, p. 33. http://eur-lex.europa.eu/LexUriServ/LexUriServ.do?uri=CELEX:31994L0036:EN:HTML

European Parliament and Council Directive No 95/2/EC of 20 February 1995 on food additives other than colours and sweeteners. Official Journal L 61, 18 March 1995, pp. 1-40. consolidated version: http://eur-lex.europa.eu/LexUriServ/LexUriServ.do?uri=CONSLEG:1995L0002:20060815:EN:PDF

Council Directive 96/22/EC of 29 April 1996 concerning the prohibition on the use in stockfarming of certain substances having a hormonal or thyrostatic action and of ß-agonists, and repealing Directives 81/602/EEC, 88/146/EEC and 88/299/EEC. Official Journal L 125, 23 May 1996, pp. 3-9. consolidated version: http://eur-lex.europa.eu/LexUriServ/LexUriServ.do?uri=CONSLEG:1996L0022:20031014:EN:PDF

Council Directive 96/43/EC of 26 June 1996 amending and consolidating Directive 85/73/EEC in order to ensure financing of veterinary inspections and controls on live animals and certain animal products and amending Directives 90/675/EEC and 91/496/EEC. Official Journal L 162, 1 July 1996, pp. 1-13. http://eur-lex.europa.eu/LexUriServ/LexUriServ.do?uri=CELEX:31996L0043:EN:HTML

Directive 97/4/EC of the European Parliament and of the Council of 27 January 1997 amending Directive 79/112/EEC on the approximation of the laws of the Member States relating to the labelling, presentation and advertising of foodstuffs. Official Journal L 43, 14 February 1997, pp. 21-23. http://eur-lex.europa.eu/LexUriServ/LexUriServ.do?uri=CELEX:31997L0004:EN:HTML

Directive 98/44/EC of the European Parliament and of the Council of 6 July 1998 on the legal protection of biotechnological inventions. Official Journal L 213, 30 July 1998, pp. 13-21. http://eur-lex.europa.eu/LexUriServ/LexUriServ.do?uri=OJ:L:1998:213:0013:0021:EN:PDF

Council Directive 98/81/EC of 26 October 1998 amending Directive 90/219/EEC on the contained use of genetically modified micro-organisms. Official Journal J L 330, 5 December 1998, pp. 13-31. corrigenda in Official Journal L 3, 7 January 1999, p 23 and Official Journal L 93, 8 April 1999, p. 27. consolidated version http://eur-lex.europa.eu/LexUriServ/LexUriServ.do?uri=CONSLEG:1998L0081:19981205:EN:PDF

Council Directive 98/83/EC of 3 November 1998 on the quality of water intended for human consumption. Official Journal L 330, 5 December 1998, pp. 32-54, corrigendum in Official Journal L 111, 20 April 2001, p. 31. consolidated version: http://eur-lex.europa.eu/LexUriServ/LexUriServ.do?uri=CONSLEG:1998L0083:20031120:EN:PDF

Directive 1999/4/EC of the European Parliament and of the Council of 22 February 1999 relating to coffee extracts and chicory extracts. Official Journal L 66, 13 March 1999, pp. 26-29. consolidated version: http://eur-lex.europa.eu/LexUriServ/LexUriServ.do?uri=CONSLEG:1999L0004:20031120:EN:PDF

Directive 1999/34/EC of the European Parliament and of the Council of 10 May 1999 amending Council Directive 85/374/EEC on the approximation of the laws, regulations and administrative provisions of the Member States concerning liability for defective products. Official Journal L 141, 4 June 1999, pp. 20-21, corrigendum in Official Journal L 283, 6 November 1999, p. 20. consolidated version: http://eur-lex.europa.eu/LexUriServ/LexUriServ.do?uri=CONSLEG:1999L0034:19990604:EN:PDF

Directive 2000/13/EC of the European Parliament and of the Council on the approximation of the laws of the Member States relating to the labelling, presentation and advertising of foodstuffs. Official Journal L 109, 6 May 2000, pp. 29-42. consolidated version: http://eur-lex.europa.eu/LexUriServ/LexUriServ.do?uri=CONSLEG:2000L0013:20071129:EN:PDF

Directive 2000/36/EC of the European Parliament and of the Council relating to cocoa and chocolate products intended for human consumption. Official Journal L 197, 3 August 2000, pp. 19-25. consolidated version: http://eur-lex.europa.eu/LexUriServ/LexUriServ.do?uri=CONSLEG:2000L0036:20040501:EN:PDF

Commission Directive 2001/15/EC of 15 February 2001 on substances that may be added for specific nutritional purposes in foods for particular nutritional uses (Text with EEA relevance). Official Journal L 52, 22 February 2001, pp. 19-25, corrigendum in Official Journal L 253, 21 September 2001, pp. 34-34. consolidated version: http://eur-lex.europa.eu/LexUriServ/LexUriServ.do?uri=CONSLEG:2001L0015:20060411:EN:PDF

Directive 2001/18/EC of the European Parliament and of the Council of 12 March 2001 on the deliberate release into the environment of genetically modified organisms and repealing Council Directive 90/220/EEC - Commission Declaration. Official Journal L 106, 17 April 2001, pp. 1-39. consolidated version: http://eur-lex.europa.eu/LexUriServ/LexUriServ.do?uri=CONSLEG:2001L0018:20080321:EN:PDF

Directive 2001/82/EC of the European Parliament and of the Council of 6 November 2001 on the Community code relating to veterinary medicinal products. Official Journal L 311, 28 November 2001, pp. 1-66. consolidated version: http://eur-lex.europa.eu/LexUriServ/LexUriServ.do?uri=CONSLEG:2001L0082:20040430:EN:PDF

Council Directive 2001/110/EC of 20 December 2001 relating to honey. Official Journal L 10, 12 January 2002, pp. 47-52. http://eur-lex.europa.eu/LexUriServ/LexUriServ.do?uri=OJ:L:2002:010:0047:0052:EN:PDF

Council Directive 2001/111/EC of 20 December 2001 relating to certain sugars intended for human consumption. Official Journal L 10, 12 January 2002, pp. 53-57. http://eur-lex.europa.eu/LexUriServ/LexUriServ.do?uri=OJ:L:2002:010:0053:0057:EN:PDF

Council Directive 2001/112/EC of 20 December 2001 relating to fruit juices and certain similar products intended for human consumption. Official Journal L 10, 12 January 2002, pp. 58-66. consolidated version: http://eur-lex.europa.eu/LexUriServ/LexUriServ.do?uri=CONSLEG:2001L0112:20080101:EN:PDF

Council Directive 2001/113/EC of 20 December 2001 relating to fruit jams, jellies and marmalades and sweetened chestnut purée intended for human consumption. Official Journal L 10, 12 January 2002, pp. 67-72. consolidated version: http://eur-lex.europa.eu/LexUriServ/LexUriServ.do?uri=CONSLEG:2001L0113:20080101:EN:PDF

Council Directive 2001/114/EC of 20 December 2001 relating to certain partly or wholly dehydrated preserved milk for human consumption. Official Journal L 15, 17 January 2002, pp. 19-23. consolidated version: http://eur-lex.europa.eu/LexUriServ/LexUriServ.do?uri=CONSLEG:2001L0114:20071007:EN:PDF

Directive 2002/33/EC of the European Parliament and of the Council of 21 October 2002 amending Council Directives 90/425/EEC and 92/118/EEC as regards health requirements for animal by-products. Official Journal L 315, 19 November 2002, pp. 14-15. http://eur-lex.europa.eu/LexUriServ/LexUriServ.do?uri=OJ:L:2002:315:0014:0015:EN:PDF

Directive 2002/46/EC of the European Parliament and of the Council of 10 June 2002 on the approximation of the laws of the Member States relating to food supplements (Text with EEA relevance). Official Journal L 183, 12 July 2002, pp. 51-57. consolidated version: http://eur-lex.europa.eu/LexUriServ/LexUriServ.do?uri=CONSLEG:2002L0046:20060421:EN:PDF

Commission Directive 2002/67/EC of 18 July 2002 on the labelling of foodstuffs containing quinine, and of foodstuffs containing caffeine (Text with EEA relevance). Official Journal L 191, 19 July 2002, pp. 20-21. http://eur-lex.europa.eu/LexUriServ/LexUriServ.do?uri=OJ:L:2002:191:0020:0021:EN:PDF

Council Directive 2002/99/EC of 16 December 2002 laying down the animal health rules governing the production, processing, distribution and introduction of products of animal origin for human consumption Official Journal L 18, 23.1.2003, pp. 11-20. http://eur-lex.europa.eu/LexUriServ/LexUriServ.do?uri=OJ L:2003:018:0011:0020:EN:PDF

Directive 2003/114/EC of the European Parliament and of the Council of 22 December 2003 amending Directive 95/2/EC on food additives other than colours and sweeteners. Official Journal L 24, 29 January 2004, pp. 58-64. http://eur-lex.europa.eu/LexUriServ/LexUriServ.do?uri=OJ:L:2004:024:0058:0064:EN:PDF

Directive 2004/41/EC of the European Parliament and of the Council of 21 April 2004 repealing certain Directives concerning food hygiene and health conditions for the production and placing on the market of certain products of animal origin intended for human consumption and amending Council Directives 89/662/EEC and 92/118/EEC and Council Decision 95/408/EC. Official Journal L 157, 30 April 2004. Corrected version in Official Journal L 195, 2 June 2004, pp. 12-15. http://europa.eu.int/eur-lex/lex/LexUriServ/site/en/oj/2004/l_195/l_19520040602en00120015.pdf

Commission Directive 2008/5/EC of 30 January 2008 concerning the compulsory indication on the labelling of certain foodstuffs of particulars other than those provided for in Directive 2000/13/EC of the European Parliament and of the Council (Codified version) (Text with EEA relevance). Official Journal L 27, 31 January 2008, pp. 12-16. http://eur-lex.europa.eu/LexUriServ/LexUriServ.do?uri=OJ:L:2008:027:0012:0016:EN:PDF

Regulations

EEC Council Regulation No 23 on the progressive establishment of a common organisation of the market in fruit and vegetables. Official Journal 30, 20 April 1962, pp. 965-988. http://eur-lex.europa.eu/LexUriServ/LexUriServ.do?uri=CELEX:31962R0023:EN:HTML

Commission Regulation (EEC) No 1292/81 of 12 May 1981 laying down quality standards for leeks, aubergines and courgettes. Official Journal L 129, 15 May 1981, pp. 38-47. http://eur-lex.europa.eu/LexUriServ/LexUriServ.do?uri=CELEX:31981R1292:EN:HTML. consolidated version for aubergines: http://eur-lex.europa.eu/LexUriServ/LexUriServ.do?uri=CONSLEG:1981R1292:20050106:EN:PDF

Commission Regulation (EEC) No 2213/83 of 28 July 1983 laying down quality standards for onions and witloof chicory. Official Journal L 213, 4 August 1983, pp. 13-21. consolidated version: http://eur-lex.europa.eu/LexUriServ/LexUriServ.do?uri=CONSLEG:1983R2213:20050106:EN:PDF

Commission Regulation (EEC) No 1591/87 of 5 June 1987 laying down quality standards for cabbages, Brussels sprouts, ribbed celery, spinach and plums. Official Journal L 146, 6 June 1987, pp. 36-52. http://eur-lex.europa.eu/LexUriServ/LexUriServ.do?uri=OJ:L:1987:146:0036:038:EN:HTML. consolidated versions for groups of fruit and vegetables exist.

Commission Regulation (EEC) No 1677/88 of 15 June 1988 laying down quality standards for cucumbers. Official Journal L 150, 16 June 1988, pp. 21-25. consolidated version: http://eur-lex.europa.eu/LexUriServ/LexUriServ.do?uri=CONSLEG:1988R1677:20050106:EN:PDF

Council Regulation (EEC) No 1576/89 of 29 May 1989 laying down general rules on the definition, description and presentation of spirit drinks. Official Journal L 160, 12 June 1989, pp. 1-17. consolidated version: http://eur-lex.europa.eu/LexUriServ/LexUriServ.do?uri=CONSLEG:1989R1576:20070101:EN:PDF

Council Regulation (EEC) No 2377/90 of 26 June 1990 laying down a Community procedure for the establishment of maximum residue limits of veterinary medicinal products in foodstuffs of animal origin. Official Journal L 224, 18 August 1990, pp. 1-8. consolidated version: http://eur-lex.europa.eu/LexUriServ/LexUriServ.do?uri=CONSLEG:1990R2377:20080120:EN:PDF

Council Regulation (EEC) No 1601/91 of 10 June 1991 laying down general rules on the definition, description and presentation of aromatized wines, aromatized wine- based drinks and aromatized wine-product cocktails. Official Journal L 149, 14 June 1991, pp. 1-9. consolidated version: http://eur-lex.europa.eu/LexUriServ/LexUriServ.do?uri=CONSLEG:1991R1601:20070101:EN:PDF

Council Regulation (EEC) No 315/93 of 8 February 1993 laying down Community procedures for contaminants in food. Official Journal L 37, 13 February 1993, pp. 1-3. consolidated version: http://eur-lex.europa.eu/LexUriServ/LexUriServ.do?uri=CONSLEG:1993R0315:20031120:EN:PDF

Commission Regulation (EC) No 122/94 of 25 January 1994 laying down certain detailed rules for the application of Council Regulation (EEC) No 1601/91 on the definition, description and presentation of aromatized wines, aromatized wine-based drinks, and aromatized wine-product cocktails. Official Journal L 21, 26 January 1994, pp. 7-8. http://eur-lex.europa.eu/LexUriServ/LexUriServ.do?uri=CELEX:31994R0122:EN:HTML

Council Regulation (EC) No 3286/94 of 22 December 1994 laying down Community procedures in the field of the common commercial policy in order to ensure the exercise of the Community's rights under international trade rules, in particular those established under the auspices of the World Trade Organization. Official Journal L 349, 31 December 1994, pp. 71-78. consolidated version: http://eur-lex.europa.eu/LexUriServ/LexUriServ.do?uri=CONSLEG:1994R3286:20080305:EN:PDF

Council Regulation (EC) No 2200/96 of 28 October 1996 on the common organization of the market in fruit and vegetables. Official Journal L 297, 21 November 1996, pp. 1-28. consolidated version: http://eur-lex.europa.eu/LexUriServ/LexUriServ.do?uri=CONSLEG:1996R2200:20080101:EN:PDF

Council Regulation (EC) No 2201/96 of 28 October 1996 on the common organization of the markets in processed fruit and vegetable products. Official Journal L 297, 21 November 1996, pp. 29-48. consolidated version: http://eur-lex.europa.eu/LexUriServ/LexUriServ.do?uri=CONSLEG:1996R2201:20080101:EN:PDF

Council Regulation (EC) No 2202/96 of 28 October 1996 introducing a Community aid scheme for producers of certain citrus fruits. Official Journal L 297, 21 November 1996, pp. 49-52. consolidated version: http://eur-lex.europa.eu/LexUriServ/LexUriServ.do?uri=CONSLEG:1996R2202:20040501:EN:PDF

Regulation (EC) No 2232/96 of the European Parliament and of the Council of 28 October 1996 laying down a Community procedure for flavouring substances used or intended for use in or on foodstuffs. Official Journal L 299, 23 November 1996, pp. 1-4. consolidated version: http://eur-lex.europa.eu/LexUriServ/LexUriServ.do?uri=CONSLEG:1996R2232:20031120:EN:PDF

Regulation (EC) No 258/97 of the European Parliament and of the Council of 27 January 1997 concerning novel foods and novel food ingredients. Official Journal L 43, 14 February 1997, pp. 1-6. consolidated version: http://eur-lex.europa.eu/LexUriServ/LexUriServ.do?uri=CONSLEG:1997R0258:20040418:EN:PDF

Council Regulation (EC) No 820/97 of 21 April 1997 establishing a system for the identification and registration of bovine animals and regarding the labelling of beef and beef products. Official Journal L 117, 7 May 1997, pp. 1-8. consolidated version: http://eur-lex.europa.eu/LexUriServ/LexUriServ.do?uri=CONSLEG:1997R2630:20000928:EN:PDF

Commission Regulation (EC) No 831/97 of 7 May 1997 laying down marketing standards applicable to avocados. Official Journal L 119 8 May 1997, pp. 13-16. consolidated version: http://eur-lex.europa.eu/LexUriServ/LexUriServ.do?uri=CONSLEG:1997R0831:20050501:EN:PDF

Commission Regulation (EC) No 2288/97 of 18 November 1997 laying down marketing standards for garlic. Official Journal L 315, 19 November 1997, pp. 3-6. consolidated version: http://eur-lex.europa.eu/LexUriServ/LexUriServ.do?uri=CONSLEG:1997R2288:20050106:EN:PDF

Commission Regulation (EC) No 963/98 of 7 May 1998 laying down marketing standards for cauliflowers and artichokes. Official Journal L 135, 8 May 1998, pp. 18-25. consolidated version: http://eur-lex.europa.eu/LexUriServ/LexUriServ.do?uri=CONSLEG:1998R0963:20050106:EN:PDF

Commission Regulation (EC) No 730/1999 of 7 April 1999 laying down the marketing standard for carrots. Official Journal L 93, 8 April 1999, pp. 14-19. consolidated version: http://eur-lex.europa.eu/LexUriServ/LexUriServ.do?uri=CONSLEG:1999R0730:20050106:EN:PDF

Commission Regulation (EC) No 1168/1999 of 3 June 1999 laying down marketing standards for plums. Official Journal L 141, 4 June 1999, pp. 5-10. consolidated version: http://eur-lex.europa.eu/LexUriServ/LexUriServ.do?uri=CONSLEG:1999R1168:20050325:EN:PDF

Commission Regulation (EC) No 1455/1999 of 1 July 1999 laying down the marketing standard for sweet peppers. Official Journal L 167, 2 July 1999, pp. 22-26. consolidated version: http://eur-lex.europa.eu/LexUriServ/LexUriServ.do?uri=CONSLEG:1999R1455:20050106:EN:PDF

Council Regulation (EC) No 1493/1999 of 17 May 1999 on the common organisation of the market in wine. Official Journal L 179, 14 July 1999, pp. 1-84. consolidated version: http://eur-lex.europa.eu/LexUriServ/LexUriServ.do?uri=CONSLEG:1999R1493:20080101:EN:PDF

Commission Regulation (EC) No 1666/1999 of 28 July 1999 laying down detailed rules for the application of Council Regulation (EC) No 2201/96 as regards the minimum marketing characteristics for certain varieties of dried grapes. Official Journal L 197, 29 July 1999, pp. 32-35. http://eur-lex.europa.eu/LexUriServ/LexUriServ.do?uri=OJ:L:1999:197:0032:0035:EN:PDF

Commission Regulation (EC) No 2377/1999 of 9 November 1999 laying down the marketing standard for asparagus. Official Journal L 287, 10 November 1999, pp. 6-11. consolidated version: http://eur-lex.europa.eu/LexUriServ/LexUriServ.do?uri=CONSLEG:1999R2377:20050726:EN:PDF

Commission Regulation (EC) No 2561/1999 of 3 December 1999 laying down the marketing standard for peas. Official Journal L 310, 4 December 1999, pp. 7-10. consolidated version: http://eur-lex.europa.eu/LexUriServ/LexUriServ.do?uri=CONSLEG:1999R2561:20050106:EN:PDF

Commission Regulation (EC) No 2789/1999 of 22 December 1999 laying down the marketing standard for table grapes. Official Journal L 336, 29 December 1999, pp. 13-20. consolidated version: http://eur-lex.europa.eu/LexUriServ/LexUriServ.do?uri=CONSLEG:1999R2789:20050106:EN:PDF

Commission Regulation (EC) No 790/2000 of 14 April 2000 laying down the marketing standard for tomatoes. Official Journal L 95, 15 April 2000, pp. 24-29. consolidated version: http://eur-lex.europa.eu/LexUriServ/LexUriServ.do?uri=CONSLEG:2000R0790:20050106:EN:PDF

Commission Regulation (EC) No 851/2000 of 27 April 2000 laying down the marketing standard for apricots. Official Journal L 103, 28 April 2000, pp. 22-26. consolidated version: http://eur-lex.europa.eu/LexUriServ/LexUriServ.do?uri=CONSLEG:2000R0851:20050106:EN:PDF

Regulation (EC) No 1760/2000 of the European Parliament and of the Council of 17 July 2000 establishing a system for the identification and registration of bovine animals and regarding the labelling of beef and beef products and repealing Council Regulation (EC) No 820/97. Official Journal L 204, 11 August 2000, pp. 1-10. consolidated version: http://eur-lex.europa.eu/LexUriServ/LexUriServ.do?uri=CONSLEG:2000R1760:20070101:EN:PDF

Commission Regulation (EC) No. 1825/2000 of 25 August 2000 laying down detailed rules for the application of Regulation (EC) No. 1760/2000 of the European Parliament and of the Council as regards the labelling of beef and beef products. Official Journal L 216, 26 August 2000, pp. 8-12. consolidated version: http://eur-lex.europa.eu/LexUriServ/LexUriServ.do?uri=CONSLEG:2000R1825:20070323:EN:PDF

Commission Regulation (EC) No 175/2001 of 26 January 2001 laying down the marketing standard for walnuts in shell. Official Journal L 26, 27 January 2001, pp. 24-30. consolidated version: http://eur-lex.europa.eu/LexUriServ/LexUriServ.do?uri=CONSLEG:2001R0175:20050106:EN:PDF

Commission Regulation (EC) No 466/2001 of 8 March 2001 setting maximum levels for certain contaminants in foodstuffs (Text with EEA relevance). Official Journal L 77, 16 March 2001, pp. 1-13. consolidated version: http://eur-lex.europa.eu/LexUriServ/LexUriServ.do?uri=CONSLEG:2001R0466:20060701:EN:PDF

Commission Regulation (EC) No 912/2001 of 10 May 2001 laying down the marketing standard for beans. Official Journal L 129, 11 May 2001, pp. 4-7. consolidated version: http://eur-lex.europa.eu/LexUriServ/LexUriServ.do?uri=CONSLEG:2001R0912:20050106:EN:PDF

Commission Regulation (EC) No 1508/2001 of 24 July 2001 laying down the marketing standard for onions and amending Regulation (EEC) No 2213/83. Official Journal L 200, 25 July 2001, pp. 14-18. consolidated version: http://eur-lex.europa.eu/LexUriServ/LexUriServ.do?uri=CONSLEG:2001R1508:20050106:EN:PDF

Commission Regulation (EC) No 1543/2001 of 27 July 2001 laying down the marketing standard for lettuces and curled-leaved and broad-leaved (Batavian) endives. Official Journal L 203, 28 July 2001, pp. 9-12. consolidated version: http://eur-lex.europa.eu/LexUriServ/LexUriServ.do?uri=CONSLEG:2001R1543:20050106:EN:PDF

Commission Regulation (EC) No 1615/2001 of 7 August 2001 laying down the marketing standard for melons and amending Regulation (EC) No 1093/97. Official Journal L 214, 8 August 2001, pp. 21-25. consolidated version: http://eur-lex.europa.eu/LexUriServ/LexUriServ.do?uri=CONSLEG:2001R1615:20060725:EN:PDF

Commission Regulation (EC) No 1799/2001 of 12 September 2001 laying down the marketing standard for citrus fruit. Official Journal L 244, 14 September 2001, pp. 12-18. consolidated version: http://eur-lex.europa.eu/LexUriServ/LexUriServ.do?uri=CONSLEG:2001R1799:20050106:EN:PDF

Commission Regulation (EC) No 2065/2001 of 22 October 2001 laying down detailed rules for the application of Council Regulation (EC) No 104/2000 as regards informing consumers about fishery and aquaculture products (Text with EEA relevance). Official Journal L 278, 23 October 2001, pp. 6-8. consolidated version: http://eur-lex.europa.eu/LexUriServ/LexUriServ.do?uri=CONSLEG:2001R2065:20070101:EN:PDF

Commission Regulation (EC) No 2396/2001 of 7 December 2001 laying down the marketing standard applicable to leeks. Official Journal L 325, 8 December 2001, pp. 11-14. consolidated version: http://eur-lex.europa.eu/LexUriServ/LexUriServ.do?uri=CONSLEG:2001R2396:20050106:EN:PDF

Regulation (EC) No 178/2002 of the European Parliament and of the Council of 28 January 2002 laying down the general principles and requirements of food law, establishing the European Food Safety Authority and laying down procedures in matters of food safety. Official Journal L 31, 1 February 2002, pp. 1-24. consolidated version: http://eur-lex.europa.eu/LexUriServ/LexUriServ.do?uri=CONSLEG:2002R0178:20080325:EN:PDF

Commission Regulation (EC) No 843/2002 of 21 May 2002 laying down the marketing standard for strawberries and amending Regulation (EEC) No 899/87. Official Journal L 134, 22 May 2002, pp. 24-28. consolidated version: http://eur-lex.europa.eu/LexUriServ/LexUriServ.do?uri=CONSLEG:2002R0843:20050106:EN:PDF

Commission Regulation (EC) No 1284/2002 of 15 July 2002 laying down the marketing standard for hazelnuts in shell. Official Journal L 187, 16 July 2002, pp. 14-20. consolidated version: http://eur-lex.europa.eu/LexUriServ/LexUriServ.do?uri=CONSLEG:2002R1284:20050106:EN:PDF

Regulation (EC) No 1774/2002 of the European Parliament and of the Council of 3 October 2002 laying down health rules concerning animal by-products not intended for human consumption. Official Journal L 273, 10 October 2002, pp. 1-95. consolidated version: http://eur-lex.europa.eu/LexUriServ/LexUriServ.do?uri=CONSLEG:2002R1774:20070101:EN:PDF

Commission Regulation (EC) No 48/2003 of 10 January 2003 laying down the rules applicable to mixes of different types of fresh fruit and vegetables in the same sales package. Official Journal L 7, 11 January 2003, pp. 65-67. http://eur-lex.europa.eu/LexUriServ/LexUriServ.do?uri=OJ:L:2003:007:0065:0067:EN:PDF

Commission Regulation (EC) No 1304/2003 of 23 July 2003 on the procedure applied by the European Food Safety Authority to requests for scientific opinions referred to it. Official Journal L 185, 24 September 2003, p. 6, as corrected by Corrigendum, Official Journal L 186, 25 July 2003, p. 46. consolidated version: http://eur-lex.europa.eu/LexUriServ/LexUriServ.do?uri=CONSLEG:2003R1304:20030813:EN:PDF

Commission Regulation (EC) No 1466/2003 of 19 August 2003 laying down the marketing standard for artichokes and amending Regulation (EC) No 963/98. Official Journal L 210, 20 August 2003, pp. 6-10. consolidated version: http://eur-lex.europa.eu/LexUriServ/LexUriServ.do?uri=CONSLEG:2003R1466:20070101:EN:PDF

Commission Regulation (EC) No 1757/2003 of 3 October 2003 laying down the marketing standard for courgettes and amending Regulation (EEC) No 1292/81. Official Journal L 252, 4 October 2003, pp. 11-16. consolidated version: http://eur-lex.europa.eu/LexUriServ/LexUriServ.do?uri=CONSLEG:2003R1757:20040520:EN:PDF

Regulation (EC) No 1829/2003 of the European Parliament and of the Council of 22 September 2003 on genetically modified food and feed (Text with EEA relevance). Official Journal L 268, 18 October 2003, pp. 1-23. consolidated version: http://eur-lex.europa.eu/LexUriServ/LexUriServ.do?uri=CONSLEG:2003R1829:20080410:EN:PDF

Regulation (EC) No 1830/2003 of the European Parliament and of the Council of 22 September 2003 concerning the traceability and labelling of genetically modified organisms and the traceability of food and feed products produced from genetically modified organisms and amending Directive 2001/18/EC. Official Journal L 268, 18 October 2003, pp. 24-28. http://eur-lex.europa.eu/LexUriServ/LexUriServ.do?uri=OJ:L:2003:268:0024:0028:EN:PDF

Regulation (EC) No 1946/2003 of the European Parliament and of the Council of 15 July 2003 on transboundary movements of genetically modified organisms (Text with EEA relevance). Official Journal L 287, 5 November 2003, pp. 1-10. http://eur-lex.europa.eu/LexUriServ/LexUriServ.do?uri=OJ:L:2003:287:0001:0010:EN:PDF

Regulation (EC) No 2065/2003 of the European Parliament and of the Council of 10 November 2003 on smoke flavourings used or intended for use in or on foods. Official Journal L 309, 26 November 2003, pp. 1-8. http://eur-lex.europa.eu/LexUriServ/LexUriServ.do?uri=OJ:L:2003:309:0001:0008:EN:PDF

Council Regulation (EC) No 21/2004 of 17 December 2003 establishing a system for the identification and registration of ovine and caprine animals and amending Regulation (EC) No 1782/2003 and Directives 92/102/EEC and 64/432/EEC. Official Journal L 5, 9 January 2004, pp. 8-17. consolidated version: http://eur-lex.europa.eu/LexUriServ/LexUriServ.do?uri=CONSLEG:2004R0021:20071222:EN:PDF

Commission Regulation (EC) No 65/2004 of 14 January 2004 establishing a system for the development and assignment of unique identifiers for genetically modified organisms. Official Journal L 10, 16 January 2004, pp. 5-10. http://eur-lex.europa.eu/LexUriServ/LexUriServ.do?uri=OJ:L:2004:010:0005:0010:EN:PDF

Commission Regulation (EC) No 85/2004 of 15 January 2004 laying down the marketing standard for apples. Official Journal L 13, 20 January 2004, pp. 3-18. consolidated version: http://eur-lex.europa.eu/LexUriServ/LexUriServ.do?uri=CONSLEG:2004R0085:20050801:EN:PDF

Commission Regulation (EC) No 86/2004 of 15 January 2004 laying down the marketing standard for pears. Official Journal L 13, 20 January 2004, pp. 19-27. consolidated version: http://eur-lex.europa.eu/LexUriServ/LexUriServ.do?uri=CONSLEG:2004R0086:20040520:EN:PDF

Commission Regulation (EC) No 214/2004 of 6 February 2004 laying down the marketing standard for cherries. Official Journal L 36, 7 February 2004, pp. 6-9. http://eur-lex.europa.eu/LexUriServ/LexUriServ.do?uri=OJ:L:2004:036:0006:0009:EN:PDF

Commission Regulation (EC) No 608/2004 of 31 March 2004 concerning the labelling of foods and food ingredients with added phytosterols, phytosterol esters, phytostanols and/or phytostanol esters (Text with EEA relevance). Official Journal L 97, 1 April 2004, pp. 44-45. http://eur-lex.europa.eu/LexUriServ/LexUriServ.do?uri=OJ:L:2004:097:0044:0045:EN:PDF

Commission Regulation (EC) No 641/2004 of 6 April 2004 on detailed rules for the implementation of Regulation (EC) No 1829/2003 of the European Parliament and of the Council as regards the application for the authorisation of new genetically modified food and feed, the notification of existing products and adventitious or technically unavoidable presence of genetically modified material which has benefited from a favourable risk evaluation (Text with EEA relevance). Official Journal L 102, 7 April 2004, pp. 14-25. http://eur-lex.europa.eu/LexUriServ/LexUriServ.do?uri=OJ:L:2004:102:0014 0025:EN:PDF

Regulation (EC) No 852/2004 of the European Parliament and of the Council of 29 April 2004 on the hygiene of foodstuffs. Official Journal L 139, 30 April 4 2004. Corrected version in Official Journal L 226, 25 June 6.2004. http://eur-lex.europa.eu/LexUriServ/LexUriServ.do?uri=OJ:L:2007:204:0026:0026:EN:PDF

Regulation (EC) No 853/2004 of the European Parliament and of the Council of 29 April 2004 laying down specific hygiene rules for food of animal origin. Official Journal L 139, 30 April 2004, pp. 55-205. consolidated version: http://eur-lex.europa.eu/LexUriServ/LexUriServ.do?uri=CONSLEG:2004R0853:20071114:EN:PDF

Regulation (EC) No 854/2004 of the European Parliament and of the Council of 29 April 2004 laying down specific rules for the organisation of official controls on products of animal origin intended for human consumption. Official Journal L 139, 30 April 2004. Corrected version in Official Journal L 226, 25 June 2004. consolidated version: http://eur-lex.europa.eu/LexUriServ/LexUriServ.do?uri=CONSLEG:2004R0854:20070101:EN:PDF

Regulation (EC) No 882/2004 of the European Parliament and of the Council of 29 April 2004 on official controls performed to ensure the verification of compliance with feed and food law, animal health and animal welfare rules. Official Journal L 191, 28 May 2004, pp. 1. consolidated version: http://eur-lex.europa.eu/LexUriServ/LexUriServ.do?uri=CONSLEG:2004R0882:20080410:EN:PDF

Commission Regulation (EC) No 887/2004 of 29 April 2004 establishing the standard import values for determining the entry price of certain fruit and vegetables. Official Journal L 163, 30 April 2004, pp. 1-2. http://eur-lex.europa.eu/LexUriServ/LexUriServ.do?uri=OJ:L:2004:163:0001:0002:EN:PDF

Commission Regulation (EC) No 911/2004 of 29 April 2004 implementing Regulation (EC) No 1760/2000 of the European Parliament and of the Council as regards eartags, passports and holding registers (Text with EEA relevance). Official Journal L 163, 30 April 2004, pp. 65-70. consolidated version: http://eur-lex.europa.eu/LexUriServ/LexUriServ.do?uri=CONSLEG:2004R0911:20070101:EN:PDF

Commission Regulation (EC) No 1673/2004 of 24 September 2004 laying down the marketing standard applicable to kiwifruit. Official Journal L 300, 25 September 2004, pp. 5-10. http://eur-lex.europa.eu/LexUriServ/LexUriServ.do?uri=CELEX:32004R1673:EN:HTML

Commission Regulation (EC) No 1861/2004 of 28 October 2004 laying down the marketing standard applicable to peaches and nectarines. Official Journal L 325, 28 October 2004, pp. 10-16. http://eur-lex.europa.eu/LexUriServ/LexUriServ.do?uri=OJ:L:2004:325:0010:0016:EN:PDF

Commission Regulation (EC) No 1862/2004 of 26 October 2004 laying down the marketing standard applicable to watermelons. Official Journal L 325, 28 October 2004, pp. 17-22. http://eur-lex.europa.eu/LexUriServ/LexUriServ.do?uri=OJ:L:2004:325:0017:0022:EN:PDF

Commission Regulation (EC) No 1863/2004 of 26 October 2004 laying down the marketing standard applicable to cultivated mushrooms. Official Journal L 325, 28 October 2004, pp. 23-29. http://eur-lex.europa.eu/LexUriServ/LexUriServ.do?uri=OJ:L:2004:325:0023:0029:EN:PDF

Regulation (EC) No 1935/2004 of the European Parliament and of the Council of 27 October 2004 on materials and articles intended to come into contact with food and repealing Directives 80/590/EEC and 89/109/EEC. Official Journal L 338, 13 November 2004, pp. 4-17. http://eur-lex.europa.eu/LexUriServ/LexUriServ.do?uri=OJ:L:2004:338:0004:0017:EN:PDF

Regulation (EC) No 183/2005 of the European Parliament and of the Council of 12 January 2005 laying down requirements for feed hygiene. Official Journal L 35, 8 February 2005, pp. 1-22: http://eur-lex.europa.eu/LexUriServ/LexUriServ.do?uri=OJ:L:2005:035:0001:0022:EN:PDF

Regulation (EC) No 396/2005 of the European Parliament and of the Council of 23 February 2005 on maximum residue levels of pesticides in or on food and feed of plant and animal origin and amending Council Directive 91/414/EECText with EEA relevance. Official Journal L 70, 16 March 2005, pp. 1-16. consolidated version: http://eur-lex.europa.eu/LexUriServ/LexUriServ.do?uri=CONSLEG:2005R0396:20080410:EN:PDF

Commission Regulation (EC) No 2073/2005 of 15 November 2005 on microbiological criteria for foodstuffs (Text with EEA relevance). Official Journal L 338, 22 December 2005, pp. 1-26. consolidated version: http://eur-lex.europa.eu/LexUriServ/LexUriServ.do?uri=CONSLEG:2005R2073:20071227:EN:PDF

Commission Regulation (EC) No 2074/2005 of 5 December 2005 laying down implementing measures for certain products under Regulation (EC) No 853/2004 of the European Parliament and of the Council and for the organisation of official controls under Regulation (EC) No 854/2004 of the European Parliament and of the Council and Regulation (EC) No 882/2004 of the European Parliament and of the Council, derogating from Regulation (EC) No 852/2004 of the European Parliament and of the Council and amending Regulations (EC) No 853/2004 and (EC) No 854/2004 (Text with EEA relevance). Official Journal L 338, 22 December 2005, pp. 27-59. consolidated version: http://eur-lex.europa.eu/LexUriServ/LexUriServ.do?uri=CONSLEG:2005R2074:20061125:EN:PDF

Commission Regulation (EC) No 2075/2005 of 5 December 2005 laying down specific rules on official controls for *Trichinella* in meat (Text with EEA relevance). Official Journal L 338, 22 December 2005, pp. 60-82. consolidated version: http://eur-lex.europa.eu/LexUriServ/LexUriServ.do?uri=CONSLEG:2005R2075:20071114:EN:PDF

Commission Regulation (EC) No 2076/2005 of 5 December 2005 laying down transitional arrangements for the implementation of Regulations (EC) No 853/2004, (EC) No 854/2004 and (EC) No 882/2004 of the European Parliament and of the Council and amending Regulations (EC) No 853/2004 and (EC) No 854/2004 (Text with EEA relevance). Official Journal L 338, 22 December 2005, pp. 83-88. consolidated version: http://eur-lex.europa.eu/LexUriServ/LexUriServ.do?uri=CONSLEG:2005R2076:20071114:EN:PDF

Commission Regulation (EC) No 178/2006 of 1 February 2006 amending Regulation (EC) No 396/2005 of the European Parliament and of the Council to establish Annex I listing the food and feed products to which maximum levels for pesticide residues apply (Text with EEA relevance). Official Journal L 29, 2 February 2006, pp. 3-25. http://eur-lex.europa.eu/LexUriServ/LexUriServ.do?uri=OJ:L:2006:029:0003:0025:EN:PDF

Council Regulation (EC) No 318/2006 of 20 February 2006 on the common organisation of the markets in the sugar sector. Official Journal L 58, 28 February 2006, pp. 1-31. Corrigendum, Official Journal L 235, 30 August 2006, pp. 23. consolidated version: http://eur-lex.europa.eu/LexUriServ/LexUriServ.do?uri=CONSLEG:2006R0318:20080101:EN:PDF

Commission Regulation (EC) No 401/2006 of 23 February 2006 laying down the methods of sampling and analysis for the official control of the levels of mycotoxins in foodstuffs (Text with EEA relevance). Official Journal L 70, 9 March 2006, pp. 12-34. http://eur-lex.europa.eu/LexUriServ/LexUriServ.do?uri=OJ:L:2006:070:0012:0034:EN:PDF

Council Regulation (EC) No 509/2006 of 20 March 2006 on agricultural products and foodstuffs as traditional specialities guaranteed. Official Journal L 93, 31 March 2006, pp. 1-11. http://eur-lex.europa.eu/LexUriServ/LexUriServ.do?uri=OJ:L:2006:093:0001:0011:EN:PDF

Council Regulation (EC) No 510/2006 of 20 March 2006 on the protection of geographical indications and designations of origin for agricultural products and foodstuffs. Official Journal L 93, 31 March 2006, pp. 12-25. consolidated version: http://eur-lex.europa.eu/LexUriServ/LexUriServ.do?uri=CONSLEG:2006R0510:20070101:EN:PDF

Commission Regulation (EC) No 575/2006 of 7 April 2006 amending Regulation (EC) No 178/2002 of the European Parliament and of the Council as regards the number and names of the permanent Scientific Panels of the European Food Safety Authority. Official Journal L 100, 08 April 2006, p. 3. http://eur-lex.europa.eu/LexUriServ/LexUriServ.do?uri=OJ:L:2006:100:0003:0003:EN:PDF

Council Regulation (EC) No 1028/2006 of 19 June 2006 on marketing standards for eggs. Official Journal L 186, 7 July 2006, pp. 1-5. http://eur-lex.europa.eu/LexUriServ/LexUriServ.do?uri=OJ:L:2006:186:0001:0005:EN:PDF

Commission Regulation (EC) No 1881/2006 of 19 December 2006 setting maximum levels for certain contaminants in foodstuffs (Text with EEA relevance). Official Journal L 364, 20 December 2006, pp. 5-24. consolidated version: http://eur-lex.europa.eu/LexUriServ/LexUriServ.do?uri=CONSLEG:2006R1881:20070701:EN:PDF

Commission Regulation (EC) No 1883/2006 of 19 December 2006 laying down methods of sampling and analysis for the official control of levels of dioxins and dioxin-like PCBs in certain foodstuffs (Text with EEA relevance). Official Journal L 364, 20 December 2006, pp. 32-43. http://eur-lex.europa.eu/LexUriServ/LexUriServ.do?uri=OJ:L:2006:364:0032:0043:EN:PDF

Regulation (EC) No 1907/2006 of the European Parliament and of the Council of 18 December 2006 concerning the Registration, Evaluation, Authorisation and Restriction of Chemicals (REACH), establishing a European Chemicals Agency, amending Directive 1999/45/EC and repealing Council Regulation (EEC) No 793/93 and Commission Regulation (EC) No 1488/94 as well as Council Directive 76/769/EEC and Commission Directives 91/155/EEC, 93/67/EEC, 93/105/EC and 2000/21/EC. Official Journal L 396, 30 December 2006, pp. 1-849. consolidated version: http://eur-lex.europa.eu/LexUriServ/LexUriServ.do?uri=CONSLEG:2006R1907:20071123:EN:PDF

Regulation (EC) No 1924/2006 of the European Parliament and of the Council of 20 December 2006 on nutrition and health claims made on foods. Official Journal L 404, 30 December 2006, pp. 9-25. Corrigendum in Official Journal L 12, 18 January 2007, pp. 3-18. consolidated version: http://eur-lex.europa.eu/LexUriServ/LexUriServ.do?uri=CONSLEG:2006R1924:20080304:EN:PDF

Commission Regulation (EC) No 333/2007 of 28 March 2007 laying down the methods of sampling and analysis for the official control of the levels of lead, cadmium, mercury, inorganic tin, 3-MCPD and benzo(a)pyrene in foodstuffs (Text with EEA relevance). Official Journal L 88, 29 March 2007, pp. 29-38. http://eur-lex.europa.eu/LexUriServ/LexUriServ.do?uri=OJ:L:2007:088:0029:0038:EN:PDF

Commission Regulation (EC) No 557/2007 of 23 May 2007 laying down detailed rules for implementing Council Regulation (EC) No 1028/2006 on marketing standards for eggs. Official Journal L 132, 24 May 2007, pp. 5-20. consolidated version: http://eur-lex.europa.eu/LexUriServ/LexUriServ.do?uri=CONSLEG:2007R0557:20071119:EN:PDF

Council Regulation (EC) No 700/2007 of 11 June 2007 on the marketing of the meat of bovine animals aged 12 months or less. Official Journal L 161, 22 June 2007, pp. 1-8. http://eur-lex.europa.eu/LexUriServ/LexUriServ.do?uri=OJ:L:2007:161:0001:0008:EN:PDF

Commission Regulation (EC) No 782/2007 of 3 July 2007 amending Regulation (EC) No 634/2006 laying down the marketing standard applicable to headed cabbages. Official Journal L 174, 4 July 2007, pp. 7-7 . http://eur-lex.europa.eu/LexUriServ/LexUriServ.do?uri=OJ:L:2007:174:0007:0007:EN:PDF

Council Regulation (EC) No 834/2007 of 28 June 2007 on organic production and labelling of organic products and repealing Regulation (EEC) No 2092/91. Official Journal L 189, 20 July 2007, pp. 1-23. http://eur-lex.europa.eu/LexUriServ/LexUriServ.do?uri=OJ:L:2007:189:0001:0023:EN:PDF

Commission Regulation (EC) No 884/2007 of 26 July 2007 on emergency measures suspending the use of E 128 Red 2G as food colour, Official Journal L 195, 27 July 2007, pp. 8-9 http://eur-lex.europa.eu/LexUriServ/LexUriServ.do?uri=OJ:L:2007:195:0008:0009:EN:PDF

Council Regulation (EC) No 1182/2007 of 26 September 2007 laying down specific rules as regards the fruit and vegetable sector, amending Directives 2001/112/EC and 2001/113/EC and Regulations (EEC) No 827/68, (EC) No 2200/96, (EC) No 2201/96, (EC) No 2826/2000, (EC) No 1782/2003 and (EC) No 318/2006 and repealing Regulation (EC) No 2202/96. Official Journal L 273, 17 October 2007, pp. 1-30. http://eur-lex.europa.eu/LexUriServ/LexUriServ.do?uri=OJ:L:2007:273:0001:0030:EN:PDF

Council Regulation (EC) No 1234/2007 of 22 October 2007 establishing a common organisation of agricultural markets and on specific provisions for certain agricultural products (Single CMO Regulation). Official Journal L 299, 16 November 2007, pp. 1-149. http://eur-lex.europa.eu/LexUriServ/LexUriServ.do?uri=OJ:L:2007:299:0001:0149:EN:PDF

Commission Regulation (EC) No 1580/2007 of 21 December 2007 laying down implementing rules of Council Regulations (EC) No 2200/96, (EC) No 2201/96 and (EC) No 1182/2007 in the fruit and vegetable sector. Official Journal L 350, 31 December 2007, pp. 1-98. consolidated version: http://eur-lex.europa.eu/LexUriServ/LexUriServ.do?uri=CONSLEG:2007R1580:20080501:EN:PDF

Commission Regulation (EC) No 149/2008 of 29 January 2008 amending Regulation (EC) No 396/2005 of the European Parliament and of the Council by establishing Annexes II, III and IV setting maximum residue levels for products covered by Annex I thereto (Text with EEA relevance). Official Journal L 58, 1 March 2008, pp. 1-398. http://eur-lex.europa.eu/LexUriServ/LexUriServ.do?uri=OJ:L:2008:058:0001:0398:EN:PDF

Commission Regulation (EC) No 202/2008 of 4 March 2008 amending Regulation (EC) No 178/2002 of the European Parliament and of the Council as regards the number and names of the Scientific Panels of the European Food Safety Authority (Text with EEA relevance) Official Journal L 60, 5 March 2008, pp. 17-17. http://eur-lex.europa.eu/LexUriServ/LexUriServ.do?uri=OJ:L:2008:060:0017:0017:EN:PDF

Council Regulation (EC) No 361/2008 of 14 April 2008 amending Regulation (EC) No 1234/2007 establishing a common organisation of agricultural markets and on specific provisions for certain agricultural products (Single CMO Regulation). Official Journal L 121, 7 May 2008, pp. 1-31. http://eur-lex.europa.eu/LexUriServ/LexUriServ.do?uri=OJ:L:2008:121:0001:0031:EN:PDF

Decisions

Commission Decision 76/642/EEC of 9 June 1976 relating to a proceeding under Article 86 of the Treaty establishing the European Economic Community (IV/29.020 - Vitamins) (Only the German text is authentic). Official Journal L 223, 16 August 1976, pp. 27-38. http://eur-lex.europa.eu/LexUriServ/LexUriServ.do?uri=CELEX:31976D0642:EN:HTML

Council Decision 88/389/EEC of 22 June 1988 on the establishment, by the Commission, of an inventory of the source materials and substances used in the preparation of flavourings. Official Journal L 184, 15 July 1988, pp. 67-67. http://eur-lex.europa.eu/LexUriServ/LexUriServ.do?uri=CELEX:31988D0389:EN:HTML

Council Decision, (93/591/EU, Euratom, ECSC, EC), OJ 1993, L 281/18, rectified OJ 1993, L 285/41. http://eur-lex.europa.eu/Notice.do?val=294326:cs&lang=en&list=294326:cs,294325:cs,&pos=1&page=1&nbl=2&pgs=10&hwords=

Decision 292/97/EC of the European Parliament and of the Council of 19 December 1996 on the maintenance of national laws prohibiting the use of certain additives in the production of certain specific foodstuffs. Official Journal L 48, 19 February1997, pp. 13-15. http://eur-lex.europa.eu/LexUriServ/LexUriServ.do?uri=CELEX:31997D0292:EN:HTML

Commission Decision 1999/217 of 23 February 1999 adopting a register of flavouring substances used in or on foodstuffs drawn up in application of Regulation (EC) No 2232/96 of the European Parliament and of the Council of 28 October 1996 (notified under number C(1999) 399) (text with EEA relevance). Official Journal L 84, 27 March 1999, pp. 1-137. consolidated version: http://eur-lex.europa.eu/LexUriServ/LexUriServ.do?uri=CONSLEG:1999D0217:20060329:EN:PDF

Council Decision 1999/468/EC of 28 June 1999 laying down the procedures for the exercise of implementing powers conferred on the Commission, Official Journal L 184, 17 July 1999, pp. 23-26. consolidated version: http://eur-lex.europa.eu/LexUriServ/LexUriServ.do?uri=CONSLEG:1999D0468:20060723:EN:PDF

Commission Decision 2000/418/EC of 29 June 2000 regulating the use of material presenting risks as regards transmissible spongiform encephalopathies and amending Decision 94/474/EC (notified under document number C(2000) 1735) (Text with EEA relevance). Official Journal L 158, 30 June 2000, pp. 76-82. consolidated version: http://eur-lex.europa.eu/LexUriServ/LexUriServ.do?uri=CONSLEG:2000D0418:20010331:EN:PDF

Commission Decision 2000/500/EC of 24 July 2000 on authorising the placing on the market of 'yellow fat spreads with added phytosterol esters' as a novel food or novel food ingredient under Regulation (EC) No 258/97 of the European Parliament and of the Council (notified under document number C(2000) 2121) (Only the English text is authentic). Official Journal L 200 , 08 August 2000, pp. 59-60. http://eur-lex.europa.eu/LexUriServ/LexUriServ.do?uri=OJ:L:2000:200:0059:0060:EN:PDF

Commission Decision 2000/678/EC of 23 October 2000 laying down detailed rules for registration of holdings in national databases for porcine animals as foreseen by Council Directive 64/432/EEC (notified under document number C(2000) 3075) (Text with EEA relevance). Official Journal L 281, 7 November 2000, pp. 16-17. http://eur-lex.europa.eu/LexUriServ/LexUriServ.do?uri=OJ:L:2000:281:0016:0017:EN:PDF

Council Decision 2003/822/EC of 17 November 2003 on the accession of the European Community to the Codex Alimentarius Commission. Official Journal L 309, 26 November 2003, pp. 14-21. http://eur-lex.europa.eu/LexUriServ/LexUriServ.do?uri=OJ:L:2003:309:0014:0021:EN:PDF

Commission Decision of 6 August 2004 concerning the creation of an advisory group on the food chain and animal and plant health, OJ L 275, 25.8.2004, pp. 17-19. Commission of the European Communities, Draft: Communication from the Commission, concerning the creation of an advisory group on the food chain and animal and plant health and the establishment of a consultation procedure on the food chain and animal and plant health through representative European bodies, no date, but prepared Commission Decision (2004/613/EC). Official Journal L 275, 25 August 2004, pp. 17-19. http://eur-lex.europa.eu/LexUriServ/LexUriServ.do?uri=CELEX:32004D0613:EN:HTML

Council Decision 2006/512/EC of 17 July 2006 amending Decision 1999/468/EC laying down the procedures for the exercise of implementing powers conferred on the Commission. Official Journal L 200, 22 July 2006, pp. 11-13. http://eur-lex.europa.eu/LexUriServ/LexUriServ.do?uri=OJ:L:2006:200:0011:0013:EN:PDF

Council Decision (2007/5/EC,Euratom) of 1 January 2007 determining the order in which the office of President of the Council shall be held. Official Journal L 1, 4 January 2007, pp. 11-12. http://eur-lex.europa.eu/LexUriServ/LexUriServ.do?uri=OJ:L:2007:001:0011:0012:EN:PDF

Commission Decision 2007/308/EC of 25 April 2007 on the withdrawal from the market of products derived from GA21xMON810 (MON-ØØØ21-9xMON-ØØ81Ø-6) maize (notified under document number C(2007) 1810). Official Journal L 117, 5 May 2007, pp. 25-26. http://eur-lex.europa.eu/LexUriServ/LexUriServ.do?uri=OJ:L:2007:117:0025:0026:EN:PDF

Council Decision 2008/486/EC of 23 June 2008 appointing half of the members of the Management Board of the European Food Safety Authority http://eur-lex.europa.eu/LexUriServ/LexUriServ.do?uri=OJ:L:2008:165:0008:0009:EN:PDF

Registers and lists

Commission - List of committees which assist the Commission in the exercise of its implementing powers. Official Journal C 225, 08 August 2000, 2-18. http://eur-lex.europa.eu/LexUriServ/LexUriServ.do?uri=OJ:C:2000:225:0002:0018:EN:PDF

Community Register of GM Food and Feed. http://ec.europa.eu/food/dyna/gm_register/index_en.cfm

Community Register for National Guides to Good Practice. http://ec.europa.eu/food/food/biosafety/hygienelegislation/register_national_guides_en.pdf

Community Register of approved food establishments. http://ec.europa.eu/food/food/biosafety/establishments/list_en.htm

Community Register of national Guides to Good Practice http://ec.europa.eu/food/food/biosafety/hygienelegislation/register_national_guides_en.pdf

EFSA decisions and other documents

European Food Safety Authority, Advisory Forum AF 25.11.2005- 5, INA-AFWG-Outline for 20 January-document, Ad Hoc Advisory Forum Working Group on the input of national authorities into the work of EFSA's Scientific Committee, Panels and other expert groups (INA-AFWG). http://www.efsa.eu.int/cs/BlobServer/DocumentSet/5reportofafwg-ina1.pdf

European Food Safety Authority, Evaluation of EFSA, Final Report, Contract FIN0105, Bureau van Dijk Ingénieurs Conseils with Arcadia International EEIG, Brussels, 5 December 2005. http://www.efsa.europa.eu/cs/BlobServer/Non_Scientific_Document/final_report_evaluation1.pdf

EFSA Management Board Decision MB 21.01.2003 concerning the operation of the Advisory Forum. http://www.efsa.europa.eu/cs/BlobServer/DocumentSet/decision_af_mb_06_en11,0.pdf?ssbinary=true

EFSA Management Board Decision MB 11.09.2003 – Implementing measures of transparency and confidentiality requirements 10.03.2005 – 10. http://www.efsa.europa.eu/cs/BlobServer/DocumentSet/mb_transparency_confidentiality_requirements1,4.pdf?ssbinary=true

EFSA Management Board Decision MB 16.09.2003-11-Adopted, EFSA Code of good administrative behaviour, 16 September 2003. http://www.efsa.europa.eu/cs/BlobServer/DocumentSet/mboard_meeting_010_doc13_adopted_en11,0.pdf?ssbinary=true

EFSA Management Board Decision MB 16.09.2003 – 13, Agreed Openness, transparency and confidentiality - general principles. http://www.efsa.europa.eu/cs/BlobServer/DocumentSet/mboard_meeting_010_doc14_adopted_en11,4.pdf?ssbinary=true

EFSA Management Board Decision MB 16.09.2003 – adopted, concerning access to documents. http://www.efsa.europa.eu/cs/BlobServer/DocumentSet/mboard_meeting_010_doc15_adopted_en11,0.pdf?ssbinary=true

EFSA Management Board, Annual work programme AWP

EFSA Management Board Decision MB – Adopted by written procedure on 7 March 2008, Annual Work Programme for Grants 2008. http://www.efsa.europa.eu/cs/BlobServer/Non_Scientific_Document/efsa_annual_work_programme_2008_grants,0.pdf?ssbinary=true

EFSA Management Board, Multi-annual work programme

EFSA Management Board Decision, Financial Regulation of the European Food Safety Authority. http://www.efsa.europa.eu/cs/BlobServer/DocumentSet/efsa_financiaregulation_final,0.pdf?ssbinary=true

EFSA Management Board Decision, Implementing Rules for the Financial Regulation. http://www.efsa.europa.eu/cs/BlobServer/DocumentSet/financialregulation_implementingrules,0.pdf?ssbinary=true

EFSA Management Board Decision MB 24.1.2006 on implementing rules concerning the tasks, duties and powers of the Data Protection Officer. http://www.efsa.europa.eu/cs/BlobServer/DocumentSet/mb_implementingrules_24meet_en2,1.pdf?ssbinary=true

EFSA Management Board Decision, MB 10.05.2006, Rules of Procedure of the Management Board of the European Food Safety Authority, As last amended by the Management Board on 10 May 2006. http://www.efsa.europa.eu/cs/BlobServer/DocumentSet/rules_proc_mb_en11,0.pdf?ssbinary=true

EFSA Management Board of the European Food Safety Authority, MB 20.06.2006-4, Proposal for Management Board Conclusions of the External Evaluation of EFSA and Recommendations Arising from The Report. www.efsa.europa.eu/EFSA/DocumentSet/mb_recommendations_evaluation_final_30062006,0.pdf

EFSA Management Board Decision MB 12.09.2006 – Adopted by written procedure on 8 November 2006, EFSA Risk Communications Strategy and Plans. http://www.efsa.europa.eu/cs/BlobServer/DocumentSet/mb_commstrategy_final_20061108,0.pdf?ssbinary=true

EFSA Management Board Decision MB 11.09.2007 concerning the establishment and operations of the Scientific Committee and Panels. http://www.efsa.europa.eu/cs/BlobServer/DocumentSet/mb_32ndmeet_annex_a_en_4,0.pdf?ssbinary=true

EFSA Management Board Decision, Document providing the predicted work of the Authority during 2008 both in relation to its annual and multi-annual work programmes.

EFSA Annual Report 2007 http://www.efsa.europa.eu/cs/BlobServer/DocumentSet/comm_annual_report_2007_en.pdf?ssbinary=true

Management Board Decision MB 11.09.2007, Guidance Document on Declarations of Interests, Annex 1 Declaration of Commitment EFSA Management Board. http://www.efsa.europa.eu/cs/BlobServer/General/mb_annex_procedure_doi_en%20030408.pdf?ssbinary=true

Management Board Decision MB 11.09.2007, Guidance Document on Declarations of Interests, Annex 2, Annual Declaration of Interests. http://www.efsa.europa.eu/cs/BlobServer/General/mb_policy_doi_en.pdf?ssbinary=true

Management Board Decision MB 11.09.2007, Guidance Document on Declarations of Interests, Annex 3, Specific Declaration of Interests. http://www.efsa.europa.eu/cs/BlobServer/General/doi_guidance_allannexes.pdf?ssbinary=true

EFSA Management Board Decision MB 11.09.07 – 4.2 Proposal to divide the tasks of the AFC panel. http://www.efsa.eu.int/cs/BlobServer/DocumentSet/mb_32ndmeet_panel_afc_split_en_4_2,0.pdf

EFSA Management Board Decision MB 13.12.07 – Adopted by written procedure on 21 December 2007., Management Plan of the European Food Safety Authority for 2008. http://www.efsa.europa.eu/cs/BlobServer/DocumentSet/mb_managementplan2008-adopted,3.pdf?ssbinary=true

Proposals for new legislation and preparatory documents

COM(2000) 716 final. Proposal for a Regulation of the European Parliament and of the Council laying down the general principles and requirements of food law, establishing the European Food Authority, and laying down procedures in matters of food. Official Journal C 96 E, 27 March 2001, pp. 247-268. http://eur-lex.europa.eu/LexUriServ/LexUriServ.do?uri=OJ:C:2001:096E:0247:0268:EN:PDF

COM(2003) 52 final. Proposal for a Regulation of the European Parliament and of the Council on official feed and food controls 5.2.2003. http://eur-lex.europa.eu/LexUriServ/LexUriServ.do?uri=COM:2003:0052:FIN:EN:PDF

COM(2005) 661 final. Commission proposal for a 'Council Regulation on the indication of the country of origin of certain products imported from third countries'. http://eur-lex.europa.eu/LexUriServ/LexUriServ.do?uri=COM:2005:0661:FIN:EN:PDF

COM(2006) 427 final, Commission, Proposal for a Regulation of the European Parliament and of the Council on flavourings and certain food ingredients with flavouring properties for use in and on foods and amending Council Regulation (EEC) No 1576/89, Council Regulation (EEC) No 1601/91, Regulation (EC) No 2232/96 and Directive 2000/13/EC. http://ec.europa.eu/food/food/chemicalsafety/additives/com2006_427_en.pdf

Proposed legislation for market regulation. http://ec.europa.eu/enterprise/regulation/internal_market_package/index_en.htm

COM(2007) 36 final. Proposal for a regulation of the European parliament and of the council laying down procedures relating to the application of certain national technical rules to products lawfully marketed in another Member State and repealing Decision 3052/95/EC. http://eur-lex.europa.eu/LexUriServ/site/en/com/2007/com2007_0036en01.pdf

COM(2007) 37 final. Proposal for a Regulation of the European Parliament and of the Council setting out the requirements for accreditation and market surveillance relating to the marketing of products. http://eur-lex.europa.eu/LexUriServ/site/en/com/2007/com2007_0037en01.pdf

COM(2007) 90 final. Proposal for a Regulation of the European Parliament and of the Council amending Regulation No 11 concerning the abolition of discrimination in transport rates and conditions, in implementation of Article 79 (3) of the Treaty establishing the European Economic Community and Regulation (EC) No 852/2004 of the European Parliament and the Council on the hygiene of foodstuffs. http://eur-lex.europa.eu/LexUriServ/LexUriServ.do?uri=COM:2007:0090:FIN:EN:PDF

COM(2007) 670 final. Amended Proposal for a Regulation of the European Parliament and of the Council on food enzymes and amending Council Directive 83/417/EEC, Council Regulation (EC) No 1493/1999, Directive 2000/13/EC of the European Parliament and of the Council, and Council Directive 2001/112/EC and Regulation (EC) No 258/97 of the European Parliament and of the Council (presented by the Commission pursuant to article 250 (2) of the EC Treaty). http://eur-lex.europa.eu/LexUriServ/LexUriServ.do?uri=COM:2007:0670:FIN:EN:PDF

COM(2007) 671 final. Amended proposal for a Regulation of the European Parliament and of the Council on flavourings and certain food ingredients with flavouring properties for use in and on foods and amending Council Regulation (EEC) No 1576/89, Council Regulation (EEC) No 1601/91, Regulation (EC) No 2232/96 and Directive 2000/13/EC (presented by the Commission pursuant to Article 250 (2) of the EC Treaty). http://eur-lex.europa.eu/LexUriServ/LexUriServ.do?uri=COM:2007:0671:FIN:EN:PDF

COM(2007) 672 final. Amended Proposal for a Regulation of the European Parliament and of the Council establishing a common authorisation procedure for food additives, food enzymes and food flavourings (presented by the Commission pursuant to Article 250 (2) of the EC Treaty). http://eur-lex.europa.eu/LexUriServ/LexUriServ.do?uri=COM:2007:0672:FIN:EN:PDF

COM(2007) 673 final. Amended proposal for a Regulation of the European Parliament and of the Council on food additives (presented by the Commission pursuant to Article 250 (2) of the EC Treaty). http://eur-lex.europa.eu/LexUriServ/LexUriServ.do?uri=COM:2007:0673:FIN:EN:PDF

COM(2007) 872. Proposal for a Regulation of the European Parliament and of the Council on novel foods and amending Regulation (EC) No XXX/XXXX [common procedure]. http://ec.europa.eu/food/food/biotechnology/novelfood/COM872_novel_food_proposal_en.pdf

http://ec.europa.eu/food/food/biotechnology/novelfood/initiatives_en.htm

Proposed legislation on pre-market approval schemes of food enzymes, flavourings and additives. http://ec.europa.eu/food/food/chemicalsafety/additives/prop_leg_en.htm

COM(2008)40 final. Proposal for a Regulation of the European Parliament and of the Council on the provision of food information to consumers. http://eur-lex.europa.eu/LexUriServ/LexUriServ.do?uri=COM:2008:0040:FIN:EN:PDF

Council, Common Position (EC) No 9/2008 of 10 March 2008 adopted by the Council, acting in accordance with the procedure referred to in Article 251 of the Treaty establishing the European Community, with a view to the adoption of a Regulation of the European Parliament and of the Council on flavourings and certain food ingredients with flavouring properties for use in and on foods and amending Council Regulations (EEC) No 1576/89 and (EEC) No 1601/91, Regulation (EC) No 2232/96 and Directive 2000/13/EC (Text with EEA relevance). Official Journal C 111E, 6 May 2008, pp. 46-67. http://eur-lex.europa.eu/LexUriServ/LexUriServ.do?uri=OJ:C:2008:111E:0046:0067:EN:PDF

Case law

ECJ 5 February 1963, Case 26/62, NV Algemene Transport en Expeditie Onderneming Van Gend en Loos v. Nederlandse Administratie der belastingen. European Court Reports (ECR) 1. http://eur-lex.europa.eu/LexUriServ/LexUriServ.do?uri=CELEX:61962J0026:EN:HTML

ECJ 15 July 1964, Case 6/64, Flaminio Costa v. ENEL, ECR 585. http://eur-lex.europa.eu/LexUriServ/LexUriServ.do?uri=CELEX:61964J0006:EN:HTML

ECJ 16 June 1966, Case 54/65, Compagnie des forges de Châtillon, Commentry & Neuves-Maisons v High Authority of the ECSC. ECR 185 at 195. http://eur-lex.europa.eu/LexUriServ/LexUriServ.do?uri=CELEX:61965J0054:EN:HTML

ECJ 3 April 1968, Case 28/67, Firma Molkerei-Zentrale Westfalen Lippe GmbH v. Hauptzollamt Paderborn. ECR 143 at 152. http://eur-lex.europa.eu/LexUriServ/LexUriServ.do?uri=CELEX:61967J0028:EN:HTML

ECJ 7 February 1972, Case 39/72, Commission v. Italy, Premiums for slaughtering cows, ECR 1973, pp. 101. http://eur-lex.europa.eu/LexUriServ/LexUriServ.do?uri=CELEX:61972J0039:EN:HTML

ECJ 11 July 1974, Case 8/74, Procureur du Roi v Benoît and Gustave Dassonville, ECR 1974, pp. 837. http://eur-lex.europa.eu/LexUriServ/LexUriServ.do?uri=CELEX:61974J0008:EN:HTML

ECJ 14 July 1976, Combined cases 3, 4 and 6/76, Cornelis Kramer and others. - References for a preliminary ruling: Arrondissementsrechtbank Zwolle et Arrondissementsrechtbank Alkmaar - Netherlands. - Biological resources of the sea. ECR 1976, pp. 1279. http://eur-lex.europa.eu/LexUriServ/LexUriServ.do?uri=CELEX:61976J0003:EN:HTML

ECJ 1 February 1977, Case 51/76, Verbond van Nederlandse Ondernemingen v Inspecteur der Invoerrechten en Accijnzen. ECR 1977, pp. 113. http://eur-lex.europa.eu/LexUriServ/LexUriServ.do?uri=CELEX:61976J0051:EN:HTML

ECJ 13 February 1979, Case 85/76, Hoffmann – La Roche & Co. AG v. Commission. ECR 1979, pp. 461. http://eur-lex.europa.eu/LexUriServ/LexUriServ.do?uri=CELEX:61976J0085:EN:HTML

ECJ 20 February 1979, Case 120/78, Rewe-Zentral AG v Bundesmonopolverwaltung für Branntwein (Cassis de Dijon), ECR 1979, pp. 649. http://eur-lex.europa.eu/LexUriServ/LexUriServ.do?uri=CELEX:61978J0120:EN:HTML

ECJ 5 April 1979, Case 148/78, Criminal proceedings against Tullio Ratti. ECR 1979, pp. 1629. http://eur-lex.europa.eu/LexUriServ/LexUriServ.do?uri=CELEX:61978J0148:EN:HTML

ECJ 10 November 1982, Case 261/81, Walter Rau Lebensmittelwerke v De Smedt PVBA. ECR 1982, pp. 3961. http://eur-lex.europa.eu/LexUriServ/LexUriServ.do?uri=CELEX:61981J0261:EN:HTML

ECJ 25 April 1985, Case 207/83, Commission of the European Communities v United Kingdom of Great Britain and Northern Ireland. ECR 1985 pp. 1201. http://eur-lex.europa.eu/LexUriServ/LexUriServ.do?uri=CELEX:61983J0207:EN:HTML

ECJ 12 March 1987, Case 178/84 Commission v Germany ('Reinheitsgebot' or 'German beer'). ECR 1987, pp. 1227. http://eur-lex.europa.eu/LexUriServ/LexUriServ.do?uri=CELEX:61984J0178:EN:HTML

ECJ 8 October 1987, Case 80/86 Criminal proceedings against Kolpinghuis Nijmegen BV. ECR 1987, pp. 3969. http://eur-lex.europa.eu/LexUriServ/LexUriServ.do?uri=CELEX:61986J0080:EN:HTML

ECJ 4 February 1988, Case 255/86, Commission of the European Communities v Kingdom of Belgium, Failure of a State to fulfil its obligations, ECR 1988, pp. 693. http://eur-lex.europa.eu/LexUriServ/LexUriServ.do?uri=CELEX:61986J0255:EN:HTML

ECJ 19 November 1991, Joined Cases C-6/90 and C-9/90, Andrea Francovich and Danila Bonifaci and others v Italian Republic. ECR 1991, I-5357. http://eur-lex.europa.eu/LexUriServ/LexUriServ.do?uri=CELEX:61990J0006:EN:HTML

ECJ 5 March 1996, Joined Cases C-46/93 and C-48/93, Brasserie du Pêcheur SA v Bundesrepublik Deutschland and The Queen v Secretary of State for Transport, ex parte: Factortame Ltd and others, ECR 1996, I-01029. http://eur-lex.europa.eu/LexUriServ/LexUriServ.do?uri=CELEX:61993J0046:EN:HTML

ECJ 5 May 1998, Case C-157/96, The Queen v Ministry of Agriculture, Fisheries and Food, Commissioners of Customs & Excise, ex parte National Farmers' Union, David Burnett and Sons Ltd, R. S. and E. Wright Ltd, Anglo Beef Processors Ltd, United Kingdom Genetics, Wyjac Calves Ltd, International Traders Ferry Ltd, MFP International Ltd, Interstate Truck Rental Ltd and Vian Exports Ltd. ECR 1998, I-02211. http://eur-lex.europa.eu/LexUriServ/LexUriServ.do?uri=CELEX:61996J0157:EN:HTML

ECJ 5 May 1998, Case C-180/96, U.K. Great Britain and Northern Ireland v. Commission of European Communities, ECR 1996, I-03903. http://eur-lex.europa.eu/LexUriServ/LexUriServ.do?uri=CELEX:61996J0180:EN:HTML

ECJ 1 October 1998, Case C-209/96, United Kingdom of Great Britain and Northern Ireland v. Commission of the European Communities. EAGGF - Clearance of accounts - 1992 and 1993 - Beef and veal. ECR 1998, I-05655. http://eur-lex.europa.eu/LexUriServ/LexUriServ.do?uri=CELEX:61996J0209:EN:HTML

CFI 19 July 1999, Case T-188/97, Rothmans v Commission. ECR 1999, II-2463. http://eur-lex.europa.eu/LexUriServ/LexUriServ.do?uri=CELEX:61997A0188:EN:HTML

ECJ 5 December 2000, Case C-448/98, Criminal proceedings against Jean-Pierre Guimont (Emmenthal cheese case), ECR 2000, I-10663. http://eur-lex.europa.eu/LexUriServ/LexUriServ.do?uri=CELEX:61998J0448:EN:HTML

ECJ 25 April 2002, Case C-154/00, Commission of the European Communities v Hellenic Republic. ECR 2002, I-03879. http://eur-lex.europa.eu/LexUriServ/LexUriServ.do?uri=CELEX:62000J0154:EN:HTML

ECJ 5 November 2002, Case C-325/00, Commission v. Germany, ECR 2002, I-09977. http://eur-lex.europa.eu/LexUriServ/LexUriServ.do?uri=CELEX:62000J0325:EN:HTML

CFI 14 December 2005, Case T-383/00, Beamglow Ltd v European Parliament, Council of the European Union and Commission of the European Communities, ECR 2005, II-05459. http://eur-lex.europa.eu/LexUriServ/LexUriServ.do?uri=CELEX:62000A0383:EN:HTML

ECJ 6 March 2003, Case C-6/02, Commission of the European Communities v French Republic. ECR 2003, I-02389http://eur-lex.europa.eu/LexUriServ/LexUriServ.do?uri=CELEX:62002J0006:EN:HTML

ECJ 9 June 2005, Joined Cases C-211/03, C-299/03, C-316/03, C-317/03 to C-318/03. HLH Warenvertriebs GmbH and Orthica BV v Bundesrepublik Deutschland. ECR 2005, I-05141. http://eur-lex.europa.eu/LexUriServ/LexUriServ.do?uri=CELEX:62003J0211:EN:HTML

ECJ 28 September 2006, Cases C-129/05 and C-130/05, NV Raverco (C-129/05), Coxon & Chatterton Ltd (C-130/05) v. Minister van Landbouw, Natuur en Voedselkwaliteit (NL). ECR 2006, I-09297. http://eur-lex.europa.eu/LexUriServ/LexUriServ.do?uri=CELEX:62005J0129:EN:HTML

ECJ 23 November 2006 case C-315/05, Lidl Italia Srl v. Comune di Arcole (VR). http://curia.europa.eu/jurisp/cgi-bin/gettext.pl?where=&lang=en&num=79938876C19050315&doc=T&ouvert=T&seance=ARRET

ECJ 15 November 2007, Case C-319/05, Commission v. Federal Republic of Germany. ECR 2007, pp. 00000. http://eur-lex.europa.eu/LexUriServ/LexUriServ.do?uri=CELEX:62005J0319:EN:HTML

ECJ 13 March 2008, Cases 383/06 to 385/06, Vereniging Nationaal Overlegorgaan Sociale Werkvoorziening (C-383/06) and Gemeente Rotterdam (C-384/06) v Minister van Sociale Zaken en Werkgelegenheid and Sociaal Economische Samenwerking West-Brabant (C-385/06) v Algemene Directie voor de Arbeidsvoorziening. ECR 2008, p. 0000. http://eur-lex.europa.eu/LexUriServ/LexUriServ.do?uri=CELEX:62006J0383:EN:HTML

Soft law, policy documents, reports and general information

Inter-institutional

Spaak Report: Rapport des Chefs de Délégations aux Ministres des Affaires Etrangères. Secretariat of the Intergovernmental Conference Brussels, 21 April 1956. http://www.ena.lu/report_heads_delegation_foreign_ministers_brussels_21_april_1956-022300010.html

Joint Practical Guide of the European Parliament, the Council and the Commission, for persons involved in the drafting of legislation within the Community institutions, Brussels 16 March 2000. http://eur-lex.europa.eu/en/techleg/pdf/en.pdf

Agreement between the European Parliament and the Commission on procedures for implementing Council Decision 1999/468/EC of 28 June 1999 laying down the procedures for the exercise of implementing powers conferred on the Commission. Official Journal L 256, 10 October 2000, pp. 19-20. http://eur-lex.europa.eu/LexUriServ/LexUriServ.do?uri=OJ:L:2000:256:0019:0020:EN:PDF

The interinstitutional agreement on better law-making of the European Parliament, Council and Commission. Official Journal C 321, 31 December 2003, pp 1-5. http://eur-lex.europa.eu/LexUriServ/LexUriServ.do?uri=OJ:C:2003:321:0001:0005:EN:PDF

Council and European Parliament

Conclusions of Luxembourg Summit 1997, 13 December 1997, nr. 57. http://www.vm.ee/est/euro/aken_prindi/2658.html#environment

European Council Presidency Conclusions 1994-2008. http://europa.eu/european-council/index_en.htm

Manuel Medina Ortega, Report of the Temporary Committee of Inquiry into BSE, set up by the Parliament in July 1996, on the alleged contraventions or maladministration in the implementation of Community law in relation to BSE, without prejudice to the jurisdiction of the Community and the national courts of 7 February 1997, A4-0020/97/A, PE 220.544/fin/A. http://www.mad-cow.org/final_EU.html

Minority opinions to Medina Ortega Report: http://www.europarl.europa.eu/sides/getDoc.do;jsessionid=57EFC6E4B222427727B7EA925F7E90BB.node1?language=EN&pubRef=-//EP//NONSGML+REPORT+A4-1997-0020+0+DOC+PDF+V0//EN

European Parliament Fact Sheets 4.10.1. Consumer Policy: principles and instruments, chapter 3 Reform in the wake of the BSE crisis. http://www.europarl.europa.eu/factsheets/4_10_1_en.htm

European Commission, agencies and comitology

COM(85) 310 Final. White Paper Completing the Internal Market. http://ec.europa.eu/comm/off/pdf/1985_0310_f_en.pdf

COM (1997) 176. Green Paper on the General Principles of Food Law in the European Union. http://www.foodlaw.rdg.ac.uk/eu/green-97.doc

COM(97) 183 final. Communication of the European Commission, Consumer Health and Food Safety. http://ec.europa.eu/food/fs/sc/comec1en.pdf

COM (1999) 719. White Paper on Food Safety. http://ec.europa.eu/dgs/health_consumer/library/pub/pub06_en.pdf

COM(2000) 1 final. Communication on the use of the precautionary principle Brussels 2.2.2000. http://ec.europa.eu/dgs/health_consumer/library/pub/pub07_en.pdf

COM(2001) 428 final. European Governance. A White Paper. http://eur-lex.europa.eu/LexUriServ/site/en/com/2001/com2001_0428en01.pdf

COM(2001) 593. Communication from the commission to the council the European parliament and the economic and social committee. Community Strategy for Dioxins, Furans and Polychlorinated Biphenyls. http://ec.europa.eu/food/food/chemicalsafety/contaminants/com2001_0593en01.pdf

COM(2005) 9 final. Report from the European Commission to the Council and the European Parliament on the Possibility of Introduction of Electronic Identification for Bovine Animals, Jan. 25, 2005. http://eur-lex.europa.eu/LexUriServ/LexUriServ.do?uri=COM:2005:0009:FIN:EN:PDF

COM(2007) 640 final. Commission of the European Communities, Communication from the Commission to the European Parliament the Council, the European Economic and Social Committee and the Committee of the Regions, Commission Legislative and Work Programme 2008, Brussels, 23.10.2007. http://ec.europa.eu/atwork/programmes/docs/clwp2008_en.pdf

COM(2007) 842 final. Commission of the European Communities, Report from the Commission on the working of Committees during 2006, Brussels, 20.12.2007. http://eur-lex.europa.eu/LexUriServ/LexUriServ.do?uri=COM:2007:0842:FIN:EN:PDF

Commission of the European Communities, Bulletin of the European Union; http://europa.eu/bulletin/en/welcome.htm

Commission of the European Communities, General Report on the Activities of the European Union; http://europa.eu/generalreport/en/welcome.htm

Commission of the European Communities, Health & Consumer Protection Directorate-General, Healthy democracy. Conclusions and Actions following the DG SANCO 2006 Peer Review Group on Stakeholder Involvement, February 2007. http://ec.europa.eu/health/ph_overview/Documents/stakeholders_en.pdf

Commission of the European Communities, Health & Consumer Protection Directorate-General, Stakeholder Involvement Event, The Report, Brussels, 23 May 2007. http://www.sanco-stakeholderinvolvement.eu/

Commission of the European Communities, Health & Consumer Protection Directorate-General, 03 - Science and stakeholder relations Joint meeting of the stakeholder dialogue group and the advisory group on the food chain and animal and plant health, summary record, Brussels, SANCO.03, 30 November 2007. http://ec.europa.eu/food/committees/advisory/summary_30112007.pdf

Communication from the Commission concerning the consequences of the judgment given by the Court of Justice on 20 February 1979 in case 120/78 ('Cassis de Dijon'). Official Journal C 256, 03 October 1980, pp 2-3. http://eu.pravo.hr/fileadmin/Europsko/dokumenti/EU_razno/Communication_from_the_Commission_concerning_the_consequences_of_the_judgment_given_by_the_Court_of_Justice_on_20_Fe.doc

Consumer Voice September 2002, 7/02, FVO at Home and Away. http://ec.europa.eu/dgs/health_consumer/newsletter/200209/consumervoice_en.pdf

Health & Consumer Voice November 2007, Safer Food for Europe – over a decade of achievement for the FVO. http://ec.europa.eu/dgs/health_consumer/consumervoice/cvsp_112007_en.pdf

GMO public comments. http://ec.europa.eu/food/food/biotechnology/autorisation/public_comments_en.htm.

Guidance document for Competent Authorities for the control of compliance with EU legislation on aflatoxins. http://ec.europa.eu/food/food/chemicalsafety/contaminants/aflatoxin_guidance_en.pdf

Guidance on the Implementation of Articles 11, 12, 16, 17, 18, 19 and 20 of Regulation (EC) n° 178/2002 on General Food Law, Conclusions of the Standing Committee on the Food Chain and Animal Health (2004). http://ec.europa.eu/food/food/foodlaw/guidance/guidance_rev_7_en.pdf

Guidance document on certain key questions related to import requirements and the new rules on food hygiene and on official food controls. http://ec.europa.eu/food/international/trade/interpretation_imports.pdf

Guidance document on the implementation of certain provisions of Regulation (EC) No 852/2004 On the hygiene of foodstuffs http://ec.europa.eu/food/food/biosafety/hygienelegislation/guidance_doc_852-2004_en.pdf

Guidance document on the implementation of certain provisions of Regulation (EC) No 853/2004 on the hygiene of food of animal origin. http://ec.europa.eu/food/food/biosafety/hygienelegislation/guidance_doc_853-2004_en.pdf

Guidance document on the implementation of procedures based on the HACCP principles, and on the facilitation of the implementation of the HACCP principles in certain food businesses. http://ec.europa.eu/food/food/biosafety/hygienelegislation/guidance_doc_haccp_en.pdf

Guidelines regarding/relating to Article 6, paragraph 10 of Directive 2000/13/EC as amended by Directive 2003/89/EC. http://ec.europa.eu/food/food/labellingnutrition/foodlabelling/guidelines_6_10.pdf

Guidelines from the Commission' services for the contents of the notifications requested by new paragraph 11 of Directive 2000/13/EC, as amended by Directive 2003/89/EC. http://ec.europa.eu/food/food/labellingnutrition/foodlabelling/guidelines.pdf

Second administrative guidance from the Commission' services for the application of Article 6 paragraph 11 of Directive 2000/13/EC. http://ec.europa.eu/food/food/labellingnutrition/foodlabelling/2nd_guid_art6_11_200013ec_en.pdf

General guidelines for implementing the principle of Quantitative Ingredients Declaration (QUID) – Article 7 of Directive 79/112/EEC as amended by Directive 97/4/EC. http://ec.europa.eu/food/food/labellingnutrition/resources/fl02_en.pdf

Guidelines for the development of community guides to good practice for hygiene and for the application of the HACCP principles, in accordance with Article 9 of Regulation (EC) No 852/2004 on the hygiene of foodstuffs and Article 22 of Regulation (EC) No 183/2005 laying down requirements for feed hygiene. http://ec.europa.eu/food/food/biosafety/hygienelegislation/guidelines_good_practice_en.pdf

Modus Operandi for the management of new food safety incidents with a potential for extension involving a chemical substance, January 2006; Standing Committee on the Food Chain and Animal health (section Toxicological Safety). http://ec.europa.eu/food/food/foodlaw/procedures/modus_operandi.pdf

Notice to applicants F2/AW D(2003). Guideline on the categorisation of extenson applications (ea) versus variations applications (v) medicinal products for human and veterinary use. http://ec.europa.eu/enterprise/pharmaceuticals/eudralex/vol-6/newdoc/v6c_ea_v%20_10_2003b.pdf

Novel foods (approved and other). http://ec.europa.eu/food/food/biotechnology/novelfood/index_en.htm

Rapid Alert System for food and Feed (RASFF) annual report 2006. http://ec.europa.eu/food/food/rapidalert/report2006_en.pdf

Commission Recommendation 97/618/EC of 29 July 1997 concerning the scientific aspects and the presentation of information necessary to support applications for the placing on the market of novel foods and novel food ingredients and the preparation of initial assessment reports under Regulation (EC) No 258/97 of the European Parliament and of the Council. Official Journal L 253, 16 September 1997, pp. 1-36. http://eur-lex.europa.eu/LexUriServ/LexUriServ.do?uri=CELEX:31997H0618:EN:HTML

Commission Recommendation of 23 July 2003 on guidelines for the development of national strategies and best practices to ensure the coexistence of genetically modified crops with conventional and organic farming (notified under document number C(2003) 2624). Official Journal L 189, 29 July 2003, pp. 36-47. http://eur-lex.europa.eu/LexUriServ/LexUriServ.do?uri=CELEX:32003H0556:EN:HTML

Commission Recommendation of 4 February 2005 on the further investigation into the levels of polycyclic aromatic hydrocarbons in certain foods (notified under document number C(2005) 256) (Text with EEA relevance). Official Journal L 34, 8 February 2005, pp. 43-45. http://eur-lex.europa.eu/LexUriServ/LexUriServ.do?uri=OJ:L:2005:034:0043:0045:EN:PDF

Commission Recommendation of 6 February 2006 on the reduction of the presence of dioxins, furans and PCBs in feedingstuffs and foodstuffs (notified under document number C(2006) 235) (Text with EEA relevance). Official Journal L 42, 14 February 2006, pp. 26-28. http://europa.eu.int/eur-lex/lex/LexUriServ/site/en/oj/2006/l_042/l_04220060214en00260028.pdf

Technical Specifications in Relation to the Master List and the Lists of EU Approved Food Establishments (SANCO/2179/2005 Revision 5). http://ec.europa.eu/food/food/biosafety/establishments/techspecs_en.pdf

Trade Barriers Regulation (brochure). http://trade.ec.europa.eu/doclib/docs/2005/april/tradoc_122567.pdf

European Economic and Social Committee

Opinion of the European Economic and Social Committee on 'Hygiene rules and artisanal food processors' (2006/C 65/25). Official Journal C 65 17 March 2006, pp. 141-148. http://eur-lex.europa.eu/LexUriServ/LexUriServ.do?uri=OJ:C:2006:065:0141:0148:EN:PDF

Other sources of law

International documents

Agreement on the Application of Sanitary and Phytosanitary Measures (WTO). http://www.wto.org/english/docs_e/legal_e/15-sps.pdf

Agreement on Technical Barriers to Trade (WTO). http://www.wto.org/english/docs_e/legal_e/17-tbt.pdf

Agreement on Trade Related Aspects of Intellectual Property Rights (WTO). http://www.wto.org/english/docs_e/legal_e/27-trips pdf

Biosafety Clearing House (OECD). http://bch.cbd.int/

Cartagena Protocol on Biosafety to the Convention on Biological Diversity. Official Journal L 201, 31 july 2002, pp. 50-55. http://eur-lex.europa.eu/LexUriServ/LexUriServ.do?uri=CELEX:22002A0731(01):EN:HTML

Charter of the United Nations (UN). http://www.un.org/aboutun/charter/

Codex Alimentarius. Codex Alimentarius Commission, Procedural Manual, 17th edition, Rome 2007. http://www.codexalimentarius.net/web/procedural_manual.jsp

Codex Alimentarius, Basis texts on Food Hygiene, 3rd edition Rome, 2003. ftp://ftp.fao.org/codex/Publications/Booklets/Hygiene/FoodHygiene_2003e.pdf

Codex Alimentarius Procedural Manual, Ninth Edition, pages 150–151, Terms of Reference Codex Committee on Fresh Fruits and Vegetables (CX-731).

Convention on Biological Diversity. http://www.cbd.int/doc/legal/cbd-un-en.pdf

Convention establishing an International Organisation of Legal Metrology, done at Paris - France, the 12th of October 1955. Official translation in English made by the British Government and published under Treaty series No 60 of 1962. http://www.oiml.org/publications/B/B001-e55.pdf

Committee on Economic, Social and Cultural Rights, General Comment nr. 12. http://www.unhchr.ch/tbs/doc.nsf/0/3d02758c707031d58025677f003b73b9?Opendocument and http://www.fao.org/righttofood/common/ecg/51635_en_General_Comment_No.12.pdf

Dispute Settlement Understanding (WTO). http://www.wto.org/english/tratop_e/dispu_e/dsu_e.htm

Food and Agriculture Organization of the United Nations, Constitution of the Food and Agriculture Organization of the United Nations, http://www.fao.org/docrep/x5584e/x5584e0i.htm

FAO, Voluntary Guidelines to support the progressive realization of the right to adequate food in the context of national food security http://www.fao.org/docrep/meeting/009/y9825e/y9825e00.htm

General Agreement on trade in Services (WTO). http://www.wto.org/english/docs_e/legal_e/26-gats.pdf

General Agreement on Tariffs and Trade (WTO). http://www.wto.org/english/docs_e/legal_e/06-gatt.pdf

Revised Geneva Protocol on Standardization of Fresh Fruit and Vegetables and Dry and Dried Fruit, published 1958 and revised 1985. http://www.unece.org/trade/agr/info/gevprot/gevprot.htm

Standard layout for UNECE standards concerning the marketing and commercial quality control of Fresh Fruit and Vegetables. The 2003 version is based on document TRADE/WP.7/2002/9/Add.13 of 23 January 2003. The Standard Layout 2007 will replace the 2003 version after the completion of the recommendation phase in November 2008 if all agree. Both versions can be found at http://www.unece.org/trade/agr/standard/fresh/fresh_e.htm.

Understanding on Rules and Procedures Governing the Settlement of Disputes http://www.wto.org/english/docs_e/legal_e/28-dsu_e.htm.

United Nations, Charter, San Francisco, 26 June 1945. http://www.un.org/aboutun/charter/

United Nations, The Millennium Development Goals Report 2006, New York, 2006. http://www.unmillenniumproject.org/ and http://www.unmillenniumproject.org/documents/MainReportComplete-lowres.pdf

United Nations and Food and Agriculture Organization of the United Nations, specialised agency agreement A/78, 30 September 1946, Item 24 of the provisional agenda for the second part of the first session of the General Assembly, http://www.unsystemceb.org/reference/system/agreements

United Nations General Assembly Resolution 50 (I) approving the first four specialised agency agreements, among which FAO's, at the Sixty-fifth plenary meeting, 14 December 1946. http://www.unsystemceb.org/reference/system/agreements

Vienna Convention on the Law of Treaties, Vienna 1969, United Nations Treaty Series, (UNTS)vol. 1155, p. 331. http://untreaty.un.org/ilc/texts/instruments/english/conventions/1_1_1969.pdf

WHO/FAO. World Health Organisation in cooperation with the Food and Agricultural Organisation of the United Nations, The International Food Safety Authorities Network (INFOSAN) Users Guide, October 2006. http://www.who.int/foodsafety/publications/fs_management/INFOSAN_User_Guide_Final.pdf

World Health Organization, Constitution of the World Health Organization, Basic Documents, Forty-fifth edition, Supplement, October 2006. http://www.who.int/governance/eb/who_constitution_en.pdf

World Trade Organization, Agreement establishing the World Trade Organization http://www.wto.org/english/thewto_e/whatis_e/tif_e/agrm1_e.htm

World Trade Organization, organization chart, http://www.wto.org/english/thewto_e/whatis_e/tif_e/org2_e.htm

WTO. WTO International Trade Statistics 2007. http://www.wto.org/english/res_e/statis_e/its2007_e/its07_toc_e.htm

International case law

EC hormones case. WTO appellate body 16 January 1998; WT/DS48/AB/R. http://www.wto.org/english/tratop_e/dispu_e/cases_e/ds26_e.htm.

EC Biotech case. WTO dispute settlement body 29 September 2006; WT/DS291/R, WT/DS292/R, WT/DS293/R. http://www.wto.org/english/news_e/news06_e/291r_e.htm http://www.trade-environment.org/page/theme/tewto/biotechcase.htm.

Second EC hormones case. WTO dispute settlement body 31 March 2008; WT/DS320/R. http://www.wto.org/english/news_e/news08_e/320r_321r_e.htm

Private standards

BRC. http://www.brc.org.uk

Dutch HACCP. http://www.foodsafetymanagement.info

Fair trade. http://www.fairtrade.nl/main_en.php?language=en
GFSI. http://www.cies-net.com
GlobalGAP (EurepGAP). http://www.globalgap.org
IFS. http://www.food-care.info
ISO 22.000. http://www.22000-tools.com
SQF. http://www.sqfi.com
ICC Official Rules for the Interpretation of Trade Terms, ICC Publication No. 560, 2000 Edition. http://www.searates.com/reference/incoterms/

EU member states' and third countries' legislation

Constitution of the United States of America. http://www.constitution.org/indexco_.htm
Constitution for the Kingdom of The Netherlands 2002. Source of translation: the Ministry of Interior and Kingdom Relations, http://www.minbzk.nl/uk/constitution
Constitution for the Federal Republic of Germany (in German). www.bundesregierung.de/Gesetze
Lebensmittel-, Bedarfsgegenstände- und Futtermittelgesetzbuch (German Code on food, food contact materials and feed) http://www.bundesrecht.juris.de/bundesrecht/lfgb/gesamt.pdf
Italy, Repubblica Italiana, the Italian Republic, Costituzione della Repubblica Italiana (Constitution of the Italian Republic).

Literature

Abaitua Borda, I., Philen, R.M., Posada de la Paz, M., De la Cámara, A.G., Ruiz-Navarro, M.D. Giménez Ribota, O., Alvargonzález Soldevilla, J., Terracini, B., Peña, S.S., Fuentes Leal, C. and Kilbourne, E.M., Toxic Oil Syndrome Mortality: The First Thirteen Years. Int. J. Epidemiology 27 (1998): 1057-1063. http://ije.oxfordjournals.org/cgi/content/abstract/27/6/1057
Ammendrup, S. and Füssell, A.E., Legislative Requirements for the Identification and Traceability of Farm Animals within the European Union. Revue Scientifique et Technique (International Office of Epizootics), 20 (2001): 437-444. http://www.oie.int/eng/publicat/RT/2002/AMMENDRU.PDF
Berends, G. and Carreno, I., Safeguards in food law – ensuring food scares are scarce. European Law Review 30 (2005): 386-405.
Bevilacqua, D., The Codex Alimentarius Commission and its Influence on European and National Food Policy. EFFL 1/1/2006, p. 3-16.
Bevilacqua, D., The EC-Biotech Case. EFFL 1/6/2006, 331-347.
Broberg, M.P., Transforming the European Community's Regulation of Food Safety. Sieps 2008 (e-book). http://www.sieps.se/publ/rapporter/2008/bilagor%202008/2008-5.pdf
Cheftel, J.C., Food and nutrition labelling in the European Union. Food Chemistry 93 (2005): 531-550. http://www.sciencedirect.com/science?_ob=ArticleURL&_udi=B6T6R-4FH4V4G-2&_user=10&_rdoc=1&_fmt=&_orig=search&_sort=d&view=c&_acct=C000050221&_version=1&_urlVersion=0&_userid=10&md5=f62c5b54141255539687b1f52e1c85220

Chia-Hui Lee, G., Private Food Standards and their Impacts on Developing Countries. European Commission, DG Trade Unit G2. http://trade.ec.europa.eu/doclib/docs/2006/november/tradoc_127969.pdf

Coffee Jr., J.C., The Rise of Dispersed Ownership: The Roles of Law & the State in the Separation of Ownership and Control. Yale Law Journal 111 (2001): 62-63. http://yalelawjournal.org/111/1/1_john_c_coffee_jr.html

Coutrelis, N., Product Liability in the Food Sector. http://ec.europa.eu/enterprise/regulation/goods/docs/liability/1999-greenpaper-replies/046.pdf

Eide, W.B. and Kracht, U., Food and Human Rights in Development. Vol. I. Legal and Institutional Dimensions and Selected Topics, Itersentia Antwerpen – Oxford, 2005.

Eide, W.B. and Kracht, U., Food and Human Rights in Development. Vol. II. Evolving Issues and Emerging Applications, Itersentia Antwerpen – Oxford, 2007.

FAO Committee On Agriculture, Development of a Framework for Good Agricultural Practices, Seventeenth Session, Rome, 31 March-4 April 2003. http://www.fao.org/docrep/meeting/006/y8704e.htm

FAO, Understanding the Codex Alimentarius, Rome 2005. http://www.fao.org/docrep/008/y7867e/y7867e00.htm

FAO/WHO, Report of the Evaluation of the Codex Alimentarius and other FAO aAnd WHO Food Standards Work. http://www.who.int/foodsafety/codex/eval_report/en/index.html

Fogden, M., Hygiene. In: K. Goodburn (ed.) EU food law. A practical guide. Woodhead Publishing Cambridge UK, 2001.

Gelpí, E., Posada de la Paz, M., Terracini, B., Abaitua, I., de la Cámara, A.G., Kilbourne, E.M., Lahoz, C., Nemery, B., Philen, R.M., Soldevilla, L., Tarkowski, S. and WHO/CISAT Scientific Committee for the Toxic Oil Syndrome. The Spanish Toxic Oil Syndrome Twenty Years After Its Onset: A Multidisciplinary Review of Scientific Knowledge. Environ. Health Perspect. 110 (2002): 457-464. http://www.pubmedcentral.nih.gov/articlerender.fcgi?artid=1240833

European Food and Feed Law Review (EFFL) is not electronically available. http://www.lexxion.eu/effl/ or http://www.effl.eu/

Goodburn, K. (ed.), EU food law. A practical guide. Woodhead Publishing Cambridge UK, 2001. http://www.woodheadpublishing.com/en/book.aspx?bookID=420#sec1

Gormley, L.W., Introduction to the Law of the European Communities. 3th ed., London, 1998.

Hampton, P., Reducing administrative burdens: effective inspection and enforcement, HM Treasury, March 2005. http://www.berr.gov.uk/files/file22988.pdf

Harris, S., Swinbank, A. and Wilkinson, G., The Food and Farm Policies of the European Community. Chichester, 1983. http://ideas.repec.org/a/eee/jfpoli/v9y1984i2p171-172.html

ICTSD Bridges weekly. http://www.ictsd.org/weekly/index.htm

Journal of International Biotechnology Law (JIBL). http://www.degruyter.de/journals/jibl/

James, P., Kemper, F. and Pascal, G., A European Food and Public Health Authority. The future of scientific advice in the EU, 1999. http://ec.europa.eu/food/fs/sc/future_food_en.pdf

Kent, G. Freedom from Want. The human right to adequate food, Georgetown University Press Washington, D.C. 2005. http://press.georgetown.edu/pdfs/9781589010550.pdf

Kimbrell, E., What is Codex Alimentarius. AgBioForum 3 (2000): 197-202. http://www.agbioforum.org/v3n4/v3n4a03-kimbrell.pdf

Knipschild, K., Lebensmittelsicherheit als Aufgabe des Veterinär- und Lebensmittelrechts. (diss.) Nomos Verlagsgesellschaft Baden-Baden, Germany, 2003.

Knudsen, G. and Matikainen-Kallström, M., Joint Parliamentary Committee Report on food safety in the EEA, 1999. secretariat.efta.int/Web/EuropeanEconomicArea/eea_jpc_resolutions/1999FoodSafety.doc

Korver, O., Kühn, M.C. and Richardson, D., The Functional Foods Dossier: Building Solid Health Claims. Bennekom (The Netherlands), 2nd ed. 2006. http://www.foodapplication.net/foodbookstore/ffdossier/

Lawrence, D., Kennedy, J. and Hattan, E., New Controls on the Deliberate Release of GMOs. European Environmental Law Review 11 (2002): 51-56.

Lelieveld, H. and Keener, L., Global harmonization of food regulations and legislation - the Global Harmonization Initiative. Trends in Food Science & Technology 18 (2007): S15-S19. http://www.icc.or.at/international_research/2007_EHEDG_Yearbook-TIFS18.pdf

Liang C.F. and A.R. Ferguson, The botanical nomenclature of the kiwifruit and related taxa. New Zealand Journal of Botany 24 (1986): 183-184. www.rsnz.org/publish/nzjb/1986/10.pdf

Luning, P.A., Marcelis, W.J. and Jongen, W.M.F., Food Quality Management. A techno-managerial approach, Wageningen Academic Publishers, the Netherlands, 2002. http://www.wageningenacademic.com/quality

MacRae, R., A history of sustainable agriculture. 1990. Ecological Agriculture Projects. Excerpt from thesis, 'Strategies for overcoming the barriers to the transition to sustainable agriculture' www.eap.mcgill.ca.

Malanczuk, P., Akehurst's Modern Introduction to International Law, 7th ed. London, 1997.

Masson-Matthee, M.D., The Codex Alimentarius Commission and Its Standards. An examination of the legal aspects of the Codex Alimentarius Commission. Asser Press, the Netherlands, 2007.

Navarro, S. and Wood, R., Codex Deciphered. Leatherhead, Surry UK, 2001.

Nöhle, U., Risikokommunication und Risikomanagement in der erweiterten EU. ZLR 3 (2005): 297-305.

Riedl, R. and Riedl, C., Shortcomings of the New European Food Hygiene Legislation from the Viewpoint of a Competent Authority, EFFL, 3/2/2008: 64-83.

Roosevelt, F.D. Four Freedoms Address to the USA Congress, January 6, 1941. http://www.ourdocuments.gov.

Rosso Grossman, M., Animal Identification and Traceability under the US National Animal Identification System. Journal of Food Law & Policy 2 (2006): 231-315.

Rosso Grossman, M., Traceability and Labeling of Genetically Modified Crops, Food and Feed in the European Union. Journal of Food Law & Policy 1 (2005): 43-85.

Recuerda Girela, M.A. Food Safety, Politics and the Law, EFFL, 1/1/2006, p. 33-38..

Recuerda Girela, M.A. Risk and Reason in European Food Law, EFFL, 1/5/2006, p. 270-2856.

Schermers, H.G. and Blokker, N.M., International Institutional Law. Unity within Diversity, 4th ed., The Hague, 2004.

Senden, L.A.J., Soft Law in European Community Law. Oxford, 2004.

Study Group on a European Civil Code and the Research Group on EC Private Law (Acquis Group), Principles, Definitions and Model Rules of European Private Law, Draft Common Frame of Reference (DCFR). http://www.law-net.eu/en_index.htm

Van den Bossche, P., Schrijver, N. and Faber, G., Unilateral Measures Addressing non-Trade Concerns, Ministry of Foreign Affairs, The Hague 2007. http://www.minbuza.nl/binaries/en-pdf/thema-s-en-dossiers/beleidscoherentie/boek-wto.pdf

Van der Meulen, B.M.J. The Right to Adequate Food. Food Law between the Market and Human Rights, Elsevier The Hague 2004.

Van der Meulen, B.M.J., The new EU regulatory framework for GM food (Part I) Procedural aspects: safety assessment, authorisation and administrative review. Journal of International Biotechnology Law 2 (2005): 117-122.

Van der Meulen, B.M.J., The new EU regulatory framework for GM food (Part II) Traceability, labelling & enforcement. Journal of International Biotechnology Law 2 (2005): 158-162.

Van der Meulen, B.M.J., Regulating GM food: three levels, three issues. In: H. Somsen (ed.) The Regulatory Challenge of Biotechnology. Human Genetics, Food and Patents, Biotechnology Regulation Series, Edward Elgar, Cheltenham UK/Northampton, MA, USA, 2007, pp. 139-155.

Van der Meulen, B., The EU Regulatory Approach to GM Foods. The Kansas Journal of Law & Public Policy 14 (2007): 286-323.

Van der Meulen, B.M.J. and Freriks, A.A., 'Beastly Bureaucracy' Animal Traceability, Identification and Labeling in EU Law. Journal of Food Law & Policy 2 (2006) 317-359.

Van der Meulen, B.M.J. and Freriks, A.A., Millefeuille. The emergence of a multi-layered controls system in the European food sector. Utrecht Law Review 2 (2006): 156-176. http://www.utrechtlawreview.org/publish/articles/000022/english.html

Van der Spiegel, M., Measuring effectiveness of food quality management (diss.) Wageningen University, The Netherlands, 2004.

Van Plaggenhoef, W., Batterink, M. and Trienekens, J.H., International Trade and Food Safety. Overview of legislation and standards, Wageningen University, 2003

Will, M. and Guenther, D., Food Quality and Safety Standards, as required by EU Law and the Private Industry With special reference to the MEDA countries' exports of fresh and processed fruits & vegetables, herbs & spices A Practitioners' Reference Book. 2nd edition GTZ 2007. http://www2.gtz.de/dokumente/bib/07-0800.pdf

WIPO Intellectual Property Handbook: Policy, Law and Use, WIPO Publication No.489 (E). http://www.wipo.int/about-ip/en/iprm/index.html

Wijnands, J.H.M., Van der Meulen, B.M.J. and Poppe, K.J., Competitiveness of the European Food Industry. An economic and legal assessment. Office for Official Publications of the European Communities, 2007. http://ec.europa.eu/enterprise/food/competitiveness_study.pdf

Working Party on Agricultural Policies and Markets, Final Report on Private Standards and the Shaping of the Agro-Food System, OECD 2006. http://www.olis.oecd.org/olis/2006doc.nsf/linkto/agr-ca-apm(2006)9-final

Press

BBC 16 may 1990 on BSE. http://news.bbc.co.uk/onthisday/hi/dates/stories/may/16/newsid_2913000/2913807.stm

References

BBC News, June 5, 2002. Belgian Hormone Killers Jailed, http://news.bbc.co.uk/2/low/europe/2027719.stm

Butler, K., Why the Mafia is into Your Beef: The EU Ban on Growth Hormones for Cows has Created a Lucrative Black Market, Independent (London), Mar. 19, 1996, at 13. http://findarticles.com/p/articles/mi_qn4158/is_19960319/ai_n14035042

Butler, K., Four Men Found Guilty of Contract Hit on Vet. Independent (London), June 5, 2002, at 11. http://findarticles.com/p/articles/mi_qn4158/is_20020605/ai_n12618881

Graff, J., One Sweet Mess, Time, July 21, 2002. www.time.com/time/nation/article/0,8599,322596,00.htm

IFIC on functional foods. http://ific.org/nutrition/functional/index.cfm

Nutriwatch on functional foods. http://www.nutriwatch.org/04Foods/ff.html

Whitney, C., Brussels Journal, Food Scandal Adds to Belgium's Image of Disarray, New York Times, June 9, 1999. http://query.nytimes.com/gst/fullpage.html?res=9F06E0DC1139F93AA35755C0A96F958260

Appendix A

The General Food Law

►B REGULATION (EC) No 178/2002 OF THE EUROPEAN PARLIAMENT AND OF THE COUNCIL

of 28 January 2002

laying down the general principles and requirements of food law, establishing the European Food Safety Authority and laying down procedures in matters of food safety

(OJ L 31, 1.2.2002, p. 1)

Amended by:

		Official Journal		
		No	page	date
►M1	Regulation (EC) No 1642/2003 of the European Parliament and of the Council of 22 July 2003	L 245	4	29.9.2003
►M2	Commission Regulation (EC) No 575/2006 of 7 April 2006	L 100	3	8.4.2006
►M3	Commission Regulation (EC) No 202/2008 of 4 March 2008	L 60	17	5.3.2008

▼B

REGULATION (EC) No 178/2002 OF THE EUROPEAN PARLIAMENT AND OF THE COUNCIL

of 28 January 2002

laying down the general principles and requirements of food law, establishing the European Food Safety Authority and laying down procedures in matters of food safety

THE EUROPEAN PARLIAMENT AND THE COUNCIL OF THE EUROPEAN UNION,

Having regard to the Treaty establishing the European Community, and in particular Articles 37, 95, 133 and Article 152(4)(b) thereof,

Having regard to the proposal from the Commission ([1]),

Having regard to the opinion of the Economic and Social Committee ([2]),

Having regard to the opinion of the Committee of the Regions ([3]),

Acting in accordance with the procedure laid down in Article 251 of the Treaty ([4]),

Whereas:

(1) The free movement of safe and wholesome food is an essential aspect of the internal market and contributes significantly to the health and well-being of citizens, and to their social and economic interests.

(2) A high level of protection of human life and health should be assured in the pursuit of Community policies.

(3) The free movement of food and feed within the Community can be achieved only if food and feed safety requirements do not differ significantly from Member State to Member State.

(4) There are important differences in relation to concepts, principles and procedures between the food laws of the Member States. When Member States adopt measures governing food, these differences may impede the free movement of food, create unequal conditions of competition, and may thereby directly affect the functioning of the internal market.

(5) Accordingly, it is necessary to approximate these concepts, principles and procedures so as to form a common basis for measures governing food and feed taken in the Member States and at Community level. It is however necessary to provide for sufficient time for the adaptation of any conflicting provisions in existing legislation, both at national and Community level, and to provide that, pending such adaptation, the relevant legislation be applied in the light of the principles set out in the present Regulation.

(6) Water is ingested directly or indirectly like other foods, thereby contributing to the overall exposure of a consumer to ingested substances, including chemical and microbiological contaminants. However, as the quality of water intended for human consumption is already controlled by Council Directives 80/778/EEC ([5]) and 98/83/EC ([6]), it suffices to consider water after the point of compliance referred to in Article 6 of Directive 98/83/EC.

([1]) OJ C 96 E, 27.3.2001, p. 247.
([2]) OJ C 155, 29.5.2001, p. 32.
([3]) Opinion delivered on 14 June 2001 (not yet published in the Official Journal).
([4]) Opinion of the European Parliament of 12 June 2001 (not yet published in the Official Journal), Council Common Position of 17 September 2001 (not yet published in the Official Journal) and Decision of the European Parliament of 11 December 2001 (not yet published in the Official Journal). Council Decision of 21 January 2002.
([5]) OJ L 229, 30.8.1980, p. 11. Directive repealed by Directive 98/83/EC.
([6]) OJ L 330, 5.12.1998, p. 32.

▼B

(7) Within the context of food law it is appropriate to include requirements for feed, including its production and use where that feed is intended for food-producing animals. This is without prejudice to the similar requirements which have been applied so far and which will be applied in the future in feed legislation applicable to all animals, including pets.

(8) The Community has chosen a high level of health protection as appropriate in the development of food law, which it applies in a non-discriminatory manner whether food or feed is traded on the internal market or internationally.

(9) It is necessary to ensure that consumers, other stakeholders and trading partners have confidence in the decision-making processes underpinning food law, its scientific basis and the structures and independence of the institutions protecting health and other interests.

(10) Experience has shown that it is necessary to adopt measures aimed at guaranteeing that unsafe food is not placed on the market and at ensuring that systems exist to identify and respond to food safety problems in order to ensure the proper functioning of the internal market and to protect human health. Similar issues relating to feed safety should be addressed.

(11) In order to take a sufficiently comprehensive and integrated approach to food safety, there should be a broad definition of food law covering a wide range of provisions with a direct or indirect effect on the safety of food and feed, including provisions on materials and articles in contact with food, animal feed and other agricultural inputs at the level of primary production.

(12) In order to ensure the safety of food, it is necessary to consider all aspects of the food production chain as a continuum from and including primary production and the production of animal feed up to and including sale or supply of food to the consumer because each element may have a potential impact on food safety.

(13) Experience has shown that for this reason it is necessary to consider the production, manufacture, transport and distribution of feed given to food-producing animals, including the production of animals which may be used as feed on fish farms, since the inadvertent or deliberate contamination of feed, and adulteration or fraudulent or other bad practices in relation to it, may give rise to a direct or indirect impact on food safety.

(14) For the same reason, it is necessary to consider other practices and agricultural inputs at the level of primary production and their potential effect on the overall safety of food.

(15) Networking of laboratories of excellence, at regional and/or inter-regional level, with the aim of ensuring continuous monitoring of food safety, could play an important role in the prevention of potential health risks for citizens.

(16) Measures adopted by the Member States and the Community governing food and feed should generally be based on risk analysis except where this is not appropriate to the circumstances or the nature of the measure. Recourse to a risk analysis prior to the adoption of such measures should facilitate the avoidance of unjustified barriers to the free movement of foodstuffs.

(17) Where food law is aimed at the reduction, elimination or avoidance of a risk to health, the three interconnected components of risk analysis — risk assessment, risk management, and risk communication — provide a systematic methodology for the determination of effective, proportionate and targeted measures or other actions to protect health.

▼B

(18) In order for there to be confidence in the scientific basis for food law, risk assessments should be undertaken in an independent, objective and transparent manner, on the basis of the available scientific information and data.

(19) It is recognised that scientific risk assessment alone cannot, in some cases, provide all the information on which a risk management decision should be based, and that other factors relevant to the matter under consideration should legitimately be taken into account including societal, economic, traditional, ethical and environmental factors and the feasibility of controls.

(20) The precautionary principle has been invoked to ensure health protection in the Community, thereby giving rise to barriers to the free movement of food or feed. Therefore it is necessary to adopt a uniform basis throughout the Community for the use of this principle.

(21) In those specific circumstances where a risk to life or health exists but scientific uncertainty persists, the precautionary principle provides a mechanism for determining risk management measures or other actions in order to ensure the high level of health protection chosen in the Community.

(22) Food safety and the protection of consumer's interests is of increasing concern to the general public, non-governmental organisations, professional associations, international trading partners and trade organisations. It is necessary to ensure that consumer confidence and the confidence of trading partners is secured through the open and transparent development of food law and through public authorities taking the appropriate steps to inform the public where there are reasonable grounds to suspect that a food may present a risk to health.

(23) The safety and confidence of consumers within the Community, and in third countries, are of paramount importance. The Community is a major global trader in food and feed and, in this context, it has entered into international trade agreements, it contributes to the development of international standards which underpin food law, and it supports the principles of free trade in safe feed and safe, wholesome food in a non-discriminatory manner, following fair and ethical trading practices.

(24) It is necessary to ensure that food and feed exported or re-exported from the Community complies with Community law or the requirements set up by the importing country. In other circumstances, food and feed can only be exported or re-exported if the importing country has expressly agreed. However, it is necessary to ensure that even where there is agreement of the importing country, food injurious to health or unsafe feed is not exported or re-exported.

(25) It is necessary to establish the general principles upon which food and feed may be traded and the objectives and principles for the contribution of the Community to developing international standards and trade agreements.

(26) Some Member States have adopted horizontal legislation on food safety imposing, in particular, a general obligation on economic operators to market only food that is safe. However, these Member States apply different basic criteria for establishing whether a food is safe. Given these different approaches, and in the absence of horizontal legislation in other Member States, barriers to trade in foods are liable to arise. Similarly such barriers may arise to trade in feed.

(27) It is therefore necessary to establish general requirements for only safe food and feed to be placed on the market, to ensure that the internal market in such products functions effectively.

▼B

(28) Experience has shown that the functioning of the internal market in food or feed can be jeopardised where it is impossible to trace food and feed. It is therefore necessary to establish a comprehensive system of traceability within food and feed businesses so that targeted and accurate withdrawals can be undertaken or information given to consumers or control officials, thereby avoiding the potential for unnecessary wider disruption in the event of food safety problems.

(29) It is necessary to ensure that a food or feed business including an importer can identify at least the business from which the food, feed, animal or substance that may be incorporated into a food or feed has been supplied, to ensure that on investigation, traceability can be assured at all stages.

(30) A food business operator is best placed to devise a safe system for supplying food and ensuring that the food it supplies is safe; thus, it should have primary legal responsibility for ensuring food safety. Although this principle exists in some Member States and areas of food law, in other areas this is either not explicit or else responsibility is assumed by the competent authorities of the Member State through the control activities they carry out. Such disparities are liable to create barriers to trade and distort competition between food business operators in different Member States.

(31) Similar requirements should apply to feed and feed business operators.

(32) The scientific and technical basis of Community legislation relating to the safety of food and feed should contribute to the achievement of a high level of health protection within the Community. The Community should have access to high-quality, independent and efficient scientific and technical support.

(33) The scientific and technical issues in relation to food and feed safety are becoming increasingly important and complex. The establishment of a European Food Safety Authority, hereinafter referred to as 'the Authority', should reinforce the present system of scientific and technical support which is no longer able to respond to increasing demands on it.

(34) Pursuant to the general principles of food law, the Authority should take on the role of an independent scientific point of reference in risk assessment and in so doing should assist in ensuring the smooth functioning of the internal market. It may be called upon to give opinions on contentious scientific issues, thereby enabling the Community institutions and Member States to take informed risk management decisions necessary to ensure food and feed safety whilst helping avoid the fragmentation of the internal market through the adoption of unjustified or unnecessary obstacles to the free movement of food and feed.

(35) The Authority should be an independent scientific source of advice, information and risk communication in order to improve consumer confidence; nevertheless, in order to promote coherence between the risk assessment, risk management and risk communication functions, the link between risk assessors and risk managers should be strengthened.

(36) The Authority should provide a comprehensive independent scientific view of the safety and other aspects of the whole food and feed supply chains, which implies wide-ranging responsibilities for the Authority. These should include issues having a direct or indirect impact on the safety of the food and feed supply chains, animal health and welfare, and plant health. However, it is necessary to ensure that the Authority focuses on food safety, so its mission in relation to animal health, animal welfare and plant health issues that are not linked to the safety of the food

▼B

supply chain should be limited to the provision of scientific opinions. The Authority's mission should also cover scientific advice and scientific and technical support on human nutrition in relation to Community legislation and assistance to the Commission at its request on communication linked to Community health programmes.

(37) Since some products authorised under food law such as pesticides or additives in animal feed may involve risks to the environment or to the safety of workers, some environmental and worker protection aspects should also be assessed by the Authority in accordance with the relevant legislation.

(38) In order to avoid duplicated scientific assessments and related scientific opinions on genetically modified organisms (GMOs), the Authority should also provide scientific opinions on products other than food and feed relating to GMOs as defined by Directive 2001/18/EC ([1]) and without prejudice to the procedures established therein.

(39) The Authority should contribute through the provision of support on scientific matters, to the Community's and Member States' role in the development and establishment of international food safety standards and trade agreements.

(40) The confidence of the Community institutions, the general public and interested parties in the Authority is essential. For this reason, it is vital to ensure its independence, high scientific quality, transparency and efficiency. Cooperation with Member States is also indispensable.

(41) To that effect the Management Board should be appointed in such a way as to secure the highest standard of competence, a broad range of relevant expertise, for instance in management and in public administration, and the broadest possible geographic distribution within the Union. This should be facilitated by a rotation of the different countries of origin of the members of the Management Board without any post being reserved for nationals of any specific Member State.

(42) The Authority should have the means to perform all the tasks required to enable it to carry out its role.

(43) The Management Board should have the necessary powers to establish the budget, check its implementation, draw up internal rules, adopt financial regulations, appoint members of the Scientific Committee and Scientific Panels and appoint the Executive Director.

(44) The Authority should cooperate closely with competent bodies in the Member States if it is to operate effectively. An Advisory Forum should be created in order to advise the Executive Director, to constitute a mechanism of exchange of information, and to ensure close cooperation in particular with regard to the networking system. Cooperation and appropriate exchange of information should also minimise the potential for diverging scientific opinions.

(45) The Authority should take over the role of the Scientific Committees attached to the Commission in issuing scientific opinions in its field of competence. It is necessary to reorganise these Committees to ensure greater scientific consistency in relation to the food supply chain and to enable them to work more effectively. A Scientific Committee and Permanent Scientific Panels should therefore be set up within the Authority to provide these opinions.

([1]) Directive 2001/18/EC of the European Parliament and of the Council of 12 March 2001 on the deliberate release into the environment of genetically modified organisms and repealing Council Directive 90/220/EEC (OJ L 106, 17.4.2001, p. 1).

▼B

(46) In order to guarantee independence, members of the Scientific Committee and Panels should be independent scientists recruited on the basis of an open application procedure.

(47) The Authority's role as an independent scientific point of reference means that a scientific opinion may be requested not only by the Commission, but also by the European Parliament and the Member States. In order to ensure the manageability and consistency of the process of scientific advice, the Authority should be able to refuse or amend a request providing justification for this and on the basis of predetermined criteria. Steps should also be taken to help avoid diverging scientific opinions and, in the event of diverging scientific opinions between scientific bodies, procedures should be in place to resolve the divergence or provide the risk managers with a transparent basis of scientific information.

(48) The Authority should also be able to commission scientific studies necessary for the accomplishment of its duties, while ensuring that the links established by it with the Commission and the Member States prevent duplication of effort. It should be done in an open and transparent fashion and the Authority should take into account existing Community expertise and structures.

(49) The lack of an effective system of collection and analysis at Community level of data on the food supply chain is recognised as a major shortcoming. A system for the collection and analysis of relevant data in the fields covered by the Authority should therefore be set up, in the form of a network coordinated by the Authority. A review of Community data collection networks already existing in the fields covered by the Authority is called for.

(50) Improved identification of emerging risks may in the long term be a major preventive instrument at the disposal of the Member States and the Community in the exercise of its policies. It is therefore necessary to assign to the Authority an anticipatory task of collecting information and exercising vigilance and providing evaluation of and information on emerging risks with a view to their prevention.

(51) The establishment of the Authority should enable Member States to become more closely involved in scientific procedures. There should therefore be close cooperation between the Authority and the Member States for this purpose. In particular, the Authority should be able to assign certain tasks to organisations in the Member States.

(52) It is necessary to ensure that a balance is struck between the need to use national organisations to carry out tasks for the Authority and the need to ensure for the purposes of overall consistency that such tasks are carried out in line with the criteria established for such tasks. Existing procedures for the allocation of scientific tasks to the Member States, in particular with regard to the evaluation of dossiers presented by industry for the authorisation of certain substances, products or procedures, should be re-examined within a year with the objective of taking into account the establishment of the Authority and the new facilities it offers, the evaluation procedures remaining at least as stringent as before.

(53) The Commission remains fully responsible for communicating risk management measures. The appropriate information should therefore be exchanged between the Authority and the Commission. Close cooperation between the Authority, the Commission and the Member States is also necessary to ensure the coherence of the global communication process.

(54) The independence of the Authority and its role in informing the public mean that it should be able to communicate autonomously

▼B

in the fields falling within its competence, its purpose being to provide objective, reliable and easily understandable information.

(55) Appropriate cooperation with the Member States and other interested parties is necessary in the specific field of public information campaigns to take into account any regional parameters and any correlation with health policy.

(56) In addition to its operating principles based on independence and transparency, the Authority should be an organisation open to contacts with consumers and other interested groups.

(57) The Authority should be financed by the general budget of the European Union. However, in the light of experience acquired, in particular with regard to the processing of authorisation dossiers presented by industry, the possibility of fees should be examined within three years following the entry into force of this Regulation. The Community budgetary procedure remains applicable as far as any subsidies chargeable to the general budget of the European Union are concerned. Moreover, the auditing of accounts should be undertaken by the Court of Auditors.

(58) It is necessary to allow for the participation of European countries which are not members of the European Union and which have concluded agreements obliging them to transpose and implement the body of Community law in the field covered by this Regulation.

(59) A system for rapid alert already exists in the framework of Council Directive 92/59/EEC of 29 June 1992 on general product safety ([1]). The scope of the existing system includes food and industrial products but not feed. Recent food crises have demonstrated the need to set up an improved and broadened rapid alert system covering food and feed. This revised system should be managed by the Commission and include as members of the network the Member States, the Commission and the Authority. The system should not cover the Community arrangements for the early exchange of information in the event of a radiological emergency as defined in Council Decision 87/600/Euratom ([2]).

(60) Recent food safety incidents have demonstrated the need to establish appropriate measures in emergency situations ensuring that all foods, whatever their type and origin, and all feed should be subject to common measures in the event of a serious risk to human health, animal health or the environment. Such a comprehensive approach to emergency food safety measures should allow effective action to be taken and avoid artificial disparities in the treatment of a serious risk in relation to food or feed.

(61) Recent food crises have also shown the benefits to the Commission of having properly adapted, more rapid procedures for crisis management. These organisational procedures should make it possible to improve coordination of effort and to determine the most effective measures on the basis of the best scientific information. Therefore, revised procedures should take into account the Authority's responsibilities and should provide for its scientific and technical assistance in the form of advice in the event of a food crisis.

(62) In order to ensure a more effective, comprehensive approach to the food chain, a Committee on the Food Chain and Animal Health should be established to replace the Standing Veterinary Committee, the Standing Committee for Foodstuffs and the Standing Committee for Feedingstuffs. Accordingly, Council

([1]) OJ L 228, 11.8.1992, p. 24.
([2]) OJ L 371, 30.12.1987, p. 76.

▼B

Decisions 68/361/EEC ([1]), 69/414/EEC ([2]), and 70/372/EEC ([3]), should be repealed. For the same reason the Committee on the Food Chain and Animal Health should also replace the Standing Committee on Plant Health in relation to its competence (for Directives 76/895/EEC ([4]), 86/362/EEC ([5]), 86/363/EEC ([6]), 90/642/EEC ([7]) and 91/414/EEC ([8])) on plant protection products and the setting of maximum residue levels.

(63) The measures necessary for the implementation of this Regulation should be adopted in accordance with Council Decision 1999/468/EC of 28 June 1999 laying down the procedures for the exercise of implementing powers conferred on the Commission ([9]).

(64) It is necessary that operators should have sufficient time to adapt to some of the requirements established by the present Regulation and that the European Food Safety Authority should commence its operations on 1 January 2002.

(65) It is important to avoid confusion between the missions of the Authority and the European Agency for the Evaluation of Medicinal Products (EMEA) established by Council Regulation (EEC) No 2309/93 ([10]). Consequently, it is necessary to establish that this Regulation is without prejudice to the competence conferred on the EMEA by Community legislation, including powers conferred by Council Regulation (EEC) No 2377/90 of 26 June 1990 laying down a Community procedure for the establishment of maximum residue limits of veterinary medicinal products in foodstuffs of animal origin ([11]).

(66) It is necessary and appropriate for the achievement of the basic objectives of this Regulation to provide for the approximation of the concepts, principles and procedures forming a common basis for food law in the Community and to establish a European Food Safety Authority. In accordance with the principle of proportionality as set out in Article 5 of the Treaty, this Regulation does not go beyond what is necessary in order to achieve the objectives pursued,

HAVE ADOPTED THIS REGULATION:

([1]) OJ L 255, 18.10.1968, p. 23.
([2]) OJ L 291, 19.11.1969, p. 9.
([3]) OJ L 170, 3.8.1970, p. 1.
([4]) OJ L 340, 9.12.1976, p. 26. Directive as last amended by Commission Directive 2000/57/EC (OJ L 244, 29.9.2000, p. 76).
([5]) OJ L 221, 7.8.1986, p. 37. Directive as last amended by Commission Directive 2001/57/EC (OJ L 208, 1.8.2001, p. 36).
([6]) OJ L 221, 7.8.1986, p. 43. Directive as last amended by Commission Directive 2001/57/EC.
([7]) OJ L 350, 14.12.1990, p. 71. Directive as last amended by Commission Directive 2001/57/EC.
([8]) OJ L 230, 19.8.1991, p. 1. Directive as last amended by Commission Directive 2001/49/EC (OJ L 176, 29.6.2001, p. 61).
([9]) OJ L 184, 17.7.1999, p. 23.
([10]) OJ L 214, 24.8.1993, p. 1. Regulation amended by Commission Regulation (EC) No 649/98 (OJ L 88, 24.3.1998, p. 7).
([11]) OJ L 224, 18.8.1990, p. 1. Regulation as last amended by Commission Regulation (EC) No 1553/2001 (OJ L 205, 31.7.2001, p. 16).

▼B

CHAPTER I

SCOPE AND DEFINITIONS

Article 1

Aim and scope

1. This Regulation provides the basis for the assurance of a high level of protection of human health and consumers' interest in relation to food, taking into account in particular the diversity in the supply of food including traditional products, whilst ensuring the effective functioning of the internal market. It establishes common principles and responsibilities, the means to provide a strong science base, efficient organisational arrangements and procedures to underpin decision-making in matters of food and feed safety.

2. For the purposes of paragraph 1, this Regulation lays down the general principles governing food and feed in general, and food and feed safety in particular, at Community and national level.

It establishes the European Food Safety Authority.

It lays down procedures for matters with a direct or indirect impact on food and feed safety.

3. This Regulation shall apply to all stages of production, processing and distribution of food and feed. It shall not apply to primary production for private domestic use or to the domestic preparation, handling or storage of food for private domestic consumption.

Article 2

Definition of 'food'

For the purposes of this Regulation, 'food' (or 'foodstuff') means any substance or product, whether processed, partially processed or unprocessed, intended to be, or reasonably expected to be ingested by humans.

'Food' includes drink, chewing gum and any substance, including water, intentionally incorporated into the food during its manufacture, preparation or treatment. It includes water after the point of compliance as defined in Article 6 of Directive 98/83/EC and without prejudice to the requirements of Directives 80/778/EEC and 98/83/EC.

'Food' shall not include:

(a) feed;

(b) live animals unless they are prepared for placing on the market for human consumption;

(c) plants prior to harvesting;

(d) medicinal products within the meaning of Council Directives 65/65/EEC [1] and 92/73/EEC [2];

(e) cosmetics within the meaning of Council Directive 76/768/EEC [3];

(f) tobacco and tobacco products within the meaning of Council Directive 89/622/EEC [4];

(1) OJ 22, 9.2.1965, p. 369. Directive as last amended by Directive 93/39/EEC (OJ L 214, 24.8.1993, p. 22).
(2) OJ L 297, 13.10.1992, p. 8.
(3) OJ L 262, 27.9.1976, p. 169. Directive as last amended by Commission Directive 2000/41/EC (OJ L 145, 20.6.2000, p. 25).
(4) OJ L 359, 8.12.1989, p. 1. Directive as last amended by Directive 92/41/EEC) (OJ L 158, 11.6.1992, p. 30).

▼B

(g) narcotic or psychotropic substances within the meaning of the United Nations Single Convention on Narcotic Drugs, 1961, and the United Nations Convention on Psychotropic Substances, 1971;

(h) residues and contaminants.

Article 3

Other definitions

For the purposes of this Regulation:

1. 'food law' means the laws, regulations and administrative provisions governing food in general, and food safety in particular, whether at Community or national level; it covers any stage of production, processing and distribution of food, and also of feed produced for, or fed to, food-producing animals;

2. 'food business' means any undertaking, whether for profit or not and whether public or private, carrying out any of the activities related to any stage of production, processing and distribution of food;

3. 'food business operator' means the natural or legal persons responsible for ensuring that the requirements of food law are met within the food business under their control;

4. 'feed' (or 'feedingstuff') means any substance or product, including additives, whether processed, partially processed or unprocessed, intended to be used for oral feeding to animals;

5. 'feed business' means any undertaking whether for profit or not and whether public or private, carrying out any operation of production, manufacture, processing, storage, transport or distribution of feed including any producer producing, processing or storing feed for feeding to animals on his own holding;

6. 'feed business operator' means the natural or legal persons responsible for ensuring that the requirements of food law are met within the feed business under their control;

7. 'retail' means the handling and/or processing of food and its storage at the point of sale or delivery to the final consumer, and includes distribution terminals, catering operations, factory canteens, institutional catering, restaurants and other similar food service operations, shops, supermarket distribution centres and wholesale outlets;

8. 'placing on the market' means the holding of food or feed for the purpose of sale, including offering for sale or any other form of transfer, whether free of charge or not, and the sale, distribution, and other forms of transfer themselves;

9. 'risk' means a function of the probability of an adverse health effect and the severity of that effect, consequential to a hazard;

10. 'risk analysis' means a process consisting of three interconnected components: risk assessment, risk management and risk communication;

11. 'risk assessment' means a scientifically based process consisting of four steps: hazard identification, hazard characterisation, exposure assessment and risk characterisation;

12. 'risk management' means the process, distinct from risk assessment, of weighing policy alternatives in consultation with interested parties, considering risk assessment and other legitimate factors, and, if need be, selecting appropriate prevention and control options;

13. 'risk communication' means the interactive exchange of information and opinions throughout the risk analysis process as regards hazards and risks, risk-related factors and risk perceptions, among risk assessors, risk managers, consumers, feed and food businesses,

▼B

the academic community and other interested parties, including the explanation of risk assessment findings and the basis of risk management decisions;

14. 'hazard' means a biological, chemical or physical agent in, or condition of, food or feed with the potential to cause an adverse health effect;

15. 'traceability' means the ability to trace and follow a food, feed, food-producing animal or substance intended to be, or expected to be incorporated into a food or feed, through all stages of production, processing and distribution;

16. 'stages of production, processing and distribution' means any stage, including import, from and including the primary production of a food, up to and including its storage, transport, sale or supply to the final consumer and, where relevant, the importation, production, manufacture, storage, transport, distribution, sale and supply of feed;

17. 'primary production' means the production, rearing or growing of primary products including harvesting, milking and farmed animal production prior to slaughter. It also includes hunting and fishing and the harvesting of wild products;

18. 'final consumer' means the ultimate consumer of a foodstuff who will not use the food as part of any food business operation or activity.

CHAPTER II

GENERAL FOOD LAW

Article 4

Scope

1. This Chapter relates to all stages of the production, processing and distribution of food, and also of feed produced for, or fed to, food-producing animals.

2. The principles laid down in Articles 5 to 10 shall form a general framework of a horizontal nature to be followed when measures are taken.

3. Existing food law principles and procedures shall be adapted as soon as possible and by 1 January 2007 at the latest in order to comply with Articles 5 to 10.

4. Until then, and by way of derogation from paragraph 2, existing legislation shall be implemented taking account of the principles laid down in Articles 5 to 10.

SECTION 1

GENERAL PRINCIPLES OF FOOD LAW

Article 5

General objectives

1. Food law shall pursue one or more of the general objectives of a high level of protection of human life and health and the protection of consumers' interests, including fair practices in food trade, taking account of, where appropriate, the protection of animal health and welfare, plant health and the environment.

▼B

2. Food law shall aim to achieve the free movement in the Community of food and feed manufactured or marketed according to the general principles and requirements in this Chapter.

3. Where international standards exist or their completion is imminent, they shall be taken into consideration in the development or adaptation of food law, except where such standards or relevant parts would be an ineffective or inappropriate means for the fulfilment of the legitimate objectives of food law or where there is a scientific justification, or where they would result in a different level of protection from the one determined as appropriate in the Community.

Article 6

Risk analysis

1. In order to achieve the general objective of a high level of protection of human health and life, food law shall be based on risk analysis except where this is not appropriate to the circumstances or the nature of the measure.

2. Risk assessment shall be based on the available scientific evidence and undertaken in an independent, objective and transparent manner.

3. Risk management shall take into account the results of risk assessment, and in particular, the opinions of the Authority referred to in Article 22, other factors legitimate to the matter under consideration and the precautionary principle where the conditions laid down in Article 7(1) are relevant, in order to achieve the general objectives of food law established in Article 5.

Article 7

Precautionary principle

1. In specific circumstances where, following an assessment of available information, the possibility of harmful effects on health is identified but scientific uncertainty persists, provisional risk management measures necessary to ensure the high level of health protection chosen in the Community may be adopted, pending further scientific information for a more comprehensive risk assessment.

2. Measures adopted on the basis of paragraph 1 shall be proportionate and no more restrictive of trade than is required to achieve the high level of health protection chosen in the Community, regard being had to technical and economic feasibility and other factors regarded as legitimate in the matter under consideration. The measures shall be reviewed within a reasonable period of time, depending on the nature of the risk to life or health identified and the type of scientific information needed to clarify the scientific uncertainty and to conduct a more comprehensive risk assessment.

Article 8

Protection of consumers' interests

1. Food law shall aim at the protection of the interests of consumers and shall provide a basis for consumers to make informed choices in relation to the foods they consume. It shall aim at the prevention of:

(a) fraudulent or deceptive practices;

(b) the adulteration of food; and

(c) any other practices which may mislead the consumer.

▼B

SECTION 2

PRINCIPLES OF TRANSPARENCY

Article 9

Public consultation

There shall be open and transparent public consultation, directly or through representative bodies, during the preparation, evaluation and revision of food law, except where the urgency of the matter does not allow it.

Article 10

Public information

Without prejudice to the applicable provisions of Community and national law on access to documents, where there are reasonable grounds to suspect that a food or feed may present a risk for human or animal health, then, depending on the nature, seriousness and extent of that risk, public authorities shall take appropriate steps to inform the general public of the nature of the risk to health, identifying to the fullest extent possible the food or feed, or type of food or feed, the risk that it may present, and the measures which are taken or about to be taken to prevent, reduce or eliminate that risk.

SECTION 3

GENERAL OBLIGATIONS OF FOOD TRADE

Article 11

Food and feed imported into the Community

Food and feed imported into the Community for placing on the market within the Community shall comply with the relevant requirements of food law or conditions recognised by the Community to be at least equivalent thereto or, where a specific agreement exists between the Community and the exporting country, with requirements contained therein.

Article 12

Food and feed exported from the Community

1. Food and feed exported or re-exported from the Community for placing on the market of a third country shall comply with the relevant requirements of food law, unless otherwise requested by the authorities of the importing country or established by the laws, regulations, standards, codes of practice and other legal and administrative procedures as may be in force in the importing country.

In other circumstances, except in the case where foods are injurious to health or feeds are unsafe, food and feed can only be exported or re-exported if the competent authorities of the country of destination have expressly agreed, after having been fully informed of the reasons for which and the circumstances in which the food or feed concerned could not be placed on the market in the Community.

2. Where the provisions of a bilateral agreement concluded between the Community or one of its Member States and a third country are applicable, food and feed exported from the Community or that Member State to that third country shall comply with the said provisions.

▼B

Article 13

International standards

Without prejudice to their rights and obligations, the Community and the Member States shall:

(a) contribute to the development of international technical standards for food and feed and sanitary and phytosanitary standards;

(b) promote the coordination of work on food and feed standards undertaken by international governmental and non-governmental organisations;

(c) contribute, where relevant and appropriate, to the development of agreements on recognition of the equivalence of specific food and feed-related measures;

(d) give particular attention to the special development, financial and trade needs of developing countries, with a view to ensuring that international standards do not create unnecessary obstacles to exports from developing countries;

(e) promote consistency between international technical standards and food law while ensuring that the high level of protection adopted in the Community is not reduced.

SECTION 4

GENERAL REQUIREMENTS OF FOOD LAW

Article 14

Food safety requirements

1. Food shall not be placed on the market if it is unsafe.

2. Food shall be deemed to be unsafe if it is considered to be:

(a) injurious to health;

(b) unfit for human consumption.

3. In determining whether any food is unsafe, regard shall be had:

(a) to the normal conditions of use of the food by the consumer and at each stage of production, processing and distribution, and

(b) to the information provided to the consumer, including information on the label, or other information generally available to the consumer concerning the avoidance of specific adverse health effects from a particular food or category of foods.

4. In determining whether any food is injurious to health, regard shall be had:

(a) not only to the probable immediate and/or short-term and/or long-term effects of that food on the health of a person consuming it, but also on subsequent generations;

(b) to the probable cumulative toxic effects;

(c) to the particular health sensitivities of a specific category of consumers where the food is intended for that category of consumers.

5. In determining whether any food is unfit for human consumption, regard shall be had to whether the food is unacceptable for human consumption according to its intended use, for reasons of contamination, whether by extraneous matter or otherwise, or through putrefaction, deterioration or decay.

▼B

6. Where any food which is unsafe is part of a batch, lot or consignment of food of the same class or description, it shall be presumed that all the food in that batch, lot or consignment is also unsafe, unless following a detailed assessment there is no evidence that the rest of the batch, lot or consignment is unsafe.

7. Food that complies with specific Community provisions governing food safety shall be deemed to be safe insofar as the aspects covered by the specific Community provisions are concerned.

8. Conformity of a food with specific provisions applicable to that food shall not bar the competent authorities from taking appropriate measures to impose restrictions on it being placed on the market or to require its withdrawal from the market where there are reasons to suspect that, despite such conformity, the food is unsafe.

9. Where there are no specific Community provisions, food shall be deemed to be safe when it conforms to the specific provisions of national food law of the Member State in whose territory the food is marketed, such provisions being drawn up and applied without prejudice to the Treaty, in particular Articles 28 and 30 thereof.

Article 15

Feed safety requirements

1. Feed shall not be placed on the market or fed to any food-producing animal if it is unsafe.

2. Feed shall be deemed to be unsafe for its intended use if it is considered to:

— have an adverse effect on human or animal health;

— make the food derived from food-producing animals unsafe for human consumption.

3. Where a feed which has been identified as not satisfying the feed safety requirement is part of a batch, lot or consignment of feed of the same class or description, it shall be presumed that all of the feed in that batch, lot or consignment is so affected, unless following a detailed assessment there is no evidence that the rest of the batch, lot or consignment fails to satisfy the feed safety requirement.

4. Feed that complies with specific Community provisions governing feed safety shall be deemed to be safe insofar as the aspects covered by the specific Community provisions are concerned.

5. Conformity of a feed with specific provisions applicable to that feed shall not bar the competent authorities from taking appropriate measures to impose restrictions on it being placed on the market or to require its withdrawal from the market where there are reasons to suspect that, despite such conformity, the feed is unsafe.

6. Where there are no specific Community provisions, feed shall be deemed to be safe when it conforms to the specific provisions of national law governing feed safety of the Member State in whose territory the feed is in circulation, such provisions being drawn up and applied without prejudice to the Treaty, in particular Articles 28 and 30 thereof.

Article 16

Presentation

Without prejudice to more specific provisions of food law, the labelling, advertising and presentation of food or feed, including their shape, appearance or packaging, the packaging materials used, the manner in which they are arranged and the setting in which they are displayed, and

▼B

the information which is made available about them through whatever medium, shall not mislead consumers.

Article 17

Responsibilities

1. Food and feed business operators at all stages of production, processing and distribution within the businesses under their control shall ensure that foods or feeds satisfy the requirements of food law which are relevant to their activities and shall verify that such requirements are met.

2. Member States shall enforce food law, and monitor and verify that the relevant requirements of food law are fulfilled by food and feed business operators at all stages of production, processing and distribution.

For that purpose, they shall maintain a system of official controls and other activities as appropriate to the circumstances, including public communication on food and feed safety and risk, food and feed safety surveillance and other monitoring activities covering all stages of production, processing and distribution.

Member States shall also lay down the rules on measures and penalties applicable to infringements of food and feed law. The measures and penalties provided for shall be effective, proportionate and dissuasive.

Article 18

Traceability

1. The traceability of food, feed, food-producing animals, and any other substance intended to be, or expected to be, incorporated into a food or feed shall be established at all stages of production, processing and distribution.

2. Food and feed business operators shall be able to identify any person from whom they have been supplied with a food, a feed, a food-producing animal, or any substance intended to be, or expected to be, incorporated into a food or feed.

To this end, such operators shall have in place systems and procedures which allow for this information to be made available to the competent authorities on demand.

3. Food and feed business operators shall have in place systems and procedures to identify the other businesses to which their products have been supplied. This information shall be made available to the competent authorities on demand.

4. Food or feed which is placed on the market or is likely to be placed on the market in the Community shall be adequately labelled or identified to facilitate its traceability, through relevant documentation or information in accordance with the relevant requirements of more specific provisions.

5. Provisions for the purpose of applying the requirements of this Article in respect of specific sectors may be adopted in accordance with the procedure laid down in Article 58(2).

Article 19

Responsibilities for food: food business operators

1. If a food business operator considers or has reason to believe that a food which it has imported, produced, processed, manufactured or distributed is not in compliance with the food safety requirements, it shall immediately initiate procedures to withdraw the food in question

▼B

from the market where the food has left the immediate control of that initial food business operator and inform the competent authorities thereof. Where the product may have reached the consumer, the operator shall effectively and accurately inform the consumers of the reason for its withdrawal, and if necessary, recall from consumers products already supplied to them when other measures are not sufficient to achieve a high level of health protection.

2. A food business operator responsible for retail or distribution activities which do not affect the packaging, labelling, safety or integrity of the food shall, within the limits of its respective activities, initiate procedures to withdraw from the market products not in compliance with the food-safety requirements and shall participate in contributing to the safety of the food by passing on relevant information necessary to trace a food, cooperating in the action taken by producers, processors, manufacturers and/or the competent authorities.

3. A food business operator shall immediately inform the competent authorities if it considers or has reason to believe that a food which it has placed on the market may be injurious to human health. Operators shall inform the competent authorities of the action taken to prevent risks to the final consumer and shall not prevent or discourage any person from cooperating, in accordance with national law and legal practice, with the competent authorities, where this may prevent, reduce or eliminate a risk arising from a food.

4. Food business operators shall collaborate with the competent authorities on action taken to avoid or reduce risks posed by a food which they supply or have supplied.

Article 20

Responsibilities for feed: feed business operators

1. If a feed business operator considers or has reason to believe that a feed which it has imported, produced, processed, manufactured or distributed does not satisfy the feed safety requirements, it shall immediately initiate procedures to withdraw the feed in question from the market and inform the competent authorities thereof. In these circumstances or, in the case of Article 15(3), where the batch, lot or consignment does not satisfy the feed safety requirement, that feed shall be destroyed, unless the competent authority is satisfied otherwise. The operator shall effectively and accurately inform users of the feed of the reason for its withdrawal, and if necessary, recall from them products already supplied when other measures are not sufficient to achieve a high level of health protection.

2. A feed business operator responsible for retail or distribution activities which do not affect the packaging, labelling, safety or integrity of the feed shall, within the limits of its respective activities, initiate procedures to withdraw from the market products not in compliance with the feed-safety requirements and shall participate in contributing to the safety of food by passing on relevant information necessary to trace a feed, cooperating in the action taken by producers, processors, manufacturers and/or the competent authorities.

3. A feed business operator shall immediately inform the competent authorities if it considers or has reason to believe that a feed which it placed on the market may not satisfy the feed safety requirements. It shall inform the competent authorities of the action taken to prevent risk arising from the use of that feed and shall not prevent or discourage any person from cooperating, in accordance with national law and legal practice, with the competent authorities, where this may prevent, reduce or eliminate a risk arising from a feed.

4. Feed business operators shall collaborate with the competent authorities on action taken in order to avoid risks posed by a feed which they supply or have supplied.

▼B

Article 21

Liability

The provisions of this Chapter shall be without prejudice to Council Directive 85/374/EEC of 25 July 1985 on the approximation of the laws, regulations and administrative provisions of the Member States concerning liability for defective products [1].

CHAPTER III

EUROPEAN FOOD SAFETY AUTHORITY

SECTION 1

MISSION AND TASKS

Article 22

Mission of the Authority

1. A European Food Safety Authority, hereinafter referred to as the 'Authority', is hereby established.

2. The Authority shall provide scientific advice and scientific and technical support for the Community's legislation and policies in all fields which have a direct or indirect impact on food and feed safety. It shall provide independent information on all matters within these fields and communicate on risks.

3. The Authority shall contribute to a high level of protection of human life and health, and in this respect take account of animal health and welfare, plant health and the environment, in the context of the operation of the internal market.

4. The Authority shall collect and analyse data to allow the characterisation and monitoring of risks which have a direct or indirect impact on food and feed safety.

5. The mission of the Authority shall also include the provision of:

(a) scientific advice and scientific and technical support on human nutrition in relation to Community legislation and, at the request of the Commission, assistance concerning communication on nutritional issues within the framework of the Community health programme;

(b) scientific opinions on other matters relating to animal health and welfare and plant health;

(c) scientific opinions on products other than food and feed relating to genetically modified organisms as defined by Directive 2001/18/EC and without prejudice to the procedures established therein.

6. The Authority shall provide scientific opinions which will serve as the scientific basis for the drafting and adoption of Community measures in the fields falling within its mission.

7. The Authority shall carry out its tasks in conditions which enable it to serve as a point of reference by virtue of its independence, the scientific and technical quality of the opinions it issues and the information it disseminates, the transparency of its procedures and methods of operation, and its diligence in performing the tasks assigned to it

(1) OJ L 210, 7.8.1985, p. 29. Directive as last amended by Directive 1999/34/EC of the European Parliament and of the Council (OJ L 141, 4.6.1999, p. 20).

▼B

It shall act in close cooperation with the competent bodies in the Member States carrying out similar tasks to these of the Authority.

8. The Authority, Commission and Member States shall cooperate to promote the effective coherence between risk assessment, risk management and risk communication functions.

9. The Member States shall cooperate with the Authority to ensure the accomplishment of its mission.

Article 23

Tasks of the Authority

The tasks of the Authority shall be the following:

(a) to provide the Community institutions and the Member States with the best possible scientific opinions in all cases provided for by Community legislation and on any question within its mission;

(b) to promote and coordinate the development of uniform risk assessment methodologies in the fields falling within its mission;

(c) to provide scientific and technical support to the Commission in the areas within its mission and, when so requested, in the interpretation and consideration of risk assessment opinions;

(d) to commission scientific studies necessary for the accomplishment of its mission;

(e) to search for, collect, collate, analyse and summarise scientific and technical data in the fields within its mission;

(f) to undertake action to identify and characterise emerging risks, in the fields within its mission;

(g) to establish a system of networks of organisations operating in the fields within its mission and be responsible for their operation;

(h) to provide scientific and technical assistance, when requested to do so by the Commission, in the crisis management procedures implemented by the Commission with regard to the safety of food and feed;

(i) to provide scientific and technical assistance, when requested to do so by the Commission, with a view to improving cooperation between the Community, applicant countries, international organisations and third countries, in the fields within its mission;

(j) to ensure that the public and interested parties receive rapid, reliable, objective and comprehensible information in the fields within its mission;

(k) to express independently its own conclusions and orientations on matters within its mission;

(l) to undertake any other task assigned to it by the Commission within its mission.

SECTION 2

ORGANISATION

Article 24

Bodies of the Authority

The Authority shall comprise:

(a) a Management Board;

(b) an Executive Director and his staff;

▼B

(c) an Advisory Forum;

(d) a Scientific Committee and Scientific Panels.

Article 25

Management Board

1. The Management Board shall be composed of 14 members appointed by the Council in consultation with the European Parliament from a list drawn up by the Commission which includes a number of candidates substantially higher than the number of members to be appointed, plus a representative of the Commission. Four of the members shall have their background in organisations representing consumers and other interests in the food chain.

The list drawn up by the Commission, accompanied by the relevant documentation, shall be forwarded to the European Parliament. As soon as possible and within three months of such communication, the European Parliament may make its views available for consideration by the Council, which will then appoint the Management Board.

The members of the Board shall be appointed in such a way as to secure the highest standards of competence, a broad range of relevant expertise and, consistent with these, the broadest possible geographic distribution within the Union.

2. Members' term of office shall be four years, and may be renewed once. However, for the first mandate, this period shall be six years for half of the members.

3. The Management Board shall adopt the Authority's internal rules on the basis of a proposal by the Executive Director. These rules shall be made public.

4. The Management Board shall elect one of its members as its Chair for a two-year period, which shall be renewable.

5. The Management Board shall adopt its rules of procedure.

Unless otherwise provided, the Management Board shall act by a majority of its members.

6. The Management Board shall meet at the invitation of the Chair or at the request of at least a third of its members.

7. The Management Board shall ensure that the Authority carries out its mission and performs the tasks assigned to it under the conditions laid down in this Regulation.

8. Before 31 January each year, the Management Board shall adopt the Authority's programme of work for the coming year. It shall also adopt a revisable multi-annual programme. The Management Board shall ensure that these programmes are consistent with the Community's legislative and policy priorities in the area of food safety.

Before 30 March each year, the Management Board shall adopt the general report on the Authority's activities for the previous year.

▼M1

9. The financial rules applicable to the Authority shall be adopted by the Management Board after the Commission has been consulted. They may not depart from Commission Regulation (EC, Euratom) No 2343/2002 of 19 November 2002 on the framework Financial Regulation for the bodies referred to in Article 185 of Council Regulation (EC, Euratom) No 1605/2002 on the Financial Regulation applicable to the general budget of the European Communities [1] unless such departure is specifically required for the Authority's operation and the Commission has given its prior consent.

[1] OJ L 357, 31.12.2002, p. 72; corrigendum in OJ L 2, 7.1.2003, p. 39.

▼B

10. The Executive Director shall take part in the meetings of the Management Board, without voting rights, and shall provide the Secretariat. The Management Board shall invite the Chair of the Scientific Committee to attend its meetings without voting rights.

Article 26

Executive Director

1. The Executive Director shall be appointed by the Management Board, on the basis of a list of candidates proposed by the Commission after an open competition, following publication in the *Official Journal of the European Communities* and elsewhere of a call for expressions of interest, for a period of five years which shall be renewable. Before appointment the candidate nominated by the Management Board shall be invited without delay to make a statement before the European Parliament and answer questions put by members of this institution. The Executive Director may be removed from office by a majority of the Management Board.

2. The Executive Director shall be the legal representative of the Authority and shall be responsible for:

(a) the day-to-day administration of the Authority;

(b) drawing up a proposal for the Authority's work programmes in consultation with the Commission;

(c) implementing the work programmes and the decisions adopted by the Management Board;

(d) ensuring the provision of appropriate scientific, technical and administrative support for the Scientific Committee and the Scientific Panels;

(e) ensuring that the Authority carries out its tasks in accordance with the requirements of its users, in particular with regard to the adequacy of the services provided and the time taken;

▼M1

(f) the preparation of the Authority's draft statement of estimates of revenue and expenditure, and the execution of its budget;

▼B

(g) all staff matters;

(h) developing and maintaining contact with the European Parliament, and for ensuring a regular dialogue with its relevant committees.

▼M1

3. Each year, the Executive Director shall submit to the Management Board for approval:

(a) a draft general report covering all the activities of the Authority in the previous year;

(b) draft programmes of work.

The Executive Director shall, following adoption by the Management Board, forward the programmes of work to the European Parliament, the Council, the Commission and the Member States, and shall have them published.

The Executive Director shall, following adoption by the Management Board and by 15 June, forward the Authority's general report to the European Parliament, the Council, the Commission, the Court of Auditors, the European Economic and Social Committee and the Committee of the Regions, and shall have it published.

The Executive Director shall forward annually to the budgetary authority all information relevant to the outcome of the evaluation procedures.

▼M1

————

▼B

Article 27

Advisory Forum

1. The Advisory Forum shall be composed of representatives from competent bodies in the Member States which undertake tasks similar to those of the Authority, on the basis of one representative designated by each Member State. Representatives may be replaced by alternates, appointed at the same time.

2. Members of the Advisory Forum may not be members of the Management Board.

3. The Advisory Forum shall advise the Executive Director in the performance of his duties under this Regulation, in particular in drawing up a proposal for the Authority's work programme. The Executive Director may also ask the Advisory Forum for advice on the prioritisation of requests for scientific opinions.

4. The Advisory Forum shall constitute a mechanism for an exchange of information on potential risks and the pooling of knowledge. It shall ensure close cooperation between the Authority and the competent bodies in the Member States in particular on the following items:

(a) avoidance of duplication of the Authority's scientific studies with Member States, in accordance with Article 32;

(b) in those circumstances identified in Article 30(4), where the Authority and a national body are obliged to cooperate;

(c) in the promoting of the European networking of organisations operating within the fields of the Authority's mission, in accordance with Article 36(1);

(d) where the Authority or a Member State identifies an emerging risk.

5. The Advisory Forum shall be chaired by the Executive Director. It shall meet regularly at the invitation of the Chair or at the request of at least a third of its members, and not less than four times per year. Its operational procedures shall be specified in the Authority's internal rules and shall be made public.

6. The Authority shall provide the technical and logistic support necessary for the Advisory Forum and provide the Secretariat for its meetings.

7. Representatives of the Commission's departments may participate in the work of the Advisory Forum. The Executive Director may invite representatives of the European Parliament and from other relevant bodies to take part.

Where the Advisory Forum discusses the matters referred to in Article 22(5)(b), representatives from competent bodies in the Member States which undertake tasks similar to those referred to in Article 22(5)(b) may participate in the work of the Advisory Forum, on the basis of one representative designated by each Member State.

Article 28

Scientific Committee and Scientific Panels

1. The Scientific Committee and permanent Scientific Panels shall be responsible for providing the scientific opinions of the Authority, each within their own spheres of competence, and shall have the possibility, where necessary, of organising public hearings.

▼B

2. The Scientific Committee shall be responsible for the general coordination necessary to ensure the consistency of the scientific opinion procedure, in particular with regard to the adoption of working procedures and harmonisation of working methods. It shall provide opinions on multisectoral issues falling within the competence of more than one Scientific Panel, and on issues which do not fall within the competence of any of the Scientific Panels.

Where necessary, and particularly in the case of subjects which do not fall within the competence of any of the Scientific Panels, the Scientific Committee shall set up working groups. In such cases, it shall draw on the expertise of those working groups when establishing scientific opinions.

3. The Scientific Committee shall be composed of the Chairs of the Scientific Panels and six independent scientific experts who do not belong to any of the Scientific Panels.

4. The Scientific Panels shall be composed of independent scientific experts. When the Authority is established, the following Scientific Panels shall be set up:

▼M3

(a) the Panel on food additives and nutrient sources added to food;

▼B

(b) the Panel on additives and products or substances used in animal feed;

▼M2

(c) the Panel on plant protection products and their residues;

▼B

(d) the Panel on genetically modified organisms;

(e) the Panel on dietetic products, nutrition and allergies;

(f) the Panel on biological hazards;

(g) the Panel on contaminants in the food chain;

(h) the Panel on animal health and welfare ;

▼M2

(i) the Panel on plant health;

▼M3

(j) the Panel on food contact materials, enzymes, flavourings, and processing aids.

▼B

The number and names of the Scientific Panels may be adapted in the light of technical and scientific development by the Commission, at the Authority's request, in accordance with the procedure referred to in Article 58(2).

5. The members of the Scientific Committee who are not members of Scientific Panels and the members of the Scientific Panels shall be appointed by the Management Board, acting upon a proposal from the Executive Director, for a three-year term of office, which shall be renewable, following publication in the *Official Journal of the European Communities*, in relevant leading scientific publications and on the Authority's website of a call for expressions of interest.

6. The Scientific Committee and the Scientific Panels shall each choose a Chair and two Vice-Chairs from among their members.

7. The Scientific Committee and the Scientific Panels shall act by a majority of their members. Minority opinions shall be recorded.

8. The representatives of the Commission's departments shall be entitled to be present in the meetings of the Scientific Committee, the

▼B

Scientific Panels and their working groups. If invited to do so, they may assist for the purposes of clarification or information but shall not seek to influence discussions.

9. The procedures for the operation and cooperation of the Scientific Committee and the Scientific Panels shall be laid down in the Authority's internal rules.

These procedures shall relate in particular to:

(a) the number of times that a member can serve consecutively on a Scientific Committee or Scientific Panel;

(b) the number of members in each Scientific Panel;

(c) the procedure for reimbursing the expenses of members of the Scientific Committee and the Scientific Panels;

(d) the manner in which tasks and requests for scientific opinions are assigned to the Scientific Committee and the Scientific Panels;

(e) the creation and organisation of the working groups of the Scientific Committee and the Scientific Panels, and the possibility of external experts being included in those working groups;

(f) the possibility of observers being invited to meetings of the Scientific Committee and the Scientific Panels;

(g) the possibility of organising public hearings.

SECTION 3

OPERATION

Article 29

Scientific opinions

1. The Authority shall issue a scientific opinion:

(a) at the request of the Commission, in respect of any matter within its mission, and in all cases where Community legislation makes provision for the Authority to be consulted;

(b) on its own initiative, on matters falling within its mission.

The European Parliament or a Member State may request the Authority to issue a scientific opinion on matters falling within its mission.

2. Requests referred to in paragraph 1 shall be accompanied by background information explaining the scientific issue to be addressed and the Community interest.

3. Where Community legislation does not already specify a time limit for the delivery of a scientific opinion, the Authority shall issue scientific opinions within the time limit specified in the requests for opinions, except in duly justified circumstances.

4. Where different requests are made on the same issues or where the request is not in accordance with paragraph 2, or is unclear, the Authority may either refuse, or propose amendments to a request for an opinion in consultation with the institution or Member State(s) that made the request. Justifications for the refusal shall be given to the institution or Member State(s) that made the request.

5. Where the Authority has already delivered a scientific opinion on the specific topic in a request, it may refuse the request if it concludes there are no new scientific elements justifying the re-examination. Justifications for the refusal shall be given to the institution or Member State (s) that made the request.

▼B

6. The implementing rules for the application of this Article shall be established by the Commission after consulting the Authority, in accordance with the procedure provided for in Article 58(2). These rules shall specify in particular:

(a) the procedure to be applied by the Authority to the requests referred to it;

(b) the guidelines governing the scientific evaluation of substances, products or processes which are subject under Community legislation to a system of prior authorisation or entry on a positive list, in particular where Community legislation makes provision for, or authorises, a dossier to be presented for this purpose by the applicant.

7. The Authority's internal rules shall specify requirements in regard to format, explanatory background and publication of a scientific opinion.

Article 30

Diverging scientific opinions

1. The Authority shall exercise vigilance in order to identify at an early stage any potential source of divergence between its scientific opinions and the scientific opinions issued by other bodies carrying out similar tasks.

2. Where the Authority identifies a potential source of divergence, it shall contact the body in question to ensure that all relevant scientific information is shared and in order to identify potentially contentious scientific issues.

3. Where a substantive divergence over scientific issues has been identified and the body in question is a Community agency or one of the Commission's Scientific Committees, the Authority and the body concerned shall be obliged to cooperate with a view to either resolving the divergence or presenting a joint document to the Commission clarifying the contentious scientific issues and identifying the relevant uncertainties in the data. This document shall be made public.

4. Where a substantive divergence over scientific issues has been identified and the body in question is a Member State body, the Authority and the national body shall be obliged to cooperate with a view to either resolving the divergence or preparing a joint document clarifying the contentious scientific issues and identifying the relevant uncertainties in the data. This document shall be made public.

Article 31

Scientific and technical assistance

1. The Authority may be requested by the Commission to provide scientific or technical assistance in any field within its mission. The tasks of providing scientific and technical assistance shall consist of scientific or technical work involving the application of well-established scientific or technical principles which does not require scientific evaluation by the Scientific Committee or a Scientific Panel. Such tasks may include in particular assistance to the Commission for the establishment or evaluation of technical criteria and also assistance to the Commission in the development of technical guidelines.

2. Where the Commission refers a request for scientific or technical assistance to the Authority, it shall specify, in agreement with the Authority, the time limit within which the task must be completed.

▼B

Article 32

Scientific studies

1. Using the best independent scientific resources available, the Authority shall commission scientific studies necessary for the performance of its mission. Such studies shall be commissioned in an open and transparent fashion. The Authority shall seek to avoid duplication with Member State or Community research programmes and shall foster cooperation through appropriate coordination.

2. The Authority shall inform the European Parliament, the Commission and the Member States of the results of its scientific studies.

Article 33

Collection of data

1. The Authority shall search for, collect, collate, analyse and summarise relevant scientific and technical data in the fields within its mission. This shall involve in particular the collection of data relating to:

(a) food consumption and the exposure of individuals to risks related to the consumption of food;

(b) incidence and prevalence of biological risk;

(c) contaminants in food and feed;

(d) residues.

2. For the purposes of paragraph 1, the Authority shall work in close cooperation with all organisations operating in the field of data collection, including those from applicant countries, third countries or international bodies.

3. The Member States shall take the necessary measures to enable the data they collect in the fields referred to in paragraphs 1 and 2 to be transmitted to the Authority.

4. The Authority shall forward to the Member States and the Commission appropriate recommendations which might improve the technical comparability of the data it receives and analyses, in order to facilitate consolidation at Community level.

5. Within one year following the date of entry into force of this Regulation, the Commission shall publish an inventory of data collection systems existing at Community level in the fields within the mission of the Authority.

The report, which shall be accompanied, where appropriate, by proposals, shall indicate in particular:

(a) for each system, the role which should be assigned to the Authority, and any modifications or improvements which might be required to enable the Authority to carry out its mission, in cooperation with the Member States;

(b) the shortcomings which should be remedied to enable the Authority to collect and summarise at Community level relevant scientific and technical data in the fields within its mission.

6. The Authority shall forward the results of its work in the field of data collection to the European Parliament, the Commission and the Member States.

▼B

Article 34

Identification of emerging risks

1. The Authority shall establish monitoring procedures for systematically searching for, collecting, collating and analysing information and data with a view to the identification of emerging risks in the fields within its mission.

2. Where the Authority has information leading it to suspect an emerging serious risk, it shall request additional information from the Member States, other Community agencies and the Commission. The Member States, the Community agencies concerned and the Commission shall reply as a matter of urgency and forward any relevant information in their possession.

3. The Authority shall use all the information it receives in the performance of its mission to identify an emerging risk.

4. The Authority shall forward the evaluation and information collected on emerging risks to the European Parliament, the Commission and the Member States.

Article 35

Rapid alert system

To enable it to perform its task of monitoring the health and nutritional risks of foods as effectively as possible, the Authority shall be the recipient of any messages forwarded via the rapid alert system. It shall analyse the content of such messages with a view to providing the Commission and the Member States with any information required for the purposes of risk analysis.

Article 36

Networking of organisations operating in the fields within the Authority's mission

1. The Authority shall promote the European networking of organisations operating in the fields within the Authority's mission. The aim of such networking is, in particular, to facilitate a scientific cooperation framework by the coordination of activities, the exchange of information, the development and implementation of joint projects, the exchange of expertise and best practices in the fields within the Authority's mission.

2. The Management Board, acting on a proposal from the Executive Director, shall draw up a list to be made public of competent organisations designated by the Member States which may assist the Authority, either individually or in networks, with its mission. The Authority may entrust to these organisations certain tasks, in particular preparatory work for scientific opinions, scientific and technical assistance, collection of data and identification of emerging risks. Some of these tasks may be eligible for financial support.

3. The implementing rules for the application of paragraphs 1 and 2 shall be laid down by the Commission, after consulting the Authority, in accordance with the procedure referred to in Article 58(2). Those rules shall specify, in particular, the criteria for inclusion of an institute on the list of competent organisations designated by the Member States, arrangements for setting out harmonised quality requirements and the financial rules governing any financial support.

4. Within one year following the entry into force of this Regulation, the Commission shall publish an inventory of Community systems existing in the fields within the mission of the Authority which make provision for Member States to carry out certain tasks in the field of scientific evaluation, in particular the examination of authorisation dossiers. The report, which shall be accompanied, where appropriate, by proposals,

▼B

shall indicate in particular, for each system, any modifications or improvements which might be required to enable the Authority to carry out its mission, in cooperation with the Member States.

SECTION 4

INDEPENDENCE, TRANSPARENCY, CONFIDENTIALITY AND COMMUNICATION

Article 37

Independence

1. The members of the Management Board, the members of the Advisory Forum and the Executive Director shall undertake to act independently in the public interest.

For this purpose, they shall make a declaration of commitment and a declaration of interests indicating either the absence of any interests which might be considered prejudicial to their independence or any direct or indirect interests which might be considered prejudicial to their independence. Those declarations shall be made annually in writing.

2. The members of the Scientific Committee and the Scientific Panels shall undertake to act independently of any external influence.

For this purpose, they shall make a declaration of commitment and a declaration of interests indicating either the absence of any interests which might be considered prejudicial to their independence or any direct or indirect interests which might be considered prejudicial to their independence. Those declarations shall be made annually in writing.

3. The members of the Management Board, the Executive Director, the members of the Advisory Forum, the members of the Scientific Committee and the Scientific Panels, as well as external experts participating in their working groups shall declare at each meeting any interests which might be considered prejudicial to their independence in relation to the items on the agenda.

Article 38

Transparency

1. The Authority shall ensure that it carries out its activities with a high level of transparency. It shall in particular make public without delay:

(a) agendas and minutes of the Scientific Committee and the Scientific Panels;

(b) the opinions of the Scientific Committee and the Scientific Panels immediately after adoption, minority opinions always being included;

(c) without prejudice to Articles 39 and 41, the information on which its opinions are based;

(d) the annual declarations of interest made by members of the Management Board, the Executive Director, members of the Advisory Forum and members of the Scientific Committee and Scientific Panels, as well as the declarations of interest made in relation to items on the agendas of meetings;

(e) the results of its scientific studies;

(f) the annual report of its activities;

▼B

(g) requests from the European Parliament, the Commission or a Member State for scientific opinions which have been refused or modified and the justifications for the refusal or modification.

2. The Management Board shall hold its meetings in public unless, acting on a proposal from the Executive Director, it decides otherwise for specific administrative points of its agenda, and may authorise consumer representatives or other interested parties to observe the proceedings of some of the Authority's activities.

3. The Authority shall lay down in its internal rules the practical arrangements for implementing the transparency rules referred to in paragraphs 1 and 2.

Article 39

Confidentiality

1. By way of derogation from Article 38, the Authority shall not divulge to third parties confidential information that it receives for which confidential treatment has been requested and justified, except for information which must be made public if circumstances so require, in order to protect public health.

2. Members of the Management Board, the Executive Director, members of the Scientific Committee and Scientific Panels as well as external experts participating in their working groups, members of the Advisory Forum and members of the staff of the Authority, even after their duties have ceased, shall be subject to the requirements of confidentiality pursuant to Article 287 of the Treaty.

3. The conclusions of the scientific opinions delivered by the Authority relating to foreseeable health effects shall on no account be kept confidential.

4. The Authority shall lay down in its internal rules the practical arrangements for implementing the confidentiality rules referred to in paragraphs 1 and 2.

Article 40

Communications from the Authority

1. The Authority shall communicate on its own initiative in the fields within its mission without prejudice to the Commission's competence to communicate its risk management decisions.

2. The Authority shall ensure that the public and any interested parties are rapidly given objective, reliable and easily accessible information, in particular with regard to the results of its work. In order to achieve these objectives, the Authority shall develop and disseminate information material for the general public.

3. The Authority shall act in close collaboration with the Commission and the Member States to promote the necessary coherence in the risk communication process.

The Authority shall publish all opinions issued by it in accordance with Article 38.

4. The Authority shall ensure appropriate cooperation with the competent bodies in the Member States and other interested parties with regard to public information campaigns.

▼M1

Article 41

Access to documents

1. Regulation (EC) No 1049/2001 of the European Parliament and of the Council of 30 May 2001 regarding access to European Parliament, Council and Commission documents ([1]) shall apply to documents held by the Authority.

2. The Management Board shall adopt the practical arrangements for implementing Regulation (EC) No 1049/2001 within six months after the entry into force of Regulation (EC) No 1642/2003 of the European Parliament and of the Council of 22 July 2003 amending Regulation (EC) No 178/2002 laying down the general principles and requirements of food law, establishing the European Food Safety Authority and laying down procedures in matters of food safety ([2]).

3. Decisions taken by the Authority pursuant to Article 8 of Regulation (EC) No 1049/2001 may form the subject of a complaint to the Ombudsman or of an action before the Court of Justice, under the conditions laid down in Articles 195 and 230 of the EC Treaty respectively.

▼B

Article 42

Consumers, producers and other interested parties

The Authority shall develop effective contacts with consumer representatives, producer representatives, processors and any other interested parties.

SECTION 5

FINANCIAL PROVISIONS

Article 43

Adoption of the Authority's budget

1. The revenues of the Authority shall consist of a contribution from the Community and, from any State with which the Community has concluded the agreements referred to in Article 49 and charges for publications, conferences, training and any other similar activities provided by the Authority.

2. The expenditure of the Authority shall include the staff, administrative, infrastructure and operational expenses, and expenses resulting from contracts entered into with third parties or resulting from the financial support referred to in Article 36.

▼M1

3. The Executive Director shall draw up, in good time before the date referred to in paragraph 5, a draft statement of estimates of the Authority's revenue and expenditure for the following financial year and shall forward it to the Management Board, together with the establishment plan.

4. Revenue and expenditure shall be in balance.

5. Each year the Management Board, on the basis of a draft statement of estimates of revenue and expenditure, shall produce a statement of estimates of revenue and expenditure of the Authority for the following financial year. This statement of estimates, which shall include a draft establishment plan together with the provisional work programmes, shall be forwarded by 31 March at the latest by the Management Board to the

([1]) OJ L 145, 31.5.2001, p. 43.
([2]) OJ L 245, 29.9.2003, p. 4.

▼M1

Commission and to the countries with which the Community has concluded agreements in accordance with Article 49.

6. The statement of estimates shall be forwarded by the Commission to the European Parliament and the Council (hereinafter referred to as the budgetary authority) together with the preliminary draft general budget of the European Union.

7. On the basis of the statement of estimates, the Commission shall enter in the preliminary draft general budget of the European Union the estimates it deems necessary for the establishment plan and the amount of the subsidy to be charged to the general budget, which it shall place before the budgetary authority in accordance with Article 272 of the Treaty.

8. The budgetary authority shall authorise the appropriations for the subsidy to the Authority.

The budgetary authority shall adopt the establishment plan for the Authority.

9. The budget shall be adopted by the Management Board. It shall become final following final adoption of the general budget of the European Union. Where appropriate, it shall be adjusted accordingly.

10. The Management Board shall, as soon as possible, notify the budgetary authority of its intention to implement any project which may have significant financial implications for the funding of the budget, in particular any projects relating to property such as the rental or purchase of buildings. It shall inform the Commission thereof.

Where a branch of the budgetary authority has notified its intention to deliver an opinion, it shall forward its opinion to the Management Board within a period of six weeks from the date of notification of the project.

Article 44

Implementation of the Authority's budget

1. The Executive Director shall implement the Authority's budget.

2. By 1 March at the latest following each financial year, the Authority's accounting officer shall communicate the provisional accounts to the Commission's accounting officer together with a report on the budgetary and financial management for that financial year. The Commission's accounting officer shall consolidate the provisional accounts of the institutions and decentralised bodies in accordance with Article 128 of the general Financial Regulation.

3. By 31 March at the latest following each financial year, the Commission's accounting officer shall forward the Authority's provisional accounts to the Court of Auditors, together with a report on the budgetary and financial management for that financial year. The report on the budgetary and financial management for the financial year shall also be forwarded to the European Parliament and the Council.

4. On receipt of the Court of Auditors' observations on the Authority's provisional accounts under Article 129 of the general Financial Regulation, the Executive Director shall draw up the Authority's final accounts under his own responsibility and submit them to the Management Board for an opinion.

5. The Management Board shall deliver an opinion on the Authority's final accounts.

6. The Executive Director shall, by 1 July at the latest following each financial year, forward the final accounts to the European Parliament, the Council, the Commission and the Court of Auditors, together with the Management Board's opinion.

▼M1

7. The final accounts shall be published.

8. The Executive Director shall send the Court of Auditors a reply to its observations by 30 September at the latest. He shall also send this reply to the Management Board.

9. The Executive Director shall submit to the European Parliament, at the latter's request, all information necessary for the smooth application of the discharge procedure for the financial year in question, as laid down in Article 146(3) of the general Financial Regulation.

10. The European Parliament, on a recommendation from the Council acting by a qualified majority, shall, before 30 April of year N + 2, give a discharge to the Executive Director in respect of the implementation of the budget for year N.

▼B

Article 45

Fees received by the Authority

Within three years following the date of entry into force of this Regulation and after consulting the Authority, the Member States and the interested parties, the Commission shall publish a report on the feasibility and advisability of presenting a legislative proposal under the co-decision procedure and in accordance with the Treaty and for other services provided by the Authority.

SECTION 6

GENERAL PROVISIONS

Article 46

Legal personality and privileges

1. The Authority shall have legal personality. In all Member States it shall enjoy the widest powers granted by law to legal persons. In particular, it may acquire and dispose of movable and immovable property and institute legal proceedings.

2. The Protocol on the privileges and immunities of the European Communities shall apply to the Authority.

Article 47

Liability

1. The contractual liability of the Authority shall be governed by the law applicable to the contract in question. The Court of Justice of the European Communities shall have jurisdiction to give judgment pursuant to any arbitration clause contained in a contract concluded by the Authority.

2. In the case of non-contractual liability, the Authority shall, in accordance with the general principles common to the laws of the Member States, make good any damage caused by it or its servants in the performance of their duties. The Court of Justice shall have jurisdiction in any dispute relating to compensation for such damage.

3. The personal liability of its servants towards the Authority shall be governed by the relevant provisions applying to the staff of the Authority.

▼B

Article 48

Staff

1. The staff of the Authority shall be subject to the rules and regulations applicable to officials and other staff of the European Communities.

2. In respect of its staff, the Authority shall exercise the powers which have been devolved to the appointing authority.

Article 49

Participation of third countries

The Authority shall be open to the participation of countries which have concluded agreements with the European Community by virtue of which they have adopted and apply Community legislation in the field covered by this Regulation.

Arrangements shall be made under the relevant provisions of those agreements, specifying in particular the nature, extent and manner in which these countries will participate in the Authority's work, including provisions relating to participation in the networks operated by the Authority, inclusion in the list of competent organisations to which certain tasks may be entrusted by the Authority, financial contributions and staff.

CHAPTER IV

RAPID ALERT SYSTEM, CRISIS MANAGEMENT AND EMERGENCIES

SECTION 1

RAPID ALERT SYSTEM

Article 50

Rapid alert system

1. A rapid alert system for the notification of a direct or indirect risk to human health deriving from food or feed is hereby established as a network. It shall involve the Member States, the Commission and the Authority. The Member States, the Commission and the Authority shall each designate a contact point, which shall be a member of the network. The Commission shall be responsible for managing the network.

2. Where a member of the network has any information relating to the existence of a serious direct or indirect risk to human health deriving from food or feed, this information shall be immediately notified to the Commission under the rapid alert system. The Commission shall transmit this information immediately to the members of the network.

The Authority may supplement the notification with any scientific or technical information, which will facilitate rapid, appropriate risk management action by the Member States.

3. Without prejudice to other Community legislation, the Member States shall immediately notify the Commission under the rapid alert system of:

(a) any measure they adopt which is aimed at restricting the placing on the market or forcing the withdrawal from the market or the recall of food or feed in order to protect human health and requiring rapid action;

▼B

(b) any recommendation or agreement with professional operators which is aimed, on a voluntary or obligatory basis, at preventing, limiting or imposing specific conditions on the placing on the market or the eventual use of food or feed on account of a serious risk to human health requiring rapid action;

(c) any rejection, related to a direct or indirect risk to human health, of a batch, container or cargo of food or feed by a competent authority at a border post within the European Union.

The notification shall be accompanied by a detailed explanation of the reasons for the action taken by the competent authorities of the Member State in which the notification was issued. It shall be followed, in good time, by supplementary information, in particular where the measures on which the notification is based are modified or withdrawn.

The Commission shall immediately transmit to members of the network the notification and supplementary information received under the first and second subparagraphs.

Where a batch, container or cargo is rejected by a competent authority at a border post within the European Union, the Commission shall immediately notify all the border posts within the European Union, as well as the third country of origin.

4. Where a food or feed which has been the subject of a notification under the rapid alert system has been dispatched to a third country, the Commission shall provide the latter with the appropriate information.

5. The Member States shall immediately inform the Commission of the action implemented or measures taken following receipt of the notifications and supplementary information transmitted under the rapid alert system. The Commission shall immediately transmit this information to the members of the network.

6. Participation in the rapid alert system may be opened up to applicant countries, third countries or international organisations, on the basis of agreements between the Community and those countries or international organisations, in accordance with the procedures defined in those agreements. The latter shall be based on reciprocity and shall include confidentiality measures equivalent to those applicable in the Community.

Article 51

Implementing measures

The measures for implementing Article 50 shall be adopted by the Commission, after discussion with the Authority, in accordance with the procedure referred to in Article 58(2). These measures shall specify, in particular, the specific conditions and procedures applicable to the transmission of notifications and supplementary information.

Article 52

Confidentiality rules for the rapid alert system

1. Information, available to the members of the network relating to a risk to human health posed by food and feed shall in general be available to the public in accordance with the information principle provided for in Article 10. In general, the public shall have access to information on product identification, the nature of the risk and the measure taken.

However, the members of the network shall take steps to ensure that members of their staff are required not to disclose information obtained for the purposes of this Section which by its nature is covered by professional secrecy in duly justified cases, except for information which must be made public, if circumstances so require, in order to protect human health.

▼B

2. Protection of professional secrecy shall not prevent the dissemination to the competent authorities of information relevant to the effectiveness of market surveillance and enforcement activities in the field of food and feed. The authorities receiving information covered by professional secrecy shall ensure its protection in conformity with paragraph 1.

SECTION 2

EMERGENCIES

Article 53

Emergency measures for food and feed of Community origin or imported from a third country

1. Where it is evident that food or feed originating in the Community or imported from a third country is likely to constitute a serious risk to human health, animal health or the environment, and that such risk cannot be contained satisfactorily by means of measures taken by the Member State(s) concerned, the Commission, acting in accordance with the procedure provided for in Article 58(2) on its own initiative or at the request of a Member State, shall immediately adopt one or more of the following measures, depending on the gravity of the situation:

(a) in the case of food or feed of Community origin:

(i) suspension of the placing on the market or use of the food in question;

(ii) suspension of the placing on the market or use of the feed in question;

(iii) laying down special conditions for the food or feed in question;

(iv) any other appropriate interim measure;

(b) in the case of food or feed imported from a third country:

(i) suspension of imports of the food or feed in question from all or part of the third country concerned and, where applicable, from the third country of transit;

(ii) laying down special conditions for the food or feed in question from all or part of the third country concerned;

(iii) any other appropriate interim measure.

2. However, in eMERGENCIES, the Commission may provisionally adopt the measures referred to in paragraph 1 after consulting the Member State(s) concerned and informing the other Member States.

As soon as possible, and at most within 10 working days, the measures taken shall be confirmed, amended, revoked or extended in accordance with the procedure referred to in Article 58(2), and the reasons for the Commission's decision shall be made public without delay.

Article 54

Other emergency measures

1. Where a Member State officially informs the Commission of the need to take emergency measures, and where the Commission has not acted in accordance with Article 53, the Member State may adopt interim protective measures. In this event, it shall immediately inform the other Member States and the Commission.

2. Within 10 working days, the Commission shall put the matter before the Committee set up in Article 58(1) in accordance with the procedure provided for in Article 58(2) with a view to the extension, amendment or abrogation of the national interim protective measures.

▼B

3. The Member State may maintain its national interim protective measures until the Community measures have been adopted.

SECTION 3

CRISIS MANAGEMENT

Article 55

General plan for crisis management

1. The Commission shall draw up, in close cooperation with the Authority and the Member States, a general plan for crisis management in the field of the safety of food and feed (hereinafter referred to as 'the general plan').

2. The general plan shall specify the types of situation involving direct or indirect risks to human health deriving from food and feed which are not likely to be prevented, eliminated or reduced to an acceptable level by provisions in place or cannot adequately be managed solely by way of the application of Articles 53 and 54.

The general plan shall also specify the practical procedures necessary to manage a crisis, including the principles of transparency to be applied and a communication strategy.

Article 56

Crisis unit

1. Without prejudice to its role of ensuring the application of Community law, where the Commission identifies a situation involving a serious direct or indirect risk to human health deriving from food and feed, and the risk cannot be prevented, eliminated or reduced by existing provisions or cannot adequately be managed solely by way of the application of Articles 53 and 54, it shall immediately notify the Member States and the Authority.

2. The Commission shall set up a crisis unit immediately, in which the Authority shall participate, and provide scientific and technical assistance if necessary.

Article 57

Tasks of the crisis unit

1. The crisis unit shall be responsible for collecting and evaluating all relevant information and identifying the options available to prevent, eliminate or reduce to an acceptable level the risk to human health as effectively and rapidly as possible.

2. The crisis unit may request the assistance of any public or private person whose expertise it deems necessary to manage the crisis effectively.

3. The crisis unit shall keep the public informed of the risks involved and the measures taken.

▼B

CHAPTER V

PROCEDURES AND FINAL PROVISIONS

SECTION 1

COMMITTEE AND MEDIATION PROCEDURES

Article 58

Committee

1. The Commission shall be assisted by a Standing Committee on the Food Chain and Animal Health, hereinafter referred to as the 'Committee', composed of representatives of the Member States and chaired by the representative of the Commission. The Committee shall be organised in sections to deal with all relevant matters.

2. Where reference is made to this paragraph, the procedure laid down in Article 5 of Decision 1999/468/EC shall apply, in compliance with Articles 7 and 8 thereof.

3. The period provided for in Article 5(6) of Decision 1999/468/EC shall be three months.

Article 59

Functions assigned to the Committee

The Committee shall carry out the functions assigned to it by this Regulation and by other relevant Community provisions, in the cases and conditions provided for in those provisions. It may also examine any issue falling under those provisions, either at the initiative of the Chairman or at the written request of one of its members.

Article 60

Mediation procedure

1. Without prejudice to the application of other Community provisions, where a Member State is of the opinion that a measure taken by another Member State in the field of food safety is either incompatible with this Regulation or is likely to affect the functioning of the internal market, it shall refer the matter to the Commission, which will immediately inform the other Member State concerned.

2. The two Member States concerned and the Commission shall make every effort to solve the problem. If agreement cannot be reached, the Commission may request an opinion on any relevant contentious scientific issue from the Authority. The terms of that request and the time limit within which the Authority is requested to give its opinion shall be established by mutual agreement between the Commission and the Authority, after consulting the two Member States concerned.

SECTION 2

FINAL PROVISIONS

Article 61

Review clause

1. Before 1 January 2005 and every six years thereafter, the Authority, in collaboration with the Commission, shall commission an

▼B

independent external evaluation of its achievements on the basis of the terms of reference issued by the Management Board in agreement with the Commission. The evaluation will assess the working practices and the impact of the Authority. The evaluation will take into account the views of the stakeholders, at both Community and national level.

The Management Board of the Authority shall examine the conclusions of the evaluation and issue to the Commission such recommendations as may be necessary regarding changes in the Authority and its working practices. The evaluation and the recommendations shall be made public.

2. Before 1 January 2005, the Commission shall publish a report on the experience acquired from implementing Sections 1 and 2 of Chapter IV.

3. The reports and recommendations referred to in paragraphs 1 and 2 shall be forwarded to the Council and the European Parliament.

Article 62

References to the European Food Safety Authority and to the Standing Committee on the Food Chain and Animal Health

1. Every reference in Community legislation to the Scientific Committee on Food, the Scientific Committee on Animal Nutrition, the Scientific Veterinary Committee, the Scientific Committee on Pesticides, the Scientific Committee on Plants and the Scientific Steering Committee shall be replaced by a reference to the European Food Safety Authority.

2. Every reference in Community legislation to the Standing Committee on Foodstuffs, the Standing Committee for Feedingstuffs and the Standing Veterinary Committee shall be replaced by a reference to the Standing Committee on the Food Chain and Animal Health.

Every reference to the Standing Committee on Plant Health in Community legislation based upon and including Directives 76/895/EEC, 86/362/EEC, 86/363/EEC, 90/642/EEC and 91/414/EEC relating to plant protection products and the setting of maximum residue levels shall be replaced by a reference to the Standing Committee on the Food Chain and Animal Health.

3. For the purpose of paragraphs 1 and 2, 'Community legislation' shall mean all Community Regulations, Directives and Decisions.

4. Decisions 68/361/EEC, 69/414/EEC and 70/372/EEC are hereby repealed.

Article 63

Competence of the European Agency for the Evaluation of Medicinal Products

This Regulation shall be without prejudice to the competence conferred on the European Agency for the Evaluation of Medicinal Products by Regulation (EEC) No 2309/93, Regulation (EEC) No 2377/90, Council Directive 75/319/EEC [1] and Council Directive 81/851/EEC [2].

(1) OJ L 147, 9.6.1975, p. 13. Directive amended by Directive 2001/83/EC of the European Parliament and of the Council (OJ L 311, 28.11.2001, p. 67).
(2) OJ L 317, 6.11.1981, p. 1. Directive amended by Directive 2001/82/EC of the European Parliament and of the Council (OJ L 311, 28.11.2001, p. 1).

▼B

Article 64

Commencement of the Authority's operation

The Authority shall commence its operations on 1 January 2002.

Article 65

Entry into force

This Regulation shall enter into force on the 20th day following that of its publication in the *Official Journal of the European Communities*.

Articles 11 and 12 and Articles 14 to 20 shall apply from 1 January 2005.

Articles 29, 56, 57 and 60 and Article 62(1) shall apply as from the date of appointment of the members of the Scientific Committee and of the Scientific Panels which shall be announced by means of a notice in the 'C' series of the Official Journal.

This Regulation shall be binding in its entirety and directly applicable in all Member States.

Appendix B. Tables of equivalences referred to in Article 5 of the Treaty of Lisbon

Treaty on European Union

Old numbering of the Treaty on European Union	New numbering of the Treaty on European Union
Title I – Common provisions	***Title I – Common provisions***
Article 1	Article 1
	Article 2
Article 2	Article 3
Article 3 (repealed)	
	Article 4
	Article 5
Article 4 (repealed)	
Article 5 (repealed)	
Article 6	Article 6
Article 7	Article 7
	Article 8
Title II – Provisions amending the treaty establishing the european economic community with a view to establishing the european community	***Title II – Provisions on democratic principles***
Article 8 (repealed)	Article 9
	Article 10
	Article 11
	Article 12
Title III – Provisions amending the treaty establishing the european coal and steel community	***Title III – Provisions on the institutions***
Article 9 (repealed)	Article 13
	Article 14
	Article 15
	Article 16
	Article 17
	Article 18
	Article 19

Old numbering of the Treaty on European Union	New numbering of the Treaty on European Union
Title IV – Provisions amending the treaty establishing the european atomic energy community	***Title IV – Provisions on enhanced cooperation***
Article 10 (repealed) *Articles 27 A to 27 E (replaced) Articles 40 to 40 B (replaced) Articles 43 to 45 (replaced)*	Article 20
Title V – Provisions on a common foreign and security policy	***Title V – General provisions on the union's external action and specific provisions on the common foreign and security policy***
	Chapter 1 – General provisions on the Union's external action
	Article 21
	Article 22
	Chapter 2 – Specific provisions on the common foreign and security policy
	Section 1 – Common provisions
	Article 23
Article 11	Article 24
Article 12	Article 25
Article 13	Article 26
	Article 27
Article 14	Article 28
Article 15	Article 29
Article 22 (moved)	Article 30
Article 23 (moved)	Article 31
Article 16	Article 32
Article 17 (moved)	*Article 42*
Article 18	Article 33
Article 19	Article 34
Article 20	Article 35
Article 21	Article 36
Article 22 (moved)	*Article 30*
Article 23 (moved)	*Article 31*
Article 24	Article 37
Article 25	Article 38
	Article 39
Article 47 (moved)	Article 40
Article 26 (repealed)	
Article 27 (repealed)	

Old numbering of the Treaty on European Union	New numbering of the Treaty on European Union
Article 27 A (replaced)	*Article 20*
Article 27 B (replaced)	*Article 20*
Article 27 C (replaced)	*Article 20*
Article 27 D (replaced)	*Article 20*
Article 27 E (replaced)	*Article 20*
Article 28	Article 41
	Section 2 – Provisions on the common security and defence policy
Article 17 (moved)	Article 42
	Article 43
	Article 44
	Article 45
	Article 46
Title VI – Provisions on police and judicial cooperation in criminal matters (repealed)	
Article 29 (replaced)	
Article 30 (replaced)	
Article 31 (replaced)	
Article 32 (replaced)	
Article 33 (replaced)	
Article 34 (repealed)	
Article 35 (repealed)	
Article 36 (replaced)	
Article 37 (repealed)	
Article 38 (repealed)	
Article 39 (repealed)	
Article 40 (replaced)	*Article 20*
Article 40 A (replaced)	*Article 20*
Article 40 B (replaced)	*Article 20*
Article 41 (repealed)	
Article 42 (repealed)	
Title VII – Provisions on enhanced cooperation (replaced)	**Title IV – Provision on enhanced cooperation**
Article 43 (replaced)	*Article 20*
Article 43 A (replaced)	*Article 20*
Article 43 B (replaced)	*Article 20*
Article 44 (replaced)	*Article 20*
Article 44 A (replaced)	*Article 20*
Article 45 (replaced)	*Article 20*

Old numbering of the Treaty on European Union	**New numbering of the Treaty on European Union**
Titre VIII – Final provisions	***Title VI – Final provisions***
Article 46 (repealed)	
	Article 47
Article 47 (moved)	*Article 40*
Article 48	Article 48
Article 49	Article 49
	Article 50
	Article 51
	Article 52
Article 50 (repealed)	
Article 51	Article 53
Article 52	Article 54
Article 53	Article 55

Old numbering of the Treaty establishing the European Community	***New numbering of the Treaty on the Functioning of the European Union***
Part one – Principles	***Part one – Principles***
Article 1 (repealed)	
	Article 1
Article 2 (repealed)	
	Title I – Categories and areas of union competence
	Article 2
	Article 3
	Article 4
	Article 5
	Article 6
	Title II – Provisions having general application
	Article 7
Article 3, paragraph 1 (repealed)	
Article 3, paragraph 2	Article 8
Article 4 (moved)	*Article 119*
Article 5 (replaced)	
	Article 9
	Article 10
Article 6	Article 11

Old numbering of the Treaty establishing the European Community	***New numbering of the Treaty on the Functioning of the European Union***
Article 153, paragraph 2 (moved)	Article 12
	Article 13
Article 7 (repealed)	
Article 8 (repealed)	
Article 9 (repealed)	
Article 10 (repealed)	
Article 11 (replaced)	*Articles 326 to 334*
Article 11a (replaced)	*Articles 326 to 334*
Article 12 (repealed)	*Article 18*
Article 13 (moved)	*Article 19*
Article 14 (moved)	*Article 26*
Article 15 (moved)	*Article 27*
Article 16	Article 14
Article 255 (moved)	Article 15
Article 286 (moved)	Article 16
	Article 17
Part two – Citizenship of the union	***Part two – Non-discrimination and citizenship of the union***
Article 12 (moved)	Article 18
Article 13 (moved)	Article 19
Article 17	Article 20
Article 18	Article 21
Article 19	Article 22
Article 20	Article 23
Article 21	Article 24
Article 22	Article 25
Part three – Community policies	***Part three – Policies and internal actions of the union***
	Title I – The internal market
Article 14 (moved)	Article 26
Article 15 (moved)	Article 27
Title I – Free movement of goods	***Title II – Free movement of goods***
Article 23	Article 28
Article 24	Article 29
Chapter I – The customs union	***Chapter I – The customs union***
Article 25	Article 30
Article 26	Article 31
Article 27	Article 32

Old numbering of the Treaty establishing the European Community	***New numbering of the Treaty on the Functioning of the European Union***
Part Three, Title X, Customs cooperation (moved)	***Chapter 2 – Customs cooperation***
Article 135 (moved)	Article 33
Chapter 2 – Prohibition of quantitative restrictions between Member States	***Chapter 3 – Prohibition of quantitative restrictions between Member States***
Article 28	Article 34
Article 29	Article 35
Article 30	Article 36
Article 31	Article 37
Title II – Agriculture	***Title III – Agriculture and fisheries***
Article 32	Article 38
Article 33	Article 39
Article 34	Article 40
Article 35	Article 41
Article 36	Article 42
Article 37	Article 43
Article 38	Article 44
Title III – Free movement of persons, services and capital	***Title IV – Free movement of persons, services and capital***
Chapter 1 – Workers	***Chapter 1 – Workers***
Article 39	Article 45
Article 40	Article 46
Article 41	Article 47
Article 42	Article 48
Chapter 2 – Right of establishment	***Chapter 2 – Right of establishment***
Article 43	Article 49
Article 44	Article 50
Article 45	Article 51
Article 46	Article 52
Article 47	Article 53
Article 48	Article 54
Article 294 (moved)	Article 55
Chapter 3 – Services	***Chapter 3 – Services***
Article 49	Article 56
Article 50	Article 57
Article 51	Article 58
Article 52	Article 59
Article 53	Article 60
Article 54	Article 61
Article 55	Article 62

Old numbering of the Treaty establishing the European Community	***New numbering of the Treaty on the Functioning of the European Union***
Chapter 4 – Capital and payments	***Chapter 4 – Capital and payments***
Article 56	Article 63
Article 57	Article 64
Article 58	Article 65
Article 59	Article 66
Article 60 (moved)	*Article 75*
Title IV – Visas, asylum, immigration and other policies related to free movement of persons	***Title V – Area of freedom, security and justice***
	Chapter 1 – General provisions
Article 61	Article 67
	Article 68
	Article 69
	Article 70
	Article 71
Article 64, paragraph 1 (replaced)	Article 72
	Article 73
Article 66 (replaced)	Article 74
Article 60 (moved)	Article 75
	Article 76
	Chapter 2 – Policies on border checks, asylum and immigration
Article 62	Article 77
Article 63, points 1 et 2, and Article 64, paragraph 2	Article 78
Article 63, points 3 and 4	Article 79
	Article 80
Article 64, paragraph 1 (replaced)	*Article 72*
	Chapter 3 – Judicial cooperation in civil matters
Article 65	Article 81
Article 66 (replaced)	*Article 74*
Article 67 (repealed)	
Article 68 (repealed)	
Article 69 (repealed)	
	Chapter 4 – Judicial cooperation in criminal matters
	Article 82
	Article 83
	Article 84

Old numbering of the Treaty establishing the European Community	**New numbering of the Treaty on the Functioning of the European Union**
	Article 85
	Article 86
	Chapter 5 – Police cooperation
	Article 87
	Article 88
	Article 89
Title V – Transport	***Title VI – Transport***
Article 70	Article 90
Article 71	Article 91
Article 72	Article 92
Article 73	Article 93
Article 74	Article 94
Article 75	Article 95
Article 76	Article 96
Article 77	Article 97
Article 78	Article 98
Article 79	Article 99
Article 80	Article 100
Title VI – Common rules on competition, taxation and approximation of laws	***Title VII – Common rules on competition, taxation and approximation of laws***
Chapter 1 – Rules on competition	***Chapter 1 – Rules on competition***
Section 1 – Rules applying to undertakings	*Section 1 – Rules applying to undertakings*
Article 81	Article 101
Article 82	Article 102
Article 83	Article 103
Article 84	Article 104
Article 85	Article 105
Article 86	Article 106
Section 2 – Aids granted by States	*Section 2 – Aids granted by States*
Article 87	Article 107
Article 88	Article 108
Article 89	Article 109
Chapter 2 – Tax provisions	***Chapter 2 – Tax provisions***
Article 90	Article 110
Article 91	Article 111
Article 92	Article 112
Article 93	Article 113
Chapter 3 – Approximation of laws	***Chapter 3 – Approximation of laws***
Article 95 (moved)	Article 114

Old numbering of the Treaty establishing the European Community	***New numbering of the Treaty on the Functioning of the European Union***
Article 94 (moved)	Article 115
Article 96	Article 116
Article 97	Article 117
	Article 118
Title VII – Economic and monetary policy	***Title VIII – Economic and monetary policy***
Article 4 (moved)	Article 119
Chapter 1 – Economic policy	***Chapter 1 – Economic policy***
Article 98	Article 120
Article 99	Article 121
Article 100	Article 122
Article 101	Article 123
Article 102	Article 124
Article 103	Article 125
Article 104	Article 126
Chapter 2 – monetary policy	***Chapter 2 – monetary policy***
Article 105	Article 127
Article 106	Article 128
Article 107	Article 129
Article 108	Article 130
Article 109	Article 131
Article 110	Article 132
Article 111, paragraphs 1 to 3 and 5 (moved)	*Article 219*
Article 111, paragraph 4 (moved)	*Article 138*
	Article 133
Chapter 3 – Institutional provisions	***Chapter 3 – Institutional provisions***
Article 112 (moved)	*Article 283*
Article 113 (moved)	*Article 294*
Article 114	Article 134
Article 115	Article 135
	Chapter 4 – Provisions specific to Member States whose currency is the euro
	Article 136
	Article 137
Article 111, paragraph 4 (moved)	Article 138
Chapter 4 – Transitional provisions	***Chapter 5 – Transitional provisions***
Article 116 (repealed)	
	Article 139

Old numbering of the Treaty establishing the European Community	***New numbering of the Treaty on the Functioning of the European Union***
Article 117, paragraph 2, first five indents (moved)	*Article 141, paragraph 2*
Article 117, paragraphs 1, 2, sixth indent, and 3 to 9 (repealed)	
Article 121, paragraph 1 (moved) Article 122, paragraph 2, second sentence (moved) Article 123, paragraph 5 (moved)	Article 140
Article 118 (repealed)	
Article 123, paragraph 3 (moved) Article 117, paragraph 2, first five indents (moved)	Article 141
Article 124, paragraph 1 (moved)	Article 142
Article 119	Article 143
Article 120	Article 144
Article 121, paragraph 1 (moved)	*Article 140, paragraph 1*
Article 121, paragraphs 2 to 4 (repealed)	
Article 122, paragraphs 1, 2, first sentence, 3, 4, 5 and 6 (repealed)	
Article 122, paragraph 2, second sentence (moved)	*Article 140, paragraph 2, first subparagraph*
Article 123, paragraphs 1, 2 and 4 (repealed)	
Article 123, paragraph 3 (moved)	*Article 141, paragraph 1*
Article 123, paragraph 5 (moved)	*Article 140, paragraph 3*
Article 124, paragraph 1 (moved)	*Article 142*
Article 124, paragraph 2 (repealed)	
Title VIII – Employment	***Title IX – Employment***
Article 125	Article 145
Article 126	Article 146
Article 127	Article 147
Article 128	Article 148
Article 129	Article 149
Article 130	Article 150
Title IX – Common commercial policy (moved)	**Part Five, Title II, common commercial policy**
Article 131 (moved)	*Article 206*
Article 132 (repealed)	
Article 133 (moved)	*Article 207*
Article 134 (repealed)	
Title X – Customs cooperation (moved)	**Part Three, Title II, Chapter 2, Customs cooperation**
Article 135 (moved)	*Article 33*

Old numbering of the Treaty establishing the European Community	***New numbering of the Treaty on the Functioning of the European Union***
Title XI – Social policy, education, vocational training and youth	***Title X – Social policy***
Chapter 1 – social provisions (repealed)	
Article 136	Article 151
	Article 152
Article 137	Article 153
Article 138	Article 154
Article 139	Article 155
Article 140	Article 156
Article 141	Article 157
Article 142	Article 158
Article 143	Article 159
Article 144	Article 160
Article 145	Article 161
Chapter 2 – The European Social Fund	***Title XI – The European Social Fund***
Article 146	Article 162
Article 147	Article 163
Article 148	Article 164
Chapter 3 – Education, vocational training and youth	***Title XII – Education, vocational training, youth and sport***
Article 149	Article 165
Article 150	Article 166
Title XII – Culture	***Title XIII – Culture***
Article 151	Article 167
Title XIII – Public health	***Title XIV – Public health***
Article 152	Article 168
Title XIV – Consumer protection	***Title XV – Consumer protection***
Article 153, paragraphs 1, 3, 4 and 5	Article 169
Article 153, paragraph 2 (moved)	*Article 12*
Title XV – Trans-European networks	***Title XVI – Trans-European networks***
Article 154	Article 170
Article 155	Article 171
Article 156	Article 172
Title XVI – Industry	***Title XVII – Industry***
Article 157	Article 173
Title XVII – Economic and social cohesion	***Title XVIII – Economic, social and territorial cohesion***
Article 158	Article 174
Article 159	Article 175
Article 160	Article 176

Old numbering of the Treaty establishing the European Community	*New numbering of the Treaty on the Functioning of the European Union*
Article 161	Article 177
Article 162	Article 178
Title XVIII – Research and technological development	***Title XIX – Research and technological development and space***
Article 163	Article 179
Article 164	Article 180
Article 165	Article 181
Article 166	Article 182
Article 167	Article 183
Article 168	Article 184
Article 169	Article 185
Article 170	Article 186
Article 171	Article 187
Article 172	Article 188
	Article 189
Article 173	Article 190
Title XIX – Environment	***Title XX – Environment***
Article 174	Article 191
Article 175	Article 192
Article 176	Article 193
	Title XXI – Energy
	Article 194
	Title XXII – Tourism
	Article 195
	Title XXIII – Civil protection
	Article 196
	Title XXIV – Administrative cooperation
	Article 197
Title XX – Development cooperation (moved)	**Part Five, Title III, Chapter 1, Development cooperation**
Article 177 (moved)	*Article 208*
Article 178 (repealed) I	
Article 179 (moved)	*Article 209*
Article 180 (moved)	*Article 210*
Article 181 (moved)	*Article 211*
Title XXI – Economic, financial and technical cooperation with third countries (moved)	**Part Five, Title III, Chapter 2, Economic, financial and technical cooperation with third countries**
Article 181a (moved)	*Article 212*

Old numbering of the Treaty establishing the European Community	***New numbering of the Treaty on the Functioning of the European Union***
Part four – Association of the overseas countries and territories	***Part four – Association of the overseas countries and territories***
Article 182	Article 198
Article 183	Article 199
Article 184	Article 200
Article 185	Article 201
Article 186	Article 202
Article 187	Article 203
Article 188	Article 204
	Part five – External action by the union
	Title I – General provisions on the union's external action
	Article 205
Part three, Title IX, Common commercial policy (moved)	***Title II – Common commercial policy***
Article 131 (moved)	Article 206
Article 133 (moved)	Article 207
	Title III – Cooperation with third countries and humanitarian aid
Part Three, Title XX, Development cooperation (moved)	***Chapter 1 – development cooperation***
Article 177 (moved)	Article 208
Article 179 (moved)	Article 209
Article 180 (moved)	Article 210
Article 181 (moved)	Article 211
Part Three, Title XXI, Economic, financial and technical cooperation with third countries (moved)	***Chapter 2 – Economic, financial and technical cooperation with third countries***
Article 181a (moved)	Article 212
	Article 213
	Chapter 3 – Humanitarian aid
	Article 214
	Title IV – Restrictive measures
Article 301 (replaced)	Article 215
	Title V – International agreements
	Article 216
Article 310 (moved)	Article 217
Article 300 (replaced)	Article 218
Article 111, paragraphe 1 to 3 and 5 (moved)	Article 219

Old numbering of the Treaty establishing the European Community	***New numbering of the Treaty on the Functioning of the European Union***
	Title VI – The Union's relations with international organisations and third countries and the Union delegations
Articles 302 to 304 (replaced)	Article 220
	Article 221
	Title VII – Solidarity clause
	Article 222
Part five – Institutions of the community	***Part six – Institutional and budgetary provisions***
Title I – Institutional provisions	***Title I – Institutional provisions***
Chapter I – The institutions	***Chapter I – The institutions***
Section I – The European Parliament	*Section I – The European Parliament*
Article 189 (repealed)	
Article 190, paragraphs 1 to 3 (repealed)	
Article 190, paragraphs 4 and 5	Article 223
Article 191, first paragraph (repealed)	
Article 191, second paragraph	Article 224
Article 192, first paragraph (repealed)	
Article 192, second paragraph	Article 225
Article 193	Article 226
Article 194	Article 227
Article 195	Article 228
Article 196	Article 229
Article 197, first paragraph (repealed)	
Article 197, second, third and fourth paragraphs	Article 230
Article 198	Article 231
Article 199	Article 232
Article 200	Article 233
Article 201	Article 234
	Section 2 – The European Council
	Article 235
	Article 236
Section 2 – The Council	*Section 3 – The Council*
Article 202 (repealed)	
Article 203 (repealed)	
Article 204	Article 237
Article 205, paragraphs 2 and 4 (repealed)	
Article 205, paragraphs 1 and 3	Article 238
Article 206	Article 239

Old numbering of the Treaty establishing the European Community	***New numbering of the Treaty on the Functioning of the European Union***
Article 207	Article 240
Article 208	Article 241
Article 209	Article 242
Article 210	Article 243
Section 3 – The Commission	*Section 4 – The Commission*
Article 211 (repealed)	
	Article 244
Article 212 (moved)	*Article 249, paragraph 2*
Article 213	Article 245
Article 214 (repealed)	
Article 215	Article 246
Article 216	Article 247
Article 217, paragraphs 1, 3 and 4 (repealed)	
Article 217, paragraph 2	Article 248
Article 218, paragraph 1 (repealed)**4**	
Article 218, paragraph 2	Article 249
Article 219	Article 250
Section 4 – The Court of Justice	*Section 5 – The Court of Justice of the European Union*
Article 220 (repealed)	
Article 221, first paragraph (repealed)	
Article 221, second and third paragraphs	Article 251
Article 222	Article 252
Article 223	Article 253
Article 224	Article 254
	Article 255
Article 225	Article 256
Article 225a	Article 257
Article 226	Article 258
Article 227	Article 259
Article 228	Article 260
Article 229	Article 261
Article 229a	Article 262
Article 230	Article 263
Article 231	Article 264
Article 232	Article 265
Article 233	Article 266
Article 234	Article 267
Article 235	Article 268
	Article 269

Old numbering of the Treaty establishing the European Community	***New numbering of the Treaty on the Functioning of the European Union***
Article 236	Article 270
Article 237	Article 271
Article 238	Article 272
Article 239	Article 273
Article 240	Article 274
	Article 275
	Article 276
Article 241	Article 277
Article 242	Article 278
Article 243	Article 279
Article 244	Article 280
Article 245	Article 281
	Section 6 – The European Central Bank
	Article 282
Article 112 (moved)	Article 283
Article 113 (moved)	Article 284
Section 5 – The Court of Auditors	*Section 7 – The Court of Auditors*
Article 246	Article 285
Article 247	Article 286
Article 248	Article 287
Chapter 2 – Provisions common to several institutions	***Chapter 2 – Legal acts of the Union, adoption procedures and other provisions***
	Section 1 – The legal acts of the Union
Article 249	Article 288
	Article 289
	Article 290
	Article 291
	Article 292
	Section 2 – Procedures for the adoption of acts and other provisions
Article 250	Article 293
Article 251	Article 294
Article 252 (repealed)	
	Article 295
Article 253	Article 296
Article 254	Article 297
	Article 298
Article 255 (moved)	*Article 15*
Article 256	Article 299

Old numbering of the Treaty establishing the European Community	***New numbering of the Treaty on the Functioning of the European Union***
	Chapter 3 – The Union's advisory bodies
	Article 300
Chapter 3 – The economic and social committee	***Section 1 – The economic and social committee***
Article 257 (repealed)	
Article 258, first, second and fourth paragraphs	Article 301
Article 258, third paragraph (repealed)	
Article 259	Article 302
Article 260	Article 303
Article 261 (repealed)	
Article 262	Article 304
Chapter 4 – The Committee of the Regions	***Section 2 – The Committee of the Regions***
Article 263, first and fifth paragraphs (repealed)	
Article 263, second to fourth paragraphs	Article 305
Article 264	Article 306
Article 265	Article 307
Chapter 5 – The European Investment Bank	***Chapter 4 – The European Investment Bank***
Article 266	Article 308
Article 267	Article 309
Title II – Financial provisions	***Title II – Financial provisions***
Article 268	Article 310
	Chapter 1 – The Union's own resources
Article 269	Article 311
Article 270 (repealed)	
	Chapter 2 – The multiannual financial framework
	Article 312
	Chapter 3 – The Union's annual budget
Article 272, paragraph 1 (moved)	Article 313
Article 271 (moved)	*Article 316*
Article 272, paragraph 1 (moved)	*Article 313*
Article 272, paragraphs 2 to 10	Article 314
Article 273	Article 315
Article 271 (moved)	Article 316

Old numbering of the Treaty establishing the European Community	*New numbering of the Treaty on the Functioning of the European Union*
	Chapter 4 – Implementation of the budget and discharge
Article 274	Article 317
Article 275	Article 318
Article 276	Article 319
	Chapter 5 – Common provisions
Article 277	Article 320
Article 278	Article 321
Article 279	Article 322
	Article 323
	Article 324
	Chapter 6 – Combating fraud
Article 280	Article 325
	Title III – Enhanced cooperation
Articles 11 and 11 A (replaced)	Article 326
Articles 11 and 11 A (replaced)	Article 327
Articles 11 and 11 A (replaced)	Article 328
Articles 11 and 11 A (replaced)	Article 329
Articles 11 and 11 A (replaced)	Article 330
Articles 11 and 11 A (replaced)	Article 331
Articles 11 and 11 A (replaced)	Article 332
Articles 11 and 11 A (replaced)	Article 333
Articles 11 and 11 A (replaced)	Article 334
Part six – General and final provisions	***Part seven – General and final provisions***
Article 281 (repealed)	
Article 282	Article 335
Article 283	Article 336
Article 284	Article 337
Article 285	Article 338
Article 286 (replaced)	*Article 16*
Article 287	Article 339
Article 288	Article 340
Article 289	Article 341
Article 290	Article 342
Article 291	Article 343
Article 292	Article 344
Article 293 (repealed)	
Article 294 (moved)	*Article 55*
Article 295	Article 345

Old numbering of the Treaty establishing the European Community	***New numbering of the Treaty on the Functioning of the European Union***
Article 296	Article 346
Article 297	Article 347
Article 298	Article 348
Article 299, paragraph 1 (repealed)	
Article 299, paragraph 2, second, third and fourth subparagraphs	Article 349
Article 299, paragraph 2, first subparagraph, and paragraphs 3 to 6 (moved)	*Article 355*
Article 300 (replaced)	*Article 218*
Article 301 (replaced)	*Article 215*
Article 302 (replaced)	*Article 220*
Article 303 (replaced)	*Article 220*
Article 304 (replaced)	*Article 220*
Article 305 (repealed)	
Article 306	Article 350
Article 307	Article 351
Article 308	Article 352
	Article 353
Article 309	Article 354
Article 310 (moved)	*Article 217*
Article 311 (repealed)	
Article 299, paragraph 2,first subparagraph, and paragraphs 3 to 6 (moved)	Article 355
Article 312	Article 356
Final Provisions	
Article 313	Article 357
	Article 358
Article 314 (repealed)	

Index

A

B

C

D

F

G

J

K

L

T

W

Z